MARKETING MANAGEMENT
A STRATEGIC DECISION-MAKING APPROACH

Alreck & Settle
The Survey Research Handbook
Third Edition

Anderson, Beveridge, Lawton & Scott
Merlin: A Marketing Simulation
First Edition

Arens
Contemporary Advertising
Ninth Edition

Arnould, Price & Zinkhan
Consumers
Second Edition

Bearden, Ingram & LaForge
Marketing: Principles & Perspectives
Fourth Edition

Belch & Belch
Advertising & Promotion: An Integrated Marketing Communications Approach
Sixth Edition

Bingham & Gomes
Business Marketing
Third Edition

Cateora & Graham
International Marketing
Twelfth Edition

Cole & Mishler
Consumer and Business Credit Management
Eleventh Edition

Cravens & Piercy
Strategic Marketing
Seventh Edition

Cravens, Lamb & Crittenden
Strategic Marketing Management Cases
Seventh Edition

Crawford & Di Benedetto
New Products Management
Seventh Edition

Duncan
Principles of Advertising and IMC
Second Edition

Dwyer & Tanner
Business Marketing
Second Edition

Eisenmann
Internet Business Models: Text and Cases
First Edition

Etzel, Walker & Stanton
Marketing
Thirteenth Edition

Forrest
Internet Marketing Intelligence
First Edition

Futrell
ABC's of Relationship Selling
Eighth Edition

Futrell
Fundamentals of Selling
Eighth Edition

Gourville, Quelch & Rangan
Cases in Health Care Marketing
First Edition

Hair, Bush & Ortinau
Marketing Research
Second Edition

Hawkins, Best & Coney
Consumer Behavior
Ninth Edition

Johansson
Global Marketing
Third Edition

Johnston & Marshall
Churchill/Ford/Walker's Sales Force Management
Seventh Edition

Johnston & Marshall
Relationship Selling and Sales Management
First Edition

Kerin, Hartley & Rudelius
Marketing: The Core
First Edition

Kerin, Berkowitz, Hartley & Rudelius
Marketing
Seventh Edition

Lehmann & Winer
Analysis for Marketing Planning
Fifth Edition

Lehmann & Winer
Product Management
Third Edition

Levy & Weitz
Retailing Management
Fifth Edition

Mason & Perreault
The Marketing Game!
Third Edition

McDonald
Direct Marketing: An Integrated Approach
First Edition

Mohammed, Fisher, Jaworski & Paddison
Internet Marketing: Building Advantage in a Networked Economy
Second Edition

Monroe
Pricing
Third Edition

Mullins, Walker & Boyd
Marketing Management: A Strategic Decision-Making Approach
Fifth Edition

Nentl & Miller
SimSeries Simulations:
    SimSell
    SimSales Management
    SimMarketing
    SimMarketing Research
    SimCRM
First Edition

Pelton, Strutton, Lumpkin & Cooper
Marketing Channels: A Relationship Management Approach
Third Edition

Perreault & McCarthy
Basic Marketing: A Global Managerial Approach
Fifteenth Edition

Perreault & McCarthy
Essentials of Marketing: A Global Managerial Approach
Ninth Edition

Peter & Donnelly
A Preface to Marketing Management
Ninth Edition

Peter & Donnelly
Marketing Management: Knowledge and Skills
Seventh Edition

Peter & Olson
Consumer Behavior
Seventh Edition

Purvis & Burton
Which Ad Pulled Best?
Ninth Edition

Quelch, Rangan & Lal
Marketing Management Text and Cases
First Edition

Rayport & Jaworski
Introduction to e-Commerce
Second Edition

Rayport & Jaworski
e-Commerce
First Edition

Rayport & Jaworski
Cases in e-Commerce
First Edition

Richardson
Internet Marketing
First Edition

Roberts
Internet Marketing: Integrating Online and Offline Strategies
First Edition

Spiro, Stanton & Rich
Management of a Sales Force
Eleventh Edition

Stock & Lambert
Strategic Logistics Management
Fourth Edition

Ulrich & Eppinger
Product Design and Development
Third Edition

Walker, Boyd, Mullins & Larreche
Marketing Strategy: A Decision-Focused Approach
Fourth Edition

Weitz, Castleberry & Tanner
Selling: Building Partnerships
Fifth Edition

Zeithaml & Bitner
Services Marketing
Third Edition

MARKETING MANAGEMENT
A STRATEGIC DECISION-MAKING APPROACH

FIFTH EDITION

JOHN W. MULLINS
Associate Professor of Management Practice
London Business School

ORVILLE C. WALKER JR.
James D. Watkins Professor of Marketing, Emeritus
University of Minnesota

HARPER W. BOYD JR.
Donaghey Distinguished Professor of Marketing
University of Arkansas–Little Rock

JEAN-CLAUDE LARRÉCHÉ
Alfred H. Heineken Professor of Marketing
European Institute of Business Administration
INSEAD

Boston   Burr Ridge, IL   Dubuque, IA   Madison, WI   New York   San Francisco   St. Louis
Bangkok   Bogotá   Caracas   Kuala Lumpur   Lisbon   London   Madrid   Mexico City
Milan   Montreal   New Delhi   Santiago   Seoul   Singapore   Sydney   Taipei   Toronto

 **McGraw-Hill**
Irwin

MARKETING MANAGEMENT: A STRATEGIC DECISION-MAKING APPROACH
Published by McGraw-Hill/Irwin, a business unit of The McGraw-Hill Companies, Inc. 1221 Avenue of the
Americas, New York, NY, 10020. Copyright © 2005, 2002, 1998, 1995, 1990, by The McGraw-Hill Companies,
Inc. All rights reserved. No part of this publication may be reproduced or distributed in any form or by any
means, or stored in a database or retrieval system, without the prior written consent of The McGraw-Hill
Companies, Inc., including, but not limited to, in any network or other electronic storage or transmission, or
broadcast for distance learning.

Some ancillaries, including electronic and print components, may not be available to customers outside the
United States.

This book is printed on acid-free paper.

domestic   2 3 4 5 6 7 8 9 0 QPD/QPD 0 9 8 7 6 5 4
international   1 2 3 4 5 6 7 8 9 0 QPD/QPD 0 9 8 7 6 5 4

ISBN: 0-07-286370-6

Vice president and editor-in-chief: *Robin J. Zwettler*
Editorial director: *John E. Biernat*
Sponsoring editor: *Barrett Koger*
Editorial assistant: *Jill M. O'Malley*
Media producer: *Craig Atkins*
Project manager: *Laura Griffin*
Production supervisor: *Gina Hangos*
Coordinator freelance design: *Artemio Ortiz Jr.*
Photo research coordinator: *Jeremy Cheshareck*
Photo researcher: *Kelly Mountain*
Lead supplement producer: *Cathy L. Tepper*
Senior digital content specialist: *Brian Nacik*
Cover and interior design: *Ryan Brown*
Typeface: *10/12 Times Roman*
Compositor: *GAC Indianapolis*
Printer: *Quebecor World Dubuque Inc.*

Library of Congress Cataloging-in-Publication Data

Mullins, John W. (John Walker)
    Marketing management : a strategic decision-making approach / John W. Mullins,
 Orville C. Walker, Jr., Jean-Claude Larréché. — 5th ed.
        p. cm. — (McGraw-Hill/Irwin series in marketing)
    Rev. ed. of: Marketing management : a strategic, decision-making approach / Harper W.
 Boyd, Jr. ... [et al.].
    ISBN 0-07-286370-6 (alk. paper)
    1. Marketing—Management. I. Walker, Orville C. II. Larréché, Jean-Claude. III.
 Marketing management : a strategic, decision-making approach. IV. Title. V. Series.
 HF5415.13.M845 2005
 658.8—dc22
                                                            20030066459

INTERNATIONAL EDITION ISBN 0-07-111169-7
Copyright © 2005. Exclusive rights by The McGraw-Hill Companies, Inc. for manufacture and export. This
book cannot be re-exported from the country to which it is sold by McGraw-Hill. The International Edition is
not available in North America.

www.mhhe.com

ABOUT THE AUTHORS

JOHN W. MULLINS

John W. Mullins is Associate Professor of Management Practice at London Business School, where he heads the entrepreneurship group. He earned his MBA at the Stanford Graduate School of Business and, considerably later in life, his Ph.D. in marketing from the University of Minnesota. An award-winning teacher, John brings to his teaching and research 20 years of executive experience in high-growth firms, including two ventures he founded, one of which he took public. Since becoming a business school professor in 1992, John has published more than 30 articles in a variety of outlets, including *Harvard Business Review*, the *Journal of Product Innovation Management*, and the *Journal of Business Venturing*. His research has won national and international awards from the Marketing Science Institute, the American Marketing Association, and the Richard D. Irwin Foundation. He is the author of *The New Business Road Test: What Entrepreneurs and Executives Should Do* Before *Writing a Business Plan*, and coauthor of *Marketing Strategy: A Decision-Focused Approach*, 4th edition.

ORVILLE C. WALKER JR.

Orville C. Walker Jr. is Professor Emeritus in the University of Minnesota's Carlson School of Management, where he served until recently as the James D. Watkins Professor of Marketing and Director of the Ph.D. Program. He holds a master's degree in social psychology from The Ohio State University and a Ph.D. in marketing from the University of Wisconsin–Madison. Orville has coauthored three books and has published more than 50 research articles in scholarly and business journals. He has won several awards for his research, including the O'Dell award from the *Journal of Marketing Research*, the Maynard award from the *Journal of Marketing*, and a lifetime achievement award from the Sales Management Interest Group of the American Marketing Association. Orville has been a consultant to a number of business firms and not-for-profit organizations, and he has taught in executive development programs around the world, including programs in Poland, Switzerland, Scotland, and Hong Kong. Perhaps his biggest business challenge, however, is attempting to turn a profit as the owner-manager of a small vineyard in western Wisconsin.

JEAN-CLAUDE LARRÉCHÉ

Jean-Claude Larréché is Alfred Heineken Professor of Marketing at the European Institute of Business Administration, INSEAD, in Fontainebleau, France. He holds an MBA from INSEAD and a Ph.D. from the Stanford Graduate School of Business. As a popular executive development teacher and consultant to major international firms, Jean-Claude has worked with top management teams in Europe, North America, and Asia. He is founder and chairman of StratX, a publisher of marketing simulations and other tools for strategic marketing. An award-winning teacher, Jean-Claude is also a two-time winner of the overall case competition of the European Case Clearing House, and coauthor of *Marketing Strategy: A Decision-Focused Approach*, 4th edition.

BRIEF CONTENTS

PREFACE xviii

SECTION ONE

THE ROLE OF MARKETING IN DEVELOPING
SUCCESSFUL BUSINESS STRATEGIES 1

1 The Marketing Management
Process 2

2 The Marketing Implications of
Corporate and Business
Strategies 30

SECTION TWO

MARKET OPPORTUNITY ANALYSIS 65

3 Environmental Analysis: Tools to
Identify Attractive Markets 66

4 Industry Analysis and Competitive
Advantage 84

5 Understanding Consumer Buying
Behavior 106

6 Understanding Organizational Markets
and Buying Behavior 130

7 Measuring Market Opportunities:
Forecasting and Marketing
Research 152

8 Market Segmentation and Target
Marketing 180

9 Differentiation and Positioning 200

SECTION THREE

DEVELOPING STRATEGIC MARKETING
PROGRAMS 219

10 Business Strategies: A Foundation for
Marketing Program Decisions 220

11 Product Decisions 242

12 Pricing Decisions 268

13 Distribution Channel Decisions 294

14 Integrated Promotion
Decisions 326

SECTION FOUR

STRATEGIC MARKETING PROGRAMS FOR SELECTED
SITUATIONS 353

15 Marketing Strategies for the New
Economy 354

16 Strategies for New and Growing
Markets 384

17 Strategic Choices for Mature and
Declining Markets 418

SECTION FIVE

IMPLEMENTING AND CONTROLLING MARKETING
PROGRAMS 447

18 Organizing and Planning for Effective
Implementation 448

19 Measuring and Delivering Marketing
Performance 474

INDEX 496

CONTENTS

PREFACE xviii

SECTION ONE
THE ROLE OF MARKETING IN DEVELOPING
SUCCESSFUL BUSINESS STRATEGIES 1

1 The Marketing Management
Process 2

RedEnvelope—Marketing Upscale Gifts Online 2

A New Mission and Strategy 2
The New Marketing Plan 2
The Results 4

Marketing Challenges Addressed in Chapter 1 4

Why Are Marketing Decisions Important? 4

The Importance of the Top Line 5

Marketing Creates Value by Facilitating Exchange
Relationships 5

What Factors Are Necessary for a Successful
Exchange Relationship? 6
1. Who Markets and Who Buys? The Parties in
an Exchange? 6
2. Customer Needs and Wants 7
3. What Gets Exchanged? Products and
Services 10
4. How Exchanges Create Value 10
5. Defining a Market 12

What Does Effective Marketing Practice Look
Like? 13

Marketing Management—A Definition 13
Integrating Marketing Plans with the Company's
Strategies and Resources 15
Market Opportunity Analysis 16
Formulating Strategic Marketing Programs 17
Formulating Strategic Marketing Programs for
Specific Situations 18
Implementation and Control of the Marketing
Program 19

The Marketing Plan—a Blueprint for
Action 20

Who Does What? 21

Marketing Institutions 21
Who Pays the Cost of Marketing Activities—and
Are They Worth It? 22
Room for Improvement in Marketing
Efficiency 23
The Role of the Marketing Decision Maker 24

Some Recent Developments Affecting Marketing
Management 24

Globalization 25
Increased Importance of Service 25
Information Technology 25
Relationships across Functions and Firms 27

Take-aways 27

Endnotes 28

2 The Marketing Implications of
Corporate and Business
Strategies 30

IBM Switches Strategies 30

Technology Changes and Competitor Actions
Require a Shift in Strategy 30
A New Corporate Strategy 32
New Business and Marketing Strategies 32
The Bottom Line 33

Marketing Challenges Addressed in Chapter 2 33

What Is Marketing's Role in Formulating and
Implementing Strategies? 34

Market-Oriented Management 35
Does Being Market-Oriented Pay? 36
Factors That Mediate Marketing's Strategic
Role 37

Three Levels of Strategy: Similar Components, but
Different Issues 39

Strategy: A Definition   39
The Components of Strategy   40
The Hierarchy of Strategies   40
Corporate Strategy   40
Business-Level Strategy   42
Marketing Strategy   42

The Marketing Implications of Corporate Strategy
Decisions   42

Corporate Scope—Defining the Firm's
Mission   43
Corporate Objectives   46
Corporate Growth Strategies   48
Allocating Corporate Resources   51

The Marketing Implications of Business-Unit
Strategy Decisions   56

How Should Strategic Business Units Be
Designed?   58
The Business Unit's Objectives   58
The Business Unit's Competitive Strategy   58

Take-aways   60

Endnotes   61

Appendix 2.1 The American Marketing Association's
Code of Ethics   63

SECTION TWO

MARKET OPPORTUNITY ANALYSIS   65

**3   Environmental Analysis: Tools to
Identify Attractive Markets   66**

The Changing American Menswear Market   66

The Impact of Macroenvironmental Trends   66
What's Next? Will Suits Come Back?   67

Marketing Challenges Addressed in Chapter 3   67

Swimming Upstream or Downstream: An Important
Strategic Choice   68

Macro Trend Analysis: A Framework for Assessing
Market Attractiveness   68

The Demographic Environment   69
The Sociocultural Environment   70
The Economic Environment   72
The Political/Legal Environment   73
The Technological Environment   75
The Physical Environment   77

Environmental Analysis Guides Marketing Decision
Making   78

Prioritizing Trend Categories   78
Information Sources and Outputs of Macro
Trend Analysis   79
Anticipating and Responding to Environmental
Change   80

Take-aways   81

Endnotes   81

**4   Industry Analysis and Competitive
Advantage   84**

The Cellular Telephone Business: Increasing
Competition in a Growing Market   84

Cell Phone Manufacturing   84
Cell Phone Service Providers   84

Marketing Challenges Addressed in Chapter 4   85

Markets and Industries: What's the Difference?   85

Defining Markets and Industries: Levels of
Analysis   86
Challenges in Market and Industry
Definition   86

Your Market Is Attractive: What About Your
Industry?   88

Driving Forces   88
Porter's Five Competitive Forces   91
A Five Forces Analysis of the Cellular Phone
Service Industry   91
Changing Competition and Industry
Evolution   91
Critical Success Factors: Who Wins *within* an
Industry?   92

Industry Analysis Locally: How Intense Is the
Immediate Competition?   93

Rate of Diffusion of Innovations: Another Factor in
Assessing Opportunity Attractiveness   94

The Adoption Process   94
The Rate of Adoption   94
Adopter Categories   95
Implications of Diffusion of Innovation Theory
for Forecasting Sales of New Products and New
Firms   96

Sustaining Competitive Advantage over the Product
Life Cycle   97

Life-Cycle Curves 97
Market and Competitive Implications of Product Life-Cycle Stages 99
Strategic Implications and Limitations of the Product Life Cycle 102

Take-aways 103

Endnotes 103

5 Understanding Consumer Buying Behavior 106

Cruise Ships—Not Just for Grandma and Grandpa Anymore 106

Savvy Marketing Helped Fuel Industry Growth 106
Future Challenges 107

Marketing Challenges Addressed in Chapter 5 108

The Psychological Importance of the Purchase Affects the Decision-Making Process 109

How Do Consumers Make High-Involvement Purchase Decisions? 109
Low-Involvement Purchase Decisions 116
Understanding the Target Consumer's Level of Involvement Enables Better Marketing Decisions 117

Why People Buy Different Things—the Marketing Implications of Psychological and Personal Influences 119

Perception and Memory 119
Needs and Attitudes 121
Demographics and Lifestyle 123

Why People Buy Different Things: Part 2—the Marketing Implications of Social Influences 125

Culture 125
Social Class 126
Reference Groups 126
The Family 127

Take-aways 127

Endnotes 128

6 Understanding Organizational Markets and Buying Behavior 130

Exel: Building Long-Term Relationships with Organizational Buyers 130

Delivering Printing Systems in the Netherlands 130

Marketing Challenges Addressed in Chapter 6 131

Who Is the Customer? 132

A Comparison of Organizational versus Consumer Markets 132
What Do the Unique Characteristics of Organizational Markets Imply for Marketing Programs? 134
The Organizational Customer Is Usually a Group of Individuals 134

How Organizational Members Make Purchase Decisions 137

Types of Buying Situations 137
The Purchase Decision-Making Process 138
The Marketing Implications of Different Organizational Purchasing Situations 144
Purchasing Processes in Government Markets 145

Selling Different Kinds of Goods and Services to Organizations Requires Different Marketing Programs 146

Raw Materials 146
Component Materials and Parts 148
Installations 148
Accessory Equipment 149
Operating Supplies 149
Business Services 149

Take-aways 150

Endnotes 150

7 Measuring Market Opportunities: Forecasting and Market Research 152

African Communications Group: Bringing Modern Telecommunications to Tanzania 152

Market Analysis 152
Industry Analysis 153
Consumer Needs and Behavior 153
The Business Idea 153
Determining Market Potential and Preparing a Sales Forecast 153

Marketing Challenges Addressed in Chapter 7 154

Every Forecast Is Wrong! 154

A Forecaster's Toolkit: A Tool for Every Forecasting Setting   155

   Statistical and Other Quantitative Methods   156
   Observation   157
   Surveys   157
   Analogy   158
   Judgment   159
   Market Tests   159
   Mathematics Entailed in Forecasting   160

Cautions and Caveats in Forecasting   161

   Keys to Good Forecasting   161
   Biases in Forecasting   162

Why Data? Why Marketing Research?   162

Market Knowledge Systems: Charting a Path toward Competitive Advantage   163

   Internal Records Systems   163
   Marketing Databases   164
   Competitive Intelligence Systems   166
   Client Contact and Salesforce Automation Systems   166
   Other Kinds of Market Knowledge Systems   168

Marketing Research Resolves Specific Marketing Challenges   168

   Step 1:   Identify the Managerial Problem and Establish Research Objectives   168
   Step 2:   Determine the Data Sources and Types of Data Required   169
   Step 3:   Design the Research   172
   Step 4:   Collect the Data   174
   Step 5:   Analyze the Data   175
   Step 6:   Report the Results to the Decision Maker   175

What Users of Marketing Research Should Ask   176

Rudimentary Competence: Are We There Yet?   176

Take-aways   177

Endnotes   177

8   Market Segmentation and Target Marketing   180

Blue Ribbon Sports Targets Distance Runners   180

   The Unique Needs of Distance Runners   180
   The Waffle Revolution   180
   Launching and Expanding the Nike Brand   181
   World Cup 2002   181

Marketing Challenges Addressed in Chapter 8   181

Why Do Market Segmentation and Target Marketing Make Sense?   182

   Most Markets Are Heterogeneous   182
   Today's Market Realities Often Make Segmentation Imperative   183

How Are Market Segments Best Defined?   184

   Demographic Descriptors   184
   Geographic Descriptors   186
   Geodemographic Descriptors   186
   Behavioral Descriptors   187
   Innovative Segmentation: A Key to Marketing Breakthroughs   189

Choosing Attractive Market Segments: A Five-Step Process   190

   Step 1:   Select Market-Attractiveness and Competitive-Position Factors   191
   Step 2:   Weight Each Factor   193
   Step 3:   Rate Segments on Each Factor, Plot Results on Matrices   193
   Step 4:   Project Future Position for Each Segment   194
   Step 5:   Choose Segments to Target, Allocate Resources   195

Different Targeting Strategies Suit Different Opportunities   196

   Niche-Market Strategy   197
   Mass-Market Strategy   197
   Growth-Market Strategy   197
   Global Market Segmentation   197

Take-aways   198

Endnotes   198

9   Differentiation and Positioning   200

Repositioning French Wine   200

Marketing Challenges Addressed in Chapter 9   200

Differentiation: One Key to Customer Preference and Competitive Advantage   201

   Differentiation in Business Strategies   202
   Differentiation among Goods and Services   203

Physical Positioning   203

   Limitations of Physical Positioning   204

Perceptual Positioning   204

Levers Marketers Can Use to Establish
Positioning   205

Preparing the Foundation for Marketing Strategies:
The Positioning Process   206

   Step 1:   Identify a Relevant Set of Competitive
   Products   207
   Step 2:   Identify Determinant Attributes   207
   Step 3:   Collect Data about Customers'
   Perceptions for Products in the Competitive
   Set   209
   Step 4:   Analyze the Current Positions of
   Products in the Competitive Set   209
   Step 5:   Determine Customers' Most Preferred
   Combination of Attributes   211
   Step 6:   Consider Fit of Possible Positions
   with Customer Needs and Segment
   Attractiveness   212
   Step 7:   Write Positioning Statement or Value
   Proposition to Guide Development of Marketing
   Strategy   214

Analytical Tools for Positioning Decision
Making   216

Take-aways   218

Endnotes   218

SECTION THREE
DEVELOPING STRATEGIC MARKETING PROGRAMS   219

10   Business Strategies: A Foundation for Marketing Program Decisions   220

Business Strategies and Marketing Programs
at 3M   220

Marketing Challenges Addressed in Chapter 10   221

How Do Businesses Compete?   223

   Generic Business-Level Competitive
   Strategies   223
   Do the Same Competitive Strategies Work for
   Single-Business Firms and Start-ups?   225
   Do the Same Competitive Strategies Work for
   Service Businesses?   226
   Do the Same Competitive Strategies Work for
   Global Competitors?   227
   Will the Internet Change Everything?   228

How Do Competitive Strategies Differ from One
Another?   229

   Differences in Scope   229
   Differences in Goals and Objectives   230
   Differences in Resource Deployments   231
   Differences in Sources of Synergy   231

Deciding When a Strategy Is Appropriate:
The Fit between Business Strategies and the
Environment   232

   Appropriate Conditions for a Prospector
   Strategy   232
   Appropriate Conditions for an Analyzer
   Strategy   234
   Appropriate Conditions for a Defender
   Strategy   234

How Different Business Strategies Influence
Marketing Decisions   235

   Product Policies   237
   Pricing Policies   238
   Distribution Policies   238
   Promotion Policies   238

What If the Best Marketing Program for a
Product Does Not Fit the Business's Competitive
Strategy?   239

Take-aways   240

Endnotes   241

11   Product Decisions   242

Product Decisions in a Services Business   242

Marketing Challenges Addressed in Chapter 11   243

Product Design Decisions for Competitive
Advantage   244

   Goods and Services: Are the Product Decisions
   the Same?   245
   Product Quality and Features Decisions   247
   Branding Decisions   248
   Packaging Decisions   251
   Services Decisions and Warranties   251

Managing Product Lines for Customer Appeal and
Profit Performance   252

   Line Filling   253
   Line Stretching   254
   Line Extensions   254

Brand Extensions   254
Dropping Products   255
Product Systems   255

New Product Development Process Decisions   255

The Importance of New Products to Long-Term
Profitability   256
New Product Success and Failure   256
Organizing for New Product Development   257
Key Decisions in the New Product Development
Process   258

Take-aways   265

Endnotes   266

12   Pricing Decisions   268

Ryanair: Low Prices but High Profits—So Far   268

Marketing Challenges Addressed in Chapter 12   269

A Process for Making Pricing Decisions   270

Strategic Pricing Objectives   270
Estimating Demand and Perceived Value   274
Estimating Costs   276
Analyzing Competitors' Costs and Prices   278

Methods Managers Use to Determine an Appropriate
Price Level   278

Cost-Oriented Methods   278
Competition-Oriented Methods   281
Customer-Oriented Methods   283

Deciding on a Price Structure: Adapting Prices to
Market Variations   286

Geographic Adjustments   286
Global Adjustments   287
Discounts and Allowances   288
Differential Pricing   290
Product-Line Pricing Adjustments   291

Take-aways   292

Endnotes   293

13   Distribution Channel Decisions   294

Changing Global Retail Trends Send a "Get Well"
Greeting to Hallmark   294

Marketing Challenges Addressed in Chapter 13   295

Why Do Multifirm Marketing Channels Exist?   296

Designing Distribution Channels: What Are the
Objectives to Be Accomplished?   297

Product Availability   299
Meeting Customers' Service Requirements   299
Promotional Effort   300
Market Information   300
Cost-Effectiveness   300
Flexibility   301

Designing Distribution Channels: What Kinds of
Institutions Might Be Included?   301

Merchant Wholesalers   301
Agent Middlemen   302
Retailers   302
Nonstore Retailing   303

Channel Design Alternatives   305

Alternative Consumer Goods Channels   305
Alternative Industrial Goods Channels   306

Which Alternative Is Best? It Depends on the Firm's
Objectives and Resources   307

Availability and the Satisfaction of Customer
Service Requirements   307
Promotional Effort, Market Information, and
Postsale Service Objectives   309
Cost-Effectiveness   310
Flexibility   312
Multichannel Distribution   312

Channel Design for Global Markets   313

Market Entry Strategies   313
Channel Alternatives   314

Channel Design for Services   315

Channel Management Decisions   316

Vertical Marketing Systems   316
Sources of Channel Power   319
Channel Control Strategies   320
Trade Promotions—Incentives for Motivating
Channel Members   321
Channel Conflicts and Resolution
Strategies   323

Take-aways   324

Endnotes   325

**14   Integrated Promotion
Decisions   326**

Integrated Marketing Communication Takes on Some
New Twists   326

Larazade   326

Big Brother   326
What's Next?   327

Marketing Challenges Addressed in Chapter 14   327

The Promotion Mix: A Communication Toolkit   328

Developing an Integrated Marketing Communications Plan   329

Step 1:   Define the Audience(s) to Be Targeted   329
Step 2:   Set the Promotional Objectives   330
Step 3:   Set the Promotion Budget   331
Step 4:   Design the Promotion Mix   332
Step 5:   Evaluate the Results   333

The Nitty-Gritty of Promotional Decision Making   334

Making Advertising Decisions   334
Making Personal Selling Decisions   344
Organizing the Sales Effort in Global Markets   344
Customer Service: An Increasingly Important Personal Selling Function   346

Using Technology to Enhance Sales and Customer Service Performance   347

Recruiting, Training, and Compensating Salespeople: The Keys to Salesforce Performance   348

Evaluating and Controlling Salesforce Performance to Ensure Delivery of Budgeted Results   348

Making Sales Promotion Decisions   349
Making Public Relations Decisions   350

Take-aways   351

Endnotes   351

SECTION FOUR
STRATEGIC MARKETING PROGRAMS FOR SELECTED SITUATIONS   353

15   Marketing Strategies for the New Economy   354

Chocolate Company Sweetens the Web   354

Thorntons Goes Online   354
Sweet Rewards   354

Marketing Challenges Addressed in Chapter 15   355

Does Every Company Need a New-Economy Strategy?   356

Threats or Opportunities? The Inherent Advantages and Disadvantages of the New Economy for Marketers   358

The Syndication of Information   358
Increasing Returns to Scale of Network Products   359
The Ability to Efficiently Personalize and Customize Market Offerings   360
Disintermediation and Restructuring of Distribution Channels   361
Global Reach, 24×7 Access, and Instantaneous Delivery   361
Are These New-Economy Attributes Opportunities or Threats?   362
First-Mover Advantage: Fact or Fiction?   365

Developing a New-Economy Strategy: A Decision Framework   365

Marketing Applications for New-Economy Tools   366
Developing New-Economy Marketing Strategies: The Critical Questions   375

Developing Strategies to Serve New-Economy Markets   378

What Lessons Can We Learn from the Dot.com Crash?   379
What Are the Key Success Factors in Serving the Dot.com Markets of Tomorrow?   380

Take-aways   382

Endnotes   382

16   Strategies for New and Growing Markets   384

Canon, Inc.—Success That Is Hard to Copy   384

Marketing Challenges Addressed in Chapter 16   385

How New Is New?   386

Market Entry Strategies: Is It Better to Be a Pioneer or a Follower?   388

Pioneer Strategy   388
Not All Pioneers Capitalize on Their Potential Advantages   390
Follower Strategy   390
Determinants of Success for Pioneers and Followers   391

Strategic Marketing Programs for Pioneers   393

Mass-Market Penetration   393

Niche Penetration   395
Skimming and Early Withdrawal   395
Marketing Program Components for a Mass-
Market Penetration Strategy   396
Marketing Program Components for a Niche
Penetration Strategy   400
Marketing Program Components for a Skimming
Strategy   400

Growth-Market Strategies for Market Leaders   401

Marketing Objectives for Share Leaders   401
Marketing Actions and Strategies to Achieve
Share-Maintenance Objectives   402
Fortress, or Position Defense, Strategy   402
Flanker Strategy   406
Confrontation Strategy   407
Market Expansion   408
Contraction or Strategic Withdrawal   408

Share-Growth Strategies for Followers   409

Marketing Objectives for Followers   409
Marketing Actions and Strategies to Achieve
Share Growth   409
Frontal Attack Strategy   411
Leapfrog Strategy   413
Flanking and Encirclement Strategies   414
Supporting Evidence   415

Take-aways   416

Endnotes   417

**17   Strategic Choices for Mature and
Declining Markets   418**

Johnson Controls—Making Money in Mature
Markets   418

Marketing Challenges Addressed in Chapter 17   419

Challenges in Mature Markets   420
Challenges in Declining Markets   420

Strategic Choices in Mature Markets   420

Strategies for Maintaining Competitive
Advantage   421
Methods of Differentiation   422
Methods of Maintaining a Low-Cost
Position   427
Customers' Satisfaction and Loyalty Are Crucial
for Maximizing Their Lifetime Value   429

Marketing Strategies for Mature Markets   431

Strategies for Maintaining Current Market
Share   431

Strategies for Extending Volume Growth   433

Strategies for Declining Markets   438

Relative Attractiveness of Declining
Markets   439
Divestment or Liquidation   441
Marketing Strategies for Remaining
Competitors   441

Take-aways   445

Endnotes   445

**SECTION FIVE
IMPLEMENTING AND CONTROLLING MARKETING
PROGRAMS   447**

**18   Organizing and Planning for Effective
Implementation   448**

Hewlett-Packard—Reorganizing to Implement a New
Strategy   448

The Internet Changed the Firm's Market
Environment   448
Reorganizing to Implement a New
Strategy   449

Marketing Challenges Addressed in Chapter 18   450

Designing Appropriate Administrative Relationships
for the Implementation of Different Competitive
Strategies   451

Business-Unit Autonomy   452
Shared Programs and Facilities   453
Evaluation and Reward Systems   454

Designing Appropriate Organizational Structures
and Processes for Implementing Different
Strategies   454

Functional Competencies and Resource
Allocation   455
Additional Considerations for Service
Organizations   455
Organizational Structures   457
Recent Trends in Organizational Design   461
Organizational Adjustments as Firms Grow and
Markets Change   462
Organizational Designs for Selling in Global
Markets   463

Marketing Plans: The Foundation for Implementing
Marketing Actions   465

The Situational Analysis   468

Key Issues   470
Objectives   470
Marketing Strategy   470
Action Plans   470
Projected Profit-and-Loss Statement   471
Contingency Plans   471

Take-aways   471

Endnotes   472

19   Measuring and Delivering Marketing Performance   474

Controls Pay for Wal-Mart   474

Marketing Challenges Addressed in Chapter 19   475

Designing Control Systems Step by Step   476

Setting Standards of Performance   477
Specifying and Obtaining Feedback Data   482
Evaluating Feedback Data   482
Taking Corrective Action   483

Design Decisions for Strategic Control Systems   484

Identifying Key Variables   484

Tracking and Monitoring   485
Strategy Reassessment   485

Design Decisions for Marketing Performance Measurement   486

Who Needs What Information?   486
When and How Often Is the Information Needed?   489
In What Media and in What Format(s) or Levels of Aggregation Should the Information Be Provided?   490
What Contingencies Should Be Planned For?   490
Global Marketing Control   492

A Tool for Periodic Assessment of Marketing Performance: The Marketing Audit   493

Types of Audits   493

Take-aways   495

Endnotes   495

INDEX   496

PREFACE

WHY THIS BOOK?

WHY DID YOUR INSTRUCTOR CHOOSE THIS BOOK? Chances are, it was for one or more of the following reasons:

- Among your instructor's objectives is to give you the necessary tools and frameworks to enable you to be an effective contributor to marketing decision making—regardless of whether you follow a career in marketing positions *per se*, in another functional area, or as an entrepreneur or in other general management roles. This book's focus on **strategic decision making** sets it apart from other texts that place greater emphasis on *description* of marketing phenomena than on the strategic and tactical marketing *decisions* that managers and entrepreneurs must make each and every day.

- Your instructor wants to use the most current and most **Internet-savvy** book available. We integrate the latest developments in Internet-based communication and distribution technology into every chapter, and we devote an entire chapter, Chapter 15, to the development of marketing strategies for the new economy. In addition, we supplement the book with an interactive website to help you self-test what you learn and to help your instructor choose the best cases and other materials and in-class activities.

  Although the stock market bubble built on dot.com start-ups burst several years ago, the proportion of goods and services marketed over the Internet continues to grow rapidly around the world. And increasing numbers of dot.com start-ups are finally achieving profitability. Therefore, our goal—and probably that of your instructor as well—is to make both the latest Internet-based tools as well as time-tested marketing principles relevant to those of you who will work in either old- or new-economy companies.

- Your instructor appreciates and believes you will benefit from the **real-world, global perspectives** offered by the authors of this book. Our combined entrepreneurial, marketing management, and consulting experience spans a broad variety of manufacturing, service, software, and distribution industries and has taken us—and thereby you, the reader—around the world many times.

As the reader will see from the outset in Chapter 1, marketing decision making is a critical activity in every firm, from start-ups to big companies with traditional marketing departments. Further, it is not just marketing managers who make marketing decisions. People in nearly every role in every company can have powerful influence on how happy customers are, or are not, with the goods and services the company provides. Stockbrokers must attract new customers. Accounting and consulting firms must find ways to differentiate their services from other providers so their customers have reasons to give them their business. Software engineers must understand how their technology can benefit the intended customer, for without such benefits, customers will not buy. Thus, we have written this book to meet the marketing needs of readers who hope to make a difference in the long-term strategic success of their organizations—whether their principal roles are in marketing or otherwise.

In this brief preface, we want to say a bit more about each of the three distinctive benefits, listed above, that this book offers its readers. We also point out the key changes in this edition compared to previous ones; and we thank our many students, colleagues, and others from whom we have learned so much, without whom this book would not have been possible.

A FOCUS ON STRATEGIC DECISION MAKING

Previous editions of this book have been known for their strategic approach, an approach that helps clarify the relationships among corporate, business-level, and marketing strategies for firms large and small; the relationships between marketing strategies and the marketing environment; and the relationships between marketing and other functional areas in the firm. This fifth edition retains this strategic perspective while providing the reader with specific tools and frameworks for making marketing decisions that take best advantage of the conditions in which the firm finds itself—both internally, in terms of the firm's mission and competencies, and externally, in terms of the market and competitive context in which it operates.

This decision-focused approach is important to students and executives who are our readers, because, in most marketing management classes and executive courses, the students or participants will be asked to make numerous decisions—decisions in case studies about what the protagonist in the case should do; decisions in a course project, such as those entailed in developing a marketing plan; or decisions in a marketing simulation.

Our decision-focused approach is also important to employers, who tell us they want today's graduates to be prepared to "hit the ground running" and contribute to the firm's decision making from day one. The ability to bring thoughtful and disciplined tools and frameworks—as opposed to seat-of-the-pants hunches or blind intuition—to marketing decision making is one of the key assets today's business school graduates offer their employers. This book puts the tools in the toolbox to make this happen. In the end, employers want to know what their new hires can *do*, not just what they *know*.

WEB-SAVVY INSIGHTS

This book brings a realistic and informed perspective to an important question many students are asking: "Has the advent of the Internet changed all the rules?" Our answer is, "Well, yes and no." On one hand, the Internet has made available a host of new marketing tools, from banner ads to e-mail marketing to delivery of digital goods and services over the Internet, all of which are available to companies in the so-called old and new economies alike. On the other hand, time-tested marketing fundamentals, such as understanding one's customers and competitors and meeting customer needs in ways that are differentiated from the offerings of those competitors, have become even more important in the fast-moving digital world, as the many recent dot.com failures attest.

Thus, throughout the book, we integrate examples of new-economy companies—both successful and otherwise—to show how both yesterday's and today's marketing tools and decision frameworks can most effectively be applied. Because the advent of the Internet, mobile telephony, and other new-economy technologies is so important in its own right, however, we also devote Chapter 15 to new-economy strategies. This chapter provides for marketers in all kinds of companies a road map for decisions about where, when, and how to deploy new-economy tools.

A REAL-WORLD, GLOBAL PERSPECTIVE

Theory is important, because it enhances our understanding of business phenomena and helps managers think about what they should do. It is in the *application* of theory—the world of marketing practice—where we believe this book excels. Our decision focus is all about application. But we don't just bring an academic perspective to the party, important as that perspective is.

Two of us on the author team, Jean-Claude Larréché and John Mullins, have started successful entrepreneurial companies. One of these firms has "gone public." Two of us, Orv Walker and John, have worked in the United States, at the University of Minnesota and University of Denver, respectively. Two, Jean-Claude and John, work in Europe, Jean-Claude at IN-SEAD and John at the London Business School. All of us, including Harper Boyd, who passed away in 1999 but whose legacy lives on in this edition, have contributed the fruits of our research to the growing body of knowledge in the marketing management, marketing strategy, new products, and entrepreneurship arenas. The result of our collective and varied experience and expertise is a book filled with examples of real people from around the world making real decisions, examples of start-ups and high-growth companies as well as the more common examples of larger, more established firms.

WHAT'S NEW IN THIS EDITION?

Compared to the extensive changes we undertook last time, the revisions in this edition are largely a matter of fine-tuning rather than major restructuring. But no chapter escaped untouched. All have been updated with the most recent marketing tools, techniques, and examples, although the basic flow, sequence, and strategic focus of the book have remained unchanged. We did, however, make a couple more extensive changes worth noting to those familiar with previous editions.

- Many of the new examples we have added throughout the book were chosen for the express purpose of increasing its global focus and international perspective. We have made an extensive effort to find and incorporate examples of marketing strategies and actions from firms and not-for-profit organizations all around the world, not just in the United States. Even many of the extensive case vignettes that open each chapter now focus on firms in Europe, Asia, and Africa.
- We have combined the two former chapters discussing promotion decisions and personal selling decisions into a single chapter that examines the choices involved in designing integrated marketing communications programs. Our rationale was simple: We think integrated communications programs can be understood best when the various components of such programs, together with their strengths and shortcomings, are examined in an integrated way within a single comprehensive chapter.

THANKS!

Simply put, this book is not solely our work—far from it. Many of our students, colleagues, and those we work with in industry have made contributions that have significantly shaped our perspectives on marketing decision making. We are grateful to all of them.

There are several people, though, who have played more direct roles in making this edition what it is, by providing detailed and constructive suggestions on one or more chapters or by helping us develop the related materials that make this book readable and useful for students and instructors alike. They include:

- Rhonda Bakke, Flathead Valley Community College–Kalispell
- Sarah Hickey, London Business School
- Nicola Lee, London Business School
- Nancy Jane Marlow, Eastern Illinois University
- Abi Murthy, London Business School
- Prema Nakra, Marist College
- Rosalyn S. Rufer, SUNY Empire State College
- Khaled Sartawi, Fort Valley State University

We also thank a small army of talented people at McGraw-Hill/Irwin for their work that has turned our rough manuscript into an attractive and readable book. In particular, our editors, Barrett Koger, Sarah Crago, and Jill O'Malley, have been instrumental in giving birth to this edition. Without them, we'd probably still be writing!

Finally, we thank Harper Boyd, without whom this book would not exist, and our parents, without whom, of course, none of us would be here. To all of you we extend our love, our respect, and our gratitude for passing on to us your curiosity and your passion for learning. We therefore dedicate this book to Harper Boyd, to Jeannette and Orville Walker, Sr., to Alice and Jack Mullins, and to Odette and Pierre Larréché.

John W. Mullins
Orville C. Walker Jr.
Jean-Claude Larréché
London, Minneapolis, and Fontainebleau
Summer 2003

Walkthrough

Case Vignette

These vignettes have been chosen to increase the book's global focus and international perspective.

options and characteristics, but also offer tutorials about how to use the product, help lines, and other information geared to helping customers obtain full value from their purchases. For instance, the outdoor gear retailer REI provides 45,000 pages of product use information and tips, such as a clinic on backpacking, on its site, www.rei.com.

KEY OBSERVATION

Many new sites have taken over much of the search for information about alternative offerings in a product category in exchange for a small fee from the consumer or advertising from manufacturers or dealers in the category.

More important, many new sites have taken over much of the search for information about alternative offerings in a product category in exchange for a small fee from the consumer or advertising from manufacturers or dealers in the category. For example, www.cruisecompany.net provides detailed information on cruises organized by type of cruise, itinerary, or cruise line, in exchange for a commission on any cruise a consumer books through the site.

While such sites facilitate the consumer's search for information about high-involvement products and services, they do not solve all the consumer's problems. Most of the information provided by such sites is obtained from commercial and public, rather than personal, sources. Therefore, some consumers may not consider it very useful for evaluating alternative choices, particularly when it comes to choosing intangible services. This shortcoming helps explain why some sites, such as www.amazon.com, publish product reviews and evaluations submitted by individual customers. Also, sensory information such as touch and smell, which can be important for evaluating foods, fashion items, and similar products, cannot be displayed on the Web. Finally, the effort by some sites to collect information for free from other sites has raised ethical and legal questions concerning who "owns" product information. These questions have yet to be resolved. An example is summarized in Ethical Perspective 5.1.

ETHICAL PERSPECTIVE 5.1
Who Owns Product Information on the Internet?

The Internet may substantially reduce consumers' costs of collecting extensive information about product or service alternatives through the development of Web-crawling robots, or "bots," software that trolls through many Internet sites collecting information about items in a given product category. For instance, Bidder's Edge, a small start-up in Burlington, Massachusetts, developed a bot that crawls through online auction sites searching for whatever product a customer is interested in. The bot compiled information on the status of, say, Furby auctions and ranked them in order of expiration date. Without the bot, a consumer would have to click through more than 200 sites to collect the same information.

However, eBay, the biggest Web auction site, sued Bidder's Edge seeking to prevent its bots from trolling eBay's site without prior approval. The auction site argued that the bots take up valuable bandwidth the firm should have the right to use for its own purposes. As the company's lawyer argued, bots are "like 100 people in a store, taking pictures and interfering with the regular customers." The trial judge agreed with

eBay's argument, ruling that Bidder's Edge had violated eBay's "fundamental property right to exclude others from its computer system."

Many other online retailers applauded the ruling. As the chairwoman of Shop.org, a trade group of online retailers, points out, "Most don't like to be compared on price alone." On the other hand, opponents argue that if bots must obtain permission from all sites they enter and/or pay for the information they collect, their usefulness to the consumer will be severely compromised and it will be much more difficult for them to find the best deal. As an opposing lawyer argues, "Property laws weren't meant to be applied to something as ambiguous as cyberspace." And even if the doctrines are applied, he argues, trespass laws are often suspended for the common good.

The initial ruling will undoubtedly be appealed through higher courts, and at this writing it is too early to tell how the issues will ultimately be resolved. One thing that is clear, however, is that the question of who owns the rights to product information on the Web will take many forms—and be the subject of many related court cases—for years into the future.

Source: Daniel Roth, "Meet eBay's Worst Nightmare," Fortune, June 26, 2000, pp. 199–206.

Ethical Perspectives

These mini-cases highlight ethical issues that commonly arise in marketing management.

KEY OBSERVATION

Five interactive competitive forces collectively determine an industry's long-term attractiveness—present competitors, potential competitors, the bargaining power of suppliers, the bargaining power of buyers, and the threat of substitute products.

adopted to be succe
of an industry's a
Porter's seminal wo
The strength of
and, over time, with
forces are present
King versus McDon

Key Observations

Highlight critical information and crucial questions throughout each chapter.

 Government Deregulation
out much of the world have bec
ciencies, restricts entry by new
United States, airlines, trucking
deregulated. Markets are also b
many of the developing countrie
technological innovation.

Global Perspective and Internet Icons

Identify global examples as well as effective Internet marketing for both new and economic marketers.

 manufactured goods for loc
countries have created grow
home repair, and home m
homes.[4] Demographic trenc
keting programs targeted a

Take-aways

End-of-chapter bulleted points review the most important "lessons learned" from each chapter.

TAKE-AWAYS

- Decisions about product design—including product features, brand names, related services, and warranties, for both goods and services—are among the most

critical in differentiating one's product from others to achieve competitive advantage. Factors to consider in making product decisions are provided in this chapter.

Supplements

Online Learning Center

Favorite cases and supplementary readings selected by the authors can be found at www.mhhe.com/mullins05.

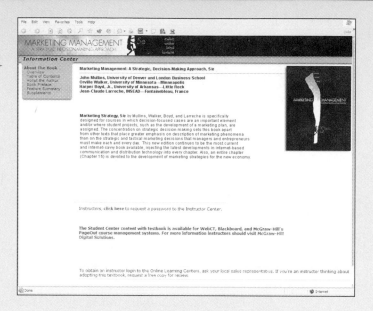

Instructor's Resource CD-ROM

The author-prepared instructor package provides everything a new or experienced marketing management instructor needs to hit the ground running.

Instructor's Manual

Contents include PowerPoint slides, test bank, web-based Discussion questions, and videos.

SECTION ONE

THE ROLE OF MARKETING IN DEVELOPING SUCCESSFUL BUSINESS STRATEGIES

CHAPTER 1   The Marketing
             Management Process

CHAPTER 2   The Marketing
             Implications of Corporate
             and Business Strategies

CHAPTER ONE

The Marketing Management Process

RedEnvelope—Marketing Upscale Gifts Online[1]

IN 1997 TWO RECENT MBA GRADUATES started a company called 911Gifts. The firm combined a website and a toll-free customer service center with gifts provided by two established merchants to cater to last-minute crisis shoppers. Although the new company attracted gift-givers, it also had some weaknesses: The company name, with its connotation of wailing ambulances, turned off many potential customers; the firm's suppliers provided an uninspired assortment of gifts; and a lack of capital inhibited the company's ability to grow. As a result, by early 1999 the firm was treading water. The site had managed only about $1 million in sales the previous year. Consequently, the owners decided to reinvent the company.

A New Mission and Strategy

The owners' first move was to hire a marketing-savvy chief executive officer. They attracted Hilary Billings, a 36-year-old manager, away from Williams-Sonoma where she had successfully developed the firm's Pottery Barn catalog operation.

After analyzing 911Gifts' strengths and weaknesses, she crafted a new mission and competitive strategy for the company. Instead of positioning itself as a center for emergency gifts, the firm would aim for upscale elegance. Further, it would try to broaden the definition of gift-giving opportunities. "Most online retailers are inherently self-purchase," Ms. Billings says. They "repurpose themselves just before Christmas as gift companies. There's a big difference between that and a company that thinks only about gifts."

Within six weeks of becoming CEO, Ms. Billings had developed marketing and business plans detailing how the firm would accomplish its new strategic mission and had hired the core of a new management team. She then made the rounds of Silicon Valley's venture capitalists with a slide show detailing the company's new plans and subsequently obtained $21 million in new financing from Sequoia Capital and $10 million from Weston Presidio in exchange for approximately a one-third ownership of the company.

The New Marketing Plan

The Target Market Consistent with the firm's new strategic mission, it targeted its marketing efforts at a more selective segment of potential customers. The new target market was similar to the one Ms. Billings knew from her days at Williams-Sonoma: high income (over $85,000 per year), well-educated professionals, including both men and women. The focus was also on people who were connected to the Internet and had a history of buying online.

To understand the needs and preferences of the firm's target customers, managers did a little qualitative marketing research, informally interviewing some prospective customers and analyzing past sales patterns. But initially the firm relied more heavily on the customer knowledge its managers had gained through past experience. "We talked about our [target] customer in a very intimate way," one manager recalls. "What kind of clothes they wore, what kind of car they drove. We put up a poster labeled 'him' and 'her' and we'd put Post-it Notes under each with products we thought they'd want to buy."

The New Product Line and Company Brand

Armed with information and intuition concerning the desires of the target market, company managers set about upgrading the product line. A variety of suppliers were contracted to provide products that reflected a high-quality, upscale point of view: things such as amber heart necklaces, old-fashioned thermometers, and seven stalks of bamboo—an Asian symbol of good luck—in a crystal vase for $46. The firm also partnered with suppliers to develop its first wave of exclusive merchandise: a series of gift baskets that might be described as "lifestyle kits." For instance, for fishing fanatics they developed a fishing creel filled with 12 hand-cut fish-shaped cookies for $48.

Another criterion the firm used to reorganize its product offerings was a high gross margin. Most of the firm's products carry margins of 50 percent or more, a necessary offset for lavish spending on customer service, which Ms. Billings says is unavoidable. "You have to own your customer's experience—and that comes at a price." About half of the 450 stock keeping units (SKUs) that 911Gifts had been selling were dropped, and more than 300 items were added.

To simplify a customer's search for the perfect gift, the company also redesigned its website. The new website allowed customers to navigate through the offerings by type of recipient, by gift-giving occasion, or by product category.

Finally, to more clearly reflect the firm's new upscale positioning, the company name was changed to RedEnvelope. The name derives from an Asian custom of marking special occasions by giving cash or small presents enclosed in a red envelope. It also suggested a distinctive packaging approach: all RedEnvelope gifts are delivered in a red gift box with a hand-tied bow.

Advertising and Promotion

With only a few weeks to go before the peak holiday selling season, RedEnvelope decided to devote a third of its new capital to advertising aimed at building customer awareness of the site. Rather than costly TV ads, the firm concentrated its money on a series of print ads to be run in newspapers and magazines, such as the *New York Times,* with readerships similar to RedEnvelope's target market. The company also paid to establish partnerships with a number of online hubs such as America Online, web portals like Yahoo! and Excite, and a select group of more narrowly focused websites such as iVillage.com. It devoted $2 million to these partnerships—paid for through either a flat fee or a percentage of sales—for a simple reason: "To be where people are shopping online means being on the portals," says RedEnvelope's vice president for business development.

Distribution and Order Fulfillment

RedEnvelope owns its own inventory, marketing, systems management, and customer service operations. But it does not yet have sufficient capital to develop its own physical logistics and order fulfillment operation. Consequently, the company contracted with ComAlliance, a fulfillment firm in Ohio, to provide warehouse space and everything that goes with it, including the workers expected to produce scads of smartly wrapped packages. The ComAlliance facility is located at the end of an Airborne Express runway. Thus, merchandise that leaves the warehouse by 2 A.M. can be in the air by 4:30 and to its destination by noon. This setup allowed RedEnvelope to make a promise that was the core of its early brand-building efforts: Christmas Eve delivery of gifts ordered by midnight on December 23.

Customer Feedback

Once the site was up and running, managers were able to track purchases hourly and quickly reformulate the product mix. For example, a line of wines was not selling as quickly as expected, generating only six purchases an hour. It was replaced with a Zen fountain that sold reliably at a rate of one every five minutes.

The Results

RedEnvelope's new management team brought the new operation online 60 days before Christmas in 1999. In two months the company shipped 20,000 packages and generated more revenue than the firm had managed in the preceding two years. Its Web alliances and ads were particularly effective. Most important, the firm lived up to its promises. It filled 98 percent of its orders accurately, shipped 99 percent of its packages on time, and only 2 percent of recipients wanted to return their gifts.

On the minus side, during the first two months of its existence the company shelled out nearly $4 in marketing for every $1 in gross sales. But as awareness of the firm's brand began to grow within its target market, RedEnvelope was able to reduce its heavy media advertising budget and lower the cost of acquiring each new customer to only $30, far below the $55 thought to be average for online retailers. And while many dot.coms went bust during the first years of the new century, RedEnvelope continued to grow, reaching $50 million in sales—and even managing a profit—by the end of 2001.

Marketing Challenges Addressed in Chapter 1

The activities of RedEnvelope's managers as they worked to redefine the company's marketing plan clearly demonstrate that marketing involves decisions crucial to the success of every organization, whether large or small, profit or nonprofit, manufacturer, retailer, or service firm. The CEO of a start-up such as RedEnvelope must decide what goods or services to sell, to whom, with what features and benefits, at what price, and so on. A chief financial officer for a large multinational corporation must market the merits of the company to the capital markets to obtain the resources needed for continued growth. The executive director of a nonprofit community agency must pursue the resources necessary for the agency to achieve its mission, whether those resources come from fees for the services it delivers or from grants and contributions. And all of those managers must market their ideas for improving their organizations' prospects and performance to their colleagues inside the firm as well as to customers, suppliers, strategic partners, and prospective employees. Thus, most managers engage in tasks involving marketing decisions virtually every day.

This book provides prospective managers and entrepreneurs with the marketing tools, perspectives, and analytical frameworks they'll need to play an effective role in the marketing life and overall strategic development of their organizations, regardless of whether or not they occupy formal marketing jobs. Chapter 1 addresses a number of broad but important questions all managers must resolve in their own minds: Are marketing decisions important? Does marketing create value for customers and shareholders? What constitutes effective marketing practice? Who does what in marketing and how much does it cost? And finally, what decisions go into the development of a strategic marketing program for a particular good or service and how can those decisions be summarized in an action plan?

Why Are Marketing Decisions Important?

The improved performance of RedEnvelope following the retooling of its strategic marketing plan illustrates the importance of good marketing decisions in today's business organizations. And according to many managers and expert observers around the world, a strong customer focus and well-conceived and executed marketing strategies will be even more crucial for the success of most organizations as the global marketplace becomes more crowded and competitive.[2]

The importance of marketing in a company's ongoing success can be better appreciated when you consider the activities marketing embraces. Marketing attempts to measure and anticipate the needs and wants of a group of customers and respond with a flow of need-satisfying goods and services. Accomplishing this requires the firm to

- Target those customer groups whose needs are most consistent with the firm's resources and capabilities.
- Develop products and/or services that meet the needs of the target market better than competitors.
- Make its products and services readily available to potential customers.
- Develop customer awareness and appreciation of the value provided by the company's offerings.
- Obtain feedback from the market as a basis for continuing improvement in the firm's offerings.
- Work to build long-term relationships with satisfied and loyal customers.

The most important characteristic of marketing as a business function is its focus on customers and their needs. This is a focus that all managers—not just marketers—need to adopt to ensure their organizations can build and sustain a healthy "top line."

The Importance of the Top Line

In the financial markets it is a company's bottom line—its profitability—that is most important. In the long run, all firms—even Internet start-ups—must make a profit to survive. But as the managers at RedEnvelope are well aware, there can never be a positive bottom line—nor financing, employees, or anything else—without the ability to build and sustain a healthy top line: sales revenue. As a wise observer once said, nothing happens until somebody sells something. Or to paraphrase management guru Peter Drucker, everything a company does internally is a cost center. The only *profit* center is a customer whose check doesn't bounce.

That is why the customer focus inherent in the marketing function is important. When properly implemented, a customer focus enables firms to enjoy success by exploiting changes in the marketplace, by developing products and services that have superiority over what is currently available, and by taking a more focused and integrated cross-functional

KEY OBSERVATION

A customer focus enables firms to enjoy success by exploiting changes in the marketplace, by developing products and services that have superiority over what is currently available, and by taking a more focused and integrated cross-functional approach to their overall operations.

approach to their overall operations. RedEnvelope, for example, started down the road to bottom line success by developing a unique and appealing line of gift products and backing them up with a user-friendly website and quick and reliable delivery. All the firm's activities are focused on satisfying its target market because, as Hilary Billings points out, "Success . . . lies in creating a memorable experience for the customer."[3]

Marketing Creates Value by Facilitating Exchange Relationships

While we have described marketing activities from an individual organization's perspective, marketing also plays an important role in the broader context of the global economy. It helps facilitate exchange relationships among people, organizations, and nations.

Marketing is a social process involving the activities necessary to enable individuals and organizations to obtain what they need and want through exchanges with others and to develop ongoing exchange relationships.[4]

Increased division and specialization of labor are some of the most important changes that occur as societies move from a primitive economy toward higher levels of economic development. But while increased specialization helps improve a society's overall standard of living, it leads to a different problem: Specialists are no longer self-sufficient. Artisans who specialize in making pots become very skilled and efficient at pot making, producing a surplus of pots, but they do not make any of the many other goods and services they need to survive and to improve their lifestyle. A society cannot reap the full benefits of specialization until it develops the means to facilitate the trade and exchange of surpluses among its members. Similarly, a nation cannot partake of the full range of goods and services available around the world or penetrate all potential markets for the economic output of its citizens unless exchanges can occur across national boundaries.

What Factors Are Necessary for a Successful Exchange Relationship?

Many exchanges are necessary for people and organizations to reap the benefits of the increased specialization and productivity that accompanies economic development. But such exchanges do not happen automatically, nor does every exchange necessarily lead to a mutually satisfying long-term relationship. The conditions for a successful exchange transaction can be met only after the parties themselves—or marketing intermediaries such as a wholesale distributor or a retailer like RedEnvelope—have performed several tasks. These include identifying potential exchange partners, developing offerings, communicating information, delivering products, and collecting payments. This is what marketing is all about. Before we take a closer look at specific marketing activities and how they are planned and implemented by marketing managers, we will discuss some terms and concepts in our definition of marketing and the conditions necessary for exchange. Let's examine the following questions:

1. Who are the *parties* involved in exchange relationships? Which organizations and people market things, and who are their customers?
2. Which *needs and wants* do parties try to satisfy through exchange, and what is the difference between the two?
3. *What* is exchanged?
4. How does exchange create *value?* Why is a buyer better off and more satisfied following an exchange?
5. How do potential exchange partners become a *market* for a particular good or service?

1. Who Markets and Who Buys? The Parties in an Exchange

Virtually every organization and individual with a surplus of *anything* engages in marketing activities to identify, communicate, and negotiate with potential exchange partners. Some are more aggressive—and perhaps more effective—in their efforts than others. When considering extensive marketing efforts aimed at stimulating and facilitating exchange, we think first of the activities of goods manufacturers (Intel, BMW, Sony), service producers (Air France, McDonald's, 20th Century Fox), and large retailers (Zara, Marks & Spencer, Wal-Mart).

However, museums, hospitals, theaters, universities, and other social institutions—whether for profit or nonprofit—also carry out marketing activities to attract customers, students, and donors. In the past, their marketing efforts were not very extensive or well organized. Now, increasing competition, changing customer attitudes and demographics,

What's old time-religion to do? At a time when the search for spiritual guidance is on the rise, angels, crystals, and shamans are more engaging to many people than organized religion.

Amid the competition for a piece of America's soul, denominations such as the Southern Baptists, Lutherans, and Roman Catholics are searching for ways to reach baby boomers—without seeming too evangelical. Those religions, along with the Mormon Church, which is starting its 50th advertising campaign, have introduced national public-service campaigns focused on children and families. They are also producing cable and network television specials that incorporate Christian themes in their story lines. The Lutherans of the Missouri Synod are even studying how best to use the Internet to get their spiritual message across.

The Lutheran Hour Ministries, which spends about half of its $20 million budget on marketing, produced an advertising campaign with themes about family, instead of specific religious messages. A print, radio,

and TV campaign that recently appeared in Chicago shows two children with the words "Drugs. Violence. Peer Pressure. The world is tough. Being a kid shouldn't be." The rest of the text includes a toll-free number to call to receive a free audio cassette and booklet on how to "talk with your kids about today's issues and the Christian values they need in today's world."

Some observers have expressed doubts about the ethics of the Lutheran Hour approach, fearing that it may be just a well-disguised attempt to identify prospects for recruiting new church members. It is true that a person who calls the toll-free number can request a visit from members of a local Lutheran church. But "there's no hit made [to recruit]. It's not a bait-and-switch," says Dr. Dale Meyer, speaker for the Lutheran Hour Ministries. "We know we have to be more sophisticated than just saying, 'Go to church on Sunday,' or being evangelistic."

Source: Fara Warner, "Churches Develop Marketing Campaigns," *The Wall Street Journal,* April 17, 1995, p. B4. Copyright 1995 Dow Jones & Co., Inc. Reprinted by permission of Dow Jones & Co., Inc. via the Copyright Clearance Center.

and rising costs have caused many nonprofit organizations to look to more extensive marketing efforts to solve their problems.[5] For example, some churches are using marketing techniques to address social problems, as well as to increase church attendance. But as discussed in Ethical Perspective 1.1, such efforts have also raised ethical questions.

Customers Both individuals and organizations seek goods and services obtained through exchange transactions. **Ultimate customers** buy goods and services for their own personal use or the use of others in their immediate household. These are called **consumer goods and services. Organizational customers** buy goods and services (1) for resale (as when RedEnvelope buys several gross of Zen Fountains for resale to individual consumers); (2) as inputs to the production of other goods or services (as when Toyota buys sheet steel to be stamped into car body parts); or (3) for use in the day-to-day operations of the organization (as when a university buys paper and printer cartridges). These are called **industrial goods and services.** Throughout this book we examine differences in the buying behavior of these two types of customers and the marketing strategies and programs relevant for each.[6]

2. Customer Needs and Wants

Needs are the basic forces that drive customers to take action and engage in exchanges. An unsatisfied **need** is a gap between a person's actual and desired states on some physical or psychological dimension. We all have *basic physical needs* critical to our survival, such as food, drink, warmth, shelter, and sleep. We also have *social and emotional needs* critical to our psychological well-being, such as *security, belonging, love, esteem,* and *self-fulfillment.* Those needs that motivate the consumption behavior of individuals are few and basic. They are not created by marketers or other social forces; they flow from our basic biological and psychological makeup as human beings.

Organizations also must satisfy needs to assure their survival and well-being. Shaped by the organization's strategic objectives, these needs relate to the resource inputs, capital equipment, supplies, and services necessary to meet those objectives.

Wants reflect a person's desires or preferences for specific ways of satisfying a basic need. Thus, a person wants particular products, brands, or services to satisfy a need. A person is thirsty and wants a Coke. A company needs office space and its top executives want an office at a prestigious address in midtown Manhattan.

Basic needs are relatively few, but people's many wants are shaped by social influences, their past history, and consumption experiences. Different people may have very different wants to satisfy the same need. Everyone *needs* to keep warm on cold winter nights, for instance. But some people *want* electric blankets, while others prefer old-fashioned down comforters.

This distinction between needs and wants helps put into perspective the charge that "marketers create needs," or that "marketers make people want things they don't need." Neither marketers nor any other single social force can create needs deriving from the biological and emotional imperatives of human nature. On the other hand, marketers—and many other social forces—influence people's wants. A major part of a marketer's job is to develop a new product or service and then to stimulate customer wants for it by convincing people it can help them better satisfy one or more of their needs.

Do Customers Always Know What They Want?   Some managers—particularly in high-tech firms—question whether a strong focus on customer needs and wants is always a good thing. They argue that customers cannot always articulate their needs and wants, in part because they do not know what kinds of products or services are technically possible. As Akio Morita, the late visionary CEO of Sony, once said:

> Our plan is to lead the public with new products rather than ask them what kind of products they want. The public does not know what is possible, but we do. So instead of doing a lot of marketing research, we refine our thinking on a product and its use and try to create a market for it by educating and communicating with the public.[7]

Others have pointed out that some very successful new products, such as the Chrysler minivan and Compaq's pioneering PC network server, were developed with little or no market research. On the other hand, some famous duds, like Ford's Edsel, New Coke, and McDonald's McLean low-fat hamburger, were developed with a great deal of customer input.[8]

The laws of probability dictate that some new products will succeed and more will fail regardless of how much is spent on marketing research. But the critics of a strong customer focus argue that paying too much attention to customer needs and wants can stifle innovation and lead firms to produce nothing but marginal improvements or line extensions of products and services that already exist. How do marketers respond to this charge?

While many consumers may lack the technical sophistication necessary to articulate their needs or wants for cutting-edge technical innovations, the same is not true for industrial purchasers. About half of all manufactured goods in most countries are sold to other organizations rather than individual consumers. Many high-tech industrial products are initiated at the urging of one or more major customers, developed with their cooperation (perhaps in the form of an alliance or partnership), and refined at customer beta sites.

As for consumer markets, one way to resolve the conflict between the views of technologists and marketers is to consider the two components of R&D. First there is basic research and then there is development—the conversion of technical concepts into actual salable products or services. Most consumers have little knowledge of scientific advancements and emerging technologies. Therefore, they usually don't—and probably shouldn't—play a role in influencing how firms allocate their basic research dollars.

Exhibit 1.1   Iomega Zip Drive—Helping Customers Store Their "Stuff"

In the late 1980s Iomega Corporation pioneered a nifty technological innovation. The Bernoulli Box was a portable, add-on storage unit for personal computers (PCs). Resembling a gray shoebox with a hole in the front, it could hold 150 megabytes of data on one disk—the equivalent of 107 floppy disks.

But by late 1993 the product was in trouble. Its $600 unit price and $100 disk price had proven too high to attract many individual PC users, the 52-page user's manual was hard for customers to decipher, and a competitor had already introduced a cheaper, faster alternative. Consequently, the firm reported an $18 million loss for the year and its stock price was at an all-time low.

The struggling company brought in a new CEO whose first priority was to convert the Bernoulli Box technology into a product line that would succeed in the marketplace. He appointed a cross-functional development team with representatives from engineering, marketing, operations, and other areas. The team, together with designers from Fitch PLC, an industrial design firm, started by interviewing more than 1,000 people who used computers in large companies, small organizations, or at home. Based on the information gathered, they created several generations of prototype products, which were further refined in response to reactions from additional samples of potential customers.

Based on the extensive customer feedback received, the development team streamlined the old Bernoulli Box, reducing its weight to about a pound so it could fit in a briefcase. To appeal to different segments of individual and business users, the team designed three models with different storage capacities and prices. All three were given bright colors to make them stand out from their environment and to signal that they were different from the "gray" competition. The most basic model—the Zip drive—held 100 megabytes and was initially priced at $200 per unit and $20 per disk (prices that have fallen substantially since) to appeal to individual PC owners for their personal use. Finally, a promotional campaign was crafted around the theme that Zip could help people organize their "stuff" to make it more accessible and portable.

Within three years of its introduction, more than 3 million Zip drives were sold. Consequently, Iomega's share price soared from $2 to $150 (before stock splits), and the firm made it to the top 50 of *Fortune*'s list of fastest-growing companies.

Source: "The Right Stuff." Reprinted with permission from *@issue: The Journal of Business and Design,* vol. 2, no. 2 (Fall 1996), pp. 6–11. Published by Corporate Design Foundation and sponsored by Sappi Fine Paper; "America's Fastest Growing Companies," *Fortune,* October 14, 1996, pp. 90–104. © 1996 Time, Inc. All rights reserved; Paul Eng, "What to Do When You Need More Space." Reprinted from the November 4, 1996 issue of *Business Week* by permission. Copyright The McGraw-Hill Companies.

However, a customer focus is critical to development. Someone within the organization must either have the insight and market experience (as was the case with Hilary Billings at RedEnvelope) or the substantial customer input necessary to decide what product to develop from a new technology, what benefits it will offer to customers, and whether customers will value those benefits sufficiently to make the product a commercial success. Iomega's experiences in developing the Zip drive into a commercially successful product—as described in Exhibit 1.1—illustrate this point.

Often, as was the case with the Zip drive, a new technology must be developed into a concrete product concept before consumers can react to it and its commercial potential can be assessed. In other cases, consumers can express their needs or wants for specific benefits even though they do not know what is technically feasible. They can tell you what problems they are having with current products and services and what additional benefits they would like from new ones. For instance, before Sony introduced the Walkman, few consumers would have asked for such a product because they were unfamiliar with the possibilities of miniaturization in the electronics industry. But if they had been asked whether they would buy a battery-driven product small enough to hook on their belt that could produce sound nearly as good as the full-sized stereo system in their home, many probably would have said, "Sure!"

A strong customer focus is not inconsistent with the development of technically innovative products, nor does it condemn a firm to concentrate on satisfying only current, articulated customer wants. More important, while firms can sometimes succeed in the short run even though they ignore customer desires, a strong customer focus usually pays big dividends in terms of market share and profit over the long haul,[9] as we'll see in the next chapter. As Iomega's CEO points out, "I don't know how else you can sell in a consumer marketplace without understanding product design and usage. You have to know what the end user wants."[10]

3. What Gets Exchanged? Products and Services

Products and services help satisfy a customer's need when they are acquired, used, or consumed. **Products** are essentially tangible physical objects (such as cars, watches, and computers) that provide a benefit. For example, a car provides transportation; a watch tells the time. **Services** are less tangible and, in addition to being provided by physical objects, can be provided by *people* (doctors, lawyers, architects), *institutions* (the Roman Catholic Church, the United Way), *places* (Walt Disney World, Paris), and *activities* (a contest or a stop-smoking program).

4. How Exchanges Create Value

Customers Buy Benefits, Not Products   As argued earlier, when people buy products to satisfy their needs, they are really buying the **benefits** they believe the products provide, rather than the products per se. For instance, you buy headache relief, not aspirin. The specific benefits sought vary among customers depending on the needs to be satisfied and the situations where products are used. Because different customers seek different benefits, they use different choice criteria and attach different importance to product features when choosing models and brands within a product category. (This is diagrammed in Exhibit 1.2.) For example, a car buyer with strong needs for social acceptance and esteem might seek a socially prestigious automobile. Such a buyer would be likely to attach great importance to criteria relating to social image and engineering sophistication such as a high-powered motor, European-road-car styling, all-leather interior, and a state-of-the-art sound system.

Exhibit 1.2

CUSTOMERS BUY BENEFITS, NOT PRODUCTS

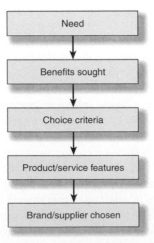

Keep in mind, too, that services offered by the seller can also create benefits for customers by helping them reduce their costs, obtain desired products more quickly, or use those products more effectively. Such services are particularly important for satisfying organizational buyers. For example, a few years ago the Massachusetts Institute of Technology discovered that it was doing business with about 20,000 vendors of office and laboratory supplies each year. To improve the efficiency of its purchasing system, MIT developed a computerized catalog that staff members can access via the school's intranet. It then formed alliances with two main suppliers—Office Depot Inc. and VWR Corp.— who won the bulk of MIT's business by promising to deliver superior service. Both firms deliver purchases within a day or two right to the purchaser's desk rather than to a building's stockroom.[11]

Product Benefits, Service, and Price Determine Value

A customer's estimate of a product's or service's benefits and capacity to satisfy specific needs and wants determines the value he or she will attach to it. Generally, after comparing alternative products, brands, or suppliers, customers choose those they think provide the most need-satisfying benefits per dollar. Thus, **value** is a function of intrinsic product features, service, and price, and it means different things to different people.[12]

Customers' estimates of products' benefits and value are not always accurate. For example, after buying an air-conditioning installation for its premises, a company may find that the product's cost of operation is higher than expected, its response time to changes in the outside temperature is slow, and the blower is not strong enough to heat or cool remote areas in the building.

A customer's ultimate *satisfaction* with a purchase, then, depends on whether the product actually lives up to expectations and delivers the anticipated benefits. This is why customer services—particularly those occurring *after* a sale, such as delivery, installation, operating instruction, and repair—are often critical for maintaining satisfied customers.

Also it is essential that companies handle customer complaints effectively. The average business never hears from 96 percent of its dissatisfied customers. This is unfortunate, for 50 percent of those who complain would do business with the company again if their complaints were handled satisfactorily—95 percent if the complaints were resolved quickly.[13]

The Value of Long-Term Customer Relationships

Firms have traditionally focused on the individual transaction with a customer as the fruition of their marketing efforts. But as global markets have become increasingly competitive and volatile, many firms have turned their attention to building a continuing long-term *relationship* between the organization and the customer as the ultimate objective of a successful marketing strategy. They are taking action to increase **lifetime customer value**—the present value of a stream of revenue that can be produced by a customer over time. For an automobile manufacturer, for instance, the lifetime value of a first-time car buyer who can be kept satisfied and loyal to the manufacturer—buying all future new cars from the same company—is well over a million dollars.

KEY OBSERVATION

Many firms have turned their attention to building a continuing long-term relationship between the organization and the customer as the ultimate objective of a successful marketing strategy.

Throughout this book we will discuss marketing decisions and activities geared to increasing the satisfaction and loyalty—and therefore the lifetime value—of customers. While such activities can add to a company's marketing costs, they can also produce big dividends, not only in terms of long-term revenues and market share, but also in terms of profitability. The reason is simple: It costs more to attract a new customer than to keep an existing one.[14] To persuade a customer to leave a competitor and buy your product or service instead usually takes either a financial inducement (a lower price or special promotional deal) or an extensive and convincing communication program (advertising or sales

Exhibit 1.3

BIG PAYOFFS FROM KEEPING LOYAL CUSTOMERS

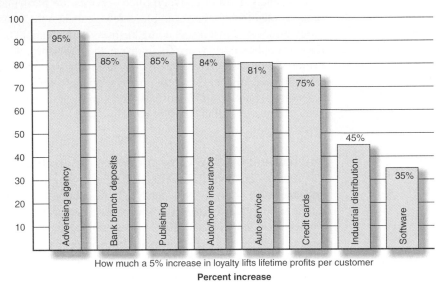

How much a 5% increase in loyalty lifts lifetime profits per customer

Percent increase

force effort), all of which are costly. Consequently, the increased loyalty that comes through developing long-term customer relationship translates into higher profits. Exhibit 1.3 shows how much a 5 percent improvement in customer loyalty is estimated to increase the lifetime profits per customer in a variety of goods and service industries.

5. Defining a Market

A **market** consists of *(a) individuals and organizations* who *(b)* are *interested and willing* to buy a particular product to obtain benefits that will satisfy a specific need or want, and who *(c)* have the *resources (time, money)* to engage in such a transaction. Some markets are sufficiently homogeneous that a company can practice undifferentiated marketing in them. That is, the company attempts to market a line of products using a single marketing program. But because people have different needs, wants, and resources, the entire population of a society is seldom a viable market for a single product or service. Also, people or organizations often seek different benefits to satisfy needs and wants from the same type of product (e.g., one car buyer may seek social status and prestige while someone else wants economical basic transportation).

The total market for a given product category thus is often fragmented into several distinct **market segments.** Each *segment* contains people who are relatively homogeneous in their needs, their wants, and the product benefits they seek. Also, each segment seeks a different set of benefits from the same product category.

Strategic marketing management involves a seller trying to determine the following points in an effort to define the target market:

1. Which customer needs and wants are currently not being satisfied by competitive product offerings.

Exhibit 1.4 Hanna Andersson—Pursuing a Segment of the Kids' Clothing Market

Socially conscious parents who like to shop from home to save time, but who want a knowledgeable salesperson all to themselves—this is the market segment targeted by Hanna Andersson, a Portland, Oregon, mail-order firm. The company specializes in endlessly washable, 100 percent cotton clothing for kids and in providing excellent service from highly trained phone representatives. The firm has also developed some innovative service policies to appeal to its target customers. Most innovative is the company's policy on returned clothing that no longer fits. Ship it back, and the firm credits 20 percent of the original price toward your next purchase. It then donates the returned clothes to charities and relief organizations, thus touching a desire in many consumers to do good works—even though they lack the time.

Source: Adapted from "The Fine Art of Niche Picking," by Jaclyn Fierman, *Fortune,* Special Issue, Autumn–Winter 1993, pp. 82–83.

2. How desired benefits and choice criteria vary among potential customers and how to identify the resulting segments by demographic variables such as age, sex, lifestyle, or some other characteristics.
3. Which segments to target, and which product offerings and marketing programs appeal most to customers in those segments.
4. How to position the product to differentiate it from competitors' offerings and give the firm a sustainable competitive advantage.

Exhibit 1.4 provides an example of a small firm that has been very successful in segmenting its market, targeting a precisely defined niche within that market, and positioning its products and services to appeal to the customers in that target segment.

What Does Effective Marketing Practice Look Like?

Exchange transactions—and particularly long-term relationships—do not happen automatically. They are the result of many decisions that must be planned and carried out by somebody. Sometimes a single organization has the necessary resources to plan and execute an entire marketing strategy by itself. Usually, though, a firm's marketing program involves cooperative efforts from a network of more specialized institutions: suppliers, wholesalers, retailers, advertising agencies, and the like. RedEnvelope's marketing program, for instance, relies heavily on products supplied by a number of manufacturers or wholesale merchants, advertising developed and placed by an ad agency, warehouse and fulfillment facilities provided by ComAlliance, delivery by Airborne Express, and access to potential customers via partnerships with various Web portals. In some cases, major customers may be involved in shaping and executing parts of a firm's marketing program, such as new product development and testing.

Regardless of who is involved, we refer to the entire sequence of analyses, decisions, and activities involved in planning, carrying out, and evaluating a strategic marketing program as the marketing management process. We take a more detailed look at this process—and at the roles of different functional managers and marketing institutions in planning and executing the activities involved—next.

Marketing Management—a Definition

Our discussion suggests that marketing management occurs whenever one party has something it would like to exchange with another. Marketing management is the process that

Exhibit 1.5

THE MARKETING MANAGEMENT PROCESS

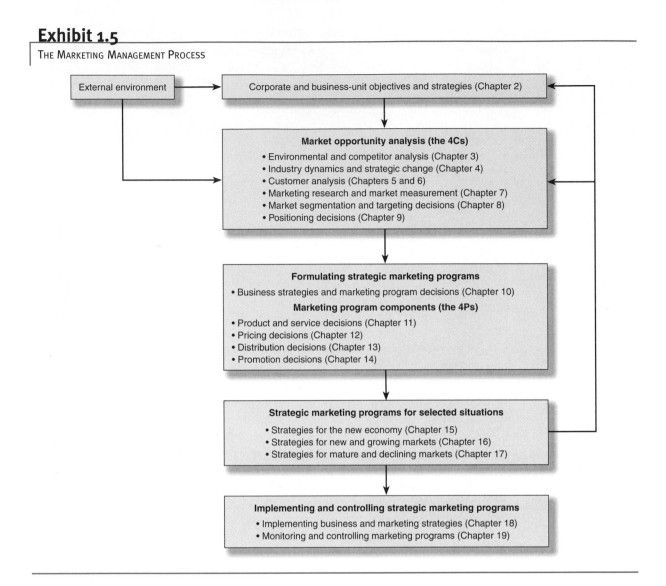

helps make such exchanges happen. More specifically, **marketing management** is the process of analyzing, planning, implementing, coordinating, and controlling programs involving the conception, pricing, promotion, and distribution of products, services, and ideas designed to create and maintain beneficial exchanges with target markets for the purpose of achieving organizational objectives.

Exhibit 1.5 diagrams the major decisions and activities involved in the marketing management process, and it also serves as the organizational framework for the rest of this book. For that reason, it is important to note the basic focus of this framework and the sequence of events within it.

A Decision-Making Focus   The framework has a distinct decision-making focus. Planning and executing an effective marketing program involves many interrelated decisions about what to do, when to do it, and how. Those decisions are the major focus of the rest of this book. Every chapter details decisions that must be made and actions taken with respect to a specific piece of a strategic marketing program and provides the analytical tools and frameworks you'll need to make those decisions intelligently.

Analyzing the 4Cs   A substantial amount of analysis of customers, competitors, and the company itself occurs *before* decisions are made concerning specific components of the marketing program. This reflects our view that successful marketing management decisions usually rest on an objective, detailed, and evidence-based understanding of the market and the environmental context. Of course, most marketing strategies never get implemented in quite the same way as they were drawn on paper. Adjustments are made and new activities undertaken in response to rapid changes in customer demands, competitive actions, or shifting economic conditions. But a thorough and ongoing analysis of the market and the broader environment enables managers to make such adjustments in a well-reasoned and consistent way rather than by the seat of the pants.

The analysis necessary to provide the foundation for a good strategic marketing plan should focus on four elements of the overall environment that may influence a given strategy's appropriateness and ultimate success: (1) the *company's* internal resources, capabilities, and strategies; (2) the environmental *context*—such as broad social, economic, and technology trends—in which the firm will compete; (3) the needs, wants, and characteristics of current and potential *customers*; and (4) the relative strengths and weaknesses of *competitors* and trends in the competitive environment. Marketers refer to these elements as **the 4Cs,** and they are described in more detail below.

Integrating Marketing Plans with the Company's Strategies and Resources

Many firms—particularly larger organizations with multiple divisions or business units—develop a hierarchy of interdependent strategies. Each strategy is formulated at varying levels within the firm and deals with a different set of issues. For example, IBM has reduced its focus and the proportion of resources it devotes to its traditional computer hardware businesses. Instead, it is seeking future growth and profits by investing heavily in developing information engineering, software, and e-commerce consulting services aimed at helping business clients integrate their old corporate databases into new online systems.[15] This change in emphasis reflects IBM's new **corporate strategy.** This level of strategy reflects the company's mission and provides direction for decisions about what businesses it should pursue, how it should allocate its available resources, and its growth policies.

Iomega's heavy investment in R&D and consumer research to develop a new generation of technically superior, attractively designed, but reasonably priced data storage products (as described in Exhibit 1.2) represents part of a **business-level (or competitive) strategy** that addresses how the business intends to compete in its industry. Iomega sought to regain a competitive advantage by offering cutting-edge technology, innovative design, and superior customer value.

Finally, interrelated decisions about market segments, product line, advertising appeals and media, prices, and partnerships with suppliers, Web portals, and fulfillment and transportation companies all reflect RedEnvelope's **marketing strategy.** This is the company's plan for pursuing its objectives within the upscale segment of the online gift market. Because RedEnvelope is a small startup with only a single product line, its business-level competitive strategy and its marketing strategy substantially overlap. This is often the case with smaller organizations.

A major part of the marketing manager's job is to monitor and analyze customers' needs and wants and the emerging opportunities and threats posed by competitors and trends in the external environment. Therefore, because all levels of strategy must consider such factors, marketers often play a major role in providing inputs to—and influencing the development of—corporate and business strategies. Conversely, general managers and senior managers in other functions need a solid understanding of marketing in order to craft effective organizational strategies.

Marketing managers also bear the primary responsibility for formulating and implementing strategic marketing plans for individual product-market entries or product lines. But as the above discussion suggests, such strategic marketing programs are not created in a vacuum. Instead, the marketing objectives and strategy for a particular product-market entry must be achievable with the company's available resources and capabilities and consistent with the direction and allocation of resources inherent in the firm's corporate and business-level strategies. In other words, there should be a good fit—or internal consistency—among the elements of all three levels of strategy. Chapter 2 describes in more detail the components of corporate and business strategies and the roles marketers and other functional managers play in shaping the strategic direction of their organizations and business units.

KEY OBSERVATION

The marketing objectives and strategy for a particular product-market entry must be achievable with the company's available resources and capabilities and consistent with the direction and allocation of resources inherent in the firm's corporate and business-level strategies.

Market Opportunity Analysis

A major factor in the success or failure of strategies at all three levels is whether the strategy elements are consistent with the realities of the firm's external environment. Thus, the next step in developing a strategic marketing plan is to monitor and analyze the opportunities and threats posed by factors outside the organization. This is an ongoing responsibility for marketing managers.

Environmental and Competitor Analysis   To understand potential opportunities and threats over the long term, marketers must first monitor and analyze broad trends in the economic and social environment. These include demographic, economic, technological, political/legal, and social/cultural developments. Of particular concern within an organization's economic environment are the actions and capabilities of its current and potential competitors. Chapter 3 identifies a number of macroenvironmental factors marketing managers should pay attention to. It discusses methods for monitoring, analyzing, and perhaps even influencing the impact of those factors on the future performance of their product-market entries.

Industry Dynamics and Strategic Change   The competitive and market environments of an industry are not static, but can change dramatically over time. For example, Iomega's initial product, the Bernoulli Box, lost much of its early momentum when SyQuest entered the market with a faster, cheaper alternative. Chapter 4 explores the competitive dynamics of an industry, emphasizing how competition and customers' buying patterns are likely to change as an industry or product-market moves through various life-cycle stages.

Customer Analysis   The primary purpose of marketing activities is to facilitate and encourage exchange transactions with potential customers. One of a marketing manager's major responsibilities is to analyze the motivations and behavior of present and potential customers. What are their needs and wants? How do those needs and wants affect the product benefits they seek and the criteria they use in choosing products and brands? Where do they shop? How are they likely to react to specific price, promotion, and service policies? To answer such questions, a marketing manager must have some notion of the mental processes customers go through when making purchase decisions and of the psychological and social factors that influence those processes. Chapter 5 discusses the processes and influences that shape consumers' buying behavior. Because some aspects of the purchase process differ for organizations, Chapter 6 examines the buying behavior of institutional customers.

Marketing Research and Market Measurements   Marketing managers must obtain objective information about potential customers, the satisfaction and loyalty of current customers, the firm's wholesale and retail partners, and the strengths and weaknesses of competitors. Consequently, even relatively small organizations such as Iomega and RedEnvelope often expend substantial financial and personnel resources studying the needs and preferences of potential customers, developing new products, and tracking the sales patterns and satisfaction of existing customers and channel members.

If managers are to make informed decisions, however, research information must be converted into estimates of the sales volume and profit the firm might reasonably expect a particular marketing program to generate within a given market segment. Chapter 7 discusses techniques and methods for collecting and analyzing marketing research information and for measuring the market potential and likely sales volumes of particular market segments. The specific research methods that marketing managers use to make decisions about elements of a marketing program—such as what price to charge or which advertising media to use—will be examined in more detail in chapters dealing with each of these program decisions.

Market Segmentation, Targeting, and Positioning Decisions   Not all customers with similar needs seek the same products or services to satisfy those needs. Their purchase decisions may be influenced by individual preferences, personal characteristics, social circumstances, and so forth. On the other hand, customers who do purchase the same product may be motivated by different needs, seek different benefits from the product, rely on different sources of information about products, and obtain the product from different distribution channels. Thus, one of the manager's most crucial tasks is to divide customers into **market segments**—distinct subsets of people with similar needs, circumstances, and characteristics that lead them to respond in a similar way to a particular product or service offering or to a particular strategic marketing program. Chapter 8 examines dimensions for measurement and analytical techniques that can help managers identify and define market segments in both consumer and organizational markets.

After defining market segments and exploring customer needs and the firm's competitive strengths and weaknesses within segments, the manager must decide which segments represent attractive and viable opportunities for the company, that is, on which segments to focus a strategic marketing program. Iomega, for instance, targeted two market segments with its new line of data storage drives. The Zip drive was aimed at individual PC owners for their personal use, while larger capacity and more expensive drives were aimed at organizational buyers. Chapter 8 discusses some of the considerations in *selecting a target segment*.

Finally, the manager must decide how to **position** the product or service offering within a target segment, that is, to design the product and its marketing program so as to emphasize attributes and benefits that appeal to customers in the target segment and at once distinguish the company's offering from those of competitors. Thus, RedEnvelope has positioned its offering as unique, high-quality, quickly delivered gifts for upscale buyers. Issues and analytical techniques involved in marketing positioning decisions are discussed in Chapter 9.

Formulating Strategic Marketing Programs

Designing an effective strategic marketing program for a product-market entry involves three interrelated sets of decisions:

1. The manager must set specific objectives to be accomplished within the target market, such as sales volume, market share, and profitability goals. Those objectives must be consistent with the firm's corporate and business-unit strategic objectives, yet specific enough to enable management to monitor and evaluate the product-market entry's performance over time.

2. The manager must decide on an overall marketing strategy to appeal to customers—and to gain a competitive advantage—in the target market. The strategy must be consistent with the firm's capabilities, its corporate and business-unit strategies, and the product-market objectives.

3. The manager must then make decisions about each element of the tactical marketing program used to carry out the strategy. These decisions must be internally consistent and integrated across all elements of the marketing program.

Specifying Marketing Objectives and Strategies

The first step in developing a strategic marketing program is to specify the objectives and the overall marketing strategy of each target market. As we've mentioned, these are partly dictated by corporate and business-level objectives, strategies, and resources. RedEnvelope's decision to rely on a partnership with ComAlliance to perform its order fulfillment, for instance, was dictated in part by the firm's small size and limited financial resources. Similarly, the design of its product line, its advertising appeals and media selection, and its pricing policies were all shaped by the firm's competitive strategy of specializing in gifts for upscale buyers and by its objectives of building a loyal customer base and earning high margins as a route to eventual profitability. Chapter 10 describes a number of generic business-level competitive strategies and examines the way such strategies influence decisions about marketing objectives and programs, as well as the role other functional managers play in implementing those marketing programs.

Marketing Program Components

Dozens of specific tactical decisions must be made in designing a strategic marketing program for a product-market entry. These decisions fall into four categories of major marketing variables that a manager has some ability to control over the short term. Often called **the 4 Ps,** the controllable elements of a marketing program are the **product offering** (including the breadth of the product line, quality levels, and customer services); **price; promotion** (advertising, sales promotion, and salesforce decisions); and **place** (or distribution). Because decisions about each element should be consistent and integrated with decisions concerning the other three, the four components are often referred to as the *marketing mix.*

> The **marketing mix** is the combination of controllable marketing variables that a manager uses to carry out a marketing strategy in pursuit of the firm's objectives in a given target market.

Exhibit 1.6 outlines some of the decisions that must be made within each of the four elements of the marketing mix. Chapters 11 through 14 discuss in more detail the various methods and criteria for making decisions about each of these program components.

Formulating Strategic Marketing Programs for Specific Situations

The strategic marketing program for a product should reflect market demand and the competitive situation within the target market. But demand and competitive conditions change over time as a product moves through its life cycle. Therefore, different marketing strategies are typically more appropriate and successful for different market conditions and at different life cycle stages. Chapter 15 explores marketing strategies for the rapidly

Exhibit 1.6

DECISIONS WITHIN THE FOUR ELEMENTS OF THE MARKETING MIX

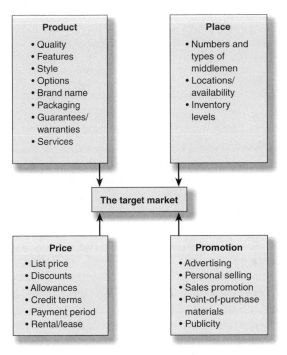

Product
- Quality
- Features
- Style
- Options
- Brand name
- Packaging
- Guarantees/ warranties
- Services

Place
- Numbers and types of middlemen
- Locations/ availability
- Inventory levels

The target market

Price
- List price
- Discounts
- Allowances
- Credit terms
- Payment period
- Rental/lease

Promotion
- Advertising
- Personal selling
- Sales promotion
- Point-of-purchase materials
- Publicity

evolving conditions being created by e-commerce and the new economy. Chapter 16 examines marketing strategies for introducing new entries and for strengthening a product's competitive position as its market grows. Chapter 17 then discusses the marketing strategies a firm might adopt in mature and declining product-markets.

Implementation and Control of the Marketing Program

A final critical determinant of a strategy's success is the firm's ability to implement it effectively. And this depends on whether the strategy is consistent with the resources, the organizational structure, the coordination and control systems, and the skills and experience of company personnel.[16] Managers must design a strategy to fit the company's existing resources, competencies, and procedures—or try to construct new structures and systems to fit the chosen strategy. For example, Iomega's attempt to develop a new generation of data storage products would not have been so successful without its substantial investments in R&D and marketing research and a team structure that encouraged communication and cooperation across functional areas throughout the development process. Chapter 18 discusses the structural variables, planning and coordination processes, and personnel and corporate culture characteristics related to the successful implementation of various marketing strategies.

The final tasks in the marketing management process are determining whether the strategic marketing program is meeting objectives and adjusting the program when performance is disappointing. This evaluation and control process provides feedback to managers and serves as a basis for a market opportunity analysis in the next planning period.

Chapter 19 examines ways to evaluate marketing performance and develop contingency plans when things go wrong.

The Marketing Plan—a Blueprint for Action

The results of the various analyses and marketing program decisions discussed above should be summarized periodically in a detailed formal marketing plan.[17]

> A **marketing plan** is a written document detailing the current situation with respect to customers, competitors, and the external environment and providing guidelines for objectives, marketing actions, and resource allocations over the planning period for either an existing or a proposed product or service.

While some firms—particularly smaller ones—do not bother to write their marketing plans, most organizations believe that "unless all the key elements of a plan are written down . . . there will always be loopholes for ambiguity or misunderstanding of strategies and objectives, or of assigned responsibilities for taking action."[18] This suggests that even small organizations with limited resources can benefit from preparing a written plan, however brief. Written plans also provide a concrete history of a product's strategies and performance over time, which aids institutional memory and helps educate new managers assigned to the product. Written plans are necessary in most larger organizations because a marketing manager's proposals must usually be reviewed and approved at higher levels of management and because the approved plan provides the benchmark against which the manager's performance will be judged. Finally, the discipline involved in producing a formal plan helps ensure that the proposed objectives, strategy, and marketing actions are based on rigorous analysis of the 4Cs and sound reasoning.

Because a written marketing plan is such an important tool for communicating and coordinating expectations and responsibilities throughout the firm, we will say more about it in Chapter 18 when we discuss the implementation of marketing programs in detail. But because the written plan attempts to summarize and communicate an overview of the marketing management process we have been examining, it is worthwhile to briefly examine the contents of such plans here.

Marketing plans vary in timing, content, and organization across companies. In general, marketing plans are developed annually; though planning periods for some big-ticket industrial products, such as commercial aircraft, may be longer, and in some highly volatile industries, such as telecommunications or e-commerce, they can be shorter. Plans typically follow a format similar to that outlined in Exhibit 1.7.

There are three major parts to the plan. First, the marketing manager details his or her assessment of the current situation. This is the homework portion of the plan where the manager summarizes the results of his or her analysis of current and potential customers, the company's relative strengths and weaknesses, the competitive situation, the major trends in the broader environment that may affect the product and, for existing products, past performance outcomes. This section typically also includes forecasts, estimates of sales potential, and other assumptions underlying the plan, which are especially important for proposed new products or services. Based on these analyses, the manager may also call attention to several key issues—major opportunities or threats that should be dealt with during the planning period.

The second part of the plan details the strategy for the coming period. This part usually starts by detailing the objectives (e.g., sales volume, market share, profits, customer satisfaction levels, etc.) to be achieved by the product or service during the planning period. It then outlines the overall marketing strategy, the actions associated with each of the 4 Ps

Exhibit 1.7

CONTENTS OF A MARKETING PLAN

Section	Content
I. Executive summary	Presents a short overview of the issues, objectives, strategy, and actions incorporated in the plan and their expected outcomes for quick management review.
II. Current situation and trends	Summarizes relevant background information on the market, competition and the macroenvironment, and trends therein, including size and growth rates for the overall market and key segments.
III. Performance review (for an existing product or service only)	Examines the past performance of the product and the elements of its marketing program (e.g., distribution, promotions, etc.).
IV. Key issues	Identifies the main opportunities and threats to the product that the plan must deal with in the coming year, and the relative strengths and weaknesses of the product and business unit that must be taken into account in facing those issues.
V. Objectives	Specifies the goals to be accomplished in terms of sales volume, market share, and profit.
VI. Marketing strategy	Summarizes the overall strategic approach that will be used to meet the plan's objectives.
VII. Action plans	This is the most critical section of the annual plan for helping to ensure effective implementation and coordination of activities across functional departments. It specifies • The **target market** to be pursued. • **What** specific actions are to be taken with respect to each of the 4 Ps. • **Who** is responsible for each action. • **When** the action will be engaged in. • **How** much will be budgeted for each action.
VIII. Projected profit-and-loss statement	Presents the expected financial payoff from the plan.
IX. Controls	Discusses how the plan's progress will be monitored; may present contingency plans to be used if performance falls below expectations or the situation changes.
X. Contingency plans	Describes actions to be taken if specific threats or opportunities materialize during the planning period.

necessary to implement the strategy, and the timing and locus of responsibility for each action.

Finally, the plan details the financial and resource implications of the strategy and the controls to be employed to monitor the plan's implementation and progress over the period. Some plans also specify some contingencies: how the plan will be modified if certain changes occur in the market, competitive, or external environments.

Who Does What?

Marketing Institutions

A strategic marketing program involves a large number of activities aimed at encouraging and facilitating exchanges and building relationships with customers. And all of those activities must be performed by somebody for exchanges to happen. One of the few eternal truths in marketing is that "you can eliminate the middlemen, but you can't eliminate their functions." Somebody has to gather information or feedback from customers concerning their needs and wants; use that information to design product or service offerings that will provide valued benefits; communicate the existence and benefits of the offering to the

Exhibit 1.8

WHAT MUST CHANGE HANDS TO COMPLETE AN EXCHANGE BETWEEN A BUYER AND A SELLER?

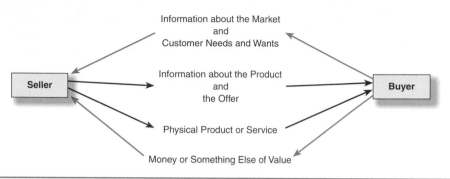

market; perform the storage, order fulfillment, and transportation activities necessary to make the product conveniently available to customers; finance purchases; collect payment; and resolve customer problems or complaints after the sale. The major flows of the physical product, payment, and information that occur during an exchange are summarized in Exhibit 1.8.

In a few cases, nearly all these activities are performed by a single organization and its employees. Such internal control of the full range of marketing functions and activities is referred to as **vertical integration.** Dell Computer's reliance on the Internet to attract customers and process orders together with a flexible manufacturing system that produces computers to order and minimizes finished inventories, and Canon's reliance on its own factories, salesforce, and distribution facilities to produce and market its copiers and printers are examples of highly integrated marketing organizations.

The majority of goods and services in most developed economies, however, are marketed through alliances or networks involving multiple institutions or middlemen. These networks are commonly referred to as **marketing channels** or **channels of distribution.** Each institution within the channel specializes in performing only a part of the activities or functions necessary to conduct exchanges with the end user. We will examine these institutions and the nature of their interactions with one another in more detail in Chapter 13. Marketing institutions fall into one of the following categories:

- **Merchant wholesalers** take title to the goods they sell and sell primarily to other resellers (retailers), industrial, and commercial customers, rather than to individual consumers.
- **Agent middlemen,** such as manufacturers' representatives and brokers, also sell to other resellers and industrial or commercial customers, but they do not take title to the goods they sell. They usually specialize in the selling function and represent client manufacturers on a commission basis.
- **Retailers** sell goods and services directly to final consumers for their personal, nonbusiness use.
- **Facilitating agencies,** such as advertising agencies, marketing research firms, collection agencies, railroads, and Web portals, specialize in one or more marketing functions on a fee-for-service basis to help their clients perform those functions more effectively and efficiently.

Who Pays the Cost of Marketing Activities—and Are They Worth It?

The final selling price of the product reflects the costs of performing the activities necessary for exchange transactions. Those costs vary widely across different products and customers. They account for a relatively high proportion of the price of frequently purchased consumer package goods such as cereals and cosmetics. Extensive transportation, storage, and promotion activities facilitate the millions of consumer purchases that occur every year. On average, roughly 50 percent of the retail price of such products is made up of marketing and distribution costs; one-half represents retailer margins, and the other half the marketing expenses of the manufacturer and wholesale middlemen.[19] On the other hand, marketing costs for nontechnical industrial goods, such as sheet steel or basic chemicals, are much lower because they are sold in large quantities directly to a small number of regular customers.

Though both individual and organizational customers pay for the marketing activities of manufacturers and their middlemen, they are still usually better off than if they were to undertake all the functions themselves. This is true for two reasons: First, the purchasing, storage, promotion, and selling activities of wholesalers and retailers allow customers to buy a wide variety of goods from a single source in one transaction, thereby increasing **transactional efficiency.** For example, a consumer may buy a week's groceries on a single trip to the supermarket (or perhaps even over the Internet from a home-delivery service) rather than engage in separate transactions with a butcher, a baker, and a variety of farmers or food processors. Thus, the number of exchanges necessary for a consumer to acquire a desired assortment of goods and services is reduced and efficiency is increased when middlemen are added to an economic system.

A second benefit of an extensive marketing system is that specialization of labor and economies of scale lead to **functional efficiency.** Manufacturers and their agents can perform the exchange activities more cheaply than can individual customers. A railroad, for instance, can ship a load of new tires from a plant in Akron to a wholesaler in Tucson more cheaply than an individual consumer in Arizona could transport them in the family minivan.

From the customer's viewpoint, then, the increased transactional and functional efficiency of exchange produced by members of the marketing system increases the value— the **utility/price** relationship—of goods and services. A product has greater utility for a potential customer when it can be purchased with a minimum of risk and shopping time (**possession utility**), at a convenient location (**place utility**), and at the time the customer is ready to use the product (**time utility**).

Room for Improvement in Marketing Efficiency

While the existence of specialized institutions in our economy's marketing system has greatly increased the efficiency and value of most exchange transactions from the customer's point of view, that does not mean the current system is nearly as efficient as it could be. Marketing is one of the few functional areas of business whose efficiency has not substantially improved in recent years. Two authorities estimate that, on average, manufacturing costs have declined from about 50 percent of total corporate costs after World War II to about 30 percent today through automation, flexible manufacturing systems, product redesign for manufacturing, just-in-time approaches, and so on. Similarly, they argue that the average costs of "management"—defined to include finance, accounting, human resources, and support functions like R&D—have fallen from about 30 percent to 20 percent as the result of downsizing, outsourcing, and process reengineering. On the other hand, they estimate that the percentage of corporate costs accounted for by marketing activities actually went up substantially over the same period.[20]

Of course, there are some good reasons why marketing costs have increased in recent years, including the greater intensity of global competition, the rapid pace of technological change, the fragmentation of the communications media, and many other factors.

Nevertheless, even modest improvements in marketing efficiency could produce dramatic cost reductions, increased profits, and improved customer value in many industries. The grocery industry alone believes it can cut $30 billion, or nearly 10 percent of its annual operating costs, by redesigning its logistics and distribution systems.[21] We will focus throughout this book on ways marketers are attempting to improve operational efficiency through (1) more effective use of telecommunications and information technologies, such as the World Wide Web, (2) the development of cooperative alliances with suppliers, middlemen, and ultimate customers, and (3) the search for new budgeting methods that are more clearly focused on improving cash flows and adding economic value.[22]

The Role of the Marketing Decision Maker

The title *marketing manager* is necessarily and intentionally vague because many people are directly involved with an organization's marketing activities. This can include people not formally located in a marketing or sales department or even within the company. The exact nature of the marketing manager's job will vary widely depending on the industry involved, the organization's structure, and its position in the managerial hierarchy.

While the marketing manager bears the primary responsibility for formulating and implementing a strategic marketing program for a product or service, a single marketing manager (1) seldom does all the analysis or makes all the decisions involved in such plans all alone and (2) almost never has the formal authority to demand that all the activities specified in the plan be carried out by subordinates exactly as they are written down.

Many marketing activities are usually contracted out to independent middlemen or facilitating agencies or are performed in concert with a firm's suppliers, major customers, or other organizational partners. A marketing manager has no formal authority over these outsiders. Thus, the development and nurturing of long-term relationships with suppliers, channel members, and major customers can do more than simply improve marketing efficiency; they can provide the information, advice, and cooperation necessary to devise and carry out successful marketing strategies.[23]

Even those marketing activities that are performed in-house are seldom all within the domain of the marketing department or under the authority of a single marketing executive. Implementing a marketing plan requires cooperation and coordination across many specialized functional areas. Marketing is—or should be—everybody's business. After all, delivering superior value to customers is the key to business success, and that superior value flows from a combination of well-designed products or services, produced with high quality; efficient operations that enable low costs and competitive prices; and reliable customer service. Creating value is a cross-functional endeavor, and marketing and nonmarketing executives alike must operate with a clear customer focus to make it happen.

KEY OBSERVATION

Creating value is a cross-functional endeavor, and marketing and nonmarketing executives alike must operate with a clear customer focus to make it happen.

Some Recent Developments Affecting Marketing Management

While many of the basic tasks involved in developing and implementing strategic marketing programs have remained unchanged for decades, recent developments in our economy and around the world have greatly changed the context in which those tasks are carried out and the information and tools that marketers have at their disposal. These developments include (1) the increased globalization of markets and competition, (2) the growth of the service sector of the economy and the importance of service in maintaining customer satisfaction and loyalty, (3) the rapid development of new information and communications technologies, and (4) the growing importance of relationships for improved coordination and increased efficiency of marketing programs and for capturing a larger portion of customers' lifetime value. Some recent impacts of these four developments on marketing management are briefly summarized below and will be continuing themes throughout this book.

Globalization

International markets account for a large and growing portion of the sales of many organizations. But while global markets represent promising opportunities for additional sales growth and profits, differences in market and competitive conditions across country boundaries can require firms to adapt their competitive strategies and marketing programs to be successful. Even when similar marketing strategies are appropriate for multiple countries, international differences in infrastructure, culture, legal systems, and the like often mean that one or more elements of the marketing program—such as product features, promotional appeals, or distribution channels—must be tailored to local conditions for the strategy to be effective.

Increased Importance of Service

A service can be defined as "any activity or benefit that one party can offer another that is essentially intangible and that does not result in the ownership of anything. Its production may or may not be tied to a physical product."[24] Service businesses such as airlines, hotels, restaurants, and consulting firms account for roughly two-thirds of all economic activity in the United States, and services are the fastest-growing sector of most other developed economies around the world. While many of the decisions and activities involved in marketing services are essentially the same as those for marketing physical goods, the intangible nature of many services can create unique challenges for marketers. We will discuss these challenges—and the tools and techniques firms have developed to deal with them—throughout this book.

As the definition suggests, services such as financing, delivery, installation, user training and assistance, and maintenance are often provided in conjunction with a physical product. Such ancillary services have become more critical to firms' continued sales and financial success in many product-markets. As markets have become crowded with global competitors offering similar products at ever-lower prices, the creative design and effective delivery of supplemental services has become a crucial means by which a company may differentiate its offering and generate additional benefits and value for customers. Those additional benefits, in turn, can justify higher prices and margins in the short term and help improve customer satisfaction, retention, and loyalty over the long term.[25] This is particularly true in organizational markets.

Information Technology

The computer revolution and related technological developments are changing the nature of marketing management in two important ways. First, new technologies are making it possible for firms to collect and analyze more detailed information about potential customers and their needs, preferences, and buying habits. Thus, it is now possible for many firms to identify and target smaller and more precisely defined market segments—sometimes segments consisting of only one or a few customers—and to customize product features, promotional appeals, prices, and financing arrangements to fit such segments.[26]

Exhibit 1.9

CATEGORIES OF E-COMMERCE

	BUSINESS	CONSUMER
Business	**Business-to-Business (B2B)** Examples: • Purchasing sites of Ford, Oracle, Cisco • Supply chain networks linking producers and distribution channel members, such as 3M and Wal-Mart	**Business-to-Consumer (B2C)** Examples: • E-tailers, such as E*Trade, Amazon, RedEnvelope • Producers' direct sales sites, such as Dell, American Airlines • Websites of traditional retailers, such as Sears, Lands' End
Consumer	**Consumer-to-Business (C2B)** Examples: • Sites that enable consumers to bid on unsold airline tickets and other goods and services, such as Priceline	**Consumer-to-Consumer (C2C)** Examples: • Auction sites, such as eBay, QXL

Source: Adapted from "A Survey of E-Commerce: Shopping Around the Web," *The Economist,* February 26, 2000, p. 11. © 2000 The Economist Newspaper Ltd. All rights reserved. Reprinted with permission. Further reproduction prohibited. www.economist.com

A second impact of information technology has been to open new channels for communications and transactions between suppliers and customers. As Exhibit 1.9 suggests, one simple way of categorizing these new channels is based on whether the suppliers and customers involved are organizations or individual consumers.

More than $600 billion in global sales were transacted over the World Wide Web in 2001.[27] Roughly 80 percent of those sales were business-to-business transactions, such as those in the upper-left quadrant of Exhibit 1.9. Many high-tech firms like Oracle Corp. and Cisco Systems, and even some low-tech companies such as General Motors, conduct all or a large portion of their purchasing activities over the Web. And many firms rely on their websites to communicate product information to potential customers, make sales, and deal with customer problems.

Perhaps even more important, though, new information and communications technologies are enabling firms to forge more cooperative and efficient relationships with their suppliers and distribution channel partners. For example, Procter & Gamble and 3M have formed alliances with major retailers—such as Kroger and Wal-Mart—to develop automatic restocking systems. Sales information from the retailer's checkout scanners is sent directly to the supplier's computers, which figure out automatically when to replenish each product and schedule deliveries direct to each of the retailer's stores. Such paperless exchanges reduce mistakes and billbacks, minimize inventory levels, improve cash flow, and increase customer satisfaction and loyalty.

In contrast, Internet sales from businesses to consumers (the upper-right quadrant in Exhibit 1.9) accounted for less than $120 billion in 2001. However, sales volumes of firms such as Amazon, Dell Computer, and RedEnvelope are expanding rapidly, and many traditional retailers are expanding their marketing efforts on the Web as well. Information available over the Internet is affecting consumer purchase patterns even when the purchases are made in traditional retail outlets. For instance, while fewer than 3 percent of car sales were actually made over the Web in 1999, an estimated 40 percent of all car buyers used the Web to compare prices or gather information about brands.[28]

Clearly, the Web is presenting marketers with new strategic options—as well as new competitive threats and opportunities—regardless of what or to whom they are selling. Therefore, we will devote all of Chapter 15 to marketing strategies for e-commerce, and discuss specific examples and their implications in every chapter.

Relationships across Functions and Firms

New information technologies and the ongoing search for greater marketing efficiency and customer value in the face of increasing competition are changing the nature of exchange between companies. Instead of engaging in a discrete series of arm's-length, adversarial exchanges with customers, channel members, and suppliers on the open market, more firms are trying to develop and nurture long-term relationships and alliances, such as the one between 3M and Wal-Mart. Such cooperative relationships are thought to improve each partner's ability to adapt quickly to environmental changes or threats, to gain greater benefits at lower costs from its exchanges, and to increase the lifetime value of its customers.[29]

Similar kinds of cooperative relationships are emerging inside companies as firms seek mechanisms for more effectively and efficiently coordinating across functional departments the various activities necessary to identify, attract, service, and satisfy customers. In many firms, the planning and execution that used to be the responsibility of a product or marketing manager are now coordinated and carried out by cross-functional teams. Thus, the boundaries between functional areas are beginning to blur, and marketing programs are increasingly a group activity. Regardless of who is responsible or who carries out the work, however, the decisions and activities involved in such marketing programs remain the same. They are the focus of the rest of this book.

TAKE-AWAYS

- Marketing is pervasive. It is a social process involving the activities that facilitate exchanges of goods and services among individuals and organizations.

- Customers buy benefits, not products. The benefits a customer receives from a firm's offering, less the costs he or she must bear to receive those benefits, determine the offering's value to that customer.

- Delivering superior value to one's customers is the essence of business success. Because delivering superior value is a multifunctional endeavor, both marketing and nonmarketing managers must adopt a strong focus on the customer and coordinate their efforts to make it happen.

- A focus on satisfying customer needs and wants is not inconsistent with being technologically innovative.

- The marketing management process requires an understanding of the 4Cs: the company and its mission, strategies, and resources; the macroenvironmental context in which it operates; customers and their needs and wants; and competitors. Obtaining an objective, detailed, evidence-based understanding of these factors is critical to effective marketing decision making.

- Marketing decisions—such as choices about what goods or services to sell, to whom, and with what strategy— are made or approved at the highest levels in most firms, whether large or small. Therefore, managers who occupy or aspire to strategic positions in their organizations need marketing perspectives and analytical skills.

Self-diagnostic questions to test your ability to apply the concepts in this chapter to marketing decision making may be found at this book's website at www.mhhe.com/mullins05.

ENDNOTES

1. This case example is based on information found in Erin White, "Emergency Overhaul," *The Wall Street Journal,* December 10, 2001, p. B-1; Dan Brekke, "The Future Is Now—or Never," *New York Times Magazine,* January 23, 2000, pp. 30–33, and at the company's website: www.redenvelope.com.

2. For example, see Frederick E. Webster, Jr., "The Future Role of Marketing in the Organization," in Donald Lehmann and Katherine E. Jocz, eds., *Reflections on the Future of Marketing* (Cambridge, MA: Marketing Science Institute, 1997), pp. 39–66; Christine Moorman and Roland T. Rust, "The Role of Marketing," *Journal of Marketing* 63 (Special Issue 1999), pp. 180–97; and Frederick E. Webster, Jr., "Marketing Management in Changing Times," *Marketing Management,* January–February 2002, pp. 18–23.

3. Brekke, "The Future Is Now—or Never," p. 30.

4. The American Marketing Association offers a similar, though more detailed, definition of marketing, as follows: "Marketing is the process of planning and executing the conception, pricing, promotion, and distributing of ideas, goods, and services to create exchanges that satisfy individual and organizational objectives."

5. For more examples, see Philip Kotler and Alan R. Andreasen, *Strategic Marketing for Nonprofit Organizations,* 5th ed. (Englewood Cliffs, NJ: Prentice Hall, 1997).

6. Some evidence indicates that differences between organizational and individual consumers account for more of the variation in the performance of a given business strategy across firms than any other environmental or organizational variable. See Donald C. Hambrick and David Lei, "Toward an Empirical Prioritization of Contingency Variables for Business Strategy," *Academy of Management Journal* 28 (1985), pp. 763–88.

7. Quoted in Gary Hamel and C. K. Prahalad, *Competing for the Future* (Cambridge, MA: Harvard Business School Press, 1994).

8. Justin Martin, "Ignore Your Customer," *Fortune,* May 1, 1995, pp. 121–26.

9. For empirical evidence, see John C. Narver and Stanley F. Slater, "The Effect of a Market Orientation on Business Profitability," *Journal of Marketing* 54 (April 1990), pp. 1–18; and Stanley F. Slater and John C. Narver, "Market Orientation, Performance, and the Moderating Influence of Competitive Environment," *Journal of Marketing* 58 (January 1994), pp. 46–55.

10. "The Right Stuff," *Journal of Business and Design* 2 (Fall 1996), p. 11.

11. John W. Verity, "Revolution in the Supply Closet," *Business Week,* June 10, 1996, p. 112.

12. Rahul Jacob, "Beyond Quality and Value," *Fortune,* Special Issue, Autumn–Winter 1993, p. 10.

13. Patricia Sellers, "How to Handle Customers' Gripes," *Fortune,* October 24, 1988, p. 88.

14. Patricia Sellers, "Keeping the Customers You Already Have," *Fortune,* Special Issue, Autumn–Winter 1993, p. 57. See also, Frederick F. Reicheld, "Loyalty and the Renaissance of Marketing," *Marketing Management* 2 (1994), pp. 10–21.

15. Spencer E. Ante, "For Big Blue, The Big Enchilada," *Business Week,* October 28, 2002, pp. 58–59; and Ira Sager, "Inside IBM: Internet Business Machines," *Business Week,* December 13, 1999, pp. EB20–40.

16. C. K. Prahalad and Gary Hamel, "The Core Competence of the Corporation," *Harvard Business Review* 68 (May–June 1990), pp. 79–91; and George S. Day, "The Capabilities of Market-Driven Organizations," *Journal of Marketing* 58 (October 1994), pp. 37–52.

17. For a more detailed discussion of formal marketing plans, see Donald R. Lehmann and Russell S. Winer, *Analysis for Marketing Planning,* 4th ed. (New York: Irwin/McGraw-Hill, 1997).

18. David S. Hopkins, *The Marketing Plan* (New York: The Conference Board, 1981), p. 2.

19. Jagdish N. Sheth and Rajendra S. Sisodia, "Feeling the Heat," *Marketing Management* 4 (Fall 1995), p. 10.

20. Ibid.

21. Ronald Henkoff, "Delivering the Goods," *Fortune,* November 28, 1994, p. 64. Also see, "A Survey of E-Commerce: Shopping Around the Web," *The Economist,* February 26, 2000.

22. Rajendra K. Srivastava, Tasadduq A. Shervani, and Liam Fahey, "Marketing, Business Processes, and Shareholder Value: An Organizationally Embedded View of Marketing Activities and the Discipline of Marketing," *Journal of Marketing* 63 (Special Issue 1999), pp. 168–79.

23. Ravi S. Achrol and Philip Kotler, "Marketing in the Network Economy," *Journal of Marketing* 63 (Special Issue 1999), pp. 146–63.

24. Philip Kotler and Gary Armstrong, *Principles of Marketing* (Englewood Cliffs, NJ: Prentice Hall, 1989), p. 575.

25. For examples, see Terry G. Vavra, *Aftermarketing* (Burr Ridge, IL: Richard D. Irwin, 1995).

26. For examples, see Faith Keenan, Stanley Holmes, Jay Greene, and Roger O. Crockett, "A Mass Market of One," *Business Week,* December 2, 2002, pp. 68–72.

27. Estimates reported in Robert D. Hoff and Steve Hamm, "How E-Biz Rose, Fell, and Will Rise Again," *Business Week Online,* May 13, 2002.

28. "A Survey of E-Commerce: Shopping around the Web," *The Economist,* February 26, 2000, p. 5.

29. Achrol and Kotler, "Marketing in the Network Economy."

CHAPTER TWO

The Marketing Implications of Corporate and Business Strategies

IBM Switches Strategies[1]

FOR DECADES International Business Machines focused most of its efforts on the hardware side of the computer industry: first on large mainframe computers, then on personal computers (PCs), and then, as the Internet began to take off in the mid-1990s, on servers and related equipment. Its target customers for that hardware were typically organizations rather than individual consumers and usually large organizations that needed lots of data processing capacity and had the financial resources to afford it. The firm did not ignore consumers or small businesses, but it relied on independent retailers, such as Circuit City, and value-added resellers to reach those segments while focusing much of its own marketing and sales effort on large organizations.

IBM's competitive strategy was also quite consistent over the years. Given that the firm was never the lowest cost producer in the industry, it did not try to compete with low prices. Instead, the firm pursued a quality differentiation strategy by offering superior products backed up by excellent technical service and selling them at premium prices.

To implement its strategy, the company tried to ensure a steady stream of cutting-edge products by allocating vast resources to R&D and product development. IBM also generally followed an "open architecture"

policy. In its PC business, for instance, the firm licensed its PC-DOS operating system (developed in collaboration with Microsoft) to other manufacturers and software developers. This helped expand the number of PC-DOS users, thereby providing incentives for IBM's licensees to develop more innovative applications software to run on PC-DOS systems, which in turn enhanced the usefulness and customer value of IBM's hardware.

On the marketing side, the firm maintained substantial advertising and promotion budgets to keep potential customers informed about its constantly evolving product lines and to burnish the identity of the IBM brand. More important, though, were the millions spent recruiting, training, and compensating one of the world's largest and most technically competent salesforces.

Technology Changes and Competitor Actions Require a Shift in Strategy

For decades IBM's corporate, business, and marketing strategies were all very successful. By the mid-1990s, however, several of IBM's traditional businesses were

Exhibit 2.1

A Print Advertisement for IBM's E-Business Services

in trouble. The company's share of the worldwide PC market fell to about 8 percent in 1999, third behind Dell and Compaq. Worse, the firm's PC business was projected to lose $400 million, on top of a $1 billion loss in 1998. Similarly, while server sales, made up mostly of UNIX-based computers, were growing rapidly around the world, IBM was able to capture only a small share of that business. Its growth rate in the server market during the late 1990s was only about one-third as fast as that of major competitors such as Sun Microsystems. Even its venerable mainframe business, which had been a low-growth but highly profitable market throughout the 1980s and early 1990s, suffered a profit squeeze due to falling prices and declining demand.

IBM's performance problems can be traced to a variety of factors, which all worked to make the firm's tried-and-true corporate, competitive, and marketing strategies less effective than they once were. For one thing, major technological changes in the macroenvironment—such as the rapid increase in power of desktop PCs, the emergence of the Internet, and the development of internal, organizationwide computer networks (or intranets)—greatly contributed to the declining demand for large mainframe computers and centralized data processing systems.

Also, IBM's quality differentiation strategy became less effective as some of its product-markets began to mature and customers' purchase criteria changed. Technical and performance differences among competing brands became less pronounced as the PC industry matured, for example, and later buyers tended to be less technically sophisticated, more price-conscious, and more interested in buying equipment that was easy to use. IBM's premium price position put it at a disadvantage in attracting such customers. Worse, a number of competitors, notably Dell, provided more benefits at lower prices by offering custom-designed systems, convenient direct purchasing over the Web, and user-friendly service and support programs.

Even IBM's traditional focus on large organizational customers contributed to the firm's problems in the newly emerging markets for servers and related equipment and software. It was slow to pursue the many small start-up businesses at the forefront of the dot.com revolution, leaving an open field for Sun, Hewlett-Packard, and other competitors. "We've had to adapt our [strategy] model to them," conceded Lou Gerstner, IBM's CEO. "We were late."

A New Corporate Strategy

When Lou Gerstner took over as IBM's chief executive in 1994, he and a task force of other executives, including many from the marketing and sales ranks, reexamined all the firm's businesses, customer segments, competitors, and potential competitors. Their conclusion: The Internet would change everything. They foresaw that "The real leadership in the [information technology] industry was moving away from the creation of the technology to the application of the technology," says Gerstner. "The explosive growth is in services." Further, "We concluded that this [the Internet] was not an information superhighway. This was all about business, doing transactions, not looking up information."

Consequently, IBM's top executives began to refocus the corporate mission, de-emphasizing the development and manufacture of high-tech hardware while increasing the emphasis on providing customers with e-business engineering, software, and outsourcing services. To leverage the firm's existing competencies and its long-term relationships with its traditional customers, many of the new services the firm developed concentrate on helping large, bricks-and-mortar firms (1) hook old corporate databases (often on mainframes) into new online systems, (2) integrate Web technology into their internal business processes to improve efficiency, and (3) develop and run company websites. For instance, Lego, the Danish toy manufacturer, pays IBM to run its entire Web operation, including contracting with the Danish post office to handle shipping.

But the corporation has also expanded the scope of both its new service and old hardware businesses to embrace smaller customers. For example, in 2002 the

firm released scaled-down versions of its database, e-mail, and network-management software that are easier to maintain and up to 80 percent cheaper than its standard versions. IBM also announced a partnership with J. D. Edwards & Co. in which the provider of tech services to midsized companies will base its entire software menu on IBM programs.

New Business and Marketing Strategies

IBM's new corporate emphasis on e-business services and software as its primary paths toward future growth has also forced some changes in the firm's competitive and marketing strategies. At the business level, the firm still seeks to differentiate itself from competitors on the basis of superior quality and to charge premium prices for that quality. But in its new service businesses, competitive superiority depends on the knowledge, experience, and expertise of its consultants—and their familiarity with a customer's operations that comes from continuing interaction—rather than the technical quality of its products. Therefore, to implement its new service-based differentiation strategy effectively, the company reorganized and reallocated many of its internal resources. For example, the firm created a stand-alone software division with its own salesforce, and a new Internet division with responsibility for ensuring that all company products work with the Web and for developing and coordinating a continuing stream of e-business services. It has also shifted over 50 percent of its $5.7 billion R&D budget into projects aimed at creating new Internet-based services and software.

Given that the success of IBM's competitive strategy depends heavily on the knowledge and expertise of its personnel and their ability to forge beneficial relationships with customers, the firm's salesforce is even more crucial than ever. Many salespeople who used to spend a portion of their time selling the company's hardware have been given additional training and turned into full-time software engineers or e-business consultants.

The superior expertise and experience of IBM's people—and the firm's ability to satisfy the e-commerce needs of customers in a variety of industries—was also effectively communicated via an advertising campaign featuring a series of ads such as that shown in Exhibit 2.1. The ads identified firms in different industries that relied on IBM to design and implement their websites and were placed in a variety of media directed at managers and entrepreneurs.

The Bottom Line

At the time of this writing, IBM's new strategies had not enabled the firm to totally avoid the worldwide downturn that shook the information technology industry in the first years of the new century, but they helped the company ride out the storm in better shape than many competitors. While the firm's revenues slipped 5 percent in 2002 compared to the previous year, they still amounted to $83 billion. More than 40 percent of those revenues were generated by the firm's service businesses, and another 15 percent came from software sales.

More importantly, IBM was gaining market share against such major competitors as Oracle, Sun, and BEA Systems in nearly every service and software segment in which it competed. As a result, IBM's stock earned more than $2 per share in 2002, a year that was much less profitable for many other information technology companies.

Marketing Challenges Addressed in Chapter 2

IBM's experiences in the information technology industry illustrate some important points about the nature of business strategy and the interrelationships among different levels of strategy in an organization. They also demonstrate the importance of timely and accurate insights into customer desires, environmental trends, and competitors' actions in formulating successful strategies at every level.

As we discussed in Chapter 1, marketing managers' familiarity with customers, competitors, and environmental trends often means they play a crucial role in influencing strategies formulated at higher levels in the firm. While the need for new corporate and competitive strategies at IBM became obvious because of stagnating sales and declining profits in some of the firm's most venerable businesses, decisions about the content of those new strategies were influenced by information and analyses supplied by the firm's marketing and sales personnel. Marketing executives were key members of the task force appointed by CEO Gerstner to analyze the firm's strengths and weaknesses and develop new directions for growth and profitability. And Gerstner himself was recruited, in part, because of his experience working for customer-oriented package goods and financial services businesses at Nabisco and American Express.

Some firms systematically incorporate such market and competitive analyses into their planning processes. They also coordinate their activities around the primary goal of satisfying unmet customer needs. Such firms are *market-oriented* and follow a business philosophy commonly called the *marketing concept*. Market-oriented firms have been shown to be among the more profitable and successful at maintaining strong competitive positions in their industries over time. As we shall see later in this chapter, however, companies do not always embrace a market orientation—nor rely as heavily on inputs from their marketing and sales personnel—in developing their strategies. Some firm's strategies are driven more by technology, production, or cost concerns.

Regardless of their participation or influence in formulating corporate and business-level strategies, marketing managers' freedom of action is ultimately constrained by those higher-level strategies. The objectives, strategies, and action plans for a specific product-market are but one part of a hierarchy of strategies within the firm. Each level of strategy must be consistent with—and therefore influenced and constrained by—higher levels within the hierarchy. For example, not only the new services developed by IBM, but also their advertising appeals, prices, and other aspects of the marketing plans were shaped by

KEY OBSERVATION

Each level of strategy must be consistent with—and therefore influenced and constrained by—higher levels within the hierarchy.

the shift in corporate strategy toward emphasizing Web-based services as the primary avenue for future growth.

These interrelationships among the various levels of strategy raise several questions of importance to marketing managers as well as managers in other functional areas and top executives. While marketing managers clearly bear the primary responsibility for developing strategic marketing plans for individual product or service offerings, what role does marketing play in formulating strategies at the corporate and divisional or business unit level? Why do some organizations pay much more attention to customers and competitors when formulating their strategies (i.e., why are some firms more market-oriented) than others, and does it make any difference in their performance? What do strategies consist of, and are they similar or different at the corporate, business, and functional levels? What specific decisions underlie effective corporate and business-level strategies, and what are their implications for marketing?

What Is Marketing's Role in Formulating and Implementing Strategies?

The essence of strategic planning at all levels is identifying threats to avoid and opportunities to pursue. The primary strategic responsibility of any manager is to look outward continuously to keep the firm or business in step with changes in the environment. Because they occupy positions at the boundary between the firm and its customers, distributors, and competitors, marketing managers are usually most familiar with conditions and trends in the market environment. Consequently, they not only are responsible for developing strategic plans for their own product-market entries, but also are often primary participants and contributors to the planning process at the business and corporate level as well.

The wide-ranging influence of marketing managers on higher-level strategic decisions is clearly shown in a recent survey of managers in 280 U.S. and 234 German business units of firms in the electrical equipment, mechanical machinery, and consumer package goods industries.[2] The study examined perceptions of marketing managers' influence relative to managers from sales, R&D, operations, and finance on a variety of strategic and tactical decisions within their businesses. Exhibit 2.2 summarizes the results.

The study found that, on average, marketing and sales executives exerted significantly more influence than managers from other functions on strategic decisions concerning traditional marketing activities, such as advertising messages, pricing, distribution, customer service and support, and measurement and improvement of customer satisfaction. Interestingly, though, the influence of sales executives was perceived to be even greater than that of marketing managers on some of these decisions. One reason—particularly in the industrial goods firms selling electronic equipment and machinery—may be that sales managers have more detailed information about customer needs and desires because they have direct and continuing contact with existing and potential buyers.

More surprisingly, marketing managers were also perceived to wield significantly more influence than managers from other functional areas on cross-functional, business-level strategic decisions. While the views of finance and operations executives carry more weight in approving major capital expenditures, marketing and sales managers exert more influence on decisions concerning the strategic direction of the business unit, expansion into new geographic markets, the selection of strategic business partners, and new product development.

Might the relative influence of the different functions become more similar as firms adopt more integrative organizational forms, such as cross-functional work teams? The study's results suggest not. Marketing's influence was not significantly reduced in companies that had instituted cross-functional structures and processes.

Exhibit 2.2

INFLUENCE OF FUNCTIONAL UNITS OVER VARIOUS BUSINESS DECISIONS

Decisions	Marketing	Sales	R&D	Operations	Finance
Business strategy decisions					
Strategic direction of the business	38	29**	11**	9**	14**
Expansion into new geographic markets	39	45**	3**	3**	10**
Choices of strategic partners	33	38*	7**	9**	12**
New product development	32	23**	29**	9**	7**
Major capital expenditures	13	11**	13	29**	35**
Marketing strategy decisions					
Advertising messages	65	29**	3**	1**	2**
Customer satisfaction measurement	48	35**	5**	8**	4**
Customer satisfaction improvement	40	37*	7**	10**	6**
Distribution strategy	34	52**	1**	6**	6**
Customer service and support	31	47**	5**	10**	7**
Pricing	30	41**	4**	9**	16**

The number in each cell is the mean of the amount of points given by responding managers to each function, using a constant-sum scale of 100. A t-test was performed to compare column 2 (mean of relative influence of marketing) with columns 3 through 6 (relative influence of sales, R&D, operations, and finance). Statistically significant differences with marketing are indicated by asterisks, where: * $p < .05$; ** $p < .01$.

Source: Adapted from Christian Homburg, John P. Workman, Jr., and Harley Krohmer, "Marketing's Influence Within the Firm," Journal of Marketing (April 1999), p. 9. Used by permission of the American Marketing Association.

But marketing managers may not play as pervasive a strategic role in other cultures as they do in the United States. The study found that marketers' influence on both tactical and strategic issues was significantly lower in German firms. As one of the study's authors points out, "Germany has traditionally stressed technology and operations more than the softer, customer-oriented aspects central to marketing. So even when the environment changes, a signal to top-level German managers that marketing should be playing a greater role, they are reluctant to give it that role."[3]

Market-Oriented Management

Even within the United States, however, marketing managers do not play an equally extensive strategic role in every firm because not all firms are equally market-oriented. Not surprisingly, marketers tend to have a greater influence on all levels of strategy in organizations that embrace a market-oriented philosophy of business. More critically, managers in other functional areas of market-oriented firms incorporate more customer and competitor information into their decision-making processes as well.

Market-oriented organizations tend to operate according to the business philosophy known as the marketing concept. As originally stated by General Electric five decades ago, the **marketing concept** holds that the planning and coordination of all company activities around the primary goal of satisfying customer needs is the most effective means to attain and sustain a competitive advantage and achieve company objectives over time.

Exhibit 2.3

GUIDELINES FOR MARKET-ORIENTED MANAGEMENT

1. Create customer focus throughout the business.
2. Listen to the customer.
3. Define and nurture your distinctive competence.
4. Define marketing as market intelligence.
5. Target customers precisely.
6. Manage for profitability, not sales volume.
7. Make customer value the guiding star.
8. Let the customer define quality.

9. Measure and manage customer expectations.
10. Build customer relationships and loyalty.
11. Define the business as a service business.
12. Commit to continuous improvement and innovation.
13. Manage culture along with strategy and structure.
14. Grow with partners and alliances.
15. Destroy marketing bureaucracy.

Source: Frederick E. Webster, Jr., "Executing the New Marketing Concept," Marketing Management 3, no. 1 (1994), p. 10. Used by permission of the American Marketing Association.

Thus, market-oriented firms are characterized by a consistent focus by personnel in all departments and at all levels on customers' needs and competitive circumstances in the market environment. They are also willing and able to quickly adapt products and functional programs to fit changes in that environment. Such firms pay a great deal of attention to customer research *before* products are designed and produced. They embrace the concept of market segmentation by adapting product offerings and marketing programs to the special needs of different target markets.

Market-oriented firms also adopt a variety of organizational procedures and structures to improve the responsiveness of their decision making, including using more detailed environmental scanning and continuous, real-time information systems; seeking frequent feedback from and coordinating plans with key customers and major suppliers; decentralizing strategic decisions; encouraging entrepreneurial thinking among lower-level managers; and using interfunctional management teams to analyze issues and initiate strategic actions outside the formal planning process.[4] For example, IBM formed a high-level cross-functional task force to reevaluate its market environment, develop a new strategic focus, and map new avenues toward future growth. The company has also formed alliances with enterprise software developers, such as PeopleSoft and Great Plains Software, to improve its ability to help customers integrate Web technology into their business processes. These and other actions recommended to make an organization more market-driven and responsive to environmental changes are summarized in Exhibit 2.3.

Does Being Market-Oriented Pay?

Since an organization's success over time hinges on its ability to provide benefits of value to its customers—and to do that better than its competitors—it seems likely that market-oriented firms should perform better than others. By paying careful attention to customer needs and competitive threats—and by focusing activities across all functional departments on meeting those needs and threats effectively—organizations should be able to enhance, accelerate, and reduce the volatility and vulnerability of their cash flows.[5] And that should enhance their economic performance and shareholder value. Indeed, profitability is the third leg, together with a customer focus and cross-functional coordination, of the three-legged stool known as the marketing concept.

Sometimes the marketing concept is interpreted as a philosophy of trying to satisfy all customers' needs regardless of the cost. That would be a prescription for financial disaster.

Instead, the marketing concept is consistent with the notion of focusing on only those segments of the customer population that the firm can satisfy both effectively *and* profitably. Firms might offer less extensive or costly goods and services to unprofitable segments or avoid them. For example, the Buena Vista Winery website (**www.buenavistawinery.com**) does not accept orders of less than a half case because they are too costly to process and ship.

Substantial evidence supports the idea that being market-oriented pays dividends, at least in a highly developed economy such as the United States. A number of studies involving more than 500 firms or business units across a variety of industries indicate that a market orientation has a significant positive effect on various dimensions of performance, including return on assets, sales growth, and new product success.[6]

KEY OBSERVATION

A market orientation has a significant positive effect on various dimensions of performance, including return on assets, sales growth, and new product success.

Factors That Mediate Marketing's Strategic Role

Despite the evidence that a market-orientation boosts performance, many companies around the world are not very focused on their customers or competitors. Among the reasons firms are not always in close touch with their market environments are these:

- Competitive conditions may enable a company to be successful in the short run without being particularly sensitive to customer desires.
- Different levels of economic development across industries or countries may favor different business philosophies.
- Firms can suffer from strategic inertia—the automatic continuation of strategies successful in the past, even though current market conditions are changing.

Competitive Factors Affecting a Firm's Market Orientation   The competitive conditions some firms face enable them to be successful in the short term without paying much attention to their customers, suppliers, distributors, or other organizations in their market environment. Early entrants into newly emerging industries, particularly industries based on new technologies, are especially likely to be internally focused and not very market-oriented. This is because there are likely to be relatively few strong competitors during the formative years of a new industry, customer demand for the new product is likely to grow rapidly and outstrip available supply, and production problems and resource constraints tend to represent more immediate threats to the survival of such new businesses.

Businesses facing such market and competitive conditions are often **product-oriented** or **production-oriented.** They focus most of their attention and resources on such functions as product and process engineering, production, and finance in order to acquire and manage the resources necessary to keep pace with growing demand. The business is primarily concerned with producing more of what it wants to make, and marketing generally plays a secondary role in formulating and implementing strategy. Other functional differences between production-oriented and market-oriented firms are summarized in Exhibit 2.4.

As industries grow, they become more competitive. New entrants are attracted and existing producers attempt to differentiate themselves through improved products and more-efficient production processes. As a result, industry capacity often grows faster than demand and the environment shifts from a seller's market to a buyer's market. Firms often respond to such changes with aggressive promotional activities—such as hiring more salespeople, increasing advertising budgets, or offering frequent price promotions—to maintain market share and hold down unit costs.

Unfortunately, this kind of **sales-oriented** response to increasing competition still focuses on selling what the firm wants to make rather than on customer needs. Worse, competitors

Exhibit 2.4

DIFFERENCES BETWEEN PRODUCTION-ORIENTED AND MARKET-ORIENTED ORGANIZATIONS

Business activity or function	Production orientation	Marketing orientation
Product offering	Company sells what it can make; primary focus on functional performance and cost.	Company makes what it can sell; primary focus on customers' needs and market opportunities.
Product line	Narrow.	Broad.
Pricing	Based on production and distribution costs.	Based on perceived benefits provided.
Research	Technical research; focus on product improvement and cost cutting in the production process.	Market research; focus on identifying new opportunities and applying new technology to satisfy customer needs.
Packaging	Protection for the product; minimize costs.	Designed for customer convenience; a promotional tool.
Credit	A necessary evil; minimize bad debt losses.	A customer service; a tool to attract customers.
Promotion	Emphasis on product features, quality, and price.	Emphasis on product benefits and ability to satisfy customers' needs or solve problems.

can easily match such aggressive sales tactics. Simply spending more on selling efforts usually does not create a sustainable competitive advantage.

As industries mature, sales volume levels off and technological differences among brands tend to disappear as manufacturers copy the best features of each other's products. Consequently, a firm must seek new market segments or steal share from competitors by offering lower prices, superior services, or intangible benefits other firms cannot match. At this stage, managers can most readily appreciate the benefits of a market orientation, and marketers are often given a bigger role in developing competitive strategies.[7]

The Influence of Different Stages of Development across Industries and Global Markets

The previous discussion suggests that the degree of adoption of a market orientation varies not only across firms but also across entire industries. Industries that are in earlier stages of their life cycles, or that benefit from barriers to entry or other factors reducing the intensity of competition, are likely to have relatively fewer market-oriented firms. For instance, in part because of governmental regulations that restricted competition, many service industries—including banks, airlines, physicians, lawyers, accountants, and insurance companies—were slow to adopt the marketing concept. But with the trend toward deregulation and the increasingly intense global competition in such industries, many service organizations are working much harder to understand and satisfy their customers.[8]

Given that entire economies are in different stages of development around the world, the popularity—and even the appropriateness—of different business philosophies may also vary across countries. A production orientation was the dominant business philosophy in the United States, for instance, during the industrialization that occurred from the mid-1800s through World War I.[9] Similarly, a primary focus on developing product and production technology may still be appropriate in developing nations that are in the midst of industrialization.

International differences in business philosophies can cause some problems for the globalization of a firm's strategic marketing programs, but it can create some opportunities as well, especially for alliances or joint ventures. Consider, for example, General Electric's joint venture with the Mexican appliance manufacturer Organization Mabe. The arrangement benefits GE by providing direct access to Mexico's rapidly growing market for household appliances and its low-cost supply of labor. But it also benefits Mabe—and the Mexican economy—by giving the firm access to cutting-edge R&D and production technology and the capital necessary to take advantage of its newfound know-how.[10]

Strategic Inertia   In some cases, a firm that achieved success by being in tune with its environment loses touch with its market because managers become reluctant to tamper with strategies and marketing programs that worked in the past. They begin to believe there is one best way to satisfy their customers. Such strategic inertia is dangerous because customers' needs and competitive offerings change over time. IBM's traditional focus on large organizational customers, for instance, caused the company to devote too little effort to the much faster-growing segment of small technology start-ups. And its emphasis on computer technology and hardware made it slow to respond to the explosive growth in demand for Web-based applications and services. Thus, in environments where such changes happen frequently, the strategic planning process needs to be ongoing and adaptive. All the participants, whether from marketing or other functional departments, need to pay constant attention to what is happening with their customers and competitors.

Three Levels of Strategy: Similar Components, but Different Issues

We have argued that marketing managers have primary responsibility for the marketing strategies associated with individual product or service offerings, and that their perspectives and inputs often have a major influence on the decisions that shape corporate and business-level strategies. But we haven't said much about what those strategic decisions are. Consequently, it's time to define what strategies are and how they vary across different levels of an organization.

Strategy: A Definition

Although *strategy* first became a popular business buzzword during the 1960s, it continues to be the subject of widely differing definitions and interpretations. The following definition, however, captures the essence of the term:

> A **strategy** is a fundamental pattern of present and planned objectives, resource deployments, and interactions of an organization with markets, competitors, and other environmental factors.[11]

Our definition suggests that a strategy should specify (1) *what* (objectives to be accomplished), (2) *where* (on which industries and product-markets to focus), and (3) *how* (which resources and activities to allocate to each product-market to meet environmental opportunities and threats and to gain a competitive advantage).

The Components of Strategy

A well-developed strategy contains five components, or sets of issues:

1. *Scope.* The scope of an organization refers to the breadth of its strategic domain—the number and types of industries, product lines, and market segments it competes in or plans to enter. Decisions about an organization's strategic scope should reflect management's view of the

firm's purpose, or *mission*. This common thread among its various activities and product-markets defines the essential nature of what its business is and what it should be.

2. *Goals and objectives.* Strategies should also detail desired levels of accomplishment on one or more dimensions of performance—such as volume growth, profit contribution, or return on investment—over specified time periods for each of those businesses and product-markets and for the organization as a whole.

3. *Resource deployments.* Every organization has limited financial and human resources. Formulating a strategy also involves deciding how those resources are to be obtained and allocated, across businesses, product-markets, functional departments, and activities within each business or product-market.

4. *Identification of a sustainable competitive advantage.* One important part of any strategy is a specification of *how the organization will compete* in each business and product-market within its domain. How can it position itself to develop and sustain a differential advantage over current and potential competitors? To answer such questions, managers must examine the market opportunities in each business and product-market and the company's distinctive competencies or strengths relative to its competitors.

5. *Synergy.* Synergy exists when the firm's businesses, product-markets, resource deployments, and competencies complement and reinforce one another. Synergy enables the total performance of the related businesses to be greater than it would otherwise be: The whole becomes greater than the sum of its parts.

The Hierarchy of Strategies

Explicitly or implicitly, these five basic dimensions are part of all strategies. However, rather than a single comprehensive strategy, most organizations have a hierarchy of interrelated strategies, each formulated at a different level of the firm. The three major levels of strategy in most large, multiproduct organizations are (1) **corporate strategy,** (2) **business-level strategy,** and (3) **functional strategies** focused on a particular product-market entry. In small, single-product-line companies or entrepreneurial start-ups, however, corporate and business-level strategic issues merge.

Our primary focus is on the development of marketing strategies and programs for individual product-market entries, but other functional departments, such as R&D and production, also have strategies and plans for each of the firm's product-markets. Throughout this book, therefore, we examine the interfunctional implications of product-market strategies, conflicts across functional areas, and the mechanisms that firms use to resolve those conflicts.

Strategies at all three levels contain the five components mentioned earlier, but because each strategy serves a different purpose within the organization, each emphasizes a different set of issues. Exhibit 2.5 summarizes the specific focus and issues dealt with at each level of strategy; we discuss them in the next sections.

Corporate Strategy

At the corporate level, managers must coordinate the activities of multiple business units and, in the case of conglomerates, even separate legal business entities. Decisions about the organization's scope and resource deployments across its divisions or businesses are the primary focus of corporate strategy. The essential questions at this level include, What business(es) are we in? What business(es) *should* we be in? and What portion of our total resources should we devote to each of these businesses to achieve the organization's overall goals and objectives? Thus, new CEO Gerstner and other top-level managers at IBM decided to pursue future growth primarily through the development of Web-based services and software rather than computer hardware. They shifted substantial corporate resources—

Exhibit 2.5

KEY COMPONENTS OF CORPORATE, BUSINESS, AND MARKETING STRATEGIES

Strategy components	Corporate strategy	Business strategy	Marketing strategy

Scope	• Corporate domain—"Which businesses should we be in?"
	• Corporate development strategy
	  Conglomerate diversification (expansion into unrelated businesses)
	  Vertical integration
	  Acquisition and divestiture policies
		• Business domain—"Which product-markets should we be in within this business or industry?"
		• Business development strategy
		  Concentric diversification (new products for existing customers or new customers for existing products)
			• Target market definition
			• Product-line depth and breadth
			• Branding policies
			• Product-market development plan
			• Line extension and product elimination plans

Goals and objectives	• Overall corporate objectives aggregated across businesses
	  Revenue growth
	  Profitability
	  ROI (return on investment)
	  Earnings per share
	  Contributions to other stakeholders
		• Constrained by corporate goals
		• Objectives aggregated across product-market entries in the business unit
		  Sales growth
		  New product or market growth
		  Profitability
		  ROI
		  Cash flow
		  Strengthening bases of competitive advantage
			• Constrained by corporate and business goals
			• Objectives for a specific product-market entry
			  Sales
			  Market share
			  Contribution margin
			  Customer satisfaction

Allocation of resources	• Allocation among businesses in the corporate portfolio • Allocation across functions shared by multiple businesses (corporate R&D, MIS)	• Allocation among product-market entries in the business unit • Allocation across functional departments within the business unit	• Allocation across components of the marketing plan (elements of the marketing mix) for a specific product-market entry
Sources of competitive advantage	• Primarily through superior corporate financial or human resources; more corporate R&D; better organizational processes or synergies relative to competitors across all industries in which the firm operates	• Primarily through competitive strategy, business unit's competencies relative to competitors in its industry	• Primarily through effective product positioning; superiority on one or more components of the marketing mix relative to competitors within a specific product-market
Sources of synergy	• Shared resources, technologies, or functional competencies across businesses within the firm	• Shared resources (including favorable customer image) or functional competencies across product-markets within an industry	• Shared marketing resources, competencies, or activities across product-market entries

including R&D expenditures, marketing and advertising budgets, and vast numbers of sales-people—into the corporation's service and software businesses to support the new strategic direction.

Attempts to develop and maintain distinctive competencies at the corporate level focus on generating superior human, financial, and technological resources; designing effective organization structures and processes; and seeking synergy among the firm's various businesses. Synergy can provide a major competitive advantage for firms where related businesses share R&D investments, product or production technologies, distribution channels, a common salesforce and/or promotional themes—as in the case of IBM.[12]

Business-Level Strategy

How a business unit competes within its industry is the critical focus of business-level strategy. A major issue in a business strategy is that of sustainable competitive advantage. What distinctive competencies can give the business unit a competitive advantage? And which of those competencies best match the needs and wants of the customers in the business's target segment(s)? For example, a business with low-cost sources of supply and efficient, modern plants might adopt a low-cost competitive strategy. One with a strong marketing department and a competent salesforce may compete by offering superior customer service.[13]

Another important issue a business-level strategy must address is appropriate scope: how many and which market segments to compete in, and the overall breadth of product offerings and marketing programs to appeal to these segments. Finally, synergy should be sought across product-markets and across functional departments within the business.

Marketing Strategy

The primary focus of marketing strategy is to effectively allocate and coordinate marketing resources and activities to accomplish the firm's objectives within a specific product-market. Therefore, the critical issue concerning the scope of a marketing strategy is specifying the target market(s) for a particular product or product line. Next, firms seek competitive advantage and synergy through a well-integrated program of marketing mix elements (the 4 Ps of product, price, place, promotion) tailored to the needs and wants of potential customers in that target market.

The Marketing Implications of Corporate Strategy Decisions

To formulate a useful corporate strategy, top management must address four interrelated decisions: the overall scope and mission of the organization; company goals and objectives; a development strategy for future growth; and the allocation of corporate resources across the firm's various businesses.[14] While a market orientation—and the analytical tools that marketing managers use to examine customer desires and competitors' strengths and weaknesses—can provide useful insights to guide all four of these strategic decisions, they are particularly germane for revealing the most attractive avenues for future growth and for determining which businesses or product-markets are likely to produce the greatest returns on the company's resources.

In turn, all four of these corporate decisions have major implications for the strategic marketing plans of the firm's various products or services. Together, they define the general strategic direction, objectives, and resource constraints within which those marketing plans must operate. We examine the marketing implications involved in both formulating and implementing these four components of corporate strategy next.

Corporate Scope—Defining the Firm's Mission

A well-thought-out mission statement guides an organization's managers as to which market opportunities to pursue and which fall outside the firm's strategic domain. A clearly stated mission can help instill a shared sense of direction, relevance, and achievement among employees, as well as a positive image of the firm among customers, investors, and other stakeholders.

To provide a useful sense of direction, a corporate mission statement should clearly define the organization's strategic scope. It should answer such fundamental questions as the following: What is our business? Who are our customers? What kinds of value can we provide to these customers? and What should our business be in the future? For example, several years ago PepsiCo, the manufacturer of Pepsi-Cola, broadened its mission to focus on "marketing superior quality food and beverage products for households and consumers dining out." That clearly defined mission guided the firm's managers toward the acquisition of several related companies, such as Frito-Lay, Taco Bell, and Pizza Hut.

More recently, in response to a changing global competitive environment, PepsiCo narrowed its scope to focus primarily on *package* foods (particularly salty snacks) and beverages distributed through supermarket and convenience store channels. This new, narrower mission led the firm to: (1) divest all of its fast-food restaurant chains; (2) acquire complementary beverage businesses, such as Tropicana juices and Lipton's iced teas; and (3) develop new brands targeted at rapidly growing beverage segments, such as Aquafina bottled water.[15]

Market Influences on the Corporate Mission   Like any other strategy component, an organization's mission should fit both its internal characteristics and the opportunities and threats in its external environment. Obviously, the firm's mission should be compatible with its established values, resources, and distinctive competencies. But it should also focus the firm's efforts on markets where those resources and competencies will generate value for customers, an advantage over competitors, and synergy across its products. Thus, PepsiCo's new mission reflects the firm's package goods marketing, sales, and distribution competencies and its perception that substantial synergies can be realized across snack foods and beverages within supermarket channels via shared logistics, joint displays and sales promotions, cross-couponing, and the like.

Criteria for Defining the Corporate Mission   Several criteria can be used to define an organization's strategic mission. Many firms specify their domain in *physical* terms, focusing on *products* or *services* or the *technology* used. The problem is that such statements can lead to slow reactions to technological or customer-demand changes. For example, Theodore Levitt argues that Penn Central's view of its mission as being "the railroad business" helped cause the firm's failure. Penn Central did not respond to major changes in transportation technology, such as the rapid growth of air travel and the increased efficiency of long-haul trucking. Nor did it respond to consumers' growing willingness to pay higher prices for the increased speed and convenience of air travel. Levitt argues that it is better to define a firm's mission as *what customer needs are to be satisfied and the functions the firm must perform to satisfy them.*[16] Products and technologies change over time, but basic customer needs tend to endure. Thus, if Penn Central had defined its mission as satisfying the transportation needs of its customers rather than simply being a railroad, it might have been more willing to expand its domain to incorporate newer technologies.

One problem with Levitt's advice, though, is that a mission statement focusing only on basic customer needs can be too broad to provide clear guidance and can fail to take into account the firm's specific competencies. If Penn Central had defined itself as a transportation

Exhibit 2.6

CHARACTERISTICS OF EFFECTIVE CORPORATE MISSION STATEMENTS

	Broad	Specific
Functional Based on customer needs	Transportation business	Long-distance transportation for large-volume producers of low-value, low-density products
Physical Based on existing products or technology	Railroad business	Long-haul, coal-carrying railroad

Source: Reprinted by permission from p. 43 of *Strategy Formulation: Analytical Concepts,* by C. W. Hofer and D. Schendel. Copyright © 1978. Reprinted with permission of South-Western, a division of Thomson Learning. www.thomsonrights.com, Fax 800-730-2216.

company, should it have diversified into the trucking business? Started an airline? As the upper-right quadrant of Exhibit 2.6 suggests, the most useful mission statements focus on the customer need to be satisfied and the functions that must be performed to satisfy that need. They are *specific* as to the customer groups and the products or technologies on which to concentrate. Thus, instead of seeing itself as being in the railroad business or as satisfying the transportation needs of all potential customers, Burlington Northern Santa Fe Railroad's mission is to provide long-distance transportation for large-volume producers of low-value, low-density products, such as coal and grain.

 Social Values and Ethical Principles   An increasing number of organizations are developing mission statements that also attempt to define the social and ethical boundaries of their strategic domain and the ethical principles they try to follow in dealings with customers, suppliers, and employees. Roughly two-thirds of U.S. firms have formal codes of ethics, and one in five large firms have formal departments dedicated to encouraging compliance with company ethical standards. At United Technologies, a global defense contractor and engineering firm, 160 business ethics officers monitor the firm's activities and relations with customers, suppliers, and governments around the world.[17]

Outside America, fewer firms have formal ethics bureaucracies. To some extent, this reflects the fact that in other countries governments and organized labor both play a bigger role in corporate life. In Germany, for instance, workers' councils often deal with issues such as sexual equality, race relations, and workers' rights.[18]

Ethics is concerned with the development of moral standards by which actions and situations can be judged. It focuses on those actions that may result in actual or potential harm of some kind (e.g., economic, mental, physical) to an individual, group, or organization.

Particular actions may be legal but not ethical. For instance, extreme and unsubstantiated advertising claims, such as "Our product is far superior to Brand X," might be viewed as simply legal puffery engaged in to make a sale, but many marketers (and their customers) view such little white lies as unethical. Thus, ethics is more proactive than the law. Ethical standards attempt to anticipate and avoid social problems, whereas most laws and regulations emerge only after the negative consequences of an action become apparent.[19]

KEY OBSERVATION

Unethical practices can damage the trust between a firm and its suppliers or customers, thereby disrupting the development of long-term exchange relationships and resulting in the likely loss of sales and profits over time.

Why Are Ethics Important? The Marketing Implications of Ethical Standards

One might ask why a corporation should take responsibility for providing moral guidance to its managers and employees. While such a question may be a good topic for philosophical debate, there is a compelling, practical reason for a firm to impose ethical standards to guide employees. Unethical practices can damage the trust

Exhibit 2.7

ISSUES ADDRESSED BY COMPANY ETHICS STATEMENTS

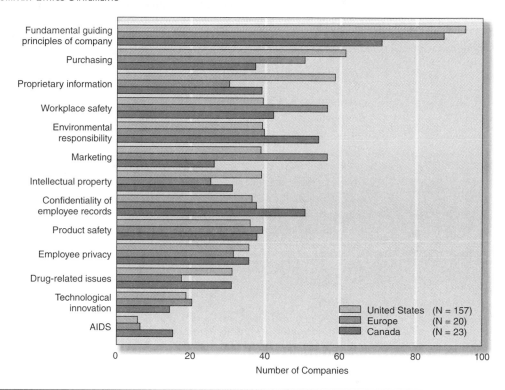

Source: Ronald E. Berenbeim, *Corporate Ethics Practices* (New York: The Conference Board, 1992). Used by permission.

between a firm and its suppliers or customers, thereby disrupting the development of long-term exchange relationships and resulting in the likely loss of sales and profits over time. For example, one survey of 135 purchasing managers from a variety of industries found that the more unethical a supplier's sales and marketing practices were perceived to be, the less eager were the purchasing managers to buy from that supplier.[20]

Unfortunately, not all customers or competing suppliers adhere to the same ethical standards. As a result, marketers sometimes feel pressure to engage in actions that are inconsistent with what they believe to be right—either in terms of personal values or formal company standards—in order to close a sale or stay even with the competition. This point was illustrated by a survey of 59 top marketing and sales executives concerning commercial bribery—attempts to influence a potential customer by giving gifts or kickbacks. While nearly two-thirds of the executives considered bribes unethical and did not want to pay them, 88 percent also felt that *not* paying bribes might put their firms at a competitive disadvantage.[21] Such dilemmas are particularly likely to arise as a company moves into global markets involving different cultures and levels of economic development where economic exigencies and ethical standards may be quite different.

Such inconsistencies in external expectations and demands across countries and markets can lead to job stress and inconsistent behavior among marketing and sales personnel, which in turn can risk damaging long-term relationships with suppliers, channel partners, and customers. A company can reduce such problems by spelling out formal social policies and ethical standards in its corporate mission statement and communicating and enforcing those standards. Unfortunately, it is not always easy to decide what those policies and standards should be. There are multiple philosophical traditions or frameworks that managers might use to evaluate the ethics of a given action. Consequently, different firms or managers can pursue somewhat different ethical standards, particularly across national cultures. Exhibit 2.7 displays a comparison (across three geographic regions) of the proportion of company ethical statements that address a set of specific issues. Note that a larger number of companies in the United States and Europe appear to be more concerned with the ethics of their purchasing practices than those of their marketing activities. Comparing firms across regions, U.S. companies are more concerned about proprietary information. Canadian firms are more likely to have explicit guidelines concerning environmental responsibility, and European companies more frequently have standards focused on workplace safety.

A general code of ethics prescribed for members of the American Marketing Association (the largest association of marketing professionals) is shown in Appendix 2.1 at the end of this chapter. Since many ethical issues in marketing are open to interpretation and debate, however, we will examine such issues and their implications individually as they arise throughout the remainder of this book.

Corporate Objectives

Confucius said, "For one who has no objective, nothing is relevant." Formal objectives provide decision criteria that guide an organization's business units and employees toward specific dimensions and performance levels. Those same objectives provide the benchmarks against which actual performance can be evaluated.

To be useful as decision criteria and evaluative benchmarks, corporate objectives must be specific and measurable. Therefore, each objective contains four components:

- A *performance dimension* or attribute sought.
- A *measure or index* for evaluating progress.
- A *target or hurdle* level to be achieved.
- A *time frame* within which the target is to be accomplished.

Exhibit 2.8 lists some common performance dimensions and measures used in specifying corporate as well as business-unit and marketing objectives.

The Marketing Implications of Corporate Objectives   Most organizations pursue multiple objectives. This is clearly demonstrated by a study of the stated objectives of 82 large corporations. The largest percentage of respondents (89 percent) had explicit profitability objectives: 82 percent reported growth objectives; 66 percent had specific market share goals. More than 60 percent mentioned social responsibility, employee welfare, and customer service objectives, and 54 percent of the companies had R&D/new product development goals.[22] These percentages add up to more than 100 percent because most firms had several objectives.

Trying to achieve many objectives at once leads to conflicts and trade-offs. For example, the investment and expenditure necessary to pursue growth in the long term is likely to reduce profitability and ROI in the short term.[23] Managers can reconcile conflicting goals by prioritizing them. Another approach is to state one of the conflicting goals as a constraint or **hurdle.** Thus, a firm attempts to maximize growth subject to meeting some minimum ROI hurdle.

In firms with multiple business units or product lines, however, the most common way to pursue a set of conflicting objectives is to first break them down into subobjectives, then

Exhibit 2.8

COMMON PERFORMANCE CRITERIA AND MEASURES THAT SPECIFY CORPORATE, BUSINESS-UNIT, AND MARKETING OBJECTIVES

Performance criteria	Possible measures or indexes
• Growth	$ sales Unit sales Percent change in sales
• Competitive strength	Market share Brand awareness Brand preference
• Innovativeness	$ sales from new products Percentage of sales from product-market entries introduced within past five years Percentage cost savings from new processes
• Profitability	$ profits Profit as percentage of sales Contribution margin* Return on investment (ROI) Return on net assets (RONA) Return on equity (ROE)
• Utilization of resources	Percent capacity utilization Fixed assets as percentage of sales
• Contribution to owners	Earnings per share Price/earnings ratio
• Contribution to customers	Price relative to competitors Product quality Customer satisfaction Customer retention Customer loyalty Customer lifetime value
• Contribution to employees	Wage rates, benefits Personnel development, promotions Employment stability, turnover
• Contribution to society	$ contributions to charities or community institutions Growth in employment

*Business-unit managers and marketing managers responsible for a product-market entry often have little control over costs associated with corporate overhead, such as the costs of corporate staff or R&D. It can be difficult to allocate those costs to specific strategic business units (SBUs) or products. Consequently, profit objectives at the SBU and product-market level are often stated as a desired *contribution margin* (the gross profit prior to allocating such overhead costs).

assign subobjectives to different business units or products. Thus, subobjectives often vary across business units and product offerings depending on the attractiveness and potential of their industries, the strength of their competitive positions, and the resource allocation decisions made by corporate managers. For example, PepsiCo's managers likely set relatively high volume and share-growth objectives but lower ROI goals for the firm's Aquafina brand, which is battling for prominence in the rapidly growing bottled water category, than for Lay's potato chips, which hold a commanding 40 percent share of a mature product category. Therefore, two marketing managers responsible for different products may face very different goals and expectations—requiring different marketing strategies to accomplish— even though they work for the same organization.

As firms emphasize developing and maintaining long-term customer relationships, *customer-focused objectives*—such as satisfaction, retention, and loyalty—are being given greater importance. Such market-oriented objectives are more likely to be consistently pursued across business units and product offerings. There are several reasons for this. First, given the huge profit implications of a customer's lifetime value, maximizing satisfaction and loyalty tends to make good sense no matter what other financial objectives are being pursued in the short term. Second, satisfied, loyal customers of one product can be leveraged to provide synergies for other company products or services. Finally, customer satisfaction and loyalty are determined by factors other than the product itself or the activities of the marketing department. A study of one industrial paper company, for example, found that about 80 percent of customers' satisfaction scores were accounted for by nonproduct factors, such as order processing, delivery, and postsale services.[24] Since such factors are influenced by many functional departments within the corporation, they are likely to have a similar impact across a firm's various businesses and products.

Corporate Growth Strategies

Often, the projected combined future sales and profits of a corporation's business units and product-markets fall short of the firm's long-run growth and profitability objectives. There is a gap between what the firm expects to become if it continues on its present course and what it would like to become. This is not surprising because some of its high-growth markets are likely to slip into maturity over time and some of its high-profit mature businesses may decline to insignificance as they get older. Thus, to determine where future growth is coming from, management must decide on a strategy to guide corporate development.

Essentially, a firm can go in two major directions in seeking future growth: **expansion** of its current businesses and activities, or **diversification** into new businesses, either through internal business development or acquisition. Exhibit 2.9 outlines some specific options a firm might pursue while seeking growth in either of these directions.

Expansion by Increasing Penetration of Current Product-Markets   One way for a company to expand is by increasing its share of existing markets. This typically requires actions such as making product or service improvements, cutting costs and prices, or outspending competitors on advertising or promotions. Amazon.com pursued a combination of all these actions—as well as forming alliances with Web portals, affinity groups, and the like—to expand its share of Web shoppers, even though the expense of such activities postponed the firm's ability to become profitable.

Even when a firm holds a commanding share of an existing product-market, additional growth may be possible by encouraging current customers to become more loyal and concentrate their purchases, use more of the product or service, use it more often, or use it in new ways. In addition to its promotional efforts, Amazon.com spent hundreds of millions of dollars on warehouses and order fulfillment activities, investments that earned the loyalty of its customers. As a result, by the year 2000 more than three-quarters of the firm's sales were coming from repeat customers.[25] Other examples include museums that sponsor special exhibitions to encourage patrons to make repeat visits and the recipes that Quaker Oats includes on the package to tempt buyers to include oatmeal as an ingredient in other foods, such as cookies and desserts.

Expansion by Developing New Products for Current Customers   A second avenue to future growth is through a product-development strategy emphasizing the introduction of product-line extensions or new product or service offerings aimed at existing

Exhibit 2.9

Alternative Corporate Growth Strategies

	Current products	New products

Current markets	**Market penetration strategies**
	• Increase market share
	• Increase product usage
	    Increase frequency of use
	    Increase quantity used
	    New applications
		Product development strategies
		• Product improvements
		• Product-line extensions
		• New products for same market

New markets	**Market development strategies**
	• Expand markets for existing products
	    Geographic expansion
	    Target new segments
		Diversification strategies
		• Vertical integration
		    Forward integration
		    Backward integration
		• Diversification into related businesses
		    (concentric diversification)
		• Diversification into unrelated businesses
		    (conglomerate diversification)

customers. For example, Arm & Hammer successfully introduced a laundry detergent, an oven cleaner, and a carpet cleaner. Each capitalized on baking soda's image as an effective deodorizer and on a high level of recognition of the Arm & Hammer brand.

Expansion by Selling Existing Products to New Segments or Countries

Perhaps the growth strategy with the greatest potential for many companies is the development of new markets for their existing goods or services. This may involve the creation of marketing programs aimed at nonuser or occasional-user segments of existing markets. Thus, theaters, orchestras, and other performing arts organizations often sponsor touring companies to reach audiences outside major metropolitan areas and promote matinee performances with lower prices and free public transportation to attract senior citizens and students.

Expansion into new geographic markets, particularly new countries, is also a primary growth strategy for many firms. For example, General Electric announced a growth strategy that shifts the firm's strategic center of gravity from the industrialized West to Asia and Latin America.[26]

While developing nations represent attractive growth markets for basic industrial and infrastructure goods and services, growing personal incomes and falling trade barriers are making them attractive potential markets for many consumer goods and services as well. Even developed nations can represent growth opportunities for products or services based on newly emerging technologies or business models. For instance, while the rapid growth of e-retailers such as Amazon.com is likely to slow in the United States over the next few years, growth in the number of online shoppers is expected to expand rapidly in Europe[27].

Expansion by Diversifying   Firms also seek growth by diversifying their operations. This is typically riskier than the various expansion strategies because it often involves

learning new operations and dealing with unfamiliar customer groups. Nevertheless, the majority of large U.S., European, and Asian firms are diversified to one degree or another.

Vertical integration is one way for companies to diversify. **Forward vertical integration** occurs when a firm moves downstream in terms of the product flow, as when a manufacturer integrates by acquiring or launching a wholesale distributor or retail outlet. For example, IBM recently withdrew its Aptiva desktop PCs from independent computer retailers and made them available only over the company's own retail website in order to improve customer service and reduce costs. **Backward integration** occurs when a firm moves upstream by acquiring a supplier.

Integration can give a firm access to scarce or volatile sources of supply or tighter control over the marketing, distribution, or servicing of its products. But it increases the risks inherent in committing substantial resources to a single industry. Also, the investment required to vertically integrate often offsets the additional profitability generated by the integrated operations, resulting in little improvement in return on investment.[28]

Related (or **concentric**) **diversification** occurs when a firm internally develops or acquires another business that does not have products or customers in common with its current businesses but that might contribute to internal synergy through the sharing of production facilities, brand names, R&D know-how, or marketing and distribution skills. Thus, PepsiCo acquired Cracker Jack to complement its salty snack brands and leverage its distribution strengths in grocery stores.

The motivations for **unrelated (or conglomerate) diversification** are primarily financial rather than operational. By definition, an unrelated diversification involves two businesses that have no commonalities in products, customers, production facilities, or functional areas of expertise. Such diversification mostly occurs when a disproportionate number of a firm's current businesses face decline because of decreasing demand, increased competition, or product obsolescence. The firm must seek new avenues of growth. Other, more fortunate, firms may move into unrelated businesses because they have more cash than they need in order to expand their current businesses, or because they wish to discourage takeover attempts.

Unrelated diversification tends to be the riskiest growth strategy in terms of financial outcomes. Most empirical studies report that related diversification is more conducive to capital productivity and other dimensions of performance than is unrelated diversification.[29] This suggests that the ultimate goal of a corporation's strategy for growth should be to develop a compatible portfolio of businesses to which the firm can add value through the application of its unique core competencies. The corporation's marketing competencies can be particularly important in this regard.

Expansion by Diversifying through Organizational Relationships or Networks

Recently, firms have attempted to gain some benefits of market expansion or diversification while simultaneously focusing more intensely on a few core competencies. They try to accomplish this feat by forming relationships or organizational networks with other firms instead of acquiring ownership.[30]

Perhaps the best models of such organizational networks are the Japanese *keiretsu* and the Korean *chaebol*—coalitions of financial institutions, distributors, and manufacturing firms in a variety of industries that are often grouped around a large trading company that helps coordinate the activities of the various coalition members and markets their goods and services around the world. As we have seen, many Western firms like IBM and RedEnvelope are also forming alliances with suppliers, resellers, and even customers to expand their product and service offerings without making major new investments or neglecting their core competencies.

Exhibit 2.10

BCG'S MARKET GROWTH RELATIVE SHARE MATRIX

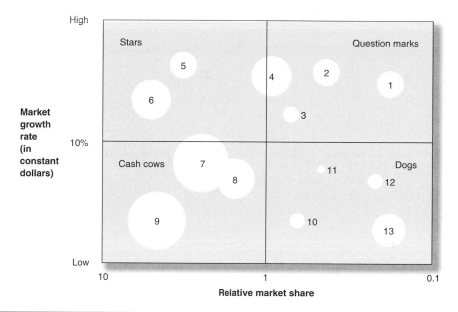

Source: Reprinted from Barry Hedley, "Strategy and the Business Portfolio," *Long Range Planning* 10. @ 1977 with permission from Elsevier.

Allocating Corporate Resources

Diversified organizations have several advantages over more narrowly focused firms. They have a broader range of areas in which they can knowledgeably invest, and their growth and profitability rates may be more stable because they can offset declines in one business with gains in another. To exploit the advantages of diversification, though, corporate managers must make intelligent decisions about how to allocate financial and human resources across the firm's various businesses and product-markets. Two sets of analytical tools have proven useful in making such decisions: **portfolio models** and **value-based planning.**

Portfolio Models   One of the most significant developments in strategic management during the 1970s and 1980s was the widespread adoption of portfolio models to help managers allocate corporate resources across multiple businesses. These models enable managers to classify and review their current and prospective businesses by viewing them as portfolios of investment opportunities and then evaluating each business's competitive strength and the attractiveness of the markets it serves.

The Boston Consulting Group's (BCG) Growth-Share Matrix   One of the first—and best known—of the portfolio models is the growth-share matrix developed by the Boston Consulting Group in the late 1960s. It analyzes the impact of investing resources in different businesses on the corporation's future earnings and cash flows. Each business is positioned within a matrix, as shown in Exhibit 2.10. The vertical axis indicates the industry's growth rate and the horizontal axis shows the business's relative market share.

The growth-share matrix assumes that a firm must generate cash from businesses with strong competitive positions in mature markets. Then it can fund investments and expenditures in industries that represent attractive future opportunities. Thus, the **market**

Exhibit 2.11

CASH FLOWS ACROSS BUSINESSES IN THE BCG PORTFOLIO MODEL

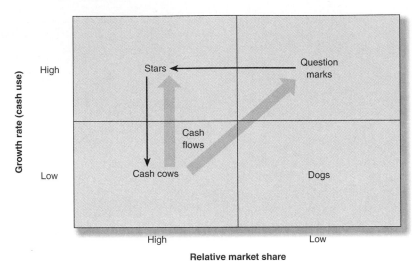

growth rate on the vertical axis is a proxy measure for the maturity and attractiveness of an industry. This model represents businesses in rapidly growing industries as more attractive investment opportunities for future growth and profitability.

Similarly, a business's relative market share is a proxy for its competitive strength within its industry. It is computed by dividing the business's absolute market share in dollars or units by that of the leading competitor in the industry. Thus, in Exhibit 2.10 a business is in a strong competitive position if its share is equal to, or larger than, that of the next leading competitor (i.e., a relative share of 1.0 or larger). Finally, in the exhibit, the size of the circle representing each business is proportional to that unit's sales volume. Thus, businesses 7 and 9 are the largest-volume businesses in this hypothetical company, while business 11 is the smallest.

Resource Allocation and Strategy Implications
Each of the four cells in the growth-share matrix represents a different type of business with different strategy and resource requirements. The implications of each are discussed below and summarized in Exhibit 2.11.

- *Question marks.* Businesses in high-growth industries with low relative market shares (those in the upper-right quadrant of Exhibit 2.11) are called *question marks* or *problem children.* Such businesses require large amounts of cash, not only for expansion to keep up with the rapidly growing market, but also for marketing activities (or reduced margins) to build market share and catch the industry leader. If management can successfully increase the share of a question mark business, it becomes a star. But if managers fail, it eventually turns into a dog as the industry matures and the market growth rate slows.

- *Stars.* A *star* is the market leader in a high-growth industry. Stars are critical to the continued success of the firm. As their industries mature, they move into the bottom-left quadrant and become cash cows. Paradoxically, while stars are critically important, they often are net users rather than suppliers of cash in the short run (as indicated by the possibility of a negative cash flow shown in Exhibit 2.11). This is because the firm must continue to invest in such businesses to keep up with rapid market growth and to support the R&D and marketing activities necessary to maintain a leading market share.

- *Cash cows.* Businesses with a high relative share of low-growth markets are called *cash cows* because they are the primary generators of profits and cash in a corporation. Such businesses do not require much additional capital investment. Their markets are stable, and their share leadership position usually means they enjoy economies of scale and relatively high profit margins. Consequently, the corporation can use the cash from these businesses to support its question marks and stars (as shown in Exhibit 2.11). However, this does not mean the firm should necessarily maximize the business's short-term cash flow by cutting R&D and marketing expenditures to the bone—particularly not in industries where the business might continue to generate substantial future sales.

- *Dogs.* Low-share businesses in low-growth markets are called *dogs* because although they may throw off some cash, they typically generate low profits, or losses. Divestiture is one option for such businesses, although it can be difficult to find an interested buyer. Another common strategy is to harvest dog businesses. This involves maximizing short-term cash flow by paring investments and expenditures until the business is gradually phased out.

Limitations of the Growth-Share Matrix

Because the growth-share matrix uses only two variables as a basis for categorizing and analyzing a firm's businesses, it is relatively easy to understand. But while this simplicity helps explain its popularity, it also means the model has limitations:

- *Market growth rate is an inadequate descriptor of overall industry attractiveness.* Market growth is not always directly related to profitability or cash flow. Some high-growth industries have never been very profitable because low entry barriers and capital intensity have enabled supply to grow even faster, resulting in intense price competition. Also, rapid growth in one year is no guarantee that growth will continue in the following year.

- *Relative market share is inadequate as a description of overall competitive strength.* Market share is more properly viewed as an outcome of past efforts to formulate and implement effective business-level and marketing strategies than as an indicator of enduring competitive strength.[31] If the external environment changes, or the SBU's managers change their strategy, the business's relative market share can shift dramatically.

- *The outcomes of a growth-share analysis are highly sensitive to variations in how growth and share are measured.*[32] Defining the relevant industry and served market (i.e., the target-market segments being pursued) can also present problems. For example, does Pepsi Cola compete only for a share of the cola market, or for a share of the much larger market for nonalcoholic beverages, such as iced tea, bottled water, and fruit juices?

- *While the matrix specifies appropriate investment strategies for each business, it provides little guidance on how best to implement those strategies.* While the model suggests that a firm should invest cash in its question mark businesses, for instance, it does not consider whether there are any potential sources of competitive advantage that the business can exploit to successfully increase its share. Simply providing a business with more money does not guarantee that it will be able to improve its position within the matrix.

- *The model implicitly assumes that all business units are independent of one another except for the flow of cash.* If this assumption is inaccurate, the model can suggest some inappropriate resource allocation decisions. For instance, if other SBUs depend on a dog business as a source of supply—or if they share functional activities, such as a common plant or salesforce, with that business—harvesting the dog might increase the costs or reduce the effectiveness of the other SBUs.

Alternative Portfolio Models

In view of the above limitations, a number of firms have attempted to improve the basic portfolio model. Such improvements have focused primarily on developing more detailed, multifactor measures of industry attractiveness and a business's competitive strength and on making the analysis more future-oriented. Exhibit 2.12 shows some factors managers might use to evaluate industry attractiveness and a

Exhibit 2.12

THE INDUSTRY ATTRACTIVENESS-BUSINESS POSITION MATRIX

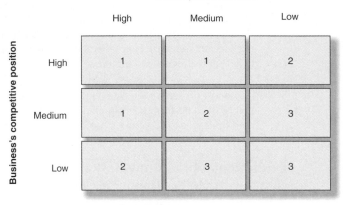

1 Invest/grow
2 Selective investment/maintain position
3 Harvest/divest

Variables that might be used to evaluate:

Business's competitive position		Industry attractivement	
Size	Distribution	Size	Profitability
Growth	Technology	Growth	Technological sophistication
Relative share	Marketing skills	Competitive intensity	Government regulations
Customer loyalty	Patents	Price levels	
Margins			

business's competitive position. Corporate managers must first select factors most appropriate for their firm and weight them according to their relative importance. They then rate each business and its industry on the two sets of factors. Next, they combine the weighted evaluations into summary measures used to place each business within one of the nine boxes in the matrix. Businesses falling into boxes numbered 1 (where both industry attractiveness and the business's ability to compete are relatively high) are good candidates for further investment for future growth. Businesses in the 2 boxes should receive only selective investment with an objective of maintaining current position. Finally, businesses in the 3 boxes are candidates for harvesting or divestiture.

These multifactor models are more detailed than the simple growth-share model and consequently provide more strategic guidance concerning the appropriate allocation of resources across businesses. They are also more useful for evaluating potential new product-markets. However, the multifactor measures in these models can be subjective and ambiguous, especially when managers must evaluate different industries on the same set of factors. Also, the conclusions drawn from these models still depend on the way industries and product-markets are defined.[33]

Value-Based Planning   As mentioned, one limitation of portfolio analysis is that it specifies how firms should allocate financial resources across their businesses without considering the competitive strategies those businesses are, or should be pursuing. Portfolio analysis provides little guidance, for instance, in deciding which of two question mark businesses—each in attractive markets but following different strategies—is worthy of the greater investment or in choosing which of several competitive strategies a particular business unit should pursue.

Exhibit 2.13

FACTORS AFFECTING THE CREATION OF SHAREHOLDER VALUE

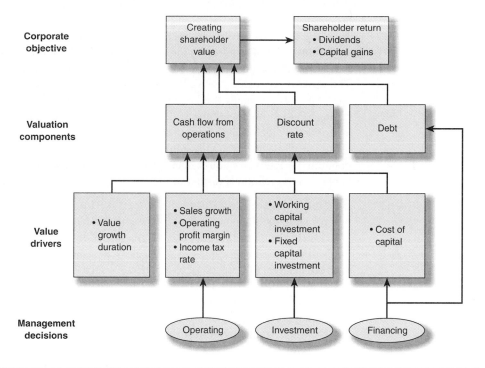

Value-based planning is a resource allocation tool that attempts to address such questions by assessing the shareholder value a given strategy is likely to create. Thus, value-based planning provides a basis for comparing the economic returns to be gained from investing in different businesses pursuing different strategies or from alternative strategies that might be adopted by a given business unit.

A number of value-based planning methods are currently in use, but all share three basic features.[34] First, they assess the economic value a strategy is likely to produce by examining the cash flows it will generate, rather than relying on distorted accounting measures, such as return on investment.[35] Second, they estimate the shareholder value that a strategy will produce by discounting its forecasted cash flows by the business's risk-adjusted cost of capital. Finally, they evaluate strategies based on the likelihood that the investments required by a strategy will deliver returns greater than the cost of capital. The amount of return a strategy or operating program generates in excess of the cost of capital is commonly referred to as its **economic value added**, or EVA.[36] This approach to evaluating alternative strategies is particularly appropriate for use in allocating resources across business units because most capital investments are made at the business-unit level, and different business units typically face different risks and therefore have different costs of capital.

Discounted Cash Flow Model Perhaps the best-known and most widely used approach to value-based planning is the discounted cash flow model proposed by Alfred Rappaport and the Alcar Group, Inc. In this model, as Exhibit 2.13 indicates, shareholder value created by a strategy is determined by the cash flow it generates, the business's cost of capital (which is used to discount future cash flows back to their present value) and the market value of the debt assigned to the business. The future cash flows generated by the strategy are, in turn, affected by six "value drivers": the rate of sales growth the strategy will produce, the operating profit margin, the income tax rate, investment in working capital, fixed capital investment required by the strategy, and the duration of value growth.

The first five value drivers are self-explanatory, but the sixth requires some elaboration. The duration of value growth represents management's estimate of the number of years over which the strategy can be expected to produce rates of return that exceed the cost of capital. This estimate, in turn, is tied to two other management judgments. First, the manager must decide on the length of the planning period (typically three to five years); he or she must then estimate the residual value the strategy will continue to produce after the planning period is over. Such decisions are tricky, for they involve predictions of what will happen in the relatively distant future.[37]

Some Limitations of Value-Based Planning   Value-based planning is not a substitute for strategic planning; it is only one tool for evaluating strategy alternatives identified and developed through managers' judgments. It does so by relying on forecasts of many kinds to put a financial value on the hopes, fears, and expectations managers associate with each alternative. Projections of cash inflows rest on forecasts of sales volume, product mix, unit prices, and competitors' actions. Expected cash outflows depend on projections of various cost elements, working capital, and investment requirements.

While good forecasts are notoriously difficult to make, they are critical to the validity of value-based planning. Unfortunately, there are natural human tendencies to overvalue the financial projections associated with some strategy alternatives and to undervalue others. For instance, managers are likely to overestimate the future returns from a currently successful strategy. Evidence of past success tends to carry more weight than qualitative assessments of future threats.

KEY OBSERVATION

Some kinds of strategy alternatives are consistently undervalued. Particularly worrisome from a marketing viewpoint is the tendency to underestimate the value of keeping current customers.

Some kinds of strategy alternatives are consistently undervalued. Particularly worrisome from a marketing viewpoint is the tendency to underestimate the value of keeping current customers. Putting a figure on the damage to a firm's competitive advantage from not making a strategic investment necessary to maintain the status quo is harder than documenting potential cost savings or profit improvements that an investment might generate. And, finally, value-based planning can evaluate alternatives, but it cannot create them. The best strategy will never emerge from the evaluation process if management fails to identify it.[38]

The Marketing Implications of Business-Unit Strategy Decisions

The components of a firm engaged in multiple industries or businesses are typically called **strategic business units,** or **SBUs.** Managers within each of these business units decide which objectives, markets, and competitive strategies to pursue. Top-level corporate managers typically reserve the right to review and approve such decisions to ensure their overall consistency with the company's mission, objectives, and the allocation of resources across SBUs in its portfolio. However, SBU-level managers, particularly those in marketing and sales, bear the primary responsibility for collecting and analyzing relevant information and generating appropriate strategies for their businesses. Those managers are more familiar with a given SBU's products, customers, and competitors and are responsible for successfully implementing the strategy. The rationale for breaking larger firms into semi-autonomous SBUs usually stems from a market-oriented desire to move strategic decision making closer to the customers the business is trying to reach.

The first step in developing business-level strategies, then, is for the firm to decide how to divide itself into SBUs. The managers in each SBU must then make recommendations about *(a)* the unit's objectives, *(b)* the scope of its target customers and offerings, *(c)* which broad competitive strategy to pursue to build a competitive advantage in its product-markets, and *(d)* how resources should be allocated across its product-market entries and functional departments.

How Should Strategic Business Units Be Designed?

Ideally, strategic business units have the following characteristics:

- *A homogeneous set of markets to serve with a limited number of related technologies.* Minimizing diversity across an SBU's product-market entries enables the unit's manager to better formulate and implement a coherent and internally consistent business strategy.

- *A unique set of product-markets,* in the sense that no other SBU within the firm competes for the same customers with similar products. Thus, the firm avoids duplication of effort and maximizes economies of scale within its SBUs.

- *Control over those factors necessary for successful performance,* such as production, R&D and engineering, marketing, and distribution. This does not mean an SBU should not share resources, such as a manufacturing plant or a salesforce, with one or more other business units. But the SBU should determine how its share of the joint resource is used to effectively carry out its strategy.

- *Responsibility for their own profitability.*

As you might expect, firms do not always meet all of these ideals when designing business units. There are usually trade-offs between having many small homogeneous SBUs versus large but fewer SBUs that top managers can more easily supervise.

What criteria should managers use to decide how product-markets should be clustered into a business unit? The three dimensions that define the scope and mission of the entire corporation also define individual SBUs:

1. *Technical compatibility,* particularly with respect to product technologies and operational requirements, such as the use of similar production facilities and engineering skills.
2. Similarity in the *customer needs* or the product benefits sought by customers in the target markets.
3. Similarity in the *personal characteristics* or behavior patterns of customers in the target markets.

In practice, the choice is often between technical/operational compatibility on the one hand and customer homogeneity on the other. Frequently management defines SBUs by product-markets requiring similar technologies, production facilities, and employee skills. This minimizes the coordination problems involved in administering the unit and increases its ability to focus on one or a few critical competencies.

In some cases, however, the marketing synergies gained from coordinating technically different products aimed at the same customer need or market segment outweigh operational considerations. In these firms, managers cluster product-market entries into SBUs based on similarities across customers or distribution systems. General Foods Corporation, for instance, includes Cool Whip and Jell-O in the same SBU even though they require different production technologies because they are marketed as dessert products.

The Business Unit's Objectives

As we discussed earlier, corporate objectives are typically broken down into subobjectives for each SBU. Those subobjectives often vary according to the attractiveness of the SBU's industry, the strength of its competitive position, and the like.

Similarly, breaking down an SBU's objectives into subobjectives for each of its product-market entries is often a major part of developing business-level strategy. Those subobjectives need to add up to the accomplishment of the SBU's overall goals; yet they should vary across product-market entries to reflect differences in the attractiveness and growth potential of individual market segments and the competitive strengths of the SBU's product in each market.

The Business Unit's Competitive Strategy

The essential question in formulating a business strategy is, How will the business unit compete to gain a sustainable competitive advantage within its industry? Achieving a competitive advantage requires a business unit to make two choices:

- What is the SBU's competitive domain or scope? Which market segments can it target, and which customer needs can it satisfy? These are stated in more general terms than is the case with marketing strategy. They serve as guidelines for the formulation of strategies for the individual product-market entries.
- How can the business unit distinguish itself from competitors in its target market(s)? What distinctive competencies can it rely on to achieve a unique position relative to its competitors?

Decisions about an SBU's Scope   A business's strategic scope can be defined either broadly or narrowly. It can pursue a range of market segments within its industry or focus on only one or a few target segments. The decision about how many customer segments to serve usually hinges on a combination of factors, including the business's objectives and available resources, characteristics of the market (e.g., the number and size of different customer segments), and the SBU's strengths and weaknesses relative to its competitors. We will examine these decisions about strategic scope and the variables that influence them in more detail in Chapters 16 and 17 where we discuss strategies for different kinds of industries at varying stages in their life cycles.

For now, the important point to recognize is that the scope of a business's strategic focus has ramifications for nearly every component of its marketing program, including the breadth of its product line; the audience for its advertising, promotion, and personal selling efforts; the design of its distribution system; and the range of prices that are viable. For example, when IBM decided to expand the target market for its Web-based services to include a wider range of small business and dot.com start-ups, it had to develop many new service offerings to meet the needs of such customers. But it also had to abandon its strategy of charging only premium prices, change the content of its advertising, and redirect a significant portion of its personal selling and promotional efforts toward its new customer segments.

Allocating Resources within the Business Unit   Once SBU managers decide on the scope of market segments and product-market entries to pursue, they allocate the financial and human resources provided by corporate management across those product-markets. Because this process is similar to allocating corporate resources across SBUs, many firms use similar portfolio analysis tools for both.

Gaining a Competitive Advantage   There are many ways in which a business unit might attempt to gain an advantage over its competitors within the scope of its strategic domain. To be successful over the long haul, however, a competitive strategy should have three characteristics.[39]

- It should generate customer value. It should give potential customers a good reason to purchase from the SBU instead of its competitors. The strategy should be predicated on providing one or more superior benefits at a price similar to what competitors charge or delivering comparable benefits at lower cost.

- The superior value must be perceived by the customer. Even if an SBU's product or service is better than the competition, if the customer is not aware of that—or doesn't attach much value to the additional benefits—it does not gain a competitive advantage. For example, as the technical and performance differences among PCs narrowed, IBM's competitive strategy of charging premium prices for technically superior products became untenable.

- The advantage should be difficult for competitors to copy. The easier it is for competitors to copy a successful strategy, the more short-lived the SBU's competitive advantage. For instance, Minnetonka, Inc., gained an advantage by introducing Check-Up, the first plaque-fighting toothpaste. But because its unique ingredients could not be patented, more than two dozen competing brands reached the market within a year; many from much bigger companies such as Procter & Gamble and Colgate-Palmolive.

Marketing Resources and Competitive Advantage
To be sustainable, a competitive advantage must be based on resources that other firms do not have and which are hard to acquire.[40] Many such unique resources are marketing-related. For example, some businesses have highly developed information systems, extensive market research operations, and/or cooperative long-term relationships with customers that give them a superior ability to identify and respond to emerging customer needs and desires. Others have a brand name that customers recognize and trust, cooperative alliances with suppliers or distributors that enhance efficiency, or a body of satisfied and loyal customers who are predisposed to buy related products or services.[41]

The trick is for the business unit to develop a competitive strategy that converts one or more of its unique resources or competencies into something of value to customers. While one can conceive of a nearly infinite assortment of such strategies, most can be classified into a few "generic" types. For example, Treacy and Wiersema argue that market leaders tend to pursue one of three categories of competitive strategy. They either stress operational excellence, which typically translates into lower costs and prices, or differentiate themselves through product leadership or customer intimacy and superior service.[42] These generic strategies are summarized in Exhibit 2.14, together with some traits and competencies of businesses that are able to implement each strategy effectively. Note how many of the core business processes underlying all three strategy types are related to the marketing function.

Other authors suggest additional ways to categorize business strategies.[43] No matter how such strategies are defined, though, the key points are (a) that competitive strategies are built—at least in part—on marketing resources and competencies and (b) the competitive strategy pursued by an SBU, in turn, helps determine what strategic marketing programs are viable for its various product-market entries. We examine this symbiotic relationship between marketing resources and competencies, business-level competitive strategies, and marketing programs for individual products and services in more detail in Chapter 10.

Competitive Strategies for Entrepreneurial Start-ups
Much of the above discussion of competitive strategies for individual SBUs within large corporations also applies to small, self-contained firms and start-ups. However, most successful start-ups have a narrow strategic scope, at least in the beginning. Their limited financial, human, and marketing

Exhibit 2.14

THREE COMPETITIVE STRATEGIES AND THE TRAITS AND COMPETENCIES OF BUSINESSES THAT IMPLEMENT THEM EFFECTIVELY

	DISCIPLINES		
Company traits	Operational excellence	Product leadership	Customer intimacy
Core business processes	Sharpen distribution systems and provide no-hassle service	Nurture ideas, translate them into products, and market them skillfully	Provide solutions and help customers run their businesses
Structure	Has strong, central authority and a finite level of empowerment	Acts in an ad hoc, organic, loosely knit, and ever-changing way	Pushes empowerment close to customer contact
Management systems	Maintain standard operating procedures	Reward individuals' innovative capacity and new product success	Measure the cost of providing service and of maintaining customer loyalty
Culture	Acts predictably and believes "one size fits all"	Experiments and thinks "out-of-the-box"	Is flexible and thinks "have it your way"

Source: Michael Treacy and Fred Wiersema, "How Market Leaders Keep Their Edge," *Fortune,* February 6, 1995, p. 96. © 1995 Time, Inc. All rights reserved.

resources (e.g., unknown brands, lack of established distribution channels, lack of a loyal customer base, etc.) force them to focus on one or a few tightly defined target segments. They simply don't have the resources to be all things to all people.

Those same resource limitations make it very wise to avoid direct confrontations with larger, more established competitors. Thus, successful start-ups tend to concentrate on niche segments that are not being adequately served and/or on finding ways to provide unique benefits and superior value. As we saw in Chapter 1, for example, even though RedEnvelope was able to raise millions in venture capital, it focused on a narrowly defined target market of upscale gift givers. And the firm is attempting to deliver superior value by developing a unique line of gifts that cannot be found anywhere else and by achieving rigorous standards of customer service. The bottom line is that the symbiosis between market analysis and customer knowledge, competitive strategy, marketing programs, and successful performance is often stronger in small firms and new start-ups than it is in the IBMs and PepsiCos of the world.

TAKE-AWAYS

- Marketing perspectives lie at the heart of strategic decision making, whether at the corporate, business-unit, or product-market levels. All managers who aspire to general management roles need marketing concepts and tools in their repertoire.

- Market-oriented firms—those that plan and coordinate company activities around the primary goal of satisfying customer needs—tend to outperform other firms on a variety of dimensions, including sales growth, return on assets, and new product success.

- Unethical behavior by a firm's employees can damage the trust between a firm and its suppliers and customers, thereby disrupting the development of long-term relationships and reducing sales and profits over time.

- The four major paths to corporate growth—market penetration, market development, product development, and diversification strategies—imply differences in a firm's strategic scope, require different competencies and marketing actions, and involve different types and amounts of risk. Decisions about which path(s) to pursue should consider all of these factors.

- The ultimate goal in formulating business-unit strategies is to establish a basis for a sustainable competitive advantage that provides superior value to customers. Doing so requires the development of resources—often marketing resources, such as brand names, marketing information systems and databases, long-term customer relationships, and so on—that other firms do not have and that are hard to acquire.

- Successful new firm formation typically requires a competitive strategy that delivers superior value to a narrowly defined target segment in a way that either

avoids direct confrontation with established competitors or is difficult for them to emulate. Therefore, market sensing and analysis, market segmentation and targeting, and market positioning skills are usually crucial in helping new firms surmount the long odds against survival.

Self-diagnostic questions to test your ability to apply the analytical tools and concepts in this chapter to marketing decision making may be found at this book's website at www.mhhe.com/mullins05.

ENDNOTES

1. This opening case example is based on material found in Spencer E. Ante, "The New Blue," *Business Week,* March 17, 2003, pp. 80–88; Spencer E. Ante, "For Big Blue, The Big Enchilada," *Business Week,* October 28, 2002, pp. 58–59; Ira Sager, "Inside IBM: Internet Business Machines," *Business Week,* E-BIZ Section, December 13, 1999, pp. EB20–38; and the company's website at www.ibm.com. Also, some historical background information is based on Das Narayandas and V. Kasturi Rangan, "Dell Computer Corporation," Harvard Business School case # 9-596-058 (Cambridge, MA: Harvard Business School, 1995).

2. Christian Homburg, John P. Workman, Jr., and Harley Krohmer, "Marketing's Influence Within the Firm," *Journal of Marketing* 63 (April 1999), pp. 1–17.

3. Quoted in Katherine Z. Andrews, "Still a Major Player: Marketing's Role in Today's Firms," *Insights From MSI,* Winter 1999, p. 2.

4. Frederick E. Webster, Jr., "Executing the New Marketing Concept," *Marketing Management* 3 (1994), pp. 9–16.

5. Rajendra K. Srivastava, Tasadduq A. Shervani, and Liam Fahey, "Marketing, Business Processes, and Shareholder Value: An Organizationally Embedded View of Marketing Activities and the Discipline of Marketing," *Journal of Marketing* 63 (Special Issue 1999), pp. 168–79.

6. For example, see John C. Narver and Stanley F. Slater, "The Effect of a Market Orientation on Business Profitability," *Journal of Marketing* 54 (April 1990), pp. 1–18; Bernard J. Jaworski and Ajay Kohli, "Market Orientation: Antecedents and Consequences," *Journal of Marketing* 57 (July 1993); and Stanley F. Slater and John C. Narver, "Market Orientation, Performance, and the Moderating Influence of Competitive Environment," *Journal of Marketing* 58 (January 1994), pp. 46–55.

7. Slater and Narver, "Market Orientation"; and John P. Workman, Jr., "When Marketing Should Follow Instead of Lead," *Marketing Management* 2 (1993), pp. 8–19.

8. For many examples, see Valarie A. Zeithaml and Mary Jo Bitner, *Services Marketing* (New York: McGraw-Hill, 1996).

9. E. Jerome McCarthy and William D. Perreault, Jr., *Basic Marketing: A Global Managerial Approach,* 11th ed. (Burr Ridge, IL: Richard D. Irwin, 1993), chap. 2.

10. "GE's Brave New World," *Business Week,* November 8, 1993, pp. 64–70.

11. This is a slightly modified form of the definition in Charles W. Hofer and Dan Schendel, *Strategy Formulation: Analytical Concepts* (St. Paul, MN: West, 1978), p. 25. However, our definition differs in that we view the setting of objectives as an integral part of strategy formulation, whereas they see objective setting as a separate process. Because a firm or business unit's objectives are influenced and constrained by many of the same environmental and competitive factors as the other elements of strategy, however, it seems logical to treat both the determination of objectives and the resource allocations

aimed at reaching those objectives as two parts of the same strategic planning process.

12. However, while such corporate-level synergies are often used to justify mergers, acquisitions, and forays into new businesses, they sometimes prove elusive. For example, see Laura Landro, "Giants Talk Synergy But Few Make It Work," *The Wall Street Journal,* September 25, 1995, p. B1.

13. C. K. Prahalad and Gary Hamel, "The Core Competence of the Corporation," *Harvard Business Review* 68 (May–June 1990), pp. 79–91.

14. As suggested by Exhibit 2.5, corporate resource decisions should also consider the development of superior or unique resources capable of giving the firm a sustainable competitive advantage, and the possibility of generating synergy via resource sharing across business units or divisions. While such corporate concerns are largely beyond the scope of this book, interested readers can find a more detailed discussion in Orville C. Walker, Jr., Harper W. Boyd, Jr., John Mullins, and Jean-Claude Larreche, *Marketing Strategy: A Decision-Focused Approach,* 4th ed. (New York: McGraw-Hill/Irwin, 2003), chap. 2.

15. John A. Byrne, "PepsiCo's New Formula," *Business Week,* April 10, 2000, pp. 172–84.

16. Theodore Levitt, "Marketing Myopia," *Harvard Business Review* (July–August 1960), pp. 455–56.

17. "Good Grief," *The Economist,* April 8, 1995, p. 57; and "Doing Well by Doing Good," *The Economist,* April 22, 2000, pp. 65–67.

18. "Doing Well by Doing Good," p. 66.

19. Robert A. Cooke, *Ethics in Business: A Perspective* (Chicago: Arthur Andersen, 1988).

20. I. Fredrick Trawick, John E. Swan, Gail W. McGee, and David R. Rink, "Influence of Buyer Ethics and Salesperson Behavior on Intention to Choose a Supplier," *Journal of the Academy of Marketing Science* 19 (Winter 1991), pp. 17–23.

21. Dawn Bryan, "Using Gifts to Make the Sale," *Sales & Marketing Management,* September 1989, pp. 48–53. See also, "The Destructive Cost of Greasing Palms," *Business Week,* December 6, 1993, pp. 133–38.

22. Y. K. Shetty, "New Look at Corporate Goals," *California Management Review* 12 (Winter 1979), pp. 71–79; see also Robert S. Kaplan and David P. Norton, "Using the Balanced Scorecard as a Strategic Management System," *Harvard Business Review* 74 (January–February 1996), pp. 75–85.

23. Gordon Donaldson, *Managing Corporate Wealth* (New York: Praeger, 1984). See also, Kaplan and Norton, "Using the Balanced Scorecard," and Srivastava, Shervani, and Fahey, "Marketing, Business Processes, and Shareholder Value."

24. Daniel P. Finkelman, "Crossing the 'Zone of Indifference,'" *Marketing Management* 2, no. 3 (1993), pp. 22–31.

25. Heather Green, "Shakeout: E–tailers," *Business Week*, May 15, 2000, pp. EB102–108; and Heather Green, "How Hard Should Amazon Swing?" *Business Week,* January 14, 2002, p. 38.

26. "GE's Brave New World," *Business Week*, November 8, 1993, pp. 64–70.

27. Jennifer L. Schenker, "The Future Is Now," *Time*, April 10, 2000, pp. 85–86; and "2002 Marketing Factbook," *Marketing News,* July 8, 2002, p. 19.

28. Robert D. Buzzell and Bradley T. Gale, *The PIMS Principles: Linking Strategy to Performance* (New York: Free Press, 1987), chap. 8.

29. For a more comprehensive review of the evidence concerning the effects of diversification on firm performance, see Roger A. Kerin, Vijay Mahajan, and P. Rajan Varadarajan, *Contemporary Perspectives on Strategic Market Planning* (Boston: Allyn and Bacon, 1990), chap. 6.

30. For example, see Ravi S. Achrol and Philip Kotler, "Marketing in the Network Economy," *Journal of Marketing* 63 (Special Issue 1999), pp. 146–63.

31. Robert Jacobson argues that market share and profitability are joint outcomes from successful strategies and, further, that management skills likely have the greatest impact on profitability. See "Distinguishing Among Competing Theories of the Market Share Effect," *Journal of Marketing* 52 (October 1988), pp. 68–80.

32. Yoram Wind, Vijay Mahajan, and Donald J. Swire, "An Empirical Comparison of Standardized Portfolio Models," *Journal of Marketing* 47 (Spring 1983), pp. 89–99.

33. For a more detailed discussion of the uses and limitations of multifactor portfolio models, see Kerin, Mahajan, and Varadarajan, *Contemporary Perspectives on Strategic Market Planning*, chap. 3.

34. The discounted cash flow model is the approach focused on in this chapter. It is detailed in Alfred Rappaport, *Creating Shareholder Value: A New Standard for Business Performance* (New York: Free Press, 1986).

35. For a detailed discussion of the shortcomings of accounting data for determining the value created by a strategy, see Rappaport, *Creating Shareholder Value*, chap. 2.

36. For a more detailed discussion of EVA and some practical examples, see Shawn Tully, "The Real Key to Creating Wealth," *Fortune*, September 20, 1993, pp. 38–50; and Terrence P. Pare, "The New Champ of Wealth Creation," *Fortune*, September 18, 1995, pp. 131–32.

37. A more in-depth discussion of the forecasts and other procedures used in value-based planning can be found in Rappaport, *Creating Shareholder Value*, or Kerin, Mahajan, and Varadarajan, *Contemporary Perspectives on Strategic Market Planning*, chap. 9.

38. The limitations of value-based planning are discussed in more detail in George S. Day and Liam Fahey, "Putting Strategy into Shareholder Value Analysis," *Harvard Business Review*, March–April, 1990, pp. 156–62.

39. David A. Aaker, *Strategic Market Management*, 5th ed. (New York: Wiley, 1998), chap. 8.

40. Jay B. Barney, "Firm Resources and Sustained Competitive Advantage," *Journal of Management* 17 (1991), pp. 99–120; and Margaret A. Peteraf, "The Cornerstone of Competitive Advantage: A Resource-Based View," *Strategic Management Journal*, 14 (1993), pp. 179–92.

41. George S. Day, "The Capabilities of Market-Driven Organizations," *Journal of Marketing* 58 (October 1994), pp. 37–52; and George S. Day and Prakash Nedungadi, "Managerial Representations of Competitive Advantage," *Journal of Marketing* 58 (April 1994), pp. 31–44.

42. Michael Treacy and Fred Wiersema, *The Discipline of Market Leaders* (Reading, MA: Addison-Wesley, 1995).

43. For example, see Michael E. Porter, *Competitive Advantage* (New York: Free Press, 1985); and Robert E. Miles and Charles C. Snow, *Organizational Strategy, Structure, and Process* (New York: McGraw-Hill, 1978).

APPENDIX 2.1

THE AMERICAN MARKETING ASSOCIATION'S CODE OF ETHICS

CODE OF ETHICS

Members of the American Marketing Association (AMA) are committed to ethical professional conduct. They have joined together in subscribing to this Code of Ethics embracing the following topics:

Responsibilities of the Marketer

Marketers must accept responsibility for the consequences of their activities and make every effort to ensure that their decisions, recommendations, and actions function to identify, serve, and satisfy all relevant publics: customers, organizations, and society.

Marketers' professional conduct must be guided by:

1. The basic rule of professional ethics: not knowingly to do harm.
2. The adherence to all applicable laws and regulations.
3. The accurate representation of their education, training and experience.
4. The active support, practice, and promotion of this Code of Ethics.

Honesty and Fairness

Marketers shall uphold and advance the integrity, honor, and dignity of the marketing profession by:

1. Being honest in serving consumers, clients, employees, suppliers, distributors, and the public.
2. Not knowingly participating in a conflict of interest without prior notice to all parties involved.
3. Establishing equitable fee schedules including the payment or receipt of usual, customary, and/or legal compensation for marketing exchanges.

Rights and Duties of Parties in the Marketing Exchange Process

Participants in the marketing exchange process should be able to expect that:

1. Products and services offered are safe and fit for their intended uses.
2. Communications about offered products and services are not deceptive.
3. All parties intend to discharge their obligations, financial and otherwise, in good faith.

4. Appropriate internal methods exist for equitable adjustment and/or redress of grievances concerning purchases.

It is understood that the above would include, *but is not limited to,* the following responsibilities of the marketer.

In the area of product development and management:

- Disclosure of all substantial risks associated with product or service usage.
- Identification of any product component substitution that might materially change the product or impact on the buyer's purchase decision.
- Identification of extra-cost added features.

In the area of promotions:

- Avoidance of false and misleading advertising.
- Rejection of high-pressure manipulations or misleading sales tactics.
- Avoidance of sales promotions that use deception or manipulation.

In the area of distribution:

- Not manipulating the availability of a product for purpose of exploitation.
- Not using coercion in the marketing channel.
- Not exerting undue influence over the reseller's choice to handle a product.

In the area of pricing:

- Not engaging in price fixing.
- Not practicing predatory pricing.
- Disclosing the full price associated with any purchase.

In the area of marketing research:

- Prohibiting selling or fund-raising under the guise of conducting research.
- Maintaining research integrity by avoiding misrepresentation and omission of pertinent research data.
- Treating outside clients and suppliers fairly.

Organizational Relationships

Marketers should be aware of how their behavior may influence or impact on the behavior of others in organizational relationships. They should not demand, encourage, or apply coercion to obtain unethical behavior in their relationships with others, such as employees, suppliers, or customers.

1. Apply confidentiality and anonymity in professional relationships with regard to privileged information.

2. Meet their obligations and responsibilities in contracts and mutual agreements in a timely manner.

3. Avoid taking the work of others, in whole, or in part, and representing this work as their own or directly benefiting from it without compensation or consent of the originator or owner.

4. Avoid manipulation to take advantage of situations to maximize personal welfare in a way that unfairly deprives or damages the organization or others.

Any AMA members found to be in violation of any provision of this Code of Ethics may have his or her Association membership suspended or revoked.

SECTION TWO

MARKET OPPORTUNITY ANALYSIS

CHAPTER 3   Environmental Analysis: Tools to Identify Attractive Markets

CHAPTER 4   Industry Analysis and Competitive Advantage

CHAPTER 5   Understanding Consumer Buying Behavior

CHAPTER 6   Understanding Organizational Markets and Buying Behavior

CHAPTER 7   Measuring Market Opportunities: Forecasting and Marketing Research

CHAPTER 8   Market Segmentation and Target Marketing

CHAPTER 9   Differentiation and Positioning

Environmental Analysis: Tools to Identify Attractive Markets

The Changing American Menswear Market[1]

FROM JEANS TO KHAKIS, from tailored suits to business casual, clothing preferences among American men have been changing. A trend toward casual dress in the workplace that got its start during the 1980s in high-tech firms in California has become pervasive. One day in early 2000, some 350 lawyers and staffers from the old-line New York law firm of Cadwalader, Wickersham, and Taft crowded into the Polo mansion on New York's posh upper east side to get some advice on how to enter the "business casual" era. And in the City of London, in the staid investment banking hallways of Goldman Sachs, Merrill Lynch, and Morgan Stanley, business casual was the order of the day.

The Impact of Macroenvironmental Trends

For companies serving the men's tailored clothing market, the challenges brought about by the business casual trend have been daunting. Manufacturers of tailored men's clothing have stumbled, and some have attempted to reposition themselves as purveyors of more casual attire. Retailers of men's suits have also struggled, and some, such as the Kuppenheimer chain, a unit of Hartmarx, the leading manufacturer of tailored menswear in the United States, have closed their doors.

What happens when unexpected trends, like that toward more casual dress in the workplace, cause demand for a category of goods or services to shrink? First, providers of such goods feel a softening in their sales. As sales grow softer, firms find they have excess capacity and expense levels that cannot be supported by reduced levels of revenue. Often, the performance figures that result paint a picture that is anything but pretty. In 1999 the bankrupt American retailer Edison Brothers liquidated its 295 Riggings stores because none of 250 interested parties was willing to buy the ailing chain. In 2000 Moss Brothers, the British high street menswear retailer, plunged into the red, losing £3.4 million in its year ended January 2001 compared to a £6.7 million profit the prior year. In response the company announced plans to convert its tailored clothing stores—operating under the Savoy Taylors Guild, Suit Company, and Blazer brands—to a new casual clothing format called Code.

The widespread troubles experienced by menswear retailers and manufacturers in the 1990s are typical of what can happen when unforeseen trends cause consumer demand to drop rapidly. Simply put, the market for tailored men's apparel shrunk like a cheap suit, and the ensuing competitive pressures in the menswear manufacturing and retailing industries made this market and these industries far less attractive than they had once been.

What's Next? Will Suits Come Back?

When the dot-com bubble burst in 2000, the time seemed right for a return to more formal business attire. The logic was that laid-off dot.com workers would be interviewing again, and those who had kept their jobs would begin dressing better out of fear. By 2002, signs indicated that a reversal of the casual trend was under way. Spending on men's casual wear in the UK was down 9 percent compared to the prior year, and spending on men's formal wear and suits were both up. Moss Bros, whose development of its Code stores had not gone well, decided to close the Code stores and refocus on formal wear and tailored clothing as well as its upmarket Hugo Boss and Cecil Gee businesses. As Moss Brothers CEO Adrian Wright put it, "If my job were under threat, I'd work harder, get in earlier, and smarten up." Will suits come back, or will they simply be one option, to be worn when appropriate, for client meetings or to make one's employer think you have a job interview? Time will tell. For marketing strategists in the menswear industry, it's a question not to be ignored.

Marketing Challenges Addressed in Chapter 3

As the story of the changing menswear market shows, unfavorable trends that negatively influence market demand can have a devastating effect on the performance of firms serving that market. Similarly, favorable trends exert positive forces that make it easier for firms to perform well. As discussed in Exhibit 3.1, retailers and manufacturers of casual clothing suitable for today's workplace fared well in the late 1990s but have stumbled in the new millennium. Entrepreneurs wanting to start new firms, investors seeking to find favorable returns, and managers working in existing firms are well-advised to consider the presence and strength of such trends in deciding where to place their bets. Thus, decisions about whether to enter or invest in a new business or a new market, whether to continue to serve the firm's current market, or whether to adopt new strategies to take advantage of favorable trends or mitigate the effects of unfavorable ones require that such trends be identified and understood.

In this chapter, we address the second of the 4Cs—the **environmental context** in which the business operates—that were identified in Chapter 1 as the analytical foundation of the marketing management process. We provide a framework to help managers, entrepreneurs, and investors comprehensively assess the environment in which they operate or propose to operate, in order to assess market attractiveness and enhance their likelihood of achieving success. Thus, this chapter addresses three important questions: Does it really matter whether we swim upstream or downstream? How can we be sure we've identified and understood the key trends? And finally, how does macro trend analysis play out in assessing markets and in making marketing decisions?

KEY OBSERVATION

Does it really matter whether we swim upstream or downstream? How can we be sure we've identified and understood the key trends?

Exhibit 3.1   Casual Clothing Comes and Goes

In the late 1990's casual dress in the workplace was all the rage. Dot.com entrepreneurs dressed in Aerosmith T-shirts raised millions in venture capital, and office workers everywhere put their suits in the back of the closet. Khakis' share of young men's sportswear reached 15 percent by 1999, as khaki sales doubled over 1998. Casual dress was here to stay, or so it seemed.

By 2002, however, the pendulum was moving the other way. At an international law firm with 650 lawyers, Coudert Brothers, a memo went out reminding the firm's New York employees what was and was not appropriate office wear. The trend toward more formal office dress embraced women, too. "As of late, I think there's a lot more importance being placed on looking polished and appropriate at work," said Kim Roy, President of Ann Taylor, the women's fashion apparel chain. The company's new line of man-styled women's suits—nearly forgotten relics from the 1980's—was racking up double-digit increases in suit sales in autumn 2002 compared with suit sales the year before.

Where will trends in office attire move next? Time will tell, and casual apparel retailers like Gap, along with purveyors of more formal apparel like Ann Taylor and Moss Brothers, will be watching closely.

Sources: Jackie Kuntz, "Khaki Sales Up, Jeans Sales Down," *Daily News Record,* February 11, 2000; Ginia Bellafonte, "A Swing to More Suitable Attire," *The Hamilton Spectator,* November 8, 2002.

Swimming Upstream or Downstream: An Important Strategic Choice

Casual dress in the workplace was a social trend. The graying of the world population is a demographic one. Global warming is a trend in our physical environment. All these trends influence the fortunes of some companies, but not others. As we have seen, the influence of **macroenvironmental trends**—or **macro trends,** for short—like these can be pervasive and powerful. In general, life is better swimming downstream, accompanied by favorable trends, than upstream, running counter to such trends.

KEY OBSERVATION

Like mosquitoes or cooling breezes on a humid summer evening, trends will always be present, whether marketing managers like them or not. The question is what managers can do about them.

Like mosquitoes or cooling breezes on a humid summer evening, trends will always be present, whether marketing managers like them or not. The question is what managers can do about them. For some trends, marketers and other managers can do little but react and adapt. In the 1990s, manufacturers of products sold in spray containers were required to find new propellants less harmful to the ozone layer. Governments concerned about global warming mandated this change. For other trends, like the shift toward or away from casual dress in the workplace, favorable moves can be reinforced through effective marketing. Similarly, sometimes, unfavorable ones can be mitigated. But doing these things requires that important trends be noticed and understood. The sociocultural, demographic, and physical environments are but three of six major components of the **macroenvironment.** The other three are the political/legal, economic, and technological components. We deal with the competitive environment in Chapter 4.

Macro Trend Analysis: A Framework for Assessing Market Attractiveness

In this section, we examine each of the six macroenvironmental components in terms of how the dynamics of change affect the attractiveness of particular markets and influence marketing strategies and programs. Analysis of such macro trends is one of the most fundamental tools in the marketing manager's toolkit.[2]

The Demographic Environment

The world's population in 2002 was 6.23 billion versus 2.56 billion in 1950, and is expected to grow to 7.83 billion by 2025. Some 80 percent of the world's population lives in the less-developed countries, and 98 percent of the increase in population is expected to be concentrated in Asia, Africa, and Latin America. If current trends continue, the proportion of world population living in Sub-Saharan Africa, the Near East, and North Africa will rise through year 2025 because of the above-average growth rates of these regions. On the other hand, because the growth rates of today's more developed countries are slower than the global average, the share of world population living in today's more-affluent nations will continue to shrink, from 20 percent to about 15 percent of the total during the first quarter of this century. Thus, the biggest markets of this century will be Asia, Africa, and Latin America, although their purchasing power per person may not follow this trend.[3]

Over the course of the next 25 years, the age structure of world population will continue to shift, with older age groups making up an increasingly larger share of the total. For example, during the 1998–2025 period, the world's elderly population (ages 65 and above) will more than double while the world's youth (population under age 15) will grow by 6 percent, and the number of children under age 5 will increase by less than 5 percent.

Because of population aging, elderly dependency ratios—the ratio of the population ages 65 and over to the working age population (ages 15 to 64)—will rise in every major world region during the next 25 years. And the world community as a whole will face an elderly support burden nearly 50 percent larger in 2025 than in 1998. A significant factor impacting population growth and dependency ratios negatively in Sub-Saharan countries is the HIV/AIDS pandemic (see Exhibit 3.2).

Another global trend is the rapid shift of the populations in Asia, Africa, and Latin America from rural to urban. By 2025, 60 percent of the world population will be urban versus 37 percent currently. From 1998 to 2025 the share of total world urban population found in the United States and the other more developed countries making up the rest of the world will drop from about 24 percent to about 16 percent of the total. By the year 2015, seven cities will have populations in excess of 20 million (see Exhibit 3.3).

Exhibit 3.2   The Impact of the HIV/AIDS Pandemic

Less developed countries in Africa and Asia are facing an unprecedented crisis caused by the rapid permeation and spread of HIV/AIDS. Average life expectancy in Sub-Saharan Africa has been dramatically reduced to 47 from 62 years. Africa remains by far the worst affected region in the world: 3.5 million new infections occurred in Africa in 2001, bringing to 28.5 million the total number of people living with HIV/AIDS in the region. In contrast to the developed world, where up to 30 percent of all infected people receive antiretroviral therapy, fewer than 30,000 people (0.1 percent) of the 28.5 million infected Africans were estimated to have received antiretroviral therapy. Although this represents a huge market opportunity for pharmaceutical companies, they also have to incorporate the vastly lower financing capabilities in these nations and the almost nonexistent medical and patient-monitoring infrastructure prevalent there.

Source: The Global HIV/AIDS Pandemic 2002: A Status Report, at the Johns Hopkins AIDS Service, http://www.hopkins-aids.edu/publications/report/sept02_5html#global.

Exhibit 3.3

POPULATIONS OF THE 10 LARGEST URBAN AREAS—1994 VERSUS 2015 (IN MILLIONS)

Urban area	1994	Urban area	2015
1. Tokyo	26.5	1. Tokyo	28.4
2. New York	16.3	2. Bombay	27.4
3. Sao Paulo	16.1	3. Lagos	24.4
4. Mexico City	15.5	4. Shanghai	23.4
5. Shanghai	14.7	5. Jakarta	21.2
6. Bombay	14.5	6. Sao Paulo	20.8
7. Los Angeles	12.2	7. Karachi	20.6
8. Beijing	12.0	8. Beijing	19.4
9. Calcutta	11.5	9. Dhaka	19.0
10. Seoul	11.5	10. Mexico City	18.8

Source: United Nations Population Division, World Urbanization Prospects: The 1999 Revision, Data Tables and Highlights, ESA/P/WP.161 (New York: United Nations, 2000).

Implications of Demographic Trends for Market Attractiveness   The demographic trends discussed in this section have resulted in rapidly growing markets for a diverse array of products and services. Rapid economic development and a growing middle class in Asia have been a boon for capital goods manufacturers in the United States and Europe, as they export capital equipment to the Asian factories seeking to satisfy Asia's growing demand for manufactured goods for local as well as export markets. Aging populations in developed countries have created growing demand for senior housing of many types and for in-home, home repair, and home modification services to enable older persons to stay in their homes.[4] Demographic trends have also led marketers to develop products and special marketing programs targeted at minority and other demographic groups whose numbers are growing.

KEY OBSERVATION

Rapid economic development and a growing middle class in Asia have been a boon for capital goods manufacturers.

The Sociocultural Environment

This environment represents the values, attributes, and general behavior of the individuals in a given society. Compared with economic, political, and technological changes, the sociocultural environment evolves slowly. People grow up in a system of values they tend to carry throughout their lifetimes. Transformation in the structure of society, in its institutions, and in the distribution of wealth occur gradually in democratic countries. Even so, we have in recent years seen a substantial change in individual values, family structure, minority rights, leisure-time activities, and conservation.

During the 1960s, North American society moved away from previously held values of hard work, thriftiness, and faith in others and in institutions, to social activism for causes such as civil rights and the end of the Vietnam War, and nonconformism. This era is often referred to as the "Age of Us."

More recently, individual values have shifted again, particularly in the younger generation (20–29 years of age), often referred to as Generation X[5] who have been more influenced by the advent of the knowledge society, the electronic/computer revolution, the

Exhibit 3.4

SHIFTING VALUES IN WESTERN SOCIETIES

Traditional values	New values
Self-denial ethic	Self-fulfillment ethic
Higher standard of living	Better quality of life
Traditional sex roles	Blurring of sex roles
Accepted definition of success	Individualized definition of success
Traditional family life	Alternative families
Faith in industry, institutions	Self-reliance
Live to work	Work to live
Hero worship	Love of ideas
Expansionism	Pluralism
Patriotism	Less nationalistic
Unparalleled growth	Growing sense of limits
Industrial growth	Information/service growth
Receptivity to technology	Technology orientation

Developed Western societies are gradually moving away from traditional values and toward the emerging new values being embraced on an ever-widening scale, says author Joseph Plummer.

Source: "Changing Values: The New Emphasis on Self-Actualization," *The Futurist,* January–February 1989, p. 15. Used by permission.

transience of jobs, the changing structure of the American family, and the growing influence of minority groups.

Because of these experiences, members of this generation are greatly concerned with simplifying their lives, with obtaining a college education, with their relations with their families and the opposite sex, and with economic security. Their coping includes living at home (particularly men), postponing marriage, and delaying having children. They are realistic and pragmatic about surviving yet do not define success solely in terms of money. They place considerable emphasis on the family life they missed as children. While generally turned off by big government, they care a great deal about such issues as AIDS, abortion, and the environment.[6] For one professional's list of the shifting values in Western societies, see Exhibit 3.4.

Although sociocultural changes are slow to happen in any individual country, there are fundamental differences between countries that are driven by their cultural histories. For example, a study of the physical form of housing prevalent today in England and Japan reveals that the English homes are built around personal privacy and home-centered living whereas the Japanese homes emphasize familial privacy and family-centered living.[7]

Implications of Sociocultural Trends for Market Attractiveness   Along with broader sociocultural trends come changes in consumer tastes and behavior. Natural foods are in. Exercise for both genders is in. Fat and cholesterol are out. The increasing importance of the individual has also given rise to a plethora of customized products, from made-to-measure jeans to business suits. Thus, sociocultural changes, such as those described in this section and at the beginning of the chapter, influence the markets for a broad array of consumer products such as natural foods, exercise equipment and sports beverages, low-fat food products, and apparel. Sociocultural trends have also influenced how marketing activities are carried out in some markets. For example, advertising programs now accommodate more joint decision making in households.

The Economic Environment

The economic performance of a country is measured by **gross domestic product (GDP)**—usually on a per-capita basis after accounting for inflation. To realistically compare incomes across countries, it is necessary to use a **purchasing power parity (PPP)** approach that considers the cost of a standard basket of products (expressed in U.S. dollars) for each country.

Thus, using a PPP analysis helps to compare the relative purchasing power of a given country with other countries. Historically, Japan had the world's highest average if GDP per capita is calculated on the basis of exchange rates. But America's figure is the highest if purchasing power parity is used.[8]

Using PPP values typically produces lower GDP per capita income for the wealthier countries and higher ones for the poorer nations. Despite this "leveling," the gap in real GDP (less inflation) has increased between rich and poor countries—mainly because of higher population growth.[9] But PPP does not take into account the subsidies provided by many countries for such essentials as food, utilities, shelter, transportation, education, and medical care, which account for about half of the average household expenditures in developed countries.

The world's economic growth continues to increase as measured by total gross domestic product (GDP). In the last part of the 1990s, America experienced impressive growth in productivity that seems to be continuing despite the overall economic slowdown, which is attributed to the huge investments in technology and capital equipment made in the last decade. A similar, but smaller growth in productivity is also seen in Europe, which is consistent with the slower percolation of technology investments in these countries.

Favorable economic trends never last forever, however. The terrorist attacks of September 11, 2001, dealt a significant blow to the already weakened U.S. economy, sharply affecting consumer and business confidence. The recovery was consumer-led, driven by consumer spending, low interest rates, tax cuts, and significant buildup in home equity, as consumers took advantage of their homes appreciating in value and refinanced their home mortgages.[10]

As we write, however, the advanced economies of the world are struggling to recover from a slowdown, and future economic forecasts are dependent on how quickly the United States and Europe recover. In the years ahead, the developing countries are expected to have substantially higher rates of economic growth than the developed ones. Asia has experienced the strongest growth—over 6 percent (primarily because of China and India's impressive growth)—and is expected to continue at a 5+ percent rate near-term.[11] In South America, Argentina is still recovering from its crisis, but its effects do not seem to have spread to other countries.

On a brighter note, discretionary spending is on the rise globally. For example, the average person in the United Kingdom spends £114 per month just to free up time—opt for takeaways rather than cooking, take taxis instead of walking, hire cleaners, dog-walkers, and baby-sitters.[12] Another important trend is the rise of household financial debt and increasing levels of credit card spending. This rise is of more concern in developing nations, because of their lower ability to repay these debts as compared to more advanced economies. In South Korea, household debt had increased 88 percent since 1997.[13] In the United Kingdom, credit card debt doubled in four years, from £20 to £40 billion in 2002.[14]

International Trade   Increasingly countries have become more economically interdependent as have many of their industries. Free-trade agreements are in place today in several regions of the world—Andean Common Market (ANDEAN), Asia-Pacific Economic
Cooperation (APEC), Association of South-East Asian Nations (ASEAN), the European
Union (EU), the North American Free Trade Agreement (NAFTA), the Central European
Free Trade Agreement (CEFTA), and the Southern Common Market (MERCOSUR). The
21 APEC countries logged the highest level of intraregion trade, followed by 15 countries
in the European Union. Apart from eliminating or reducing the tariffs on imports and exports within the region, these agreements also set a common standard that companies can
develop products for. Thus, companies achieve instant marketability in several countries
with a single product.[15]

The United States is by far the largest national market, representing about 25 percent of
the total world market for goods and services (Europe is second with 10 percent). As such,
the U.S. market is a high priority target for the business firms of most countries, especially
those of Japan and Europe. Inevitably, the United States is a highly competitive market for
many goods and services. It is not only the biggest importer of goods and services, but also
the biggest exporter, with the European Union a close second.[16] Germany, Japan, and the
United Kingdom are the next largest nations who are the largest importers and exporters
behind the United States.[17]

Canada receives the largest share of exports from the United States, which is followed
very closely by the European Union. The United States in turn receives its largest share of
imports from Canada, the European Union, Japan, and Mexico. Chemicals, machinery, and
transport equipment form the bulk of imports from the EU, whereas automotive products
and office and telecommunication equipment are the major imports from Japan.[18] Many
U.S. companies are foreign-owned—for example, DaimlerChrysler (German), Carnation
(Swiss), Firestone (Japanese), and Universal (French).

Fluctuating exchange rates can significantly change the relative price competitiveness
of firms manufacturing in different countries. For example, the devaluation of the yen versus the U.S. dollar (from 108.95 in June 1996 to 122.78 in February 1997) enabled Japanese automakers to offer better deals in selling and leasing their cars in the United States,
especially those made in Japan. The big three U.S. automakers (General Motors, Ford, and
Chrysler) complained about the U.S. policy of strengthening the value of the dollar against
the yen and the German mark and forecast lower profits—even a decline in market share.

Implications of Economic Trends for Market Attractiveness   Economic
trends influence the level of demand in most markets, but they are particularly important in
capital goods markets, real estate, and other markets where sensitivity to interest rates and

the level of household or corporate income can be extreme. Economic
trends often combine with other macro trend categories, with powerful
effects. For example, the growth of the baby boomers,[19] a demographic
trend, combined with the strong American economy and low interest
rates in the late 1990s, both economic trends, resulted in rapidly growing demand for con-
dominiums and second homes in resort areas. Some who foresaw these trends made a
killing during this period.

The Political/Legal Environment

In every country there is a legislative or **regulatory environment** within which both local and foreign firms must operate. As with any other external force, the political/legal
environment presents a firm with strategic opportunities as well as threats. The business

regulations in a country reflect its economic maturity and political philosophy. At the extreme, political risk for the firm includes confiscation (seizure without compensation as happened in Iran several years ago), expropriation (seizure with some compensation), and domestication (requiring transfer of ownership to the host country and local management and sourcing).

Other risks include changes in exchange control (which can take a variety of forms), local content laws, import restrictions, taxes, and price controls—all of which usually operate to the advantage of local industry. Clearly, many third world countries present an array of political risks to companies seeking to do business in them. (See Exhibit 3.5 for a discussion of the risks of investing in China.) On the other hand, governments can encourage foreign investment through policies such as tax concessions and tariff protection. Indeed, countries commonly encourage certain kinds of investments while simultaneously restricting others. For example, governments may encourage local firms to export to countries that have considerable political risk by providing insurance against losses from such risk (for instance, the U.S. Export-Import Bank).

An increasingly important issue in political/legal terms is the protection of intellectual property. Controversies over copyright infringement involve the highest stakes. In China, pirate factories often under the protection of senior politicians and high-ranking military officials engage in counterfeiting such items as videos, compact disks, computer software, prescription drugs, herbicides, and Rolex watches. A study of the impact of software piracy reports that in China alone, the loss of retail software sales is estimated to be US$1.6 billion in 2001.[20]

Government Regulation   The number and intricacy of laws and regulations make it difficult to understand regulatory elements affecting marketing. Most countries have regulations concerning food and drugs, as well as price, products, promotion, and distribution, but these vary considerably in their applicability to marketing. For example, the European Union has phased in thousands of rules to provide uniform safety, health, and environmental standards for its member countries. These rules now favor companies producing a variety of products for several countries, but in the future some exporters will be required to make costly design changes, to substantially retool, and to add new quality control systems.

It has long been argued that regulations cripple the economy and stifle innovation. This is often true, but effects are frequently overstated since business will strive to find innovative ways to adhere to regulations at less than the anticipated costs. For example, when the U.S. Occupational Safety and Health Administration issued a higher standard for avoiding

---

Exhibit 3.5   Hungary's Changing Landscape

After the collapse of the Iron Curtain in 1990, several U.S. companies rushed to invest in Hungary. Over the last decade, General Electric invested more than US$1.1 billion into Hungary, making it one of the country's largest investors. In that time, GE turned around a state-owned dinosaur, built three new plants, and recruited dozens of scientists.

Yet the Hungary that GE discovered more than a decade ago bears little resemblance to the country that stood in 2003 on the brink of joining the EU. The economy is more stable, the legal and regulatory environment is more transparent, and local suppliers are more reliable. But doing business here is getting more expensive with every passing year, as wages rise and as officials are forced to phase out big tax breaks to comply with EU rules. IBM announced that it would shut one factory, and Flextronics Corp. moved hundreds of jobs to China.

Source: "No Hungarian Rhapsody for GE." Reprinted from the November 25, 2002 issue of *Business Week* by permission. Copyright The McGraw-Hill Companies.

worker exposure to the toxic chemical formaldehyde, industry costs were expected to be $10 million yearly. But by modifying the resins and reducing the amount of formaldehyde, costs were negligible. Further, the changes enhanced the global competitiveness of the U.S. foundry supply and equipment industry.[21]

Government Deregulation   Government, business, and the general public throughout much of the world have become increasingly aware that overregulation protects inefficiencies, restricts entry by new competitors, and creates inflationary pressures. In the United States, airlines, trucking, railroads, telecommunications, and banking have been deregulated. Markets are also being liberated in Western and Eastern Europe, Asia, and many of the developing countries. Trade barriers are crumbling due to political unrest and technological innovation.

Deregulation has typically changed the structure of the affected industries as well as lowered prices. For example, the period following deregulation of the U.S. airline industry (1978–1985), gave rise to a new airline category—the budget airline. The rise of Southwest and other budget airlines led to lower fares across all routes, and forced the major carriers to streamline operations and phase out underperforming routes.[22] A similar story has followed in the European market, where discount airlines Ryan Air and EasyJet continued to grow at double-digit rates through the economic and travel downturn, post September 11.[23] The early actions of firms following deregulation include improving pricing capabilities, finding new ways to differentiate their services, increasing their marketing skills, and conserving capital to maintain flexibility. Later, the strategies of the surviving companies center on fine-tuning their pricing capabilities, cutting costs, preempting competitors via strategic alliances, and developing their marketing skills.[24]

Implications of Regulation and Deregulation for Market Attractiveness

As regulatory practices wax and wane, the attractiveness of markets often follows suit. For example, the deregulation of telecommunications in Europe, following earlier deregulation in the United States, is opening markets to firms seeking to offer new services and take market share from the established monopolies. The rise of Internet retailing and Internet telephony has policy makers arguing over the degree to which these Internet activities should be subject to state and federal tax in the United States. The outcome of these arguments may have considerable effect on consumers' interest in buying and calling on the Web. Further, the U.S. government's effort to force a breakup of Microsoft has left high-tech firms wondering about the extent to which their successful innovations will cause them to run afoul of government antitrusters.[25]

The Technological Environment

Technology can have a substantial impact on an industry's performance. Consider the effect of genetic engineering on pharmaceuticals, of transistors on telecommunications, and of plastics on metals. Identification of the commercial potential of technological developments has dramatically accelerated, and the lag between ideas, invention and commercialization has decreased.

In the past three decades, an amazing number of new technologies have brought forth such products as video recorders, compact disks, ever-more-powerful and ever-smaller computers, fax machines, new lightweight materials, and highly effective genetically engineered drugs. Technological progress over the next 10 years is predicted to be several times that experienced during the past 10 years, and much of it will be spurred by the need to find solutions to our environmental problems. Major technological innovations can be expected in a variety of fields, especially in biology and electronics/telecommunications.[26]

Exhibit 3.6   The Search Engine Revolution

As the Internet and the World Wide Web grew, it became increasingly difficult to find what you were looking for. Early search engines started off as directories of web pages or links, for example Yahoo. Most early search engines evolved into net portals—places that people begin their search for information. Today search is a sophisticated science, measured more by the relevance of the answers to a query rather than the number of web pages returned.

In the aftermath of September 11, news sites such as CNN were overwhelmed by people looking for the latest information. The search engine Google stepped in, by saving copies of the news pages and serving them up from its cache. Search services are now a vital intermediary, and among the most frequented sites on the web with millions of hits or visits every day. Because of this many search engines have morphed into advertising engines, driven by the need to become profitable. Companies can purchase "key words" with search engines, and when users search on these key words, the advertiser's web page is displayed first in the results.

Source: Ben Elgin, Jim Kerstetter, with Linda Himelstein, "Why They Are Agog over Google," Reprinted from the September 24, 2001 issue of *Business Week* by permission. Copyright The McGraw-Hill Companies.; and Glen Farrelly "Search Engines, Evolution and Revolution" at http://webhome.idirect.com/~glenjenn/search/history1.htm.

Trends in Electronics/Telecommunications   Electronics have played an important role in our society since the 1950s. They were first used primarily in radio and television and lately in digital watches, automatic cameras, video games, and microcomputers. Probably nothing has changed the workplace more in recent years than the spread of the Internet and the World Wide Web, now numbering 3,083,324,652 web pages, as tabulated by the popular search engine Google. See Exhibit 3.6 for a description of search engines and their role in the Internet.

Technology is also changing the nature and scope of the telecommunications industry. The changes are revolutionizing how businesses operate (banks, airlines, retail stores, and marketing research firms), how goods and services as well as ideas are exchanged, and how individuals learn and earn as well as interact with one another. Consumers today enjoy check-free banking, the death of the invoice, and ticketless air travel.

These innovations are the result not only of changes in computing systems but also of reduced costs in communicating (voice or data). For example, the cost of processing an additional telephone call is so small it might as well be free. And distance is no longer a factor—it costs about the same to make a trans-Atlantic call as one to your next-door neighbor.[27]

At the dawn of the new millennium, developments in telecommunications and computing have led to the rapid convergence of the telecommunications, computing, and entertainment industries. Music-hungry consumers have been downloading music from legal and illegal sites, and have forced the music industry to change the way they distribute music. In June 2002, three of the five major music labels—Universal, Sony, and Warner Music announced that they would make thousands of songs available for download over the Internet at the discount price of 99 cents each.[28] Cell phone users in Europe and Asia check sports scores, breaking news, stock quotes, and more using text messaging or SMS.[29] Savvy marketers and entrepreneurs who follow technological trends are able to foresee new and previously unheard of applications such as these and thereby place themselves and their firms at the forefront of the innovation curve, sometimes earning entrepreneurial fortunes in the process.

Implications of Technological Trends for Market Attractiveness   Changes in technology have always created attractive new markets. Think of all the markets created or made more attractive by Henry Ford's invention of the automobile. Such changes have also swept away old ones, such as the market for buggy whips. Today's venture capital investors monitor such changes, and many seek to invest their funds to serve markets that are growing exponentially as a result of technological developments, such as providing services for e-commerce firms. Some would say that choosing attractive markets or industries for investment is one of the most important criteria for venture capital success.[30]

In addition to creating attractive new markets, technological developments are having a profound impact on all aspects of marketing practice, including marketing communication (ads on the Web or via e-mail), distribution (books and other consumer and industrial goods bought and sold via the Web), packaging (use of new materials), and marketing research (monitoring supermarket purchases with scanners or Internet activity with digital "cookies"). We explore the most important of these changes in the ensuing chapters in this book.

The Physical Environment

Beyond the depletion of many of the earth's valuable resources, there are indications that the earth's overall health is declining. Deserts are growing while forests are shrinking, lakes are dying, the quality and quantity of groundwater are declining, and the planet may be experiencing a rising temperature.

One of the more frightening environmental scenarios concerns the buildup of carbon dioxide in the atmosphere that has resulted from heavy use of fossil fuels. This carbon dioxide "blanket" traps the sun's radiation, which leads to an increase in the earth's average temperature. One computer model of the climate predicts a cooling of Europe; Africa, East Asia, and South America warming a lot; and less rain in East Asia, Southern Africa, most of South America, Mexico, and parts of the United States. While the evidence is increasing that greenhouse gases are changing the climate, there is considerable disagreement over the details of the warming effects. Still, various concerned groups (including insurance companies) are demanding that governments take strong remedial action.[31] Among other undesirable eventualities, the greenhouse effect might trigger the infection of nontropical populations with such diseases as malaria, hepatitis, yellow fever, cholera, and meningitis.[32]

Worldwide, there are inadequate supplies of municipal water, which has forced European cities to use tertiary sewage treatments to purify water for household use. And, in a recent move towards water self-sufficiency, Singapore will start adding reclaimed and treated used water to its raw water supply.[33] Elsewhere, bottled water consumption has increased steadily for the last 30 years, becoming the most dynamic sector in the food and beverage industry, one now worth $22 billion.[34]

Pollution problems exist throughout the world, especially in Eastern Europe, China, and the developing countries. Germany is spending tens of billions of dollars to clean up eastern Germany, where under communist rule forests were blighted, drinking water badly polluted, and the air fouled such that motorists were forced to use their headlights during the day. China is the world's worst polluter, dumping billions of tons of industrial pollutants into waterways and hundreds of millions of tons of carbon emissions into the atmosphere.[35] It is encouraging to note that pollution regulations are becoming stricter throughout the world, including China, where investment in environmental protection projected to nearly double in real terms, from 0.7 percent of gross domestic product in the five years from 1990–95 to 1.3 percent in 2000–05.[36] And consumers the world over are buying more "green" or eco-friendly products.[37]

Development of Green Products as a Response to Environmental Problems

In general, discussion of the problems in the physical environment has stressed the threats and penalties facing business throughout the world. But business can do a number of things to turn problems into opportunities. One is to invest in research to find ways to save energy in heating and lighting. Another is to find new energy sources such as low-cost wind farms and hydroelectric projects. Businesses have also seen opportunities in developing hundreds of **green products** (those that are environmentally friendly) such as phosphate-free detergents, recycled motor oil, tuna caught without netting dolphins, organic fertilizers, high-efficiency light bulbs, recycled paper, and men's and women's casual clothes made from 100 percent organic cotton and colored with nontoxic dyes.[38] Other innovations include using smaller packages for many consumer goods (such as compact containers for superconcentrated soaps and collapsible pouches for cleaners once packed in plastic jugs), discontinuing the use of cardboard packages for deodorants, and selling teabags without tags and strings.[39] For the public, prices of eco (green) products are in line with ordinary products, especially when the quantity offered (tissues per roll of toilet tissue and loads of laundry per liter of concentrated detergent) is considered.[40]

Many companies are using recycled materials to save costs and improve profit margins—fast-food giant McDonald's is testing containers made from recycled juice boxes.[41] A Japanese company has developed the world's first car airconditioner that uses carbon dioxide as refrigerant to reduce the impact on the environment.[42]

Implications of Trends in the Physical Environment for Market Attractiveness

Global warming can create attractive opportunities for green products that are earth-friendly. On the other hand, if global warming continues, it may play havoc with markets for winter vacationers, snowmobiles, and other products and services whose demand depends on the reliable coming of Old Man Winter. Other physical trends, such as the depletion of natural resources and fresh groundwater may significantly impact firms in many industries serving a vast array of markets. Tracking such trends and understanding their effects is an important task.

Environmental Analysis Guides Marketing Decision Making

Macro trends can have powerful influence on the attractiveness of markets, as well as on marketing practice. What should managers charged with strategic responsibilities do to take advantage of or cope with such trends? First, they need to prioritize trend categories, so they know what to watch for. Second, they need to identify, and then monitor, sources of relevant information about macro trends. Third, as key developments are noted, they need to anticipate impacts and be prepared to change strategies if necessary.

Prioritizing Trend Categories

Apparel marketers closely watch sociocultural trends so as to provide garments in tune with today's changing lifestyles. For example, specialized undergarments for female athletes have become a growing market, as more and more women participate in athletic pursuits.

Real estate investors closely monitor economic trends; changes in interest rates or income can dramatically impact demand for both commercial and residential properties. Venture capitalists and high-tech entrepreneurs watch technological trends. Food marketers study demographic and sociocultural trends to provide new food products that fit modern lifestyles and satisfy rapidly growing demand for ethnic foods. The list goes on and on. What's important is for business people to understand which macro trend categories are

ETHICAL PERSPECTIVE 3.1
Ethical Issues in Macro Trend Analysis

Because there are myriad ways in which business and the environment interact, it is not surprising that firms find it difficult to cope with environmental issues. More and more companies, however, are taking an active role in dealing with the environmental issues that face society today, not only making sure they are in compliance with environmental regulations, but also taking a strong proenvironmental stance that includes abandoning products that are environmentally harmful.

Most companies make an effort to develop a proenvironment attitude among their employees, customers, and the general public—a substantial majority have ethical codes of behavior to guide their employees regarding the environment. Many support green organizations such as the National Wildlife Federation, the Sierra Club, and the Environmental Defense Fund. Since the public demands it, more and more resource conservation and recycling receive considerable support from many members of the business community. McDonald's, for example, has switched from plastic and styrofoam packaging to cardboard and paper.

Another ethical problem area lies in treatment of third world countries. Concern for such countries has a long history; witness the campaigns against South Africa's apartheid and, more recently, for civil rights in China. U.S. companies have come under severe criticism for contracting with suppliers that use child labor or that provide unhealthy working environments and for charging high prices in third world countries for goods such as pharmaceutical drugs.

Dealing with environmental problems can seem intractable because of difficulty in defining their severity (e.g., the greenhouse effect), let alone knowing how to solve them (replenishing underground water supplies). When we think we have found a solution, we are not sure of its long-term versus short-term effects and the extent to which the solution may be dysfunctional. In some areas, however, the picture is clearer, and a positive response may even be good business.

KEY OBSERVATION

What's important is for business people to understand which macro trend categories are likely to have the most impact on their fortunes and monitor those categories accordingly.

likely to have the most impact on their fortunes and monitor those categories accordingly. Similarly, managers need to monitor changes in ethical standards and expectations, so they do not run afoul of their customers' expectations. Ethical Perspective 3.1 discusses ethical issues that have arisen in this arena.

Information Sources and Outputs of Macro Trend Analysis

There is an endless supply of information about macro trends, including the popular and business press, the Internet, supplier and customer contacts, and so on. Thus, gathering relevant data is not difficult, but it does take time and effort. A good place to start is with trade associations and trade magazines, both of which typically track and report on trends relevant to the industries they serve. Most local, state, and federal governments provide demographic data easily accessible at their websites, such as **www.census.gov** in the United States. Government sources and the business press are good places to look for economic trends and data from Eurostat, the statistical office of the European Union (**europa.eu.int/comm/eurostat**). Almost all sources of information are now readily available on the web. Search engines such as Google are a powerful tool in the quest for information.

The key outputs of a competent macro trend analysis for any market should include both quantitative and qualitative data. Quantitative data should provide evidence of the market's size and growth rate, for the overall market as well as for key segments. Qualitative data should include factors that will likely influence these figures in the future, whether favorably or unfavorably.

Exhibit 3.7

OPPORTUNITY/THREAT MATRIX FOR A TELECOMMUNICATIONS COMPANY

	PROBABILITY OF OCCURRENCE (2010)	
Level of Impact on Company*	High	Low
High	4	1
Low	2	3

1. Wireless communications technology will make networks based on fiber and copper wires redundant.
2. Technology will provide for the storage and accessing of vast quantities of data at affordable costs.
3. The prices of large-screen (over 36-inch) digitalized TV sets will be reduced by 50 percent (constant dollars).
4. Telephone companies will emerge as the dominant force in the telecommunications industry.

*Profits or market share or both.

Anticipating and Responding to Environmental Change

Critical changes in macroenvironmental conditions often call for changes in the firm's strategy. Such changes can be proactive or reactive, or both. To the extent that a firm identifies and effectively deals with key trends before its competitors do, it is more likely to win and retain competitive advantage. In any case, management needs systems to help identify, evaluate, and respond to environmental events that may affect the firm's longer-term profitability and position. One such approach uses an opportunity/threat matrix to better assess the impact and the timing of an event, followed by the development of an appropriate response strategy. This approach is discussed below.

Impact and Timing of Event   In any given period, many environmental events that could have an impact on the firm—either positively or negatively—may be detected. Somehow, management must determine the probability of their occurrence and the degree of impact (profitability and/or market share) of each event. One relatively simple way to accomplish these tasks is to use a 2 × 2 dimensional **opportunity/threat matrix** such as that shown in Exhibit 3.7. This example contains four potential environmental events that the high-speed access division of a large U.K. telecommunications company might have identified as worthy of concern in the early 2000s. The probability of each occurring by the year 2010 was rated as was the impact on the company in terms of profitability or market share. The event likely both to occur by 2010 and to have the greatest impact appears in the upper left-hand box. At the very least, such an event should be examined closely, including estimating with as much precision as possible its impact on profitability and market share.

The opportunity/threat matrix enables the examination of a large number of events in such a way that management can focus on the most important ones. Thus, events such as number 4 in the exhibit with a high probability of occurring and having a high impact should be closely monitored. Those with a low probability of occurrence and low impact, such as number 3 in the exhibit, should probably be dropped, at least for the moment. Events with a low probability/high impact (number 1) should be reexamined less frequently to determine whether the impact rating remains basically sound.

TAKE-AWAYS

- Trends can and often will profoundly influence the success of any business. Serving attractive markets, where trends are favorable—swimming with the current—is likely to yield more success than serving those where trends are unfavorable—swimming against the current. Thus, context, the second of the 4 Cs, matters and is central to the assessment of any opportunity.

- Taken together, the six macro trend categories constitute a useful analytical framework to ensure that all bases are covered when scanning environmental conditions.

- Paying regular and systematic attention to the highest priority macro trend categories permits timely decision making, perhaps ahead of competitors.

- Gathering hard data on macro trends is not difficult. Trade associations and trade magazines provide a good place to start.

  Self-diagnostic questions to test your ability to apply the analytical tools and concepts in this chapter to marketing decision making may be found at this book's website at www.mhhe.com/mullins05.

ENDNOTES

1. This section on the changing men's apparel market is based on information found in AnnMarie Dodd, "Clothing Consultation Addresses the Variable Dress Code," *DNR,* April 7, 2000, p. 16; Melanie Kletter, "Tough 4th Quarter for Three Men's Merchants," *DNR,* March 19, 1999, p. FC; Jean Palmieri, "George Zimmer Is Gradually Zeroing in on US$10B for Men's Wearhouse," *DNR,* June 23, 1999, p. 24; Vicki M. Young, "Edison Bros. to Liquidate Riggings, JeansWest," *DNR,* April 26, 1999, p. A1; the 1999 annual reports of Hartmarx Corp., and The Men's Wearhouse, Inc.; Andrew Ward, "Austin Reed Reveals Takeover Talks as Sales Suffer 5% Fall," *Financial Times,* April 7, 2000, p. 23; Susanna Voyle, "Moss Bros to Rebrand Outlets in Radical Overhaul," *Financial Times,* October 3, 2000, p. 27; Gautam Malkani, "Overhaul Sees Moss Bros Dive into Red," *Financial Times,* April 3, 2001, p. 24; Lucy Farndon, "Dress Sense Suits Moss Bros," *Daily Mail,* October 17, 2001, source: FT Intelligence, Financial Times Information Limited FDM; Chairman's Statement, Moss Bros PLC website at www.mossbros .com/chairman.asp.

2. See John Mullins, *The New Business Road Test* (London: Prentice-Hall/FT, 2003) for a worksheet that's useful for conducting a macro trend analysis.

3. Total Midyear Population for the World: 1950–2050, http://www.census.gov/ipc/www/worldpop.html. The majority of the text for the world demographics was drawn from World Population Profile: 1998. Report WP/98, available on the web at http://www.census.gov/ipc/www/wp98.html.

4. For a closer look at the implications of America's graying population, see Ken Dychtwald, *The Age Wave* (New York: Bantam Books, 1990), and Ken Dychtwald, *Age Power* (New York: J. P. Tarcher, 1999).

5. Early research on this group reported their behavior as being strange and unexplainable and hence the name "Generation X," which derived from a novel of that name written by Douglas Copeland (New York: St. Martin's Press, 1991). Subsequent research reveals this stereotype to be highly inaccurate in describing this generation's values and beliefs.

6. Material summarized in this section comes from "A Trend Analysis Report on Youth," *Nachus Ov Realities,* no. 1 (New York: BKG Young, n.d.); Chiat/Day, "Notes from the Emerging Media Frontier," *Fame and Flame,* January 6, 1994; "The New Femininity," *Mademoiselle,* Spring 1994; Karen Ritchie, "Marketing to Generation X," *American Demographics,* April 1995, p. 34; Karen Cooperman, "Marketing to Generation X—A Special Report," *Advertising Age,* February 6, 1994, p. 27; John Naisbitt's *Trendletter* 14, no. 9 (April 27, 1995); and Diedre R. Schwieslow, "Sixties Legacy: This Monstrous Bureaucracy," *USA Today,* July 26, 1995, p. 1.

7. Housing as a Reflection of Culture: Privatised Living and Privacy in England and Japan by Ritsuko Ozaki, Housing Studies, Vol. 17, No. 2, 209–227, 2002.

8. GDP per capita, 2001, at current prices, in U.S. dollars published by the OECD. Luxembourg's inflated GDP is an anomaly contributed by its high population of temporary workers who are not counted as part of the resident population. http://www.oecd.org/pdf/M00018000/M00018516.pdf.

9. Ibid.

10. Source IMF http://www.imf.org/external/pubs/ft/weo/2002/01/pdf/chapter1.pdf.

11. Source IMF http://www.imf.org/external/pubs/ft/weo/2002/01/pdf/chapter1.pdf.

12. November 19, 2002, The *Express* newspaper, UK.

13. Household Debts Increase Over 88 Pct Since 1997, November 19, 2002, Yonhap English News.

14. "Plethora of Plastic, and Low Interest Rates Lead to Debt Culture That Is Likely to Stay," *Financial Times,* November 19, 2002.

15. International Trade Statistics 2002, published by the World Trade Organization. Regional integration agreements ANDEAN: Bolivia, Colombia, Ecuador, Peru and Venezuela. APEC: Australia; Brunei Darussalam; Canada; Chile; China; Hong Kong, China; Indonesia; Japan; Republic of Korea; Malaysia; Mexico; New Zealand; Papua New Guinea; Peru; Philippines; Russian Federation; Singapore; Taipei, Chinese; Thailand; United States of America and Viet Nam. ASEAN: Brunei Darussalam, Cambodia, Indonesia, Lao People's Democratic Republic, Malaysia, Myanmar, Philippines, Singapore, Thailand and Vietnam. CEFTA: Bulgaria, Czech Republic, Hungary, Poland, Romania, Slovenia and the Slovak Republic. EUROPEAN UNION: Austria, Belgium, Denmark, Finland, France, Germany, Greece, Ireland, Italy, Luxembourg, Netherlands, Portugal, Spain, Sweden, and the United Kingdom. MERCOSUR: Argentina, Brazil, Paraguay and Uruguay. NAFTA: Canada, Mexico and the United States of America. http://www.wto.org/english/res_e/statis_e/its2002_e/its02_overview_e.htm.

16. The OECD Observer *OECD in Figures,* Volume 2002, Supplement 1, http://www1.oecd.org/publications/e-book/0102071E.pdf.

17. Leading importers and exporters in world merchandise trade 2001, World Trade Organization, http://www.wto.org/english/res_e/statis_e/its2002_e/section1_eh05.xls.

18. Merchandise trade by product, region and major trading partner 1999–01—United States, WTO Statistics.

19. The generation of Americans born between 1946 and 1964, starting after the end of the Second World War. http://www.unt.edu/cpe/module1/deffile/def7-02.htm.

20. Bill Montague, "China Deal Unlikely to Halt Piracy," *USA Today,* June 18, 1996. p. A1. Seventh Annual BSA Global Software Piracy Study, http://www.bsa.org/resources/2002-06-10.130.pdf.

21. John Carey and Mary Beth Regan, "Are Regs Bleeding the Economy," *Business Week,* June 17, 1995, p. 75. Also, see Michael E. Porter and Clas Van der Linde, "Green and Competitive," *Harvard Business Review,* September–October 1995, p. 123. American companies have long insisted they were over-regulated. For a discussion of why this may not be true—at least as far as Germany and Japan are concerned—see "To All U.S. Managers Upset by Regulations: Try Germany or Japan," *The Wall Street Journal,* December 14, 1995, p. A5.

22. Peter R. Dickson, *Marketing Management* (Ft. Worth, TX: The Dryden Press, 1994), p. 92.

23. WSJ.COM/Middle Seat: Industry Veteran Mulls Airlines Woes, November 19, 2002; "Low-Cost Carriers Steal the European Show," *Aviation Week & Space Technology,* 59 Vol. 57, No. 21, November 18, 2002.

24. Joel A. Bleeke, "Strategic Choices for Newly Opened Markets," *Harvard Business Review,* September–October 1990, p. 163.

25. N. Gregory Mankiw, "D.C, Stay Out of the Economy," Fortune, May 15, 2000, p. 70.

26. These were among the top technologies in importance ranked by scientists at a leading research institute. Others include those concerned with high-density energy sources (fuel cells), miniaturization (supercomputer that fits in a pocket), antiaging products (making the process less traumatic), and sensors that can detect diseases at an early stage (lung cancer from breath measurements). See Douglas E. Olesen, "The Top Technologies for the Next 10 Years," *The Futurist,* September–October 1995, p. 9.

27. "The Death of Distance," *The Economist,* September 30, 1995, p. 5; and Bill Gates, *The Road Ahead* (New York: Viking Penguin, 1995), p. 6.

28. "The Labels Start Turning Up the Volume," *Business Week,* Special Report on Digital Music's Future, August 12, 2002.

29. "Chinese Portals Near Profitability, Boosted by Text Message Services," *The Wall Street Journal,* November 6, 2002, and "T-Mobile, Sony Unit Set Deal to Distribute Digital Content," *The Wall Street Journal,* November 11, 2002.

30. Bob Zider, "How Venture Capital Works," *Harvard Business Review,* November–December 1998, p. 133.

31. "Science and Technology: Reading the Patterns," *The Economist,* April 1, 1995, p. 65.

32. George F. Sanderson, "Climate Change: The Threat to Human Health," *The Futurist,* March–April 1992, p. 34.

33. Water—Flush With Pride: Technology that allows Singapore to reclaim used tap and flushing water will move the nation closer to water self-sufficiency; But will it wash with the masses? *Far Eastern Economic Review,* September 26, 2002.

34. "Bottled-Water Market Keeps Burgeoning Around the World," *The Nation* (Thailand), October 14, 2002.

35. Jane H. Lii, "Boom at a Glance," *New York Times Magazine,* February 18, 1995, p. 27.

36. "How Hong Kong Can Lead the Way in Sustainability," *Environmental Challenges, South China Morning Post,* December 5, 2002.

37. Examples: "Chinese Environmental Friendly Products Form a RMB 55 Billion Market," *SinoCast China Business Daily News,* November 14, 2002. "Dutch Green Power Imports +28.5% in 2001," *Agency,* November 12, 2002; Dow Jones International News Money Spent Going Green Up Almost 20% on Last Year (UK), *The Herald,* November 2, 2002.

38. Pat Sloan, "Where-O-Where Can You Get 'Green' Garb?" *Advertising Age,* June 5, 1992, p. 3.

39. Gary Strauss, "Big Trend: Smaller Packaging," *USA Today,* April 1, 1993, p. B1.

40. Kristen Clark, "The Frugal Environmentalist," *The Environmental Magazine,* May–June 1994. For a discussion of how concern for the environment has affected exporting products to Europe, see Kristen Bergstrom, "The Eco-Label and Exporting to Europe," *Business America,* November 29, 1993, p. 21.

41. "Maybe It's Not So Hard Being Eco-Friendly," *Business Week,* April 16, 2001.

42. "Denso Develops Eco-Friendly Car Air Conditioner," Jiji Press English News Service, December 4, 2002.

CHAPTER FOUR

Industry Analysis and Competitive Advantage

The Cellular Telephone Business: Increasing Competition in a Growing Market[1]

FROM LONDON TO TOKYO to Chicago, cell phones have become a "can't do without it" tool of time-pressed business people, hip teenagers, and just about anyone else who wants to stay in touch. The market for mobile telephone service is growing rapidly. In 1983, when the first cellular phone system began operations, it was projected that by 2000, less than one million people would subscribe. As a result of dramatic growth among both business and household users, however, by 2002, the number of cell phone users had reached more than 1 billion worldwide! In Finland and Taiwan, the number of cell phone subscribers is higher than the total population of the country; and Hong Kong is expected to join them soon.

The rapidly growing market for mobile telephony is served by two principal industries: cell phone manufacturers and cell phone service providers. How attractive are these apparently booming industries?

Cell Phone Manufacturing

Rapid-fire technological advances from Qualcomm, Ericsson, Nokia, and others have brought countless new features to the market, including software to access the World Wide Web, the ability to send and receive photographic images, and various location-based services that take advantage of global positioning technology. In Europe, new phones enable mobile users to check the weather forecast, their e-mail, stock quotes, and more. Finland's Nokia has rocketed to world leadership in cell phones, leaving early and longtime leader Motorola in the dust. From year to year, market share figures for leading cell phone manufacturers can double or be halved, depending on whose latest technology catches the fancy of users. To investors' joy or dismay, stock prices follow suit. Qualcomm's shares soared 2,600 percent in 1999, only to fall back by more than 60 percent by mid-2000, and a further 50 percent by mid-2002. Nokia, too, saw its share price tumble in 2001.

This recent history in the hotly competitive cell phone manufacturing industry suggests that a rapidly growing market does not necessarily provide a smooth path to success. Growing markets are one thing, but turbulent industries serving those markets are quite another.

Cell Phone Service Providers

Industry conditions for service providers have run wild as well. The race to win global coverage has led to mergers of large players such as Europe's Vodafone with America's AirTouch in 1999. Vodafone did not stop there, however, going on to acquire Germany's

Mannesmann in 2000. Other marketers with well-known brands have also jumped into the fray. Richard Branson's Virgin Group bought idle capacity from a British also-ran and launched Virgin Telecom, picking up 150,000 customers in his first six weeks. All over Europe, where cell phone penetration is far higher than in the United States, market-by-market battles for market share have raged. Prices for cell phone service have slid, given the competitive pressures. To make matters worse, the cost of obtaining new government licenses to support new third-generation (3G) services has skyrocketed. Britain's auction in early 2000 of 3G licenses wound up raising some $35 billion in license fees, roughly 10 times what was expected. Other European governments took notice and followed in the U.K.'s path.

Thus, the rapidly growing market for cell phone service has attracted so much interest from competing firms and some governments eager to get their hands on a share of the money that the long-term ability of the industry to be profitable is being questioned by some.

Marketing Challenges Addressed in Chapter 4

As the examples of the cellular phone manufacturing and service industries show, serving a growing market hardly guarantees smooth sailing. Equally or more important are industry conditions and the degree to which specific players in the industry can establish and sustain competitive advantage. Thus, as entrepreneurs and marketing decision makers ponder an **opportunity** to enter or attempt to increase their share of a growing market like that for mobile phones, they also must carefully examine a host of other issues, including the conditions that are currently prevailing in the industry in which they would compete and the likelihood that favorable conditions will prevail in the future.

In this chapter, we provide analytical frameworks to enable prospective entrepreneurs and marketing strategists to address four critical questions pertinent to such an examination: How can we assess the attractiveness of an industry? If we aim to compete on the basis of innovation, how can we determine how quickly our innovation is likely to win market acceptance? What does the overall attractiveness of the market and industry context imply for chances for future success? Finally, how can we establish and then sustain competitive advantage over the duration of our product's life cycle? First, however, we clarify the difference between two oft-confused terms: **market** and **industry.**

KEY OBSERVATION

How can we assess the attractiveness of an industry? If we aim to compete on the basis of innovation, how can we determine how quickly our innovation is likely to win market acceptance?

Markets and Industries: What's the Difference?

In Chapter 1, we defined a market as being comprised of individuals and organizations who are interested and willing to buy a good or service to obtain benefits that will satisfy a particular need or want and who have the resources to engage in such a transaction. One such market consists of college students who get hungry in the middle of the afternoon and have a few minutes and enough spare change to buy a snack between classes.

An industry is a group of firms that offer a product or class of products that are similar and are close substitutes for one another. What industries serve the student snack market? At the producer level, there are the salty snack industry (makers of potato and corn chips and similar products); the candy industry; the fresh produce industry (growers of apples, oranges, bananas, and other easy-to-eat fruits); and others too numerous to mention. Distribution channels for these products include the supermarket industry, the food service industry, the coin-operated vending industry, and so on. Clearly, these industries are different and offer varying bundles of benefits to hungry students.

KEY OBSERVATION

Markets are comprised of buyers, industries are comprised of sellers.

Thus, markets are comprised of buyers, industries are comprised of sellers. The distinction is an important one because industries can vary substantially in their attractiveness and overall profitability.

Sellers who look only to others in their own industry as competitors are likely to overlook other very real rivals and risk having their markets undercut by innovators from other industries. Should Kodak be more concerned with Fuji, Agfa, and other longtime players in the film and photoprocessing industries, or should it be worrying about Hewlett-Packard, Sony, and others whose digital technologies may make photography's century-old silver halide chemistry go the way of the buggy whip? Only time will tell.

Defining Markets and Industries: Levels of Analysis

Assessing the attractiveness of markets and industries requires clarity about which consumers and which of their needs or which sellers of which products are to be included in the assessment. Confusion between market and industry can result since consumer needs are often thought of in product terms—"I'm hungry. I need a candy bar"—in the same way that industries are typically described by the products they sell. Thus, *markets* are often defined both in demographic and/or geographic terms (who and/or where the customers are) and in terms of a particular good or service demanded by the consumer, expressed at the generic category, product class, or product type level.

Challenges in Market and Industry Definition

Markets and industries can be defined at several **levels of analysis: generic category, product class,** or **product type** are most common. The level chosen for a particular analysis can have important implications for strategic and marketing planning. Defining a market or industry at too broad a level can cause the analyst to overlook important market–industry interactions in a particular market segment or for a particular product class or type. But defining the market or industry too narrowly can cause the analyst to miss potentially important competitive developments.

The problem with using the **generic category level** is that it typically includes an array of noncompeting products. For example, within the motor vehicle market, is a Toyota Echo in competition with a BMW or a Mack truck? Within chemical markets, do polymers that substitute for natural materials compete with gasoline additives, dyestuffs, and industrial coatings? Probably not. For an entrepreneur seeking to market a new chemical compound that enhances the depth of color when cotton yarns are dyed, understanding the state of the overall chemical industry is probably less important than understanding dyestuffs competitors.

Using **product class** as one's level of analysis suffers from this same type of problem since the products involved may serve diverse markets or market segments. The more generic the definition of a product class, the higher the aggregation level of products (for instance, all cars versus convertibles) and the more stable is market demand, as well as the product life-cycle curve, a concept we explore later in this chapter. Thus, basic needs for automobiles (at least, in developed countries) typically change slowly, though demand patterns for convertibles or pickup trucks or compact cars may be more volatile. The more generically the product class is defined, the less useful it is for strategic planning, which seeks to identify opportunities and threats for specific product-market relationships.

Product types are subsets of a product class and contain items that are technically similar, although they may vary in such aspects as appearance and price. In the case of cereals, for example, the product types could be defined as hot or cold cereals. Hot cereals would include at least two subtypes—regular and instant. Cold cereals would include regular, presweetened, natural, and fortified. Regular could be broken down into such categories as corn flakes, raisin brans, and shredded wheat. Other examples of product hierarchies abound, especially when different processing technologies are involved—frozen, canned, fresh, dehydrated, and freeze-dried fruits and vegetables, for example.

Most marketers select product type as their level of analysis for marketing planning because, while products within a product type may serve different subsets of needs, they are typically close substitutes for one another. The product-type level of aggregation is considerably more sensitive than the other levels to environmental changes—such as those driven by macro trends, as discussed in Chapter 3—that create opportunities or threats for individual product-market entries. The danger in restricting one's market and competitive

KEY OBSERVATION

The danger in restricting one's market and competitive analysis to a particular product type is that other product types may be overlooked.

analysis to a particular product type is that other product types, such as bagels or a trip through the drive-through at McDonald's in the breakfast market, may be overlooked. Focusing on the true **consumer need** (i.e., a fast breakfast, rather than cereal, a product) can help avoid this problem.

Doing so appears to be uncommon, however. A recent study found that managers tended to rely on supply-based attributes (i.e., what companies sell) in identifying competitors, rather than demand- or customer need-based attributes (i.e., what customers need).[2] Further, managers tend to identify too few firms as competitors and are especially likely to omit new firms or potential competitors. Stories of experienced managers who "know their business" and are surprised by the sudden emergence of a new competitor that operates in a different way are legion.[3] For an example of how firms create new market space not bound by old industry definitions, see Exhibit 4.1.

Exhibit 4.1   Creating New Market Space

W. Chan Kim and Reneé Mauborgne argue that one way to avoid cutthroat, head-to-head competition, in rapidly growing markets as well as those that are flat or growing slowly, is to find new "market space," as they call it, that defies conventional boundaries of industry competition. By looking across substitute industries or to complementary product and service offerings that go beyond what an industry has traditionally offered, companies can rethink the functional and emotional orientation of their industry and help shape industry trends to their own advantage. Cisco Systems created new market space in this way when it recognized that the doubling of the number of Internet users every 100 days was creating demand for high-speed data exchange that was not being adequately served by existing industries. By 1999, more than 75 percent of all traffic on the Internet flowed through Cisco's routers, switches, and other network devices, on which Cisco earned margins in the 60 percent range. Creating new market space can be attractive, indeed!

Source: Reprinted by permission of *Harvard Business Review.* From "Creating New Market Space," by W. Chan Kim and Reneé Mauborgne, January–February 1999. pp. 83–89. Copyright © 1999 by the Harvard Business School Publishing Corporation, all rights reserved.

Notwithstanding its intuitive appeal, defining markets or industries based on consumer needs—instead of based on generic category, product class, or product type—brings its own difficulties. For example, should airlines view themselves as being in the business of facilitating human contact? If they did, they might be tempted to enter the videoconferencing business (as American Airlines did with a brief and unsuccessful foray in the 1990s) or the telecommunications business, industries where they are probably poorly equipped to compete.

The best way to avoid ill-advised temptation or confusion over how broadly or narrowly to define one's market and industry is to carefully examine *both* one's market (using the frameworks in Chapter 3) *and* one's industry (as we address in this chapter). It's also important to take the time to think *both* broadly (motor vehicles, food processing) *and* narrowly (pickup trucks, fortified cold cereals) in defining and examining the attractiveness of one's industry and one's immediate competitive environment, as the remainder of this chapter will illustrate.

Your Market Is Attractive: What About Your Industry?

As consumers and business people have become hooked on cell phones, the market for mobile communication has grown rapidly. By most measures, this is a large, growing, and attractive *market*. But are cell phone manufacturing and cellular services attractive *industries?* An industry's attractiveness at a point in time can best be judged by analyzing its driving forces, and especially the five major competitive forces: rivalry among present competitors, potential competitors, the bargaining power of suppliers, the bargaining power of buyers, and the threat of substitute products.

Driving Forces

Just as macroenvironmental trends are important in shaping market attractiveness, they are similarly important in shaping the attractiveness of industries. Michael Porter calls these trends driving forces.[4] These include (1) changes in the industry's long-term growth rate, which directly affect investment decisions and intensity of competition; (2) changes in key buyer segments, which affect demand and strategic marketing programs; (3) diffusion of proprietary knowledge, which controls both the rate at which products become more alike and the entry of new firms; (4) changes in cost and efficiency, derived from scale and learning effects, which have the potential of making entry more difficult; and (5) changes in government regulations, which can affect entry, costs, bases of competition, and profitability.

Collecting and examining trend data in each of these areas helps an entrepreneur or marketer determine whether an industry is sufficiently attractive to enter or remain in and helps shape strategic marketing decisions that enable the firm to compete effectively. The profusion of data now available on the Internet has made the gathering of this data much easier than was true several years ago.

Porter's Five Competitive Forces[5]

Five interactive competitive forces collectively determine an industry's long-term attractiveness—present competitors, potential competitors, the bargaining power of suppliers, the bargaining power of buyers, and the threat of substitute products (see Exhibit 4.2). This mix of forces explains why some industries are consistently more profitable than others and provides further insights into which resources are required and which strategies should be

Exhibit 4.2

THE MAJOR FORCES THAT DETERMINE INDUSTRY ATTRACTIVENESS

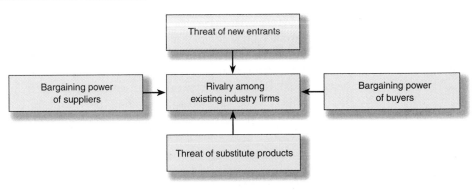

---

adopted to be successful. A useful way to conduct a five forces analysis of an industry's attractiveness is to construct a checklist based on Porter's seminal work.[6]

The strength of the individual forces varies from industry to industry and, over time, within the same industry. In the fast-food industry the key forces are present competitors (for example, Wendy's versus Burger King versus McDonald's), substitute products (neighborhood delis, salad bars, all-you-can-eat buffet restaurants, and frozen meals), and buyers who are concerned about health and nutrition and who see fast foods as a symbol of a throw-away society. The growing popularity of healthier fast-food alternatives has brought new entrants like Prêt A Manger in the United Kingdom and Panera in the United States.

Rivalry among Present Competitors

Rivalry occurs among firms that produce products that are close substitutes for each other, especially when one competitor acts to improve its standing or protect its position. Thus, firms are mutually dependent: What one firm does affects others, and vice versa. Ordinarily, profitability decreases as rivalry increases. Rivalry is greater under the following conditions:

- *There is high investment intensity; that is, the amount of fixed and working capital required to produce a dollar of sales is large.* High intensity requires firms to operate at or near capacity as much as possible, thereby putting strong downward pressure on prices when demand slackens. Thus, high investment–intensity businesses are, on average, much less profitable than those with a lower level of investment. Bob Crandall, the former CEO of American Airlines, once described the airline business as being "intensely, vigorously, bitterly, savagely competitive."[7]
- *There are many small firms in an industry or no dominant firms exist.* The restaurant industry is a good example.
- *There is little product differentiation*—for example, major appliances, TV sets, and passenger-car tires.
- *It's easy for customers to switch from one seller's products to those of others* (low switching cost for buyers).
- *There is a high cost to changing suppliers (switching costs)* as would be the case in changing a major computer software system.[8]

The greater the competitive rivalry in an industry, the less attractive it is to current players or would-be entrants. Though the cellular service industry is capital intensive, there are several dominant firms whose products are differentiated through rapid technological change, and switching costs to change cell phone suppliers are low. Thus, rivalry in this industry might be judged as moderately unfavorable.

Threat of New Entrants

A second force affecting industry attractiveness is the threat of new entrants. New competitors add capacity to the industry and bring with them the need to gain market share, thereby making competition more intense. The threat of new entrants, such as firms using new packet-switching technology that allows the user to always be connected, is a very real concern to present cellular industry players.[9] On the other hand, the huge cost of obtaining bandwidth in government auctions makes threat of entry into the cellular service industry relatively low. The greater the threat of new entrants, the less will be an industry's attractiveness. Entry is more difficult under the following conditions:

- *When strong economies of scale and learning effects are present,* since it takes time to obtain the volume and learning required to yield a low relative cost per unit. If firms already present are vertically integrated, entry becomes even more expensive. Also, if the existing firms share their output with their related businesses, the problem of overcoming the cost disadvantage is made even more difficult.
- *If the industry has strong capital requirements at the outset.*
- *When strong product differentiation exists among current players.*
- *If gaining distribution is particularly difficult.*

Bargaining Power of Suppliers

The bargaining power of suppliers over firms in an industry is the third major determinant of industry attractiveness. It is exercised largely through increased prices. Its impact can be significant, particularly when a limited number of suppliers service several different industries. Their power is increased if switching costs and prices of substitutes are high and they can realistically threaten forward integration.[10] Supplier power is also increased when the supplier's product is a large part of the buyer's value added—as is the case with metal cans, where the cost of tin plate is over 60 percent of the value added.

In recent years, the bargaining power of suppliers in many industries has changed dramatically as more companies seek a partnership relationship with their suppliers. What was once an arm's-length adversarial relationship has turned into a cooperative one resulting in lower transaction costs, improved quality derived primarily from using a supplier's technological skills to design and manufacture parts, and decreased transaction time in terms of inventory replenishments through just-in-time procurement systems.

The greater the bargaining power of the key suppliers to an industry, the less will be the overall attractiveness of the industry. The newly discovered power that European governments have exerted by auctioning bandwidth for new cellular services has raised their bargaining power as suppliers of bandwidth to the cellular industry, thereby reducing the attractiveness of this industry.

Bargaining Power of Buyers

An industry's customers constantly look for reduced prices, improved product quality, and added services and thus can affect competition within an industry. Buyers play individual suppliers against one another in their efforts to obtain these and other concessions. This is certainly the case with some large retailers such as Wal-Mart and Carrefour in their dealings with many of their suppliers.

The extent to which buyers succeed in their bargaining efforts depends on several factors, among others, including these:

- The extent of buyer concentration, as when a few large buyers that account for a large portion of industry sales can gain concessions.
- Switching costs that reduce the buyer's bargaining power.

- The threat of backward integration, thereby alleviating the need for the supplier.
- The product's importance to the performance of the buyer's product—the greater the importance, the lower their bargaining power.
- Buyer profitability—if buyers earn low profits and the product involved is an important part of their costs, then bargaining will be more aggressive.

The greater the power of the high-volume customers served by an industry, the less attractive will be that industry. One attractive dimension of the cellular phone service industry is that its customers have relatively little power to set terms and conditions for cellular phone service. Buyers are numerous and not very concentrated and their cell phone costs are typically not of great importance or expense, relatively speaking.

Threat of Substitute Products   Substitutes are alternative product types (not brands) that perform essentially the same functions, as plastic bottles versus aluminum cans, oleomargarine versus butter, and the faxing of documents versus overnight express delivery. Substitute products put a ceiling on the profitability of an industry by limiting the price that can be charged, especially when supply exceeds demand. Thus, in the plastic food packaging industry, aluminum cans are substitutes for plastic bottles and conversely, constrain the prices that can be charged. For cellular phone service providers, possible substitutes include personal digital assistants (PDAs) such as the ubiquitous Palm Pilot,[11] possible new multimedia devices from the likes of Sony, Matsushita, and Samsung,[12] or new mobile digital products not yet imagined.

A Five Forces Analysis of the Cellular Phone Service Industry

A useful way to summarize a five forces industry analysis is to construct a chart like that shown in Exhibit 4.3. There, we summarize one analyst's judgment of the favorability of the five forces for the cellular phone service industry in the year 2003. This analysis indicates that, consistent with the preceding discussion, compared to earlier in the industry's history when there were fewer players (thus, less rivalry), no threatening substitutes on the horizon, and a cozier relationship with governments to provide bandwidth, the industry in 2003 was probably less attractive than some industries, for which four or five of the forces might be favorable.

Thus, strategists who must decide whether to enter or continue to invest in this industry must make a judgment as to whether the rapid growth of the *market*—a *favorable* **environmental context**—is sufficient to offset the deteriorating attractiveness of the *industry*—the *not-so-favorable* **competitive situation.** Given this mixed outlook, strategists would consider other factors, including the degree to which they believe they are likely to be able to establish and sustain competitive advantage. We develop this theme further later in this chapter.

Changing Competition and Industry Evolution

As we shall see later in this chapter, most products and product categories pass through a series of stages in their life cycles: introduction, growth, shakeout, maturity, and decline. All five competitive forces just discussed are affected by the passage of time; therefore, their strength varies as the industry passes from its introductory stage to its growth stage and on to maturity, followed by decline. Competitive forces are apt to be weakest during the fast-growth period; thus, there are substantial opportunities for gaining market share. During the shakeout period, competitive forces are at their strongest, and many competitors are forced

Exhibit 4.3

FIVE FORCES ANALYSIS OF THE WORLDWIDE CELL PHONE SERVICE INDUSTRY IN EARLY 2003

Five Forces	Score	Rationale
Rivalry among present competitors	Rivalry is high leading to high customer churn: unfavorable	Products are differentiated through new features and services, customer switching costs are low.
Threat of new entrants	Threat of new entrants is low: moderately favorable	While rapid pace of technological change may bring new entrants based on new technologies: (i.e., packet switching, satellites) new service providers must purchase a bandwidth license by spending billions.
Supplier power	Supplier power is high: moderately unfavorable	Governments have raised the price of additional bandwidth through auctions.
Buyer power	Buyer power is low: very favorable	Even large customers have little power to set terms and conditions in this oligopolistic industry.
Threat of substitutes	Threat of substitutes is high: moderately unfavorable	PDAs and laptops using WiFi networks to access the web could cannibalize expected sales of 2.5G and 3G wireless network cell phones.

Overall conclusion: Only two of the five forces are favorable, while three are unfavorable. Thus, the cellular phone service industry is not particularly attractive at this time.

to exit the industry. During maturity, competition typically slackens, but only if the industry leader holds a strong relative share position. An industry will experience more price competition during maturity if the leader holds a weak *relative* share position. Kellogg and General Mills have for many years held two-thirds of the U.S. domestic cereal market, but because Kellogg does not hold a dominant relative share, the industry experiences considerable price competition. A declining industry usually witnesses considerable rivalry, the extent of which depends on the strength of the exit barriers and the rate of decline.

Critical Success Factors: Who Wins *within* an Industry?

The **critical success factors** that differentiate between the success and failure of firms *within* an industry differ from industry to industry. These factors often are concerned with one or more of the elements in the marketing mix—product (e.g., the capability to generate successful new products), price (be a low-cost producer), place (obtain widespread product distribution), and promotion (strong relationship with large customers). As the old saying goes in the retailing industry, three things are critical to success: location, location, and location. Thus, location, a potentially powerful source of competitive advantage, often makes the difference between which retailers are successful and which are not.

KEY OBSERVATION

Assessing the fit between an industry's critical success factors and the presence of those factors in a firm or a proposed management team is a good way to assess whether an industry is attractive to that particular firm or management team.

Assessing the fit between an industry's critical success factors and the presence of those factors in a firm or a proposed management team is a good way to assess whether an industry is attractive to that particular firm or management team and to determine whether that firm or team is likely to be attractive to investors or other suppliers of resources. Thus, before deciding whether or not to invest in a start-up, most venture capitalists want to know whether the start-up team has the necessary competencies to be successful in the industry it proposes to enter.

Industry Analysis Locally: How Intense Is the Immediate Competition?

As we have seen, assessing an industry's driving forces and Porter's five forces and understanding its critical success factors are important to industry analysis. These are macro-level issues, similar to the macro trends we examined in Chapter 3. To most firms, immediate product-class and product-type competitive conditions are equally if not more important. Such conditions are particularly salient for firms, such as retailers, that operate on a local basis.

If an entrepreneur wants to open a fly-fishing shop near a blue-ribbon trout stream in Montana, he or she will be pleased that fly-fishing is on the rise, that consumers have adequate income to pursue such a sport, and that leisure activities are becoming more important to many people. But it also matters if there are already a couple of fly-fishing shops serving the local market, and whether those shops serve their customers effectively.

KEY OBSERVATION

Assessing an industry must typically be done locally and at the product-class and product-type levels, as well as more globally, and relevant information about specific competitors must be obtained.

If so, the overall trends and industry conditions probably do not matter much, for the local fly-fishing pie can be sliced only so many ways! Thus, assessing an industry must typically be done locally and at the product-class and product-type levels, as well as more globally, and relevant information about specific competitors must be obtained.

In Chapter 7, we'll address the market knowledge systems that many firms use to gather competitive information as well as other relevant market and industry data. As we shall see, gathering this information is important, and ethical issues having to do with how competitive information is obtained are likely to arise. For a discussion of ethical issues in gathering information to perform competitive analyses, see Ethical Perspective 4.1.

ETHICAL PERSPECTIVE 4.1
SCIP: Setting Standards for Gathering Competitive Intelligence

SCIP, the Society of Competitive Intelligence Professionals (www.scip.org), is an organization of consultants and business people whose job it is to monitor the competitive environment for their firms. Competitive intelligence (CI) enables senior managers in companies of all sizes to make informed decisions about everything from marketing, R&D, and investing tactics to long-term business strategies. Effective CI is a continuous process involving the legal and ethical collection of information, analysis that doesn't avoid unwelcome conclusions, and controlled dissemination of actionable intelligence to decision makers. SCIP's code of ethics provides a useful guide for anyone charged with gathering information about competitors.

SCIP Code of Ethics for CI Professionals

To continually strive to increase the recognition and respect of the profession.

To comply with all applicable laws, domestic and international.

To accurately disclose all relevant information, including one's identity and organization, prior to all interviews.

To fully respect all requests for confidentiality of information.

To avoid conflicts of interest in fulfilling one's duties.

To provide honest and realistic recommendations and conclusions in the execution of one's duties.

To promote this code of ethics within one's company, with third-party contractors, and within the entire profession.

To faithfully adhere to and abide by one's company policies, objectives, and guidelines.

Source: "SCIP: Setting Standards for Gathering Competitive Intelligence," www.scip.org. Used by permission.

Rate of Diffusion of Innovations: Another Factor in Assessing Opportunity Attractiveness

Before entrepreneurs or established marketers invest in the development and introduction of an innovation, they should evaluate how rapidly the innovation is likely to be adopted by the target market. The faster the adoption rate, the more attractive an innovative good or service is to the marketer, as competitors are caught short while consumers build loyalty to the new product. **Diffusion of innovation** theory seeks to explain the adoption of an innovative product or service over time among a group of potential buyers. Lack of awareness and limited distribution typically limit early adoption. As positive word about the product spreads, the product is adopted by additional consumers. Diffusion theory is useful to managers in predicting the likely adoption rate for new and innovative goods or services.

The Adoption Process

The **adoption process** involves the attitudinal changes experienced by individuals from the time they first hear about a new product, service, or idea until they adopt it. Not all individuals respond alike; some tend to adopt early, some late, and some never. The five stages in the adoption process are awareness, interest, evaluation, trial, and adoption:

1. *Awareness.* In this stage, the person is only aware of the existence of the new product and is insufficiently motivated to seek information about it.
2. *Interest.* Here the individual becomes sufficiently interested in the new product but is not yet involved.
3. *Evaluation.* This is sometimes referred to as the *mental rehearsal* stage. At this point, the individual is mentally applying the new product to his or her own use requirements and anticipating the results.
4. *Trial.* Here the individual actually uses the product, but, if possible, on a limited basis to minimize risk. Trial is not tantamount to adoption; only if the use experience is satisfactory will the product stand a chance of being adopted.
5. *Adoption.* In this stage, the individual not only continues to use the new product but also adopts it in lieu of substitutes.

The Rate of Adoption

If plotted on a cumulative basis, the percentage of people adopting a new product over time resembles an S curve. Although the curve tends to have the same shape regardless of the product involved, the length of time required differs among products—often substantially.

The time dimension is a function of the rate at which people in the target group (those ultimately adopting) move through the five stages in the adoption process. Generally, the speed of the adoption process depends on the following factors: (1) the risk (cost of product failure or dissatisfaction), (2) the relative advantage over other products, (3) the relative simplicity of the new product, (4) its compatibility with previously adopted ideas and behavior, (5) the extent to which its trial can be accomplished on a small-scale basis, and (6) the ease with which the central idea of the new product can be communicated.[13] Some new products move quickly through the adoption process (a new breakfast cereal), while others take years. Risk minimization via guarantees and reliable and prompt service can be critical as can the ability to demonstrate the product's uniqueness in meeting the customer's needs. Source credibility is also important.

The rate at which a product passes through the adoption process is also a function of the actions taken by the product's supplier. Thus, the diffusion process is faster when there is strong competition among members of the supplier group, when they have favorable reputations, and when they allocate substantial sums to R&D (to improve performance) and marketing (to build awareness).[14] Early cellular telephones scored high on most of the key adoption factors.

Adopter Categories

Early adopters differ from later adopters. Using time of adoption as a basis for classifying individuals, five major groups can be distinguished: innovators, early adopters, early majority, late majority, and laggards. (Note that these are different from the five stages of adoption for a given individual just discussed.) See Exhibit 4.4 for the approximate size and characteristics of each group.[15] Because each category comprises individuals who have similar characteristics and because individuals differ substantially across categories, these adopter groups can be considered market segments. Thus, one would use a different set of strategies to market a new product to the early adopter group than to market it to the late majority group. For a discussion of the challenges in transitioning marketing efforts from group to group, see Exhibit 4.5.

The differences cited in the Exhibits 4.4 and 4.5 are important because they help in the development of strategic marketing programs. In organizational markets, suppliers can identify innovative firms by reputation, profitability, size, and the suppliers' experiences in dealing with them. As evident from earlier discussion, information alone about the product or service is not usually a sufficient reason to adopt. Commercial sources of information (such as salespeople and mass media advertising) are important at the outset, but less-commercial and more-professional sources are sought to validate the proclaimed merits of the new product, especially during the evaluation stage. Advice from opinion leaders is more critical as a legitimizing agent than as a source of information. A classic study of how doctors reacted to the introduction of a new "miracle drug" found that only 10 percent

Exhibit 4.4

SIZE AND CHARACTERISTICS OF INDIVIDUAL ADOPTER GROUP

- **Innovators** represent the first 2.5 percent of all individuals who ultimately adopt a new product. They are more venturesome than later adopters, more likely to be receptive to new ideas, and tend to have high incomes, which reduces the risk of a loss arising from an early adoption.
- **Early adopters** represent the next 13 to 14 percent who adopt. They are more a part of the local scene, are often opinion leaders, serve as vital links to members of the early majority group (because of their social proximity), and participate more in community organizations than do later adopters.
- The **early majority** includes 34 percent of those who adopt. These individuals display less leadership than early adopters, tend to be active in community affairs (thereby gaining respect from their peers), do not like to take unnecessary risks, and want to be sure that a new product will prove successful before they adopt it.
- The **late majority** represents another 34 percent. Frequently, these individuals adopt a new product because they are forced to do so for either economic or social reasons. They participate in community activities less than the previous groups and only rarely assume a leadership role.
- **Laggards** comprise the last 16 percent of adopters. Of all the adopters, they are the most "local." They participate less in community matters than members of the other groups and stubbornly resist change. In some cases, their adoption of a product is so late it has already been replaced by another new product.

Exhibit 4.5   Crossing the Chasm: A Difficult Transition in the Diffusion Process

In Geoffrey Moore's classic book on the marketing of high-technology products, Moore explores the challenges of crossing the "chasm," as he calls it, in the diffusion process between the early adopters and the early majority. For many high-tech products, innovators and early adopters have quite different needs from early majority customers. They are often willing to adopt a revolutionary new product that is not yet very user-friendly or whose product features have not yet been fully developed. Their own technical skill enables them to adapt such a product to their needs and resolve some of the uncertainties inherent in the product's perhaps still-unclear potential. Their self-percep-

tion as an innovator gives them comfort in trying new products before others do. Early majority buyers, on the other hand, typically require easier-to-use products, whose benefits are clearly defined, and for which there is proof that the product will perform. Taking a product from the first group of buyers to the second is a difficult challenge, one that is compounded by the fact that buyers in the innovator and early adopter groups are not likely to associate or talk with buyers in the early majority group.

Source: From *Crossing the Chasm* by Geoffrey A. Moore. Copyright © 1991 by Geoffrey A. Moore. Reprinted by permission of Harper-Collins Publishers Inc.

---

adopted on the basis of data provided by their initial source of information, indicating that data alone will not cause adoption.[16]

Thus, commercial sources are most important at the awareness stage in the adoption process, while personal influence is most important at the evaluation stage. In the interest stage, both are important. In the trial stage, marketers should attempt to make it relatively easy for a prospect to try a product under conditions that minimize risk. Therefore, strategic marketing programs should accommodate the various stages in the adoption process as well as the different adoption audiences.

Implications of Diffusion of Innovation Theory for Forecasting Sales of New Products and New Firms

KEY OBSERVATION

Optimistic entrepreneurs or new product managers sometimes naively forecast that their innovations will capture 10 percent or 20 percent of the market in its first year.

Optimistic entrepreneurs or new product managers sometimes wax euphoric about the prospects for the innovations they plan to bring to market. They naively forecast that their innovations will capture 10 percent or 20 percent of the market in its first year. How likely is it that a truly innovative new product, even a compellingly attractive one, will win all of the innovators plus most of the early adopters in its first year on the market? History suggests that such penetration levels are rare at the outset. More typically, first-year penetration levels include some but not all of the innovators, well under 2½ percent of those who, it is hoped, will ultimately adopt!

A good way to estimate how quickly an innovation is likely to move through the diffusion process is to construct a chart that rates the adoption on the six key factors influencing adoption speed, as shown in Exhibit 4.6. An innovation that is risky for the prospective user to try or buy, has little competitive advantage, is complex or incompatible with current user behavior, and is difficult or expensive to try or to understand its benefits is likely to face tough sledding, regardless of the attractiveness of the industry. Personal robots, introduced in the early 1980s with great fanfare following the introduction of personal computers, were such an innovation. Thus, introducing a new product that delivers no real benefits or lacks competitive advantage into *any* industry, regardless of its high-tech profile, is likely to be an unpleasant experience!

Exhibit 4.6

COMPARISON OF RATE OF ADOPTION OF CELLULAR PHONES AND PERSONAL COMPUTERS FOR HOME USE

Adoption factor	Cell phones		Home computers	
Risk	+/−	Moderate risk: Cell phones were given away to attract early adopters who agreed to one year's usage.	−	An expensive investment wasted, if it turned out not to be useful.
Relative advantage	+	Enabled people to make and receive phone calls from anywhere—in the car or at the beach!	−	It was not clear, in the early days of personal computing, what the advantages of a PC were in the home.
Relative simplicity	+	Early cell phones were easy to use.	−	Early PCs were inordinately complex to use.
Compatibility with current behavior	+	Just like making or receiving a phone call at home or office.	−	Lots of learning required to use.
Ease of small-scale trial	1	Contracts required only modest minutes of use.	+/−	One could visit a store for hands-on trial, but couldn't understand the "bits, bites, and RAM."
Ease of communication of benefits	+	"Make or receive calls anywhere" is easy to understand.	−	Benefits were not clear, thus not communicable.

Key:

+ Favorable for rapid adoption

− Unfavorable for rapid adoption

Sustaining Competitive Advantage over the Product Life Cycle

The **product life cycle** or (PLC) is concerned with the sales history of a product or product class. The concept holds that a product's sales change over time in a predictable way and that products go through a series of five distinct stages: introduction, growth, shakeout, maturity, and decline (see Exhibit 4.7). Each of these stages provides distinct opportunities and threats, thereby affecting the firm's strategy as well as its marketing programs. Despite the fact that many new products do not follow such a prescribed route because of failure, the PLC concept is extremely valuable in helping management look into the future and better anticipate what changes will need to be made in strategic marketing programs.

KEY OBSERVATION

The PLC concept is extremely valuable in helping management look into the future and better anticipate what changes will need to be made in strategic marketing programs.

Life-Cycle Curves

Many products do not go through the product life-cycle curve shown in Exhibit 4.7 because a high percentage are aborted after an unsatisfactory introductory period. Other products seemingly never die (Scotch whiskey, TVs, automobiles). The shape of the life-cycle curve varies considerably between and within industries but is typically described as "S"-shaped. One study identified 12 different types of curves.[17] In general, however, only one or a very few curves typify an industry (see Exhibit 4.8 for the common types).

Exhibit 4.7

GENERALIZED PRODUCT LIFE CYCLE

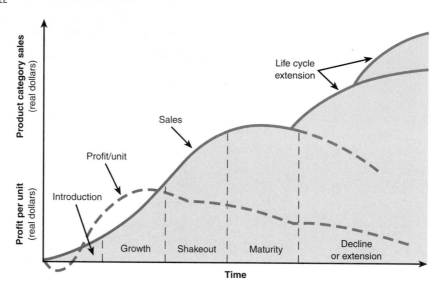

Exhibit 4.8

COMMON PRODUCT LIFE-CYCLE CURVES

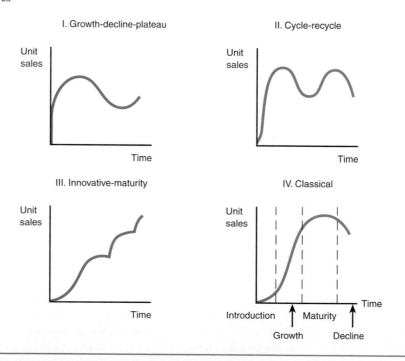

Source: Adopted from J. E. Swan and D. R. Rink, "Effective Use of Industrial Product Life Cycle Trends," in *Marketing in the '80s* (New York: American Marketing Association, 1980), pp. 198–99. Used by permission of the American Marketing Association.

Market and Competitive Implications of Product Life-Cycle Stages

The various stages of the product life cycle present different opportunities and threats to the firm. By understanding the characteristics of the major stages, a firm can do a better job of setting forth its objectives and formulating its strategies as well as developing its action plans (see top half of Exhibit 4.9). Our discussion here is generalized; in Chapters 16 and 17 we present a comprehensive examination of specific marketing-strategy programs and do so for both leaders and followers.

KEY OBSERVATION

By understanding the characteristics of the major stages, a firm can do a better job of setting forth its objectives and formulating its strategies.

Marketing Mix Decisions in the Introductory Stage The length of the product line should typically be relatively short to reduce production costs and hold down inventories. Efforts to establish competitive advantage are typically focused on differentiating the new product or product line from solutions customers previously employed to satisfy the targeted want or need. Many early PCs were purchased to perform spreadsheet analyses on the computer, instead of running the calculations by hand, with all the potential for error and difficulty in making changes that the previous manual procedures entailed. Where

KEY OBSERVATION

Efforts to establish competitive advantage are typically focused on differentiating the new product or product line from solutions customers previously employed.

Exhibit 4.9

EXPECTED CHARACTERISTICS AND RESPONSES BY MAJOR LIFE-CYCLE STAGES

STAGES IN PRODUCT LIFE CYCLE

Stage characteristics	Introduction	Growth	Shakeout	Maturity	Decline
Market growth rate (constant dollars)	Moderate	High	Leveling off	Insignificant	Negative
Technical change in product design	High	Moderate	Limited	Limited	Limited
Segments	Few	Few to many	Few to many	Few to many	Few
Competitors	Small	Large	Decreasing	Limited	Few
Profitability	Negative	Large	Low	Large for high market-share holders	Low

Firm's normative responses					
Strategic marketing objectives	Stimulate primary demand	Build share	Build share	Hold share	Harvest
Product	Quality	Continue quality improvements	Rationalize	Concentrate on features	No change
Product line	Narrow	Broad	Rationalize	Hold length of line	Reduce length of line
Price	Skimming versus penetration	Reduce	Reduce	Hold or reduce selectively	Reduce
Channels	Selective	Intensive	Intensive	Intensive	Selective
Communications	High	High	High	High to declining	Reduce

service is important, the firm must be able to provide it promptly (as in postpurchase service and spare-parts availability).

Pricing in the introductory stage is strongly affected by a variety of factors: the product's value to the end user; how quickly it can be imitated by competitors; the presence of close substitutes; and the effect of price on volume (elasticity) and, in turn, on costs. Basic strategy choices involve skimming and penetration. **Skimming** is designed to obtain as much margin per unit as possible. This enables the company to recover its new product investments more quickly. Such a strategy is particularly appropriate in niche markets and where consumers are relatively insensitive to price, as was the case in the sale of cellular phones to business executives early in the product life cycle. **Penetration pricing** enables the firm to strive for quick market development and makes sense when there is a steep experience curve, which lowers costs, a large market, and strong potential competition.

Distribution decisions can vary widely, depending in part on whether the new product is intended for consumer or industrial markets, and whether the producer adopts a mass market or niche focus. Achieving distribution is particularly important with consumer goods because of the large amounts sometimes spent on promotion to make consumers aware of the product and to induce trial of the product. Distribution is easier to obtain if the company enjoys established channels for its other products and has a successful track record with new product introductions.

During the introductory period, **promotion** expenditures involving advertising and salesforce are a high percentage of sales, especially for a mass-market, small-value product. Some dot.coms spent themselves to failure for promotional purposes. For industrial goods, personal selling costs are apt to be much higher than advertising costs. The communications task at the outset is to build awareness of the new product's uniqueness, which is typically an expensive undertaking. Further, the promotional expenditures (such as in-store displays, premiums, coupons, samples, and off-list pricing) required to obtain product availability and trial are substantial. For industrial products, the time required to develop awareness of the product's uniqueness is often extensive due to the number of people in the buying center and the complexity of the buying systems.

Marketing Mix Decisions in the Growth Stage   In the growth stage of the PLC, the product line often expands to attract new market segments. It does so by offering an array of prices and different product features, as we have seen in the fast-growing market for mobile phones. The quest for competitive advantage now shifts to differentiation from other entrants in the product class.

Prices tend to decline during the growth period (the average cost of servicing cellular subscribers dropped by about 20 percent annually as that market developed), and price differences between brands decrease. The extent of the decline depends on cost—volume relationships, industry concentration, and the volatility of raw material costs. If growth is so strong it outpaces supply, there is little or no pressure on price; indeed, it may enable sellers to charge premium prices.

During this period sellers of both industrial and consumer goods strive to build a channel or a direct-sales system that provides maximum product availability and service at the lowest cost. If this can be accomplished, rivals are placed at a disadvantage, even to the extent of being excluded from some markets. This is particularly the case with some industrial goods for which the number of intermediaries in any one market is limited. A brand must attain some degree of distribution success in advance of the mature stage, because channel members then tend to disinvest in less-successful brands.

Promotion costs (advertising and personal selling) become more concerned with building demand for a company's brand (selective demand) than demand for the product class or type (primary demand). Firms strive to build favorable attitudes toward their brand on the basis of its unique features. Communications are also used to cultivate new segments. Even though promotion costs remain high, they typically decline as a percentage of sales.

Marketing Mix Decisions in the Shakeout Stage

The advent of this period is signaled by a drop in the overall growth rate and is typically marked by substantial price cuts. As weaker competitors exit the market, the stronger firms gain shares. Thus, major changes in the industry's competitive structure occur. During shakeout the firm must *rationalize* its product line by eliminating weaker items, emphasize creative promotional pricing, and strengthen its channel relationships. At the turn of the millennium, the global personal computer industry became mired in a global price war in its efforts to adjust to a slowing market. The entire industry was experiencing higher inventories and simultaneously intensifying competitive environment. Dell was eating its competitors' lunch.[18] Several firms have dropped out of the retail computer market. To a considerable extent, what happens during a shakeout has been predetermined by how well each brand has been positioned in relation to its targeted segments, its distribution system, and its relative costs per unit.

Marketing Mix Decisions in the Maturity Stage

Because of technical maturity, the various brands in the marketplace become more similar; therefore, any significant breakthroughs by R&D or engineering that help to differentiate the product or redirect its cost can have a substantial payout. Not all innovations achieve their goals, however, as Exhibit 4.10 demonstrates. One option is to add value to the product that benefits the customer by improving the ease of use (voice-activated dialing with cellular phones), by incorporating labor-saving features, or by selling systems rather than single products (adding extended service contracts).

KEY OBSERVATION

Service becomes a way of differentiating the offering in the maturity stage.

Increasingly, in many product classes *service* becomes a way of differentiating the offering in the maturity stage. *Promotion* expenditures and *prices* tend to remain stable during the mature stage. But the nature of the former is apt to change; media advertising for consumer goods declines and in-store promotions, including price deals, increase. The price premium attainable by the high-quality producer tends to erode. The effect of experience on costs and

---

Exhibit 4.10   What the Bicycle Industry Needs Is Innovation

In the early 80s mountain bikes gave the bicycle industry a much-needed boost in sales. But the demand for such bikes peaked and most firms in the industry soon experienced flat or declining sales. Clearly what the industry needs, and is attempting, to do is reinvent the bike. An attempt to do so via the use of a battery-powered motor to propel the bike failed, but one entrepreneur is working on a foldable bike that weighs less than 3.5 pounds.

Recumbent bikes are another innovation that has experienced success in a niche market. The latest innovation is a two-wheel-drive mountain bike, designed to give the rider more control when climbing steep hills. While each of these innovations represents a radical engineering innovation, a visit to your local bicycle shop will prove that even the combined effect of all of these innovations has not significantly altered the bicycle industry.

Source: "Reinventing the Bicycle," *The Economist,* November 18, 1995, p. 76; Meryl Davids Landau, "Easy Rider," *The Wall Street Journal,* March 19, 2001, p. R4; David Rocks, "A Cyclist's New Best Friend," *Business Week Online,* December 16, 2002.

prices becomes smaller and smaller. Competition may force prices down, especially when the two leading competitors hold similar shares. For consumer goods, distribution and in-store displays (shelf facings) become increasingly important, as does effective cost management.

Marketing Mix Decisions in the Decline Stage   Eventually most products enter the decline stage, which may be gradual (canned vegetables/hot cereals) or extremely fast (some prescription drugs). Products enter this stage primarily because of technologically superior substitutes (jet engines over piston engines) and a shift in consumer tastes, values, and beliefs (cholesterol-free margarine over butter).

KEY OBSERVATION

Marketing expenditures, especially those associated with promotion, usually decrease as a percentage of sales in the decline stage.

Marketing expenditures, especially those associated with *promotion,* usually decrease as a percentage of sales in the decline stage. *Prices* tend to remain stable if the rate of decline is slow, there are some enduring profitable segments and low exit barriers, customers are weak and fragmented, and there are few single-product competitors. Conversely, aggressive pricing is apt to occur when decline is fast and erratic, there are no strong unique segments, there are high exit barriers, a number of large single-product competitors are present, and customers have strong bargaining power. For consumer goods, marketing activity centers on distribution—persuading intermediaries to continue to stock the item even though they may not promote it. For industrial products the problem may center around maintaining the interest of the salesforce in selling the item.

As the decline stage unfolds, some brands find it necessary to harvest any limited value that remains in the brand or even withdraw from the market (see Exhibit 4.11). **Harvesting** or withdrawal has as its objective an increase in cash flow that can be accomplished by milking (making only the essential investments), internal transfer of assets, and sales of the business or its assets. In any milking operation, management looks for ways to reduce assets, costs, and the number of items in the product line.

Strategic Implications and Limitations of the Product Life Cycle

KEY OBSERVATION

The product life-cycle model is a framework that helps signal the occurrence of opportunities and threats in the marketplace and the industry, thereby helping the business better anticipate change in the product's strategic market objective, its strategy, and its marketing program.

The product life-cycle model is a framework that helps signal the occurrence of opportunities and threats in the marketplace and the industry, thereby helping the business better anticipate change in the product's strategic market objective, its strategy, and its marketing program. By considering the stage in which a product sits in the PLC, one can identify the most typical responses that marketing decision makers make to the changing circumstances faced by the product (see the bottom half of Exhibit 4.9).

Exhibit 4.11   GM Sinks Its Big Boats

In the early 1990s, General Motors announced plans to stop producing its Chevrolet Caprice Classic—a large, rear-wheel-drive car that had long been the favorite of police departments and taxis—and its gargantuan Cadillac Fleetwood, which was the model of choice for stretch limos and hearses. The factory where the cars were built was to be used to assemble a more trendy line of cars and pickup trucks. In dropping this duo, GM turned their markets over to Ford, which had been considering abandoning its big rear-wheel-drive Crown-Victoria. Not everyone at GM agreed with the company's decision. Some wanted to continue these models "as is," while others argued for small-volume production, even if it required an outside contractor.

Source: Gabriella Stern and Neal Timplin, "GM Turns Away from Cop-Car, Limo Markets," *The Wall Street Journal,* May 16, 1995, p. B1.

Note however, that generalizing from such typical responses to those necessary in a particular situation is fraught with risk. The product life-cycle model's major weakness lies in its normative approach to prescribing strategies based on assumptions about the features or characteristics of each stage. It fails to take into account that the product life cycle is, in reality, driven by market forces expressing the evolution of consumer preferences (the market), technology (the product), and competition (the supply side).[19] Mary Lambkin and George Day argue strongly that greater emphasis on competitive issues helps to better understand the evolution of a product-market. This is especially the case in understanding the dynamics of competitive behavior in evolving market structures.[20]

KEY OBSERVATION

The product life-cycle model's major weakness lies in its normative approach to prescribing strategies based on assumptions about the features or characteristics of each stage. It fails to take into account that the product life cycle is, in reality, driven by market forces.

TAKE-AWAYS

- Companies are more likely to be successful in generating sales and profits if the opportunities they pursue are blessed with the following conditions:

  - Driving forces for the industry are favorable.

  - The industry's five forces are, on balance, favorable.

  - The capabilities of the firm and/or the management team are sufficient to perform with respect to the industry's critical success factors.

  - Local competitive conditions are favorable.

  In other words, choosing an attractive industry, as well as a growing market, is important!

- An innovation is more likely to be successful if it will diffuse at a rate rapid enough to quickly establish customer loyalty and advantage over competitors. This chapter provides a framework for assessing this likelihood.

- Regardless of the nature of the playing field, developing and regularly updating winning marketing strategies are important, too! In developing strategies to build and sustain competitive advantage, marketing decision makers are more likely to win the competitive war by adjusting their strategies as the markets and industries in which they compete evolve through the stages of the product life cycle. Specific tools and frameworks for managing this task are provided in the balance of this book.

Self-diagnostic questions to test your ability to apply the analytical tools and concepts in this chapter to marketing decision making may be found at this book's website at www.mhhe.com/mullins05.

ENDNOTES

1. Information on the cellular telephone business at the turn of the 21st century comes from the following sources: Moon Ihlwan, "Asia Gets Hooked on Wireless," *Business Week,* June 19, 2000, p. 109; "Commentary: Europe Shouldn't Squander this Telecom Windfall," *Business Week,* May 22, 2000; Stephen Baker, "The Race to Rule Mobile," *Business Week* International Edition, February 21, 2000; Stephen Baker, "Smart Phones," *Business Week* International Edition, October 18, 1999; "Online Overseas," *New York Times,* June 7, 2000, p. H8; Steve Frank, "Darling to Dog to . . . ," *The Wall Street Journal Sunday,* June 18, 2000; Peter Elstrom, "More Americans Are Packing Finnish Phones," *Business Week,* December 21, 1998; "Nokia Chmn Sees Rise in Global Handset Mkt in 2003-FT," Dow Jones Newswires, November 17, 2002; "Asia Leads Growth in Telecommunications," *Asia Computer Weekly.* December 16, 2002. http://finance. yahoo.com/q?s=QCOM&d=c&k=cl&a=v&p=s&t=5y&l=off&z=l&q=l.

2. Bruce H. Clark and David B. Montgomery, "Managerial Identification of Competitors," *Journal of Marketing* 63 (July 1999), pp. 67–83.

3. Adrian J. Slywotzky, *Value Migration* (Boston: Harvard Business School Press, 1996).

4. Michael Porter, *Competitive Strategy* (New York: Free Press, 1980).

5. Ibid, chap. 3.

6. For an example of such a checklist, see John Mullins, *The New Business Road Test,* Appendix 3 (London: Prentice-Hall/FT, 2003).

7. Wendy Zellner, Andrea Rothman, and Eric Schine, "The Airlines Mess," *Business Week,* July 6, 1992.

8. Myron Magnet, "Meet the New Revolutionaries," *Fortune,* February 24, 1992, pp. 98–99.

9. Baker, "The Race to Rule Mobile."

10. For an interesting case study involving a PC chip-maker and its strategy to forward integrate by entering the PC business, see P. B. Campbell, "Chip-Maker Cyrex Plans to Enter Tough PC Business," *The Wall Street Journal,* March 6, 1996, p. B4.

11. Baker, "Smart Phones."

12. Ibid.

13. Everett M. Rogers, *Diffusion of Innovations* (New York: Free Press, 1983).

14. Thomas S. Robertson and Hubert Gatignon, "Competitive Effects on Technological Diffusion," *Journal of Marketing,* July 1986, pp. 1–12.

15. Rogers, *Diffusion of Innovations.*

16. Frederick E. Webster, Jr., *Industrial Marketing Strategy* (New York: John Wiley & Sons, 1991), pp. 158–74.

17. J. E. Swan and D. R. Rink, "Effective Use of Industrial Life Cycle Trends," in *Marketing in the '80s* (New York: American Marketing Association, 1980), pp. 198–99.

18. Steve Hamm, Faith Keenan, and Andy Reinhardt, "Making the Tech Slump Pay Off," *Business Week Online,* June 24, 2002; Cliff Edwards, "Everyone Loves a Freebie—Except Dell's Rivals," *Business Week Online,* July 22, 2002.

19. Frederick E. Webster, Jr., *Industrial Marketing Strategy* (New York: John Wiley & Sons, 1991), p. 128.

20. Mary Lambkin and George S. Day, "Evolutionary Processes in Competitive Markets beyond the Product Life Cycle," *Journal of Marketing,* July 1989, pp. 8–9.

CHAPTER FIVE

Understanding Consumer Buying Behavior

Cruise Ships—Not Just for Grandma and Grandpa Anymore[1]

NOT TOO LONG AGO, a sea cruise was widely viewed as a rather dull and sedate vacation alternative, appealing mostly to well-to-do elderly people who enjoyed playing shuffleboard, sipping tea, and dressing for dinner. But that perception began to change about a decade ago. As a result, the global cruise industry averaged an 8.5 percent annual growth in bookings throughout the 1990s. And thanks in part to the low taxes and operating costs gained from registering their ships in countries such as Panama and Liberia, cruise lines were among the most profitable of all service businesses during that decade. Carnival Corporation, the industry's market share leader and parent of several lines, including Carnival, Holland America, and Cunard, earned nearly $1 billion on sales of $4.5 billion in 2001.

Savvy Marketing Helped Fuel Industry Growth

A number of factors helped change consumer perceptions and build demand for cruise vacations. Some were fortuitous events beyond the companies' control. For instance, Royal Caribbean experienced the largest volume of bookings in its history during the month following the release of *Titanic,* a somewhat surprising

impact for a movie about a passenger ship that sank. More importantly, the major players in the industry strengthened all aspects of their marketing programs to appeal to a wider variety of customer segments.

First, firms invested heavily in improving their physical facilities. Many new ships were built that were not only much bigger and steadier than their predecessors, but also incorporated amenities such as casinos, shopping arcades, theaters, health spas, Internet access in every stateroom, suites with private balconies, and even a skating rink. Shorter and cheaper cruises were added to attract more price-sensitive customers. Ships were located in more ports around the world—from Southampton in the United Kingdom to Hong Kong, Majorca, and even Galveston, Texas—to draw passengers from a wider geographic area. And major sums were devoted to advertising and promotion programs. For instance, Carnival, Royal Caribbean, and Princess, the three biggest cruise lines, spent more than $100 million annually on TV advertising during the late 1990s.

Perhaps the biggest factor underlying the industry's growth, however, was the ability of the major competitors to understand and cater to the differing needs, desires, and purchase criteria of different customer segments. Ship designs, onboard amenities and activities, food and beverage options, itineraries, and prices

Exhibit 5.1

TYPES OF CRUISES, BENEFITS OFFERED, AND MAJOR COMPETITORS

Type of Cruise	Rates	Amenities/benefits	Major competitors
Contemporary/ Resort class	$100 to $200 (per person per day)	Value-oriented cruises of 3–7 days; casual environment; newer or recently renovated ships; lots of open deck and pool space; organized activities, sports, etc.; "Vegas" or "Broadway"-style productions, dancing, etc.; both sit-down and buffet-style meals.	Carnival, Royal Caribbean, Norwegian Cruise Line
Premium	$150 to $400	Semiformal, premium quality cruises of 7 days or longer; ships designed to offer more space per passenger; more attentive service; theme lounges, theaters, cigar bars, etc.; supervised activities, games, fitness facilities; premium food and beverage offerings.	Holland America, P&O Princess
Luxury	$400 to $1,000	Cruises emphasize greater choice of food, beverage, and entertainment options in a more formal atmosphere; more spacious and luxurious accommodations; more exotic itineraries.	Cunard Line; Crystal Cruises
Exclusive	$700 plus	Exclusive, yacht-like environment with only 100–200 passengers; high staff-to-customer ratio allows highly individualized service	Seabourn Cruise Line, Silversea Cruises, Swan Hellenic

Source: "Cruises by Cruise Line," The Cruise Company, www.cruisecompany.net. Used by permission.

were all tailored to specific demographic, social, and lifestyle groups. For instance, P&O Princess launched "Ocean Village" cruises in the Mediterranean in 2003. They are targeted at younger couples who enjoy sports and educational activities and offer passengers the chance to participate in such things as scuba diving, gourmet cooking, and wine tasting. Some lines offer "romantic" cruises targeted at honeymooners; others appeal to the singles crowd; and many lines, including the ships launched by Disney in 1998, focus on families with young children by offering multiroom suites and lots of supervised activities for various age groups. Even within the traditional target audience for cruises—relatively upscale couples in their 50s and 60s—lines offer cruises with unique benefits to appeal to subsegments with different interests and preferences. Some categories of cruises, the benefits they

promise, and major lines that offer them, are summarized in Exhibit 5.1.

Future Challenges

As the global cruise industry steams into the twenty-first century, however, there may be some icebergs on the horizon. Terrorist attacks and political unrest around the world disrupted industry revenues in 2002 and may continue to do so in the future. One of the industry's biggest potential challenges, though, is overcapacity. You might think that the extensive capital investment required to launch a new cruise ship would raise substantial barriers to entry and restrain industry competitiveness, but the substantial growth and profits cruise lines enjoyed during the 1990s spurred them to build more and bigger ships at an increasing rate. Carnival alone is scheduled to bring 14 new ships into service by 2006, raising its total to 59. Overall, the worldwide cruise fleet numbers about 220 vessels, and capacity is expected to grow another 12 percent or so by 2006, which is problematic given that volume growth has been relatively flat since 2001.

The primary challenge, then, is for firms in the industry to further increase the growth in passenger bookings to fill the growing capacity. One way to do this is to develop long-term relationships with past customers in the hopes of generating more repeat business. Carnival, for instance, offers substantial discounts to past customers. Given that the vast majority of vacationers around the world have never gone on a cruise, however, the greatest potential for growth involves converting nonusers into new customers. But that feat will require an even better understanding of what those people want from a vacation and how they make their leisure purchase decisions.

Marketing Challenges Addressed in Chapter 5

The ability of the global cruise industry to generate substantial new and profitable growth in a market that had been stagnant for years illustrates why examining the needs, desires, and purchasing behavior of existing and potential customers is a critical step in analyzing market opportunities. Consumers buy goods and services as means to an end, as potential solutions to their unsatisfied needs and wants. And they select particular brands or deal with a specific supplier (Carnival Cruise Line) because they perceive them to offer desirable benefits (an interesting itinerary, great food, attentive service, romantic atmosphere, programs for the kids, etc.) and superior value.

Consumer decision making is essentially a problem-solving process. Most customers, whether individual consumers or organizational buyers, go through similar mental processes in deciding which products and brands to buy. Despite this similarity, different customers often end up buying different things. Some vacationers take two-week luxury cruises, some take four-day "contemporary" cruises, while many others go to Disney World or camp in Yellowstone instead. These differences reflect variations in consumers' **personal characteristics**—their needs, benefits sought, attitudes, values, past experiences, and lifestyles—and their **social influences**—their social class, reference groups, and family situations.

The more marketers know about the factors affecting their customers' buying behavior, the greater their ability to design attractive product or service offerings, to define and target meaningful market segments, and to develop marketing programs to fit the concerns and desires of those segments. This chapter provides a framework to help organize an analysis of the mental processes individual consumers go through when making purchase decisions and the individual and environmental factors affecting those decisions.

Not all purchase decisions are equally important or psychologically involved. The decision to spend several thousand dollars on a cruise is a bigger deal for most people than the decision to add Cheerios to their shopping cart. The first question we explore, then, is whether consumers' mental processes are different when they purchase high-involvement goods or services than when they buy more mundane, low-involvement products. If so, what are the implications of those decision-making differences for the marketing manager or entrepreneur charged with developing the strategic marketing plan for a particular product or service?

Regardless of their involvement with a particular purchase decision, different people often choose different products or brands. This fact raises two important questions that we'll explore later in the chapter. How do a person's psychological processes and traits—such as perception, memory, attitudes, and lifestyle—affect his or her buying behavior? And what impact do social influences—like culture, social class, reference groups, and the family—have on purchase decisions?

The Psychological Importance of the Purchase Affects the Decision-Making Process

From an individual consumer's point of view, some purchase decisions are more important, and therefore more psychologically involving, than others. **High-involvement** purchases involve goods or services that are psychologically important to the buyer because they address social or ego needs and therefore carry social and psychological risks (e.g., the risk of looking foolish to one's family or friends). They may also involve a lot of money and therefore financial risk. Because a consumer's level of involvement with a particular purchase depends on the needs to be satisfied and the resources available, however, a high-involvement product for one buyer may be a low-involvement product for another.

The decision processes involved in purchasing high- and low-involvement products and services are quite different. As Exhibit 5.2 indicates, the decision process pursued by a given consumer can be classified into one of four categories depending on whether (1) the consumer has a high or low level of product involvement, and (2) he or she engages in an extensive search for information and evaluation of alternative brands or makes the decision routinely.[2]

KEY OBSERVATION

The decision processes involved in purchasing high- and low-involvement products and services are quite different.

How Do Consumers Make High-Involvement Purchase Decisions?

When purchasing high-involvement products or services, consumers go through a problem-solving process involving five mental steps: (1) problem identification, (2) information search, (3) evaluation of alternatives, (4) purchase, and (5) postpurchase evaluation. These five steps are diagrammed in Exhibit 5.3 and discussed in the context of buying a Caribbean cruise by a hypothetical person—Paul MacDonald, who is 33 years old and single.

Problem Identification   Consumers' purchase-decision processes are triggered by unsatisfied needs or wants. Individuals perceive differences between ideal and actual states on some physical or sociopsychological dimension. This motivates them to seek products or services to help bring their current state more into balance with the ideal.

Exhibit 5.2

TYPES OF CONSUMER DECISION MAKING

	EXTENT OF INVOLVEMENT	
Extent of analysis	**High**	**Low**
Extended (information search; consideration of brand alternatives)	Complex decision making (cars, homes, vacations)	Limited decision making, including variety seeking and impulse purchasing (adult cereals and snack foods)
Habit/routine (little or no information search; focus on one brand)	Brand loyalty (athletic shoes, adult cereals, cologne, deodorant)	Inertia (frozen vegetables, paper towels)

Exhibit 5.3

STEPS IN THE HIGH-INVOLVEMENT, COMPLEX DECISION-MAKING PROCESS

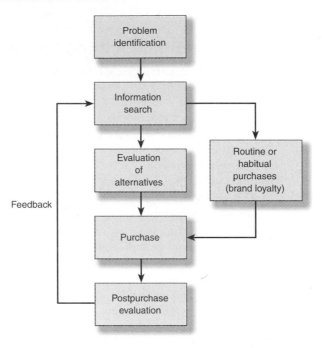

Given that most of us have limited time and financial resources, it is impossible for us to satisfy all our needs at once. Instead, we tend to focus on those that are strongest. The size of the gap between our current and our desired state largely determines the strength of a particular need. A need can become stronger and be brought to our attention by a deterioration of our actual state or an upward revision of our ideal state.

A change in a consumer's actual state can occur for several reasons:

- For physical needs, a natural deterioration of the actual state occurs all the time. A person's body burns energy and nutrients. Thus, periodically we get hungry and tired and are motivated to find something to eat and go to sleep.

- A person's actual state may change as the result of the depletion of the current solution to a need. Our hypothetical consumer might be motivated to buy a cruise package because the condo in Florida he usually rents for his winter vacation is not available this year.

- In some cases consumers can anticipate a decline in their actual state. If Paul MacDonald knew that the condo owner was trying to find someone to lease the condo for the entire season, he might decide to investigate alternatives for his winter vacation.

Similarly, a change in a consumer's desired state may occur for several reasons:

- The desired state may be revised upward because of new information or the development of an old need. Thus, MacDonald may have seen an ad showing how much fun a person can have on a cruise for a small amount of money or received such information from a friend.

- As one need is satisfied, the desired state on other need dimensions increases and becomes more demanding.

Information Search
Having recognized that a problem exists and might be satisfied by the purchase and consumption of a product or service, the consumer's next step is to

Exhibit 5.4

FACTORS THAT ARE LIKELY TO INCREASE PREPURCHASE SEARCH

Product factors

Long interpurchase time (a long-lasting or infrequently used product); frequent changes in product styling; frequent price changes, volume purchasing (large number of units); high price; many alternative brands; much variation in features.

Situational factors

Experience:

First-time purchase; no past experience because the product is new; unsatisfactory past experience within the product category.

Social acceptability:

The purchase is for a gift; the product is socially visible.

Value-related considerations:

Purchase is discretionary rather than necessary; all alternatives have both desirable and undesirable consequences; family members disagree on product requirements or evaluation of alternatives; product usage deviates from important reference group; the purchase involves ecological considerations; many sources of conflicting information.

Personal factors

Demographic characteristics of consumer:

Well-educated; high income; white-collar occupation; under 35 years of age.

Personality:

Low dogmatic (open-minded); low-risk perceiver (broad categorizer); other personal factors, such as high product involvement and enjoyment of shopping and search.

---

refer to information gained from past experience and stored in memory for possible later use. To continue with our example, MacDonald's knowledge about cruises derives primarily from advertising, his mother and father who recently took a cruise, and friends—most of whom are married. Since he has no firsthand knowledge of cruises, he will need to seek additional information, especially regarding accommodations, schedules, and fares. For a listing of the factors that are likely to increase the information search, see Exhibit 5.4.

Because services are intangible, difficult to standardize, and their production and consumption inseparable, they are more difficult to evaluate than products. Thus, most services are hard to assess until they are being consumed after purchase (cruises and restaurant meals). Some services are difficult to assess even after they have been consumed (legal services, medical diagnosis, etc.). These assessment difficulties can force consumers to rely on different cues, such as the provider's credentials or reputation, when evaluating services.[3]

How Much Information Will a Consumer Seek? People seek additional information about alternative brands until they perceive that the *costs* of obtaining more information are equal to the additional *value* or *benefit* derived from the information. Information is valuable to consumers to the extent that it helps make a more satisfying purchase and avoids the negative consequences associated with a poor choice. Thus, consumers are likely to place a higher value on—and seek more—information when the purchase is important. This importance derives from (*a*) the strength of a person's need for the product; (*b*) the person's ego-involvement with the product; and (*c*) the severity of the social and financial consequences of making a poor choice. This is why people tend to seek more information about high-priced, socially visible products that reflect their self-image (cars, home, clothing, and, for some, cruises) than for lower-priced products that other people seldom notice, such as furnace filters or paper towels.

Even when products are very expensive and ego-involving, some consumers are unlikely to conduct an exhaustive search for information before making a decision because of the costs involved. Perhaps the biggest cost for most people is the **opportunity cost** of the time involved in seeking information. They give up the opportunity to use that time for other, more important or interesting activities, such as working or taking trips. For some people, however, the opportunity costs of shopping are low because they enjoy wandering through stores or scanning newspaper ads or websites for bargains. Also, as we'll see later, the Web is reducing the opportunity costs of obtaining at least some kinds of product information.

There are also **psychological costs** involved in searching for information. Collecting information can be a frustrating task, often involving crowded stores, rude salespeople, or slow websites. Also, some consumers become frustrated and confused when they have a lot of complex information to evaluate before making a choice. Consequently they cut their information search short.

Because services, more than products, are associated with greater perceived risk, the individual involved is likely to use more information sources in the attempt to better cope with the risk. This often leads to an extended information-acquisition process, which may include purchase postponement. It also means that consumers are less likely to make a trial purchase than with some products.[4]

Sources of Information   Assume that switching from renting a condo to a cruise is important and costly enough for Paul Macdonald to seek additional information before doing so. Which sources can he use? The three broad categories of information sources are personal, commercial, and public. **Personal sources** include family members, friends, and members of the consumer's reference group.

Commercial sources refer to various information disseminated by service providers, marketers, and manufacturers and their dealers. They include media advertising, promotional brochures, package and label information, salespersons, and various in-store information, such as price markings and displays. **Public sources** include noncommercial and professional organizations and individuals who provide advice for consumers, such as doctors, lawyers, governmental agencies, travel agencies, and consumer-interest groups.

Consumers are usually exposed to more information from commercial sources than from personal or public sources. However, many consumers are influenced more by personal sources when deciding which service, product, or brand to buy. Consumers use information from different sources for different purposes and at different stages within the decision process. In general, commercial sources perform an **informing function** for consumers. Personal and public sources serve an **evaluating and legitimizing function.** Thus, MacDonald might rely on advertising and discussions with his travel agent to learn what cruises are available, what the schedules are for each, the kind and size ship used, how much each cruise costs, and the details concerning the various types of entertainment offered. It is highly likely that MacDonald would also seek the opinions of friends in deciding whether to take a cruise and in selecting a particular one. In doing so, he is consistent with the general proposition that consumers choose more personal sources for services than for goods because service consumption is highly personal and must be experienced to be understood.[5]

How Is the Web Affecting Consumers' Search for Information?   The World Wide Web is reducing the opportunity costs of information gathering, thus making it easier for people to make informed decisions. Many manufacturers and service providers have established their own sites. Some of these sites not only provide information about product options and characteristics, but also offer tutorials about how to use the product, help lines, and other information geared to helping customers obtain full value from their purchases. For instance, the outdoor gear retailer REI provides 45,000 pages of product use information and tips, such as a clinic on backpacking, on its site, www.rei.com.

KEY OBSERVATION

Many new sites have taken over much of the search for information about alternative offerings in a product category in exchange for a small fee from the consumer or advertising from manufacturers or dealers in the category.

More important, many new sites have taken over much of the search for information about alternative offerings in a product category in exchange for a small fee from the consumer or advertising from manufacturers or dealers in the category. For example, www.cruisecompany.net provides detailed information on cruises organized by type of cruise, itinerary, or cruise line, in exchange for a commission on any cruise a consumer books through the site.

While such sites facilitate the consumer's search for information about high-involvement products and services, they do not solve all the consumer's problems. Most of the information provided by such sites is obtained from commercial and public, rather than personal, sources. Therefore, some consumers may not consider it very useful for evaluating alternative choices, particularly when it comes to choosing intangible services. This shortcoming helps explain why some sites, such as www.amazon.com, publish product reviews and evaluations submitted by individual customers. Also, sensory information such as touch and smell, which can be important for evaluating foods, fashion items, and similar products, cannot be displayed on the Web. Finally, the effort by some sites to collect information for free from other sites has raised ethical and legal questions concerning who "owns" product information. These questions have yet to be resolved. An example is summarized in Ethical Perspective 5.1.

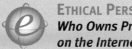

ETHICAL PERSPECTIVE 5.1
Who Owns Product Information on the Internet?

The Internet may substantially reduce consumers' costs of collecting extensive information about product or service alternatives through the development of Web-crawling robots, or "bots," software that trolls through many Internet sites collecting information about items in a given product category. For instance, Bidder's Edge, a small start-up in Burlington, Massachusetts, developed a bot that crawls through online auction sites searching for whatever product a customer is interested in. The bot compiled information on the status of, say, Furby auctions and ranked them in order of expiration date. Without the bot, a consumer would have to click through more than 200 sites to collect the same information.

However, eBay, the biggest Web auction site, sued Bidder's Edge seeking to prevent its bots from trolling eBay's site without prior approval. The auction site argued that the bots take up valuable bandwidth the firm should have the right to use for its own purposes. As the company's lawyer argued, bots are "like 100 people in a store, taking pictures and interfering with the regular customers." The trial judge agreed with

eBay's argument, ruling that Bidder's Edge had violated eBay's "fundamental property right to exclude others from its computer system."

Many other online retailers applauded the ruling. As the chairwoman of Shop.org, a trade group of online retailers, points out, "Most don't like to be compared on price alone." On the other hand, opponents argue that if bots must obtain permission from all sites they enter and/or pay for the information they collect, their usefulness to the consumer will be severely compromised and it will be much more difficult for them to find the best deal. As an opposing lawyer argues, "Property laws weren't meant to be applied to something as ambiguous as cyberspace." And even if the doctrines are applied, he argues, trespass laws are often suspended for the common good.

The initial ruling will undoubtedly be appealed through higher courts, and at this writing it is too early to tell how the issues will ultimately be resolved. One thing that is clear, however, is that the question of who owns the rights to product information on the Web will take many forms—and be the subject of many related court cases—for years into the future.

Source: Daniel Roth, "Meet eBay's Worst Nightmare," *Fortune,* June 26, 2000, pp. 199–206. © 2000 Time, Inc. All rights reserved.

Evaluation of Alternatives   Consumers find it difficult to make overall comparisons of many alternative brands because each brand might be better in some ways but worse in others. Instead, consumers simplify their evaluation in several ways. First, they seldom consider all possible brands; rather, they focus on their **evoked set**—a limited number they are familiar with that are likely to satisfy their needs.

Second, consumers evaluate each of the brands in the evoked set on a limited number of **product dimensions or attributes.** They also judge the *relative importance* of these attributes, or the minimum acceptable performance of each. The set of attributes used by a particular consumer and the relative importance of each represent the consumer's **choice criteria.** In the case of our cruise example, the dates of the cruise, the ports of call, the entertainment offered, and the costs are examples of MacDonald's choice criteria for selecting a specific cruise.

Third, consumers combine evaluations of each brand across attributes, taking into account the relative importance of those attributes. This multiattribute assessment of a brand results in an overall **attitude** toward that brand. The brand toward which consumers have the most favorable attitude is the one they are most likely to buy.

Product Attributes and Their Relative Importance   Consumers use many dimensions or attributes when evaluating alternative products and services. Thus, in addition to the above service attributes, MacDonald might also use the newness and size of ship, types of food served, availability of an exercise room, and kinds of gambling as additional ways of comparing his options. Usually, however, consumers base their evaluations on half a dozen dimensions or less. Exhibit 5.5 contains a general list of product attributes consumers might use to evaluate alternatives.

Different consumers may use different sets of attributes to evaluate brands within the same product category. But even when two people use the same set of attributes, they may arrive at different decisions because they attach varying degrees of importance to the attributes. Paul MacDonald is primarily interested in entertainment, demographics of those taking the cruise, and cost, whereas another traveler might attach greater importance to gambling, ports of call, and food.

A consumer's personal characteristics and social influences—needs, values, personality, social class, and reference groups, among other things—help determine which attributes are considered and their relative importance. Environmental factors and the usage situation can also affect the perceived importance of various product benefits. For instance, some people buy more prestigious and expensive brands of beer or wine for their party guests than for their own everyday consumption.

Exhibit 5.5

SELECTED ATTRIBUTES CONSUMERS USE TO EVALUATE ALTERNATIVE PRODUCTS OR SERVICES

Category	Specific attributes
Cost attributes	Purchase price, operating costs, repair costs, cost of extras or options, cost of installation, trade-in allowance, likely resale value.
Performance attributes	Durability, quality of materials, construction, dependability, functional performance (acceleration, nutrition, taste), efficiency, safety.
Social attributes	Reputation of brand, status image, popularity with friends, popularity with family members, style, fashion.
Availability attributes	Carried by local stores, credit terms, quality of service available from local dealer, delivery time.

Forming Attitudes toward Alternative Brands Even if two consumers use the same attributes and attach the same relative importance to them when evaluating product offerings, they may not necessarily prefer the same brand. They might rate the various brands differently on specific attributes. Differences in brand perceptions are based on past experience, the information collected, and how that information is perceived and processed. And as we shall see later, technology is making it increasingly possible for consumers to interact with manufacturers and suppliers during the production process so that product and service offerings can be customized to meet a customer's preferences on important attributes.[6] Consequently, brand attitudes may also depend on which manufacturer can be most flexible in customizing its product.

Purchase Even after a consumer has collected information about alternative brands, evaluated them, and decided which is the most desirable, the decision process still is not complete. The consumer must now decide where to buy the product. Choosing a source from which to buy the product involves essentially the same mental processes as does a product-purchase decision. The source is usually a retail store but may also be a mail-order catalog such as L. L. Bean or a website like RedEnvelope.com. Consumers obtain information about alternative sources from personal experience, advertising, comments of friends, and the like. Then they use this information to evaluate sources on such attributes as lines of merchandise carried, services rendered, price, convenience, personnel, and physical characteristics. Consumers usually select the source they perceive to be best on those attributes most important to them. If their experiences with a source are positive over time they may develop patronage loyalty and routinely shop that source—similar to the way consumers develop brand loyalties.

Consumers shopping in a retail store intent on purchasing one brand sometimes end up buying something different. MacDonald, for example, could be switched from one cruise to another by the travel agent. This happens because the consumer's ultimate purchase can be influenced by such factors as out-of-stocks (no outside cabins on a particular cruise), a special display, or a message from a salesperson ("I can get you a better deal on a similar cruise if you can go two weeks later").

Postpurchase Evaluation Whether a particular consumer feels adequately rewarded following a purchase depends on two things: (1) the person's **aspiration or expectation level**—how well the product was expected to perform (delivery of a quality pizza while it is hot)—and (2) the consumer's evaluation of how well the product actually did perform (the pizza arrived cold).

Consumers' expectations about a product's performance are influenced by several factors. These include the strength and importance of each person's need and the information collected during the decision-making process. In the case of MacDonald, a persuasive ad or an enthusiastic endorsement of a given cruise by a friend who is a frequent cruise-goer may have caused him to expect more from his cruise than he would have otherwise. He may, however, attribute part of any dissatisfaction to his own actions—an unwillingness to participate in some of the entertainment. The fact that consumers are part of the service production process makes self-blame a real possibility.[7] Nevertheless, even with services there is a danger for marketers in using exaggerated claims in product advertising. Such claims can produce inflated expectations the product cannot live up to—resulting in dissatisfied customers.

It is important to note that, as the diagram in Exhibit 5.3 indicates, the consumer's evaluation of a purchase feeds back into memory where the information can be recalled for a similar purchase decision. Stored information about one or more negative past experiences with a brand or supplier will reduce the odds that the consumer will make the same purchase again. Consistent positive experiences can ultimately lead to **brand loyalty**—the routine repurchase of the same brand with little consideration of any alternatives.

Some experts argue that consumers more often develop loyalty to service providers than to physical products because of the difficulty of evaluating alternatives before actually experiencing the service. Also, repeated patronage can bring additional benefits, such as discounts, or more customized service as the provider gains more insights into the customer's preferences.[8] This helps explain why about 25 percent of all cruise passengers are repeat customers.

Low-Involvement Purchase Decisions

Because low-involvement products are not very important to consumers, the search for information to evaluate alternative brands is likely to be minimal. As a result, decisions to buy products such as cookies or cereals often are made within the store, either *impulsively* on the basis of brand familiarity, or as a result of comparisons of the brands on the shelf. The consumers' involvement and their risks associated with making poor decisions are low for such products. Therefore, consumers are less likely to stay with the same brand over time. They have little to lose by switching brands in a search for variety. Even so, many consumers develop loyalty to a given brand, as in the continued popularity of such low-involvement products as Wrigley Doublemint chewing gum and Gold Medal flour, which have been around for years.

Most purchase decisions are low in consumer involvement—the consumer thinks the product or service is insufficiently important to identify with it. Thus, the consumer does not engage in an extensive search for information for such a purchase. Information involving such products is received passively as in, for example, seeing an ad for Green Giant frozen vegetables, which is neither interpreted or evaluated, but simply noticed and filed away in memory.

Later, the consumer identifies a need to buy some frozen vegetables. On the next trip to the supermarket, the consumer sees the Green Giant brand in the frozen-foods section and buys several packages. The familiarity generated by exposure to earlier advertising (and/or word-of-mouth information) was sufficient to stimulate the purchase of Green Giant though the consumer does not have a strong, positive brand association.

After buying and using the product, the consumer may decide Green Giant vegetables are either good or bad. This attitude will be likely to affect future purchases of frozen vegetables. However, such brand evaluations occur only *after* an initial purchase has been made. This is the opposite of complex decision making.

Inertia   As Exhibit 5.2 indicated, there are two low-involvement buying decisions. When there are few differences between brands and little risk associated with making a poor choice, consumers either buy brands at random or buy the same brand repetitively to avoid making a choice. Marketers must be careful not to confuse such repeat *inertial* purchasing with brand loyalty because it is relatively easy for competitors to entice such customers to switch brands by offering cents-off coupons, special promotions, or in-store displays. Highly brand-loyal customers, on the other hand, resist such efforts on account of their strong brand preference.

Impulse Purchasing and Variety Seeking   The second low-involvement purchase process is **impulse buying,** when consumers impulsively decide to buy a different brand from their customary choice or some new variety of a product. The new brand is probably one they are familiar with through passive exposure to advertising or other information, however. Their motivation for switching usually is not dissatisfaction but a desire for change and variety.

Understanding the Target Consumer's Level of Involvement Enables Better Marketing Decisions

The preceding discussion clearly indicates that consumers employ different decision-making processes and may be influenced by different psychological, social, and situational factors, depending on their level of involvement with the product or service they are buying. These differences between high- and low-involvement consumer behavior are summarized in Exhibit 5.6.

Such behavioral differences have a major implication for marketers. A given marketing strategy, or decisions concerning any of the 4Ps in a marketing plan, will not be equally effective for both high- and low-involvement products. Even though consumers may have differing degrees of psychological involvement with a given product category, the marketer needs to determine whether the majority of potential customers in his or her target segment are likely to be highly involved with the purchase decision or not. The various elements of the strategic marketing plan can then be tailored to the overall level of involvement of people in the target market. Exhibit 5.7 summarizes some major differences in marketing actions appropriate for high- versus low-involvement product or service offerings. These differences are briefly discussed in the following sections.

KEY OBSERVATION

A given marketing strategy, or decisions concerning any of the 4Ps in a marketing plan, will not be equally effective for both high- and low-involvement products.

Product Design and Positioning Decisions   Consumers evaluate both high- and low-involvement products on criteria that reflect the *benefits* they seek. Both types of products and services must offer at least one compelling and valued benefit to continue to win acceptance in the market. Because consumers tend to evaluate high-involvement products

Exhibit 5.6

HIGH-INVOLVEMENT VERSUS LOW-INVOLVEMENT CONSUMER BEHAVIOR

High-involvement consumer behavior	Low-involvement consumer behavior
• Consumers are information processors.	• Consumers learn information at random.
• Consumers are information seekers.	• Consumers are information gatherers.
• Consumers represent an active audience for advertising.	• Consumers represent a passive audience for advertising.
• Consumers evaluate brands before buying.	• Consumers buy first. If they do evaluate brands, it is done after the purchase.
• Consumers seek to maximize expected satisfaction. They compare brands to see which provides the most benefits related to their needs and buy based on a multiattribute comparison of brands.	• Consumers seek an acceptable level of satisfaction. They buy the brand least likely to give them problems and buy based on a few attributes. Familiarity is the key.
• Personality and lifestyle characteristics are related to consumer behavior because the product is closely tied to the person's self-identity and belief system.	• Personality and lifestyle are not related to consumer behavior because the product is not closely tied to the person's self-identity and beliefs.
• Reference groups influence consumer behavior because of the importance of the product to group norms and values.	• Reference groups exert little influence on consumer behavior because products are not strongly related to their norms and values.

Source: From *Consumer Behavior and Marketing Action*, 5th edition, by Henry Assael. © 1995. Reprinted with permission of South-Western, a division of Thomson Learning; www.thomsonrights.com, Fax 800-730-2215.

Exhibit 5.7

MARKETING DECISIONS FOR HIGH-INVOLVEMENT VERSUS LOW-INVOLVEMENT PRODUCTS OR SERVICES

Marketing mix element	Marketing decisions where the consumer exhibits high involvement	Marketing decisions where the consumer exhibits low involvement
Product decisions	For long-term success, one or more compelling product benefits are necessary, regardless of the level of consumer involvement.	For long-term success, one or more compelling product benefits are necessary, regardless of the level of consumer involvement.
Pricing decisions	Price, unless substantially lower, is likely to be of secondary importance to performance criteria. High price may suggest high quality or status, to the seller's benefit. Demonstrable consumer benefits are more likely than price to drive consumer choice.	Price offers can be effective in gaining trial. A sustained low price, compared to competitors (such as for private-label goods in super-markets), may provide sufficient inertia for repeat purchase.
Promotional decisions	Consumers *are* interested in the information that sellers provide. Promotional vehicles that communicate in greater detail (e.g., print advertising, Internet, infomercials, personal selling) are likely to be effective.	Consumers *are not* interested in the information that sellers provide. Large advertising budgets and a clear focus on a single demonstrable consumer benefit are probably necessary to get the message across.
Distribution decisions	Consumers will be relatively *less* concerned with convenience in purchasing. Relatively less extensive distribution is necessary.	Consumers will be relatively *more* concerned with convenience in purchasing. Relatively more extensive distribution is necessary.

and services *before* purchasing, however, it is particularly important that such offerings be designed to provide at least some benefits that are demonstrably superior to those offered by major competitors, and that marketing communications are effective in making potential customers aware of those benefits.

For low-involvement goods and services, on the other hand, much brand evaluation occurs *after* the purchase is made. Consumers tend to be most positive about—and more likely to repurchase—brands that don't disappoint them or cause unexpected problems. Consequently, firms that market low-involvement products or services need to pay particular attention to basic use-related attributes, such as consistent product quality, reliability, convenient packaging, and user-friendliness.

Pricing Decisions   Highly involved consumers generally buy the brand they believe will deliver the greatest value. They are willing to pay a higher price for a brand if they believe it will deliver enough superior benefits relative to cheaper competitors to justify the difference. They may even use high price as an indicator of a brand's superior quality or prestige, particularly in categories where quality is hard to evaluate objectively before purchase, such as professional services.

Many consumers buy low-involvement products largely or solely on the basis of low price. Therefore, special sales or coupon offers can be effective in gaining trial of such goods and services. If no problems are experienced during consumption, consumers may continue to buy the brand out of inertia, at least until a competitor offers an attractive price promotion.

Advertising and Promotion Decisions   Highly involved consumers typically seek at least some information about alternative brands, retail outlets, and so on, before making a purchase decision. Therefore, promotional vehicles that communicate in greater detail—such as print advertising, company websites, infomercials, or a salesperson—are more likely to be attended to and be effective in marketing high-involvement goods and services.

On the other hand, because low-involvement customers are usually passive information gatherers, advertising needs to focus on only a few main points and to deliver the message frequently in order to make it easy for consumers to gain familiarity and positive associations with a brand. Television is often the primary medium for low-involvement products because it facilitates passive learning. Distinctive package design is also important for such products since it helps consumers recognize brands they've seen advertised.

Distribution Decisions   Extensive retail distribution is particularly important for low-involvement products because most consumers are unwilling to search for, or expend extra effort to obtain, a particular brand. Thus, the larger the proportion of available retail outlets, including websites, vending machines, and the like, a marketer can induce to carry a brand, the larger that brand's market share is likely to be.

Because consumers are more willing to spend some time and effort to acquire their favorite brand in a high-involvement category, extensive retail coverage is less critical for such products. The marketer may be better off being relatively choosy in selecting retailers to carry a brand, particularly if those retailers will play an important role in promoting the product or servicing it after the sale. The value of some exclusive, prestigious brands is clearly enhanced by the fact they are *not* available from every mass merchandiser in town.

Strategies to Increase Consumer Involvement   In some cases, a firm may try to increase consumers' involvement with its brand as a way to increase revenues. Increased customer involvement can be attempted in several ways. *The product might be linked to some involving issue,* as when makers of bran cereals associate their products with a high-fiber diet that may reduce the incidence of colon cancer. Or *the product can be tied to a personally involving situation,* such as advertising a sleeping aid late in the evening when insomniacs are interested in finding something to help them sleep. Finally, *an important new feature might be added to an unimportant product* as when Revlon introduced its ColorStay Lipcolor, which promised a miracle for women—unsmeared lipstick all day long. Despite being double the price of other lipsticks, women responded to the claim that it "won't smear off on your teeth, your glass, or him" so well that ColorStay became the number-one-selling brand in drugstores and other mass merchandisers.[9]

Why People Buy Different Things—the Marketing Implications of Psychological and Personal Influences

Even when two consumers have equal involvement with a product, they often purchase different brands for varying reasons. The information they collect, the way they process and interpret it, and their evaluation of alternative brands are all influenced by psychological and personal characteristics. Some of the important psychological, or thought, variables that affect a consumer's decision-making process include *perception, memory, needs,* and *attitudes.* The consumer's personal characteristics, such as *demographic and lifestyle variables,* influence these psychological factors.

Perception and Memory

Perception is the process by which a person selects, organizes, and interprets information. When consumers collect information about a high-involvement service such as a cruise, they follow a series of steps, or a hierarchy of effects. **Exposure** to a piece of information, such as a new product, an ad, or a friend's recommendation, leads to **attention,** then to **comprehension,** and finally to **retention** in memory. Once consumers have fully perceived the information, they use it to evaluate alternative brands and to decide which to purchase.

The perception process is different for low-involvement products. Here, consumers have information in their memories without going through the sequence of attention and comprehension. Exposure may cause consumers to retain enough information so that they are familiar with a brand when they see it in a store.

Two basic factors—*selectivity* and *organization*—guide consumers' perceptual processes and help explain why different consumers perceive product information differently. **Selectivity** means that even though the environment is full of product information, consumers pick and choose only selected pieces of information and ignore the rest. For high-involvement purchases, consumers pay particular attention to information related to the needs they want to satisfy and the particular brands they are considering for purchase. This **perceptual vigilance** helps guarantee that consumers have the information needed to make a good choice. For low-involvement products, consumers tend to selectively screen out much information to avoid wasting mental effort. The average consumer is exposed to over 1,000 ads every day plus information from other sources such as catalogs, websites, and friends. Consumers must be selective in perceiving this information to cope with the clutter of messages.

Consumers also tend to avoid information that contradicts their current beliefs and attitudes. This **perceptual defense** helps them avoid the psychological discomfort of reassessing or changing attitudes, beliefs, or behaviors central to their self-images. For example, many smokers avoid antismoking messages, or play down their importance, rather than admit that smoking may be damaging to their health.

Memory Limitations   Even though consumers are selective in perceiving product information, they remember only a small portion of it. This limitation of the human memory concerns marketers since much marketing activity deals with communicating information to potential consumers to improve their attitudes toward a given brand. What can marketers do—if anything—to improve the memorability of their messages?

There are different theories of how the human memory operates, but most agree that it works in two stages. Information from the environment is first processed by the **short-term memory,** which forgets most of it within 30 seconds or less because of inattention or displacement of new incoming information. Some information, however, is transferred to **long-term memory,** from which it can be retrieved later. Long-term memory has a nearly infinite storage capacity, but the amount of product information actually stored there is quite limited. For information to be transferred to long-term memory for later recall, it must be *actively rehearsed and internalized.* It takes from 5 to 10 seconds of rehearsal to place a chunk of information in long-term memory. This is a long time relative to the fraction of a second necessary to perceive that piece of information. Therefore, new pieces of information swamp the old one before it can be transferred unless consumers find it sufficiently relevant to warrant focusing their attention.

This is why print media and interactive electronic media, such as websites, are good for communicating complex or technical information about high-involvement products. Consumers can control the pace at which such information is received and can take the time necessary to comprehend, rehearse, and remember it. Similarly, this explains why television advertising for low-involvement products should focus on a few simple pieces of information, such as brand name, symbol, or key product attributes, and be repeated frequently. Otherwise, the information will never make into the consumer's long-term memory.

Perceptual Organization   Another mental factor determining how much product information consumers remember and use is the way they organize the information. People do not view and remember each piece of information they receive in isolation. Instead, they organize information through the processes of categorization and integration. **Categorization** helps consumers process known information quickly and efficiently: "I've seen this ad before so I don't have to pay much attention." It also helps people classify new information by generalizing from past experience. An ad for a new cereal with a high vitamin and mineral content, for instance, is interpreted in light of consumers' experience with other nutritional cereals. This can cause a problem if consumers' experiences have not been very favorable: "Other nutritional cereals I've tried have tasted lousy."

Integration means that consumers perceive separate pieces of related information as an organized whole. For example, the picture, headline, copy, and location of a magazine ad interact to produce a single overall reaction to the ad and the brand advertised. Similarly, consumers integrate information about various characteristics of a brand, such as its price and the retail stores that carry it, to form an overall image of the brand.

Effects of Stimulus Characteristics on Perception   Consumers' personal characteristics—such as their particular needs, attitudes, beliefs, and past experiences with a product category—influence the information they pay attention to, comprehend, and remember. The characteristics of the message itself and the way it is communicated also influence consumers' perceptions. The ad's color, size, and position within a magazine or a TV program influence consumers' attention to the message and the brand image the ad produces in consumers' minds. We examine these factors in Chapter 15 when we discuss advertising and promotion decisions.

Needs and Attitudes

An **attitude** is a positive or negative feeling about an object (say, a brand) that predisposes a person to behave in a particular way toward that object. Attitudes derive from a consumer's evaluation that a given brand provides the benefits necessary to help satisfy a particular need. These evaluations are multidimensional; consumers judge each brand on a set of dimensions or attributes weighted by their relative importance.

Fishbein Model   Martin Fishbein pioneered a model that specified how consumers combine evaluations of a brand across multiple attributes to arrive at a single overall attitude toward that brand. His model is expressed as follows:

$$\text{Attitude}_A = \sum_{i=1}^{k} B_i i_i$$

where

Attitude_A = Consumer's overall attitude toward Brand A

B_i = Consumer's belief concerning the extent to which attribute i is associated with Brand A

I_i = The importance of attribute i to the consumer when choosing a brand to buy

k = The total attributes considered by the consumer when evaluating alternative brands in the product category

i = Any specific product attribute

Exhibit 5.8 applies the Fishbein model to Paul MacDonald's evaluation of alternative cruises. This application is **compensatory** because it assumes that MacDonald's overall

Exhibit 5.8

A COMPENSATORY MULTIATTRIBUTE MODEL OF ATTITUDES TOWARD ALTERNATIVE CRUISES

Our hypothetical consumer, Paul MacDonald, is interested in taking a Caribbean cruise lasting not more than seven days sometime during the months of January or February at a reasonable price. As the table indicates, he uses five attributes (choice criteria) to make a comparison between three alternative cruises. On the basis of information gathered from advertising, travel agents, promotional materials received from a number of cruiselines, and friends, he rates the three different cruises on each of the five attributes as follows:

Service attribute	Importance weight (0–10)	RATINGS		
		A	B	C
Demographics—other passengers	10	8	8	8
Entertainment	10	8	10	9
Ports of call	8	8	9	9
Low fares	7	9	8	8
Size/steadiness of ship	6	9	8	8

Using the formula in the text, MacDonald calculates that an overall attitude score for Cruise A equals $(10 \times 8) + (10 \times 8) + (8 \times 8) + (7 \times 9) + (6 \times 9) = 341$. His overall attitude scores for the other two cruises: Cruise B = 356 and Cruise C = 346.

Consequently, MacDonald prefers and will be predisposed to buy Cruise B, the cruise toward which he has the most positive attitude. Although the demographics of other passengers was one of the most important attributes, it played no significant role in determining which cruise he would buy because there were no significant differences between the three cruises on that attribute. Instead the *determinant attribute*—that which had the biggest impact on which cruise MacDonald would prefer—was *entertainment*.

attitude toward a given cruise is determined by the weighted sum of the ratings for that cruise on all relevant attributes. Thus, a poor evaluation on one attribute is compensated for by a strong evaluation of another attribute. It also assumes that the cruise with the highest total score is the one MacDonald is predisposed to buy.

Noncompensatory Attitude Models   As suggested by Exhibit 5.8, the mental processes involved in forming an attitude are quite complex because consumers must evaluate each alternative brand on every attribute. In some purchase situations, particularly with low-involvement products, consumers may adopt a simpler approach and evaluate alternative brands on only one attribute at a time. Such an approach is **noncompensatory** because a poor evaluation of a brand on one attribute cannot be offset by a strong evaluation on another. For instance, one noncompensatory model, the lexicographic model, suggests that consumers evaluate brands on the most important attribute first. If one brand appears clearly superior on that dimension, the consumer selects it as the best possible choice. If no brand stands out on the most important attribute, the consumer evaluates the alternative brands on the second most important attribute, and so forth.[10]

Marketing Implications of Attitude Models   Although the different attitude models provide insights into the ways consumers evaluate competitive product offerings, their implications for marketers are similar. The models suggest that to design appealing product offerings and structure effective marketing programs, marketers must have information about (1) the attributes or decision criteria consumers use to evaluate a particular product category; (2) the relative importance of those attributes to different consumers; and (3) how consumers rate their brand relative to competitors' offerings on important attributes.

Multiattribute models are especially helpful in formulating marketing strategies. They do so by showing the consumer's ideal combination of product/service attributes, each of which is weighted as to its relative importance. Clustering those respondents with similar "ideals" enables the marketer to better understand not only what different sets of consumers want, but also how they perceive the various brands relative to the ideal brand. The firm can then decide which segments to target and how best to position its product-market entries.

Attitude Change   The multiattribute attitude models of consumer choice suggest various ways marketers might change consumer attitudes favorably for their brands versus competing brands. These are discussed briefly below.

1. *Changing attitudes toward the product class or type to increase the total market*—thereby increasing sales for a particular brand. For example, a frozen-orange-juice seller once attempted to make its product acceptable as a refreshing drink throughout the day. This type of attitude change involves primary demand and is difficult to accomplish.

2. *Changing the importance consumers attach to one or more attributes.* For instance, a number of food manufacturers have spent large sums warning about the dangers of high cholesterol. After increasing the importance consumers attach to lowering their cholesterol, they can then promote their brands as an appropriate part of a low-cholesterol diet.

3. *Adding a salient attribute to the existing set.* For instance, Colgate-Palmolive added triclosan, an antibiotic that fights gingivitis, to its Total brand of toothpaste and promoted it heavily.

4. *Improving consumers' ratings of the brand on one or more salient attributes via more extensive or effective advertising and promotion.* This is the most common attempt, particularly during a brand's introduction to the market or after product improvements have been made.

5. *Lowering the ratings of the salient product characteristics of competing brands.* This can be attempted via comparative advertising, which has increased in recent years. For example, one nutritional cereal regularly compares the amount of vitamins and minerals its brand provides in an average serving with those provided by specific other brands.

Demographics and Lifestyle

Demographics   Demographics influence (1) the nature of consumers' needs and wants, (2) their ability to buy products or services to satisfy those needs, (3) the perceived importance of various attributes or choice criteria used to evaluate alternative brands, and (4) consumers' attitudes toward and preferences for different products and brands. For example, older consumers spend more on medical care and travel and less on home furnishings and clothing than do younger groups; the presence of young children obviously affects the purchasing of a variety of goods and services; and better-educated people spend more on reading materials and foreign travel than do those with less education.

Lifestyles   Two people of similar age, income, education, and even occupations do not necessarily live their lives in the same way. They may have different opinions, interests, and activities. As a result, they are likely to exhibit different patterns of behavior—including buying different products and brands and using them in different ways and for different purposes. These broad patterns of activities, interests, and opinions—and the behaviors that result—are referred to as **lifestyles.** To obtain lifestyle data, consumers are asked to indicate the extent to which they agree/disagree with a series of statements having to do with such things as price consciousness, family activities, spectator sports, traditional values, adventuresomeness, and fashion.

Lifestyle typologies or psychographic profiles have been developed by several advertising agencies and market research firms. Global Scan, developed by Backer Spielvogel & Bates ad agency, measures a variety of consumer attitudes, activities, and values among

Exhibit 5.9

GLOBAL SCAN'S LIFESTYLE PSYCHOGRAPHIC SEGMENTS AND THE PROPORTION OF PEOPLE IN EACH SEGMENT
ACROSS THREE COUNTRIES

- Strivers: Young people (median age 31) who live hectic, time-pressured lives. They strive hard for success. They are materialistic, seek pleasure, and demand instant gratification.

- Achievers: They have achieved some of the success that strivers aim for. They are affluent, assertive, arid upward bound. They are very status conscious and buy for quality and are slightly older than strivers.

- Pressured: This group cuts across age groups and is composed mainly of women who face constant financial and family pressure. They do not enjoy life as much as they could and feel generally downtrodden.

- Adapters: These are older people who maintain time-honored values but keep an open mind. They live comfortably in a changing world.

- Traditional : They hold onto the oldest values of their countries and cultures. They resist change and prefer routines and familiar products.

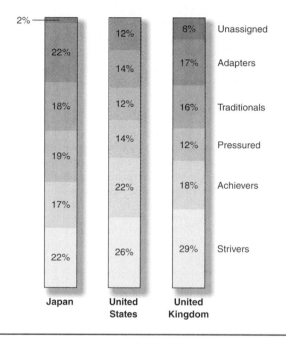

Source: Going Global: International Psychographics (Ithaca, NY: American Demographics Books, 1991). Used by permission.

a sample of 3,500 consumers in the United States and 1,000 respondents from other countries.[11] These measures are then matched against respondents' media viewing habits, product use, and purchase patterns. With this survey data, Global Scan has identified five lifestyle segments, summarized in Exhibit 5.9. The exhibit also shows the proportion of consumers that fall into each segment in the United States, the United Kingdom, and Japan. The size of the various segments varies across countries. For instance, Japan's more traditional and stable culture includes a larger proportion of "Traditionals" and "Adapters" than the United States.

An alternative lifestyle typology, called VALS 2, has been developed by the research firm SRI International. We will examine the lifestyle profiles identified by these various typologies, and their usefulness for defining and understanding market segments, in greater detail in Chapter 8.

Exhibit 5.10

SIMPLIFIED HIERARCHY OF SOCIAL FORCES AFFECTING CONSUMER BEHAVIOR

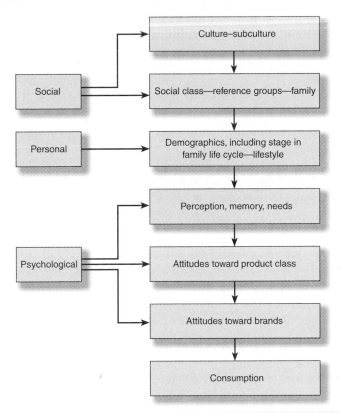

Why People Buy Different Things: Part 2—The Marketing Implications of Social Influences

Information and social pressures received from other people influence a consumer's needs, wants, evaluations, and product or brand preferences. Social influences are particularly apparent when consumers purchase high-involvement, socially visible goods or services. The social influences affecting consumers' purchase decisions include culture, subculture, social class, reference groups, and family. These five categories represent a hierarchy of social influences, ranging from broad, general effects on consumption behavior—such as those imposed by the culture we live in—to more specific influences that directly affect a consumer's choice of a particular product or brand. For a simplified view of this hierarchy of social influences, see Exhibit 5.10.

Culture

Culture is the set of beliefs, attitudes, and behavior patterns (customs and folkways) shared by members of a society and transmitted from one generation to the next through socialization. Cultural values and beliefs tend to be relatively stable over time, but they can change from one generation to the next in response to changing conditions in society. For example, the baby boomers born in the United States between 1946 and 1960 have somewhat different values and behavior patterns from those of their parents. They tend to live a more health-conscious lifestyle (e.g., to eat less red meat) and to concern themselves more with personal grooming than did their parents at the same age.

Cultural differences across countries create both problems and opportunities for international marketers. For example, Pillsbury wanted to take advantage of the cultural evolution concerning working women in Japan. About 50 percent of married women in Japan now work outside the home. Consequently, they represent an attractive market for convenience foods, such as Pillsbury's Green Giant frozen vegetables. The problem is that many feel guilty about using such products because they seem inconsistent with traditional cultural values. Therefore, in addition to touting the convenience of Green Giant vegetables, Pillsbury's advertising also stressed the nutrition and flavor benefits of freezing vegetables at the peak of ripeness. As a result, Green Giant's Japanese sales increased 50 percent in the first year of the ad campaign.[12]

Subculture   There are many groups of people in the United States who share common geographic, ethnic, racial, or religious backgrounds. They continue to hold some values, attitudes, and behavior patterns that are uniquely their own. Such groups are referred to as **subcultures.** For example, the average American family now has two wage earners who probably share decisions relating to vacations, car, financial instruments, and major furniture items. In contrast, Korean-Americans as a subculture in America are much more inclined to favor the male in almost all decisions, including food.[13]

Social Class

Every society has its status groupings largely based on similarities in income, education, and occupation. Because researchers have long documented the values of the various classes (typically thought of as five—upper, upper-middle, middle, working, and lower), it is possible to infer certain behavior concerning some products and services, including class members' reactions to advertising. For example, higher-status people are more critical of advertising, react better to more individualized messages, appreciate humor and sophistication, and look down a bit on ads that stress economy. Lower-status people respond to ads that are strongly visual and show practical solutions to their everyday problems.

Reference Groups

These include a variety of groups that affect consumer behavior through normative compliance, value-expressed influence, and informational influence. The first is most effective when there are strong normative pressures (for instance, from a college fraternity or exclusive club); when social acceptance is important (serving of certain foods to guests); and when the use of a product is conspicuous (women's fashion clothing). Value-expressive influence involves conforming to gain status within one's group.

Informational influence involves the use of certain influentials to help assess the merits of a given product/service. The opinions of such individuals often legitimize the purchase of a certain product or service. Over 40 percent of Americans seek the advice of family and friends when shopping for doctors, lawyers, and auto mechanics. Word of mouth is also important with respect to restaurants, entertainment, banking, and personal services. Young adults are more willing to seek referrals than are older people.[14]

KEY OBSERVATION

Over 40 percent of Americans seek the advice of family and friends when shopping for doctors, lawyers, and auto mechanics. Word of mouth is also important with respect to restaurants, entertainment, banking, and personal services.

The Family

The family is a reference group, but because of its importance, we discuss it separately. First, it serves as the primary socialization agent, helping members acquire the skills, knowledge, and attitudes to function as consumers in the marketplace. Consequently, it has a great and lasting influence on its younger members' attitudes toward various brands and stores. It is likely that many of the product-purchase decisions by a given generation are influenced by parents, even grandparents. Crest toothpaste, Tide laundry detergent, various brands of cars, and various insurance companies are examples of long-lived preferences that can be handed down. Children can also socialize their parents by introducing them to new products such as food, personal care items, and the personal computer. For example, nearly half of all young people age 12 to 19 sometimes cook meals for their family.[15]

Family members tend to specialize in the purchase of certain products either because of their interest or expertise or the role structure of the family. Wives, in most marriages, have the most say in the purchases of food and household products, children's clothes and toys, and over-the-counter drugs. In a similar vein, joint decisions apply on the purchase of cars, homes, vacations, major appliances, furniture, home electronics, and long-distance telephone carriers. As education increases, more joint decision making occurs.

The influence of various family members varies substantially across countries. Generally, the more traditional the society, the more men hold the power. In the more egalitarian countries, such as the Scandinavian nations, decisions are more likely to be made jointly. As women become better educated and more influential as wage earners in developing nations, more joint decision making will happen.

Family Life Cycle   When people leave home and start their own households, they progress through distinct phases of a **family life cycle.** The traditional cycle in the most industrialized nations includes young singles, young marrieds without children, young marrieds with children, middle-aged marrieds with children, middle-aged marrieds without dependent children, older marrieds, and older unmarrieds.

Each phase of the life cycle brings changes in family circumstances and purchasing behavior. For example, young singles' purchases tend to concentrate on nondurable items, including food away from home, clothing, and entertainment. Young marrieds without children are typically more affluent because both spouses usually work away from home. They are a major market for such durables as automobiles, furniture, and appliances. Young marrieds with children probably have the least disposable income, but they are the major market for single family dwellings, infant products and clothing, and child care services. Middle-aged couples without children usually have the most discretionary income. They are a major market for many luxury goods and services, such as expensive cars and international travel. Finally, the older marrieds and unmarrieds typically have less disposable income but are nevertheless an important market for medical products and services as well as hobby and craft items.

Of course, there are exceptions to and elaborations of the traditional family life cycle, especially the growing number of single-parent families and affluent seniors. These groups are of increasing importance to marketers.[16]

TAKE-AWAYS

- Not all purchase decisions are equally important or psychologically involving for the consumer. People

engage in a more extensive decision-making process, involving a more detailed search for information and comparison of alternatives, when buying high-involvement goods and services than when purchasing more mundane, low-involvement items.

- Because of the differences in the decision-making process, a given marketing strategy will not be equally effective for both high- and low-involvement products. The consumer marketer's first task, then, is to determine whether the majority of potential customers in the target segment are likely to be highly involved with the purchase decision or not.

- Because consumers are generally unwilling to spend much time or effort evaluating alternative brands in a low-involvement product category before making a purchase, marketers need to focus their promotional messages on only a few frequently repeated points and to distribute such products extensively to make them convenient for customers to buy.

- Regardless of the consumer's level of involvement with a product category, consumers often prefer different brands because of differences in their psychological or personal characteristics, such as their perceptions,

memories, attitudes, and lifestyles. Understanding how such characteristics influence consumers' decisions in a product category provides an important foundation for marketing decisions concerning the definition of market segments, the selection of target markets, and the design of marketing programs to appeal to those markets.

- Regardless of the consumer's level of involvement with a product category, consumers often prefer different brands because of differences in their social relationships, such as their culture, social class, reference groups, and family circumstances. Understanding how such social influences impact consumers' decisions in a product category provides an important foundation for marketing decisions concerning the definition of market segments, the selection of target markets, and the design of marketing programs to appeal to those markets.

Self-diagnostic questions to test your ability to apply the concepts and analytical tools in this chapter to marketing decision making may be found at this book's website at www.mhhe.com/mullins05.

ENDNOTES

1. Shelly Branch, "Sea Monsters," *Fortune,* July 6, 1998, pp. 157–62; Jeff Wise, "How Cruise Ships Shortchange the Caribbean," *Fortune,* March 29, 1999, pp. 44–46; Nanette Byrnes, "For Carnival, Few Icebergs on the Horizon," *Business Week Online,* June 14, 1999, www.businessweek.com, keyword: Cruise lines; Aixa M. Pascual, "Carnival Isn't Shipshape These Days," *Business Week Online,* April 24, 2000, www.businessweek.com, keyword: Cruise lines; "Cruise Industry," *Campaign (UK),* August 23, 2002, p. 5; Bill Glenton, "Bargains Across the Ocean," *Financial Times,* November 24, 2002, p. 2; and www.carnivalcorp.com.

2. Henry Assael, *Consumer Behavior and Marketing Action* (Cincinnati: South Western College Publishing, 1995), chap. 1.

3. For a detailed discussion of how consumers perceive, evaluate, and buy services, see Valarie A. Zeithaml and Mary Jo Bitner, *Services Marketing* (New York: McGraw-Hill, 1996), chaps. 3–5.

4. Keith B. Murray, "A Test of Services Marketing Theory: Consumer Information Acquisition Activities," *Journal of Marketing* 55 (January 1991), pp. 10–26.

5. Ibid., p. 13.

6. "All Yours," *The Economist,* April 1, 2000, pp. 57–58; and Faith Keenan, Stanley Holmes, Jay Greene, and Roger O. Crockett, "A Mass Market of One," *Fortune,* December 2, 2002, pp. 68–72.

7. Zeithaml and Bitner, *Services Marketing,* chap. 13.

8. Ibid., chap. 7.

9. Yumiko Ono, 'Non-smearing' Lipstick Makes a Vivid Imprint for Revlon," *The Wall Street Journal,* November 16, 1995, p. B1.

10. There are several other noncompensatory models that suggest consumers follow somewhat different mental processes in arriving at their preferred brand. For a more detailed discussion of attitude models, see J. Paul Peter and Jerry Olson, *Consumer Behavior* (Burr Ridge, IL: Richard D. Irwin, 1996), chap. 6.

11. American Demographics, *Going Global: International Psychographics* (Ithaca, NY: American Demographics, 1991).

12. Jack Russell, "Working Women Give Japan Culture Shock," *Advertising Age,* January 1995, pp. 1, 24.

13. John Steere, "How Asian-Americans Make Purchasing Decisions," *Marketing News,* March 24, 1996, p. 9.

14. Chip Walker, "Word of Mouth," *American Demographics,* July 1995, p. 38.

15. "The Microwave Generation," *American Demographics,* September 1995, p. 24.

16. "Over 60 and Overlooked," *The Economist,* August 10, 2002, pp. 51–52.

CHAPTER SIX

Understanding Organizational Markets and Buying Behavior

Exel: Building Long-Term Relationships with Organizational Buyers[1]

THE EXEL COMPANY is a global leader in supply chain management services. Its service offerings range from truck leasing and freight forwarding, to warehousing and distribution services, to integrated information management and e-commerce support. Headquartered in the United Kingdom, the firm employs more than 60,000 people in 1,300 locations in over 120 countries. Sales revenues exceeded £4.5 billion ($6.5 billion) in 2001, with about one-third coming from the United Kingdom and Ireland, one-third from the Americas, and one-quarter from continental Europe.

Exel's competitive strategy is to differentiate itself by offering customers the broadest range of integrated and efficient logistics services. To that end it has invested heavily to build capabilities in air, sea, and land transportation, warehousing and materials handling, and information technology. The firm's salespeople attempt to convince large potential customers in target industry segments—such as retailing, the auto industry, and technical equipment manufacturing—that some of their necessary logistics activities could be performed more effectively or efficiently if they were outsourced to Exel. Account representatives work closely with customers to develop custom-tailored programs of integrated services, monitor the performance of those programs, and suggest areas for improvement and expansion.

Delivering Printing Systems in the Netherlands

Key aspects of Exel's competitive and marketing strategies, and of the evolution of its relationships with customers over time, are illustrated by the firm's long-running association with the Dutch printing systems manufacturer Océ. The relationship began in the mid-1970s when Exel transported a consignment of printing systems from the company's manufacturing plant in Venlo in the Netherlands to a domestic customer. In the intervening years, the relationship has expanded dramatically. Today, the services Exel performs for Océ include freight management, inventory control, and technical and customer support.

The nerve center that integrates those services is a state-of-the-art 25,000-square-meter distribution center in Veghel in the Netherlands. Exel transports new printing systems from the manufacturing plant to Veghel, where parts or systems are preconfigured, tested, and shipped on to Océ's customers as they are sold. Erik van Engelen, Exel's Business Unit Manager, Technical Distribution, Benelux, says: "Twenty internal technical services personnel at the distribution center undertake the necessary predelivery inspection and testing work on behalf of Océ and other customers.

This includes . . . ensuring that each machine displays the correct language for its intended market, and is supplied with the right manuals. Prior to installation, the hardware is assembled, and functionality is programmed and tested in accordance with the manufacturers' instructions."

When a new printing system is delivered to one of Océ's customers, an Exel technical driver gives on-site instruction on how to use the machine and perform simple maintenance tasks. And the firm's mobile technicians are available to perform equipment testing and repair on customer premises.

Finally, Exel developed a "reverse logistics" service for Océ after a customer asked the firm to take back its old printing system when a new one was delivered. Exel technicians examine all returned systems and, with approval from Océ, undertake an appropriate course of action, from cleaning, to refurbishing, to recycling of the machine's component materials.

One reason the relationship between the two companies has continued to grow over the years is that it is formally reviewed and updated frequently. According to Exel's account representative, the two parties hold quarterly business reviews where Océ's and Exel's management and logistics personnel review performance for the previous three months, identify areas for improvement or expansion, and negotiate adjustments to Exel's fee schedule and service contract. So far, Océ has been a satisfied customer—at least in part because Exel has helped keep their own customers satisfied. As Jos Klerks, Logistics Manager for Océ points out, "Alliances with strategic partners such as Exel play an important role in the total solution we offer our customers."

Marketing Challenges Addressed in Chapter 6

The fact that Exel markets its logistics services to organizational customers rather than individual consumers makes it like the great majority of business firms. Worldwide, organizational markets account for more than twice the dollar value of purchases as consumer markets. About half of all manufactured goods in most countries are sold to organizational buyers. In addition, organizations such as Cargill, Nestlé, and BP buy nearly all minerals, farm and forest products, and other raw materials for further processing. Finally, organizations buy many services from accounting firms, banks, financial advisers, advertising agencies, law firms, consultants, railroads, airlines, security firms, and other suppliers.

As we'll see later, organizational customers are different in some ways from consumers, and those differences have important implications for designing effective marketing programs. But at the most basic level, marketers need to answer the same set of questions about organizational markets as about consumer markets in order to develop a solid foundation for their marketing plans. Who are the target customers and what are their needs and wants? How do those customers decide what to buy and what suppliers to buy from? Do their decision processes vary depending on their past experiences, the nature of the product being purchased, and other situational factors? If so, what are the marketing implications of those variations? This chapter provides a framework to help you address these questions.

We begin our examination of "who is the customer?" by comparing organizational markets to consumer markets and pointing out differences between the two types of customers, differences that often dictate varying marketing approaches. One of those differences is

KEY OBSERVATION

Marketers need to answer the same set of questions about organizational markets as about consumer markets in order to develop a solid foundation for their marketing plans.

simply the number of participants in the purchase decision. While consumers are influenced by family and friends, they often decide what to buy—and make the actual purchase—on their own. That is typically not the case in organizational purchasing, especially when the product or service involved is relatively complex and expensive. For instance, managers from several levels within Océ are involved in reviewing and renegotiating the service agreement with Exel each quarter. Therefore, we will discuss the different kinds of participants in organizational purchase decisions, the roles they play, and the different kinds of marketing messages and activities appropriate for each group.

Next, we examine the process that organizational customers go through in deciding what to buy and from whom. As with individual consumers, this process varies depending on the past experience the organization has in buying the particular product or service and with a given supplier. As illustrated by the association between Excel and Océ, a primary goal should be to develop long-term relationships—and ideally cooperative alliances—with customers to ensure repeat purchases and capture full lifetime value. We discuss these issues and their implications for marketing programs, as well as the impact the Internet and other information technologies are having on firms' strategies for strengthening customer relationships.

Finally, organizational purchasing processes also vary depending on the kinds of goods or services being purchased. Océ's purchase of integrated logistics services costing millions of euros was more complex, required more information, and focused on different criteria than the company's more routine purchase of office supplies or copper wire. Therefore, we conclude this chapter with an examination of how organizational purchasing processes differ across various categories of goods and services and the implications of those differences for designing effective marketing programs.

Who Is the Customer?

A Comparison of Organizational versus Consumer Markets

Organizations—including manufacturing firms, service producers, wholesalers, retailers, nonprofit organizations such as churches and museums, and governments—all buy things. They buy many of the same goods and services as households, such as computers, office supplies, cars, airline tickets, and telephone service. Thus, what distinguishes organizational markets from consumer markets is often not the kinds of products being purchased. Instead, the crucial differences from a marketing viewpoint are (1) the motivations of the buyer: what the organization will do with the product and the benefits it seeks to obtain, (2) the demographics of the market, and (3) the nature of the purchasing process and the relationship between buyer and seller. Some of these differences are summarized in Exhibit 6.1 and discussed below.

Purchase Motives—Derived Demand   Individual consumers and households buy goods and services for their own personal use and consumption. Organizational buyers purchase things for one of three reasons: (1) to facilitate the production of another product or service, as when Ford buys sheet steel, engine components, or computerized welding machines; (2) for use by the organization's employees in carrying out its operations (office supplies, computer software, advertising agency services); or (3) for resale to other customers, as when a retailer such as Target buys a truckload of towels to be distributed to its many stores and sold to individual consumers.

Exhibit 6.1

DIFFERENCES BETWEEN ORGANIZATIONAL AND CONSUMER MARKETS

Demand characteristics

The demand for industrial goods and services is

1. Derived from the demand for consumer goods and services.
2. Relatively inelastic—price changes in the short run are not likely to affect demand drastically.
3. More erratic because small increases or decreases in consumer demand can, over time, strongly affect the demand for manufacturing plants and equipment.
4. More cyclical.

Market demographics

Organizational buyers, when compared with buyers of consumer goods, are

1. Fewer in number.
2. Larger.
3. Geographically concentrated.

Buyer behavior and buyer-seller relationships

Organizational markets are characterized by the following when compared with the markets for consumer goods:

1. Use of professional buying specialists following prescribed procedures.
2. Closer buyer–seller relationships.
3. Presence of multiple buying influences.
4. More apt to buy on specifications.

Given these reasons for purchasing, organizational demand for goods and services is in many cases **derived** from underlying consumer demand. Océ's demand for Exel's logistics services, for instance, depends on the number of printing systems purchased by its customers. Fluctuating economic conditions in an industry can change a firm's production schedule, plant and equipment utilization, and materials and parts inventories. These changes affect the firm's demand for materials, components, equipment, logistics services, and more. In other words, derived demand tends to be relatively erratic and cyclical, making accurate sales forecasting and planning more difficult.

Market Demographics   Another major difference between consumer and organizational markets is the number, size, and geographic dispersion of customers. Organizational markets tend to have fewer potential customers, but on average they buy much larger volumes than consumers do. In many industries, the largest organizations also tend to cluster in one or a few geographic areas, as with the concentration of major banks and financial service firms in New York, London, Frankfurt, Zurich, and Tokyo.

Purchasing Processes and Relationships   Because of the complexity of many of the goods and services and of the large volumes typically involved, organizational purchase decisions often involve evaluation processes focused on detailed, formally specified criteria. These processes are typically carried out by specialized purchasing managers with a great deal of input and influence from other members of the organization.

What Do the Unique Characteristics of Organizational Markets Imply for Marketing Programs?

The fact that the demand for many organizational goods and services is derived from underlying consumer demand not only makes it harder to forecast sales, but it also limits the marketer's ability to influence demand among organizational buyers. Ford's demand for steel is unlikely to be increased in the short term by price cuts, persuasive advertising messages, or quantity discounts and other kinds of promotions. Until consumer demand for the firm's cars and trucks expands, increasing steel purchases would simply produce bigger materials inventories, tie up more working capital, and lower profitability.

Therefore, the forward-looking company selling to organizational markets needs to keep one eye on possible changes in organizations' buying behavior for its product and another eye on trends in the underlying consumer markets. Some firms even engage in marketing actions aimed at stimulating demand in those consumer markets in hopes of increasing demand from their organizational customers. For instance, Monsanto aggressively promoted its warranty for Wear-Dated carpets made from its high-quality synthetic fibers in hopes of stimulating consumers' selective demand for such carpets. The bottom line is that even organizational marketers need a solid understanding of consumer behavior.

The complexity of many of the goods and services organizations buy, the extensive decision process involved, and the demographics of organizational markets also have marketing implications. These factors facilitate the use of **direct selling,** with its emphasis on personal communications through company salespeople and vertically integrated distribution channels. Organizational marketers also tend to be heavy users of "high-involvement" media, such as trade journals, product brochures, and websites.

Another upshot of the derived nature of demand in organizational markets, as well as of the complex products and large dollar values involved, is that interdependence between buyers and sellers tends to be greater. The economic success of the marketer depends greatly on the economic success of the organizational customer. The marketer is part of the customer's **supply chain** and is therefore relied on for services such as coordinated delivery schedules, maintenance, spare parts availability, and efficient order handling. This high level of mutual interdependence encourages the development and maintenance of long-term relationships and alliances between the parties.[2] It also demands that supplier firms be customer-oriented and have all their functional activities—including production, R&D, finance, logistics, and customer service—focused on providing superior customer value. As one authority argues, "By its very nature, [organizational] marketing requires that all parts of the business be customer-oriented and that all marketing decisions be based on a complete and accurate understanding of customer needs."[3]

KEY OBSERVATION

High level of mutual interdependence encourages the development and maintenance of long-term relationships and alliances between the parties.

The Organizational Customer Is Usually a Group of Individuals

Organizations are social constructions. Organizations do not buy things. Rather, individual members, usually more than one, make purchase decisions on the organization's behalf. Similarly, organizations do not form relationships with other organizations. Relationships are built and maintained among their individual members. Consequently, to understand how organizational purchasing decisions are made, the marketer must first understand the roles performed by different individuals within the organization and their personal interests and concerns.

Participants in the Organizational Purchasing Process

Organizational purchasing often involves people from various departments. These participants in the buying process can be grouped as users, influencers, gatekeepers, buyers, and deciders.[4]

> *Users:* The people in the organization who must use or work with the product or service often have some influence on the purchase decision. For example, drill-press operators might request that the purchasing agent buy a particular brand of drills because they stay sharp longer and reduce downtime in the plant.
>
> *Influencers:* Influencers provide information for evaluating alternative products and suppliers. They are usually technical experts from various departments within the organization. Influencers help determine which specifications and criteria to use in making the purchase decision.
>
> *Gatekeepers:* Gatekeepers control the flow of information to other people in the purchasing process. They primarily include the organization's purchasing agents and the suppliers' salespeople. Gatekeepers influence a purchase by controlling the information that reaches other decision makers. An organization does not decide to buy a new product, for example, unless information about its existence and advantages over alternatives is brought to the decision makers' attention.
>
> *Buyers:* The buyer is usually referred to as a **purchasing agent** or **purchasing manager.** In most organizations, buyers have the authority to contact suppliers and negotiate the purchase transaction. In some cases they exercise wide discretion in carrying out their jobs. In other cases, they are tightly constrained by specifications and contract requirements determined by technical experts and top administrators. And more recently, as we shall see, technology has enabled some firms to automate parts of the buyer's role in the form of computerized reorder and logistics management systems and Web auctions.
>
> *Deciders:* The decider is the person with the authority to make a final purchase decision. Sometimes buyers have this authority, but often lower-level purchasing managers carry out the wishes of more powerful decision makers.

The Organizational Buying Center

For routine purchases with a small dollar value, a single buyer or purchasing manager may make the purchase decision. For most high-value organizational purchases, several people from different departments participate in the decision process. The individuals in this group, called a **buying center,** share knowledge and information relevant to the purchase of a particular product or service.

A buyer or purchasing manager is almost always a member of the buying center. The inclusion of people from other functional areas, however, depends on what is being purchased. When the purchase is a major new installation, the high dollar value of the purchase usually dictates that the firm's chief executive and its top financial officer actively participate in the final decision. For purchases of key fabricating parts for the manufacture of the final product, R&D, engineering, production, and quality-control people are likely to be added. For accessory equipment, such as new office equipment, an experienced user of the equipment (say, a secretary or office manager) might participate in the decision.

Different members of the buying center may participate—and exert different amounts of influence—at different stages in the decision process. For example, people from engineering and R&D often exert the greatest influence on the development of specifications and criteria that a new component must meet, while the purchasing manager often has more influence when it comes time to choose among alternative suppliers. The makeup of the buying center also varies with the amount of past experience the firm has in buying a particular product or service. The buying center tends to be smaller—and the relative influence of the purchasing manager greater—when reordering items the firm has purchased in the past than when buying a new product.[5]

Exhibit 6.2

THE RELATIVE INFLUENCE OF VARIOUS FUNCTIONAL DEPARTMENTS AT DIFFERENT STAGES IN TWO TYPES OF ORGANIZATIONAL
PURCHASING DECISIONS

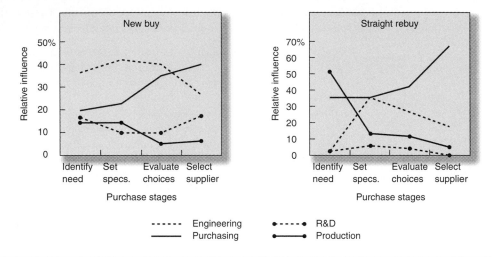

Source: Reprinted from *Industrial Marketing Management,* E. Nauman, D. J. Lincoln, and R. D. McWilliams, "The Purchase of Components: Functional Areas of Influence," pp. 113–22. © 1984, with permission of Elsevier. See also R. D. McWilliams, E. Naumann, and S. Scott," Determining Buying Center Size," *Industrial Marketing Management* 21 (February 1992), pp. 43–50.

These variations in the relative influence of different members of the buying center across types of purchase decisions and stages in the buying process as illustrated in Exhibit 6.2. The exhibit summarizes the results of a survey of 231 manufacturing firms where managers were asked to indicate the relative influence of various functional departments at different stages in the procurement of component parts. The influence of each department not only varied across stages in the buying process but also depended on whether the purchase was a new buy or a reorder.

Marketing Implications   Because employees of a customer's firm may be active at different stages of the purchase process and have different interests and concerns, an important part of planning a marketing program aimed at organizational customers involves determining which individuals to target, how and when each should be contacted, and what kinds of information and appeals each is likely to find most useful and persuasive. Fortunately, in many cases the roles played by various members of the buying center are sufficiently consistent across similar types of firms in an industry that a marketing manager can tailor different promotional messages and sales policies for specific members. For example, in smaller firms in the construction industry (those with sales volumes under $25 million) presidents and vice presidents exert significantly more influence at all stages in the decision process than do purchasing agents or construction engineers, while the situation is reversed in large firms, reflecting increasing job specialization and decentralization of purchasing in bigger companies.[6] A manager marketing to this industry might develop account management policies directing the salesforce to seek appointments with top executives when calling on smaller firms, but to initiate contacts through the purchasing department in larger organizations. Another example involving the development of different

---

Exhibit 6.3   **Communicating Value to Different Members of a Buying Center with Tailored Advertisements**

Different members of a firm's buying center value different things when choosing suppliers and products. At Honeywell's MICRO SWITCH Division, the marketing staff responsible for fiber-optic products develops customized advertisements for the different members of customers' buying centers—design engineers, production engineers, engineering managers, and purchasing agents. Design and production engineers see value in leading-edge technologies and products that are easy to design, install, and use. Engineering management is concerned with supplier capabilities, including a proven track record and good service. Purchasing agents see value in low cost and reliable delivery.

Recognizing that different business and technical functions value different things, Bob Procsal, marketing manager for fiber-optic products, carefully chooses different messages and media to communicate to each buying center member. For instance, ads stressing the products' advanced technical features and high performance levels run in technical magazines aimed at design and production engineers, while messages emphasizing Honeywell's years of experience and position as a worldwide leader in advanced switching technology are targeted at engineering managers.

Does the added effort and expense of customized advertisements pay? Bob Procsal thinks it does. He reports that inquiries about the company's line of fiber-optic products increased 50 percent after this practice was implemented.

Source: Adapted from Eric N. Berkowitz, Roger A. Kerin, Steven W. Hartley, and William Rudelius, *Marketing,* 5th ed. (Burr Ridge, IL: Richard D. Irwin, 1997), pp. 190–91. Reprinted with permission from The McGraw-Hill Companies.

---

advertising appeals and the use of different media to reach buying center members is summarized in Exhibit 6.3.

Similarly, customers' buying centers are likely to involve a wider variety of participants when they are considering the purchase of a technically complex, expensive product, such as a computer network, than when the purchase involves a simpler product or service. Consequently, firms such as IBM selling technically complex capital equipment often deploy multifunctional sales teams or utilize "multilevel" selling, with different salespeople calling on different members of the buying center to give each the kinds of information that person will find most relevant.[7]

How Organizational Members Make Purchase Decisions

Organizational purchase decisions often involve extensive information search and evaluation processes similar to those consumers use when buying high-involvement items. As with individual consumers, however, the way specific organizational purchase decisions are made can vary with the firm's level of past experience and other aspects of the buying situation.

Types of Buying Situations

Organizations encounter three kinds of buying tasks or situations: the straight rebuy, the modified rebuy, and new-task buying.[8]

A **straight rebuy** involves purchasing a common product or service the organization has bought many times before. Such purchases are often handled routinely by the purchasing department with little participation by other departments. Such purchases are almost automatic, with the firm continuing to purchase proven products from reliable, established vendors. In straight rebuy situations, all phases of the buying process tend to be short and routine. Even so, when large quantities are involved, the need for quality assurance, parity pricing, and on-time delivery to minimize inventory requires a competent salesforce to help the supplier maintain a continually satisfying relationship with the buyer over time. The rapid spread of computerized reordering systems, logistical alliances, and the like have made the development and maintenance of long-term relationships between suppliers and their customers increasingly important in the purchase of familiar goods and services. We shall examine the nature of such relationships, and how recent technological developments have facilitated their development, in a later section of this chapter.

A **modified rebuy** occurs when the organization's needs remain unchanged, but buying center members are not satisfied with the product or the supplier they have been using. They may desire a higher-quality product, a better price, or better service. Here buyers need information about alternative products and suppliers to compare with their current product and vendor. And as we'll see, Web-based technology—such as business-to-business auctions organized by firms like FreeMarkets, Inc. (www.FreeMarkets.com.) or by industry sites like e-Steel.com (www.e-Steel.com) or PlasticsNet.com (www.PlasticsNet.com)—is making it easier for organizational buyers to make such comparisons, at least on the price dimension. Therefore, modified rebuys present good opportunities for new suppliers to win the organization's business if they can deliver better value than the firm's current vendor.

New-task buying occurs when an organization faces a new and unique need or problem—one in which buying center members have little or no experience and, thus, must expend a great deal of effort to define purchasing specifications and to collect information about alternative products and vendors. Each stage of the decision process is likely to be extensive, involving many technical experts and administrators. The supplier's reputation for meeting delivery deadlines, providing adequate service, and meeting specifications is often a critical factor in selling a product or service to an organization for the first time. Because the buying center members have limited knowledge of the product or service involved, they may choose a well-known and respected supplier to reduce the risk of making a poor decision.

The Purchase Decision-Making Process

As Exhibit 6.4 suggests, the stages in the organizational purchase decision-making process—at least for modified rebuy and new-task purchases—correspond quite closely with consumers' high-involvement purchases. However, the exhibit also suggests that some activities at each stage and their execution differ. More people are involved in organizational purchase decisions; the capability of potential suppliers is more critical; and the post-purchase evaluation process is more formalized. We examine other unique features of each stage of the organizational purchase decision process next.[9]

Recognition of a Problem or Need   The organizational purchasing process starts when someone in the firm recognizes a need that can be satisfied by buying some good or service. As we have seen, though, while consumers may buy things impulsively to satisfy psychological or social needs, most of an organization's needs are derived from the demand for the goods or services they produce or resell to their own customers. In other words, most organizational purchases are motivated by the needs of the firm's production processes and its day-to-day operations.

In some cases, need recognition may be almost automatic, as when a computerized inventory system reports that an item has fallen below the reorder level or when a piece of equipment wears out. In other cases, a need arises when someone identifies a better way of

Exhibit 6.4

THE ORGANIZATIONAL DECISION-MAKING PROCESS FOR NEW-TASK PURCHASES

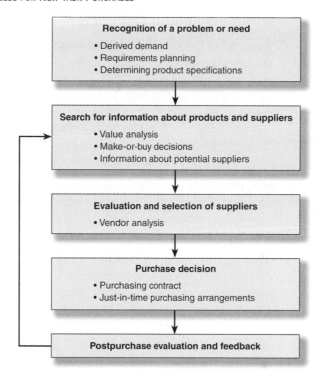

Recognition of a problem or need
- Derived demand
- Requirements planning
- Determining product specifications

Search for information about products and suppliers
- Value analysis
- Make-or-buy decisions
- Information about potential suppliers

Evaluation and selection of suppliers
- Vendor analysis

Purchase decision
- Purchasing contract
- Just-in-time purchasing arrangements

Postpurchase evaluation and feedback

carrying out day-to-day operations. Océ has expanded the range of logistics services it buys from Exel over the years, for instance, as it has discovered activities that Exel can perform more effectively or efficiently.

Finally, changes in the organization's operations can create new needs; for instance, top management may decide to produce a new product line that requires new components or raw materials. Or there may be changes in the firm's objectives, resources, market conditions, government regulations, or competition. Needs, then, may be recognized by many people within the organization, including users, technical personnel, top management, and purchasing agents.

Requirements Planning Instead of simply monitoring inventories and reordering when they run low, some firms attempt to forecast future requirements so as to plan their purchases in advance. Requirements planning governs the purchase of raw materials and fabricating components as well as supplies and major installations. One result of such planning is often the signing of long-term purchase contracts, particularly for products projected to be in short supply or to increase in price. Requirements planning can also lead to lower costs and better relations between a purchaser and its suppliers.

Determining Product Specifications The need for particular goods and services is usually derived from a firm's production or operation requirements and, therefore, must meet specific technical requirements. Technical experts from the firm's R&D, engineering, and production departments are often involved early in the purchase decision. When the firm needs a unique component or piece of equipment, it might even seek help from potential suppliers in setting the appropriate specifications. For example, automobile manufacturers consult their parts suppliers before finalizing specs for a new model. Increasingly, suppliers are active participants in the design and development of new components or systems.

Search for Information about Products and Suppliers   Once specifications for the desired product/service are developed, purchasing (and possibly other departments) performs a **value analysis.** This systematic appraisal of an item's design, quality, and performance requirements helps to minimize procurement costs. It includes an analysis of the extent to which the product might be redesigned, standardized, or processed using less-expensive production methods. A cost analysis that attempts to determine what the product costs a supplier to produce is also part of a value analysis. Such information helps the purchasing agent better evaluate alternative bids or negotiate favorable prices with suppliers.

Make-or-Buy Decisions   Sometimes a firm has the option of producing some components and services internally (advertising, marketing research) or buying them from outside suppliers. Economic considerations typically dominate such decisions, although in the long run other factors may be important (for instance, overdependence on a single supplier).

Information about Potential Suppliers   Because many firms evaluate a supplier's performance on a regular basis, there is often considerable information about that supplier's quality of performance on file. Where new suppliers are involved, the purchasing department typically engages in an in-depth investigation before qualifying that firm as a potential supplier. An investigation would include such information as the firm's finances, reputation for reliability, and the ability to meet quality standards, information that can be obtained from personal sources (such as salespersons, trade shows, other firms, and consultants) and nonpersonal sources including catalogs, advertising, and trade literature.

Evaluation and Selection of Suppliers   Like individual consumers, organizational buyers evaluate alternative suppliers and their offerings by using a set of **choice criteria** reflecting the desired benefits. The criteria used and the relative importance of each attribute vary according to the goods and services being purchased and the buyer's needs. Always important are the supplier's ability to meet quality standards and delivery schedules. Price is critical for standard items such as steel desks and chairs, but for more technically complex items, such as computers, a broader range of criteria enters the evaluation process.

Vendor Analysis   Some purchasing departments construct quantitative ratings of potential suppliers to aid in the selection process. These ratings look very much like the multi-attribute, compensatory attitude model we discussed for individual consumers. The procedure involves selecting a set of salient attributes and assigning to each a weight reflecting its relative importance. Suppliers are then rated by summing their weighted scores across all attributes.

Such ratings serve several useful purposes, including facilitating the comparison of alternative suppliers, providing a basis for discussions with suppliers about their performance, and controlling the number of qualified suppliers. The end result of a vendor analysis is typically the development of a list of approved suppliers. General Electric, for example, works only with vendors that are top-rated in an analysis of quality, technology, price, and other factors. The company finds regular vendor analysis a more efficient way to ensure the quality of the components it buys than waiting to inspect parts when they are received.[10]

This step in the buying process, along with the previous steps, seems to imply that the individuals making up the buying center respond only to economic arguments. But industrial buyers are social entities *in addition* to being interested in the economics of the situation. For example, producers of marine diesel engines for large boats understand the need to make such engines aesthetically appealing since the owners of such craft take pride in opening an engine hatch to reveal a sleek, chromed engine. In general, the more similar the suppliers and their offerings, the more likely it is that social factors will affect the buying decision.

What If the Customer Makes Unethical Demands of Its Suppliers? As we saw in Chapter 2, a supplier's ethics can have a direct effect on its success in the marketplace because organizational buyers are more likely to purchase from firms they consider ethical.[11] Ethical behavior plays a crucial role in establishing the trust and cooperation necessary for the development and maintenance of long-term relationships with customers. But what if members of the buying organization engage in or demand unethical practices?

One questionable practice that some buyers engage in is **reciprocity,** which occurs when an organization favors a supplier that is also a customer or potential customer for the organization's own products or services. Although this situation is relatively common, it can cause serious problems, including undermining the morale of purchasing and sales personnel who are constrained in the way they do their jobs. Also, reciprocal buying is illegal when it substantially injures free competition among alternative suppliers.

Another unethical practice that causes headaches for many suppliers—particularly in global markets where there are great differences in cultural values and legal restrictions—is the demand for bribes as a precondition for winning a purchase. Ethical Perspective 6.1 examines this issue.

Even in the United States, it is not always easy to know when a bribe is a bribe. For example, one common practice in high-tech industries has been for small start-ups planning an initial public offering (IPO) of common stock to give shares to executives in firms that are potential customers. While giving away such "friends and family" shares prior to an IPO is not illegal, one likely motive for the practice is the hope that the favored executives will help steer big purchase contracts to the companies in which they hold stock, thereby increasing the value of their holdings.[12]

ETHICAL PERSPECTIVE 6.1
Bribery in Organizational Purchasing

Bribery can take many forms ranging from small-value Christmas gifts to large sums of money. In the United States, gifts of high value are typically condemned. Most organizations do not want the decisions of their purchasing personnel unduly influenced by large gifts from a prospective supplier. Bribery is not officially condoned anywhere in the world. Most countries' laws concerning bribery are not as restrictive as those in the United States, however, nor are they always so rigorously enforced.

U.S. laws, on the other hand, have real teeth, including hefty fines and prison sentences. Consequently, most U.S. firms avoid paying major bribes to foreign customers and have sought other ways to influence people and win contracts. Some take foreign officials on junkets to Disney World. Others use local

agents or distributors who—known to them or not—do the dirty work. And most multinationals do make small "facilitation" payments to hasten building inspections, telephone installations, customs clearances, and the like.

Despite such actions, the ethics of U.S. suppliers and the strict U.S. antibribery laws appear to leave American firms at a competitive disadvantage in many countries around the world. One recent government report indicates that bribes were allegedly offered by foreign competitors on 294 international contracts worth $145 billion between 1994 and 1999, and that is probably just the tip of the iceberg.

Source: Dana Milbank and Marcus Brauchli, "How U.S. Concerns Compete in Countries Where Bribes Flourish," *The Wall Street Journal,* September 25, 1995, p. A1; and Robert Greenberger, "Foreigners Use Bribes to Beat U.S. Rivals, New Report Concludes," *The Wall Street Journal,* October 12, 1995, p. B1; and *Addressing the Challenges of International Bribery and Fair Competition* (Washington DC.: U.S. Department of Commerce, July 1999).

The Purchase   The purchase agreement between a supplier and an organizational customer can take several forms, ranging from individual spot contracts on the open market, to long-term purchasing contracts covering a year or more, to ongoing informal relationships based on cooperation and trust rather than legal agreements. In the past, long-term purchasing contracts were popular because they enabled an organization to concentrate its purchases with one or a few suppliers, reduce transaction costs, and gain scale economies through quantity discounts and the like. For example, an **annual requirements contract** obligated a supplier to fill all of a buyer's needs for a specific product at a consistent, usually discounted, price over a year.

One problem with long-term legal contracts, though, is that they must precisely specify all the details of a purchase agreement, including technical specifications, prices, credit terms, and so on. But in today's rapidly changing economic and technical environments, it can be difficult for the parties to foresee what their needs and market conditions will be like months or years into the future. It can be difficult to adjust the terms of a formal contract in response to unforeseen technical improvements, cost changes, or market conditions. This inflexibility of long-term contracts is a major reason their popularity has declined in favor of increased reliance on spot market contracts, or auctions, on one hand and less formal long-term relationships between customers and suppliers on the other.[13] The increased reliance on both of these approaches has been facilitated by a common factor: the growth of telecommunications technology and the Internet.

One Impact of Technology: The Growth of Auctions or E-exchanges   Over the past few years, a number of Internet firms have emerged to help organizations cut their purchasing costs. The earliest entrants, such as Commerce One and Ariba, focused on improving the efficiency of organizations' search for information and evaluation of alternative products and suppliers. They developed electronic catalogs that reduced clients' transaction costs by automating the collection of product information, orders, and payments.

More recently, sellers' auction websites have emerged in a number of industries. These provide lively global spot markets for standard processed materials such as steel, chemicals, and plastics. On MetalSite (www.metalsite.com), for instance, a steelmaker such as LTV can offer a block of sheet or rolled steel whenever its plants have excess capacity. Buyers then enter bids for the steel over two or three days, and the highest bid wins.

The websites that may have the greatest future impact on organizational purchasing behavior, however, are those that facilitate buyers' auctions. Such auctions invite qualified competing suppliers to submit bids to win a contract where the buyer has specified all of the purchase criteria in great detail, except the price. By enabling all suppliers to see what the competition is bidding in real time, these auctions have the potential to greatly increase price competition and lower buyers' acquisition costs in some cases by as much as 30 or 40 percent.[14]

However, because buyers' auctions are feasible only when the buyer is able to specify *all* its requirements except price—including all technical and performance attributes of the good or service, delivery schedules, inventory arrangements, payment schedules, and the like—they work best for purchases where the buyer has experience to draw upon, and where those requirements are unlikely to change rapidly. One service offered by auction sites such as FreeMarkets (www.FreeMarkets.com) is to help clients examine their needs and clearly spell out every aspect of their request for quotes (RFQs) so potential suppliers will know exactly what they're bidding for. Thus, buyers' auctions are like "modified rebuy" situations where the buyer knows the physical requirements of the purchase but wants to see whether an alternative supplier might offer a better price.

Because auctions throw every purchase up for grabs among alternative suppliers, they work against the development of a cooperative long-term relationship with a given supplier. And they are unlikely to replace such relationships where the product or service being purchased is very technically complex or innovative, is highly customized to the buyer's unique requirements, or requires specialized equipment or other investments to produce. Auctions are also unlikely to replace long-term cooperation between a buyer and a trusted supplier where there are substantial savings to be gained from logistical alliances, as discussed in the next section. Consequently, while the proportion of global business-to-business online sales volume accounted for by auctions or e-exchanges is predicted to increase steadily through the first decade of the 21st century, other forms of purchasing arrangements, including long-term alliances and partnerships, will continue to dominate.[15]

Logistical Alliances   Technology also has changed organizational purchasing over the past decade by facilitating logistical alliances involving the sharing of sales and inventory data and computerized reordering. Initially, such systems involved electronic data interchange through dedicated telephone or satellite links and were mainly limited to large firms. More recently, software for developing such systems on the Web and protecting the security of proprietary data has improved substantially, thereby lowering costs and increasing their availability to smaller firms.

Consumer package goods manufacturers such as Procter & Gamble have formed **supply chain management alliances** with mass merchandisers such as Wal-Mart and Target. Sales information from the retailer's checkout scanners is shared directly with the supplier's computers, which figure out when to replenish the stock of each item and schedule deliveries to appropriate distribution centers or even individual stores. Such paperless exchanges reduce sales and purchasing expenses, cut mistakes and billbacks, minimize inventories, decrease out-of-stocks, and improve cash flow. Another example involving much smaller retail partners is described in Exhibit 6.5.

Performance Evaluation and Feedback   When a purchase is made and the goods delivered, the buyer's evaluation of both product and supplier begins. The buyer inspects the goods on receipt to determine whether they meet the required specifications. Later, the department using the product judges whether it performs to expectations. Similarly, the buyer evaluates the supplier's performance on promptness of delivery and postsale service.

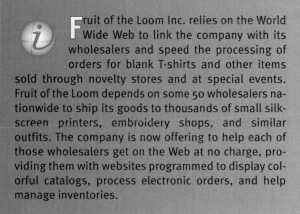

Exhibit 6.5   Fruit of the Loom Inc. Links its Wholesalers via the Internet

Fruit of the Loom Inc. relies on the World Wide Web to link the company with its wholesalers and speed the processing of orders for blank T-shirts and other items sold through novelty stores and at special events. Fruit of the Loom depends on some 50 wholesalers nationwide to ship its goods to thousands of small silk-screen printers, embroidery shops, and similar outfits. The company is now offering to help each of those wholesalers get on the Web at no charge, providing them with websites programmed to display colorful catalogs, process electronic orders, and help manage inventories.

One of Fruit of the Loom's major goals is to avoid losing sales when one of its wholesalers is out of stock. For example, if a silk screener needs 1,000 black T-shirts for a Metallica concert and the local wholesaler is running low, Fruit of the Loom can make up the difference either from its own finished goods inventory or from wholesalers in other parts of the country.

Source: John W. Verity, "Invoice? What's an Invoice?" Reprinted from the June 10, 1996 issue of *Business Week* by permission. Copyright The McGraw-Hill Companies.

In many organizations this process is done formally through reports submitted by the user department and other persons involved in the purchase. This information is used to evaluate proposals and select suppliers the next time a similar purchase is made.

The Marketing Implications of Different Organizational Purchasing Situations

The extensive purchasing process we have been talking about applies primarily to new-task purchases, where an organization is buying a relatively complex product or service for the first time. Buyers in such circumstances tend to collect a lot of information about alternative products and suppliers and to engage in extensive comparisons before making a final purchase decision. Such situations are relatively favorable to potential new suppliers who have never sold to the organization. Such newcomers can win the organization's business *if* they can provide superior product benefits, superior customer service, or better prices—in other words, better customer value—*and if* they can convince the customer of their superiority through an effective sales pitch, a user-friendly website, and/or other promotional efforts. (Good value means nothing if nobody knows about it.) Potential new suppliers may even be able to engage in product development efforts aimed at winning the new customer. This is why entrepreneurial start-ups tend to prosper in emerging categories where product designs are still in flux and there are few entrenched competitors with close ties to potential customers; they are more likely to get a full hearing and have a better chance to differentiate themselves from other suppliers.

One major reason for establishing long-term cooperative relationships with major customers is to become an active partner in designing—and setting the specifications for—the next generation of the customer's products. In the process, the supplier may have a major influence on the purchase criteria for major materials and components of the new product, thereby gaining the inside track on winning the purchase contract for those new-task purchases.

At the other extreme is the straight rebuy, where the customer is reordering an item it has purchased many times before. These purchases tend to be more routine and computerized. From the seller's viewpoint, being the established or "in" supplier in such purchase situations provides a major competitive advantage because the customer spends little or no effort evaluating alternatives. Therefore, established suppliers should develop procedures to maintain and enhance their favored position with current customers. As we'll discuss in Chapter 14, for instance, many firms have developed "key account" policies and appoint cross-functional teams to service major customers to help ensure their satisfaction and retention. New technologies have made it easier for established suppliers to strengthen their ties to customers through supply chain management systems and logistical alliances.

For "out" suppliers who do not have well-established relationships with an organizational customer, however, the marketing challenge is more difficult. Such competitors must try to move the buyer away from the relatively routine reordering procedures of the straight rebuy toward the more extensive evaluation processes of a modified rebuy purchase decision. They must attempt to interest the buyer in modifying the purchase criteria either by promising superior product performance, better service on one or more dimensions, or an equivalent package at a better price.[16] Historically, "out" suppliers—particularly small, unknown start-ups with few marketing resources—had a hard time surmounting this challenge. As with congressional elections, incumbents were firmly entrenched. But the emergence of Web-based auctions may help level the playing field for such suppliers, at least for those efficient enough to compete largely on price.

Developing Long-Term Buyer–Supplier Relationships   From a supplier's perspective, developing logistical alliances and computerized reorder systems can help tie major customers to the firm and increase the proportion of purchases they make from the supplier.[17] But as Exel's evolving relationship with Océ illustrates, long-term relationships between suppliers and their organizational customers often involve much more than merely linking their computer systems and sharing inventory data. Exel frequently gets involved in improvement projects aimed at developing customized services to meet Océ's specific needs.

Trust between Supplier and Customer Develops Person-to-Person   Such complex relationships not only involve a great deal of cooperation between the parties, but they also require *mutual trust*. Before making a substantial investment in training its employees to perform pre-installation testing of Océ's printing systems, Exel had to trust Océ to continue purchasing its services long enough to recoup that investment. Similarly, Océ had to trust Exel to measure up to its own high standards when servicing its customers. In other words, both parties must trust one another to avoid opportunistic behaviors that would advance their own short-term self-interest at their partner's expense.[18]

Organizations develop trust through the actions of individual members of the firm. Therefore, company salespeople, account teams, logistics managers, and customer service personnel often play crucial roles in winning customer trust and loyalty. Unfortunately, this can make buyer–supplier relationships vulnerable to personnel turnover. Suppliers can minimize such problems by (1) developing effective corporate policies and performance standards with respect to customer service, (2) instituting training programs and succession planning for customer contact personnel, and (3) fostering and rewarding a strong customer orientation within the corporate culture.

Conditions Favoring Trust and Commitment   While mutual trust is important for the development and maintenance of long-term commitments between suppliers and their organizational customers, it is not always easy to develop. First, trust tends to build slowly.[19] Thus, the parties must have some history of satisfying experiences with one another to provide a foundation for trust. It also helps if each party brings an established reputation for fair-dealing within its industry.[20]

From the customer's perspective, a firm is more likely to trust and develop a long-term commitment to a supplier when that supplier makes dedicated, customer-specific investments, as Excel has done in developing customized services for individual customers. Such investments send a powerful signal about the vendor's credibility and commitment to the relationship since the assets are not easily deployable elsewhere.

In markets characterized by complex and uncertain technical environments, such as where competing technologies are emerging simultaneously, as in the networking software industry, customers are less likely to develop a long-term orientation toward a single supplier. Because firms in such circumstances cannot tell which supplier's technology will eventually become the industry standard, they are more likely to keep their options open by spreading their purchases across multiple suppliers if it is economically feasible to do so.[21]

Purchasing Processes in Government Markets

Federal, state, and local governments and their various agencies are major buyers of many goods and services. However, a government's purchasing processes tend to be different in some respects from those of a business organization. For one thing, government organizations tend to require more documentation and paperwork from their suppliers because their spending decisions are subject to public review. Thus, although most governments provide would-be suppliers with detailed guides describing their procedures and requirements, some suppliers complain about excessive bureaucracy, costly paperwork, and red tape.

Another difference is that government organizations typically require suppliers to submit bids, and contracts are usually awarded to the lowest bidder who meets the minimum standards specified in the contract. In some cases, though, a government unit will make allowances for a supplier's superior product quality or customer service. They also sometimes purchase on a negotiated or "cost-plus" contract basis, particularly when the product being purchased will require a lengthy development period (a hydroelectric dam) or major and uncertain R&D investments (a new weapons system), or when there are few alternative suppliers to compete for the contract.

These differences in governmental purchasing processes make many standard marketing strategies and tools less relevant and effective than in other organizational markets. For example, since a government purchase contract usually describes the desired product specifications in great detail, and since contracts are usually awarded to the lowest bidder, a strategy of product differentiation via superior features or performance would not likely be successful, particularly if it resulted in higher costs. For the same reason, comparative advertising appeals or personal sales demonstrations have little impact. Nevertheless, many organizations—such as Rockwell, Goodyear, and 3M—have created separate government marketing departments or sales teams. Their task is to anticipate government needs and projects, participate in or influence the development of product specifications, gather competitive intelligence, carefully prepare bids, and expedite postsale activities and services.[22] The lessons learned in selling to governments may become much more relevant in private-sector markets as Web-based buyers' auctions for standardized materials and components proliferate.

Selling Different Kinds of Goods and Services to Organizations Requires Different Marketing Programs

Organizational buying processes tend to vary dramatically depending on what is being bought. Different types of goods and services require sellers to employ varying marketing strategies and actions to be successful in organizational markets. Marketers commonly classify industrial goods according to the uses made of the product by organizational purchasers. With this in mind, *six categories of industrial goods and services* can be identified: raw materials, component materials and parts, installations, accessory equipment, operating supplies, and business services. Exhibit 6.6 describes these categories and their major characteristics and marketing implications.

Raw Materials

Raw materials are goods receiving little or no processing before they are sold, except what is necessary for handling and shipping. Purchased primarily by processors and manufacturers, they are inputs for making other products. The two types of raw materials are *natural products* (fish, lumber, iron ore, and crude petroleum) and *farm products* (fruits, vegetables, grains, beef, cotton, and wool). Processors and manufacturers purchase nearly all natural products and about 80 percent of all farm products. Retailers or consumers buy the remaining 20 percent directly without any processing.

Implications for Marketing Decision Makers   The supply of most natural products is limited; in recent decades, there have been some shortages. Often only a few large

Exhibit 6.6

CATEGORIES, CHARACTERISTICS, AND MARKETING IMPLICATIONS OF GOODS AND SERVICES BOUGHT BY ORGANIZATIONS

Category	Description	Characteristics and marketing implications
Raw material	Relatively unprocessed goods that become a portion of a final product (farm products, lumber, etc.)	Limited supply, few producers; distribution is a key function, price is a critical competitive variable
Component parts and materials	Processed goods that become a portion of a final product (engines, microchips, etc.)	High-volume purchases, long-term contracts; fierce competition among suppliers, requires good service and nurturing of relationships with buyers; Web auctions also important for standard components
Installations	Major capital goods used to produce final product, but not part of the final product (plant installations, production machinery, etc.)	Long-lasting; involved in production of many units of the final product over several years; involve large dollar outlays; capital budgeting committee involved in purchase decision; sold directly from manufacturer; personal selling and system design services are crucial
Accessory equipment	Finished goods that facilitate production of a final product (trucks, hand tools, etc.)	Enduring but less so than installations; more standardized, more frequently purchased, and less costly than capital equipment; less complex buying; intermediaries may be involved
Operating supplies	Finished goods that facilitate repair, maintenance, and ongoing operations (office supplies, repair parts, etc.)	Analogous to consumer convenience goods, frequently purchased and consumed in a short time; standardized; broad market; heavy use of channel intermediaries; Web-based wholesalers and catalog sites becoming important
Business services	Provide special expertise to facilitate ongoing operations (law firms, adv. agencies, etc.)	Long-term relationships with customers; supplier's qualifications, experience, and reputation critical to success; purchase decision often made by top executives

firms produce particular natural products, and in some countries those producers have been nationalized. These supply conditions give producers the power to limit supplies and administer prices, as with the Organization of Petroleum Exporting Countries (OPEC). Such supply conditions encourage processors and manufacturers to seek ways to ensure adequate supplies for the future by negotiating long-term purchase contracts (often at premium prices) or by purchasing the raw materials sources. For example, many large steel manufacturers own iron ore mining and processing operations.

Natural materials are generally bulky and low in unit value; therefore, producers try to minimize their handling and transportation costs. Distribution channels for natural materials tend to have few middlemen; most materials are marketed directly to processors and manufacturers.

The marketing problems associated with natural products are quite different from those of agricultural products, which are produced by many relatively small farms located far from consumer markets. Also, many of these products are produced seasonally. Thus, the distribution channels for most agricultural materials involve many middlemen who buy products from a large number of farmers, collect them in a central location (such as a grain elevator), and store them for shipment throughout the year to processors and exporters. Since there is little difference among the products grown by different farmers, branding is relatively unimportant. There is usually little promotional activity, except for cooperative advertising campaigns funded by trade groups to stimulate primary demand for a product. An example is a promotional campaign to persuade health-conscious adults to drink more milk.

Component Materials and Parts

As with raw materials, component materials and parts are purchased by manufacturers as inputs for making other products. *Component materials* differ, though, in that they have been processed to some degree before they are sold (for instance, flour bought by a baker). *Component parts* are manufactured items assembled as part of another product without further changes in form (electric motors for washing machines, batteries for new cars).

Implications for Marketing Decision Makers
Manufacturers buy most component materials and parts in large quantities; therefore, they are usually sold direct, without the use of middlemen. However, wholesale distributors sell to smaller manufacturers in some lines of trade.

To avoid disrupting production runs, sellers must ensure a steady, reliable supply of materials and parts, especially when a JIT management system is being used by the buyer. This system's objective is to eliminate inventories at the customer's manufacturing site, which requires the delivery of 100 percent quality (zero-defect) products. This relieves the customer of any incoming inspection. A vendor's failure on quality or delivery can close a customer's operation so the resulting penalties are severe.

A JIT system is costly to set up and cannot be effectively implemented without a continuing and close working relationship between buyer and seller. This may explain why a growing proportion of the purchases of component materials and parts, particularly in situations where the components are standardized and the buyer is able to specify all requirements in detail, are being made through electronic buyer auctions such as FreeMarkets, Inc.[23] (www.FreeMarkets.com). Competitive bidding by suppliers can provide some of the cost saving benefits of JIT systems without the time and effort necessary to build close cooperation.

Installations

Installations are the buildings and major capital equipment that manufacturers and service producers use to carry out their operations. They are expensive and long-lived; examples are factory buildings constructed for a manufacturer, office buildings built for government agencies, computers used by the Internal Revenue Service, presses used by an automobile manufacturer, and airplanes purchased by Ryan Air.

Implications for Marketing Decision Makers
The marketing of installations presents a real challenge because there are few potential customers at any one time, and the average sale is very large. Many installations are custom-made to fit a particular customer's needs; therefore, sellers must provide some engineering and design services before making a sale. Often a long period of negotiation precedes the final transaction. Firms selling installations must usually provide many postsale services, such as installing the equipment, training the customer's personnel in its use, providing maintenance and repair services, and sometimes financing.

Because of the small number of buyers, the large dollar volume of each sale, and the custom engineering involved, distribution is usually direct from producer to customer. Sometimes wholesale distributors provide replacement parts and repair services for equipment already in operation. For similar reasons, promotional emphasis is usually on personal selling versus advertising. High-caliber, well-trained salespeople are critically important in the marketing of installations.

Accessory Equipment

As with installations, **accessory equipment i**ncludes industrial machines and tools that manufacturers, services producers, and governments use to carry out their operations. The difference is that although installations determine the scale of operations of the firms that buy and use them, accessory equipment has no such impact since it consists of tools and machines with relatively short lives and small price tags. They consist of such goods as personal computers, desks, file cabinets, and hand tools.

Implications for Marketing Decision Makers   Because this product category includes a wide range of specific items, it is hard to generalize about the most common or appropriate marketing strategies for accessory equipment. In some cases, as with Hyster forklifts and Xerox office equipment, the producers sell accessory equipment directly. Their presale and postsale service requirements are substantial, but the dollar value of the average sale is high enough to justify direct distribution. When there are many different types of potential customers scattered around the country, the average order size is small, and the product does not require much technical service, producers use wholesale distributors (for instance, Black and Decker hand tools). Web-based catalog sites, such as Commerce One (**www.CommerceOne.com**), are also becoming increasingly important in this category.

Personal selling, either by the producer's or a distributor's salesforce, remains the most important promotional method for accessory equipment, but because most products in this category are standardized and not technically complex, advertising, brand name promotions, and company websites are also important.

Operating Supplies

Operating supplies do not become a part of the buyer's product or service, nor are they used directly in producing it. Instead, these supplies facilitate the buying organization's day-to-day operations. They are usually low-priced items purchased frequently with a minimum of decision-making effort. Examples include heating fuel, floor wax, typing paper, order forms, paper clips, and pencils.

Implications for Marketing Decision Makers   These supplies are purchased in small quantities by many different organizations, so wholesale middlemen, including those with extensive websites such as Office Depot, are typically used to distribute them. Price is usually the critical decision variable, and there tends to be little brand loyalty.

Business Services

Many business services producers, or facilitating agencies, have special areas of expertise used and paid for by other organizations. These include security and guard services, janitorial services, equipment repair services, public warehouses, transportation agencies, consulting and marketing research services, advertising agencies, and legal and accounting services.

Implications for Marketing Decision Makers   Services are intangible and are purchased before they can be evaluated by the buyer. Thus, the supplier's qualifications, past performance, and reputation become critical determinants of the success of the marketing effort. Price is less important in selling business services because a lawyer or consultant with an outstanding reputation can often charge much more for a given service than one who is less well known. Also, price often serves as an indicator of quality, especially when there are no other quality cues.[24]

Because services are often tailored to the specific needs of a given customer, personal selling and negotiation are important elements in most services producers' marketing programs. This selling is often done by high-level executives in the service producer's organization. The negotiation process can be lengthy; for instance, an ad agency team spends months developing proposals and making presentations to a prospective client before finding out whether it has landed the new account. This selling task is often worth the effort, though, for once a relationship is established between a service supplier and a customer, it tends to be maintained over a long time, as in the case of Exel and Océ. Many companies employ the same law firm, advertising agency, or logistics services firm for years or even decades.

TAKE-AWAYS

- While organizational customers are different in some ways from consumers, marketers need to answer a similar set of questions to develop a solid foundation for their marketing plans. Who are our target customers? What are their needs, wants, and preferences? How do those customers decide what to buy and what suppliers to buy from?

- Organizations buy things for one of three reasons: (1) to facilitate the production of another product or service, (2) for use by the organization's employees in carrying out its operations, or (3) for resale to other customers.

- Organizations are social constructions. Therefore, "organizations" do not buy things. Rather, individual employees—usually more than one from different departments and organizational levels—make purchase decisions on the organization's behalf. Understanding the personal motivations of these individuals, and their influence on different stages of the purchasing process, is essential for marketing success.

- The Internet is simultaneously encouraging two opposing trends in organizational purchasing: (1) the

growing use of short-term spot market contracts via Web-based auctions and (2) the strengthening of long-term buyer–supplier relationships via the sharing of sales and inventory data and the development of supply chain alliances.

- The mutual interdependence of organizational buyers and their suppliers makes long-term cooperative relationships crucial for customer retention and marketing success. For firms that sell a significant portion of their output to a few large customers, the stakes are very high. Building trust and commitment at multiple levels in both firms—on an individual-to-individual basis—can be a key factor in establishing and maintaining long-term customer relationships that are profitable to both parties.

Self-diagnostic questions to test your ability to apply the analytical tools and concepts in this chapter to marketing decision making may be found at this book's website at www.mhhe.com/mullins05.

ENDNOTES

1. This opening case example is based on material found on Exel's website, www.exel.com; and "A Moving Story," *The Economist,* December 7, 2002, pp. 65–66.

2. For example, see F. Robert Dwyer, Paul H. Schurr, and Sejo Oh, "Developing Buyer-Seller Relationships," *Journal of Marketing* 51 (April 1987), pp. 11–27; and Shankar Ganesan, "Determinants of Long-Term Orientation in Buyer–Seller Relationships," *Journal of Marketing* 58 (April 1994), pp.1–19.

3. Frederick E. Webster, Jr., *Industrial Marketing Strategy* (New York: John Wiley & Sons, 1991), p. 14. Also see Bob Donath, "To Perform Marketing, Think Purchasing," *Marketing News,* July 17, 2000, p. 12.

4. Thomas V. Bonoma, "Major Sales: Who Really Does the Buying?" *Harvard Business Review,* May–June 1982, pp. 111–19. Also see Susan Lynn, "Identifying Buying Influences for a Professional Service: Implications for Marketing Efforts," *Industrial Marketing Management,* May 1987, pp. 119–30.

5. For a comprehensive review of buying-center research, see Morry Ghingold and David T. Wilson, "Buying Center Structure: An Extended Framework for Research," in *A Strategic Approach to Business Marketing,* Robert Spekman and David T. Wilson, eds. (Chicago: American Marketing Association, 1985), pp. 18–93. See also Robert D. McWilliams, Earl Naumann, and Stan Scott, "Determining Buying Center Size," *Industrial Marketing*

Management 21 (February 1992), pp. 43–50; and Richard G. Jennings and Richard E. Plank, "When the Purchasing Agent Is a Committee: Implications for Industrial Marketing," *Industrial Marketing Management* 24 (November 1995), pp. 411–19.

6. Joseph A. Bellizzi, "Organizational Size and Buying Influences," *Industrial Marketing Management* 10 (1981), pp. 17–21.

7. For a more detailed discussion of these and other account management policies aimed at reaching the various members of a customer's buying center, see Mark W. Johnson and Greg W. Marshall, *Churchill/Ford/Walker's Sales Force Management,* 7th ed. (Burr Ridge, IL: McGraw-Hill Irwin, 2003), chaps. 3 and 4.

8. Patrick J. Robinson, Charles W. Faris, and Yoram Wind, *Industrial Buying and Creative Marketing* (Boston: Allyn and Bacon, 1967). See also Erin Anderson, Wujin Chu, and Barton Weitz, "Industrial Buying: An Empirical Exploration of the Buyclass Framework," *Journal of Marketing* 51 (July 1987), pp. 71–86.

9. For a more detailed discussion of the organizational purchase decision-making process, see Wesley J. Johnson and Jeffrey E. Lewin, "Organizational Buying Behavior: Toward and Integrative Framework," *Journal of Business Research* 35 (1996), pp. 1–15.

10. Robin Y. Bergstrom, "Hanging a Vision on Quality," *Production,* July 1993, pp. 56–61.

11. I. Frederick Trawick, John E. Swan, Gail W. McGee, and David R. Rink, "Influence of Buyer Ethics and Salesperson Behavior on Intention to Choose a Supplier," *Journal of the Academy of Marketing Science* 19 (Winter 1991), pp. 17–23.

12. Linda Himelstein and Ben Elgin, "Tech's Kickback Culture," *Business Week,* February 10, 2003, pp. 74–77.

13. Jan B. Heide, "Interorganizational Governance in Marketing Channels," *Journal of Marketing* 58 (January 1994), pp. 71–85; and Ganesan, "Determinants of Long-Term Orientation in Buyer–Seller Relationships."

14. Shawn Tully, "Going, Going, Gone! The B2B Tool That Really Is Changing the World," *Fortune,* March 20, 2000, pp. 132–45.

15. "2000 Marketing Fact Book," *Marketing News,* July 3, 2000, p. 19; and "2002 Marketing Fact Book," *Marketing News,* July 8, 2002, p. 18.

16. Jan B. Heide and Allan M. Weiss, "Vendor Consideration and Switching Behavior for Buyers in High-Technology Markets," *Journal of Marketing* 59 (July 1995), pp. 30–43.

17. Sang-Lin Han, David T. Wilson, and Shirish P. Dant, "Buyer–Supplier Relationships Today," *Industrial Marketing Management* 22 (1993), pp. 331–38.

18. Robert M. Morgan and Shelby D. Hunt, "The Commitment-Trust Theory of Relationship Marketing," *Journal of Marketing* 58 (July 1994), pp. 20–38.

19. Dwyer, Schurr, and Oh, "Developing Buyer-Seller Relationships."

20. Ganesan, "Determinants of Long-Term Orientation in Buyer–Seller Relationships."

21. Ibid. Also see, Jan B. Heide and George John, "Alliances in Industrial Purchasing: The Determinants of Joint Action in Buyer-Supplier Relationships," *Journal of Marketing Research,* February 27, 1990, pp. 24–36.

22. Don Hill, "Who Says Uncle Sam's a Tough Sell?" *Sales and Marketing Management,* July 1988, pp. 56–60.

23. Tully, "Going, Going, Gone!"

24. Valarie A. Zeithaml and Mary Jo Bitner, *Services Marketing* (New York: McGraw-Hill, 1996), chap. 5.

CHAPTER SEVEN

Measuring Market Opportunities: Forecasting and Marketing Research

African Communications Group: Bringing Modern Telecommunications to Tanzania[1]

g N TANZANIA IN THE EARLY 1990s, many towns and villages had no access to telecommunications services. Even in the capital, Dar es Salaam, a city of almost 2 million people, on average only one telephone line had been installed per hundred residents. The waiting time to obtain service from the Tanzania Telecommunications Company Limited (TTCL) was 7 to 10 years. Monique Maddy and Côme Laguë, two recent MBA graduates from a leading U.S. business school, saw in these and other market and industry data an opportunity not only to bring telecommunications services to Tanzania, but also long term to bring a variety of telecommunications services—pay phones, paging, voice mail, and other voice and data communications services—to sub-Saharan Africa. After three months of on-site research in late 1993, Maddy and Laguë decided that building a pay phone network in Tanzania was the most promising opportunity for entering this market. They knew that, to obtain financing as well as the necessary licenses to operate in Tanzania, they would have to prepare a credible business plan. They also knew that among the most critical elements of any business plan was the sales forecast. Not only would

the sales number be the starting point from which all the other numbers in the plan would be developed, but it would be a key litmus test for prospective investors. If the sales forecast were well supported and credible, Maddy and Laguë believed the rest of the pieces would fall into place. But how could such a forecast be prepared with any confidence for a largely new and underdeveloped market?

Market Analysis

As a result of their research, Maddy and Laguë had concluded that the market for building a pay phone system in Tanzania was extremely attractive. In addition to those on the waiting list for phone service, there was huge "unofficial" demand from individuals who had not bothered to apply for service. Maddy and Laguë estimated that, by 1996, there would be 500,000 potential subscribers for telephone service, and even with a planned doubling of its capacity, TTCL could satisfy only perhaps half this demand. Also, on most Tanzanian phones, it took several minutes to receive a dial tone. Once a dial tone was received, it could take 40

minutes to connect with cities in Africa or 20 minutes with Europe. Of the 300 coin-operated pay phones in Tanzania, many were inoperative, and some took only coins that no longer were in circulation and were virtually worthless due to Tanzania's high rate of inflation. The market for phone service looked promising.

Industry Analysis

TTCL, Tanzania's central telephone company, was state-owned, though it was expected that TTCL would be privatized at some point. TTCL offered neither paging, fax, cellular, nor data services. There were several small private telecommunications companies, including one radio-calling service with 105 subscribers, and two high-end cellular phone companies. New licenses were likely to be issued in the next couple of years for cellular services, paging, and pay phones, and Maddy and Laguë hoped to be among those who would win these licenses.

Maddy and Laguë's analysis told them that industry conditions overall were attractive. The bureaucratic TTCL did not seem likely to be a very vigorous competitor. Though new competitors would likely enter the market, Maddy and Laguë's head start would put them in a good position. Numerous suppliers were eager to expand in the African market, and buyers currently had few options to obtain phone service of any kind. There were no substitutes other than cellular service, which was extremely expensive, due to the high cost of building the infrastructure.

Consumer Needs and Behavior

Not only was Tanzania's telecommunications infrastructure poorly developed, but the same also was true for its electricity and water services and its roads. It took three days to travel from Dar es Salaam to Mwanza, Tanzania's second-largest city, only 751 miles away.

Most telephone calls in cities were made by business people, who accounted for 70 percent of telecommunications revenue. Because most residences had no phones, misuse of business phones was common. Employees were generally required to use pay phones for all types of long-distance calls. Most retail shops—known as *dukas,* which were makeshift open-air stalls made of wood and tin—had no phones. Maddy and Laguë believed their pay phone network, together with the voice mail and paging services they planned to offer, would provide more efficient ways of doing business to these small merchants who constituted the backbone of the Tanzanian economy. The biggest challenge they would face would probably be to educate Tanzanians on how to use their proposed system. Since the literacy rate in Tanzania was about 70 percent, they felt optimistic about their ability to do so.

The Business Idea

The idea for African Communications Group (ACG), their proposed venture, was innovative, but simple. Maddy and Laguë would build a network of pay phones based on wireless radio technology, with a central platform for routing calls and connecting with the TTCL network. The phones would accept prepaid cards sold in retail establishments located near the phone booths. The retailers would get a margin on the sale of the phone cards and might help watch over the phones to discourage vandalism. Paging and voice mail would soon be added to the system at low incremental cost. These features would provide quick communication to parties that did not have regular phone service. Subscribers could receive voice-mail messages and leave messages for other voice-mail subscribers. The pagers could be used to signal the subscriber that a message had been received.

Determining Market Potential and Preparing a Sales Forecast

Maddy and Laguë liked the opportunity that lay before them, and they felt their business skills and contacts made them a good team to pursue it. But how could they translate all the market and industry data they had gathered into a credible estimate of market potential and an evidence-based sales forecast? Proving that the market and industry were attractive and that consumers would see benefits from using their network was one thing. Coming up with hard numbers for market potential and sales revenue was quite another.

Marketing Challenges Addressed in Chapter 7

Entrepreneurs such as Maddy and Laguë and managers in established firms need to develop knowledge about their market and industry and synthesize that knowledge into tangible plans that their organizations can act on. These plans can take many forms. For Maddy and Laguë, a business plan was needed to raise the necessary capital and obtain the operating licenses to start the venture. For new product managers in established firms, marketing plans must be developed to win support and resources to permit the product's launch. In organizations of all kinds, annual budgets are prepared to guide decision making for the coming year.[2] These decisions determine staffing, investments in productive capacity, levels of operating expense, and so on. In almost every case, these planning and budgeting activities begin with a sales forecast. Once a sales figure is agreed to, the various activities and investments needed to support the planned sales level are budgeted.

In Chapter 7, we deal with two key issues that enable managers and entrepreneurs to bring life to their dreams. First, we address the challenges in estimating **market potential** and **forecasting** sales, for both new and existing products or businesses. We provide a menu of evidence-based forecasting methods, each of which is useful in some situations, but not others, and we discuss their limitations. Then, we address the informational needs of the forecasting task—as well as the tasks addressed in the first six chapters of this book that enable managers and entrepreneurs to understand their market and competitive contexts—to provide guidance on to how to gather, collect, and report data relevant to marketing decision making (i.e., **marketing research**). The portion of the chapter that deals with marketing research has two objectives. First, we want to enable every reader to be an informed and critical user of marketing research since most strategic decision makers rely, in part, on such research to guide key corporate-level and business-level decisions, as was discussed in Chapter 2. Second, we want to provide readers with at least a rudimentary level of competence in designing and carrying out marketing research studies of various kinds, so that they can, even on minimal budgets, obtain useful market and competitive insights to inform their decision making. Depending on hunches—instead of carefully thought-out research inquiries, even modest ones done quickly—can be risky.

KEY OBSERVATION

We provide a menu of evidence-based forecasting methods, each of which is useful in some situations, but not others.

KEY OBSERVATION

We want to enable every reader to be an informed and critical user of marketing research.

Every Forecast Is Wrong!

We know of no manager who has ever seen a forecast that came in *exactly* on the money. Some forecasts turn out too high, others too low. Forecasting is an inherently difficult task, because no one has a perfect crystal ball. The future is inherently uncertain, especially in today's rapidly changing markets. Consumer wants and needs shift, buffeted by the winds of ever-changing macro trends. Competitors come and go. New technologies sweep away old ones. Some forecasts are based on extensive and expensive research, others on small-scale inquiries, still others on uninformed hunches. As we have seen, however, forecasting plays a central role in all kinds of planning and budgeting in all kinds of businesses and other organizations.[3] Given the stakes and the risks entailed in being *very* wrong with a forecast, some effort to prepare an **evidence-based forecast,** instead of a wild guess, is almost always called for, even if time and money are scarce. So forecast we must, but how?

A Forecaster's Toolkit: A Tool for Every Forecasting Setting

Before choosing a method to prepare a forecast, one first must know what is to be estimated or forecasted. First, there's the size of the potential market, that is, the likely demand from all actual and potential buyers of a product or product class. An estimate of **market potential** often serves as a starting point for preparing a sales forecast, which we explore in more detail later in this chapter. For Maddy and Laguë's venture in Tanzania, prospective investors will want to know how large the potential market for telephone services will be in the coming years, measured perhaps in several ways: in numbers of telephone users, in numbers and/or minutes of calls, and in dollars or Tanzanian shillings. This market is comprised of those consumers who are likely to have both the willingness and ability to buy and use a phone card or one of ACG's other services at one of ACG's pay phones. There's also the size of the currently **penetrated market,** those who are actually using pay phones in Tanzania at the time of the forecast. Investors will also want to know these figures—the size of the potential and penetrated markets for the market segments Maddy and Laguë intend to serve, their **target market.** They will also need a **sales forecast,** in which they predict sales revenues for ACG, for five years or so. How might Maddy and Laguë do these things?

Established organizations employ two broad approaches for preparing a sales forecast: top-down and bottom-up. Under the top-down approach, a central person or persons take the responsibility for forecasting and prepare an overall forecast, perhaps using aggregate economic data, current sales trends, or other methods we describe shortly.[4] Under the bottom-up approach, common in decentralized firms, each part of the firm prepares its own sales forecast, and the parts are aggregated to create the forecast for the firm as a whole. For an example of how managers at Gap Inc. retailing divisions combine both methods to forecast next-year sales, see Exhibit 7.1.

The bottom-up logic also applies to Maddy and Laguë's task. They can break their anticipated demand into pieces and sum the components to create the summary forecast. These pieces could be market segments, such as small retailers, mobile business people, consumers, and so on, or product lines, such as revenue from phone cards or individual pay phones, voice-mail fees, pager fees, and the like. Using the bottom-up approach presents numerous advantages. First, this approach will force them to think clearly about the drivers of demand for each market segment or product line, and thus better understand the real potential of their business and its parts.[5] Second, they will be forced to make explicit assumptions about the drivers of demand in each category, assumptions they can debate—and support with evidence gathered from their research—with prospective investors and which they can later verify as the business unfolds. Third, such an approach facilitates "what if" planning. Various combinations of market segments and/or product lines can be combined to build a business plan that looks viable.

What forecasting methods, or tools, can Maddy and Laguë choose from? There are six major evidence-based methods for estimating market potential and forecasting sales:

Exhibit 7.1   Forecasting Next Year's Sales at Gap

At international retailer Gap Inc., forecasting sales for the next year for each of its divisions—Gap, Banana Republic, and Old Navy—is an important process that drives a host of decisions, including how much merchandise to plan to buy for the coming year. Both top-down and bottom-up approaches are used. At Old Navy, for example, each merchandiser generates a forecast of what level of sales his or her category—women's knit tops, men's jeans, and so on—can achieve for the next year. Group merchandise managers then provide their input and sum these numbers to create a total forecast from a merchandising perspective. A second bottom-up forecast is generated by the store operations organization, summing stores and groups of stores. Simultaneously, a top-down figure is prepared at headquarters in California, using macroeconomic data, corporate growth objec-

tives, and other factors. The three forecasts are then compared, differences debated, and a final figure on which to base merchandise procurement and expense budgets is determined. Though the effort to prepare such a forecast is considerable, the broad involvement in the process helps to ensure both knowledgeable input to the forecast as well as subsequent commitment to "make the numbers." Most important, Old Navy finds that the different processes together with the ensuing discussion lead to substantially better forecasts.

Source: Reprinted by permission of *Harvard Business Review.* From "Rocket Science Retailing Is Almost Here: Are You Ready?" by Marshall L. Fisher, Ananth Raman, and Anna Sheen McClelland, July–August 2000. Copyright © 2000 by the Harvard Business School Publishing Corporation, all rights reserved.

statistical methods, observation, surveys, analogy, judgment, and market tests.[6] A seventh method, not evidenced-based—the SWAG method (Silly Wild-@*# Guess)—is not condoned here, though there is little else to support some forecasts!

Statistical and Other Quantitative Methods

Statistical methods use past history and various statistical techniques, such as multiple regression or time series analysis, to forecast the future based on an extrapolation of the past.[7] This method is typically not useful for ACG or other entrepreneurs or new product managers charged with forecasting sales for a new product or new business. There is no history in their venture on which to base a statistical forecast.

In established firms, for established products, statistical methods are extremely useful. When Michelin, the tire maker, wants to forecast demand for the replacement automobile tire market in Asia for the next year, it can build a statistical model using such factors as the number and age of vehicles currently on the road in Asia, predictions of GDP for the region, the last few years' demand, and other relevant factors to forecast market potential as well as Michelin's own replacement tire sales for the coming year. Such a procedure is likely to result in a more accurate forecast than other methods, especially if Michelin has years of experience with which to calibrate its statistical model.

KEY OBSERVATION

Statistical methods generally assume that the future will look very much like the past. Sometimes this is not the case.

As with all forecasting methods, statistical methods have important limitations. Most important of these is that statistical methods generally assume that the future will look very much like the past. Sometimes this is not the case. US WEST (now Qwest Communications), the regional Bell telephone company serving the Rocky Mountain and Northwest regions of the United States, ran into trouble in the 1990s when its statistical models used to predict needs for telephone capacity failed to allow for rapidly increasing use of computer modems, faxes, and second lines for teenagers in American homes. Suddenly, the average number of lines per home skyrocketed, and there was not enough physical plant—cable in the ground, switches, and so on—to accommodate the growing demand. Consumers had to wait, sometimes for months, to get additional lines, and they were not happy about it! Similarly, if product or market characteristics change, statistical models used without adequate judgment may not keep pace. When tire makers produce automobile tires that last 80,000 miles instead of 30,000 to 50,000 miles, the annual demand for replacement tires is reduced. If automobile manufacturers were to change the number of wheels on the typical car from four, the old statistical models would also be in trouble. For example, many large capacity pickup trucks sold in the United States feature six wheels.

Other quantitative forecasting methods, especially for new product forecasting, have also been developed. These include methods to mathematically model the diffusion of innovation process for consumer durables[8] (discussed in Chapter 4) and conjoint analysis,[9] a method to forecast the impact on consumer demand of different combinations of attributes that might be included in a new product.

Observation

Another method for preparing an evidence-based forecast is to directly observe or gather existing data about what real consumers do in the product-market of interest. Maddy and Laguë conducted a study of pay phone use in Tanzania to find out how many minutes per day the typical pay phone was used. Their study showed that an average of 150 three-minute calls were made per day at the 60 working pay phones then provided by other companies in Dar es Salaam. Revenue for most pay phones fell into the US$100 to $150 range.[10]

Like statistical methods, **observation-based forecasting** is attractive because it is based on what people actually *do*. If behavioral or usage data can be found from existing secondary sources—in company files, at the library, or on the Internet—data collection is both faster and cheaper than if a new study like the one Maddy and Laguë conducted must be designed and carried out. For new-to-the-world products, however, observation is typically not possible and secondary data are not available, since the product often does not yet exist, except in concept form. Had there been no pay phones in Tanzania or a similar country, observation would not have been possible. Market tests, which we discuss later in this section, are one way to get real purchase data about new-to-the-world products.

Surveys

Another common way to forecast sales or estimate market potential is to conduct surveys. These surveys can be done with different groups of respondents. Consumers, after being shown a statement of the product concept[11] or a prototype or sample of the product, can be asked how likely they are to buy, creating a **survey of buyers' intentions.** Buyers can also be asked about their current buying behavior: what they currently buy, how often, or how much they use. The salespeople can be asked how much they are likely to sell, completing a **survey of salesforce opinion.** Experts of various kinds—members of the distribution channel, suppliers, consultants, trade association executives, and so on—can also be surveyed.

As part of their research in Dar es Salaam, Maddy and Laguë surveyed pay phone customers to find out more about them. A whopping 65 percent were using a pay phone because they lacked access to another working phone—good news for the ACG concept! Sixty-three percent were business customers, 20 percent were students or teachers, and 17 percent were other nonbusiness customers. Business customers spent an average of US$10 per week for 14 pay phone calls, and nonbusiness customers spent US$6 per week for 12 calls.[12] By combining these data with demographic data on the Tanzanian population,

Exhibit 7.2

A Survey of Buyers' Intentions: What People Say Is Not What They Do

When Nestlé's refrigerated foods division in the United States was considering whether to acquire Lambert's Pasta and Cheese, a fresh pasta maker, it wanted to forecast the likely first-year sales volume if the acquisition were completed. To do so, Nestlé used a concept test in which consumers were asked, among other things, how likely they were to *try* the fresh pasta product. The results were as shown in the first two columns in the table below:

Purchase intent	% Response	Rule of thumb reduction for forecasting purposes	Percentage of market deemed likely to actually buy
Definitely would buy	27%	Multiply by .8	27% $\times$ **.8** = 21.6%
Probably would buy	43%	Multiply by .3	43% $\times$ **.3** = 12.9%
Might or might not buy	22%	Count as zero	
Probably or definitely would not buy	8%	Count as zero	
Totals	100%		21.6% + 12.9% = 34.5%

Even though 70% of consumers surveyed indicated they were likely to buy, Nestlé's experience indicated that these "top two box" percentages should be cut sharply: "Definitely" responses were reduced by 20%, while "Probably" responses were reduced by 70%. "Maybe" responses were considered as "No." These adjustments, shown in columns three and four, reduced the 70% figure by more than half, to 34.5%. Most consumer product manufacturers who employ concept tests use similar rules of thumb when interpreting purchase intent data for forecasting purposes, because they have learned that what people *say* they will buy exceeds what they will *actually* buy. Similar logic is useful in a variety of forecasting situations.

Source: Originally published as Marie Bell and V. Kasturi Rangan, *Nestlé Refrigerated Foods: Contadina Pasta and Pizza* (Boston: Harvard Business School Publishing, 1995). Reproduced by permission of Nestlé USA, Inc.

Maddy and Laguë now had what they needed to prepare an evidence-based, bottom-up forecast of market potential, market segment by market segment.

KEY OBSERVATION

Surveys possess important limitations, however. For one, what people say is not always what people do.

Surveys possess important limitations, however. For one, what people *say* is not always what people *do*. Consumer surveys of buyer intention are always heavily discounted to allow for this fact. For one common approach to doing so, see Exhibit 7.2. Second, the persons who are surveyed may not be knowledgeable, but if asked for their opinion, they will probably provide it! Third, what people imagine about a product concept in a survey may not be what is actually delivered once the product is launched. If consumers are asked if they will buy an "old world pasta sauce with homemade flavor," they will surely provide a response. Whether they will actually *like* the taste and texture of the sauce that the lab develops is another story! In general, statistical and observational methods, where adequate data or settings are available in which to apply them, are superior to survey methods of forecasting, because such methods are based, at least in part, on what people have *actually done* or bought (e.g., the number of old cars actually on the road, or the length of pay phone calls in Tanzania), while survey methods (Are you likely to buy replacement tires this year? How often are you likely to use a pay phone?) are based on what people *say*, a less reliable indicator of their future behavior.

Analogy

An approach often used for new product forecasting where neither statistical methods nor observations are possible is to forecast the sales or market potential for a new product or product class by **analogy.** Under this method, the product is compared with similar products for which historical data *are* available. When Danone, the leading marketer of yogurt in Europe, plans to introduce a new flavor, its managers will likely look at the sales history of earlier introductions to forecast the sales for the newest flavor. This method is also used for new-to-the-world high-technology products, for which product prototypes are often either not available or extremely expensive to produce. Rather than conduct surveys to ask consumers about their likelihood to buy a product they can hardly imagine (What would someone have said in 1978 about his or her likelihood to buy a personal computer?), forecasters consider related product introductions with which the new product may be compared. Early forecasts for high-definition television (HDTV) were done this way, comparing HDTV with historical penetration patterns for color TV, videocassette recorders (VCRs), camcorders, and other consumer electronic products.[13]

As always, there are limitations. First, the new product is never exactly like that to which the analogy is drawn. Early VCRs penetrated American households at a much faster rate than did color TV. Which analogy should be used for HDTV? Why? Second, market and competitive conditions may differ considerably from when the analogous product was launched. Such conditions need to be taken into account.

Judgment

While we hesitate to call this a forecasting method of its own, since capable and informed judgment is required for *all* methods, sometimes forecasts are made *solely* on the basis of experienced **judgment,** or intuition. Some decision makers are intuitive in their decision processes and cannot always articulate the basis for their judgments. Said a footwear buyer at Nine West Group, an international manufacturer and retailer of shoes and fashion accessories, "Trend forecasting is a visceral thing that cannot be trained. I rely on my sense of color and texture, but at times I cannot explain why I feel a certain way . . . I just know."[14] Those with sufficient forecasting experience in a market they know well may

be quite accurate in their intuitive forecasts. Unfortunately, it is often difficult for them to defend their forecasts against those prepared by evidence-based methods when the two differ. Nonetheless, the importance of experienced judgment in forecasting, whether it is used solely and intuitively or in concert with evidence-based methods, cannot be discounted.

Market Tests

Market tests of various kinds are the last of our most commonly used methods. We address market testing in more detail in Chapter 11, but a few observations are pertinent here.

Used largely for new products, market tests such as **experimental test markets** may be done under controlled experimental conditions in research laboratories, or in live **test markets** with real advertising and promotion and distribution in stores.

Use of test markets has declined over the past two decades for two reasons. First, they are expensive to conduct because significant quantities of the new product must be produced and marketing activities of various kinds must be paid for. More importantly, in today's data-intensive environment, especially for consumer products sold through supermarkets and mass merchants, competitors can buy the data collected through scanners at the checkout and learn the results of the test market without bearing the expense. More diabolically, competitors can engage in marketing tactics to mislead the company conducting the test, by increasing sampling programs, offering deep discounts or buy-one-get-one-free promotions, or otherwise distorting normal purchasing patterns in the category. Experimental test markets, on the other hand, are still commonly used.

The coming of the Internet has made possible a new kind of market test: an offer directly to consumers on the Web. Offers to chat rooms, interest groups, or e-mail lists of current customers are approaches that have been tried. Use of such techniques has increased, due to companies' ability to carry out such tests quickly and at low cost. We explore these and other Internet marketing strategies in greater detail in Chapter 15.

Mathematics Entailed in Forecasting

Regardless of the method used, the ultimate purpose of the forecasting exercise is to end up with numbers that reflect what the forecaster believes is the most likely outcome, or sometimes a range of outcomes under different assumptions, in terms of future market potential or for the sales of a product or product line. The combination of judgment and other methods often leads to the use of either of two mathematical approaches to determine the ultimate numbers: the chain ratio calculation or the use of indices. See Exhibits 7.3 and 7.4 for examples applying these mathematical calculations to arrive at sales forecasts. Both mathematical approaches begin with an estimate of market potential (the number of households in the target market in Exhibit 7.3; the national market potential for a product category in Exhibit 7.4). The market potential is then multiplied by various fractional factors that, taken together, predict the portion of the overall market potential that one firm or product can expect to obtain. In Exhibit 7.3, which shows the more detailed of the two approaches, the factors reflect the appeal of the product to consumers, as measured by marketing research data, and the company's planned marketing program.

Exhibit 7.3

CHAIN RATIO FORECAST: TRIAL OF FRESH PASTA

Once Nestlé's research on fresh pasta had been completed (see Exhibit 7.2), it used the chain ratio method to calculate the total number of households who would try their fresh pasta. The chain ratio calculation went like this:

Research results for:	Data from research	Chain ratio calculation	Result
Number of households in target market	77.4 million		
Concept purchase intent: adjusted figure from Exhibit 7.2	34.5% will try the product	77.4 million × 34.5%	26.7 million households will try *if aware*
Awareness adjustment: based on planned advertising level	48% will be aware of the product	26.7 million × 48%	12.8 million households will try *if they find product at their store*
Distribution adjustment: based on likely extent of distribution in supermarkets, given the introductory trade promotion plan	The product will obtain distribution reaching 70% of U.S. households	12.8 million × 70%	9.0 million will try the product

Similar chain ratio logic is useful in a variety of forecasting settings.

Source: Originally published as Marie Bell and V. Kasturi Rangan, *Nestlé Refrigerated Foods: Contadina Pasta and Pizza* (Boston: Harvard Business School Publishing, 1995). Reproduced by permission of Nestlé USA, Inc.

Exhibit 7.4   Estimating Market Potential Using Indices

In many countries there are published indices of buying behavior, including the "Annual Survey of Buying Power" published by *Sales and Marketing Management* in the United States. The Buying Power Index (BPI) is a weighted sum of a geographical area's percentage of national buying power for the area, based on census income data (weight = .5), plus the percentage of national retail sales for the area (weight = .3), plus the percentage of national population located in the area (weight = .2). If this calculation comes to 3.50 for a given state or region, one might expect 3.5% of sales in a given category (toys, power tools, or whatever) to come from that geographical area.

Category development indices (CDIs) are similar indices that report the ratio of consumption in a certain *category* (say, restaurant sales) to population in a defined geographical area. Trade associations or trade magazines relevant to the category typically publish such indices. Ratios greater than 1.0 for a particular geographic area, say metropolitan Chicago, indicate that the area does more business than average (compared to the country as a whole) in that category. **Brand development indices** (BDIs) compare sales for a given *brand* (say, Pizza Hut restaurants) to population. Companies that use BDI indices typically calculate them for their own use. The ratio of the BDI to the CDI for a given area is an indicator of how well a brand is doing, compared to its category overall, in that area. These various indices are useful for estimating market potential in defined geographic areas. They are, however, crude numbers, in that they do not consider differences in consumer behavior from region to region. The CDI or BDI for snowmobiles in Minnesota (with its freezing winters) is far higher than in balmy Texas, for example. Attempting to rectify this imbalance by increasing the snowmobile advertising budget in Texas would be difficult!

Cautions and Caveats in Forecasting

Keys to Good Forecasting

There are two important keys to improve the credibility and accuracy of forecasts of sales and market potential. The first of these is to make explicit the **assumptions** on which the forecast is based. This way, if there is debate or doubt about the forecast, the *assumptions* can be debated, and data to support the assumptions can be obtained. The resulting conversation is far more useful than stating mere opinions about whether the forecast is too high or too low.

For ACG, the combination of observational and survey forecasting methods enabled Maddy and Laguë to articulate the assumptions on which their revenue forecasts were based, and to support those assumptions with data. Their evidence-based forecast was instrumental in their obtaining US$3.5 million in start-up capital to get their venture off the ground.[15]

The second key to effective forecasting is to use multiple methods. When forecasts obtained by different methods converge near a common figure, greater confidence can be placed in that figure. The procedure used at Gap Inc., to forecast next-year sales (see Exhibit 7.1) is an example of such an approach. Where forecasts obtained by multiple methods diverge, the assumptions inherent in each can be examined to determine which set of assumptions can best be trusted. Ultimately, however, any forecast is almost certainly wrong. Contingency plans should be developed to cope with the reality that ultimately unfolds.[16]

Biases in Forecasting

Several sources of potential bias in forecasts should be recognized. First, forecasters are subject to anchoring bias, where forecasts are perhaps inappropriately "anchored" in recent historical figures, even though market conditions have markedly changed, for better or worse.[17]

Second, capacity constraints are sometimes misinterpreted as forecasts. Someone planning to open a car wash that can process one car every seven minutes would probably be amiss in assuming sufficient demand to actually run at that rate all the time. A restaurant chain that is able to turn its tables 2.5 times each night, on average, must still do local market research to ascertain how much volume a new restaurant will really produce. Putting similar 80-table restaurants in two trade areas with different population makeup and density, with different levels of competition, will result in varying sales levels.

Another source of bias in forecasting is incentive pay. Bonus plans can cause managers to artificially inflate or deflate forecasts, whether intentionally or otherwise. "Sandbagging"—setting the forecast or target at an easily achievable figure in order to earn bonuses when that figure is beaten—is common. Finally, unstated but implicit assumptions can overstate a well-intentioned forecast. While 34.5 percent of those surveyed (after adjustments, as shown in Exhibit 7.2) may indicate their willingness to buy a new grocery product, such as fresh pasta, for such a forecast to pan out requires that consumers actually are *made aware* of the new product when it is introduced, and that the product *can actually be found* on supermarket shelves. Assumptions of **awareness** and **distribution coverage** at levels less than 100 percent, depending on the nature of the planned marketing program for the product, should be applied to such a forecast, using the chain ratio method (see Exhibit 7.3).

Why Data? Why Marketing Research?

In the first portion of this chapter, we provided several approaches to forecasting, each of which requires that data be collected. Similarly, the first six chapters of this book provided frameworks for gaining a better understanding of market and competitive conditions and of what buyers in a given market want and need—what we call **market knowledge**.[18] Obtaining market knowledge also requires data, and so far we've provided little discussion of exactly how one might best find the necessary data. Without relevant and timely data, market knowledge is generally incomplete and often ill-informed, based perhaps on hunches or intuition that may or may not be correct.

Without adequate market knowledge, marketing decisions are likely to be misguided. Products for which there is little demand may be introduced, only to subsequently fail. New markets may be entered, despite market or industry conditions that make success unlikely. Attractive product-markets may be overlooked. Products may be marketed to the wrong target market, when consumers in another market segment would like the product better. Pricing may be too high, reducing sales, or too low, leaving money on the table. Advertising and promotion monies may be poorly spent. Second-best distribution channels may be chosen. These outcomes are all too common. Most often, they result from ill- or under-informed marketing decisions. Thoughtfully designed, competently executed marketing research can mitigate the chances of such unpleasant outcomes.

Thus, in the remainder of this chapter we address the challenge of obtaining market knowledge, including the development of systems to track pertinent market information inside and outside the firm, as well as the design and implementation of more targeted studies intended to collect information about a particular marketing problem. We begin by discussing the principal kinds of **market knowledge systems** used in companies large and small, and we show how such systems can improve the timeliness and quality of marketing decisions.

Market Knowledge Systems: Charting a Path toward Competitive Advantage

Marketing is rapidly becoming a game where information, rather than raw marketing muscle, wins the race for competitive advantage. There are four commonly used market knowledge systems on which companies rely to keep pace with daily developments: internal records regarding marketing performance in terms of sales and the effectiveness and efficiency of marketing programs, marketing databases, competitive intelligence systems, and systems to organize client contact. Effective use of such systems is likely to result in happier, higher volume, more loyal customers. Few of these systems existed in their current form until developments in data processing and data transmission made them cost effective.

Internal Records Systems

Every Monday morning, each retail director at the headquarters of Nine West Retail Stores, a leading operator of shoe specialty stores, receives the "Godzilla Report," a tabulation of detailed sales and inventory information about the fastest-selling items in Nine West stores from the prior week.[19] By style and color, each director learns which items in his or her stores are selling fast and need to be reordered. A similar report provides information about all other styles currently in Nine West's stores, so that slow sellers can be marked down or transferred to stores where those styles are in higher demand. Additional reports aggregate sales information by style and color; by merchandise category (e.g., dress or casual); store, area, or region; and for various time periods. The information provided by these reports constitutes the backbone of Nine West's decision making about which shoes to offer in which of its stores. Imagine how much more difficult the retail director's job would be without today's point-of-sale systems to collect and report such data! Imagine the potential advantage Nine West has over shoe retailers who lack such information.

Every marketer, not just retailers, needs information about "what's hot, what's not." Unfortunately, accounting systems generally do not collect such data. Typically, such systems just track dollars of revenue, with no information about *which* goods or services were sold. Thus, marketers need **internal records systems** to track what is selling, how fast, in which locations, to which customers, and so on. Providing input on the design of such systems so that the right data are provided to the right people at the right time is a critical marketing responsibility in any company. But what constitutes critical marketing information varies from company to company and industry to industry.

Nine West retail directors need to know which styles and colors are selling, in which stores, at what rate. Wal-Mart believes its key suppliers need to know its store-by-store item and category sales data, so it provides password-protected online access to such data to those suppliers. Telemarketers need to know which callers are producing sales, at what times of day, for which products. Marketers of kitchen gadgets through infomercials on late-night television need to know which ads on which stations in which cities are

Exhibit 7.5

DESIGNING AN INTERNAL RECORDS SYSTEM FOR MARKETING DECISION MAKERS

Questions to ask	Implications for a chain footwear retailer	Implications for an infomercial marketer of kitchen gadgets
What information is key to providing our customers with what they want?	Need to *know* which shoes sell, in which stores and markets, at what rate	Need to *know* which gadgets sell, in what markets, at what rate
What regular marketing decisions are critical to our profitability?	*Decide* which shoes and shoe categories to buy more of, which to buy less of or get rid of, in which stores and markets to sell them	*Decide* on which specific TV stations, programs, and times of day to place infomercials for which gadgets
What data are critical to managing profitability?	Inventory turnover and gross margin	Contribution margin (gross margin less media cost) per gadget sold
Who needs to know?	Buyers and managers of merchandise categories	Media buyers, product managers
When do they need to know, for competitive advantage?	For hottest sellers, need to know before competitors, to beat them to the reorder market. For dogs, need to know weekly, to mark them down.	Need to know daily, for prior night's ads, to reallocate media dollars
In what *sequence* and at what *level of aggregation* should data be reported?	Sequence of report: hot sellers first, in order of inventory turnover Aggregation: by style and color for buyers, by category for merchandise managers	Sequence of report: hot stations/programs first, in order of contribution margin per gadget sold Aggregation: By stations/programs for media buyers, by gadget for product managers

performing, in order to place media spending where they will be most productive. Companies selling their wares to industrial markets through outside salesforces need to know not only which products are selling to which customers but also which salespeople are selling how much, at what margins and expense rates, to whom. The salesforce, too, needs information about status of current orders, customer purchasing history, and so on.

For those charged with developing or updating internal record systems in their companies, we provide, in Exhibit 7.5, a series of questions to help marketing decision makers specify what internally generated sales data are needed, when, for whom, in what sequence, at what level of aggregation.

Marketing Databases

In the technology boom of the late 1990s, several companies launched extensive and expensive projects to help them better manage customer relationships through enhanced use of customer data. Although several large-scale customer relationship management (CRM) projects have failed to show an adequate return on investment, CRM has proved to be very successful in managing marketing campaigns. For a discussion of how one company has benefited from such tools, see Exhibit 7.6.

Many companies have become quite sophisticated about using marketing databases in other ways. Catalog marketers such as Lands' End and L.L. Bean, based in the United States, know who are their best customers and what categories they tend to buy. Online marketers like Amazon use "cookies," electronic signatures placed at a customer's personal

---

Exhibit 7.6   Customer Relationship Management (CRM) Projects—a Campaign Management Success Story

 Campaign management software allows marketers to design and execute marketing programs that allow them greater control and accountability and that produce better results than in the past. The veterinary charity, PDSA, in the United Kingdom uses software to manage its database of 3.5 million supporters, its 11 million transactions, and 22 million lines of previous mailing history. Because it is a charity, PDSA realizes that not every supporter wishes to be permanently included in their database, and the system allows for this to be factored in. PDSA uses the database to effectively target customers for its mailshot campaigns and pulls in between £10 and £12 million in contributions per year.

The European bank ING has used a Dutch software company to implement a CRM system that allowed it to identify its customers who never respond to mailshots, thereby reducing their mailings by 30 percent or 46 million. Other vendors help companies pinpoint customers who are most likely to defect to competitors, thereby reducing customer churn.

Source: "Ringing the Changes," *Precision Marketing,* September 20, 2002; Michael Dempsey, "FT Report—FT-IT—Getting Back to Basics in Battle to Win Customers," *Financial Times,* November 6, 2002.

---

computer, so they not only keep track of what each customer has bought, but they also recognize the customer when he or she logs on to their site. Airlines track members of their frequent flyer programs and target some with special promotions. Supermarket chain Tesco in the United Kingdom uses its loyalty cards to track and analyze customer buying patterns, and to offer customers coupons and incentives tailored to their buying behavior. Tesco uses their analysis in deciding product placement on shelves, managing coupon campaigns, and in tailoring product portfolios to individual stores.[20]

KEY OBSERVATION

Designing marketing databases that take effective advantage of customer data that companies are in a position to collect requires that several major issues be considered.

Designing marketing databases that take effective advantage of customer data that companies are in a position to collect requires that several major issues be considered: the cost of collecting the data, the economic benefits of using the data, the ability of the company to keep the data current in today's mobile society, and the rapid advances in technology that permit the data to be used to maximum advantage.

Collecting information, then storing and maintaining it, always costs money. If a company wants to know more about the demographics and lifestyles of its best customers, in addition to their purchasing histories, it must obtain demographic and lifestyle data about them. Doing so is more difficult than it sounds; most people are unwilling to spend much time filling out forms that ask nosy questions about education, income, whether they play tennis, and what kind of car they drive. The cost of collecting such information must be weighed against its value. What will be done with the information once it is in hand?

Various commercial marketing databases are available, with varying depth and quality of information. For example, the Polk Company (www.Polk.com) sells data compiled from state driver's license records in the United States, as well as a demographic and lifestyle database compiled from questionnaires returned with warranty cards for consumer durables such as toasters, stereos, and the like. Donnelley's DQI database (www.Donnelley.com) covers more than 150 million individual U.S. consumers and 90 million U.S. households and includes more than 1,600 demographic, lifestyle, purchasing power, and creditworthiness variables, among others. Claritas' PRIZM service (Potential Rating Index for Zip Markets, www.claritas.com) classifies U.S. consumers into one of 62 distinct demographic and behavioral clusters according to the Zip code and postal carrier route where they live. For the U.K. market, geo-demographic databases can be purchased from CACI,[21] known for its database called ACORN, and Experian,[22] which offers its MOSAIC database. These databases are useful tools for targeting consumers based on the area they live in. An important caveat for all geo-demographic databases, however, is that the accuracy of the data goes down as the granularity of the area increases; that is, customers may share the same Zip code or postcode, but may belong to very disparate economic segments.

Virtually every credit-card issuer, magazine publisher, affinity group (e.g., British Airways Executive Club members), and others who sell to or deal directly with consumers sell their customer databases. Marketers who consider buying lists or other services from any of these commercial database providers need to inquire exactly how and where the data are collected and when (Have 20 percent of the people on the list moved?). They should also compare the costs of databases containing names about which more is known (higher cost, but of higher value to targeted marketers, since response rates will be higher for names chosen on the basis of more relevant information) to the extra value, compared to simpler **compiled databases,** such as those taken from telephone directories or automobile registrations. Marketers planning to build their own databases need also to consider several increasingly important ethical issues, as discussed in Ethical Perspective 7.1.

For firms with deep pockets, advances in computing power and database technology, including new **data-mining** technology,[23] are permitting firms to combine databases from different sources to permit a more complete understanding of any member of the database. Keeping current with what is possible in database technology is important, as technological advances often make possible that which was only a dream a short time ago.

Competitive Intelligence Systems[24]

In today's fast-paced business climate, keeping up with competitors and the changing macroenvironment is no easy task. Competitive intelligence (CI) is a systematic and ethical approach for gathering and analyzing information about competitors' activities and related business trends. It is based on the idea that more than 80 percent of all information is public knowledge. The most important sources of CI information include companies' annual and other financial reports, speeches by company executives, government documents, online databases, trade organizations, as well as the popular and business press. The challenge is to find the relevant knowledge, analyze it, and share it with the decision makers in the organization, so they can use it. The critical questions that managers setting up a CI system should ask are:

- How rapidly does the competitive climate in our industry change? How important is it that we keep abreast of such changes?
- What are the objectives for CI in our company?
- Who are the best internal clients for CI? To whom should the CI effort report?
- What budget should be allocated to CI? Will it be staffed full- or part-time?

In companies that operate in industries with dynamic competitive contexts, the use of full-time CI staff is growing.

Client Contact and Salesforce Automation Systems

Salesforce automation software helps companies disseminate real-time product information to salespeople to enable them to be more productive and more able to satisfy customer needs. Such software also allows companies to effectively capture customer

ETHICAL PERSPECTIVE 7.1
Ethical Issues in Database Marketing, Internet Marketing, and Marketing Research

New technologies relating to the gathering and use of information about consumers and their behavior, interests, and intentions raise a host of legal and ethical questions. These new technologies have the potential to harm individuals when such information "is used without their knowledge and/or consent, leading them to be *excluded from* or *included in* activities in such a way that they are harmed economically, psychologically, or physically. Examples include the improper disclosure of a person's credit rating, denying medical insurance to an individual based on confidential information, and a person's being placed on target lists for direct mail and telemarketing. The depth of privacy concerns varies from country to country, a critical issue for Internet marketers, given their global reach.

Ethical issues in marketing research stem, in large part, from the interaction between the researcher and respondents, clients, and the general public. For instance, respondents should not be pressured to participate, should have the right to remain anonymous, and should not be deceived by fake sponsorship.

Client issues involve the confidentiality of the research findings and the obligation to strive to provide unbiased and honest results regardless of client expectations. The public is very much involved when they are exposed to a sales solicitation disguised as a marketing research study or issuing from data obtained from "volunteer surveys" using write-ins or call-ins.

In discussing the reliability of, and ethical issues involved with, marketing research studies, a *Wall Street Journal* article noted that many studies "are little more than vehicles for pitching a product or opinion. An examination of hundreds of recent studies indicated that the business of research has become pervaded by bias and distortion. More studies are being sponsored by companies or groups with a financial interest in the results. This too often leads to a bias in the way questions are asked.

Because of shortages in time and money, sample sizes are being reduced to the point that, when groups are further broken into subgroups, the margin of error becomes unacceptable—assuming a probability sample was used. In addition to sample size, the way the sampling universe is defined can bias the results. Thus, in a Chrysler study showing that people preferred Chrysler's cars to Toyota's, a sample of only 100 respondents was used in each of two tests, and none owned a foreign car. Thus, the respondents may well have been biased in favor of U.S. cars.

In addition to the problems noted above, subjective sampling procedures are often used, data analysis may be flawed, or only the best conclusions are reported. Frequently researchers are hired whose views on the subject area being researched are known to be similar to those of the client. In an attempt to regulate the marketing research industry, several codes of conduct and ethics have been developed. For the United States these include published codes by the American Marketing Association, the American Association for Public Opinion Research, the Marketing Research Association, and the Council of American Survey Research Organizations. In the United Kingdom, the Market Research Society has developed an ethical Code of Conduct that all members are required to adhere to. Similar organizations have developed localized guidelines in other countries. For one such listing of organizations in other countries, see the British Market Research Association website at http://www.bmra.org.uk.

Source: Paul N. Bloom, Robert Adler, and George R. Milne, "Identifying the Legal and Ethical Risks and Costs of Using New Information Technologies to Support Marketing Programs," in *The Marketing Information Revolution*, Robert C. Blattberg, Rashi Glazer, and John D. C. Little, eds. (Boston: Harvard Business School Press, 1994), p. 294; Cynthia Crossen, "Studies Galore Support Products and Positions, But Are They Reliable?" *The Wall Street Journal*, November 14, 1991, pp. A1 and A8; and Thomas E. Weber, "Europe and U.S. Reach Truce on Net Privacy, But What Comes Next?" *The Wall Street Journal*, June 19, 2000, p. B1.

intelligence from salespeople, keep track of it for use on later sales calls, and even transfer it to other salespeople in the event of a salesperson leaving the company. Several low-cost software applications that run on PCs are available. ACT and Goldmine are two of the best-known programs in this arena. These programs keep track of clients' names, addresses, phone and fax numbers, and so on—along with all kinds of personal tidbits, such as their spouse's and children's names and the kind of wine the client likes to drink—and they also provide an organized way to make notes about each contact with the customer.

They also can remind the user when it is time to follow up with the customer on a topic left pending. Most whose livelihood depends on face-to-face selling now use such systems to keep themselves organized.

Other Kinds of Market Knowledge Systems

We have covered but a few of the most common market knowledge systems, most of which are computer applications in today's increasingly sophisticated data-driven age. These tools make marketers better informed about their customers, potential customers, and competitors and help them be more productive, both of which help establish and sustain competitive advantage. New applications are being developed every day. Ultimately, the potential that many of these systems share is to enable marketers to serve target markets of one; that is, to know enough about any given customer and the competitive context that an offering can be tailored to fit each customer so well that the customer's needs are met perfectly. Doing so is many a marketer's dream!

Marketing Research Resolves Specific Marketing Challenges

We now turn to the **marketing research** task: the design, collection, analysis, and reporting of research intended to gather data pertinent to a *particular* marketing challenge or situation. The word *particular* is very important. Marketing research is intended to address carefully defined marketing problems or opportunities. Research carried out without carefully thought-out objectives usually means time and money down the tubes! Some marketing problems commonly addressed through marketing research include tracking customer satisfaction from unit to unit or year to year (**tracking studies**); testing consumer responses to elements of marketing programs, such as prices or proposed advertising campaigns; and assessing the likelihood that consumers will buy proposed new products.

We begin by presenting a model of the marketing research process that sets forth the many decisions that must be made to conduct effective and actionable marketing research. The steps in the marketing research process are shown in Exhibit 7.7. As this exhibit shows, the marketing research process is fraught with numerous opportunities for error. That's why it's so important that all who play influential roles in setting strategy for their firms or who use marketing research results for decision making be well-informed and critical users of the information that results from market research studies. To this end, we now address each of the steps in the marketing research process, from a decision making point of view.

Step 1: Identify the Managerial Problem and Establish Research Objectives

As for any other form of human endeavor, if you don't have clear objectives, any road will get you there! The same is true for conducting marketing research. A good place to start is to ask what the managerial problem or question is that a proposed program of research might address. Maddy and Laguë's initial inquiries about starting a telecommunications business in Tanzania had numerous managerial questions to be answered. How attractive is the telephone market in Tanzania? What segments are most attractive? How large is the

Exhibit 7.7

STEPS IN THE MARKETING RESEARCH PROCESS: WHAT CAN GO WRONG?

Steps	What frequently goes wrong?
1. Identify managerial problem and establish research objectives	Management identifies no clear objective, no decision to be made based on the proposed research.
2. Determine data sources (primary or secondary) and types of data and research approaches (qualitative or quantitative) required	Primary data are collected when cheaper and faster secondary data will do. Quantitative data are collected without first collecting qualitative data.
3. Design research: type of study, data collection approach, sample, etc.	These are technical issues best managed by skilled practitioners. Doing these steps poorly can generate misleading or incorrect results.
4. Collect data	Collector bias: hearing what you want to hear.
5. Analyze data	Tabulation errors or incorrect use or interpretation of statistical procedures may mislead the user.
6. Report results to the decision maker	Some users do not really want objective information—they want to prove what they already believe to be true.

market, and how fast is it likely to grow? Is the industry attractive? Who are the key competitors and what competitive advantages might they have and not have if we enter? What telecommunications wants and needs are not well satisfied currently, for which groups of consumers? How likely are consumers to use the system we propose to put in place? How much might they be willing to pay? What incentives would retailers or others need to sell our phone cards or to place our pay phones on their premises? Taking each of these managerial questions, one at a time, and applying appropriate analytical frameworks to each of them—such as macro trend analysis (see Chapter 3), Porter's five forces (Chapter 4), and so on—provides clear guidance for the kind of information the researcher needs. The result is a set of **research objectives** (e.g., determine market size and growth rate; assess supplier power in this industry, and so on) that will drive the research.

Step 2: Determine the Data Sources and Types of Data Required

This step is critical in determining the cost effectiveness and timeliness of the research effort. The researcher must answer two key questions at this stage: Should I gather data from primary or secondary sources? Whichever type of data sources are called for, do I need qualitative or quantitative research to satisfy my research objectives, or both?

Primary or Secondary Sources?   **Primary data** are data collected from individual research subjects using observation, a survey, interviews, or whatever. The data are then gathered and interpreted for the particular research objective at hand. **Secondary data** already exists—on the Internet, in government documents, in the business press, in company files, or wherever. Someone has already done the primary data collection and placed the data where others can access it, whether easily or with difficulty, whether free or at some cost.

KEY OBSERVATION

Which is better—primary or secondary data?

Which is better—primary or secondary data? *If* (and it's an important *if*) a research objective can be met using secondary data, that's usually the best course to follow. Why? First, it's usually quicker to find the data somewhere than to collect information from scratch. Imagine having to collect demographic data about Tanzania without the Tanzanian census! Second, it's usually less costly to simply find existing secondary data than to collect the information as primary data all over again. Third, secondary data are typically based on what people actually *do*, or how they actually *behave*. Surveys, a common form of primary data, are based on what people *say*. The two are not the same, as we saw earlier in the forecasting portion of this chapter.

For Maddy and Laguë, secondary data, if it is available, should answer several of their research questions, such as those on market and industry attractiveness, *if* Tanzania's government has made gathering and reporting such data a priority. Often, the availability and quality of a country's secondary data, from government as well as other sources, correlates closely with its degree of economic development. See Exhibit 7.8 for a list of some commonly used websites for market and industry analysis. Similar sources are available for most countries. To explore consumers' willingness to use the innovative system of pay phones and calling cards that Maddy and Laguë proposed to develop, primary data were necessary. It is unlikely that a study to evaluate the attractiveness of such a system to consumers had already been conducted.

Qualitative or Quantitative Data and Research Approaches?

Where secondary data are to be collected, the researcher needs to decide whether qualitative data, such as that concerning sociocultural trends in Tanzania, or quantitative data, such as the number of households in a particular income group in Dar es Salaam, are required. Most secondary research studies require both qualitative and quantitative data.

If primary data are necessary, a decision must be made about whether to collect that data using qualitative or quantitative research approaches. **Qualitative research** usually involves small samples of subjects and produces information that is not easily quantifiable. Qualitative data may yield deeper insights into consumer behavior than are available from quantitative research. For this reason, qualitative research is often conducted first and used to guide subsequent quantitative research. An important drawback of qualitative research, however, is that its generally small samples may not fairly represent the larger population. Most experienced marketing researchers would say, "*Never generalize* from qualitative research. Always follow up with a quantitative study to test the hunches developed in the qualitative study." Such statements presume, however, that adequate research resources are available to conduct additional studies. Often, and particularly in entrepreneurial settings, such is not the case, and decision makers are forced to rely, albeit tenuously, on small-scale qualitative studies.

KEY OBSERVATION
Never generalize from qualitative research.

Quantitative research collects data that are amenable to statistical analysis, usually from large enough samples so that inferences may be drawn with some confidence to the population from which the subjects in the sample are drawn. The principal benefit of quantitative research lies in its measurement of a population's attitudes toward or likely response to products or marketing programs. Because of their larger sample sizes and quantitative metrics, greater confidence can be placed in quantitative studies, when conducted properly, using appropriate sampling procedures and statistical techniques. We address these issues in more detail in subsequent sections of this chapter.

Qualitative Research Techniques

There are seemingly as many qualitative research techniques as there are stars in the sky.[25] The most common ones, however, are focus groups and interviews of various kinds.[26] A focus group typically consists of 8 to 12 consumers from the marketer's target market brought together at a research facility to discuss a particular marketing problem, such as attitudes toward a proposed new product and various possible features. A skilled moderator conducts the focus group, records the conversation on audio- and/or videotape, and writes a report of the findings. Typically two or

Exhibit 7.8

SOME INFORMATION SOURCES FOR MARKET AND INDUSTRY ANALYSIS

Type of information	Library sources	Internet sources
To find trade associations and trade magazines	*Gale Directory of Publications; Encyclopedia of Associations; UK Trade Association Forum;* European Trade Associations	www.gale.com www.instat.com www.taforum.org www.eurunion.org/infores/business/trade.htm
Information on specific companies	*Hoover's Online Business; Ward's Business Directory;* Dun and *Bradstreet Million Dollar Directory; Moody's Industrial Manual*	www.hoovers.com www.sec.gov/edgarhp.htm www.companylink.com
U.S. demographic and lifestyle data	*Lifestyle Market Analyst*	www.census.gov
Demographic data on a specific region or local trade area in the United States	*Sourcebook of County Demographics; Sourcebook of Zip Code Demographics;* Survey of Buying Power in *Sales and Marketing Management;* Claritas, 1-800-234-5973 (fee)	
International demographics and world trade	*Predicasts F&S Index* United States, Europe and International	www.stat-usa.gov www.odic.gov/cia/publications www.census.gov/ftp/pub/ipc/www/idbnew.html www.i-trade.com www.europa.eu.int/comm/eurostat/ (EU) www.unescap.org/stat/ (Asia)
Macro trends	*Statistical Abstract of the United States; Business Periodicals Index*	www.stat-usa.gov
E-commerce	*Red Herring* magazine	www.thestandard.com www.cyberatlas.com www.ecommercetimes.com www.comscore.com www.emarketer.com
Proprietary providers of research reports		www.forrester.com www.gartner.com www.scarborough.com www.findsvp.com
Market share information	*Market Share Reporter*	
Average financial statements by industry	*Annual Statement Studies,* Risk Management Association, formerly, Robert Morris and Associates	www.rmahq.com/Ann_Studies/asstudies.html

Given the rate of change on the web, some of the above Internet addresses may change, and some print sources may add websites.

Sources: Various web addresses as listed above. A useful guide to these and other sources of data is *Find it Fast: How to Uncover Expert Information on Any Subject—in Print or Online* (New York: HarperCollins, 1997).

KEY OBSERVATION

Focus groups have significant limitations.

more groups are conducted for a single research project. Focus groups have significant limitations: They are subject to data distortion caused by a dominant person in the group, their results are difficult to interpret, and they are neither representative of nor generalizable to a larger population, due to their small sample size and convenience samples. They are a good way, however, to begin a research inquiry or to gather at least some information when research budgets are tight.[27]

Quantitative Research Techniques   In most quantitative research, questionnaires are used that enable the researcher to measure the subjects' responses on quantitative scales. These scales enable the researcher to compare product attributes, the responses of demographically different consumers, and other differences in order to better understand what consumers prefer, how satisfied they are with one product compared to others, and so on. Where statistically significant differences are found, managers can be relatively certain at some known level of confidence that the differences uncovered in the research reflect those actually found in the whole population. Examples of several kinds of quantitative scales commonly used in such research are shown in Exhibit 7.9.

Novice researchers, or those whose budgets are limited, can sometimes obtain useful market knowledge from small-scale research that begins with some qualitative research, perhaps several interviews, and concludes with a quantitative study using measures such as those shown in Exhibit 7.9. Gaining experience with such research, even in a class project setting, provides future managers with some appreciation for the conduct of marketing research and the limitations to its interpretation.

Step 3: Design the Research

Designing secondary research is a simple matter of finding sources of information sufficient to satisfy the research objectives and ensuring that the sources are credible. For primary qualitative research, such as focus groups or interviews, detailed guides are

Exhibit 7.9

SOME COMMONLY USED TYPES OF SCALES FOR QUANTITATIVE MARKET RESEARCH

Type of scale	Description	Example
Semantic Differential Scale	A scale connecting two bipolar words or phrases	How satisfied are you with your provider of cable TV? Not at all satisfied 1 2 3 4 5 6 7 Extremely satisfied
Likert Scale	A statement with which the respondent shows the amount of agreement/disagreement	I am extremely satisfied with my provider of cable TV. Strongly agree 1 2 3 4 5 6 7 Strongly disagree
Quality Rating Scale	Rates some attribute on a scale from "excellent" to "poor"	My cable TV service, overall, is: Poor Fair Good Very Good Excellent

Importance Scale, using semantic differential format	Rates the importance of some attribute	How important are the following criteria to your satisfaction with your cable TV provider?
		
		                                                    Not at all Extremely
		                                                     important important
		    Answers the phone quickly 1 2 3 4 5 6 7
		    Prompt repair service 1 2 3 4 5 6 7
		    Cleans up after installation 1 2 3 4 5 6 7
		    Service never goes dark 1 2 3 4 5 6 7

Intention-to-Buy Scale	Measures how likely the respondent is to buy at some price	How likely are you to sign up for the new InterGalactic Channel for an extra $4.95 per month?
		
		    Definitely _____
		    Probably _____
		    Might or might not _____
		    Probably not _____
		    Definitely not _____

prepared for conducting the research to specify what questions are to be asked. For primary quantitative research, research design is the most technical and most difficult step in conducting the research. The key decisions to be made in primary research design are to determine the data collection method and prepare the research instrument, determine how to contact the participants in the research, and design the sampling plan.

Determine the Data Collection Method and Prepare the Research Instrument

The most common methods of collecting primary data are observation, survey, and experiment. Observation is just that: observing subjects using pay phones in Tanzania, in Maddy and Laguë's case. Typically, a form is prepared on which the observer records what is being observed, perhaps minutes of use and gender of the user, among other things. Many Japanese companies favor the use of observation to better understand not only consumers, but also salespeople and distribution channel members.[28]

Surveys involve writing a questionnaire, which will include questions and either scaled answers (such as those shown in Exhibit 7.9) or spaces for open-ended answers. Demographic information about the respondent is also usually requested to aid in market segmentation and market targeting decisions, which we address in Chapters 8 and 9. Constructing survey questions and formats for the answers is more difficult than one might expect and is beyond the scope of this book, but several sources cited in this chapter, as well as Exhibit 7.9, can help bring the reader up to speed on these tasks.[29]

Experiments are studies in which the researcher manipulates one or more variables, such as price or product features, either within the context of a survey or in a laboratory or field setting, in order to measure the effect of the manipulated variable on the consumer's response. One common use of experiments is to examine the consumer's likelihood to buy a new product at different price points. Different respondents are given different prices for the product, and the researcher tests differences in consumers' likelihood to buy as the price changes. This procedure entails less bias than asking consumers what they would be willing to pay for a product, the typical answer to which is "as little as possible!"

Determine the Contact Method

Once a data collection method is chosen, the researcher must decide how to contact those who will participate in the research. Common choices include face-to-face (perhaps in a shopping mall or a public place), mail, telephone, fax, e-mail, and the Internet. Exhibit 7.10 shows some of the trade-offs among these methods. A significant problem with survey research is that those who choose *not* to participate when asked ("We're eating dinner now, and please don't call back!") may differ from those who *do* participate. This nonresponse bias may distort the results of the research. Response

Exhibit 7.10

PROS AND CONS OF DIFFERENT CONTACT METHODS FOR SURVEY RESEARCH

Method	Response rate	Cost	Timeliness	Nonresponse bias
Face-to-face	High	High	Slow	Low
Mail	Low	Low	Slow	High
Telephone	Moderate	Moderate	Fast	Moderate
Fax	Moderate	Low	Fast	High
E-mail	Low	Low	Fast	High
Internet	Low	Low	Fast	High

rate can also be a problem, since many who are asked to participate will not do so. Response rates for mail surveys generally run about 10 to 15 percent. The other types are better or worse, as shown in Exhibit 7.10. Thus, for a mail survey, 6 to 10 times the number of surveys the researcher hopes to receive must be mailed.

Design the Sampling Plan   Selecting a sample of participants for observational, survey, or experimental research requires that three questions be answered:

1. Who is the population (or universe) from which the sample of **respondents** will be drawn?
2. What sample size is required to provide an acceptable level of confidence?
3. By what method, probability sampling (also called random sampling) or nonprobability sampling (such as convenience sampling), will the sample be selected?

We'll discuss each of these issues briefly.[30] First, the population from which the sample is to be drawn must be clearly specified. Typically, it consists of the target market, defined in demographic or behavioral terms (e.g., users of pay telephones in Tanzania), although excluding current nonusers might not be a good idea for Maddy and Laguë if they hope to expand the market.

Second, the sample must be large enough to provide confidence that statistical data, such as mean responses to survey questions, are *truly* within some narrow-enough range, sometimes called the **margin of error.** In general, the larger the sample size, the smaller the margin of error. If Maddy and Laguë observed only three pay phones in their research, they could not be very confident that the average daily minutes of use at those phones was representative of use for the hundreds of pay phones in Tanzania. A larger sample would give them more confidence. Exhibit 7.11 provides rough approximations of the margin of sampling error associated with different sample sizes.

Third, the idea behind **probability,** or **random, sampling** is that every person in the population has an equal chance of being selected. If **nonprobability samples,** such as **convenience samples,** are used, the sample may be biased. If Maddy and Laguë observe consumers using pay phones in the international departure lounge at the airport in Dar es Salaam, this sample would not reflect usage by the general Tanzanian population. Convenience samples are used quite often for marketing research because true random samples are more difficult and costly to reach. The nonresponse problem makes almost all samples potentially biased in the same way. An astute user should always ask about the sample selection method. If the method is not random, the user should inquire about how the sample was selected to look for any obvious source of bias that might distort the research results.

KEY OBSERVATION

An astute user should always ask about the sample selection method. If the method is not random, the user should inquire about how the sample was selected.

Step 4: Collect the Data

By now, the hardest parts of the research process are complete, though the most time-consuming parts have just begun. The data collection contributes more to overall error than any other step in the process. In some cases, especially where entrepreneurs or marketers conduct marketing research themselves instead of contracting with a third party for data collection, **collector bias** can be a problem. The person collecting the data might, in his or her enthusiasm for the product, bias the respondents so they tell the researcher what they think he or she wants to hear. Errors in face-to-face or telephone surveys include those that derive from nonresponse by some respondents; selection errors by the interviewer (i.e., selecting respondents who are not members of the specified population); the way the interviewer asks the questions; the interviewer's interpretation and recording of answers; and

Exhibit 7.11

MARGIN OF ERROR ASSOCIATED WITH DIFFERENT SAMPLE SIZES

Assume a poll of eligible voters is taken to determine which candidate is in the lead. Suppose the results are that Jones has 45% of the voters in her corner, Smith has 41%, and 14% are undecided. Can we conclude that Jones leads Smith? It depends, in part, on the sample size of the poll.

Sample size	Approximate margin of error for 95% confidence level	Implications for the Jones and Smith race (in which Jones appears to be leading)
100	10 percentage points	Jones has 45% plus or minus 10%, or 35% to 55%.
		Smith has 41% plus or minus 10%, or 31% to 51%.
		Smith could be leading by as much as 51% to 35%.
500	4.5 percentage points	Jones has 45% plus or minus 4.5%, or 40.5% to 49.5%.
		Smith has 41% plus or minus 4.5%, or 36.5% to 45.5%.
		Smith could be leading by as much as 45.5% to 40.5%.
1,000	3 percentage points	Jones has 45% plus or minus 3%, or 42% to °48%.
		Smith has 41% plus or minus 3%, or 38% to 44%.
		Smith could be leading by as much as 44% to 42%.

What will the headlines say? Probably that Jones leads Smith, 45 percent to 41 percent. If the sample size is 1,000, typical in national or statewide political polls, is this a fair conclusion?

Source: Adapted from "What Is a Survey: What Is a Margin of Error?" Copyright 1998 by the American Statistical Association. All rights reserved.

even interviewer cheating. In surveys conducted by fax, e-mail, or over the Internet, an additional problem is that the researcher does not know who actually replied to the survey. The data collection effort can be substantial. To complete 100 surveys in the United Kingdom with randomly selected homes using random digit dialing, several hundred phone numbers will likely be required and 1,000 dialings!

Step 5: Analyze the Data

When the data have been collected, the completed data forms must be processed to yield the information the project was designed to collect. The forms are checked to see that instructions were followed, that the data are complete, and that the data are logical and consistent within each respondent's form. Typically, the data are then entered into computer files, percentages and averages are computed, and comparisons are made between different classes, categories, and groups of respondents. Often, sophisticated statistical analyses are required.

Step 6: Report the Results to the Decision Maker

This is where the rubber meets the road. If the research study began with clearly defined objectives, reporting the results simply returns to those objectives and reports what was found. Where research is carried out without clear objectives, reporting can be difficult, as no clear conclusions may be available. Lots of marketing research money is wasted in some companies because of poorly specified research objectives.

What Users of Marketing Research Should Ask

The research process described in the preceding section makes clear where many of the potential stumbling blocks are in designing and conducting marketing research. The informed and critical user of marketing research should ask the following questions, ideally before implementing the research or if necessary subsequent to its completion, to ensure that the research is unbiased and the results are trustworthy.

1. What are the objectives of the research? Will the data to be collected meet those objectives?
2. Are the data sources appropriate? Is cheaper, faster secondary data used where possible? Is qualitative research planned to ensure that quantitative research, if any, is on target?
3. Are the planned qualitative and/or quantitative research approaches suited to the objectives of the research? Qualitative research is better for deep insights into consumer behavior, while quantitative research is better for measurement of a population's attitudes and likely responses to products or marketing programs.
4. Is the research designed well? Will questionnaire scales permit the measurement necessary to meet the research objectives? Are the questions on a survey or in an interview or focus group unbiased? ("Isn't this a great new product? Do you like it?") Do the contact method and sampling plan entail any known bias? Is the sample size large enough to meet the research objectives?
5. Are the planned analyses appropriate? They should be specified *before* the research is conducted.

Rudimentary Competence: Are We There Yet?

One objective we set at the outset of this chapter was to provide the reader with at least a rudimentary level of competence in designing and carrying out marketing research studies. Entire courses dealing with marketing research are offered in nearly every business school marketing curriculum and half a chapter does little justice to the detail and technical expertise involved in this important craft. Nonetheless, by reading this chapter and a few of the cited reference sources on particular research techniques, the reader should be able to conduct at least some useful research for a class project or even a low-budget entrepreneurial venture. Such research, despite its limitations, will give the reader an experiential base useful in assessing research done by others, and it will surely yield greater insights into the marketing problem than will hunches alone. Given the importance of marketing research in strategic decision making today, we encourage every business student from every business discipline to try his or her hand at it.

In the remaining chapters in this book, we shall return from time to time to the marketing research topic and show how marketing research informs not only market and competitive analysis and customer understanding, but also the design and implementation of marketing programs. In recent years, a wide variety of software applications have been developed to aid marketers in conducting marketing research and applying it and other data to specific marketing problems. In subsequent chapters, we'll point out specific applications for which such **marketing decision support systems** are commonly used. A few software applications used to aid decision making in the marketing research process itself—survey research design, sample selection, and focus group administration—are discussed in Exhibit 7.12. These and other marketing software tools can be extremely useful in helping marketing decision makers—from media buyers to brand managers to retail buyers to sales managers and more—manage their businesses better and more productively through better use of marketing information.

Exhibit 7.12   Software Tools for Marketing Research

As we have seen in this chapter, designing marketing research is a complex task. Several companies have developed software to aid marketing decision makers in designing and conducting survey and other kinds of research. They include Apian Software, Inc., (www.apian.com) and StatPac, Inc., (www.statpac.com), whose software (Survey Pro and StatPac for Windows, respectively) helps the marketing researcher build questionnaires for which the database and data entry screens are automatically programmed, and for which the data analysis is automated. Sensus, a similar application from Sawtooth Technologies (www.sawtooth.com), facilitates the development of surveys to be administered via the Web. The Genysys Sampling System (www.genesys-sampling.com) allows researchers to select samples for survey research down to the Zip code and census tract level. FocusVision Online (www.focusvision.com) permits marketing managers to conduct focus groups in more than 80 cities and watch them via the Internet without leaving their office. SPSS MR (www.spss.com/spssmr) is probably the most widely used program for the analysis of marketing research data. New applications are being developed constantly. The annual technology directory, published each summer in *Marketing News,* is a good place to find such applications.

Source: "Directory of Marketing Technology: Software & Internet Services," *Marketing News,* July 17, 2000. Used by permission of the American Marketing Association.

TAKE-AWAYS

- Every forecast and estimate of market potential is wrong! *Evidence-based* forecasts and estimates, prepared using the tools provided in this chapter, are far more credible—and generally more accurate—than hunches or wild guesses. A menu of evidence-based forecasting approaches is provided in this chapter.

- Forecasts have powerful influence on what companies do, through budgets and other planning procedures. Thus, forecasting merits significant management attention and commitment.

- Superior market knowledge is not only an important source of competitive advantage, but it also results in happier, higher volume, and more loyal customers. Thus, the systematic development of market knowledge is a critically important activity in any organization.

- Much can go wrong in marketing research and often does. Becoming an informed and critical user of marketing research is an essential skill for anyone who seeks to contribute to strategic decision making. Tools for obtaining this skill are presented in this chapter.

Self-diagnostic questions to test your ability to apply the analytical tools and concepts in this chapter to marketing decision making may be found at this book's website at www.mhhe.com/mullins05.

ENDNOTES

1. Information to prepare this section was taken from Anita M. McGahan, *African Communications Group (Condensed)* (Boston: Harvard Business School Publishing, 1999); and Dale O. Coxe, *African Communications Group* (Boston: Harvard Business School Publishing, 1996).

2. Charles Wardell, "High-Performance Budgeting," *Harvard Management Update,* January 1999.

3. Ibid.

4. Peter L. Bernstein and Theodore H. Silbert, "Are Economic Forecasters Worth Listening to," *Harvard Business Review,* July–August 1982.

5. F. William Barnett, "Four Steps to Forecast Total Market Demand," *Harvard Business Review,* July–August 1988.

6. For a more detailed look at forecasting methods, see David M. Georgeoff and Robert G. Murdick, "Manager's Guide to Forecasting," *Harvard Business Review,* January–February 1986; and John C. Chambers, Satinder K. Mullick, and Donald D. Smith, "How to Choose the Right Forecasting Technique," *Harvard Business Review,* July–August 1971.

7. Arthur Schleifer, Jr., *Forecasting with Regression Analysis* (Boston: Harvard Business School Publishing, 1996).

8. See Frank M. Bass, "A New Product Growth Model for Consumer Durables," *Management Science,* January 1969, pp. 215–27; and Trichy V. Krishnan, Frank M. Bass, and V. Kumar, "Impact of a Late Entrant on the Diffusion of a New Product/Service," *Journal of Marketing Research,* May 2000, pp. 269–78.

9. For more on conjoint analysis, see Robert J. Dolan, *Conjoint Analysis: A Manager's Guide* (Boston: Harvard Business School Publishing, 1990).

10. McGahan, *African Communications Group (Condensed).*

11. For more on concept testing, see Robert J. Dolan, *Concept Testing* (Boston: Harvard Business School Publishing, 1990).

12. McGahan, *African Communications Group (Condensed).*

13. Fareena Sultan, *Marketing Research for High Definition Television,* (Boston: Harvard Business School Publishing, 1991).

14. Colin Welch and Ananth Raman, *Merchandising at Nine West Retail Stores* (Boston: Harvard Business School Publishing, 1998).

15. Coxe, *African Communications Group.*

16. A key challenge for manufacturers is to be able to quickly adjust production schedules to adapt to demand that differs from the forecast. To read more about how to enable production to respond quickly in the face of unforeseen changes in demand, see Marshall L. Fisher, Janice H. Hammond, Walter R. Obermeyer, and Ananth Raman, "Making Supply Meet Demand in an Uncertain World," *Harvard Business Review,* May–June 1994.

17. Amos Tversky and Daniel Kahneman, "Judgment under Uncertainty," *Science* 185 (1974), pp. 1124–31.

18. Li and Calantone define market knowledge as "organized and structured information about the market." See Tiger Li and Roger J. Calantone, "The Impact of Market Knowledge Competence on New Product Advantage: Conceptualization and Empirical Examination," *Journal of Marketing,* October 1998, pp. 13–29.

19. Welch and Raman, *Merchandising at Nine West Retail Stores.*

20. "Marketing—Clubbing Together," *Retail Week,* November 8, 2002.

21. For more details see CACI's website at http://www.caci.co.uk/index.html.

22. For more details see Experian UK's website at http://www.experian.co.uk/products/products_targ_prospect.html.

23. For more on data mining and related topics, see Peter Jacobs, "Data Mining: What General Managers Need to Know," *Harvard Management Update,* October 1999; and Jeff Papows, *Enterprise.com: Market Leadership in the Information Age* (Cambridge, MA: Perseus Publishing, 1998).

24. Information in this section comes from the Society of Competitive Intelligence Professionals website at www.scip.org/images/education/ci.htm.

25. For additional qualitative research techniques, see Abbie Griffin, "Obtaining Customer Needs for Product Development," in M. D. Rosenau, ed., *The PDMA Handbook of New Product Development* (New York: John Wiley and Sons, 1996); and Gerald Zaltman, "Rethinking Marketing Research: Putting the People Back In," *Journal of Marketing Research,* November 1997, pp. 424–37.

26. The definitive guide to conducting in-depth interviews is Grant McCracken, *The Long Interview* (Newbury Park, CA: Sage Publications, 1988).

27. The survey research methods section of the American Statistical Association offers useful guides to conducting focus groups and surveys. Downloadable PDF files may be found at www.stat.ncsu.edu/info/srms/srms.html.

28. Malcolm Gladwell, "The Science of Shopping," *New Yorker,* November 4, 1996, pp. 66–67; and Gary Hamel and C. K. Prahalad, "Corporate Imagination and Expeditionary Marketing," *Harvard Business Review,* July–August 1991.

29. Any business school marketing research text, such as Dillon, Madden, and Firtle, *Marketing Research in a Marketing Environment* (Burr Ridge, IL: Irwin/McGraw-Hill, 1993) will have a chapter on questionnaire design. Also see Alreck and Settle, *The Survey Research Process* (Burr Ridge IL: Irwin/McGraw-Hill, 1994).

30. For more on sampling, see the sampling chapter of any business school marketing research text, such as Dillon, Madden, and Firtle, *Marketing Research in a Marketing Environment.*

CHAPTER EIGHT

Market Segmentation and Target Marketing

Blue Ribbon Sports Targets Distance Runners[1]

IT WAS 1964. PHIL KNIGHT, a recent graduate of Stanford's Graduate School of Business and a former University of Oregon runner with a 4:10 personal best in the mile, and the legendary Bill Bowerman, Knight's former track coach at the University of Oregon, were passionate about distance running. They believed that the German-made shoes that most competitive runners wore at the time were too expensive and not designed with *distance* runners' needs in mind. They saw an opportunity to design better running shoes in the United States, have them manufactured in Asia, and sell them in America at prices lower than the German shoes.

The Unique Needs of Distance Runners

Distance runners such as Knight and Bowerman had different footwear needs than other athletes. To become conditioned enough to run a 26-mile marathon or even a one-mile or two-mile race at an intercollegiate track meet, distance runners ran several miles per day and sometimes more than 100 miles in a week. Often, these miles were spent on rough trails, where rocks and other natural obstacles led to ankle sprains and other injuries, or along country roads, where the miles and miles of impact led sometimes to shin splints or even stress fractures of the bones in their

legs and ankles. Bowerman, a lifelong innovator who made shoes in his garage for his runners, believed that distance runners needed lighter and more flexible shoes, not heavy leather or stiff soles. They needed shoes with better lateral stability, to protect against ankle sprains, and more cushioning, to help the runner's body cope with miles and miles of repetitive impact.

The Waffle Revolution

Though real success took several years to materialize, the story of Bowerman's vision of a better shoe for distance runners is now entrepreneurial lore. With his wife's waffle iron and some latex, Bowerman invented the waffle outsole that would ultimately revolutionize the running shoe. The lightweight, yet durable and stable sole set a new standard for shoe performance for distance runners. Knight, the business person and visionary, had written in a class assignment at Stanford a plan for developing a business to sell American-designed, Asian-made shoes to distance runners. Knight and Bowerman each chipped in $500 to form Blue Ribbon Sports and found a Japanese company, Onitsuka Tiger, to manufacture the shoes they designed. For years, wherever there was running going on, Knight could be found selling his shoes out of the back of his station wagon. By 1969, Knight was able to quit his day job as an accountant and devote all of his energies to the growing

Corbis

business, which had grown to 20 employees and several retail outlets.

Launching and Expanding the Nike Brand

In 1972, Blue Ribbon Sports launched its Nike brand at the U.S. Olympic trials after a dispute between Blue Ribbon and Tiger led to a breakup of their relationship. In the 1972 Olympic marathon, four of the top seven finishers wore Nike shoes. By 1974, after 10 years of dogged effort to build the company, the Nike shoe with Bowerman's waffle sole was America's best-selling training shoe, and the Nike brand was on its way to stardom. In 1978, tennis great John McEnroe signed with the company, which had changed its name to Nike, Inc., and tennis shoes became a prominent part of the product line. In 1985, a promising Chicago Bulls basketball rookie named Michael Jordan endorsed a line of Air Jordan shoes and apparel. By 1986, Nike's worldwide sales passed the billion-dollar mark and Nike had become the acknowledged technological leader in the footwear industry.

World Cup 2002

Among Nike's target markets by the turn of the millennium was football—soccer to Americans—the world's most-played sport. With World Cup 2002 scheduled in Korea and Japan, Nike's product developers knew that extreme heat and humidity would call for uniforms that would help players compete at top speed and still keep their body temperature down. Working for two years with the Korean team, Nike developed its new Cool Motion technology, a material with a "two-layer structure designed to maximize thermal comfort and ventilation," said Nike's Creative Product Designer for Football, Craig Buglass. The uniform's inner layer pulled perspiration away from the skin and spread it over a wide area for quick evaporation. Its water-repellent outer layer helped to keep the uniform dry under extreme humidity during intense aerobic activity.

Did the uniforms perform? Korea, never known as a football power, surprised many by winning third place. Their relentless pressure and unending team speed impressed many observers. The high-tech uniforms surely didn't hurt.

Marketing Challenges Addressed in Chapter 8

The example of Nike, Inc.'s, origins and early development vividly points out how a few relatively simple decisions to clearly identify a market segment with unmet or poorly met needs—distance runners—and then develop innovative goods or services that meet the needs of the targeted segment can provide entrée into a market niche and serve as a foundation for subsequent expansion that can revolutionize a market or industry.

What Phil Knight, Bill Bowerman, and the management team they assembled understood so well is that different groups of consumers—different market segments—have different wants and needs, both tangible and intangible, in athletic footwear and in athletic apparel. In virtually any market, if different segments can be clearly identified, specific products with specific marketing programs can be developed to meet both the physical needs of the consumer (e.g., the lateral stability and the extra cushioning that distance runners need in their shoes) as well as the emotional needs that consumers attach to their athletic pursuits (e.g., to feel that they might someday soar through the air and dunk a basketball with the panache of Michael Jordan).

In Chapter 8, we draw on the foundation of market knowledge and customer understanding established in the first seven chapters to introduce what are probably the most important and fundamental tools in the marketer's toolkit: **market segmentation** and **target marketing.** Together with **product positioning,** which we address in Chapter 9, these tools provide the platform on which most effective marketing programs are built. Learning to apply these tools effectively, however, requires addressing several important questions. Why do market segmentation and target marketing make sense? Why not sell the same athletic shoes—or bicycles, airline tickets, beverages, or whatever—to everyone? How can potentially attractive market segments be identified and defined? Finally, how can these segments be prioritized so that the most attractive ones are pursued? Answering these questions should enable an entrepreneur, a venture capital investor in Silicon Valley, or a marketing manager in a multinational firm to decide which market segments should be targeted and which investments should be made.

Why Do Market Segmentation and Target Marketing Make Sense?

Market segmentation is the process by which a market is divided into distinct subsets of customers with similar needs and characteristics that lead them to respond in similar ways to a particular product offering and marketing program. Target marketing requires evaluating the relative attractiveness of various segments (in terms of market potential, growth rate, competitive intensity, and other factors) and the firm's mission and capabilities to deliver what each segment wants, in order to choose which segments it will serve. Product positioning entails designing product offerings and marketing programs that collectively establish an enduring competitive advantage in the target market by creating a unique image, or position, in the customer's mind. Knight and Bowerman founded Blue Ribbon Sports in part because they saw a market segment—distance runners—whose needs were not being fully met. They chose to target this segment because running was growing in popularity and because they had particular knowledge and expertise they could bring to the party. They positioned their innovative shoes as the ones that enhanced the performance of the best runners in the world and, by implication, of anyone else who cared about his or her running.

These three decision processes—market segmentation, target marketing, and positioning— are closely linked and have strong interdependence. All must be well considered and implemented if the firm is to be successful in managing a given product-market relationship. No matter how large the firm, however, its resources are usually limited compared with the number of alternative market segments available for investment. Thus, a firm must make choices. Even in the unusual case where a firm can afford to serve all market segments, it must determine the most appropriate allocation of its marketing effort *across* segments. But are all these analyses and conscious choices about which segments to serve really necessary?

KEY OBSERVATION

Are all these analyses and conscious choices about which segments to serve really necessary?

Most Markets Are Heterogeneous

Because markets are rarely homogeneous in benefits wanted, purchase rates, and price and promotion elasticities, their response rates to products and marketing programs differ. Variation among market segments in product preferences, size and growth in demand, media habits, and competitive structures further affect the differences and response rates. Thus, markets are complex entities that can be defined (segmented) in a variety of ways. The critical issue is to find an appropriate segmentation scheme that will facilitate target marketing, product positioning, and the formulation of successful marketing strategies and programs. By focusing their initial efforts on high-performance distance runners, a clearly defined and very narrow market segment, Knight and Bowerman put themselves in position to design shoes especially well suited to these runners' needs. Their segmentation scheme, arguably, played just as important a role in their early success as did Bowerman's wife's waffle iron!

Today's Market Realities Often Make Segmentation Imperative

Market segmentation has become increasingly important in the development of marketing strategies for several reasons. First, population growth has slowed, and more product-markets are maturing. This sparks more intense competition as firms seek growth via gains in market share (the situation in the automobile industry) as well as in an increase in brand extensions (Starbucks coffee ice cream, Colgate toothbrushes, Visa traveler's checks).

Second, such social and economic forces as expanding disposable incomes, higher educational levels, and more awareness of the world have produced customers with more varied and sophisticated needs, tastes, and lifestyles than ever before. This has led to an outpouring of goods and services that compete with one another for the opportunity of satisfying some group of consumers.

Third, there is an increasingly important trend toward microsegmentation in which extremely small market segments are targeted. For a discussion of how one company built itself into a multimillion-dollar business while serving a very small niche see Exhibit 8.1. This trend has been accelerated in some industries by new technology such as computer-aided design, which has enabled firms to mass-customize many products as diverse as designer jeans and cars.[2] For example, many automobile companies are using a flexible production system that can produce different models on the same production line. This enables the company to produce cars made to order as does General Motors in the United States, which is using its online presence to fine tune its build-to-order process.[3]

Exhibit 8.1   Can Under Armour Become Another Nike?

Kevin Plank did not set out to create a cult around athletic underwear—he simply wanted a comfortable T-shirt to wear under his football pads that would wick moisture away from his skin and protect him from heat exhaustion during practice. After hunting through all the sporting goods shops, Kevin realized that there was not a single product on the market that met his needs. He set out to create one. In March 1996, just before graduation, Kevin had some T-shirts sewn up in Lycra and found that he had solved a common problem for all of his teammates.

Under Armour, the company that was soon born in his grandmother's basement, made its first sale of 200 shirts for $12 apiece to the football team at Georgia Tech. Kevin ended his company's first year with sales of $17,000. Under Armour was marketed by word-of-mouth from happy, satisfied customers, and grew with sales to athletic teams in colleges. The company got its big break due to a product placement in the Oliver Stone football movie *Any Given Sunday*. Buzz from the movie, and a first-time ad in *ESPN Magazine* during the movie premiere, boosted Under Armour sales to $1.35 million in 1999. Under Armour's sales in 2001 drove triple-digit growth in its category and led industry peers at Sporting Goods Business to recognize the company as "Apparel Supplier of the Year." Under Armour posted sales of US$55 million in 2002.

The small underserved market segment that Kevin Plank discovered and his success have not gone unnoticed. Ironically, recent entrants to this market are Nike and Reebok. Kevin Plank's reaction? "I'll never let them see me sweat."

Sources: Company website http://www.underarmour.com; Elaine Shannon, "Tight Skivvies; They're What Everyone's Wearing This Season. Here's Why," *Time*, January 13, 2003, p. A1. © 2003 TIME Inc. Reprinted by permission.

Finally, many marketing organizations have made it easier to implement sharply focused marketing programs by more sharply targeting their own services. For example, many new media have sprung up to appeal to narrow interest groups. In the United Kingdom, these include special interest magazines, such as *Wanderlust* and *Autocar;* radio stations with formats targeted to different demographic groups, such as classical music, rock, country, and jazz, not to mention chat shows of various kinds; and cable TV channels, such as Sky Sport and the Discovery Channel. Also more broad-based magazines, such as *The Economist* and *Hello,* offer advertisers the opportunity to target specific groups of people within their subscription base. An advertiser can target specific regions, cities, or Zip codes, or even selected income groups.

How Are Market Segments Best Defined?

There are many ways of dividing a market into segments. Virtually all the variables discussed in Chapters 5 and 6 can influence customers in their purchases of different goods and services, so all of them can plausibly serve as criteria for segmenting markets. There are three important objectives entailed in the market segmentation process:

- **Identify a homogeneous segment that differs from other segments:** The process should identify one or more relatively homogeneous groups of prospective buyers with regard to their wants and needs and/or their likely responses to differences in the elements of the marketing mix—the 4 Ps (product, price, promotion, and place). For Bowerman and Knight, high-performance distance runners was such a segment. Differences within one market segment should be small compared to differences across various segments (most high-performance distance runners probably have athletic footwear needs that are quite similar to one another, but quite different from, say, the needs of basketball players).

- **Specify criteria that define the segment:** The segmentation criteria should measure or describe the segments clearly enough so that members can be readily identified and accessed, in order for the marketer to know whether a given prospective customer is or is not in the target market and in order to reach the prospective customer with advertising or other marketing communication messages. Knight and Bowerman might have defined their initial target market as being comprised of members of running clubs or distance runners on collegiate track and cross-country teams.

- **Determine segment size and potential:** Finally, the segmentation process should determine the size and market potential of each segment for use in prioritizing which segments to pursue, a topic we address in more detail later in this chapter. Knight and Bowerman could easily ascertain how many such runners there were in Oregon or the western United States, and they probably knew how many pairs of shoes per year the typical distance runner bought, at what average price.

Given these objectives, what kinds of segmentation criteria, or descriptors, are most useful? Marketers divide segmentation descriptors into three major categories for both consumer and organizational markets: **demographic descriptors** (which reflect *who* the target customers are), **geographic descriptors** (*where* they are), and **behavioral descriptors** of various kinds (*how* they behave with regard to their use and/or purchases of a given category of goods or services). We examine each of these categories below.

Demographic Descriptors

While firm demographics (age of firm, size of firm, industry, etc.) are useful in segmenting organizational markets, we usually think of demographics in terms of attributes of

Exhibit 8.2

SOME OF THE MORE COMMONLY USED DEMOGRAPHIC DESCRIPTORS*

Demographic descriptors	Examples of categories
Age	Under 2, 2–5, 6–11, 12–17, 18–24, 25–34, 35–49, 50–64, 65 and over
Sex	Male, female
Household life cycle	Young, single; newly married, no children; youngest child under 6; youngest child 6 or over; older couples with dependent children; older couples without dependent children; older couples retired; older, single
Income	Under $15,000, $15,000–24,999; $25,000–74,999, etc.
Occupation	Professional, manager, clerical, sales, supervisor, blue collar, homemaker, student, unemployed
Education	Some high school, graduated high school, some college, graduated college
Events	Birthdays, graduations, anniversaries, national holidays, sporting events
Race and ethnic origin	Anglo-Saxon, African-American, Italian, Jewish, Scandinavian, Hispanic, Asian

*Others include marital status, home ownership, and presence and age of children.

individual consumers, as shown in Exhibit 8.2. Some examples of demographic descriptors used to segment consumer markets are as follows:

Age: Since mobile phone penetration has reached almost saturation levels in Europe and the United Kingdom, mobile service providers are focusing on the 55–65 and 65-plus segment to improve usage and penetration respectively. Their high disposable incomes and their ability to devote time to new habits is seen as a lucrative market opportunity.[4] At the other end of the demographic scale, Red Bull has built a following among youth worldwide (see Exhibit 8.3).

Sex: In Australia, Toyota launched an online information service aimed at women, recognizing that women make up 50 percent of Toyota's sales and directly influence 8 out of 10 vehicle purchases.[5]

Income: Higher-income households purchase a disproportionate number of cellular phones, expensive cars, and theater tickets. In 2000, Nokia started a wholly owned subsidiary Vertu, to create an ultra-exclusive mobile telephone and services built around the phone, targeting the same customers who buy luxury watches and custom-made cars.[6]

Occupation: The sales of certain kinds of products (e.g., work shoes, automobiles, uniforms, and trade magazines) are tied closely to occupational type. The increase in the number of working women has created needs for specialized goods and services including financial services, business wardrobes, convenience foods, automobiles, and special-interest magazines.

Education: There is a strong positive correlation between the level of education and the purchase of travel, books, magazines, insurance, theater tickets, and photographic equipment.

Race and ethnic origin: More and more companies are targeting these segments via specialized marketing programs. In the United States, car companies have found ways to cater to the needs of the multicultural segment, which is estimated to be 32 percent of the U.S. population in 2010. A distinctive trend that had already emerged by 2002 was the Asian-American's affinity for upscale cars—they accounted for 15 percent of BMW and 9 percent of Mercedes Benz sales.[7]

KEY OBSERVATION

Demographic descriptors are also important in the segmentation of industrial markets.

Demographic descriptors are also important in the segmentation of industrial markets, which are segmented in two stages. The first, *macrosegmentation,* divides the market according to the characteristics of the buying organization using such descriptors as age of firm, firm size, and industry affiliation (SIC code in the United States). The international counterpart of SIC is the trade-category code.

Exhibit 8.3   Red Bull's Targeted Approach Wins across the Globe

Austria-based Red Bull is a company with one product, an energy drink containing the amino-acid taurine. While working for Unilever, Dietrich Mateschitz traveled often to Asia, where he tried syrups that Asian businessmen drank to revitalize. His experience there led him to spot a market opportunity, and after modifying the drink to appeal to Western palates, he launched Red Bull in 1987. Its signature, a slim, silver-colored, 8.3 ounce can, has been an enormous hit with its target youth segment across the globe. For the year 2001, Red Bull had sales of $51 million in the United States alone and captured 70 percent of the energy-drink market worldwide.

From Stanford University on California's West Coast to the beaches of Australia and Thailand, Red Bull has managed to maintain its hip, cool image, with virtually no mass-market advertising. It has instead opted for a grass-roots campaign. "In terms of attracting new customers and enhancing consumer loyalty, Red Bull has a more effective branding campaign than Coke or Pepsi," said Nancy F. Koehn, professor of business administration at Harvard Business School and author of *Brand New: How Entrepreneurs Earned Consumers' Trust from Wedgwood to Dell.** Red Bull used Collegiate Brand Managers to promote the drink via free samples handed out at student parties. The company also organized extreme sports events, for example cliff diving in Hawaii or skateboarding in San Francisco reinforcing the brand's extreme, on-the-edge image.

The beverage industry giants were taking note. Coke ran a stealth marketing campaign, where Coke was packaged in a slim can, reminiscent of Red Bull's packaging, and offered to customers in hip, trendy bars and clubs in Manhattan and New York City.

Source: Jill Bruss, "Alternatively Speaking: Alternative Beverages Keep the Industry Abuzz with New Products (Category Focus), *Beverage Industry* 1, November 2002.

*Nancy F. Koehn, *Brand New: How Entrepreneurs Earned Consumers' Trust from Wedgwood to Dell* (Boston: Harvard Business School Press, 2001).

The second stage, *microsegmentation,* groups customers by the characteristics of the individuals who influence the purchasing decision—for instance, age, sex, and position within the organization. International markets are segmented in a similar hierarchical fashion, starting with countries, followed by groups of individuals or buying organizations.

Geographic Descriptors

Different locations vary in their sales potential, growth rates, customer needs, cultures, climates, service needs, and competitive structures, as well as purchase rates for a variety of goods. For example, more pickup trucks are sold in the southwest United States, more vans in the Northeast, and more high-priced imports in the West. More and more advertisers are taking advantage of geographic media buys, and Uni-Marts, Inc., a convenience store operator of over 400 stores, focuses on small towns and rural areas, thereby avoiding big competitors. In the first 25 years of its history, it never recorded a loss.[8]

Geographic segmentation is used in both consumer and organizational markets and is particularly important in retailing and many services businesses, where customers are unwilling to travel very far to obtain the goods or services they require. Thus, one way to segment retail markets is by distance or driving time from a particular location. The area included within such a geographically defined region is called a **trade area.**

Geodemographic Descriptors

Many segmentation schemes involve *both* demographic and geographic factors. Thus, retailers usually want to know something about the people who live within, say, a two-mile or five-mile radius of their proposed new store. Neiman Marcus, the upscale department store, might target one demographic group within a given trade area, and Wal-Mart, a discounter, might target another. Claritas (www.claritas.com) and other sources offer low-cost reports based on census data that show the demographic profile of the population residing within any given radius of a particular street corner or shopping center location in the United States. These reports are useful in assessing the size and market potential of a market segment defined by a particular trade area. Geodemographics also attempts to predict consumer behavior by making demographic, psychographic, and consumer information available at the block and Zip code or postcode levels. Claritas's PRIZM service classifies all U.S. households into 62 demographically and behaviorally distinct clusters, each of which, in turn, is assigned to one of 15 social groups.[9] Claritas offers similar datasets for France and elsewhere.[10]

Behavioral Descriptors

There is no limit to the number of insightful ways successful marketers have segmented markets in behavioral terms. Knight and Bowerman originally targeted high-performance distance runners. Specialized and Gary Fisher target bicyclists who wish to ride on single-track trails or back-country terrain. Europe's EasyJet airline originally targeted leisure travelers. Gatorade's original target market consisted of athletes who needed to replenish water and salts lost through perspiration. This simple segmentation scheme created a whole new category of "sports beverages," which grew to include entries from Coke (Powerade) and Pepsi (All Sport), though Gatorade still dominates the category with an 80 percent market share. This onetime niche market has grown into a $2.2 billion market in the United States alone.[11]

These examples all demonstrate the power of highly specific behavioral descriptors in defining sharply focused market segments, based not on *who* the target consumers are or *where* they live, but based on what they *do*. In virtually every consumer and organizational market there are probably segments like these just waiting to be identified and targeted by insightful marketers. Behavioral descriptors can take many forms, including those based on consumer needs; on more general behavioral patterns, including lifestyle or social class; and, in organizational markets, on the structure of firms' purchasing activities and the types of buying situations they encounter.

Consumer Needs   Customer needs are expressed in **benefits sought** from a particular product or service. Different individual customers have different needs and thus attach different degrees of importance to the benefits offered by different products. In the end, the product that provides the best bundle of benefits—given the customer's particular needs—is most likely to be purchased.

Since purchasing is a problem-solving process, consumers evaluate product or brand alternatives on the basis of desired characteristics and how valuable each characteristic is to the consumer—**choice criteria.** Marketers can define segments according to these different choice criteria in terms of the presence or absence of certain characteristics and the importance attached to each. Firms typically single out a limited number of benefit segments to target. Thus, for example, different automobile manufacturers have emphasized different benefits over the years, such as Volvo's safety (presence of side-door airbags), reliability, and high mileage versus Jaguar's styling, quickness, and status.

In organizational markets, customers consider relevant benefits that include product performance in different use situations. For example, Cray computers are bought because they meet the high-speed computational requirements of a small group of customers such as governments, universities, and research labs. Other considerations in the purchase of industrial products/services include on-time delivery, credit terms, economy, spare parts availability, and training.

Product-Related Behavioral Descriptors

In addition to highly specific behavioral descriptors such as those just discussed, there are more general product-related descriptors as well. They include product usage, loyalty, purchase predisposition, and purchase influence, all of which can be used to segment both consumer and industrial markets. **Product usage** is important because in many markets a small proportion of potential customers makes a high percentage of all purchases. In organizational markets, the customers are better known, and heavy users (often called *key accounts*) are easier to identify.

Market segmentation based on sources of **purchase influence** for the product category is relevant for both consumer and organizational markets. Many products used by various family members are purchased by the wife, but joint husband–wife decisions are becoming more common. Children's products, prescription drugs, and gifts are clearly influenced by a variety of individuals. In organizational markets, several individuals or units with varying degrees of influence participate in the buying center.

Lifestyle

Segmentation by lifestyle, or psychographics, segments markets on the basis of consumers' activities, interest, and opinions. From such information it is possible to infer what types of products and services appeal to a particular group, as well as how best to communicate with individuals in the group. For example, Goodyear Tire and Rubber and Ogilvy and Mather (an advertising agency), working separately, have developed several classifications for global lifestyle segments. The Goodyear effort consists of six groups—the prestige buyer, the comfortable conservative, the value shopper, the pretender, the trusting patron, and the bargain hunter. Ogilvy and Mather proposes 10 global segments based on lifestyle characteristics—basic needs, fairer deal, traditional family life, conventional family life, look-at-me, somebody better, real conservatism, young optimist, visible achiever, and socially aware.[12]

Stanford Research Institute (SRI) has created a U.S. segmentation service (called VALS 2), which builds on the concept of self-orientation and resources for the individual. *Self-orientation* is based on how consumers pursue and acquire products and services that provide satisfaction and shape their identities. In doing so, they are motivated by the orientations of principle, status, and action. Principle-oriented consumers are motivated by abstract and idealized criteria, while status-oriented consumers shop for products that demonstrate the consumer's success. Action-oriented consumers are guided by the need for social or physical activity, variety, and risk taking.

Resources include all of the psychological, physical, demographic, and material means consumers have to draw on. They include education, income, self-confidence, health, eagerness to buy, intelligence, and energy level—on a continuum from minimal to abundant.

Based on these two dimensions, VALS 2 defines eight segments that exhibit distinctive behavior and decision making—actualizers, fulfillers, achievers, experiencers, believers, strivers, makers, and strugglers. Claritas and similar commercial organizations identify each of the respondents as to their VALS type, thereby permitting a cross-classification of VALS type with the product usage and personal information collected by such companies. Thus, users can determine what each VALS segment bought, what their media habits are, and similar data. The VALS system has been further developed in Europe and Asia.[13] Those interested in the VALS segmentation scheme can complete a short survey on the VALS website (log onto http://future.sri.com/VALS/VALSindex.shtml) and discover the VALS segment to which they belong.

Social Class Every society has its status groupings based largely on similarities in income, education, and occupation.[14] Because researchers have long documented the values of the various classes, it is possible to infer certain behavior concerning a given product. For example, the middle classes tend to place more value on education, family activities, cleanliness, and being up-to-date than do lower-class families. In the international field, one has to be careful in using social class as a segmentation variable since the differences among classes can become blurred, as they do in the Scandinavian countries.[15] In America many of the criteria used to define class status seem to some to be no longer applicable as the nation becomes increasingly fragmented into dozens of distinct subcultures, each with its own unique tastes and ambitions. As noted earlier, Claritas, Inc., has identified 62 distinct classes in the United States, each with its own set of beliefs and aspirations.[16]

Organizational or Firm Behavioral Descriptors   Purchasing structure and buying situation segmentation descriptors are unique to organizational markets. **Purchasing structure** is the degree to which the purchasing activity is centralized. In such a structure the buyer is likely to consider all transactions with a given supplier on a global basis, to emphasize cost savings, and to minimize risk. In a decentralized situation, the buyer is apt to be more sensitive to the user's need, to emphasize product quality and fast delivery, and to be less cost-conscious.

The **buying situation** descriptor includes three distinct types of situations: straight rebuy, a recurring situation handled on a routine basis; modified rebuy, which occurs when some element, such as price or delivery schedules, has changed in a client–supplier relationship; and a new buying situation, which may require the gathering of considerable information and an evaluation of alternative suppliers.

Innovative Segmentation: A Key to Marketing Breakthroughs

At the beginning of this section, we identified three objectives of the market segmentation process.

- Identify a homogeneous segment that differs from others.
- Specify criteria that define the segment.
- Determine segment size and potential.

KEY OBSERVATION

Insightful and innovative market segmentation is often the key to marketing breakthroughs.

Effective marketers, such as the creators of Nike athletic shoes and Red Bull energy drinks, know that meeting these objectives through insightful and innovative market segmentation is often the key to marketing breakthroughs. Often, combinations of different descriptors are used to more precisely target an attractive segment: perhaps some behavioral dimension together with a carefully defined demographic profile within some geographic region. Generally, it is useful to know the demographic profile of the target market to be pursued, even if the driving force behind the segmentation scheme is geographical and/or behavioral in nature. Understanding the demographic profile of a target market enables the marketer to better choose targeted advertising media or other marketing communication vehicles, as we shall see in Chapter 14.

As is the case for many kinds of marketing decision making, various computer-based decision support systems have been developed to aid marketers as they wrestle with market segmentation decisions. Some of the more widely used systems are identified in Exhibit 8.4.

As several examples in this section have shown, at the foundation of many a marketing breakthrough one often finds an insightful segmentation scheme that is sharply focused in

---

Exhibit 8.4   Software Tools for Market Segmentation

Two broad kinds of software applications are used in segmenting markets. Data mining applications enable the marketer to examine a customer database to identify patterns of variables that predict which customers buy or don't buy, as well as how much they buy. CART® and MARS™ from Salford Systems, Inc. (www.salford-systems.com) are two such applications. Various tools for analyzing the demographic makeup of a proposed target market are also available. National Decision Systems (www.ends.com) is one such supplier. Various analytical procedures in SPSS MR or other statistical software packages are also useful for market segmentation purposes.

Source: "Directory of Marketing Technology: Software & Internet Services," *Marketing News*, July 17, 2000. Used by permission of the American Marketing Association.

KEY OBSERVATION

At the foundation of many a marketing breakthrough one often finds an insightful segmentation scheme that is sharply focused in a behavioral way.

a *behavioral* way. Marketers with superior market knowledge are probably more likely to generate the insights necessary to define market segments in these innovative and meaningful ways. Knight and Bowerman, as runners themselves, had the necessary market knowledge to see how distance runners, as a market segment, were underserved. Their insight, together with the development of innovative products and the creation of effective marketing programs, led the growth of the athletic footwear market, as consumers purchased different shoes for their different athletic pursuits, and ultimately revolutionized the athletic footwear industry.

Choosing Attractive Market Segments: A Five-Step Process

KEY OBSERVATION

Most firms no longer aim a single product and marketing program at the mass market.

Most firms no longer aim a single product and marketing program at the mass market. Instead, they break that market into homogeneous segments on the basis of meaningful differences in the benefits sought by different groups of customers. Then they tailor products and marketing programs to the particular desires and idiosyncrasies of each segment. *But not all segments represent equally attractive opportunities for the firm.* To prioritize target segments by their potential, marketers must evaluate their future attractiveness and their firm's strengths and capabilities relative to the segments' needs and competitive situations.

Within an established firm, rather than allowing each business unit or product manager to develop an approach to evaluate the potential of alternative market segments, it is often better to apply a common analytical framework across segments. With this approach, managers can compare the future potential of different segments using the same set of criteria and then prioritize them to decide which segments to target and how resources and marketing efforts should be allocated. One useful analytical framework managers or entrepreneurs can use for this purpose is the **market-attractiveness/competitive-position matrix.** As we saw in Chapter 2, managers use such models at the corporate level to allocate resources across businesses, or at the business-unit level to assign resources across product-markets. We are concerned with the second application here.

Exhibit 8.5 outlines the steps involved in developing a market-attractiveness/ competitive-position matrix for analyzing current and potential target markets. Underlying such a matrix is the notion that managers can judge the attractiveness of a market (its profit potential) by examining market, competitive, and environmental factors that may influence profitability. Similarly, they can estimate the strength of the firm's competitive position by

Exhibit 8.5

STEPS IN CONSTRUCTING A MARKET-ATTRACTIVENESS/COMPETITIVE-POSITION MATRIX FOR EVALUATING POTENTIAL TARGET MARKETS

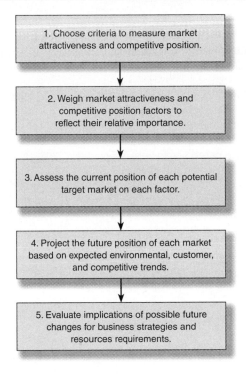

looking at the firm's capabilities or shortcomings *relative* to the needs of the market and the competencies of likely competitors. By combining the results of these analyses with other considerations, including risk, the mission of the firm, and ethical issues (see Ethical Perspective 8.1), conclusions about which markets and market segments should be pursued can be reached.

The first steps in developing a market-attractiveness/competitive-position matrix, then, are to identify the most relevant variables for evaluating alternative market segments and the firm's competitive position regarding them and to weight each variable in importance. Note, too, that Exhibit 8.4 suggests conducting a forecast of future changes in market attractiveness or competitive position in addition to, but separately from, an assessment of the current situation. This reflects the fact that a decision to target a particular segment is a strategic choice that the firm will have to live with for some time.

Step 1: Select Market-Attractiveness and Competitive-Position Factors

An evaluation of the attractiveness of a particular market or market segment and of the strength of the firm's current or potential competitive position in it builds naturally on the kind of opportunity analysis developed in Chapters 3 through 7. Managers can assess

KEY OBSERVATION

Both market and competitive perspectives are necessary.

both dimensions on the basis of information obtained from analyses of the environment, industry and competitive situation, market potential estimates, and customer needs. To make these assessments, they need to

ETHICAL PERSPECTIVE 8.1
Ethical Issues in Target Marketing

Over the years, marketing managers have confronted a number of ethical problems relating to the selection of target markets. Problems can arise from targeting consumers who because of their *inclusion* in the targeted group may be influenced to make decisions thought by some to be not in their best interest. Some would argue that advertising $150 sneakers to inner-city teenagers is ethically dubious, others that the advertising of snack foods and soft drinks to children is questionable. In other cases, *exclusion* issues are raised because the firm's marketing efforts do not include a particular group.

In the area of inclusion issues, advertisers often resort to undesirable stereotypes in an effort to simplify advertising messages. These include sex-role, race, or age stereotypes. Thus, the portrayal of women as sex objects (bikini-clad models in beer ads) or, in general, subordinate to male authority figures is thought by many to be dehumanizing and offensive. Reverse sexism with men shown as sex objects has also been on the increase to the dismay of some groups.

For exclusion issues, the concern is not only that certain groups are deprived of products and services but also that they may pay more for those they do receive. There is considerable evidence to support the latter claim. A survey in New York City found that food prices are highest in neighborhoods that can least afford them. Low-income shoppers (family of four) paid 8.8 percent more for their groceries—$350 per year. Further, inner-city stores were on average poorly stocked, had inferior foodstuffs, and offered poorer service.

Companies often face the ethical problem of whether they may exclude certain groups they would rather not serve. For example, insurance companies want only low-risk policyholders, credit-card companies only low-risk cardholders, and hospitals only patients with insurance.

Source: N. Craig Smith and John A. Quelch, *Ethics in Marketing* (Burr Ridge, IL: Richard D. Irwin, 1993), p. 183–95. Reprinted with permission from The McGraw-Hill Companies; Felix M. Freedman, "The Poor Pay More for Food in New York, Survey Finds," *The Wall Street Journal,* April 15, 1991. Copyright 1991 by Dow Jones & Co., Inc. Reprinted by permission of Dow Jones & Co., Inc. via the Copyright Clearance Center.

establish criteria, such as those shown in Exhibit 8.6, against which prospective markets or market segments can be evaluated. Both market and competitive perspectives are necessary.

Market-Attractiveness Factors   As we showed in Chapter 3, assessing the attractiveness of markets or market segments involves determining the market's size and growth rate and assessing various trends—demographic, sociocultural, economic, political/legal, technological, and physical—that influence demand in that market. An even more critical factor in determining whether to *enter* a new market or market segment, however, is the degree to which *unmet customer needs*, or needs that are currently not being well served, can be identified. In the absence of unmet or underserved needs, it is likely to be difficult to win customer loyalty, regardless of how large the market or how fast it is growing. "Me-too" products often face difficult going in today's highly competitive markets.

Competitive-Position Factors   As we showed in Chapter 4, understanding the attractiveness of the industry in which one competes is also important. Entering a segment that would place the firm in an unattractive industry or increase its exposure in an unattractive industry in which it already competes may not be wise. Of more immediate and salient concern, however, is the degree to which the firm's proposed product entry into the new market or segment will be sufficiently *differentiated* from competitors, given the critical success factors and product life-cycle conditions already prevalent in the category. Similarly, decision makers need to know whether their firm has or will be able to acquire the resources it will take—human, financial, and otherwise—to effectively compete in the new segment. Simply put, most new goods or services need to be either better from a consumer point of view or cheaper than those they hope to replace. Entering a new market or market segment without a source of competitive advantage is a trap.

Exhibit 8.6

FACTORS UNDERLYING MARKET ATTRACTIVENESS AND COMPETITIVE POSITION

Market-attractiveness factors

Customer needs and behavior

- Are there unmet or underserved needs we can satisfy?

Market or market segment size and growth rate

- Market potential in units, revenue, number of prospective customers

- Growth rate in units, revenue, number of prospective customers

- Might the target segment constitute a platform for later expansion into related segments in the market as a whole?

Macro trends: Are they favorable, on balance?

- Demographic
- Sociocultural
- Economic
- Political/legal
- Technological
- Physical

Competitive-position factors

Opportunity for competitive advantage

- Can we differentiate?
- Can we perform against critical success factors?
- Stage of competing products in product life cycle: Is the timing right?

Firm and competitor capabilities and resources

- Management strength and depth
- Financial and functional resources: marketing, distribution, manufacturing, R&D, etc.
- Brand image
- Relative market share

Attractiveness of industry in which we would compete

- Threat of new entrants
- Threat of substitutes
- Buyer power
- Supplier power
- Competitive rivalry
- Industry capacity
- Driving forces: are they favorable, on balance?

Step 2: Weight Each Factor

Next, a numerical weight is assigned to each factor to indicate its relative importance in the overall assessment. Weights that Phil Knight and Bill Bowerman might have assigned to the major factors in Exhibit 8.6 are shown in Exhibit 8.7. Some users would rate each bullet point in Exhibit 8.6 independently, assigning a weight to each one.

Step 3: Rate Segments on Each Factor, Plot Results on Matrices

This step requires that evidence—typically both qualitative and quantitative data—be collected to objectively assess each of the criteria identified in Step 1. For Blue Ribbon Sports in 1964, the assessment of the various factors might have looked such as those shown in Exhibit 8.7. While more detailed evidence than we discuss here should have been, and no doubt was, gathered, Knight and Bowerman might have reached the following conclusions:

Market-attractiveness factors

- Unmet customer needs for lateral stability, cushioning, and lightweight shoe have been identified. Score: 10.
- The distance runner segment is quite small, though growing, but it might lead to other segments in the future. Score: 7.
- Macro trends are largely favorable: fitness is "in," number of people in demographic groups likely to run is growing, global trade is increasing. Score: 8.

Exhibit 8.7

ASSESSING THE DISTANCE RUNNER MARKET SEGMENT IN 1964

	Weight	Rating (0–10 Scale)	Total
Market-attractiveness factors			
Customer needs and behavior: unmet needs?	.5	10	5.0
Segment size and growth rate	.3	7	2.1
Macro trends	.2	8	1.6
Total: Market attractiveness	**1.0**		**8.7**
Competitive-position factors			
Opportunity for competitive advantage	.6	7	4.2
Capabilities and resources	.2	5	1.0
Industry attractiveness	.2	7	1.4
Total: Competitive position	**1.0**		**6.6**

Competitive-position factors

- Opportunity for competitive advantage is somewhat favorable; proposed shoes will be differentiated, but shoe category seems mature, and Blue Ribbon Sports, as a new firm, has no track record. Score: 7.

- Resources are extremely limited, though management knows runners and distance running; Bowerman has strong reputation. Score: 5.

- Five forces are largely favorable (low buyer and supplier power, little threat of substitutes, low rivalry among existing firms), driving forces attractive. Score: 7.

Mere armchair judgments about each criterion are not very credible and run the risk of taking the manager or entrepreneur into a market segment that may turn out not to be viable. It is especially important to undertake a detailed analysis of key competitors, especially with regard to their objectives, strategy, resources, and marketing programs, as was discussed in Chapters 4 and 7. Similarly, compelling evidence that a proposed entry into a new segment will satisfy some previously unmet needs, and do so in a way that can bring about sustainable competitive advantage, is called for. Both qualitative and quantitative marketing research results, as described in Chapter 7, are typically used for this purpose. Once these assessments have been made, the weighted results can be plotted on a **market-attractiveness/competitive-position matrix** like the one shown in Exhibit 8.8.

KEY OBSERVATION

Compelling evidence that a proposed entry into a new segment will satisfy some previously unmet needs, and do so in a way that can bring about sustainable competitive advantage, is called for.

Step 4: Project Future Position for Each Segment

Forecasting a market's future is more difficult than assessing its current state. Managers or entrepreneurs should first determine how the market's attractiveness is likely to change over the next three to five years. The starting point for this assessment is to consider possible shifts in customer needs and behavior, the entry or exit of competitors, and changes in their strategies. Managers must also address several broader issues, such as possible changes in product or process technology, shifts in the economic climate, the impact of social or political trends, and shifts in the bargaining power or vertical integration of customers.

Exhibit 8.8

MARKET-ATTRACTIVENESS/COMPETITIVE-POSITION MATRIX

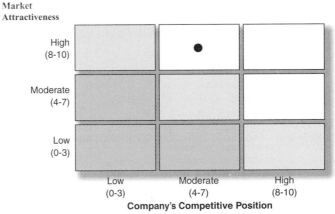

● = Market attractiveness and competitive position of distance runners segment

Managers must next determine how the business's competitive position in the market is likely to change, assuming that it responds effectively to projected environmental changes but the firm does not undertake any initiatives requiring a change in basic strategy. The expected changes in both market attractiveness and competitive position can then be plotted on the matrix in the form of a vector (arrow) that reflects the direction and magnitude of the expected changes. Anticipating such changes may be critically important in today's Internet age.

Step 5: Choose Segments to Target, Allocate Resources

Managers should consider a market to be a desirable target only if it is strongly positive on at least one of the two dimensions of market attractiveness and potential competitive position and at least moderately positive on the other. In Exhibit 8.8 this includes markets positioned in any of the three cells in the upper right-hand corner of the matrix. However, a business may decide to enter a market that currently falls into one of the middle cells under these conditions: (1) managers believe that the market's attractiveness or their competitive strength is likely to improve over the next few years; (2) they see such markets as stepping-stones to entering larger, more attractive markets in the future; or (3) shared costs or synergies are present, thereby benefiting another entry.

The market-attractiveness/competitive position matrix offers general guidance for strategic objectives and allocation of resources for segments currently targeted and suggests which new segments to enter. Thus, it can also be useful, especially under changing market conditions, for assessing markets or market segments from which to withdraw or to which allocations of resources, financial and otherwise, might be reduced. Exhibit 8.9 summarizes generic guidelines for strategic objectives and resource allocations for markets in each of the matrix cells.

Exhibit 8.9

IMPLICATIONS OF ALTERNATIVE POSITIONS WITHIN THE MARKET-ATTRACTIVENESS/COMPETITIVE-POSITION MATRIX FOR TARGET MARKET SELECTION, STRATEGIC OBJECTIVES, AND RESOURCE ALLOCATION

| | COMPETITIVE POSITION | | |
	Weak	Medium	Strong
High	Build selectively: • Specialize around limited strengths • Seek ways to overcome weaknesses • Withdraw if indications of sustainable growth are lacking	DESIRABLE POTENTIAL TARGET Invest to build: • Challenge for leadership • Build selectively on strengths • Reinforce vulnerable areas	DESIRABLE POTENTIAL TARGET Protect position: • Invest to grow at maximum digestible rate • Concentrate on maintaining strength
Medium	Limited expansion or harvest: • Look for ways to expand without high risk; otherwise, minimize investment and focus operations	Manage for earnings: • Protect existing strengths • Invest to improve position only in areas where risk is low	DESIRABLE POTENTIAL TARGET Build selectively: • Emphasize profitability by increasing productivity • Build up ability to counter competition
Low	Divest: • Sell when possible to maximize cash value • Meantime, cut fixed costs and avoid further investment	Manage for earnings: • Protect position • Minimize investment	Protect and refocus: • Defend strengths • Seek ways to increase current earnings without speeding market's decline

(Left axis label: MARKET ATTRACTIVENESS)

Source: Adapted from George S. Day, *Analysis for Strategic Market Decisions* (St. Paul: West, 1986, p. 204. © 1986. Reprinted with permission of South-Western, a division of Thomson Learning; www.thomsonrights.com; S. J. Robonson, R. E. Hitchens, and D. P. Wade, The Directional Policy Matrix: Tool for Strategic Planning," *Long Range Planning* 11 (1978), pp. 8–15. © 1987 with permission from Elsevier.

Different Targeting Strategies Suit Different Opportunities

Most successful entrepreneurial ventures target narrowly defined market segments at the outset, as did Phil Knight and Bill Bowerman, for two reasons. One, doing so puts the nascent firm in position to achieve early success in a market segment that it understands particularly well. Second, such a strategy conserves precious resources, both financial and otherwise. But segmenting the market into narrow niches and then choosing one niche to target is not always the best strategy, particularly for established firms having substantial resources. Three common targeting strategies are **niche-market, mass-market,** and **growth-market** strategies.

KEY OBSERVATION

Most successful entrepreneurial ventures target narrowly defined market segments.

Niche-Market Strategy

This strategy involves serving one or more segments that, while not the largest, consist of substantial numbers of customers seeking somewhat-specialized benefits from a product or service. Such a strategy is designed to avoid direct competition with larger firms that are pursuing the bigger segments. For example, overall coffee consumption is down in some countries, but the sales of gourmet coffees in coffee bars such as Starbucks have boomed in recent years.

Mass-Market Strategy

A business can pursue a mass-market strategy in two ways. First, it can ignore any segment differences and design a single product-and-marketing program that will appeal to the largest number of consumers. The primary object of this strategy is to capture sufficient volume to gain economies of scale and a cost advantage. This strategy requires substantial resources, including production capacity, and good mass-marketing capabilities. Consequently, it is favored by larger companies or business units or by those whose parent corporation provides substantial support. For example, when Honda first entered the American and European motorcycle markets, it targeted the high-volume segment consisting of buyers of low-displacement, low-priced cycles. Honda subsequently used the sales volume and scale economies it achieved in that mass-market segment to help it expand into smaller, more-specialized segments of the market.

A second approach to the mass market is to design separate products and marketing programs for the differing segments. This is often called **differentiated marketing.** For example, Marriott and Europe's Accor do this with their various hotel chains. Although such a strategy can generate more sales than an undifferentiated strategy, it also increases costs in product design, manufacturing, inventory, and marketing, especially promotion.

Growth-Market Strategy

Businesses pursuing a growth-market strategy often target one or more fast-growth segments, even though they may not currently be very large. It is a strategy often favored by smaller competitors to avoid direct confrontations with larger firms while building volume and share. Most venture capital firms invest only in firms pursuing growth-market strategies, because doing so is the only way they can earn the 30 percent to 60 percent annual rates of return on investment that they seek for portfolio companies. Such a strategy usually requires strong R&D and marketing capabilities to identify and develop products appealing to newly emerging user segments, plus the resources to finance rapid growth. The problem, however, is that fast growth, if sustained, attracts large competitors. This happened to Apple when IBM entered the personal computer business. The goal of the early entrant is to have developed an enduring competitive position via its products, service, distribution, and costs by the time competitors enter.

KEY OBSERVATION

The traditional approach to global market segmentation has been to view a country or a group of countries as a single segment comprising all consumers. This approach is seriously flawed.

Global Market Segmentation

The traditional approach to global market segmentation has been to view a country or a group of countries as a single segment comprising all consumers. This approach is seriously flawed because it relies on country variables rather than consumer behavior, assumes homogeneity *within* the country segment, and ignores the possibility of the existence of homogeneous groups of consumers *across* country segments.[17]

More and more companies are approaching global market segmentation by attempting to identify consumers with similar needs and wants reflected in their behavior in the marketplace in a range of countries. This intercountry segmentation enables a company to develop reasonably standardized programs requiring little change across local markets, thereby resulting in scale economies. Star TV's launch of a Pan-Asian satellite television service broadcasting throughout Asia in English and Chinese is an example of such a strategy.[18]

There are many reasons—beyond mere ambitions to grow—why companies expand internationally. Some companies go international to defend their home position against global competitors who are constantly looking for vulnerability. For example, Caterpillar, through a joint venture with Mitsubishi Heavy Industries, has for the past 30 years made a substantial investment in Japan to deny its Japanese competitor, Komatsu, strength at home, thereby taking away its profit sanctuary. Had Cat not been successful in doing so, Komatsu would have been able to compete more aggressively with Cat, not only in the United States but also in other major world markets.[19]

Another reason a firm may go overseas and target a specific country is to service customers who are also engaging in global expansion. In recent years Japanese automobile companies that have created U.S. manufacturing facilities have encouraged some of their parts suppliers to do the same. Firms also enter overseas markets to earn foreign exchange and, in some cases, are subsidized by their governments to do so.

In general, with the exception of these strategic special circumstances, the selection of overseas target markets follows essentially the same patterns as for domestic markets, although given the magnitude of economic, social, and political change in the world today, companies are paying considerably more attention to political risk.

TAKE-AWAYS

- Marketers and entrepreneurs who find new and insightful ways to segment mature markets often uncover opportunities for uncontested market entry and rapid growth.

- Sharply focused target marketing enables marketers to differentiate from mass-market leaders by giving consumers in a narrowly defined market segment what they want.

- Focused market entry strategies conserve resources and facilitate early success.

- The five-step procedure provided in this chapter identifies segments having the highest potential.

- The market-attractiveness/competitive-position matrix is a useful analytical framework for deciding which markets or market segments to enter and from which to withdraw.

Self-diagnostic questions to test your ability to apply the analytical tools and concepts in this chapter to marketing decision making may be found at this book's website at www.mhhe.com/mullins05.

ENDNOTES

1. Information to prepare this section was taken from the Nike, Inc., website at www.nikebiz.com/story/chrono.shtml; www.nikebiz.com/story/b_knight.shtml; www.nikebiz.com/story/n_bowerman.shtml; and http://www.nike.com/nikebiz/news/pressrelease.jhtml?year=2002& month=02&letter=h.

2. Joseph Pine II, Bart Victor, and Andrew C. Boynton, in the article "Making Mass Customization Work," *Harvard Business Review*, September–October 1993, pp. 108–19, discuss some of the problems involved in the implementation of a highly segmented, customized strategy.

3. David Welch, "Q&A with e-GM's Mark Hogan: Build-to-Order Is Still the End Game . . . It Takes Out a Lot of the Cost," *BusinessWeek Online,* March 26, 2001.

4. NMA WIRELESS—Silver texters," *New Media Age,* November 28, 2002, p. 35.

5. "Service for Women," *North West News,* October 10, 2001, p. 20.

6. Mark Levine, "The $19,450 Phone," *New York Times,* December 1, 2002, p. 66.

7. Jean Halliday, "Sector Survey: Pinning Down the Numbers: Automakers Attempt to Quantify Their Share of the Market," *Advertising Age,* December 2, 2002, p. 50.

8. Mora Somassundarm, "Uni-Marts Inc.'s Small Town Strategy for Convenience Stores Is Paying Off," *The Wall Street Journal,* November 20, 1995, p. B5A; Tom Dochat, "Uni-Marts Ponders Options," *Harrisburg Patriot,* November 5, 2002, p. D02.

9. Jon Goss, "We Know Who You Are and We Know Where You Live: The Instrumental Rationality of Geodemographics," *Economic Geography* 71, no. 2 (1995), p. 171.

10. JeanMarc Pichery, "Iris Opens Eyes to Geotargeting," *Precision Marketing,* September 27, 2002, p. 9.

11. Michael Arndt, "Quaker Oat is Thirsty for Even More Gatorade Hits," *www.businessweek.com/bwdaily/dnflash/feb2000/nf202c.htm,* February 2, 2000.

12. Salah S. Hassan and Lea P. Kataris, "Identification of Global Consumer Segments: A Behavioral Framework," *Journal of International Consumer Marketing* 3, no. 2 (1991), p. 16.

13. From information provided by Stanford Research Institute.

14. The relative weight of these vary across countries. In China, for example, more weight is given to occupation and education, whereas Western countries emphasize residence, income, and family background. See John D. Daniels and Lee H. Radebaugh, *International Dimensions of Contemporary International Business* (Boston: PWS-Kent, 1993), p. 136.

15. Simon Majaro, "International Marketing—the Major Issues" in *The Marketing Book,* Michael J. Baker, ed. (Oxford, England: Butterworth-Heinemann, 1992), p. 430.

16. Ned Glascock, "People Profilers," *The News & Observer,* December 6, 2000.

17. Hassan and Kataris, "Identification of Global Consumer Segments," p. 16.

18. Henry Laurence, Michael Y. Yoshino, and Peter Williamson, *STAR TV (A)* (Boston: Harvard Business School Publishing, 1994).

19. Douglas Lamont, *Winning Worldwide* (Burr Ridge, IL: Business One Irwin, 1991), pp. 59–69.

CHAPTER NINE

Differentiation and Positioning

Repositioning French Wine[1]

IN THE MID-1990S, FRENCH winemakers launched a three-year campaign in America with the objective of repositioning French wine. Traditionally these wines had been positioned as upscale—something you drink when you're dining at an elegant restaurant with a French cuisine. In an effort to broaden the appeal of their wines, French vintners were "trying to make Americans as comfortable with fumé blanc as they are with a Bud."[2] The campaign stressed that French wines can be accessible and affordable; there are plenty of such wines between $5 and $15.

Only about 12 percent of American consumers drink wine regularly. To broaden the market the industry had to appeal to more people, especially younger people. One wine marketer says the industry has only itself to blame for creating an image problem.

> For the last 20 years, the wine industry has put up huge barriers to entry. We made people choose red or white, then pick which varietal, and then which vineyard. They had to smell it and swirl it to see if it had a good mouth feel . . . The wine industry has this elitist and sophisticated image that doesn't fit with today's casual society.[3]

The campaign included consumer print ads, retail promotions, and a new website. One ad showed a group of young people enjoying some "vin rouge" as they barbecue. The headline reads, "Sizzling things happen in the 'oui' hours," which is a play on the campaign's theme, "Say yes to wines from France." The print media schedule included ads in *The Wine Spectator* and in such general interest magazines as *The New Yorker, Vanity Fair,* and *In Style.*

Retail outlets were targeted in an effort to teach retailers about French wines and encourage them to use the free in-store merchandising materials. These include self-talkers, case cards, gift bags, and guidebooks.

The winemakers' group also had a pocket guide to French wines that consumers could request through an 800 number or through the group's website. The latter included information on 40 brands of French wines complete with pictures and prices. Other sections provided data on France's grape-growing regions and how to link wines and foods. Users could even access help in pronouncing "souilly-fuisse."

The campaign generated a strong response. In its first year alone, about 10,000 calls to the toll-free number were received along with 40,000 hits on the website. And despite exchange rate changes that made the import of French wines more expensive, overall sales in America increased.

Marketing Challenges Addressed in Chapter 9

As the campaign launched by the French winemakers illustrates, the success of a product offered to a given target market depends on how well it is positioned within that market

segment—that is, how well it performs *relative to* competitive offerings and to the needs of the target audience. The campaign targeted younger consumers and included advertising, in-store promotions, and a new website. Early results suggested at least some success in stimulating members of the target group to seek out lower-priced French wines because of their quality and their ability to enhance the enjoyment of an informal event. **Positioning** (or repositioning, in the case of French wines) refers to both the place a product or brand occupies in customers' minds relative to their needs and competing products or brands and to the marketer's decision making intended to create such a position. Thus, the positioning notion comprises both competitive *and* customer need considerations.

Positioning is basically concerned with differentiation. Ries and Trout, who popularized the concept of positioning, view it as a creative undertaking whereby an existing brand in an overcrowded marketplace of similar brands can be given a distinctive position in the minds of targeted prospects. While their concept was concerned with an existing brand, it is equally applicable for new products.[4] While typically thought of in relation to the marketing of consumer goods, it has equal value for industrial goods and for services, which require essentially the same procedure as consumer goods.[5] Because services are characterized by their intangibility, perishability, consumer participation in their delivery, and the simultaneous nature of their production and consumption, they are—when compared with products—more difficult for consumers to understand, to compare with competing products, to predict in terms of their performance, and, therefore, more difficult for marketers to position successfully.

In Chapter 9, we take the final step in preparing the foundation on which effective marketing programs are based. Drawing on decisions made about target markets, as discussed in Chapter 8, we address the critical question, "How should a business position its product offering—whether goods or services—so customers in the target market perceive the offering as providing the benefits they seek, thereby giving the product an advantage over current and potential future competitors?" As we shall see, the positioning decision is a strategic one, with implications not only for how the firm's goods or services should be designed, but also for developing the other elements of the marketing strategy. Pricing decisions, promotion decisions, and decisions about how the product is to be distributed all follow from, and contribute to the effectiveness of, the positioning of the product in its competitive space. Thus, the material in this chapter provides a foundation for virtually all of the decision making that follows in the balance of this book.

Differentiation: One Key to Customer Preference and Competitive Advantage

Why do customers prefer one product over another? In today's highly competitive markets, consumers have numerous options. They can choose from dozens of best-selling novels to take along on an upcoming vacation. They can buy the novel they choose from an online merchant such as Amazon.com, from large chain booksellers such as Barnes and Noble in the United States, Waterstones in the United Kingdom, or their online counterparts, from book clubs, from a local bookstore, or in some cases from their nearby supermarket or mass merchant. They can even borrow the book at their local library and not buy it at all! Whether it's goods such as books or services such as libraries, consumers make choices such as these nearly every day. In most cases, consumers or organizational customers choose what they buy for one of two reasons: what they choose is *better*, in some sense, or *cheaper*. In either case, the good or service they choose is, in some way, almost always *different* from others they could have chosen.

Differentiation is a powerful theme in developing business strategies, as well as in marketing. As Michael Porter points out, "A company can outperform its rivals only if it can establish a difference that it can preserve. It must deliver greater value to customers or create comparable value at a lower cost, or both."[6] Most of the time, differentiation is why people buy. They buy the latest John Grisham novel because they know it will be a page-turner, different from the last Grisham they read, and hard to put down. They buy it from Amazon.com because they know Amazon's selection is enormous, and its one-click ordering system takes only a minute. Or they buy it from the megastore because it's fun to browse there or from their local bookseller because they feel good about supporting their local merchants. They buy it at the supermarket because it's convenient. All these book-selling strategies are different, and they appeal to different consumers (i.e., different market segments) at different points in time, for different book-buying purposes. If these strategies did not vary, consumers would have no reason to use some of them, and they would buy their books where they were cheapest or most convenient, though even in such a case, the cheaper pricing or greater convenience would still constitute differences.

KEY OBSERVATION

Differentiation is why people buy.

Differentiation in Business Strategies

Michael Porter's classic book on competitive advantage identified three generic strategies: cost leadership, differentiation, and focus, as shown in Exhibit 9.1.[7] These strategies, which differ in the scope of the target market and market needs they serve (broad or narrow competitive scope) and on whether they base their competitive advantage on low cost (lower prices to the customer for equivalent products) or differentiation (products that are superior on some important dimensions) represent distinctly different ways in which companies can compete for the minds and wallets of customers in their target markets. Porter argues that the worst strategy is to be "stuck in the middle," to be neither different nor lower in cost

Exhibit 9.1

GENERIC COMPETITIVE STRATEGIES

		COMPETITIVE ADVANTAGE	
		Lower Cost	Differentiation
Competitive Scope	Broad Target	**Cost Leadership Strategy**	**Differentiation Strategy**
	Narrow Target	**Focus Strategy (Cost-Based)**	**Focus Strategy (Differentiation-Based)**

Source: Adapted with the permission of The Free Press, a Division of Simon & Schuster Adult Publishing Group, from *Competitive Advantage: Creating and Sustaining Superior Performance* by Michael Porter. Copyright © 1985, 1998 by Michael E. Porter. All rights reserved.

than one's competitors. Companies in such a position offer customers little reason not to take their business elsewhere. But customers don't really buy strategies. They buy specific goods and services and effective execution: on-time delivery, proper installation, responsive customer service, and so on. Thus, strategy is implemented at the product market level, where differentiation lies at the heart of positioning.

Differentiation among Goods and Services

As we saw in the previous chapter, customers in one market segment have wants and needs that differ in some way from those of customers in other segments. Positioning allows the marketer to take advantage of and be responsive to such differences and position particular goods and services so as to better meet the needs of consumers in one or more of these segments. These differences are often physical. Nike's original waffle sole was such a difference, as we saw in Chapter 8. But differences can also be perceptual, as with Nike's later products that benefited from endorsements by John McEnroe, Michael Jordan, and other famous athletes. Creating *both* physical and perceptual differences, using all the elements of the marketing mix—product, pricing, promotion, and distribution decisions—is what effective positioning seeks to accomplish.

KEY OBSERVATION

Creating both physical and perceptual differences is what effective positioning seeks to accomplish.

Physical Positioning

One way to assess the current position of a product offering relative to competitors is on the basis of how the various offerings compare on some set of objective physical characteristics. For example, an article in *The Wall Street Journal* discussed the introduction of XC90, Volvo's first entry in the very profitable sports utility vehicle (SUV) segment in the United States. It compared the XC90 with models from the competing luxury brands, BMW, Mercedes-Benz, Acura, and Ford. It compared the models on engine/horsepower, weight, towing capacity, mileage, and price (see Exhibit 9.2).[8] In many cases a physical positioning

Exhibit 9.2

2003 VOLVO XC90 VS. OTHER ALL-WHEEL-DRIVE SUVS

Make/Model	Base Price (USD)	Engine/Horsepower	Weight (pounds)	Towing Capacity (pounds)	EPA Mileage (City/Highway)
Volvo XC90 2.5T AWD	$35,100	5-cyl./208	4,450	5,000	18/24
BMW X5 3.0	39,500	6-cyl./225	4,533	6,000	15/20
Mercedes-Benz ML350	36,950	V6/232	4,819	5,000	15/18
Acura MDX	35,700	V7/260	4,420	4,500	17/23
Ford Explorer	34,785	V6/210	4,434	5,380	15/20

Source: "Drive Buys/Volvo XC90 An SUV More Safe Than Sporty," by Jonathan Welsh. Copyright 2002 by Dow Jones & Co., Inc. Reprinted by permission of Dow Jones & Co., Inc. via the Copyright Clearance Center.

analysis can provide useful information to a marketing manager, particularly in the early stages of identifying and designing new product offerings.

Despite being based primarily on technical rather than on market data, physical comparisons can be an essential step in undertaking a positioning analysis. This is especially true with the competitive offerings of many industrial goods and services, which buyers typically evaluate largely on the basis of such characteristics. In addition, it contributes to a better marketing/R&D interface by determining key physical product characteristics; helps define the structure of competition by revealing the degree to which the various brands compete with one another; and may indicate the presence of meaningful product gaps (the lack of products having certain desired physical characteristics), which, in turn, may reveal opportunities for a new product entry.

Limitations of Physical Positioning

A simple comparison of only the physical dimensions of alternative offerings usually does *not* provide a complete picture of relative positions because, as we noted earlier, positioning ultimately occurs in customers' minds. Even though a product's physical characteristics, package, brand name, price, and ancillary services can be designed to achieve a particular position in the market, customers may attach less importance to some of these characteristics than, or perceive them differently from, what the firm expects. Also, customers' attitudes toward a product are often based on social or psychological attributes not amenable to objective comparison, such as perceptions of the product's aesthetic appeal, sportiness, or status image (for example, in the United States, French wine has traditionally been thought of as very expensive or as an accompaniment to French food). Consequently, **perceptual positioning analysis**—whether aimed at discovering opportunities for new product entries or evaluating and adjusting the position of a current offering—is critically important.

KEY OBSERVATION

A simple comparison of only the physical dimensions of alternative offerings usually does not *provide a complete picture of relative positions.*

Perceptual Positioning

Consumers often know very little about the essential physical attributes of many products, especially household products, and even if they did, they would not understand the physical attributes well enough to use them as a basis for choosing between competitive offerings. (For the major differences between physical and perceptual product positioning analyses, see Exhibit 9.3.) Many consumers do not want to be bothered about a product's physical characteristics because they are not buying these physical properties but rather the benefits they provide. While the physical properties of a product certainly influence the benefits provided, a consumer can typically evaluate a product better on the basis of what it *does* than what it *is*. Thus, for example, a headache remedy may be judged on how quickly it brings relief, a toothpaste on the freshness of breath provided, a beer on its taste, and a vehicle on how comfortably it rides.

The evaluation of many products is subjective because it is influenced by factors other than physical properties, including the way products are presented, our past experiences with them, and the opinions of others. Thus, physically similar products may be perceived as being different because of different histories, names, and advertising campaigns. For example, some people will pay considerably more for Bayer aspirin than for an unadvertised private label even though they are essentially the same product.

Exhibit 9.3

COMPARISON OF PHYSICAL AND PERCEPTUAL POSITIONING ANALYSES

Physical positioning	Perceptual positioning
• Technical orientation	• Consumer orientation
• Physical characteristics	• Perceptual attributes
• Objective measures	• Perceptual measures
• Data readily available	• Need for marketing research
• Physical brand properties	• Perceptual brand positions and positioning intensities
• Large number of dimensions	• Limited number of dimensions
• Represents impact of product specs and price	• Represents impact of product specs and communication
• Direct R&D implications	• R&D implications need to be interpreted

Levers Marketers Can Use to Establish Positioning

Customers or prospective customers perceive physical as well as other differences between goods or services within a product category, of course. Marketing decision makers seeking to win a particular position in customers' minds will seek to endow their product with various kinds of attributes, which may be categorized as follows:

- *Simple physically based attributes.* These are directly related to a single physical dimension such as price, quality, power, or size. While there is a direct correspondence between a physical dimension and a perceptual attribute, an analysis of consumers' perception of products on these attributes may unveil phenomena of interest to a marketing strategy. For instance, two cars with estimated gasoline mileage of 23.2 and 25.8 miles per gallon may be perceived as having similar gasoline consumption.

- *Complex physically based attributes.* Because of the presence of a large number of physical characteristics, consumers may use composite attributes to evaluate competitive offerings. The development of such summary indicators is usually subjective because of the relative importance attached to different cues. Examples of composite attributes are the speed of a computer system, roominess of a car, and a product's or service's being user friendly.

- *Essentially abstract attributes.* Although these perceptual attributes are influenced by physical characteristics, they are not related to them in any direct way. Examples include the sexiness of a perfume, quality of a French wine, and prestige of a car. All of these attributes are highly subjective and difficult to relate to physical characteristics other than by experience.

The importance of perceptual attributes with their subjective component varies across consumers and product classes. Thus, it can be argued that consumers familiar with a given product class are apt to rely more on physical characteristics and less on perceptual attributes than consumers who are less familiar with that product class. It can also be argued that while perceptual product positioning is essential for nondurable consumer goods, such is not the case for consumer durables (such as sport utility vehicles) and many industrial goods.

KEY OBSERVATION

Perceptual attributes must be considered in positioning most products.

Even though there is considerable truth in these statements, perceptual attributes must be considered in positioning most products. One reason is the growing similarity of the physical characteristics of more and more products. This increases the importance of other, largely subjective dimensions. Consider, for example, whether Nike's Air Jordan basketball shoes would have sold as well without basketball ace Michael Jordan's endorsement and his presence in their ads.

Preparing the Foundation for Marketing Strategies: The Positioning Process

Positioning a new product in customers' minds or repositioning a current product involves a series of steps, as outlined in Exhibit 9.4. These steps are applicable to goods and services, in domestic or international markets, and to new or existing products. This is not to suggest that the determinant product attributes and the perceptions of consumers of the various competitive offerings will remain constant across countries or other market segments; rather, they are likely to vary with most products. After managers have selected a relevant

Exhibit 9.4

STEPS IN THE POSITIONING PROCESS

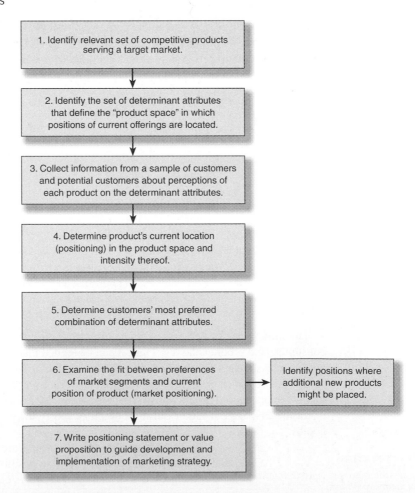

set of competing offerings serving a target market (Step 1), they must identify a set of critical or determinant product attributes important to customers in that target market (Step 2).

Step 3 involves collecting information from a sample of customers about their perceptions of the various offerings, and in Step 4 researchers analyze this information to determine the product's current position in customers' minds and the intensity thereof (Does it occupy a dominant position?), as well as those of competitors.

Managers then ascertain the customers' most preferred combinations of determinant attributes, which requires the collection of further data (Step 5). This allows an examination of the fit between the preferences of a given target segment of customers and the current positions of competitive offerings (Step 6). And finally, in Step 7, managers write a concise statement that communicates the positioning decision they have reached.

A discussion of these steps in the positioning process takes up the remainder of this chapter.

Step 1: Identify a Relevant Set of Competitive Products

Positioning analyses are useful at many levels: company, business unit, product category, and specific product line or brand. At the company or business-unit level, such analyses are useful to determine how an entire company or business unit is positioned relative to its competitors. The results of such analyses are sometimes displayed graphically by plotting competing companies or businesses in their respective quadrants of the generic strategies grid shown in Exhibit 9.1. Larger or smaller dots or circles are used to indicate relative sizes of competing firms.

At the product category level, the analysis examines customers' perceptions about types of products they might consider as substitutes to satisfy the same basic need. Suppose, for example, a company is considering introducing a new instant breakfast drink. The new product would have to compete with other breakfast foods, such as bacon and eggs, breakfast cereals, and even fast-food drive-throughs. To understand the new product's position in the market, a marketer could obtain customer perceptions of the new product concept relative to likely substitute products on various critical determinant attributes, as we describe in Steps 3 and 4 of the positioning process (see Exhibit 9.4).

Once competitors introduce several brands into the category, a positioning analysis at the product or brand level can be helpful to better understand how various brands appeal to customers, to position proposed new products or brands or reposition current ones, and to identify where new competitive opportunities might be found.

KEY OBSERVATION

Marketers who omit important substitute products or potential competitors risk being blindsided by unforeseen competition.

At whichever level the positioning analysis is to be done, the analyst's choice of competing products (or product categories or firms) is critical. Marketers who omit important substitute products or potential competitors risk being blindsided by unforeseen competition.

Step 2: Identify Determinant Attributes

Positioning can be based on a variety of attributes—some in the form of surrogates that imply desirable features or benefits as a positioning base. Some common bases are the following.[9]

- **Features** are often used in physical product positioning and, hence, with industrial products. An example of its use with a consumer good is U.S. high-end home appliance maker

Jenn-Air's claim, "This is the quietest dishwasher made in America." Amazon.com has a unique "1-click®" ordering system.

- **Benefits,** like features are directly related to a product. Examples here include Volvo's emphasis on safety and durability and Norelco's promising a "close and comfortable shave."

- **Parentage** includes who makes it (bottled by a French vintner; "At Fidelity, you're not just buying a fund, a stock, or a bond—you're buying a better way to manage it") and prior products ("Buying a car is like getting married. It's a good idea to know the family first," followed by a picture of the ancestors of the Mercedes-Benz S class model).

- **Manufacturing process** is often the subject of a firm's positioning efforts. An example is Jaeger-LeCoultre's statement about its watches—"We know it's perfect, but we take another 1,000 hours just to be sure."

- **Ingredients** as a positioning concept is illustrated by some clothing manufacturers' saying their sports shirts are made only of pure cotton.

- **Endorsements** are of two types—those by experts ("Discover why over 5,000 American doctors and medical professionals prescribe this Swedish mattress"—Tempor-Pedic) and those via emulation as with Michael Jordan using Nike shoes.

- **Comparison** with a competitor's product is common ("Tests prove Pedigree is more nutritious than IAMS, costs less than IAMS, and tastes great, too"—Pedigree Mealtime pet food).

- **Proenvironment** positioning seeks to portray a company as a good citizen ("Because we recycle over 100 million plastic bottles a year, landfills can be filled with other things, like land, for instance"—Phillips Petroleum, now part of Conoco Phillips).

- **Price/quality** is used in cases such as Wal-Mart successful positioning itself as the lowest-price seller of quality household products.

Theoretically, consumers can use many attributes to evaluate products or brands, but the number actually influencing a consumer's choice is typically small, partly because consumers can consider only attributes of which they are aware. The more variables used in positioning a given product, the greater the chance of confusion and even disbelief on the part of the consumer. The positioning effort must be kept as simple as possible and complexity should be avoided at all costs.

In using one or more attributes as the basis of a brand's positioning effort, it is important to recognize that the importance attached to these attributes often varies. For example, while the brands of soap or shampoo provided by a hotel may be an attribute that some consumers use in evaluating hotels, most are unlikely to attach much importance to it when deciding which hotel chain to patronize. Even an important attribute may not greatly influence a consumer's preference if all the alternative brands are perceived to be about equal on that dimension. Deposit safety is an important attribute to consider when choosing a bank, but most consumers perceive all banks to be about equally safe. Consequently, deposit safety is not a **determinant attribute:** It does not play a major role in helping customers to differentiate among the alternatives and to determine which bank they prefer.

Marketers should rely primarily on determinant attributes in defining the product space in a positioning analysis. The question is, "How can a marketer find out which product dimensions are determinant attributes?" Doing so typically requires conducting some kind of marketing research, using the marketing research process described in the previous chapter. This brings us to Step 3.

Step 3: Collect Data about Customers' Perceptions for Products in the Competitive Set

Having identified a set of competing products, the marketer needs to know what attributes are determinant for the target market and the product category under consideration. He or she also needs to know how different products in the competitive set are viewed on these attributes. Typically this market knowledge is developed by first conducting qualitative research, perhaps interviews or focus groups, to learn which attributes are determinant. Then quantitative research follows, perhaps a survey of consumers about their perceptions, to gather data on how competing products score on these attributes. Later in this chapter, we discuss several statistical and analytical tools that are useful in this portion of the positioning process.

Step 4: Analyze the Current Positions of Products in the Competitive Set

Whether the positioning process is directed at a new product not yet introduced or repositioning one that already exists, it is important to develop a clear understanding of the positioning of the products that have been determined to be in the competitive set (see Step 1). A useful tool for doing so is the **positioning grid,** also called a **perceptual map.**[10] The positioning grid provides a visual representation of the positions of various products or brand in the competitive set in terms of (typically) two determinant attributes. Where more than two attributes are to be considered in a positioning analysis, multidimensional grids, or multiple grids, are produced. But not all products or brands exist in the minds of most consumers.

A brand that is not known by a consumer cannot, by definition, occupy a position in that consumer's mind. Often the awareness set for a given product class is 3 or fewer brands even though the number of available brands is greater than 20. Thus, many if not most brands have little or no position in the minds of many consumers. For example, in the last 10 or so years, more than 200 new soft drinks have been introduced, most of which were not noticed or remembered by consumers. An example of a brand with a strong positioning is BMW and its powerful cars as the "Ultimate Driving Machine." Determining the attributes on which the product's positioning will be based is a key outcome of the positioning process and a driver of the marketing communication strategy, as well as the marketing strategy overall, that will ultimately be developed. Without clear guidance about the intended position of the product, advertising agencies, salesforces, and others charged with building the awareness and recognition of the product in the marketplace will be ill-equipped to do this important job.

Building a Positioning Grid   An example of what can be done with data gathered in Step 3 is found in Exhibit 9.5, which shows the results obtained from a study done by Babson College that portrays how a sample of consumers positioned a number of women's clothing retailers in the Washington, D.C., area.[11] Respondents rated the various stores on the two determinant attributes of value and fashionability. Some stores, such as Nordstrom and Kmart, occupy relatively distant positions from one another, indicating that consumers see them as very different. Other stores occupy positions comparable to one another (Neiman Marcus, Saks) and thus are considered relatively alike, meaning the intensity of competition between these stores is likely to be considerably greater than for those that occupy widely divergent positions.

Exhibit 9.5

PERCEPTUAL MAP OF WOMEN'S CLOTHING RETAILERS IN WASHINGTON, D.C.

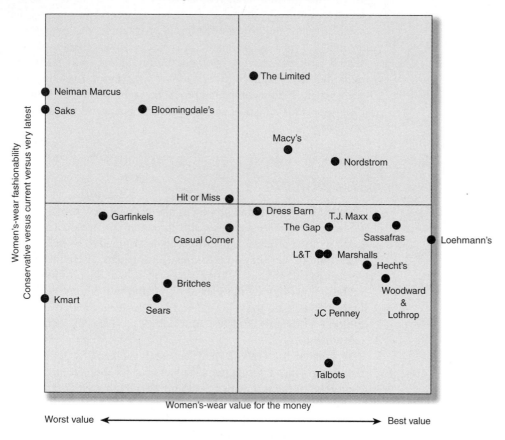

Source: Adapted from Douglas Tigert and Stephen Arnold, "Nordstrom: How Good Are They?" *Babson College Retailing Research Reports,* September 1990, as shown in Michael Levy and Barton A. Weitz, *Retailing Management* (Burr Ridge, IL: Richard D. Irwin, 1992), p. 205. Used by permission.

The store positioning shown in Exhibit 9.5 also provides useful information about possible opportunities for the launching of a new store or the repositioning of an existing one. Positioning for a new store could be done by examining the positioning map for empty spaces (competitive gaps) where no existing store is currently located. There is such a gap in the upper right quadrant of the "value/fashionability" map in Exhibit 9.5. This gap may represent an opportunity for developing a new entry or repositioning an old one that is perceived to offer greater fashionability than Nordstrom at a lower price. Of course, such gaps may exist simply because a particular position is either (1) impossible for any brand to attain because of technical constraints or (2) undesirable since there are few prospective customers for a brand with that set of attributes.

Marketing Opportunities to Gain a Distinct Position   In situations where one or a limited number of brands dominate a product class (or type) in the minds of consumers, the main opportunity for competitors generally lies in obtaining a profitable position within a market segment *not* dominated by a leading brand. Competing head-on against the leaders on the basis of attributes appropriated by larger competitors is not likely to be effective.

A better option is to concentrate on an attribute prized by members of a given market segment. Thus in the United States, Ford, having targeted women and young families, positioned its new Windstar minivan primarily on the basis of safety and cargo space (the most of any minivan). Introduced in the spring of 1994, Windstar was contesting the Dodge Caravan for the top-selling minivan spot a year later.[12]

Constraints Imposed by an Intense Position   Although marketers should seek a distinctive and intense position for their brands, attaining such a position imposes constraints on future strategies. If shifts in the market environment cause customers to reduce the importance they attach to a current determinant attribute, marketers may have difficulty repositioning a brand with an intensely perceived position on that attribute. This is the problem we discussed earlier facing the French wine industry since its wines traditionally have been perceived as upscale—expensive—and to be served with elegant food. Repositioning carries with it the threat of alienating part or all of the product's current users regardless of success with its newly targeted group. Success in its repositioning efforts may well ensure losing its current group of users.

Another concern is the dilution of an existing intense position as a result of consolidation. For example, British Leyland was formed through a series of mergers involving a number of British car manufacturers. For years, the company did not have a clear identity because it was new and manufactured a variety of brands, including Rover, Triumph, and Austin-Morris. Most Europeans had difficulty recalling spontaneously any British car manufacturer since once-strong brand names such as Austin and Morris had lost their identity and meaning. Since Leyland's 1994 acquisition by BMW and the reintroduction of the Mini Cooper, the brand's weak positioning may change.[13]

Another danger associated with an intensely positioned brand is the temptation to overexploit that position by using the brand name on line extensions and new products. The danger here is that the new products may not fit the original positioning and the brand's strong image is diluted. For example, in the late 1990s, the Holiday Inn Group offered travelers the choice of staying in Holiday Inn, Holiday Inn Express, Holiday Inn Select, or Holiday Inn Garden Court, each of which was at a different price point and service offering.[14]

Limitations of Product Positioning Analysis   The analysis depicted in Exhibit 9.5 is usually referred to as *product positioning* because it indicates how alternative products or brands are positioned relative to one another in customers' minds. The problem with this analysis, though, is that it does not tell the marketer which positions are most appealing to customers.[15] Thus, there is no way to determine if there is a market for a new brand or store that might locate in an "open" position or whether the customers in other market segments prefer brands or stores with different attributes and positions. To solve such problems it is necessary to measure customers' preferences and locate them in the product space along with their perceptions of the positions of existing brands. This is called a **market positioning analysis.** We deal with this issue in Step 5.

Step 5: Determine Customers' Most Preferred Combination of Attributes

There are several ways analysts can measure customer preferences and include them in a positioning analysis. For instance, survey respondents can be asked to think of the ideal product or brand within a product category—a hypothetical brand possessing the perfect combination of attributes (from the customer's viewpoint). Respondents could then rate their ideal product and existing products on a number of attributes. An alternative approach is to ask respondents not only to judge the degree of similarity among pairs of existing brands but also to indicate their degree of preference for each. In either case, the analyst, using the appropriate statistical techniques, can locate the respondents' ideal points relative to the positions of the various existing brands on the product space map.

Another method of assessing customers' preferences and trade-offs among them is a statistical technique called conjoint analysis.[16] Customers are surveyed and asked their preferences among various real or hypothetical product configurations, each with attributes that are systematically varied. By analyzing the resulting data, the marketer can learn which of several attributes are more important than the others. These results can then be used in positioning analyses such as those described here.

Whichever approach is used, the results will look something like Exhibit 9.6, which shows a hypothetical cluster of ideal points for one segment of women's-clothing consumers. As a group, this segment would seem to prefer Nordstrom over any other women's clothing retailer on the map.

There are, however, several reasons not all customers in this segment are likely to prefer Nordstrom. First, the ideal points of some customers are actually closer to Macy's than Nordstrom. Second, customers whose ideal point is equidistant between the two stores may be relatively indifferent in their choice of which store to patronize. And finally, customers sometimes may patronize stores somewhat further away from their ideal—particularly when buying low-involvement, nondurable goods or services—to assess the qualities of new stores, to reassess older stores from time to time, or just for the sake of variety.

Using price as one dimension of a positioning grid, or as a key dimension on which a product is positioned, is typically not very useful unless price is a key driver of the marketing strategy. This is the case for two reasons. First, price is easily imitable by competitors. Unless the firm has a clear cost advantage over its competitors, by virtue of its processes or other sources of efficiency, using low price as a basis for positioning can be a fast road to a price war that no one (except consumers) will win. Second, claims that one's product—whether a good or a service—is low-priced are sometimes not very credible, because so many marketers make such claims. It is often better to position around more enduring differentiators, and let price speak more subtly for itself. Wal-Mart, an exception, has been able to sustain its low-price positioning in the United States because its costs, compared to its chief competitors, actually are lower.

KEY OBSERVATION

Using price as one dimension of a positioning grid is typically not very useful.

Step 6: Consider Fit of Possible Positions with Customer Needs and Segment Attractiveness

An important criterion for defining market segments is the difference in the benefits sought by different customers. Because differences between customers' ideal points reflect variations in the benefits they seek, a market positioning analysis can simultaneously identify distinct market segments as well as the perceived positions of different brands. When customers' ideal points cluster in two or more locations on the product space map, the analyst can consider each cluster a distinct market segment.[17] For analytical purposes, each cluster is represented by a circle that encloses most of the ideal points for that segment; the size of the circle reflects the relative proportion of customers within a particular segment.

Exhibit 9.6

PERCEPTUAL MAP OF WOMEN'S CLOTHING RETAILERS IN WASHINGTON, D.C., SHOWING THE IDEAL POINTS OF A SEGMENT OF CONSUMERS

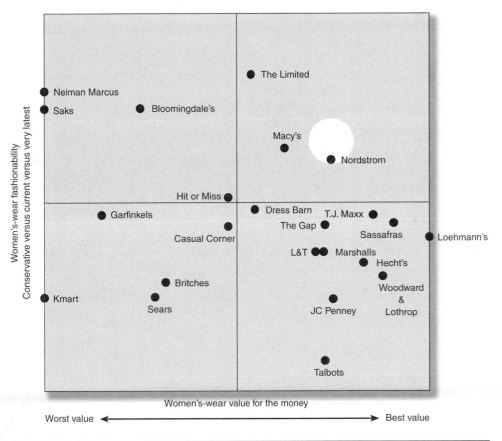

Washington 1990 Women's fashion market

Source: Adapted from Douglas Tigert and Stephen Arnold, "Nordstrom: How Good Are They?" *Babson College Retailing Research Reports,* September 1990. Used by permission.

Exhibit 9.7 groups the sample of Washington, D.C., respondents into five distinct segments on the basis of clusters of ideal points.[18] Segment 5 contains the largest proportion of customers; segment 1, the smallest.[19] By examining the preferences of customers in different segments along with their perceptions of the positions of existing brands, analyst can learn much about (1) the competitive strength of different brands in different segments, (2) the intensity of the rivalry between brands in a given segment, and (3) the opportunities for gaining a differentiated position within a specific target segment.

Step 6 not only concludes the analysis portion of the positioning process and crystallizes the decision about the positioning a product should hold, but it also can uncover locations in the product space where additional new products could be positioned to serve customer needs not well served by current competitors. Thus, Exhibit 9.4 shows that a possible side benefit of the positioning process is recognition of underserved positions where additional new products might be placed.

Exhibit 9.7

PERCEPTUAL MAP OF WOMEN'S CLOTHING RETAILERS IN WASHINGTON, D.C., SHOWING FIVE SEGMENTS BASED ON IDEAL POINTS

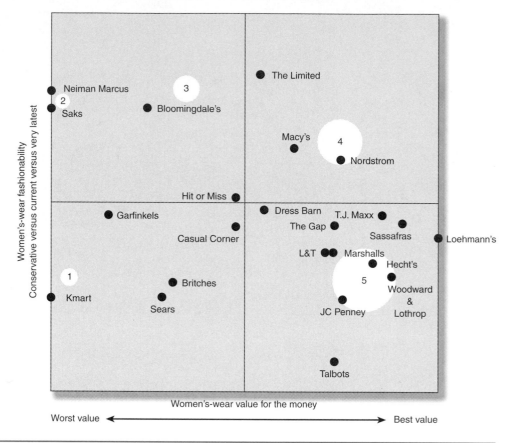

Source: Adapted from Douglas Tigert and Stephen Arnold, "Nordstrom: How Good Are They?" *Babson College Retailing Research Reports,* September 1990. Used by permission.

Step 7: Write Positioning Statement or Value Proposition to Guide Development of Marketing Strategy

The final decision about where to position a new brand or reposition an existing one should be based on both the market targeting analysis discussed in Chapter 8 and the results of a market positioning analysis. The position chosen should match the preferences of a particular market segment and should take into account the current positions of competing brands.

It should also reflect the current and *future* attractiveness of the target market (its size, expected growth, and environmental constraints) and the relative strengths and weaknesses of competitors. Such information, together with an analysis of the costs required to acquire and maintain these positions, allows an assessment of the economic implications of different market positioning strategies.

KEY OBSERVATION

*Most successful products are positioned
based on one or, at most, two determinant
attributes.*

Most successful products are positioned based on one or, at most, two determinant attributes, whether physical or perceptual. Using more simply confuses customers. Domino's Pizza in the United States, in its early days, focused its positioning solely on its fast delivery, since that was the principal dimension on which it established its competitive advantage. While there are many things Domino's could have said about the pizza itself, for example, it chose to focus its positioning on its key point of differentiation: fast delivery. Recently, when fast delivery became common in the pizza industry, Domino's added a heat retention device to its delivery containers and added a second positioning attribute: hot. Papa John's, a more recent entrant in the pizza business, positions its offering around a single attribute, the quality of its pizza, with its promotional phrase, "Better ingredients. Better pizza."

Where there are no real product differences, as in so-called **me-too products,** or no differential benefits to the user, not only is success hard to achieve, but also ethical issues may arise. For an example of ethical issues involving positioning in the pharmaceutical industry, see Ethical Perspective 9.1.

Once the desired positioning for the product has been determined, it's a good idea to write it down so those charged with developing and implementing the marketing strategy have a clear understanding of what is intended for the product and where it will fit in its competitive set. Two approaches are commonly used for doing so. In the classical approach, a **positioning statement** is written. A more recent approach, one being adopted in a growing number of firms, involves writing a **value proposition** for the product.

Writing a Positioning Statement or a Value Proposition
A positioning statement is a succinct statement that identifies the target market for which the product is intended and the product category in which it competes and states the unique benefit the product offers. An example of a positioning statement that reflects Volvo's marketing strategy in the United States is shown in Exhibit 9.8.

A value proposition is similarly explicit about what the product does for the customer (and sometimes, what it does not do) and typically also includes information about pricing relative to competitors. Both positioning statements and value propositions should reflect a **unique selling proposition** that the product embodies. In this sense, they reflect the basis on which the marketer intends to win sustainable competitive advantage by differentiating the product from others in its competitive space. In its shortest form, a value proposition typically looks like this:

ETHICAL PERSPECTIVE 9.1
*Positioning in the Pharmaceutical
Industry—An Ethical Quagmire*

Under constant and ever increasing pressure to perform, the pharmaceutical industry is frequently cited for practices that are ethically questionable. An article in the British journal *The Lancet* is an assessment of advertisements in Spanish medical journals in 1997 for antihypertensive (drugs used to treat high blood pressure) and lipid lowering (i.e., cholesterol lowering) drugs. The advertisements studied in a six-month period (264 different ads for antihypertensives and 23 different ads for lipid-lowering drugs) made a total of 125 referenced claims. After excluding the 23 claims that did not have published data, the researchers found that 44 percent of the literature did not support the statements made in the ads. This study was a note of caution for doctors who prescribe medicines based on the evidence of reported research on drugs.

Is such marketing really in the best long-term interests of the shareholders?

Source: Pilar Villanueva, Salvador Peiró, Julián Librero, Inmaculada Pereiró, "Accuracy of Pharmaceutical Advertisements in Medical Journals," *The Lancet,* January 4, 2003. Reprinted with permission from Esevier.

Exhibit 9.8

POSITIONING STATEMENT AND VALUE PROPOSITION FOR VOLVO AUTOMOBILES IN THE UNITED STATES

Positioning Statement

For upscale American families, Volvo is the automobile that offers the utmost in safety and durability.

Value Proposition

- Target market: Upscale American Families
- Benefits offered: Safety, durability
- Price range: 20% premium over similar cars

- Target market
- Benefits offered (and not offered)
- Price range (relative to competitors)

Exhibit 9.8 also provides a value proposition for Volvo. More fully developed value propositions sometimes identify the best competing alternatives available to the customer and specify the benefits, in measurable terms, that the customer can expect to receive by using the proposed product.[20] Detailed value propositions such as these are particularly helpful in positioning industrial goods and services, where quantifiable customer benefits are often essential to make the sale.

It is important that the positioning statement or value proposition states **benefits** that the user of the product will obtain, rather than **features** or attributes of the product itself, or vague or ambiguous platitudes about high quality or excellent service. By benefits, we mean the resulting end-use measurable consequences that the user will experience through the use of the product, in comparison to others.

The marketer generally writes positioning statements and value propositions for use internally and by others, such as advertising agencies, engaged to develop the marketing strategy. They are short and succinct, and are typically *not* written in catchy consumer language, though catchy **slogans** and **tag lines** for communication with customers often follow. They are commonly written for a product line or a brand, as is the case in our Volvo example, but sometimes for a single product or for a business as a whole. For products or brands, they play several important roles. They provide direction for R&D and product development about what kind of attributes should be built into the product (side door airbags, for example, in Volvo's case). They provide direction for those who create advertising campaigns about what the focus of those campaigns should be (for example, Volvo's ads almost always focus on safety or durability, even though Volvo could say other things about its cars). The value proposition provides direction for pricing decisions.

Thus, in a very real sense, the positioning statement or value proposition constitutes the foundation upon which the marketing strategy is built. More broadly, when used at the business level, as they sometimes are, these statements articulate the strategic direction toward which the company's activities in all arenas should be directed. Promising a certain sort of positioning, or value, to the target market is one thing. Delivering it is another. Clear and concise positioning statements and value propositions can play important roles in effectively executing the intended strategy.

Analytical Tools for Positioning Decision Making

Throughout the positioning process, we have advocated collecting marketing research data so positioning decisions are anchored in solid evidence, not mere supposition or naive opinion. Advances in computing power and statistical techniques have made possible a broad range of tools to help the marketing decision maker make the best use of marketing research. We briefly outline a few of these tools in Exhibit 9.9. It is beyond the scope of this book to provide detailed instruction in the use of these and other statistical techniques. Texts on marketing research and new product development are good sources for additional depth in this area.[21]

Exhibit 9.9   Software Tools for Positioning Decision Making

Software tools useful for making positioning decisions include applications that identify important determinant attributes, as well as statistical applications that can plot positioning grids from market research data.

Conjoint analysis: As was mentioned in Step 5 of the positioning process, it is important to learn which key attributes are important to consumers. Conjoint analysis is one tool for doing so. Conjoint analysis determines which combination of a limited number of attributes consumers most prefer. The technique is helpful for identifying appealing new product designs and important points that might be included in a product's advertising. Although it can provide some insights about consumer preferences, it cannot provide information about how consumers perceive the positioning of existing products in relation to product dimensions. Conjoint analysis is one way to narrow down a set of product attributes to those most important to consider in product design and positioning decisions. Most often, it is used with physical attributes, not perceptual ones. Several widely used conjoint analysis applications are available from Sawtooth Software, Inc. (www.sawtoothsoftware.com).

Factor analysis and discriminant analysis: Factor analysis and discriminant analysis are two statistical techniques useful in constructing positioning grids based on actual marketing research data. They are included in most broad-based statistical packages, such as SPSS MR (www.spss.com/spssmr). To employ factor analysis, the analyst must first identify the salient attributes consumers use to evaluate products in the category under study. The analyst then collects data from a sample of consumers concerning their ratings of each product or brand on all attributes. The factor analysis program next determines which attributes are related to the same underlying construct ("load" on the same factor). The analyst uses those underlying constructs or factors as the dimensions for a product space map, and the program indicates where each product or brand is perceived to be located on each factor.

Discriminant analysis requires the same input data as factor analysis. The discriminant analysis program then determines consumers' perceptual dimensions on the basis of which attributes best differentiate, or discriminate, among brands. Once again, those underlying dimensions can be used to construct a product space map, but they are usually not so easily interpretable as the factors identified through factor analysis. Also, as with factor analysis, the underlying dimensions may be more a function of the attributes used to collect consumer ratings than of the product characteristics that consumers actually consider to be most important.

Multidimensional scaling: Unlike the other techniques in which the underlying dimensions identified depend on the attributes supplied by the researcher when collecting data, multidimensional scaling produces dimensions based on consumer judgments about the similarity of, or their preferences for, the actual brands. These underlying dimensions are thought to be the basic dimensions that consumers actually use to evaluate alternative brands in the product class. Multidimensional scaling programs that use data on similarities construct geometrically spaced maps on which the brands perceived to be most similar are placed close together. Those that use consumer preferences produce joint space maps that show consumer ideal points and then position the most-preferred brands close to those ideal points.

Unfortunately, the underlying dimensions of the maps produced by multidimensional scaling can be difficult to interpret. Also, the dimensions identified are only those that already exist for currently available brands. This makes the technique less useful for investigating new product concepts that might involve new characteristics. Finally, the technique is subject to statistical limitations, when the number of alternative brands being investigated is small. As a rule, such techniques should be applied only when at least eight or more different products or brands are being examined.

TAKE-AWAYS

- Clear and distinctive positioning that differentiates a product from others with which it competes is usually essential for developing a winning marketing strategy.

- The positioning process outlined in this chapter helps decision makers choose a position that maximizes their chance of establishing sustainable competitive advantage.

- Distinctive and intense positioning is best accomplished when based on one or at most two attributes. More are likely to be confusing to customers.

- Writing clear and succinct positioning statements or value propositions can play an important role in ensuring effective development and execution of a marketing strategy. This chapter provides templates for writing these materials.

Self-diagnostic questions to test your ability to apply the analytical tools and concepts in this chapter to marketing decision making may be found at this book's website at www.mhhe.com/mullins05.

ENDNOTES

1. Based on an article by Cyndee Miller, "Wine for the Brew Crew," *Marketing News,* February 12, 1996, pp. 1–2.

2. Ibid.

3. Ibid.

4. Al Ries and Jack Trout, *Positioning: The Battle for Your Mind* (New York: Warner Books, 1982).

5. For a discussion of the positioning of industrial goods, see Frederick E. Webster, Jr., *Industrial Marketing Strategy* (New York: John Wiley & Sons, 1991), pp. 102–3.

6. Michael Porter, "What Is Strategy?" *Harvard Business Review,* November–December 1996, p. 62.

7. Michael Porter, *Competitive Advantage* (New York: The Free Press, 1985).

8. Jonathan Welsh, "Drive Buys/Volvo XC90 An SUV More Safe than Sporty," *The Wall Street Journal,* (U.S. Edition), November 29, 2002, p. W11C.

9. Adapted from C. Merle Crawford, *New Product Management* (Burr Ridge, IL: Richard D. Irwin, 1996), p. 348.

10. For a description of a perceptual mapping procedure that allows consumers to describe and rate the brands involved in their own terminology, see Jan-Benedict E. M. Steenkamp, Hans C. M. Van Tripp, and Jos M. F. Ten Berge, "Perceptual Mapping Based on Idiosyncratic Sets of Attributes," *Journal of Marketing Research,* February 1994, p. 15.

11. Douglas Tigert and Stephen Arnold, "Nordstrom: How Good Are They?" *Babson College Retailing Research Reports,* September 1990.

12. Steve Lyons, "The Marketing 100—Ford Windstar," *Advertising Age,* June 26, 1995, p. S-27.

13. Lindsay Brooke, "Mini: The Real Story," *Automotive Industries,* April 2002.

14. Bruce Orwall, "Multiplying Hotel Brands Puzzle Travelers," *The Wall Street Journal,* April 17, 1996, p. B1.

15. Existing brands' attractiveness can be inferred from current sales volumes and market shares. The position occupied by the share leader is obviously more appealing to a greater number of customers than are the positions occupied by lesser brands.

16. See Paul E. Green, J. Douglas Carroll, and Stephen M. Goldberg, "A General Approach to Product Design Optimization via Conjoint Analysis," *Journal of Marketing Research,* May 1985, pp. 168–84; and J. Douglas Carroll and Paul E. Green, "Psychometric Methods in Marketing Research: Part I, Conjoint Analysis," *Journal of Marketing Research,* November 1995, p. 385.

17. When using preference data to define market segments, however, the analyst should also collect information about customers' demographic characteristics, lifestyle, product usage, and other potential segmentation variables. This enables the analyst to develop a more complete picture of the differences among benefit segments. Such information can be useful for developing advertising appeals, selecting media, focusing personal selling efforts, and designing many of the other elements of a marketing program that can be effective in appealing to a particular segment.

18. The size of the individual circles in Exhibit 9.7 is fictitious and designed for illustrative purposes only.

19. The map in Exhibit 9.7 shows five distinct preference segments but only one set of perceived product positions. The implication is that consumers in this sample were similar in the way they perceived existing brands but different in the product attributes they preferred. This is the most common situation; customers tend to vary more in the benefits they seek than in how they perceive available products or brands. Sometimes, however, various segments may perceive the positions of existing brands quite differently. They may even use different determinant attributes in assessing these positions. Under such circumstances, a marketer should construct a separate market-positioning map for each segment.

20. Michael J. Lanning, *Delivering Profitable Value* (Cambridge, MA: Perseus Books, 1998).

21. For extensive critical reviews of past marketing applications of these different approaches, see John R. Hauser and Frank S. Koppleman, "Alternative Perceptual Mapping Techniques: Relative Accuracy and Usefulness," *Journal of Marketing Research,* November 1979, pp. 495–506; John W. Keon, "Product Positioning: TRINODAL Mapping of Brand Images, Ad Images, and Consumer Preference," *Journal of Marketing Research,* November 1983, pp. 380–92; Paul E. Green, J. Douglas Carroll, and Stephen M. Goldberg, "A General Approach to Product Design Optimization via Conjoint Analysis," *Journal of Marketing Research,* May 1985, pp. 168–84; Thomas W. Leigh, David M. McKay, and John O. Summers, "Reliability and Validity of Conjoint Analysis and Self-Explicated Weights," *Journal of Marketing Research,* November 1984, pp. 456–63; Paul E. Green, "Hybrid Models for Conjoint Analysis: An Expository Review," *Journal of Marketing Research,* May 1984, pp. 184–93; E. M. Steenkamp, Jan-Benedict, Hans C. M. Van Trijp, and Jos M. F. Ten Berge, "Perceptual Mapping Based on Idiosyncratic Sets of Attributes," *Journal of Marketing Research,* February 1994, p. 15; and J. Douglas Carroll and Paul E. Green, "Psychometric Methods in Marketing Research: Part I, Conjoint Analysis," *Journal of Marketing Research,* November 1995, p. 385.

SECTION THREE

DEVELOPING STRATEGIC MARKETING PROGRAMS

CHAPTER 10   Business Strategies: A
Foundation for Marketing
Program Decisions

CHAPTER 11   Product Decisions

CHAPTER 12   Pricing Decisions

CHAPTER 13   Distribution Channel
Decisions

CHAPTER 14   Integrated Promotion
Decisions

Business Strategies: A Foundation for Marketing Program Decisions

Business Strategies and Marketing Programs at 3M[1]

THE MINNESOTA MINING AND Manufacturing Company, better known as 3M, began manufacturing sandpaper nearly a century ago. Today it is the leader in dozens of technical areas from fluorochemistry to fiber optics. The firm makes more than 60,000 different products, which generated $16.3 billion in global sales in 2002. The company produced $3.1 billion in operating income, for more than an 19 percent return on invested capital.

As you might expect of a firm with so many products, 3M is organized into a large number of strategic business units (SBUs). The company contains more than 40 such SBUs or product divisions organized into seven market sectors:

- The Industrial Sector makes a variety of tapes, abrasives, adhesives, and specialty chemicals for industrial applications ranging from electronics to aerospace.
- The Health Care Sector markets a variety of medical, surgical, pharmaceutical, and dental products and services.
- The Consumer and Office Sector offers products for homes and offices, such as Post-it brand repositionable notes and Scotch brand tapes.

- The Electro and Communications Sector supplies connecting, splicing, and protective products for electronics and telecommunications markets.
- The Display and Graphics Sector is a world leader in the sale of films and reflective materials for electronic displays, touch screens, commercial graphics, and traffic control.
- The Transportation Sector markets a variety of adhesives, abrasives, filters and other products to enhance cars, trucks, airplanes, boats, and other vehicles.
- The Safety, Security and Protection Services Sector makes a wide variety of products ranging from respirators for worker safety to cleaning supplies to fire-protection products.

While 3M has acquired many smaller firms over the years, its growth strategy has focused primarily on internal new product development, emphasizing both improved products for existing customers and new products for new markets. One formal objective assigned to every business unit is to obtain at least 30 percent of annual sales from products introduced within the past four years. The company supports its growth strategy with an R&D budget of more than $1 billion, almost 7 percent of total revenues.

The company also pursues growth through the aggressive development of foreign markets for its many products. An eighth organizational sector is responsible for coordinating the firm's marketing efforts across countries. In 2002, 3M attained $8.5 billion in sales—53 percent of its total revenue—from outside the United States.

Differences in customer needs and life-cycle stages across industries, however, lead 3M's various business units to pursue their growth objectives in different ways. The Industrial Tape Division within the Industrial Sector, for example, operates in an industry where both the product technologies and the customer segments are relatively mature and stable. Growth in this group results from extending the scope of adhesive technology (for instance, attaching weather-stripping to auto doors), product improvements and line extensions targeted at existing customers, and expansion into global markets.

In contrast, the firm's Drug Delivery Systems Division within the Health Care Sector develops new medical applications for emerging technologies developed in 3M's many R&D labs. It sells a variety of technologies for the delivery of medications that are inhaled or absorbed through the skin. Most of the unit's growth comes from developing new products, often through alliances with other pharmaceutical firms, aimed at new markets.

The competitive strategies of 3M's various business units also differ. For instance, the industrial tape unit is primarily concerned with maintaining its commanding market share in existing markets while preserving or even improving its profitability. Its competitive strategy is to differentiate itself from competitors on the basis of product quality and excellent customer service.

But the drug delivery systems unit's strategy is to avoid head-to-head competitive battles by being the technological leader and introducing a stream of unique new products. To be successful, though, the unit must devote substantial resources to R&D and to the stimulation of primary demand. Thus, its main objective is volume growth; and it must sometimes sacrifice short-run profitability to fund the product development and marketing efforts needed to accomplish that goal.

These differences in competitive strategy, in turn, influence the strategic marketing programs within the various business units. For instance, the firm spends little on advertising or sales promotion for its mature industrial tape products. However, it does maintain a large, well-trained technical salesforce that provides valuable problem-solving assistance and other services to customers and informed feedback to the firm's R&D personnel about potential new applications and product improvements.

In contrast, the pioneering nature of the drug delivery unit's technologies calls for more extensive promotion to attract potential alliance partners, develop awareness among prescribing physicians, and stimulate primary demand. Consequently, the unit devotes a relatively large portion of its revenues to advertising in technical journals aimed at the pharmaceutical industry, physicians, and other medical professionals. It also supports a well-trained salesforce, but those salespeople spend much of their time demonstrating new technologies and building relationships with drug manufacturers who are prospective customers and partners.

Marketing Challenges Addressed in Chapter 10

The situation at 3M again illustrates that large firms with multiple businesses usually have a hierarchy of strategies extending from the corporate level down to the individual product-market entry. As we saw in Chapter 2, corporate strategy addresses such issues as the firm's mission and scope and the directions it will pursue for future growth. Thus, 3M's corporate growth strategy focuses primarily on developing new products and new applications for emerging technologies.

The major strategic question addressed at the business-unit level is, How should we compete in this business? For instance, 3M's industrial tape unit attempts to maintain its commanding market share and high profitability by differentiating itself on the basis of high product quality and good customer service. The drug delivery unit, on the other hand, seeks high growth via aggressive new product and market development.

Finally, the strategic marketing program for each product-market entry within a business unit attempts to allocate marketing resources and activities in a manner appropriate for accomplishing the business unit's objectives. Thus, most of the strategic marketing programs within 3M's drug delivery unit involve relatively large expenditures for marketing research and introductory advertising and promotion campaigns aimed at achieving sales growth.

One key reason for 3M's continuing success is that all three levels of strategy within the company have usually been characterized by good internal and external consistency, or **strategic fit.** The company's managers have done a good job of monitoring and adapting their strategies to the market opportunities, technological advances, and competitive threats in the company's external environment. The firm's marketing and sales managers play critical roles both in developing market-oriented strategies for individual products and in influencing and helping to formulate corporate and business-level strategies that are responsive to environmental conditions. At the same time, those strategies are usually internally compatible. Each strategy fits with those at other levels as well as with the unique competitive strengths and competencies of the relevant business unit and the company as a whole.

Recent empirical evidence shows that when there is a good fit between a business's competitive strategy and the strategic marketing programs of its various product or service offerings, the business will achieve better results in terms of sales growth, market share, and profitability than when the two levels of strategy are inconsistent with one another.[2] Therefore, this chapter focuses on what marketing decision makers can and should do to help ensure that the strategic marketing plans they develop are appropriate in light of the available resources and competitive thrust of the business that is their organizational home.

KEY OBSERVATION

When there is a good fit between a business's competitive strategy and the strategic marketing programs of its various product or service offerings, the business will achieve better results.

First, we examine the question of how a business might choose to compete. What generic competitive strategies might a business pursue, and in what environmental circumstances is each strategy most appropriate? We'll also explore whether the same kinds of competitive strategies are relevant for small, single-business organizations and entrepreneurial start-ups as for large multi-SBU firms such as 3M and whether technological shifts, such as the growth of e-commerce, are likely to give birth to new competitive strategies or make some old ones obsolete.

Next, we examine the interrelationships between different business competitive strategies and elements of the strategic marketing programs for the various products within the business. How does—or should—a particular competitive strategy influence or constrain marketing programs for the business's product offerings? And what happens if the market positioning or specific marketing actions that would be most effective for appealing to a product's target customers do not fit very well with the competitive strategy of the larger business unit? For example, as some of the products made by the drug delivery unit at 3M—such as the inhalers they make for delivering asthma medications—become well-established and mature, they may require marketing actions (e.g., more competitive pricing) that are not consistent with the aggressive product development strategy of the business unit. What should 3M and the marketing manager responsible for inhalers do under such circumstances?

How Do Businesses Compete?

As mentioned, the essential strategic question at the SBU level is, How are we going to compete in this business? Thus, business strategies are primarily concerned with allocating resources across functional activities and product-markets to give the unit a sustainable advantage over its competitors. Of course, the unit's core competencies and resources, together with the customer and competitive characteristics of its industry, determine the viability of any particular competitive strategy.[3] The 3M drug delivery unit's strategy of gaining revenue growth via technological leadership and aggressive new product and market development, for instance, will continue to work only if the firm's R&D, engineering, and marketing competencies and resources continue to outweigh those of its competitors. Consequently, most SBUs pursue a single competitive strategy—one that best fits their market environments and competitive strengths—across all or most of the product-markets in which they compete. The question is, What alternative strategies are available to a business unit? What are the basic, or generic, competitive strategies most SBUs choose to pursue?

Generic Business-Level Competitive Strategies

Researchers have identified general categories of business-level competitive strategies based on overall patterns of purpose, practice, and performance in different businesses. As we saw in Chapter 9, Michael Porter distinguishes three strategies—or competitive positions—that businesses pursue to gain and maintain competitive advantages in their various product-markets: (1) *overall cost leadership;* (2) *differentiation*—building customer perceptions of superior product quality, design, or service; and (3) *focus,* in which the business avoids direct confrontation with its major competitors by concentrating on narrowly defined market niches. Porter describes firms that lack a distinctive strategy as being "stuck in the middle" and predicts that they will perform poorly.[4]

Robert Miles and Charles Snow identified another set of business strategies based on a business's intended rate of product-market development (new product development, penetration of new markets).[5] They classify business units into four strategic types: *prospectors, defenders, analyzers,* and *reactors.* Exhibit 10.1 describes each of these business strategies briefly. As you can see, businesses pursuing a *prospector strategy* focus on growth through the development of new products and markets. 3M's drug delivery business unit illustrates this. *Defender businesses* concentrate on maintaining their positions in established product-markets while paying less attention to new product development, as is the case with 3M's industrial tape business unit. The *analyzer strategy* falls in between these two. An analyzer business attempts to maintain a strong position in its core product-market(s) but also seeks to expand into new—usually closely related—product-markets. Finally, *reactors* are businesses with no clearly defined strategy.

Even though both the Porter and Miles and Snow typologies have received popular acceptance and research support, neither is complete by itself. For example, a *defender business unit* could pursue a variety of competitive approaches to protect its market position, such as offering the lowest cost or differentiating itself on quality or service. Thus, we have combined the two typologies in Exhibit 10.2 to provide a more comprehensive overview of business strategies. Exhibit 10.2 classifies business strategies on two primary dimensions:

Exhibit 10.1

DEFINITIONS OF MILES AND SNOW'S FOUR BUSINESS STRATEGIES

Prospector

- Operates within a broad product-market domain that undergoes periodic redefinition.
- Values being a "first mover" in new product and market areas, even if not all of these efforts prove to be highly profitable.
- Responds rapidly to early signals concerning areas of opportunity, and these responses often lead to new rounds of competitive actions.
- Competes primarily by stimulating and meeting new market opportunities, but may not maintain strength over time in all markets it enters.

Defender

- Attempts to locate and maintain a secure position in relatively stable product or service areas.
- Offers relatively limited range of products or services compared with competitors.
- Tries to protect its domain by offering lower prices, higher quality, or better service than competitors.
- Usually not at the forefront of technological/new product development in its industry; tends to ignore industry changes not directly related to its area of operation.

Analyzer

- An intermediate type; makes fewer and slower product-market changes than prospectors, but is less committed to stability and efficiency than defenders.
- Attempts to maintain a stable, limited line of products or services, but carefully follows a selected set of promising new developments in its industry.
- Seldom a first mover, but often a second or third entrant in product-markets related to its existing market base—often with a lower cost or higher-quality product or service offering.

Reactor

- Lacks any well-defined competitive strategy.
- Does not have as consistent a product-market orientation as its competitors.
- Not as willing to assume the risks of new product or market development as its competitors.
- Not as aggressive in marketing established products as some competitors.
- Responds primarily when it is forced to by environmental pressures.

Source: Adapted from Raymond E. Miles and Charles C. Snow, *Organizational Strategy, Structure, and Process.* Copyright © 1978 McGraw-Hill; 2003 by the Board of Trustees of the Leland Stanford Jr. University. Used with the permission of Stanford University Press. www.sup.org.

the unit's desired rate of product-market development (expansion) and the unit's intended method of competing in its established product-markets.

Each of our strategic categories could be further subdivided according to whether a business applies the strategy across a broadly defined product-market domain or concentrates on a narrowly defined segment where it hopes to avoid direct confrontation with major competitors (the *focus* strategy of Porter). Although this distinction is useful, it is more germane to a discussion of the business's target market strategy (as discussed in Chapter 8) than to its competitive strategy. Most businesses compete in a reasonably consistent way across all of their product-markets, whether their domain is broad or narrow.

Exhibit 10.2 describes only six business strategies, rather than the eight that one might expect. We view reactor and prospector business units as two homogeneous categories.

Exhibit 10.2

COMBINED TYPOLOGY OF BUSINESS-LEVEL COMPETITIVE STRATEGIES

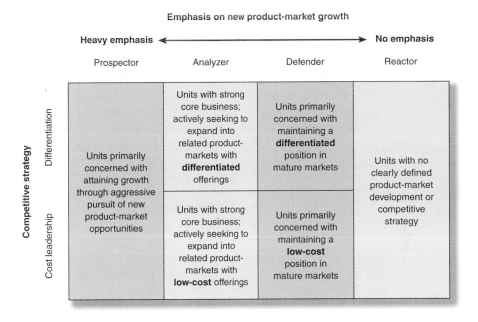

Emphasis on new product-market growth

Heavy emphasis ←————————————————→ No emphasis

	Prospector	Analyzer	Defender	Reactor
Differentiation	Units primarily concerned with attaining growth through aggressive pursuit of new product-market opportunities	Units with strong core business; actively seeking to expand into related product-markets with **differentiated** offerings	Units primarily concerned with maintaining a **differentiated** position in mature markets	Units with no clearly defined product-market development or competitive strategy
Cost leadership		Units with strong core business; actively seeking to expand into related product-markets with **low-cost** offerings	Units primarily concerned with maintaining a **low-cost** position in mature markets	

Competitive strategy

Evidence suggests that a substantial portion of businesses fall into the reactor category. One study, for instance, found that 50 out of 232 businesses examined could be classified as reactors.[6] By definition, however, such businesses do not have well-defined or consistent approaches either to new product development or to ways of competing in existing product-markets. In other words, reactors have no clear competitive strategy. Therefore, we will largely ignore them during the rest of this discussion.

Prospectors are also shown as a single strategic category in Exhibit 10.2 because the desire for rapid new product or market development is the overriding aspect of their strategy. There is little need for a prospector business to consider how it will compete in the new product-markets it develops because it will face little or no competition—at least not until those markets become established and other firms begin to enter.

Do the Same Competitive Strategies Work for Single-Business Firms and Start-ups?

Even small firms with a single business and only a few related product offerings or start-ups with a single product must decide how they will compete. And just like an SBU in a major corporation such as 3M, their competitive strategies should be tailored to their unique resources and competencies and aimed at securing a sustainable advantage over existing or potential competitors. Therefore, the same set of generic competitive strategies are just as appropriate for small firms as for business units within larger ones. For example, Belvedere vodka—made by a small distillery in Poland—has captured a substantial share of the prestige segment of the North American vodka market by stressing the five-century tradition of its production process and the superior quality of its imported product: in other words, by pursuing a very effective differentiated defender strategy.[7]

However, there is one important difference between single-business and multi-SBU organizations. In smaller single-business firms the distinction between business-level competitive strategy and marketing strategy tends to blur and the two strategies blend into one. Belvedere's competitive strategy, for instance, is essentially the same as the market positioning for its primary product: a product that offers higher quality than competing brands because it is made with old-fashioned methods and ingredients that have not changed for centuries. And the elements of its marketing strategy all flow from that competitive/market positioning: a premium price, advertising that stresses the product's long history and old-fashioned production practices, traditional packaging, and the like.

Another difference applies to entrepreneurial start-ups. Most start-ups do not have the resources to succeed by competing as a "me-too" competitor in a well-established and highly competitive product market. By definition they do not have an established market position to defend. Therefore, while the taxonomy of competitive strategies is still relevant to entrepreneurial firms, in reality most of them—at least those that stand a reasonable chance of success—begin life as prospectors. They compete primarily by developing a unique product or service that meets the needs and preferences of a customer segment that is not being well served by established competitors.

KEY OBSERVATION

While the taxonomy of competitive strategies is still relevant to entrepreneurial firms, in reality most of them—at least those that stand a reasonable chance of success—begin life as prospectors.

The critical question for a start-up firm, though, is, What happens when the new product matures and competitors arrive on the scene? This and similar issues related to strategic change are examined in more detail later in this chapter.

Do the Same Competitive Strategies Work for Service Businesses?

What is a service? Basically, *services* can be thought of as **intangibles** and *goods* as **tangibles.** The former can rarely be experienced in advance of the sale, while the latter can be experienced, even tested, before purchase.[8] Using this distinction, a **service** can be defined as "any activity or benefit that one party can offer to another that is essentially intangible and that does not result in the ownership of anything. Its production may or may not be tied to a physical product."[9]

We typically associate services with nonmanufacturing businesses, even though service is often an indispensable part of a goods producer's offering. Services such as applications engineering, system design, delivery, installation, training, and maintenance can be crucial for building long-term relationships between manufacturers and their customers, particularly in consumer durable and industrial products businesses. Thus, almost all businesses are engaged in service to some extent.

Many organizations are concerned with producing and marketing a service as their primary offering rather than as an adjunct to a physical product. These organizations include public-sector and not-for-profit service organizations, such as churches, hospitals, universities, and arts organizations. The crucial question is this: To be successful, must service organizations employ different competitive strategies than goods manufacturers?

The framework we used to classify business-level competitive strategies in Exhibit 10.2 is equally valid for service businesses. Some service firms, such as Super 8 or Days Inn in the lodging industry, attempt to minimize costs and compete largely with low prices. Other firms, like Marriott, differentiate their offerings on the basis of high service quality or unique benefits. Similarly, some service businesses adopt prospector strategies and aggressively pursue the development of new offerings or markets. For instance, American Express's Travel Related Services Division has developed a variety of new services tailored

Exhibit 10.3   Cable & Wireless Communications—Differentiation through Customer Relationships

Cable & Wireless Communications, the U.S. subsidiary of a British telecommunications firm, competes in the relatively mature and highly competitive business of providing long-distance services to business customers. Company executives knew long ago that their operation could not compete on price with larger competitors like AT&T or MCI. So they sought to differentiate themselves—and to defend their established customer base—by providing the best customer support in the industry. As a result, Cable & Wireless turned itself from a mundane commodity business into a sophisticated telemanager and partner with its customers.

Part of Cable & Wireless's success was the result of good target market selection. The firm focused on winning and holding on to small or medium-sized business clients with monthly billings of $500 to $15,000. For such small businesses, the company's 500 U.S. salespeople, working out of 36 regional offices, acted like telecommunications managers. Corporations too small to hire their own telecom specialists valued the advice and expertise Cable & Wireless people could offer, and top management gave those salespeople substantial autonomy to tailor their offerings and advice to each customer's needs.

Within its target small-business segment, however, Cable & Wireless was not content to merely maintain relationships with established customers. The firm pursued a differentiated analyzer strategy by also devoting substantial effort and resources to developing and pitching specialized services aimed at attracting new customers from new industry segments. For example, the company gained substantial business from smaller firms within the legal profession by developing functions that appealed specifically to lawyers, such as innovative ways to track and bill calls linked to specific client accounts.

Unfortunately, the corporate strategy of Cable & Wireless Communication's parent company was neither as well focused nor as effective. Like many of its global competitors—such as WorldCom and Global Crossing—the firm invested heavily during the late 1990s to build high-speed worldwide data networks to service large corporate customers. This "me too" strategy lead to excess capacity in the industry, a lack of any sustainable advantage over its competitors, and ultimately severe financial difficulties.

Source: From *The Discipline of Market Leaders* by Michael Treacy and Fred Wiersema. Copyright 1995 by Michael Treacy and Fred Wiersma (Perseus Books Publishers). Reprinted by permission via The Copyright Clearance Center.; and "Wireless and Less," *The Economist,* December 14, 2002, p. 58.

to specific segments of the firm's credit-card holders. Other service businesses focus narrowly on defending established positions in current markets. Still others can best be described as analyzers pursuing both established and new markets. For instance, Cable & Wireless Communications, a long-distance carrier whose competitive strategy is discussed in Exhibit 10.3, might best be described as a differentiated analyzer.

A study of the banking industry provides empirical evidence that service businesses actually do pursue the same types of competitive strategies as goods producers. The 329 bank CEOs who responded to the survey had little trouble categorizing their institution's competitive strategies into one of Miles and Snow's four types. Fifty-four of the executives reported that their banks were prospectors, 87 identified their firms as analyzers, 157 as defenders, and 31 as reactors.[10]

Do the Same Competitive Strategies Work for Global Competitors?

In terms of the strategies described in Exhibit 10.2, businesses that compete in multiple global markets almost always pursue one of the two types of analyzer strategy. They must continue to strengthen and defend their competitive position in their home country—and perhaps in other countries where they are well established—while simultaneously pursuing expansion and growth in new international markets.

When examined on a country-by-country basis, however, the same business unit might be viewed as pursuing different competitive strategies in different countries. For instance, while 3M's industrial tape group competes like a differentiated defender in the United States, Canada, and some European countries where it has established large market shares, it competes more like a prospector when attempting to open and develop new markets in emerging economies such as China and Mexico.

This suggests that a single SBU may need to engage in different functional activities (including different strategic marketing programs)—and perhaps even adopt different organizational structures to implement those activities—across the various countries in which it competes. For example, Huawei Technologies Co., located in Shenzhen, China, competes very effectively in its home market as a low-cost analyzer. The company earned $2.4 billion in revenues in 2001 selling Internet switches and routers patterned after the equipment manufactured by Cisco Systems and Alcatel, but at prices as much as 40 percent lower. However, only 10 percent of those revenues came from outside China. In order to compete more effectively in the developed markets of Europe and North America, Huawei will have to expand its product line and develop new equipment with more innovative features and greater functionality. In other words, it will have to compete more like a prospector in those markets. Consequently, the firm has greatly increased its R&D spending and product development efforts. It must also develop marketing programs geared to generating brand awareness and trial among potential customers. Initially, at least, Huawei plans to rely heavily on alliances with established distributors and value-added resellers to develop and implement marketing programs in developed markets. For instance, the Vierling Group has agreed to serve as Huawei's exclusive distributor in Germany.[11]

Will the Internet Change Everything?

Some analysts argue that the Internet will change the way firms compete. The Internet makes it easier for buyers and sellers to compare prices, reduces the number of middlemen necessary between manufacturers and end users, cuts transaction costs, improves the functioning of the price mechanism, and thereby increases competition.[12] One possible outcome of all these changes is that it will be harder for firms to differentiate themselves on any basis other than low price. All the business-level competitive strategies focused on differentiation will become less viable, while firms pursuing low-cost strategies will be more successful.

While we agree that the Internet has increased both efficiency and competitiveness in many product-markets, we doubt that competition will focus exclusively on price. For one thing, innovation is likely to continue—and probably accelerate—in the future. Unique new products and services will continue to emerge and provide a way for the innovator to gain a competitive advantage, at least in the short term. Thus, firms with the resources and competencies necessary to produce a continuing stream of new product or service offerings that appeal to one or more customer segments—that is, to effectively implement a prospector strategy—should be successful regardless of whether they are the lowest-cost producers in their industries. Amazon.com, the largest e-tailer as of early 2003, is generally not the lowest priced.

In addition, the Internet is primarily a communications channel. While it facilitates the dissemination of information, including price information, the goods and services themselves will continue to offer different features and benefits. As customers gather more information from the Internet and become better informed, they are less likely to be swayed by superficial distinctions between brands. But if a firm offers unique benefits that a segment of customers perceive as *meaningful,* it should still be able to differentiate its offering and command a premium price, at least until its competitors offer something similar.

Finally, the Internet will make it easier for firms to customize their offerings and personalize their relationships with their customers. Such personalization should differentiate the firm from its competitors in the customer's eyes and improve customer loyalty and retention. For instance, in Chapter 6 we discussed the role of the Internet in developing logistical alliances among organizational buyers and their suppliers. Consumer goods and services firms, and even Internet portals, are also using the Internet's interactive capabilities to acquire and communicate information and build customer relationships. For example, the My Yahoo! website allows individual consumers to personalize their Web portal in exchange for some basic demographic information. And custom-made women's jeans account for 40 percent of Lands' End's online sales even though they are 50 percent more expensive than the firm's regular offerings.[13]

How Do Competitive Strategies Differ from One Another?

In Chapter 2 we said that all strategies consist of five components or underlying dimensions: scope (or breadth of strategic domain), goals and objectives, resource deployments, a basis for achieving a sustainable competitive advantage, and synergy. But the generic strategies summarized in Exhibit 10.2 are defined largely by their differences on only one dimension: the nature of the competitive advantage sought. Each strategy also involves some important differences on the other four dimensions—differences that are outlined in Exhibit 10.4 and discussed below. Those differences provide insights concerning the conditions under which each strategy is most appropriate and about the relative importance of different marketing actions in implementing them effectively.

Differences in Scope

Both the breadth and stability of a business's domain are likely to vary with different strategies. This, in turn, can affect the variables the corporation uses to define its various businesses. At one extreme, defender businesses, whether low-cost or differentiated, tend to operate in relatively well-defined, narrow, and stable domains where both the product technology and the customer segments are mature.

At the other extreme, prospector businesses usually operate in broad and rapidly changing domains where neither the technology nor customer segments are well established. The scope of such businesses often undergoes periodic redefinition. Thus, prospector businesses are typically organized around either a core technology that might lead to the development of products aimed at a broad range of customer segments or a basic customer need that might be met with products based on different technologies. The latter is the approach taken by 3M's drug delivery systems business. Its mission is to satisfy the health needs of a broad range of patients with new products developed from technologies drawn from other business units within the firm.

Analyzer businesses, whether low-cost or differentiated, fall somewhere in between the two extremes. They usually have a well-established core business to defend, and often their domain is primarily focused on that business. However, businesses pursuing this intermediate strategy are often in industries that are still growing or experiencing technological

Exhibit 10.4

HOW BUSINESS STRATEGIES DIFFER IN SCOPE, OBJECTIVES, RESOURCE DEPLOYMENTS, AND SYNERGY

Dimensions	Low-cost defender	Differentiated defender	Prospector	Analyzer
• *Scope*	Mature/stable/ well-defined domain; mature technology and customer segments	Mature/stable/ well-defined domain; mature technology and customer segments	Broad/dynamic domains; technology and customer segments not well-established	Mixture of defender and prospector strategies
• *Goals and objectives*				
Adaptability (new product success)	Very little	Little	Extensive	Mixture of defender and prospector strategies
Effectiveness (increase in market share)	Little	Little	Large	Mixture of defender and prospector strategies
Efficiency (ROI)	High	High	Low	Mixture of defender and prospector strategies
• *Resource deployment*	Generate excess cash (cash cows)	Generate excess cash (cash cows)	Need cash for product development (question marks or stars)	Need cash for product development but less so than do prospectors
• *Synergy*	Need to seek operating synergies to achieve efficiencies	Need to seek operating synergies to achieve efficiencies	Danger in sharing operating facilities and programs— better to share technology/ marketing skills	Danger in sharing operating facilities and programs— better to share technology/ marketing skills

changes. Consequently, they must pay attention to the emergence of new customer segments and/or new product types. As a result, managers must review and adjust the domain of such businesses from time to time.

Differences in Goals and Objectives

Another important difference across generic business-level strategies with particular relevance for the design and implementation of appropriate marketing programs is that different strategies often focus on different objectives. SBU and product-market objectives might be specified on a variety of criteria, but to keep things simple, we focus on only three performance dimensions of major importance to both business-unit and marketing managers:

1. *Effectiveness.* The success of a business's products and programs relative to those of its competitors in the market. Effectiveness is commonly measured by such items as *sales growth* relative to competitors or *changes in market share.*
2. *Efficiency.* The outcomes of a business's programs relative to the resources used in implementing them. Common measures of efficiency are *profitability* as a percent of sales and *return on investment.*
3. *Adaptability.* The business's success in responding over time to changing conditions and opportunities in the environment. Adaptability can be measured in a variety of ways, but the most

common ones are the *number of successful new products* introduced relative to competitors or the *percentage of sales accounted for by products introduced within the last five years.*

However, it is very difficult for any SBU, regardless of its competitive strategy, to simultaneously achieve outstanding performance on even this limited number of dimensions, because they involve substantial trade-offs. Good performance on one dimension often means sacrificing performance on another.[14] For example, developing successful new products or attaining share growth often involves large marketing budgets, substantial up-front investment, high operating costs, and a shaving of profit margins—all of which reduce ROI. This suggests that managers should choose a competitive strategy with a view toward maximizing performance on one or two dimensions, while expecting to sacrifice some level of performance on the others, at least in the short term. Over the longer term, of course, the chosen strategy should promise discounted cash flows that exceed the business's cost of capital and thereby increase shareholder value.

As Exhibit 10.4 indicates, prospector businesses are expected to outperform defenders on both new product development and market-share growth. On the other hand, both defender strategies should lead to better returns on investment. Differentiated defenders likely produce higher returns than low-cost defenders, assuming that the greater expenses involved in maintaining their differentiated positions can be more than offset by the higher margins gained by avoiding the intense price competition low-cost competitors often face. Once again, both low-cost and differentiated analyzer strategies are likely to fall between the two extremes.[15]

Differences in Resource Deployments

Businesses following different strategies also tend to allocate their financial resources differently across product-markets, functional departments, and activities within each functional area. Prospector—and to a lesser degree, analyzer—businesses devote a relatively large proportion of resources to the development of new product-markets. Because such product-markets usually require more cash to develop than they produce short term, businesses pursuing these strategies often need infusions of financial resources from other parts of the corporation. In portfolio terms, they are "question marks" or "stars."

Defenders, on the other hand, focus the bulk of their resources on preserving existing positions in established product-markets. These product-markets are usually profitable; therefore, defender businesses typically generate excess cash to support product and market development efforts in other business units within the firm. They are the "cash cows."

Resource allocations among functional departments and activities within the SBU also vary across businesses pursuing different strategies. For instance, marketing budgets tend to be the largest as a percentage of an SBU's revenues when the business is pursuing a prospector strategy; they tend to be the smallest as a percentage of sales under a low-cost defender strategy. We discuss this in more detail later.

Differences in Sources of Synergy

Because different strategies emphasize different methods of competition and different functional activities, a given source of synergy may be more appropriate for some strategies than for others.

At one extreme, the sharing of operating facilities and programs may be an inappropriate approach to gaining synergy for businesses following a prospector strategy. And to a lesser extent, this may also be true for both types of analyzer strategies. Such sharing can reduce an SBU's ability to adapt quickly to changing market demands or competitive threats. Commitments to internally negotiated price structures and materials, as well as the use of joint resources, facilities, and programs, increase interdependence among SBUs and limit their flexibility. It is more appropriate for such businesses to seek synergy through the sharing of a technology, engineering skills, or market knowledge—expertise that can help improve the success rate of their product development efforts. Thus, 3M's drug delivery systems business attempts to find medical applications for new technologies developed in many of the firm's other business units.

At the other extreme, however, low-cost defenders should seek operating synergies that will make them more efficient. Synergies that enable such businesses to increase economies of scale and experience curve effects are particularly desirable. They help reduce unit costs and strengthen the strategy's basis of competitive advantage. The primary means of gaining such operating synergies is through the sharing of resources, facilities, and functional activities across product-market entries within the business unit or across related business units. Emerson Electric, for instance, formed an "operating group" of several otherwise autonomous business units that make different types of electrical motors and tools. By sharing production facilities, marketing activities, and a common salesforce, the group was able to reduce the costs of both per-unit production and marketing.

Deciding When a Strategy Is Appropriate: The Fit between Business Strategies and the Environment

Because different strategies pursue different objectives in different domains with different competitive approaches, they do not all work equally well under the same environmental circumstances. The question is, Which environmental situations are most amenable to the successful pursuit of each type of strategy? Exhibit 10.5 outlines some major market, technological, and competitive conditions—plus a business units' strengths relative to its competitors—that are most favorable for the successful implementation of each generic business strategy. We next discuss the reasons each strategy fits best with a particular set of environmental conditions.

Appropriate Conditions for a Prospector Strategy

A prospector strategy is particularly well suited to unstable, rapidly changing environments resulting from new technology, shifting customer needs, or both. In either case, such industries tend to be at an early stage in their life cycles and offer many opportunities for new product-market entries. Industry structure is often unstable because few competitors are present and their relative market shares can shift rapidly as new products are introduced and new markets develop.

Because they emphasize the development of new products and/or new markets, the most successful prospectors are usually strong in, and devote substantial resources to, two broad areas of competence: first, R&D, product engineering, and other functional areas that identify new technology and convert it into innovative products; second, marketing research, marketing and sales—functions necessary for the identification and development of new market opportunities.

In some cases, however, even though a prospector business has strong product development and marketing skills, it may lack the resources to maintain its early lead as product-markets grow and attract new competitors. For example, Minnetonka was the pioneer in several health and beauty-aid product categories with brands like Softsoap liquid soap and Check-Up plaque-fighting toothpaste. However, because competitors like Procter &

Exhibit 10.5

ENVIRONMENTAL FACTORS FAVORABLE TO DIFFERENT BUSINESS STRATEGIES

External factors	Prospector	Analyzer	Differentiated defender	Low-cost defender
Industry and market	Industry in introductory or early growth stage of life cycle, many potential customer segments as yet unidentified and/or undeveloped.	Industry in late growth or early maturity stage of life cycle, one or more product offerings currently targeted at major customer segments, but some potential segments may still be undeveloped.	Industry in maturity or decline stage of life cycle; current offerings targeted at all major segments; sales primarily due to repeat purchases/replacement demand.	Industry in maturity or decline stage of life cycle; current offerings targeted at all major segments; sales primarily due to repeat purchases/replacement demand.
Technology	Newly emerging technology; many applications as yet undeveloped.	Basic technology well developed but still evolving; product modifications and improvements—as well as emergence of new competing technologies—still likely.	Basic technology fully developed and stable; few major modifications or improvements likely.	Basic technology fully developed and stable; few major modifications or improvements likely.
Competition	Few established competitors; industry structure still emerging; single competitor holds commanding share of major market segments.	Large number of competitors, but future shakeout likely; industry structure still evolving; one or more competitors hold large shares in major segments but continuing growth may allow rapid changes in relative shares.	Small to moderate number of well-established competitors; industry structure stable, though acquisitions and consolidation possible; maturity of markets means relative shares of competitors tend to be reasonably stable over time.	Small to moderate number of well-established competitors; industry structure stable, though acquisitions and consolidation possible; maturity of markets means relative shares of competitors tend to be reasonably stable over time.
Business's relative strengths	SBU (or parent) has strong R&D, product engineering, and marketing research and marketing capabilities.	SBU (or parent) has good R&D, product engineering, and marketing research capabilities, but not as strong as some competitors'; has either low-cost position or strong sales, marketing, distribution, or service capabilities in one or more segments.	SBU has no outstanding strengths in R&D or product engineering; costs are higher than at least some competitors'; SBU's outstanding strengths are in process engineering and quality control and/or in marketing, sales, distribution, or customer services.	SBU (or parent) has superior sources of supply and/or process engineering and production capabilities that enable it to be low-cost producer; R&D, product engineering, marketing, sales, or service capabilities may not be as strong as some competitors'.

Gamble and Colgate-Palmolive introduced competing brands with advertising and promotion budgets much larger than Minnetonka could match, the firm was eventually forced to change its strategy and concentrate on manufacturing products under licenses from larger firms.

Appropriate Conditions for an Analyzer Strategy

The analyzer strategy is a hybrid. On the one hand, analyzers are concerned with defending—via low costs or differentiation in quality or service—a strong share position in one or more established product-markets. At the same time, the business must pay attention to new product development to avoid being leapfrogged by competitors with more technologically advanced products or being left behind in newly developing application segments within the market. This dual focus makes the analyzer strategy appropriate for well-developed industries that are still experiencing some growth and change as a consequence of evolving customer needs and desires or continuing technological improvements.

Automobile manufacturing is an example of such an industry. Competitors are relatively few and well established, the market is relatively mature, but technology continues to advance. Thus, Toyota and Honda (as well as some of their competitors) have invested many millions of dollars to develop a new generation of cars that use fuel cells to convert hydrogen gas into electricity and leave nothing but water coming out the tail pipe. Both firms introduced fuel-cell cars to the market in Japan and the United States in 2002 despite predicting it would take at least 10 years to lower costs enough to make such cars commercially viable, and despite softening global demand for their conventional cars and trucks. Both firms hoped to gain economies of scale and experience—and therefore a competitive advantage—by being the fuel-cell pioneer.[16]

The actions of Toyota and Honda illustrate one problem with an analyzer strategy. Few businesses have the resources and competencies needed to successfully defend an established core business while generating new products at the same time. Success on both dimensions requires strengths across virtually every functional area, and few businesses (or their parent companies) have such universal strengths. Therefore, analyzers are often not as innovative in new product development as prospectors. And they may not be as profitable in defending their core businesses as defenders.

Appropriate Conditions for a Defender Strategy

A defender strategy makes sense only when a business has something worth defending. It is most appropriate for units with a profitable share of one or more major segments in a relatively mature, stable industry. Consistent with the "constant improvement" principles of total quality management, most successful defenders initiate process improvements, product improvements, or line extensions to help protect and strengthen their established positions. But they devote relatively few resources to basic R&D or the development of innovative new products. Thus, a defender strategy works best in industries where the basic technology is not very complex or where it is well developed and unlikely to change dramatically over the short term. For instance, Pillsbury's prepared-dough products SBU—now part of the General Mills Company—has pursued a differentiated defender strategy for years. The unit generates substantial profits from well-established refrigerated dough products like Pillsbury Crescent rolls and Hungry Jack biscuits. But while it has introduced a number of line extensions over the years, most have been reconfigurations of the same basic dough-in-a-can technology, such as Soft Breadsticks.

Differentiated Defenders   To effectively defend its position by differentiation, a business must be strong in those functional areas critical for maintaining its particular competitive advantages over time. If a business's differentiation is based on superior product quality, those key functional areas include production, process engineering, quality control, and perhaps product engineering to develop product improvements. The effort to develop and maintain a quality differentiation can be worthwhile, though, because evidence suggests that superior product quality has a strong impact on a business's return on investment—an important performance objective for defenders.[17]

Regardless of the basis for differentiation, marketing is also important for the effective implementation of a differentiated defender strategy. Marketing activities that track changing customer needs and competitive actions and communicate the product offering's unique advantages through promotional and sales efforts to maintain customer awareness and loyalty are particularly important.

Low-Cost Defenders   Successful implementation of a low-cost defender strategy requires the business to be more efficient than its competitors. Thus, the business must establish the groundwork for such a strategy early in the growth stage of the industry. Achieving and maintaining the lowest per-unit cost usually means that the business has to seek large volume from the beginning—through some combination of low prices and promotional efforts—to gain economies of scale and experience. At the same time, such businesses must also invest in more plant capacity in anticipation of future growth and in state-of-the-art equipment to minimize production costs. This combination of low margins and heavy investment can be prohibitive unless the parent corporation can commit substantial resources to the business or unless extensive sharing of facilities, technologies, and programs with other business units is possible.

The low-cost defender's need for efficiency also forces the standardization of product offerings and marketing programs across customer segments to achieve scale effects. Thus, such a strategy is usually not so effective in fragmented markets desiring customized offerings as it is in commodity industries such as basic chemicals, steel, or flour, or in industries producing low-technology components such as electric motors or valves.

While low-cost defenders emphasize efficiency and low price as the primary focus of their competitive strategy, it is important to keep in mind that businesses pursuing other strategies should also operate as efficiently as possible given the functional activities necessary to implement those strategies. Some of the most effective businesses are those that work *simultaneously* to lower costs and improve quality and service.[18] And operating efficiency is likely to become even more critical as the Internet makes it easier for customers to compare prices across alternative suppliers or to obtain low-price bids via "buyers' auction" sites, such as www.MetalSite.com, as discussed in Chapter 6.

How Different Business Strategies Influence Marketing Decisions

Business units typically incorporate a number of distinct product-markets. A given entry's marketing manager monitors and evaluates the product's environmental situation and develops a marketing program suited to it. However, the manager's freedom to design such a program may be constrained by the business unit's competitive strategy. This is because different strategies focus on different objectives and seek to gain and maintain a competitive advantage in different ways. As a result, different functions within the SBU—and different activities within a given functional area, such as marketing—are critical for the success of different strategies.

KEY OBSERVATION

The SBU's strategy influences the amount of resources committed to marketing *and ultimately the budget available.*

There are, therefore, different key success factors inherent in the various generic business strategies. This constrains the individual marketing manager's freedom of action in two basic ways. First, because varying functions within the business unit are more important under different

Exhibit 10.6

DIFFERENCES IN MARKETING POLICIES AND PROGRAM COMPONENTS ACROSS BUSINESSES PURSUING DIFFERENT STRATEGIES

	STRATEGY		
Marketing policies and program components	Prospector	Differentiated defender	Low-cost defender
Product policies			
• Product-line breadth relative to competitors	+	+	−
• Technical sophistication of products relative to competitors	+	+	−
• Product quality relative to competitors	?	+	−
• Service quality relative to competitors	?	+	−
Price policies			
• Price levels relative to competitors	+	+	−
Distribution policies			
• Degree of forward vertical integration relative to competitors	−	+	?
• Trade promotion expenses as percent of sales relative to competitors	+	−	−
Promotion policies			
• Advertising expenses as percent of sales relative to competitors	+	?	−
• Sales promotions expenses as percent of sales relative to competitors	+	?	−
• Salesforce expenses as percent of sales relative to competitors	?	+	−

Key: Plus sign (+) = greater than the average competitor.

Minus sign (−) = smaller than the average competitor.

Question mark (?) = uncertain relationship between strategy and marketing policy or program component.

strategies, they receive different proportions of the SBU's total resources. Thus, the SBU's strategy influences *the amount of resources committed to marketing* and ultimately the budget available to an individual marketing manager within the business unit. Second, the SBU's choice of strategy influences both the kind of *market and competitive situation* that individual product-market entries are likely to face and the *objectives* they are asked to attain. Both constraints have implications for the design of marketing programs for individual products within an SBU.

It is risky to draw broad generalizations about how specific marketing policies and program elements might fit within different business strategies. While a business strategy is a general statement about how an SBU chooses to compete in an industry, that unit may comprise a number of product-market entries facing different competitive situations in various markets. Thus, there is likely to be a good deal of variation in marketing programs, and in the freedom individual marketing managers have in designing them, across products within a given SBU. Still, a business's strategy does set a general direction for the types of target markets it will pursue and how the unit will compete in those markets. And it does have some influence on marketing policies that cut across product-markets. Exhibit 10.6 outlines differences in marketing policies and program elements that occur across businesses pursuing different strategies, and those differences are discussed below.

Product Policies

One set of marketing policies defines the nature of the products the business will concentrate on offering to its target markets. These policies concern the *breadth or diversity of product lines,* their *level of technical sophistication,* and the target *level of product quality* relative to competitors.

Because prospector businesses rely heavily on the continuing development of unique new products and the penetration of new markets as their primary competitive strategy, policies encouraging broader and more technically advanced product lines than those of competitors should be positively related to performance on the critical dimension of share growth. The diverse and technically advanced product offerings of 3M's drug delivery systems SBU are a good example of this.

Whether a prospector's products should be of higher quality than competitors' products is open to question. Quality is hard to define; it can mean different things to different customers. Even so, it is an important determinant of business profitability.[19] Thus, Hambrick suggests that in product-markets where technical features or up-to-the-minute styling are key attributes in customers' definitions of quality, high-quality products may play a positive role in determining the success of a prospector strategy. In markets where the critical determinants of quality are reliability or brand familiarity, the maintenance of relatively high product quality is likely to be more strongly related to the successful performance of defender businesses, particularly differentiated defenders.[20]

Differentiated defenders compete by offering more or better choices to customers than do their competitors. For example, 3M's commercial graphics business, a major supplier of sign material for truck fleets, has strengthened its competitive position in that market by developing products appropriate for custom-designed signs. Until recently, the use of film for individual signs was not economical. But the use of computer-controlled knives and a new Scotch-brand marking film produce signs of higher quality and at lower cost than those that are hand-painted. This kind of success in developing relatively broad and technically sophisticated product lines should be positively related to the long-term ROI performance of most differentiated defender businesses.

However, broad and sophisticated product lines are less consistent with the efficiency requirements of the low-cost defender strategy. For one thing, maintaining technical sophistication in a business's products requires continuing investments in product and process R&D. For another, broad, complex lines can lead to short production runs and larger inventories. Some of the efficiency problems associated with broader, more-customized product lines may disappear, however, with continuing improvements in computer-assisted design and manufacturing, process reengineering, and the like.[21]

Instead of, or in addition to, competing on the basis of product characteristics, businesses can distinguish themselves relative to competitors on the *quality of service* they offer. Such service might take many forms, including engineering and design services, alterations, installation, training of customer personnel, or maintenance and repair services. A policy of high service quality is particularly appropriate for differentiated defenders because it offers a way to maintain a competitive advantage in well-established markets.

The appropriateness of an extensive service policy for low-cost defenders, though, is more questionable if higher operating and administrative costs offset customer satisfaction benefits. Those higher costs may detract from the business's ability to maintain the low prices critical to its strategy, as well as lowering ROI—at least in the short term. On the other hand, even low-cost defenders may have difficulty holding their position over the long term without maintaining at least competitive parity with respect to critical service attributes.[22]

Pricing Policies

Success in offering low prices relative to those of competitors should be positively related to the performance of low-cost defender businesses—for low price is the primary competitive weapon of such a strategy. However, such a policy is inconsistent with both differentiated defender and prospector strategies. The higher costs involved in differentiating a business's products on either a quality or service basis require higher prices to maintain profitability. Differentiation also provides customers with additional value for which higher prices can be charged. Similarly, the costs and benefits of new product and market development by prospector businesses require and justify relatively high prices. Thus, differentiated defenders and prospectors seldom adhere to a policy of low competitive prices.

Distribution Policies

Some observers argue that prospector businesses should show a greater degree of *forward vertical integration* than defender businesses.[23] The rationale for this view is that the prospector's focus on new product and market development requires superior market intelligence and frequent reeducation and motivation of distribution channel members. This can best be accomplished through tight control of company-owned channels. However, these arguments seem inconsistent with the prospector's need for flexibility in constructing new channels to distribute new products and reach new markets.

Attempting to maintain tight control over the behavior of channel members is a more appropriate policy for defenders who are trying to maintain strong positions in established markets. This is particularly true for defenders who rely on good customer service to differentiate themselves from competitors. Thus, it seems more likely that a relatively high degree of forward vertical integration is found among defender businesses, particularly differentiated defenders, while prospectors rely more heavily on independent channel members—such as manufacturer's representatives or wholesale distributors—to distribute their products.[24]

Because prospectors focus on new products where success is uncertain and sales volumes are small in the short run, they are likely to devote a larger percentage of sales to *trade promotions* than are defender businesses. Prospectors rely on trade promotion tools such as quantity discounts, liberal credit terms, and other incentives to induce cooperation and support from their independent channel members.

Promotion Policies

Extensive marketing communications also play an important role in the successful implementation of both prospector and differentiated defender strategies. The form of that communication, however, may differ under the two strategies. Because prospectors must constantly work to generate awareness, stimulate trial, and build primary demand for new and unfamiliar products, high advertising and sales promotion expenditures are likely to bear a positive relationship to the new product and share-growth success of such businesses. The drug delivery SBU at 3M, for instance, devotes substantial resources to advertising in professional journals and distributing samples of new products, as well as to maintaining an extensive salesforce.

Differentiated defenders, on the other hand are primarily concerned with maintaining the loyalty of established customers by adapting to their needs and providing good service. These tasks can best be accomplished—particularly in industrial goods and services industries—by an extensive, well-trained, well-supported, salesforce.[25] Therefore, differentiated defenders are likely to have higher salesforce expenditures than are competitors.

Finally, low-cost defenders appeal to their customers primarily on price. Thus, high expenditures on advertising, sales promotion, or the salesforce would detract from their basic strategy and may have a negative impact on their ROI. Consequently, such businesses are likely to make relatively low expenditures as a percentage of sales on those promotional activities.

What If the Best Marketing Program for a Product Does Not Fit the Business's Competitive Strategy?

What should a marketing manager do if the market environment facing a particular product or service demands marketing actions that are not consistent with the overall competitive strategy of the business to which it belongs? What if, for example, the product's target market is rapidly becoming more mature and competitive, but it is housed in a prospector business unit that does not have the cost structure or the personnel to allow the aggressive pricing or excellent customer service that may be needed for the product to compete successfully? Or what if newly emerging technology demands that a mature product category undergo an innovative redesign even though the defender SBU does not have extensive R&D and product development capabilities?

If a business unit is focused on a single product category or technological domain—as is the case with 3M's industrial tape unit—the ideal solution might be for the whole SBU to change its strategy in response to shifting industry circumstances. As the product category matures, for instance, the SBU might switch from a prospector to an analyzer strategy, and ultimately to one of the defender strategies.

The problem is that—as we shall see in Chapter 18—effective implementation of different business strategies requires not only different functional competencies and resources but also different organizational structures, decision-making and coordination processes, reward systems, and even personnel. Because such internal structures and processes are hard to change quickly, it can be very difficult for an entire SBU to make a successful transition from one basic strategy to another.[26] For example, many of Emerson Electric's SBUs historically were successful low-cost defenders, but accelerating technological change in their industries caused the corporation to try to convert them to low-cost analyzers who would focus more attention on new product and market development. Initially, however, this attempted shift in strategy resulted in some culture shock, conflict, and mixed performance outcomes within those units.

In view of the implementation problems involved, some firms do not try to make major changes in the basic competitive strategies of their existing business units. Instead, they might form new prospector SBUs to pursue emerging technologies and industries rather than expecting established units to handle extensive new product development efforts.

Similarly, as individual product-market entries gain successful positions in growing markets, some firms move them from the prospector unit that developed them into an existing analyzer or defender unit, or even into a newly formed SBU, better suited to reaping profits from them as their markets mature. For example, a number of innovative products developed at 3M, such as Post-it repositionable notes, have enjoyed sufficient success that new business units were formed to concentrate on defending them as their markets matured. Many successful entrepreneurial start-ups eventually reorganize into two or more business units, one to continue prospecting new products and markets and another to defend the firm's initial product offering as its market matures.

Finally, some firms that are technological leaders in their industries may divest or license individual product-market entries as they mature rather than defend them in the face

Exhibit 10.7   Jim Watkins Takes a Hike

When he was a product manager at the Pillsbury Company in the early 1970s, James D. Watkins became convinced that microwave technology represented a major opportunity for the packaged food industry. Consequently, he developed a marketing plan that proposed the pioneering development and aggressive introduction of a line of microwavable food products, starting with microwave popcorn. However, the business unit he worked for—and the entire Pillsbury Company at that time—was focused on defending strong positions in established markets, largely through incremental line extensions and product improvements. In other words, it was pursuing more of an analyzer strategy. As a result, top management rejected Watkins's proposal as being too risky and requiring resources and capabilities that were in short supply.

Watkins subsequently quit Pillsbury, founded a new firm called Golden Valley Microwave, attracted venture capital, hired some food scientists to do the necessary R&D, and began to market ActII microwave popcorn through large mass merchandisers such as Wal-Mart. As Watkins had predicted in his original marketing plan, the availability of microwavable foods spurred a rapid increase in consumer demand for microwave ovens, which in turn increased demand for more microwavable foods. His new company grew rapidly, and a few years later he sold it to Conagra for many millions of dollars.

But don't be too critical of Pillsbury. Like a good analyzer, the company avoided playing the risky role of the pioneer, but it eventually responded to the growing potential of microwave technology and successfully launched its own line of microwavable foods, including popcorn.

of increasing competition and eroding margins. This approach is relatively common at firms such as 3M and DuPont.

Because the marketing manager responsible for a given product-market entry is usually most closely tuned-in to changes in the market environment, he or she bears the responsibility for pointing out any mismatches between what is best for the product and the capabilities of the organizational unit to which it belongs. The marketer should develop a marketing strategy that makes the most sense in light of a detailed analysis of the available customer and competitive information and present a strong case for the resources necessary to implement the plan. If those resources are not available within the business unit, or if the marketing strategy is inconsistent with the SBU's objectives or competitive strategy, top management faces a choice of moving the product to a more benign unit of the firm or rejecting the recommended strategy. If the strategy is rejected, the marketer will likely have to make compromises to the strategy to make it fit better with the competitive thrust of the SBU, even though an attractive opportunity may be lost. But if the marketer has great confidence in the recommended strategy, he or she might opt to quit the firm and pursue the opportunity elsewhere, as was the case with Jim Watkins as discussed in Exhibit 10.7.

TAKE-AWAYS

- Research suggests that a business is likely to achieve superior revenue growth, market share, and profitability when there is a good fit between its competitive strategy and the strategic marketing programs of its various product or service offerings.

- Business-level competitive strategies can be usefully categorized into (1) prospector strategies focused on growth via the development of new products and markets, (2) defender strategies primarily concerned with defending strong positions in established markets through either low prices or offering customers superior value in terms of product quality or service, and (3) analyzer strategies, which are hybrids of the other two strategies.

- The generic competitive strategies described in the previous point apply equally well to services and physical products, single-product start-ups and multidivisional corporations, and global and domestic operations, and they are unlikely to change dramatically due to the rise of e-commerce.

- Because the various business-level strategies focus on different objectives and seek to gain a competitive advantage in different ways, marketing may play a different role under each of the strategies, and varying marketing actions may be called for.

- The marketing decision-maker's job is to develop a sound, evidence-based marketing strategy for his or her offering and to make a persuasive case for its support. If that strategy does not fit the objectives or available resources and competencies of the business unit in which the product is housed, top management may choose to move the product to a more amenable unit or require adjustments to the strategy.

Self-diagnostic questions to test your ability to apply the analytical tools and concepts in this chapter to marketing decision making may be found at this book's website at www.mhhe.com/mullins05.

ENDNOTES

1. Material for this example was obtained from The *3M Company 2002 Annual Report* and other information found on the company's website, www.3m.com; and Jerry Useem, "Scotch Tape Plus Innovation Equals?", *Fortune,* August 12, 2002, pp. 127–32.

2. Stanley F. Slater and Eric M. Olson, "Marketing's Contribution to the Implementation of Business Strategy: An Empirical Analysis," *Strategic Management Journal* 22 (November 2001), pp. 1055–67.

3. C. K. Prahalad and Gary Hamel, "The Core Competence of the Corporation," *Harvard Business Review* 68 (May–June 1990), pp. 79–91.

4. Michael E. Porter, *Competitive Strategy* (New York: Free Press, 1980). Also see Michael E. Porter, *Competitive Advantage: Creating and Sustaining Superior Performance* (New York: Free Press, 1985).

5. Robert E. Miles and Charles C. Snow, *Organizational Strategy, Structure, and Process* (New York: McGraw-Hill, 1978). For another taxonomy of business-level competitive strategies that incorporates elements of both the Porter and Miles and Snow frameworks, see Michael Treacy and Fred Wiersema, *The Discipline of Market Leaders* (Reading, MA: Addison-Wesley, 1995).

6. Charles C. Snow and Lawrence G. Hrebiniak, "Strategy, Distinctive Competence, and Organizational Performance," *Administrative Science Quarterly* 25 (1980), pp. 317–35.

7. Robert Szymczak, "Drinking to the Dubious Health of Privatization," *The Warsaw Voice,* business section, April 1, 2001, archived at www.warsawvoice..p1.

8. Theodore Levitt, *The Marketing Imagination* (New York: Free Press, 1986), pp. 94–95.

9. Philip Kotler and Gary Armstrong, *Principles of Marketing* (Englewood Cliffs, NJ: Prentice-Hall, 1989), p. 575.

10. Daryl O. McKee, P. Rajan Varadarajan, and William M. Pride, "Strategic Adaptability and Firm Performance: A Market-Contingent Perspective," *Journal of Marketing,* July 1989, pp. 21–35.

11. Bruce Einhorn and Ben Elgin, "The Well-Heeled Upstart on Cisco's Tail," *Business Week,* October 28, 2002, p. 91.

12. For example, see "Internet Economics: A Thinker's Guide," *The Economist,* April 1, 2000, pp. 64–66.

13. Larry Chiagouris and Brant Wansley, "Branding on the Internet," *Marketing Management* 9 (Summer 2000), pp. 35–38; and Faith Keenan, Stanley Holmes, Jay Greene, and Roger O. Crockett, "A Mass Market of One," *Business Week,* December 2, 2002, pp. 68–72.

14. Gordon Donaldson, *Managing Corporate Wealth* (New York: Praeger, 1984).

15. Donald C. Hambrick, "Some Tests of the Effectiveness and Functional Attributes of Miles and Snow's Strategic Types," *Academy of Management Journal* 26 (1983), pp. 5–26; and McKee, Varadarajan, and Pride, "Strategic Adaptability and Firm Performance."

16. Chester Dawson, "Fuel Cells: Japan's Carmakers Are Flooring It," *Business Week,* December 23, 2002, pp. 50–51.

17. Robert D. Buzzell and Bradley T. Gale, *The PIMS Principles: Linking Strategy to Performance* (New York: Free Press, 1987), chap. 6.

18. For example, see Ronald Henkoff, "Cost Cutting: How to Do It Right," *Fortune,* April 9, 1990, pp. 40–49.

19. Buzzell and Gale, *The PIMS Principles,* chap. 6.

20. Hambrick, "Some Tests of Effectiveness."

21. B. Joseph Pine II, Bart Victor, and Andrew C. Boynton, "Making Mass Customization Work," *Harvard Business Review* 71 (September–October 1993), pp. 108–19; and Keenan et al., "A Mass Market of One."

22. For additional arguments in the debate about the relative costs and competitive benefits of superior customer service, see Rahul Jacob, "Beyond Quality and Value," *Fortune,* Special Issue, Autumn–Winter 1993, pp. 8–11; and Valarie A. Zeithaml and Mary Jo Bitner, *Services Marketing* (New York: McGraw-Hill, 1996), chap. 2.

23. Miles and Snow, *Organizational Strategy, Structure, and Process;* and Hambrick, "Some Tests of Effectiveness."

24. Although Hambrick argues for the reverse relationship, data from his study of 850 SBUs actually support our contention that defenders have more vertically integrated channels than do prospectors. See Hambrick, "Some Tests of Effectiveness."

25. Leonard A. Schlesinger and James L. Heskett, "The Service-Driven Service Company," *Harvard Business Review* 69 (September–October 1991), pp. 71–81; and Jaclyn Fierman, "The Death and Rebirth of the Salesman," *Fortune,* July 25, 1994, pp. 80–91.

26. Connie J. G. Gersick, "Revolutionary Change Theories: A Multilevel Exploration of the Punctuated Equilibrium Paradigm," *Academy of Management Review* 16 (1991), pp. 10–36; and Michael L. Tushman, William H. Newman, and Elaine Romanelli, "Convergence and Upheaval: Managing the Unsteady Pace of Organizational Evolution," *California Management Review* 29 (1986), pp. 29–44.

CHAPTER ELEVEN

Product Decisions

Product Decisions in a Services Business[1]

ALMOST NO ONE LIKES BANKS. From surly tellers to long lines, from "bankers' hours" to fees for just about everything, consumers are fed up. But Prudential, the big British insurer, was convinced things didn't have to be this way. In October 1998, Prudential launched Egg, which has gone on to become one of Europe's most successful online financial services providers.

Egg, unlike many in the banking industry, believes superlative customer service is the key to growth. But can such service be delivered online? "The aim of all Egg's communication is to make the customer feel like an individual," says Patrick Muir, Egg's director of marketing. "We want to make money easier to understand and easier to manage."

Offering great customer service is easy to say, but is much harder to deliver consistently. Egg has succeeded by making a series of decisions about the product it offers—various services, in its case, rather than goods—and then managing its execution and service delivery very well through the use of technology. Banking with Egg is a far cry from conventional banking or most other applications of customer relationship management technology, for that matter, which often infuriate rather than please customers.

What were the product decisions that helped Egg succeed? First, Egg offers its customers a variety of channels of communication. There's the Internet, of course, but Egg doesn't stop there. Its Egg TV offers interactive access from the comfort of one's living room. Further, Egg's 1,200 call center associates are available round the clock to help customers who want to speak to a real person. "You actually have a conversation with someone, rather than sticking with a rigid script," says Muir. What Egg also does differently is to offer a wide variety of financial services. Checking accounts, savings, credit cards with cash-back discounts financed out of retailers' commission to Egg, mortgages, even insurance. Egg's wide range of financial services offers one-stop shopping to Egg customers. And each Egg customer can access a personal balance sheet that displays all his or her assets and liabilities on one screen. Even accounts with other online providers can be included.

Egg's multichannel strategy provides customers with more access points and enables them to access their money where, when, and as they wish. At home? Use Egg TV. At the office? Use the Internet. On holiday at a beach resort? Find an Internet café, and access your account. Egg says it's committed to mobile banking, too, as wireless technology deployment permits.

Egg's technology gives it a comprehensive customer-by-customer view which enables Egg to come up with suitable products and service to offer, based on each customer's own profile. "We want to put great offers in front of our customers that we believe are right for them rather than pushing unwanted products through hard-hitting sales campaigns," says Muir.

Egg's results speak for themselves. In 1999, it won 22 percent of net new deposits in the U.K. banking system. Within 18 months of launch, Egg had attracted more than one million customers. By 2002, brand awareness reached 88 percent and its customers numbered over 2.1 million.

"Egg was developed to make banking better," says marketing director Muir. Has Egg succeeded? Two million Brits—as well as a growing number of French consumers, following Egg's May 2002 acquisition of the French online banker Zebank—seem to think so.

Marketing Challenges Addressed in Chapter 11

As the story of Egg illustrates, decisions about product attributes—whether for goods or services—can make a huge difference in attracting customers. In this chapter, we examine the first of the four Ps—the many kinds of **product decisions** that marketers must make to provide the value that customers want. As we shall see, such decisions include those about attributes to include in the product (such as Egg's decision to offer account access via interactive TV), how to package the product (the level of access that Egg offers its customers), as well as decisions about branding, services related to the product, warranties, and so on. These decisions grow out of the need to differentiate one's products from those of competitors, as we discussed in Chapter 9, the positioning chapter. As we observed in Chapter 9, going to market with an undifferentiated product can be hazardous.

Thus, Chapter 11 addresses several critical questions that marketers face in differentiating their offerings from those of their competitors. How should our product offering, whether a good or a service, be designed to give it a chance to win sustainable competitive advantage? What product decisions must we make to deliver the benefits and value promised in our positioning statement or value proposition? How can products and product lines best be managed to satisfy the needs of different market segments, rather than simply taking market share from the firm's other products? Finally, given the importance of new products in the long-term success of most firms, how can new product development be managed, from a process perspective, to ensure a timely flow of new products that enjoy favorable reception by customers? Answering these questions thoughtfully, using evidence-based and up-to-date market knowledge as a foundation, gives the firm its best chance to offer goods and services that consumers want—as opposed to products its engineers can develop ("It's the latest technology!"), its merchants are excited about ("I have a hunch purple will be hot this year!"), or its CEO loves.

In the first portion of the chapter, we address the *content* of product decision making: decisions about product quality and features, related services, packaging, brand names, and so on. These decisions are applicable to existing and new products alike. We then broaden our focus to decisions about **product lines,** groups of related products such as Unilever's various brands of laundry detergents or Gillette's line of razors and razor blades. Then, to complete the chapter, we address the *process* of **new product development.** An abundance of recent evidence indicates that *how* the new product development process is managed—whether for **new-to-the-world products** born in high-tech research labs or simple **product modifications** or **line extensions**—can have important implications for time to market and, ultimately, for product success or failure.

Product Design Decisions for Competitive Advantage

A **product** can be defined as anything that satisfies a want or need through use, consumption, or acquisition. Thus, products include objects (TVs, radios, cars), services (medical, educational), places (New York, Moscow), people (Tony Blair and other politicians everywhere), activities (entering a contest or visiting a weight-loss clinic), and ideas (have you hugged your kids today?).

Conceptually, products should be thought of as problem solvers since they are purchased because of the core benefits they provide—not because of the product per se. For example, a student who buys a handheld calculator is buying a way to quickly solve certain mathematical problems as well as to ensure accuracy of calculations. What is important is how the *consumer* perceives the product as satisfying a need, *not* how the *seller* sees the product. The seller must turn the wanted benefits into a tangible product with **features** or attributes that will provide the intended satisfaction better than competitive products. But benefits and features are not the same. **Features** are the tangible or intangible attributes given the product by its designers. **Benefits** are the solutions to customer problems or needs delivered by the product. Some of the features that Egg offers, and the benefits they deliver, are shown in Exhibit 11.1. Ultimately, most customers are far more interested in *benefits* than they are in *features,* though marketers sometimes forget this fact in designing ads or other marketing communications messages.

KEY OBSERVATION

Most customers are far more interested in benefits *than they are in* features.

Well-managed marketers give explicit attention to all of the attributes of their products, choosing product features, packaging, warranties and services, and brand names that will help deliver the benefits sought by the product's target market (see Exhibit 11.2). We

Exhibit 11.1

SOME FEATURES OF EGG AND THE CUSTOMER BENEFITS THEY DELIVER

Feature	Benefits
Online Bank	• Available to customers 24 × 7, i.e., longer banking hours
Multiple channels to serve customers	• Use the Egg interactive TV to manage accounts from the comfort of your living room
	• Access to account available while on a holiday from an Internet café, and from your PC at home or work
	• Call center available for customers who call over the phone
Online only bank	• Bank has a lower cost basis which is transferred to customers via
	• more competitive interest rates on credit cards
	• higher interest rate on checking and savings accounts
	• Able to offer customers new products faster than bricks and mortar banks
Account aggregation, and aggregation of accounts held with other financial institutions	• Allows Egg customers to get a single snapshot of their current finances across all of their credit cards and bank accounts
	• Allows customers to more easily see savings opportunities (i.e., moving balances to a lower interest credit card)

deal with what needs to be addressed in making these decisions in the first half of this chapter.

Goods and Services: Are the Product Decisions the Same?

What is a service? As we discussed in Chapter 10, services can be thought of as *intangibles* versus goods as *tangibles*. Thus, services can rarely be experienced in advance of the sale, while tangible goods can be directly experienced, even tested, before purchase.

The service component of the U.S. economy accounts for about 75 percent of all non-farm jobs and over half the country's gross domestic product (GDP).[2] In recent years productivity of the U.S. service sector has increased dramatically to a point where it outperforms its European and Japanese counterparts by a wide margin.[3] The United States is the world's largest exporter and importer of commercial services, and commercial services account for 18 percent of total world trade.[4] Similar trends are found in most highly developed economies. (See Exhibit 11.3 for further discussion of such services from an international view.)

There are several reasons for the growing importance of services in the United States, Europe, and Japan, but the two most important are economic growth and lifestyle changes. Given the large number of women now working outside the home (in the United States, over 70 percent of women age 18 to 44), the demand for child care, housekeeping, and time-saving services has increased dramatically. Another lifestyle factor has been the growing interest in fitness, which, in turn, has increased the demand for physical fitness

Exhibit 11.2

THE AUGMENTED PRODUCT CONCEPT

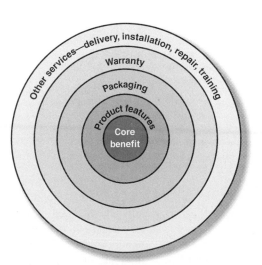

Exhibit 11.3   The International Side of Services

It is estimated that about 25 percent of all international trade is in services. But this may be an underestimate since most services are not required to have an export declaration or pass through a tariff or customs barrier. Services not being counted include advertising, accounting, consulting, legal services, and insurance—all of which are growing fast.

Originally service companies entering international markets did so primarily to satisfy their domestic clients. Today, the major reason is to seek new market opportunities. Because of the inseparability of producing and consuming services, the exporting of services is sometimes difficult. Advances in computing and telecommunications, however, have made it possible to provide customer service, software develop-

ment and programming, and many other kinds of services remotely, from wherever the requisite skills are available at lower cost.

The biggest obstacle to the continued expansion of international services is protectionism, including restrictions to favor local markets. Both direct and indirect trade barriers are increasingly being erected. They have been rationalized on a variety of levels. There is also increasing concern about how to deal with the transmission of electronic data across borders, not only in terms of human rights but also as to how best to tax the data.

Source: Philip R. Cateora, *International Marketing* (Burr Ridge, IL: Richard D. Irwin, 1996), p. 436. Reprinted with permission from The McGraw-Hill Companies.

Exhibit 11.4

MARKETING-STRATEGY IMPLICATIONS OF CONSUMER GOODS CLASSIFICATION

	Examples	Strategy elements stressed
Convenience goods and services	Dentifrice, soap, razor blades, magazines, many packaged food products, haircuts	Maximum distribution (product availability), consumer advertising (awareness and brand recognition), merchandising (in-store displays)
Shopping goods and services	Color TVs, cars, major appliances, homes, car repair, family doctors	Available in limited number of stores, personal selling important, limited to extensive advertising, seller often offers financing, warranties, and postpurchase service
Specialty goods and services	Musical instruments, stereo equipment, some brands of men's clothing, college consultants	Limited distribution, high price, strong advertising to promote brand uniqueness and to inform where available locally
Unsought goods and services	Certain medical services, personal liability insurance, encyclopedias	Strong promotion, including personal selling

and recreational services. And as populations grow older, the need for health-related services expands. Finally, the increase in the number and complexity of goods has stimulated an increase in demand for repair services. Business services (maintenance , financing, marketing research, advertising) have also grown at a high rate.[5] As we have seen with Egg, the principles entailed in product decision making apply to services as well as goods. Thus, when we say **product** in this book we mean both **goods** and **services.** As shown in Exhibit 11.4, different kinds of goods and services often call for varying marketing strategies, but the decision-making content and processes for both goods and services are similar.

KEY OBSERVATION

*When we say **product** in this book we mean both **goods** and **services**.*

Exhibit 11.5

EIGHT DIMENSIONS OF QUALITY FOR GOODS

1. *Performance* has to do with a product's basic operating characteristics. For an automobile, this translates into such traits as acceleration, miles per gallon, ease in handling, and comfort. The individual and the use environment determine what traits are important as well as how important.

2. *Features* are product characteristics that are designed to enhance the product's functioning or consumer appeal. In cars, examples include rear window defrosters, power steering, cruise control, and side-door airbags.

3. *Reliability* is the probability that a product will perform satisfactorily over a given period. Because of the cost of repair and downtime, reliability is an extremely important dimension for automobiles and heavy machinery.

4. *Conformance* is the extent to which a product's operating characteristics meet certain specifications.

5. *Durability* is a measure of the life of a product. It has both technical (replacement) and economic (repair costs) dimensions.

6. *Serviceability* is concerned with the speed and ease of obtaining competent repair.

7. *Esthetics* has to do with how a product looks, feels, sounds, tastes, and smells. These ratings are subjective and are related to how the consumer perceives quality.

8. *Perceived quality* frequently results from the use of indirect measures since the consumer may lack or not understand information about a product's attributes. Thus, perceptions may derive from such cues as price, brand name, advertising, reputation, and country of origin.

Source: Adapted with the permission of The Free Press, a Division of Simon & Schuster Adult Publishing Group from *Managing Quality: The Strategic and Competitive Edge* by David A. Garvin. Copyright © 1988 by David A. Garvin. All rights reserved.

Product Quality and Features Decisions

A well-developed positioning statement or value proposition plays an important role in designing products, whether goods or services. It tells the product's designers what benefits are to be delivered, so designers can imbue the product with the necessary features or other attributes, such as those we've seen at Egg, to deliver those benefits. Positioning makes clear how the product—an account with Egg—is to be differentiated from other products in its category.

As we have seen in the positioning chapter, products—whether goods or services—can be differentiated by both physical and perceptual means. One important dimension on which goods or services are physically differentiated is on the basis of quality—seeking to be better, in some sense, in the customers' eyes than competing products. Differentiating on quality can occur on any of the eight dimensions of quality for goods or the five dimensions of service quality, as shown in Exhibits 11.5 and 11.6.

So how should decisions about product features be made? Typically, consumers' choice criteria are limited to relatively few attributes or quality dimensions for a given product cat-

KEY OBSERVATION

How should decisions about product features be made?

egory. Thus, most products use only a few dimensions of quality as the basis on which they compete. Decisions about which dimensions of quality should be designed into a product are driven by earlier choices about the product's target market and positioning. When the product and product category, its users, and its uses are well understood, the marketing research techniques discussed in Chapter 7 can be employed to determine consumer needs and assess consumer preferences for products having various features. For example, in designing the seats for its Infinity J-30 automobile to be sold in the United States, Nissan tested more than 90 samples of leather before selecting three whose smells were most appealing to American consumers.[6] Some analytical techniques (and software packages for running them) commonly employed in determining the best set of features for a product are discussed in Exhibit 11.7.

In some situations, especially when the task is to design a breakthrough product that differs significantly from prior products, traditional marketing research is less likely to elicit

Exhibit 11.6

FIVE DIMENSIONS OF SERVICE QUALITY

1. *Tangibles* are the appearance of physical characteristics associated with the service. For a dentist, tangibles include the décor of the office, the comfort and conditions of the equipment and facilities, and the appearance of the dentist and dental assistants.

2. *Reliability* is the dependability entailed in the service performed. Does the dentist's work last over many years? Is the work pain-free once the office ordeal is over?

3. *Responsiveness* is the promptness and helpfulness of the service deliverers. Does the dentist keep patients waiting or see them on schedule? Does he or she see patients quickly in an emergency?

4. *Assurance* is the competence, courtesy, and credibility with which the service is provided. Is the dentist properly trained and certified? Is the staff courteous?

5. *Empathy* is the degree to which the service provider communicates with the customer and understands the customer's needs and concerns. Does the dentist offer and explain the merits of different treatment options? Does he or she carefully answer patients' questions?

Source: Adapted with the permission of The Free Press, a Division of Simon & Schuster Adult Publishing Group from *Delivering Quality Service: Balancing Customer Perceptions and Expectations* by Valarie A. Zeithaml, A. Parasuraman, Leonard L. Berry. Copyright © 1990 by The Free Press. All rights reserved.

Exhibit 11.7

MARKETING DECISION SUPPORT TOOLS FOR NEW PRODUCT DECISION MAKING

Tool or technique	Software packages	What they do
Brand development software	NamePro® from the Namestormers, www.namestormers.com	Helps create distinctive, memorable brands for goods or services
Quality function deployment	QFD/CAPTURE; see www.qfdcapture.com	Measures links between known customer needs, engineering characteristics, and product design features to assess product preferences
Conjoint analysis	Several Programs from Sawtooth Software, see www.sawtoothsoftware.com	Assesses consumers' preferred trade-offs among different product attributes

the information needed to design a new product. For such situations, new techniques have been developed to go beyond what consumers can easily articulate and uncover needs they may not have yet identified. Empathic design, one such technique that observes customers or prospective customers in their own environments at home, at work, or wherever, is described in Exhibit 11.8. The use of techniques such as empathic design is one way to respond to critics who charge that excessively customer-led decision processes can blind companies to the needs of customers it does not currently serve. Companies that adopt a true **market orientation** use techniques such as these to obtain a broader view of their markets than their current customers can provide.

Branding Decisions

Branding identifies and helps differentiate the goods or services of one seller from those of another. It consists of a name, sign, symbol, or some combination thereof. A **brand name** is the part that can be vocalized (BIC, Bennetton, Sony). A **brand mark** is something that cannot be verbalized, such as a symbol, design, or unique packaging (the Red Bull Silver can, the McDonald's arches, the Pillsbury Dough Boy). A **trademark** is simply a brand or some part of a brand that legally belongs exclusively to a given seller.

Exhibit 11.8

EMPATHIC DESIGN UNCOVERS NEW CUSTOMER NEEDS

Empathic design, a qualitative product design and marketing research technique, observes customers in their own environments to uncover needs that they cannot or are not likely to articulate under traditional qualitative or quantitative research settings, such as focus groups, in-depth interviews, or surveys. The empathic design process includes five steps, as follows:

1. *Observation:* Decisions about whom should be observed, who should do the observing, and what the observers should be watching are critical. A team of observers each having a different perspective—a human factors specialist, an engineer, a designer, and so on—is typically employed.

2. *Capturing data:* Most data are gathered from visual, auditory, or sensual clues, sometimes using audio or video recorders, or even rough sketches, to record the data.

3. *Reflection and analysis:* The research team gathers to reflect on what they have observed and to review their visual and textual data with other colleagues.

4. *Brainstorming for solutions:* This step is used to transform the research observations into graphic or visual representations of possible solutions to customer problems or needs.

5. *Developing prototypes:* Prototypes are used to clarify the concept and gain further feedback from others, including designers and potential customers.

A complete description of the empathic design process can be found in Leonard and Rayport (1997).

Source: Reprinted by permission of *Harvard Business Review.* From "Spark Innovation Through Empathic Design," by Dorothy Leonard and Jeffrey F. Rayport, November–December. Copyright © 1997 by the Harvard Business School Publishing Corporation, all rights reserved.

Branding is important to consumers because it simplifies shopping, facilitates the processing of information concerned with purchase options, provides confidence that the consumer has made the right decision, helps to ensure quality, and often satisfies certain status needs. Branding also benefits sellers by enhancing:[7]

- The effectiveness of their marketing programs—particularly those concerned with promotion.
- Brand loyalty, which leads to greater profitability because generally it costs less to retain customers than to acquire new ones.
- The opportunities for successfully launching brand extensions.
- Prices and margins resulting from a competitive advantage.
- Channel relationships.

Through its branding efforts, a company improves its brand equity position, which consists of four major asset categories—brand name awareness, brand loyalty, perceived quality, and brand association. Thus, given the value-enhancing power of branding, it is not surprising that more and more attention is being given to managing brands, especially in terms of developing a winning brand identity. The latter will be discussed in Chapter 14, in which we focus on advertising.

The decision issue here, of course, is what brand to give to a new product. This decision may involve developing a new brand, as Toyota did when it introduced its upscale Lexus automobiles into the United States, or using one of the firm's existing brands, as Toyota did with the introduction of its Toyota Echo models in 1999.

KEY OBSERVATION

The decision issue here, of course, is what brand to give to a new product.

Branding Strategies   A company has a number of branding-strategy options, one of which is to brand name each individual product or to use a family brand name. **Individual branding** requires the company to provide each product or product line with a distinctive name. This type of branding is practiced by such firms as Procter & Gamble (Tide and

Ariel detergent, Crest toothpaste), Diageo (Smirnoff vodka, Guiness stout, Baileys Irish Cream, Jose Cuervo tequila), and Accor hotels (Mercure, Novotel, Motel 6). Individual branding reduces a company's risk in that a failure is not readily associated with the firm's other products. Further, it enables a firm to compete via multiple entries within the same product class.

When developing a new brand, whether in a new or existing company, one key decision is whether to have the brand clearly indicate what the product is or stands for (*Burger* King, *Pizza* Hut, *Healthy* Choice cookies) or to develop a brand whose meaning must be built (BMW, Nestlé, McDonald's). The former approach may make it easier and less costly to build market awareness and gain customer trial at the outset, but it can limit the flexibility to adapt to changing market conditions (witness Kentucky Fried Chicken's name change to KFC when *fried* became a negative attribute due to trends toward healthier eating). Such an approach, however, is viewed by some as generic and boring and may make it harder to build an image for and differentiate one's brand. Positioning guru Al Ries argues that the latter approach, whereby a brand is based on its own distinctive name (eBay, Amazon.com), is probably better than the generic approach (Auction.com, Books.com) in today's rapidly changing and highly competitive marketplace.[8]

Family branding uses the same brand name to cover a group of products or product lines. There are several variations of family branding including its use primarily with related items (Campbell's soups and Dyson's vacuum cleaners), its use with all company items regardless of whether they are use-related (General Electric is an example), and the use of a family name combined with individual product names (Kellogg's Raisin Bran cereal).

The major arguments for using family branding are reduced costs and transfer of customer satisfaction from one product to another bearing the same name. The latter makes it easier to launch product modifications such as new package sizes and types, or new flavors and varieties, and new products as when Nike extended its brand to cover athletic clothing. Family branding can also increase the impact of shelf facings in stores and make feasible the promotion of a product line comprising many low-volume items.

Under certain conditions, family branding is not a good strategy. For instance, when the family brand covers products that vary in quality, consumers become confused about what quality to expect. Also, extending a brand name to an inadequate product may tarnish the quality reputation of the entire line.

Other strategies include *cobranding* and *globalization.* The former uses multiple brand names with a single product or service offering. To be successful, the new product should either open another segment or add value in existing segments. Examples are the Smart car (Mercedes-Benz and Swatch) and Häagen-Dazs' Baileys Irish Cream ice cream. Cobranding is just getting started worldwide but is expected to grow.

Building a global brand is often difficult for a variety of reasons: the meaning of the brand name evoking negative associations in some countries; the presence of strong local brands; and the heavy investments required. Still, if successful, the scale effects can dramatically enhance sales and profits. The most successful global brands include Coca-Cola, Kellogg's, Nike, Starbucks, McDonald's, Kodak, Marlboro, IBM, American Express, Sony, Mercedes-Benz, and Nescafé.[9]

Retailer and Distributor Brands   In recent years, high-quality **store brands** have gained considerable ground versus national brands. Such labels represent over $50 billion in U.S. supermarket sales and 20 percent of supermarket unit sales. Private labels are also enjoying even greater success in Europe, taking a 41 percent volume share of the market in the United Kingdom, followed by Belgium with 36.4 percent and Germany with 31 percent.[10]

The explanation for the increasing importance of store brands is that during the 1980s the national and global brands regularly increased their prices along with massive distributions of coupons, thereby training consumers to shop on price. They also undertook large numbers of line extensions and, in general, focused less on brand equity. Such fast-growing discounters as Wal-Mart and France's Carretour have moved aggressively to take advantage of the price vulnerability of many national brands. Strong retailer brands have also become very important in the soft goods trade. Ralph Lauren, The Limited, and a number of European retailers such as Burberry and Laura Ashley have opened their own U.S. stores.

But there are some countertrends to the above. A number of consumer goods companies have been acquired over the past several years at substantial multiples of their book value because of the value of their brand names (for instance, acquisition of Richardson/Vicks by Procter & Gamble and various liquor brands by Diageo). The reasoning behind such acquisitions is the high cost of creating a well-known brand and the low success rate of new products. Thus, buying popular brands can be a shortcut to growth.

Packaging Decisions

A product's package serves several functions—protecting, facilitating use of, and promoting the product, as well as providing information about the product and its use. The protection function is critical in both transport and storage. Protecting an item under a variety of temperatures and moisture conditions and against being crushed or dropped during handling is no small undertaking.

Because of increasing competition among brands within stores, packages have become an extension of the product and a way of identifying and differentiating products that can lead to increased loyalty. Packaging often facilitates use of the product, as in aerosol cans and disposable and unbreakable bottles. Packaging can also increase consumer safety, as proved by child-proof tops on drugs and tamper-resistant packages.

Packaging can give a product strong promotional support at the point of purchase. Many more potential customers may see the package than see advertising—and at more opportune times. More and more sellers are attempting to develop a common package design for their products, thereby creating a greater impact on the consumer. Because consumers purchase a high percentage of supermarket items on impulse, packaging is especially important for such items. Packaging also can play an important role in the marketing of services. The blue suits and white shirts worn by high-priced strategy consultants are an example. The distinctive store decor of the various beauty salon chains is another.

KEY OBSERVATION

Packaging can give a product strong promotional support at the point of purchase. Many more potential customers may see the package than see advertising—and at more opportune times.

Increasingly firms are recognizing the need to use environmentally sensitive packages. Given the growing concern about the disposal of solid waste, more recyclable and biodegradable materials are being used.

Services Decisions and Warranties

The service component of a product can include a variety of activities; the following are among the more common:

- Delivery reliability.
- Warranty.
- Repair and maintenance (including response time, spare parts availability, and effectiveness).

- Efficient complaint handling.
- Credit availability.
- Prompt inquires handling.
- Buyer personnel training.
- Prompt claim settlement.
- Fast price quotations.
- Fast order processing.

Companies that excel at providing service find it a substantial competitive advantage. In most markets, it is a significant part of a firm's quality rating. In many, it is more important than the product itself. Service is not just a competitive weapon; it also strongly affects the overall level of profitability since it typically costs more to get a new customer than to keep an old one. The more service-sensitive the market (the importance of service versus physical attributes), the greater the opportunity for profits. To be effective a firm's service program must contain performance standards and be monitored regularly.

Warranties can play important roles in reducing the customer's risk of purchase and enhancing quality perceptions, thereby enhancing sales. Catalog retailer Lands' End's slogan "Guaranteed, period" is such an example. Similarly, Dell's offer of extended three-year on-site warranties for computers it sells on its website helps reduce any concerns customers may have about buying Dell products sight unseen. Warranties are only part of the story in assuring customer satisfaction, however. Sometimes, products fail to perform as planned, and customers have unsatisfactory experiences with them that take the company beyond the terms of its warranties. The story of Bridgestone Corp., the makers of Firestone tires, and its handling of safety problems with Firestone's Wilderness AT tires on Ford Explorers, shows how expensive—in human lives and in financial terms—product performance and safety problems can be (see Ethical Perspective 11.1). This story also highlights how ethical issues that go beyond the original intent of a warranty can come into play.

Managing Product Lines for Customer Appeal and Profit Performance

Whether a **product line** is too short or too long depends on the extent to which the market can be segmented and how the company wants to position itself. Much also depends on what stage the product-market evolution is in. A short product line is desirable during the early stages, given the difficulties of managing a long line. It is also more profitable given the economies of scale and that it simplifies the inventories of both the company and its channel members. In the longer term, however, a short line comes under fire as competitors segment the market and develop more specialized products to meet the needs of these segments. Thus, to survive and prosper, short lines must be uniquely positioned against competitors—and the firm must be able to maintain the line's differential advantage.

In recent years more and more companies are pursuing product expansion strategies. They do so to grow by catering to more segments, to minimize competitive threats to small

lines, to satisfy the demands of some customers for a variety of goods under a single brand, and as a short-term weapon to gain more control over limited shelf space, thereby making it more difficult for a competitor to expand its line.[11] The problem is that as a line increases, it becomes

ETHICAL PERSPECTIVE 11.1

Bridgestone's Handling of Firestone Tire Recall Angers Consumers, Hammers Stock Price

In August 2000, Bridgestone/Firestone Inc. recalled 6.5 million tires that had been installed as original equipment on Ford Motor Company's hot-selling Explorer sport utility vehicles and other SUVs and light trucks. The tires had been the subject of an inquiry into a tread separation problem as a result of nearly 300 reports of tire failure, allegedly resulting in scores of injuries and 46 deaths in the United States plus other injuries and deaths elsewhere. What angered consumers and consumer advocates most, however, was not that the tires appeared to be defective, since most consumers understand that product problems do occasionally occur despite manufacturers' best efforts to prevent them. What angered them was Firestone's decision to phase the recall over many months, possibly as long a year, because it lacked sufficient inventory to replace the tires at once. If the tires were unsafe, consumers wanted replacement tires right away. Said Carlos Perdue, 79, a retired Ford facilities manager in Michigan, "I'm not going to wait for a year to get my tires replaced."

Observers of Firestone's decision to phase the recall questioned Firestone's stance in ethical terms. If the tires were unsafe (John Lampe, Firestone's executive vice president, finally acknowledged in September 2000 that it had made bad tires), why was Firestone not willing to face that fact and allow consumers to replace their tires with tires made by any manufacturer, instead of waiting for Firestone to provide its own re-

placement tires? Why had it not acted sooner, when reports of the faulty tires began to appear six months earlier. "It's about what they didn't do up to now," said Stephen Greyser, a marketing professor at Harvard Business School. "The fact that the company is just stepping up to bat tells me they've never really had the consumer as the principal focus of their thinking." As one former Bridgestone/Firestone executive remarked, "They just don't have a clue how to handle this."

Shares of Bridgestone Corp. fell to 1,849 yen on the heels of the furor over the recall, down from about 2,500 yen before news of the tires' problems began to surface. A poll of American consumers in September 2000 found that Firestone's handling of the tire recall was "extremely likely" or "very likely" to influence decisions to purchase Firestone products for a whopping 67 percent of consumers. Noriaki Hirakata of Morgan Stanley Dean Witter in Tokyo projected that global revenue for Bridgestone Corp. would fall from $19.7 billion in 2000 to $17.8 billion in 2001 as a result of the fiasco. Evidently, bad tires and bad ethical handling of the ensuing recall are likely to result in bad business performance for Firestone in the future.

Source: Timothy Aeppel, "Firestone Set to Replace 6.5 Million Tires," *The Wall Street Journal,* August 10, 2000, p. A3; John O'Dell and Edmund Sanders, "Firestone Recall May Take a Year," *Denver Post,* August 10, 2000, p. A1; Todd Zaun, "Bridgestone to Take Charge of $345 Million," *The Wall Street Journal,* August 11, 2000, p. A6; Stephen Power and Clare Ansberry, "Bridgestone/Firestone Says It Made 'Bad Tires'," *The Wall Street Journal,* September 13, 2000, p. A3; Irene M. Kunii and Dean Foust, "'They Just Don't Have a Clue How to Handle This'," *Business Week,* September 18, 2000, p. 43.

more difficult to position individual products to prevent cannibalization that reduces the scale effects realized by the older products, thus affecting the net profitability of the line. Aside from the short-line/long-line strategy issue, other product-line decisions including line filling, line stretching, **line extension,** and product abandonment. All but the last involve adding to the length of the present line.

Line Filling

This strategy lengthens the product line by adding items within the present range. Its objective is to satisfy more customers, to increase sales and profits, to placate dealers who want a full-line supplier, and to ward off competitors. Most consumer goods companies increase the length of their product lines during the growth period by adding or dropping features. Thus, for example, Mercedes has added an off-road sport utility vehicle. Because of the temptation to add items, line filling often results in too long a line from an economic viewpoint; hence the need for a periodic product-line analysis.

Line Stretching

This strategy involves lengthening the product line beyond its current range. Aircraft manufacturers such as Boeing and Airbus have typically expanded the size of their jets. Such product line stretching—literally, in this case—may be up or down or both. A stretch can also consist of trading up, as in the addition of higher price lines. JC Penney, the American soft lines retailer, has traded up many of its lines over the years. An upward stretch is not without its risks, however, since consumers may not believe that the company can produce a higher-quality product.

A downward stretch involves adding products to serve the lower end of the market; for instance, Mercedes added a minicar (in Europe) some three feet shorter than any of its other lines selling for only $20,000. The risks involved with a downward stretch are primarily that the lower quality of the new product may diminish the company's overall quality image and that channel intermediaries may not support the move because of lower margins.

Firms practice two-way stretches when they have a midrange offering and seek market dominance by expanding both up and down, as Toyota has done. Both up and down line-stretching strategies are essentially incremental. Firms can thus exploit their current technological, manufacturing, and marketing resources, reducing the risks inherent in the introduction of new products.

Line Extensions

This strategy consists of introducing new products that differ significantly from those in the existing line by more than just size and price. The commercial jet airplane industry serves as an example. Boeing aborted a line-stretching strategy based on its 727 model (involving a lengthened 200-passenger version) because of a lack of interest by several major airlines. It then successfully developed its B757, B767, and B777 models. Examples of other line extensions include Gap Kids and Time's *Sports Illustrated for Kids*.

A product-line extension strategy involves greater costs and financial risks than product-line filling or stretching strategies. It provides, however, an extended technological base for the firm and is more likely to tap new market segments. It also provides a new anchor point in the product space from which product-line filling or stretching strategies can be based, thereby minimizing the danger of cannibalizing existing products.

Brand Extensions

Brand extension involves the use of a brand name established in one product class as a vehicle to enter another product class. A majority of the new products introduced to supermarkets and drugstores fall in this category.

The rationale for an extension is that the contribution of the brand name to the extension will be positive. The critical question here is the extent to which the brand name can provide a point of differentiation, including a quality association. Examples here include Arm and Hammer Carpet Deodorizer, Duracell Durabeam flashlights, and the use of the HP (Hewlett-Packard) name on thousands of items. By providing such an association, brand extensions can facilitate the acceptance of a new product by providing it with instantaneous familiarity. Bad brand extensions occur when the name adds little or no benefit to the extension and may cause confusion and, at worst, stimulate negative attribute association. The Levi Strauss tailored classics line was said to have failed because of the negative associations with Levi's rugged materials and casualness.[12]

Dropping Products

Too few companies subject their product lines to a regular audit to determine which products, if any, should be dropped. Too often a firm rationalizes the continuation of certain

products on the basis that they are at least covering direct costs, perhaps even making a contribution to fixed costs. Such reasoning overlooks the opportunity costs of not getting rid of them, including the disproportionate amount of management time spent on weak products. Substantial profit increases can often result from the elimination of weak items. Japan's Shiseido Co., its largest cosmetics group, moved to profitability by streamlining product lines and improving inventory control.[13]

The criteria for identifying weak products focus largely on the trend of the product's contribution to profit. Each such item should then be evaluated on such considerations as future sales of the item's product type or class, its future market share assuming no changes in the product or its marketing, future market share assuming certain product and marketing changes, anticipated changes in the marketing of competitive products (including the price), the effect of dropping the product on the company's channels of distribution, the cost of dropping the item (layoffs and inventory clearances), and the effect of dropping the product on the sales and profits of the firm's other items because of joint costs or other factors.

Product Systems

This strategy consists of selling a product and providing complementary products and service as a package. For example, some airlines sell vacation packages that include airfare, rental car, hotel accommodations, meals, sight-seeing tours, and entertainment. Complex undertakings such as data processing and information retrieval also lend themselves to product systems. Many of the larger computer companies sell not only computers, but also software, operating systems, preventive maintenance (including emergency repairs), financing and employee training. Hewlett-Packard sells printers and ink cartridges. Gillette sells razors and blades.

A product-system strategy requires a strong compatibility between the various components of the system. When properly implemented, such a strategy produces scale economies (in contrast to individual consumers' attempts to put together their own systems) and a closer, more enduring relationship between buyer and seller. Implementing a product system successfully requires an in-depth understanding of customers' needs; a well-trained, high-level salesforce; and sufficient funds to finance the sale of a system, which often is a time-consuming process.

New Product Development Process Decisions

As the Egg example illustrates, a firm's growth and profitability is significantly influenced by how well it succeeds in making product decisions, improving present products, and adding new ones to serve new markets or market segments. But developing new products is a costly and risky undertaking as companies around the world have learned. This section examines a process by which a firm can better exploit the opportunities for new products and minimize the inherent risks.[14] Before detailing this process, we need to discuss the role of new products in long-term profitability, new product success rates and the major reasons new products fail.

The Importance of New Products to Long-Term Profitability

An abundance of recent research has established that new products constitute the lifeblood of long-term firm success[15] and provide a central mechanism for firms' adaptation to today's rapidly changing markets and the opportunities they offer.[16] Since 1970, one source reports, the number of new products sold through supermarkets and drugstores has increased from 1,365 to 20,076. Other sources differ from these estimates. One main reason for such differences is considerable disagreement as to what constitutes a new product.[17] There are a number of ways to classify new products. One of the simplest ways is to divide new products into four major classes: new to the world, new to the firm, product-line extensions, and product improvements. Only a small percentage (about 5 percent) of products are new to the world. Most (89 percent) are either **product-line extensions** or **product improvements.**[18] The rationale for this focus on line extensions is—Why spend a lot of time and money to introduce a new product when most fail and it's much less expensive and faster to introduce an extension or an improvement?

New Product Success and Failure

Estimates of new product failures in the United States range from as low as 25 percent to as high as 90 percent. Part of this variation in estimates comes because some studies examine the proportion of new concepts or ideas that fail to achieve commercial success, while others focus only on products that fail after being introduced into the market.[19] The consulting firm of Booz, Allen & Hamilton estimated that out of every seven ideas that enter the new product process, only one emerges as a commercial success and that nearly half of the money spent on new product development goes to products that either fail or are abandoned.[20] Unfortunately, these figures haven't improved much over the years; variants of existing products are not included in the statistics.

Differences in failure estimates are also influenced by how the new product is defined, the type of product, and the channels involved. For example, consumer goods experience higher failure rates than industrial goods primarily because the latter do a better job of segmenting their markets on the basis of need and working closely with users during the development process. Even when a new product, such as those sold by food stores, makes its way into the marketplace, very few achieve annual sales of $100 million.[21]

The biggest cause of failure, however, is the introduction of me-too products that sell for the same or for a higher price but do not outperform products already on the market.

KEY OBSERVATION

The biggest cause of failure, however, is the introduction of me-too products.

Not surprisingly, the key to developing a successful new product is to link a superior product to an attractive market where there is little or no competition. Strong marketing capabilities are also an important success determinant.

Given the high risk involved, there must be strong reasons firms spend large amounts of time and money on new product development. Most of these considerations are related to external forces that affect a firm's sales, profitability, and competitive-position objectives. Marketers identify many of these forces by market opportunity analysis, especially analyses of changes in the firm's macroenvironment. Changes in technology are among the most important driving forces in new product development because of their impact on existing products and a shortening of the product life cycle. Other macroenvironment factors affecting the development of new products are government regulations, changing costs of raw materials, demographics, and lifestyle. The introduction of new products by competitors may force a firm to respond with its own entry. Customers and suppliers can also cause a firm to develop new products, as we shall see later in this chapter.

Despite the many problems and threats involved, some companies have been consistently successful over the years in developing new products. These firms include such well-known companies as Hewlett-Packard, Intel, Merck, and 3M. All of these companies limit their search for new product ideas to areas that their resources permit them to exploit. Further, all approach new product development in a well-planned, systematic way.

Organizing for New Product Development

At the outset of the development process, the firm must decide whether to keep its development activities in-house or go outside via subcontracting or some form of joint venture. The rationale for the latter is that large integrated bureaucratic companies find it difficult during times of rapid technological changes to compete against smaller, more-focused companies that are highly flexible and can motivate their employees using stock incentives and bonuses. Large centralized companies do not, for the most part, engage in such activities.

On the other hand, managing a systemic innovation under one roof facilitates developing the needed process technology concurrent with the R&D for the new product, thereby resulting in faster introductions and lower costs to inhibit competition. Also, in-house development makes possible working out the "bugs" faster in terms of solving quality, inventory, and manufacturing problems. Finally, the development of successful innovative process technologies that can be protected by patents or that are difficult to duplicate can block or stymie a potential competitor.[22]

KEY OBSERVATION

The better the fit between the "newness" of the product concept and the organizational structure used to manage its development, the more efficient in terms of costs and time is the development process.

Empirical research suggests that relatively bureaucratic structures may be better when less-innovative products are involved such as line extensions and product improvements.[23] More participative structures such as cross-functional teams are called for when a highly innovative product is involved. The research suggests that the better the fit between the "newness" of the product concept and the organizational structure used to manage its development, the more efficient in terms of costs and time is the development process.

One of the advantages of using teams is their ability to reduce the time of the new product development process by fostering closer relations between the various functional areas. Advances in computer network technology have made it easier for team members to communicate with one another as well as members of their departments. In so doing, they minimize the time required to gain approval from one area (marketing) for another's work (product design).[24]

A reduction in **time to market** can have a strong, positive effect on the product's profitability, especially in fast-cycle industries in which product life cycles are short (three years or less). Improved profitability results from extending the product's sales life, creating opportunities to change a premium price, providing for development and manufacturing cost advantages, and reducing the risks of a marketing shift since the development process started. Reduction in time to market has been of major concern since the McKinsey new product studies, which reported that under conditions of a 20 percent growth rate, 12 percent price erosion, and a five-year product life, a six-month delay in entering the market can cost up to one-third of lifetime after-tax profit. Of course, reduction in time spent on innovation and creating new products is meaningless unless the result meets the consumer's reliability and performance expectations.[25]

Key Decisions in the New Product Development Process

Given the importance of new products—whether goods or services—in long-term firm success, much attention has been paid in recent years to the generation and assessment of new product ideas and to improving the process of getting new products to market.[26] One result of this attention has been the development of so-called **stage-gate systems** for managing new product development from **idea generation** to **product launch**.[27] A diagram of the stage-gate system is shown in Exhibit 11.9.

In a stage-gate system an idea for a new product must pass through a series of gates at each of which its merit is examined before it is allowed to continue its journey toward market introduction. Between each gate, various analyses and development activities are conducted. The point is to "kill" ideas that lack strategic or market potential early in the process, before significant resources are spent on these ideas, as well as to pave the way for high-potential ideas so that they not only get to market quickly but also have the "right" attributes to enhance their likelihood of market success. Simple new products, such as line extensions or product improvements, sometimes skip stages in the process, going directly from idea status to stage 2, 3, or 4, for example. More innovative products whose market acceptance is unclear or whose product performance is uncertain typically must pass muster at each gate. Similarly, stages in the process are sometimes conducted concurrently, and backward loops in the process are common when the results of the analysis at a given stage do not support passing the product to the next stage.

KEY OBSERVATION

The point is to "kill" ideas that lack strategic or market potential early in the process, before significant resources are spent on these ideas, as well as to pave the way for high-potential ideas.

Managing the Stage-Gate Process   Though the stage-gate process may appear lengthy and tedious, a principal goal of using such processes is to improve the speed with which a firm brings new products to market.[28] This is accomplished in three principal ways. First, clear milestones are set at each gate to encourage new product teams to move quickly through the necessary activities to get through the next gate. Second, resource commitments are made along the way to ensure that inadequate resources, whether human or

Exhibit 11.9

STAGE-GATE NEW PRODUCT DEVELOPMENT SYSTEM

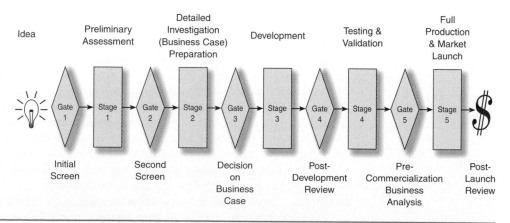

Source: Paul O'Connor, "Implementing a Stage-Gate Process: A Multi-Company Perspective," *Journal of Product Innovation Management* 11 (1994), p. 185. Blackwell Publishers.

financial, do not delay promising products. Third, concurrent engineering is employed, whereby both market analyses and technical progress proceed concurrently. Previously, it was common for R&D to develop a product and "throw it over the wall" to marketing, who were asked to sell it. Marketing would then throw it back, asking for changes to make the product more acceptable to customers, and so on, through several iterations. By the time the tossing ended, a competitor's product may have won the race to market. Thus, here, as with most other business processes, implementation is critical. In some fast-moving markets, firms seek **first-mover advantage,** whereby theirs is the first entrant in a new product category. There is much talk, especially in high technology and Internet marketing circles, about the importance of first-mover advantage. As is discussed in Exhibit 11.10, however, bringing the *right* product to market and updating it to keep it ahead of competing products are far more important in the long run than being first to market, especially with a product that does not offer what customers really want or need.

Deciding Who Staffs the Gates, and How Many Gates

In most companies or business units using stage-gate systems, a cross-disciplinary team is appointed to staff the gates. As new product ideas pass through the process, this team considers market, technical, and manufacturing or service deliverability criteria in deciding which ideas should pass through to the next stage. At minimum, marketing, R&D, and production perspectives are necessary, as is the presence of someone having the clout to commit resources needed for further development. A recent study showed that selecting gatekeepers who score high on measures of creativity, such as the MBTI® Creativity Index, enhances both the speed and productivity of the new product development process.[29]

The number of gates employed in the process varies in different firms, as some steps shown in Exhibit 11.9 can be combined or broken into additional steps.

Exhibit 11.10   How Important Is First-Mover Advantage?

The dot-com revolution that began in the late 1990s and continued into the 21st century led many to proclaim that the key to winning competitive advantage on the Internet was being first to market. Amazon.com, first to market in the online bookseller space, and others in other categories would win the game simply by virtue of being first to enter. The resulting rush to market led to huge venture capital investments in dot-com companies and a flurry of initial public offerings of fledgling dot-com enterprises, as early entrants sought to capitalize on the dot-com frenzy and raise capital in a red-hot market. Alas, the rapid fall in the valuations of many of these companies in 2000 burst the bubble.

So, how important is first-mover advantage? A candid look at business history in the 20th century indicates that being *best* in market is far more important than being *first* to market, notwithstanding the benefits that being first can bring to early leaders in any category. A 1999 review by Lambert and Slater of recent studies of first-mover advantage, as well as an abundance of anecdotal evidence (see Collins, 2000), makes it clear that first movers are often successfully leapfrogged by later competitors, who benefit from the ability to observe and improve upon the market offerings of the early entrants. Where is VisiCalc, the first personal computer spreadsheet, today? Where is Osborne, the first portable personal computer? Why are Palm Pilots now ubiquitous, while Apple's earlier Newton failed? Thus, while faster time to market can provide a competitive edge, entrants who fail to introduce the right product or improve on their early offerings risk being overtaken by followers whose offerings are more attractive. As Collins observes, being best is typically far better than being first.

Source: Jim Collins, "Best Beats First," *Inc.,* August 2000, pp. 48–51; Denis Lambert and Stanley F. Slater, "First, Fast, and On Time: The Path to Success. Or Is It?" *Journal of Product Innovation Management,* 1999, pp. 427–38.

Exhibit 11.11   Lead User Research Generates Breakthroughs at 3M

One way to generate breakthrough new product ideas is to conduct what MIT's Eric von Hippel calls lead user research. Lead user research draws on two major findings by innovation researchers. First, many commercially important products are initially thought of—and even prototyped—by users rather than manufacturers. Second, such innovations tend to be developed by **lead users**—companies or individuals who are ahead of market trends and have needs that go beyond those of the typical user.

In September 1996, a product development team in the Medical-Surgical Markets Division of 3M was charged with creating a breakthrough in surgical drapes, the material that prevents infections from spreading during surgery. After learning about the lead user process from Mary Sonnack, a 3M colleague who had studied with von Hippel, and after visiting surgical sites in challenging environments in India, Malaysia, Indonesia, and Korea, the team realized that what was really needed was a dramatically more cost-effective way to prevent infections from starting or

spreading. Their search for lead users took them to veterinary hospitals, where, "Our patients are covered with hair, don't bathe, and don't have medical insurance, so the infection controls we use can't cost much." It led them to makeup artists, who were experts in applying to the skin materials that don't irritate and are easy to remove. The lead user process culminated in a two-and-a-half-day lead user workshop, which generated concepts for six new product lines and a radical new approach to infection control. The company has since successfully tested the lead user method in 8 of its 55 divisions, and the line of 3M people who want to learn about the method from Mary Sonnack's group "extends out her office door and around the block," says Roger Lacey, a lead user advocate who runs 3M's Telecom Systems Division.

Gate 1: Idea Generation and Initial Screening Decisions   To have an effective new product strategy, a firm needs to establish objectives for its new product effort. In what customer markets does it wish to grow? What capabilities does it have? What product lines should be expanded? In a large multidivisional firm, which divisions should get greater R&D and new product funds? These decisions, which were addressed from a strategic perspective in Chapter 10, provide guidance for idea generation. Typically, a substantial number of new product ideas must be generated to get one successful product. Ideas for new products can come from customers; from the company's own staff, R&D people, the salesforce, product managers, marketing researchers; from members of its distribution channels; even from competitors. For a description of one way 3M, one of the world's most highly regarded new product companies, generates breakthrough ideas, see Exhibit 11.11. Whatever the source, at Gate 1, an initial screening is made to determine the idea's **strategic fit.** Does the idea align with the company's mission, does it take advantage of or strengthen its competencies, and are the resources needed to develop and market the product available? If the answer to any of these questions is, No, the idea will likely be rejected. Some ethical considerations in making these decisions are discussed in Ethical Perspective 11.2.

Gate 2: Secondary Screening Decisions   In Stage 1, prior to reaching Gate 2, managers are typically asked to undertake preliminary assessments of the idea's technical and market feasibility. First, can the product be developed and delivered? For a high-technology product, will the technology pan out? Second, how large is the market, and what is the estimated market potential for the proposed product? Will customers like it? This screening is typically based largely or entirely on secondary data and on the market and technical know-how resident in the company. The tools presented in Chapter 7 for estimat-

ETHICAL PERSPECTIVE 11.2
Issues in Idea Generation and Screening

Business is often criticized for excessive production of me-too products, which leads to waste in the economic system. This is a difficult criticism to refute except to note that under certain conditions the development of a me-too product is justified, such as when it can be produced at a lower price or made available to more people. Some consumers argue that business produces too many wasteful products. But what is such a product? Also, companies don't create the desire for wasteful products; it already exists.

There is also reverse criticism that business fails to produce products that are needed, such as products for people with unusual physical attributes (too tall, too short). In the medical field the development of new drugs is inhibited by risk (vaccines for children) and the uneconomic size of the market. In the latter case, the U.S. government provides federal funds for the development and marketing of so-called *orphan drugs* having only a very limited application.

It seems clear that sellers need to design safety into their products, but to what extent? Often consumers are not willing to pay the price of the added safety, as was initially the case with flame-resistant children's pajamas and auto seat belts. Both were finally mandated by the federal government. How a product is positioned and communicated affects how a product is used and, thus, can relate to safety (car

acceleration and braking power). And what should a company do when one of its products is designed for an innocent use but contributes to violence, like a high-powered toy water gun that shoots a variety of liquids, some not so pleasant to the person on the receiving end?

In recent years societies around the world have become increasingly concerned about the impact of products and their packaging on the environment. There are several ways in which both new and old products can harm the environment—through the use of destructive raw materials (asbestos and lead), the use of a manufacturing process that pollutes (use of chemicals in the production of paper), the use of the final product (automobiles and air pollution), and the disposal of the used product (tires, motor oil, beverage containers).

Firms vary in their response to the ecological problem. Some largely ignore the problem, while others go so far as to disinvest in businesses that may harm the environment. Since being ethically right is not always the most profitable position, firms face the question of how best to trade off the environmental benefits versus profits. Small businesses (some of which account for considerable pollution) in particular are often hard pressed to take even a reasonable environmental point of view because of their lack of funds and technological know-how.

Source: Philip R. Cateora, *International Marketing*, 7th ed. (Burr Ridge, IL: Richard D. Irwin, 1990), pp. 149–54. Reprinted with permission from The McGraw-Hill Companies.

KEY OBSERVATION

To invest new product development resources wisely, it is necessary to "kill" weak ideas at Gate 2, because significant resources in marketing research and in product development are likely to be incurred for products that pass this gate.

ing market potential are useful at this stage. A "classic" qualitative scoring model used by some companies at Gate 2 is shown in Exhibit 11.12. To invest new product development resources wisely, it is necessary to "kill" weak ideas at Gate 2, because significant resources in marketing research and in product development are likely to be incurred for products that pass this gate. Thus, a weak screening process can waste resources on obvious losers or misfits and can lead to a creeping commitment to the wrong projects. An overly rigid process, on the other hand, can lead to lost opportunities.

Gate 3: Decisions on the Business Case
If an idea successfully passes the tests at Gate 2, a more detailed investigation, the subject of Stage 2, is made into the market potential for the proposed product. Such an investigation includes a comprehensive customer, market, and competitive analysis using the tools and analytical frameworks provided in Chapters 3 through 6. Primary research is customarily done at this stage. Thus, some resources are now invested in research, and development of product prototypes is sometimes done to support these research efforts. For many technology-based products, development before this point has likely been limited to basic research, and actual development of a truly functional product has awaited confirmation of the business case. Decisions at Gate 3,

Exhibit 11.12

NEW PROD SCORING MODEL

(1)	(2)	(3) Very Good (10)		(4) Good (8)		(5) Average (6)		(6) Poor (4)		(7) Very Poor (2)		(8)	(9)
Subfactor	Subfactor weight	EP	EV	EP	EV	EP	EV	EP	EV	EP	EV	TOTAL EV	Subfactor evaluation
Product superiority	1.0	0.1	1.0	0.2	1.6	0.5	3.0	0.2	0.8	—	—	6.4	6.4
Unique features for users	1.0	0.1	1.0	0.2	1.6	0.4	2.4	0.2	0.8	0.1	0.2	6.0	6.0
Reduce customers' costs	3.0	0.3	3.0	0.4	3.2	0.2	1.2	0.1	0.4	—	—	7.8	23.4
Higher quality than competitors	1.0	0.1	1.0	0.2	1.6	0.5	3.0	0.2	0.8	—	—	6.4	6.4
Does unique task for user	2.0	0.5	5.0	0.4	3.2	0.1	0.6	—	—	—	—	8.8	17.6
Priced lower than competing products	2.0	—	—	0.2	1.6	0.5	3.0	0.3	1.2	—	—	5.8	11.6
	10.0											Total value of factor	71.4

Note: EP = estimated probability as judged by management. EV = expected value, computed by multiplying the rating's numerical value by the estimated probability.

while based on similar criteria as those at Gate 2, are based on greater depth of information and are the last chance to stop before proceeding with full-scale development of the product and of the marketing plan for introducing it.

Gate 4: Postdevelopment Review Decisions

During Stage 3, the technological development of the actual product design proceeds, and a marketing plan, including a total product/service offering (as we noted earlier in this chapter) is developed. A critical decision here is to settle on the product's design and its particular features.

An analysis of more than 200 new products revealed that product design was the most important single factor in their success for a number of reasons.[30] First, it can influence costs by its choice of materials and shapes, which strongly influence the manufacturing processes.[31] Second, it can call favorable attention to the product in a crowded marketplace, as was the case with Swatch watches, which used a number of unusual forms to call attention to its line of watches. Third, it creates impressions concerning other product attributes. For example, the first Apple MacIntosh had a simple compact form designed to emphasize that it was user friendly. And fourth, product design enhances our lives by the satisfaction we derive from seeing and using beautiful artistic products.[32]

Until recently, the major objective of industrial design was to design a product compatible with the company's manufacturing resources and attractive to the eye. But increasingly the charge to the designer is to enhance the product's usability, thereby making the product easier to market. Ideally, the design would match "a product to the target user's capabilities to maximize safety, efficiency of use, and comfort."[33]

Historically, there has been a tendency to overfunctionalize some products, which made relatively simple products overly complex for the

KEY OBSERVATION

Historically, there has been a tendency to overfunctionalize some products. Does your VCR blink 12:00 incessantly?

average consumer.[34] Thus, a high percentage of consumers admit to confusion and despair when confronted with the need to operate VCRs, hotel showers, car radios, stereo systems, and the like.[35] Does your VCR blink 12:00 incessantly?

In addition to product design and specific product features, pricing and channels are determined at this stage, along with brand name, packaging, and a planned marketing communications program. Additional marketing research may be needed to complete this process. These technological and marketing activities proceed in tandem, with considerable communication along the way, so that the "over the wall" problem is avoided. There are two possible causes why a product would fail to pass Gate 4, as many do. The first is that stumbling blocks are encountered with the technology or product design or with the projected costs of the final version of the product, thereby calling into question whether the product will actually work as planned or whether it will provide target customers with good value for the money. The second is the discovery, during marketing planning, that market or competitive conditions that now prevail raise questions about the marketability of the product. The entry of an unforeseen competitor, for example, is often the cause for abandoning or delaying a previously attractive product idea at Gate 4. Thus, gatekeepers at Gate 4 must take a careful look at whether the product is likely to perform, whether the marketing plan is likely to lead to market acceptance for the product, and whether the degree of acceptance is sufficient to merit further development. Making a "no-go" decision at this point is often difficult, however, given the considerable momentum the product already enjoys within the company. Failing to do so, however, in the face of cautionary market or product evidence, is one reason that many new products fail.

Gate 5: Precommercialization Business Analysis Decisions
Gate 5 is the last hurdle before the product is rolled out. To clear Gate 5, the product typically must pass muster in a **test market,** in companies with budgets large enough to afford this step. Two major kinds of test markets are commonly used by large consumer products firms to prepare for Gate 5: field and laboratory test markets. Smaller firms, whose budgets may not allow for formal market tests, may simply begin marketing the product, assessing early results as they go. With the advent of the Internet, some firms now turn the stage-gate process upside down and simply begin selling on the Internet or in limited channels as a form of market learning quite different from traditional marketing research. One such effort that led to a successful introduction of an upscale scooter to "hip" urban markets is described in Exhibit 11.13.

In a **field test market,** the marketing plan for the product is typically implemented in a small geographical area to ensure that it will deliver the expected results. This test seeks to obtain an estimate of the sales that will be achieved once the product is rolled out into the broader market, given the planned marketing strategy and marketing budget.

In the past, the big food-, household-, and personal care-products companies typically used a sample composed of a few small cities as the test market—and did so for between 12 and 18 months. The cost of such research was often several million dollars. Increasingly such companies want faster and less-expensive ways of testing their products, and not only for cost reasons. More importantly, and unfortunately, field test markets give competitors the opportunity to evaluate the results, even to the point of introducing their own new product. For example, General Mills was sufficiently impressed by a Procter & Gamble test market to quickly introduce its own version of the test product under the Betty Crocker brand name, which quickly became the best seller.[36] These concerns have led to increasing use of **laboratory test markets.**

KEY OBSERVATION

Test markets give competitors the opportunity to evaluate the results, even to the point of introducing their own new product.

Exhibit 11.13   Real-Time Market and Product Development Turns the Stage-Gate Process Upside Down

Sometimes it's not clear who the real target market is for an innovative new product. Such was the case for Nova Cruz Products (www.novacruz.com), whose lightweight Xootr scooter had flopped in a market test on a college campus. Puzzled about who might constitute the best target market and what product attributes might be most important, Nova Cruz management decided to launch the product in a couple of channels—in a few independent retail stores and on the Internet—and iteratively refine the product concept, design, features, and options as well as its positioning, segmentation, pricing, and channels based on user feedback and early results. The idea was to try some things and "do what works," using one-on-one e-mails and face-to-face conversations with early users. As Karl Ulrich of Nova Cruz points out, "For some products, it's better just to try selling than to conduct expensive research." What worked turned out to be targeting "urban hipsters," as well as importers in gadget-happy Japan!

When might such an approach be called for? Ulrich, also a marketing professor at a leading business school, says there are four conditions under which real-time product and market development makes sense: when the product category is new, so that obvious users and competitors can't be identified; when market timing is not likely to be critical; when there's little risk to the brand itself (Coca-Cola probably would not want to try this for a new beverage); and when tooling and development costs are low (e.g., not for a new automobile). Benefits include the ability to tinker with pricing and product features (no fancy brochures to produce, nor substantial commitments to important channel partners); the ability to reach global markets (Japanese importers found the Xootr on the Internet, providing early cash flow); and early and close interaction with users, aided by friendly e-mails to build customer relationships.

Source: Karl Ulrich, Nova Cruz Products, "Pre-Market Research vs. Real-Time Market Research," a presentation to a conference of the Marketing Science Institute, Denver, CO, June 1, 2000. Used by permission.

In laboratory test markets, which are used most commonly for packaged consumer products, the procedure measures the process by which a consumer adopts a new product, consisting of three major steps: **awareness, trial,** and **repeat buying.**

In the lab procedure, respondents representative of the target audience see commercials about the new product imbedded in a TV program. Then they are given the option of buying such a product in a simulated store also stocked with competing brands. If they choose the test product, then researchers make follow-up interviews to determine the extent of satisfaction (including preference over their regular brand) and repurchase intentions. These tests have the advantage of relatively low costs ($60,000–$80,000) *and* confidentiality. Their biggest disadvantage is the small range of products that can be accommodated and that they provide little or no information about the difficulty of obtaining and maintaining distribution. Over the years, hundreds of new products have been tested using this procedure with reasonably good results—between one and two market share points of *actual* market share.[37]

Marketing managers working toward Gate 5, or in entrepreneurial companies such as Nova Cruz Products (see Exhibit 11.13) much earlier in the process, are faced with decisions about whether and how to use scarce resources for market testing, in order to reduce the risk of a possibly unsuccessful market launch. Decisions about whether to conduct a market test, and whether to do so in the field or in a laboratory, must consider the likelihood of competitive interference with a field test, competitors' ability to benefit themselves from such a test, and the company's willingness and ability to spend money on test marketing.

Stage 5: Commercialization Decisions

At this point, the horse is "out of the barn," but key strategic decisions remain about how to roll out the product in hopes of winning competitive advantage. **Commercialization** requires considerable coordination between the various functional areas. Large sums are required even if the new product is a brand extension.[38] Because marketing is responsible for making the new product available, developing awareness of its unique properties, inducing trial, and fostering repeat purchases, its role is critical.

There are a number of different commercialization strategies. One is to forgo market testing and move directly to a rollout region by region or nationally from the outset. Such a strategy is used when there is little risk, as is usually the case with brand extensions and when copying a competitor's product that has experienced successful test marketing. For industrial products, the use of the Internet and e-mail to contact large accounts facilitates and accelerates the introduction.

Another commercialization strategy involves using a different kind of test market—one that is not necessarily representative of the target audience.[39] Some companies use a rollout test versus a more elaborate market test, provided the results from the market simulation studies are strongly positive. Thus, they launch their product in 10 percent of the country and rely on fast sales results data (by scanners when possible) to check how well the product is doing. General Mills did this with its multigrain Cheerios cereal. As global consumer goods markets become more similar, more companies are testing in a few countries, then following with a global rollout. For example, after Colgate successfully launched a new shampoo in the Philippines, Australia, Mexico, and Hong Kong, it was rolled out in Europe, Asia, Latin America, and Africa.[40]

All of the above strategies are based on the trade-offs between risk, the need to cashflow the introduction, and the speed with which competitors are likely to react. For example, faced with the high cost of building a plant for a new heat-resistant plastic, GE opted for a small-scale introduction that could be supplied by existing plants. Only after IBM approved its use in computer circuit boards did GE move to invest considerable sums in building a full-scale plant. This is in contrast to seeking national distribution as soon as possible. This strategy is often favored by large manufacturers of personal care items, food, and packaged household products because of the rapidity with which rivals can imitate any product and the substantial scale economies involved. We'll examine alternative marketing strategies for the commercialization of new products, and the market conditions where each makes most sense, in greater detail in Chapter 16.

Finally, it's a good idea in a company of any size to conduct a postimplementation review to assess how the launch is going and make any necessary adjustments. Even in small or young companies whose resources—both human and financial—are limited, the simultaneous creativity and discipline entailed in stage-gate thinking can serve as a foundation for entrepreneurial initiative while balancing these factors with some measure of discipline. Such balance can help mitigate the risk of costly new product failures that could lead a precarious young company to bankruptcy.

KEY OBSERVATION

The simultaneous creativity and discipline entailed in stage-gate thinking can serve as a foundation for entrepreneurial initiative while balancing these factors with some measure of discipline.

TAKE-AWAYS

- Decisions about product design—including product features, brand names, related services, and warranties, for both goods and services—are among the most critical in differentiating one's product from others to achieve competitive advantage. Factors to consider in making product decisions are provided in this chapter.

- While speed to market is important in today's fast-paced business climate, bringing the *right* products to market and keeping them current are far more important than seeking first-mover advantage for a product that customers don't want.

- Decisions about the depth and breadth of product lines must be carefully considered in market segmentation terms. Product lines that are too long or too short can place the company at a competitive disadvantage.

- *How* the new product development process is managed, from a process perspective, is as important as *what* product decisions are made. The stage-gate system helps companies strike a balance between entrepreneurial creativity and business discipline in their new product efforts.

- Though new products constitute the lifeblood of long-term success for most firms, most new products fail! Thus, product decisions, in both content and process terms, are critical to the successful implementation of business strategies.

Self-diagnostic questions to test your ability to apply the analytical tools and concepts in this chapter to marketing decision making may be found at this book's website at www.mhhe.com/mullins05.

ENDNOTES

1. Based on "What's Egg?" *ABA Banking Journal,* September 2002, p. 60; and "On Whose Face?" *Economist,* May 20, 2000, p. 31.

2. Bureau of Economic Analysis, US Department of Commerce, http://www.bea.gov/bea/dn/nipaweb/TableViewFixed.asp?SelectedTable=10&FirstYear=2001&LastYear=2002&Freq=Qtr; Myron Magnet, "Good News for the Service Economy," *Fortune,* May 3, 1993, p. 47.

3. Ibid.

4. World Trade Organization News, "World Trade Slows Sharply in 2001 amid the Uncertain International Situation," October 19, 2001, http://www.wto.org/English/news_e/pres01)e/pr249_e.htm.

5. For a discussion of international strategies for services, see Christopher H. Lovelock and George S. Yip, "Developing Global Strategies for Service Businesses," *California Management Review,* Winter 1996, p. 67.

6. Dorothy Leonard and Jeffrey F. Rayport, "Spark Innovation Through Empathic Design," *Harvard Business Review,* November–December 1997, pp. 102–13.

7. What follows is based largely on David A. Aaker, *Building Strong Brands* (New York: Free Press, 1996), chaps. 1 and 3. For an interesting and insightful discussion on measuring brand equity across products and markets, also see chap. 10.

8. See Al Ries and Laura Ries, *The 11 Immutable Laws of Internet Branding* (New York: HarperBusiness, 2000). See also Laura Ries and Al Ries, *The 22 Immutable Laws of Branding* (New York: HarperCollins, 1994).

9. Aaker, *Building Strong Brands,* p. 314. Also, see Leslie de Chernatony, Christ Halliburton, and Ratma Bernath, "International Branding: Demand or Supply-Driven Opportunity?" *International Marketing Review* 12, no. 2 (1995), p. 9.

10. Private Label Manufacturers Association, http://www.plma.com.

11. Bruce G. S. Hardie and Leonard Lodish, "The Logic of Product Line Extensions," *Harvard Business Review,* November–December 1994, p. 53.

12. David Aaker, *Managing Brand Equity* (New York: Free Press, 1991), chap. 9.

13. Irene M. Kunii, "Japan's Quick Studies in Survival," *Business Week Online,* November 18, 2002.

14. See "Producer Power," *The Economist,* March 4, 1995, p. 70, for a discussion of two books that throw light on the problem of product development. Both books conclude that "far from being a matter of luck and prayer, the ability to produce outstanding products can be planned and managed just like any other bit of corporate life," The two books—both recently published by the Harvard Business School Press—are *Product Development Challenge,* ed.

Kim Clark and Steven Wheelwright; and *Product Juggernauts,* by Jean-Phillipe Dischamps and P. Ranganath Nayak.

15. See Shona L. Brown and Kathleen M. Eisenhardt, "Product Development: Past Research, Present Findings, and Future Directions," *Academy of Management Review* 26, no. 2 (1995), pp. 343–78; and Albert L. Page, "Assessing New Product Development Practices and Performance: Establishing Crucial Norms," *Journal of Product Innovation Management* 1 (1993), pp. 273–90.

16. See Peter R. Dickson, "Toward a General Theory of Competitive Rationality," *Journal of Marketing* 56 (January 1992), pp. 69–83; and Robert Jacobson, "The 'Austrian' School of Strategy," *Academy of Management Journal* 17, no. 4 (1992), pp. 782–807.

17. See, for example, estimates prepared by A. C. Nielsen over the years relating to new food items. Also, see "Another 15,000 New Products Expected for U.S. Supermarkets," *Marketing News,* June 10, 1991, p. 8. But the number of new products sold through supermarkets and pharmacies declined 13 percent in 1996 to 19,572 from 22,572 (a record) in 1995. Major reasons cited are company downsizing and a heavier focus on core brands. See Bruce Horovitz, "1996 Saw 13% Fewer New Products," *USA Today,* January 9, 1997, p. 31.

18. D. A. Aaker, *Managing Brand Equity: Capitalizing on the Value of a Brand Name* (New York: The Free Press, 1991).

19. For a comparison of new product failure rates from seven studies conducted between 1980 and 1986, see C. Merle Crawford, *New Product Management* (Burr Ridge, IL: Richard D. Irwin, 1996), p. 76.

20. Booz, Allen & Hamilton, *Management of the New Products for the '80s* (Chicago: 1982).

21. Gary Strauss, "Companies Freshen Old Product Lines," *USA Today,* March 20, 1992, p. B1.

22. Gary P. Picaro and Steven C. Wheelwright, "The New Logic of High-Tech R&D," *Harvard Business Review,* September–October 1995, p. 93.

23. Eric M. Olson, Orville C. Walker, Jr., and Robert W. Rueckert, "Organizing for Effective New Product Development: The Moderating Role of Product Innovativeness," *Journal of Marketing,* January 1995, p. 48.

24. A recent study of 788 new products developed and commercialized by Japanese firms found that success was strongly affected by the level of cross-functional integration and information sharing. See Michael Song and Mark E. Parry, "The Determinants of Japanese New Product Success," *Journal of Marketing Research,* February 1997, pp. 65–76.

25. See Jerry Wind and Vijay Mahajan, "Issues and Opportunities in New Product Development: An Introduction to the Special Issue," *Journal of*

Marketing Research, pp. 1–12. One section contains 29 suggested ways of reducing time to market. Also see Brian Dumaine, "How Managers Can Succeed through Speed," *Fortune,* February 13, 1989, pp. 53–59.

26. See Brown and Eisenhardt, "Product Development: Past Research, Present Findings, and Future Directions."

27. The stage-gate system is described in R. G. Cooper, "Stage-Gate System: A New Tool for Managing New Products," *Business Horizons,* May–June 1990, pp. 44–54. A useful guide for implementing such systems is Paul O'Connor, "Implementing a Stage-Gate Process: A Multi-Company Perspective," *Journal of Product Innovation Management* 11 (1994), pp. 183–200.

28. For more on the importance of time to market, see George Stalk, Jr., "Time—The Next Source of Competitive Advantage," *Harvard Business Review,* July–August 1988, pp. 41–51; and Kathleen M. Eisenhardt and Shona L. Brown, "Time Pacing: Competing in Markets That Won't Stand Still," *Harvard Business Review,* March–April 1998, pp. 59–69.

29. See Greg Stevens, James Burley, and Richard Devine, "Creativity + Business Discipline = Higher Profits Faster from New Product Development," *Journal of Product Innovation Management* 16 (1999), pp. 455–68.

30. Robert G. Cooper and Elko Kleinschmidt, "New Products: What Separates the Winners from the Losers," *Journal of Product Innovation Management,* September 1987, p. 169.

31. For an excellent discussion on how product design can affect costs, see Robin Cooper and Bruce Chew, "Control Tomorrow's Costs through Today's Designs," *Harvard Business Review,* January–February 1996, p. 88.

32. Peter H. Bloch, "Seeking the Ideal Form: Product Design and Consumer Response," *Journal of Marketing,* July 1995, pp. 16–18.

33. Ibid, p. 18. Also, see Artemus March, "Usability, The New Dimension of Product Design," *Harvard Business Review,* September–October 1994, p. 144.

34. "The Five Deadly Sins of Japan's Expanding High Tech Syndrome," *Tokyo Business Today,* May 1992, p. 3.

35. Richard Wolkomer, "Falling into the Target Gap—and It's Not Our Fault," *Smithsonian,* October 1991, p. 65.

36. Christopher Poer, "Will It Sell in Podunk? Hard to Say," *Business Week,* August 10, 1992, p. 46.

37. See Glen L. Urban, John S. Hulland, and Bruce D. Weinberg, "Premarket Forecasting for New Consumer Goods' Modeling Categorization, Elimination, and Consideration Phenomena," *Journal of Marketing,* April 1993, p. 47, for an insightful discussion of the problems associated with premarket forecasting for new consumer goods.

38. A decision support system has been developed for managing the new product development process for line extensions. See Morris A. Cohen, Jehoshua Elias Verg, and Teck H. Ho, "An Anatomy of a Decision-Support System for Developing and Launching Line Extensions," *Journal of Marketing Research,* February 1997, pp. 117–29.

39. This discussion has benefited from Crawford, *New Product Management,* chap. 21.

40. Poer, "Will It Sell in Podunk?" p. 47.

CHAPTER TWELVE

Pricing Decisions

Ryanair: Low Prices but High Profits—So Far[1]

EUROPE'S AIR TRAVELERS often marvel at how Ryanair can make money offering €9.99 fares for trips such as London–Brussels. But in less than two decades of existence, the Irish airline has not only made money, it has grown into Europe's biggest airline as measured by market capitalization. And the share of intra-European passengers flown by the low-cost airlines—primarily Ryanair and Easy-Jet—continues to grow. Their market share reached 7 percent in 2002 and is predicted to top 14 percent by 2007.

Ryanair's competitive strategy is quite simple: offer the lowest fares of any airline operating in Europe. The firm has succeeded by holding its average fare below €50, which is about a third lower than even Easy-Jet's, its strongest low-price competitor.

Of course, a low-price competitive strategy can be profitable only when the firm's costs are also low. Therefore, all of Ryanair's functional activities and operating policies are designed with efficiency in mind. For instance, the firm owns rather than leases its airplanes, and most of those planes are older Boeing 737-200s, thereby reducing depreciation charges and allowing some standardization of maintenance activities and parts inventories. Ryanair also concentrates nearly all its flights to and from underutilized regional airports, such as Stansted outside of London and Charleroi south of Brussels. Such airports offer the company more favorable terms with respect to taxes, facilities fees, and ground handling charges than more popular and congested airports closer to major cities. The lack of congestion also helps reduce turnaround times and thereby lowers costs by increasing utilization rates for planes and flight crews.

Unfortunately, many of Ryanair's cost savings come at the expense of customer comfort and convenience. Not only do passengers have to find their way to and from small airports far from the big cities, they have to carry and stow their own bags and do without meals, drinks, and other in-flight services. And there is not much room for them to stretch out and relax during their flight since Ryanair carries 15 percent more seats per aircraft than traditional airlines. It is even harder for customers to buy their tickets because Ryanair pays no fees to computer reservation systems and no commissions to travel agents.

Advertising and promotion, however, are among the few areas where Ryanair has not tried to cut costs below its competitors. With the exception of the sales commissions mentioned above, the company's marketing costs are about the same per passenger-kilometer as those of more traditional airlines. Even the most frugal flyers will not seek out Ryanair's cheap fares without being aware—and being frequently reminded—that they exist. And the firm must also maintain an extensive website and call center to facilitate the direct sale of tickets.

While Ryanair's low-cost/low-price strategy has been very successful so far, there may be some turbulence on the company's horizon. At the time of this writing, the European Union's transport commissioner is investigating whether some of the favorable terms that regional airports like Charleroi have granted the firm might actually be illegal subsidies. More critically, some analysts question whether the firm's growth projections might be overly optimistic. Ryanair expanded its fleet by another 100 planes in 2002 in order to pursue an objective of 25 percent annual

growth. But some experts question whether the segment of travelers willing to sacrifice comfort and convenience for low fares is sufficiently large to make such an aggressive growth objective attainable. In other words, will potential customers perceive Ryanair's cheap but bare-bones service to be a good enough value to enable the firm to continue climbing its profitable growth curve?

Marketing Challenges Addressed in Chapter 12

Pricing is an area where managers "feel the most pressure to perform and the least certain that they are doing a good job. The pressure is intensified because, for the most part, managers believe that they don't have much control over price. It is dictated by [the firm's costs and by forces in] the market."[2] And those forces have increased in recent years. The maturing of many basic industries, slower growth, improved productivity, the growing power of retailers and their private labels, the increased aggressiveness of low-cost global competitors such as Ryanair, and the growing ability of customers to compare suppliers' prices on the Internet have made many markets more price competitive.

The perception that price decisions are dictated by factors beyond the marketer's control, however, is a dangerous one. As we shall see later in this chapter, many firms base their pricing decisions largely on what is necessary to recover their costs or match competitors. For instance, a company may try to determine the costs of making a product or delivering a service and then add a standard markup to achieve a target return on investment. Such an approach can be justified given that firms cannot price their products or services below cost, at least not for long.

The danger is that prices set solely on the basis of cost or competitive considerations may not reflect **customer value:** the customer's perception of what the product or service is really worth. The price may be higher than the customer is willing to pay, resulting in a loss of potential sales and market share. This may be a problem that Ryanair will face— even with its relatively low fares—as it pursues its aggressive growth objectives. Alternatively, the price may be much lower than customers think the product is worth, resulting in low margins and the sacrifice of potential profits. While pricing a product below its perceived value may delight customers and stimulate short-term demand, it may also depress the earnings the firm needs to compensate its employees, fund capital investments, and pay for the product development and other marketing activities necessary for long-term growth. Even small mistakes in this direction can have major implications for the firm. For example, for a company with 8 percent profit margins, a 1 percent improvement in price realization would boost the firm's margin dollars by 12.5 percent.[3]

KEY OBSERVATION

Prices set solely on the basis of cost or competitive considerations may not reflect **customer value:** *the customer's perception of what the product or service is really worth.*

The critical question addressed in this chapter is, How can a marketer determine a price that captures a fair share of the value customers receive from a product or service without violating the constraints imposed by its strategic objectives, cost structure, and competitive environment? To answer that question, the first part of this chapter describes a price-setting process that begins by considering a variety of strategic, market demand, cost, and competitive factors. It then discusses methods that different firms use to set a price level, with emphasis on methods geared to reflecting the product's value as perceived by customers in the target market.

Determining an appropriate price level for a product or service is complicated, and most firms do not charge the same list price to every customer all the time. Instead, they develop a **price structure** that establishes guidelines for adapting the price to variations in costs and demand across different markets. Consequently, the last half of this chapter examines some price adjustments marketers often make to accommodate differences across (1) geographic territories, (2) national boundaries, (3) levels of the distribution channel, (4) types of distribution channels, especially the Internet, (5) items within the product line, and (6) customer segments.

A Process for Making Pricing Decisions

A manager's freedom to select a price for a given good or service is constrained by several factors. First, the firm's costs determine the floor of the range of feasible prices—at least longer term. At the other extreme, the price sensitivity of demand for the product determines the ceiling of the range of acceptable prices. Beyond some price level, most potential customers seek less costly substitutes, such as private labels, or do without the good or service.

Where should managers set a product's price within the range of feasible prices? There are a number of ways to calculate a price, but whichever one is used should consider situational factors. Such factors include (1) the business strategy and the other components of the marketing mix with which it must be compatible, (2) the extent to which the product is perceived to differ from competitive offerings in quality or level of customer service, (3) competitors' costs and prices, and (4) the availability and prices of possible substitutes.

Given the variety of factors to consider when setting a price, the following paragraphs describe, and Exhibit 12.1 diagrams, a step-by-step procedure for managers to follow. This process is particularly appropriate for first-time pricing decisions, as when a firm introduces a new product or enters a bid for nonroutine contract work. It includes several steps involving detailed analyses of demand, costs, and the competition. First, however, managers must establish a pricing objective consistent with the firm's business and marketing strategies.

Strategic Pricing Objectives

The strategic pricing objective should reflect what the firm hopes to accomplish with the product in its target market. When the business strategy, the target market, and the positioning strategy for the product are all clearly defined, then formulating objectives and policies for the marketing program elements, including price, can be relatively simple. For instance, Ryanair's business strategy of being the lowest-cost competitor in Europe makes the most appropriate pricing objectives and policies rather obvious.

We examine marketing objectives for different market and competitive situations, and their implications for the marketing mix components, in more detail in Chapters 16 and 17. But to clarify the role of price in different marketing programs, we discuss some strategic pricing objectives next and summarize them in Exhibit 12.2. The exhibit also suggests the conditions under which each objective is appropriate and the implications for choosing a price level within the range of feasible prices.

Exhibit 12.1

PRICE-SETTING DECISION PROCESS

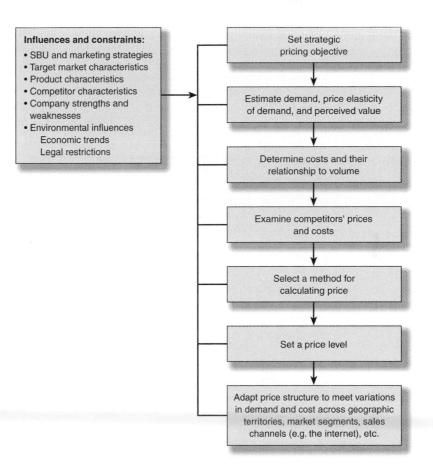

Maximize Sales Growth   When a firm is an early entrant into a new product-market with the potential for substantial growth, its objective may be to maximize its product's rate of sales growth (in units). This suggests it should set a relatively low price to attract as many new customers as quickly as possible and to capture a large share of the total market before it becomes crowded with competitors. This low-priced strategy is called **penetration pricing.** It is appropriate when, in addition to a large market,

1. Target customers are relatively sensitive to price.
2. The firm's costs are low compared to competitors' and the SBU is pursuing a low-cost strategy.
3. Production and distribution costs per unit are likely to fall substantially with increasing volume.
4. Low prices may discourage potential competitors from entering the market.

However, there is major risk in using low prices to achieve maximum sales growth in the short term as a base for future profits. If market, competitive, or technological conditions change, those future profits may never be realized.

Maintain Quality or Service Differentiation   When a firm has a strong competitive position based on superior product quality or customer service, its primary pricing

Exhibit 12.2

STRATEGIC PRICING OBJECTIVES

Objective	Conditions where most appropriate	Implications for relative price level
Maximize sales growth and penetration	Product-market is in introductory or growth stage of life cycle; firm is early entrant; target customers are sensitive to price; firm has low-cost position and is pursuing a low-cost business strategy; firm can gain experience-curve effects with increasing volume; low price may preempt potential competitors.	Set relatively low price—slightly above costs; penetration pricing policy aimed at winning new customers, expanding realized demand, and capturing as large a market share as possible.
Maintain quality or service differentiation	Product-market is in growth or maturity stage of life cycle; firm's offering is perceived to have a quality or service advantage over competitive offerings; firm does extensive advertising to maintain the product's quality image; firm has high costs; firm is pursuing differentiated defender strategy; target customers are relatively insensitive to price.	Set price high relative to competitors to cover high production, distribution, and advertising costs; price high to reinforce prestige image.
Maximize current profit		
• Skimming	Product-market is in introductory or early growth stage of life cycle; firm is the first entrant; firm is pursuing a prospector strategy; firm has limited capacity; advanced technology or other barriers prevent immediate entry by competitors.	Set price very high to appeal to only the most price-insensitive customer segment; as market matures and competitors enter, firm can (a) reduce price to attract new segments, or (b) withdraw from the product-market.
• Harvesting	Product-market is in late maturity or decline stage of life cycle; firm is pursuing differentiated defender strategy; there is no basis (e.g., product improvements, increased promotion) to sustain product demand or competitive position into the future; product is cash cow funding growth in other product-markets.	Set price to maintain margins and maximize profit or return on investment even though some customers may switch to competitive brands or substitutes.
Survival	Firm's product has a weak competitive position, but major shortcomings are correctable; firm needs to buy time and maintain cash flow to make necessary adjustments; product-market is still in growth or maturity stage of life cycle.	Reduce price, perhaps even below total cost, as long as price covers variable costs and makes a contribution to overhead.
Social objectives	Firm is a not-for-profit organization; costs are subsidized in part by tax revenues or contributions; one or more segments need the good or service but are unwilling or unable to pay full costs.	Set low price, perhaps below total cost for some segments, to stimulate or subsidize demand.

objective is to generate sufficient revenue to maintain that advantage. Such a firm usually asks a premium price for its product for two reasons: First, it needs additional revenue to cover the R&D, production, distribution, and advertising costs it takes to maintain both the reality and the perception of superior quality or service. Second, customers are usually willing to pay more for a superior offering; high quality decreases the elasticity of demand.[4]

A premium price policy is most appropriate for businesses pursuing differentiated defender strategies, as is the case with Europe's traditional, full-service airlines like British Airways and Air France. However, there are limits to the price premium customers are willing to pay for superior quality and performance. Those limits may change with shifting economic and competitive conditions. Thus, a premium price strategy is most appropriate when target customers attach relatively greater importance to quality or service attributes than to price, such as business travelers who are willing to pay more for flights convenient to major cities.

Maximize Current Profit: Skimming   When firms pioneer the development of a new product-market, sometimes their pricing objective is to maximize short-run profits. They adopt a **skimming price policy,** setting the price very high and appealing to only the least price-sensitive segment of potential customers. This can also be accomplished over time, as in "periodic discounting," when the seller prices high at the beginning of each period and low at the end. Examples include off-season travel fares, peak-load pricing by utilities, and markdowns of fashion goods.[5] Skimming is particularly appropriate for businesses pursuing prospector strategies involving investments in the development and commercialization of a stream of new products. Such businesses may not have the production capacity to fill a large initial demand for any one new product. They must try to recoup their development costs quickly so they can fund the next generation of new product ideas. Skimming works best when the new product involves proprietary technology, when the higher price reinforces the image of a superior product, or when other barriers discourage competitors from quickly entering the market and undercutting the pioneer's price. Skimming is most relevant to a small market because a large market is more apt to attract competitors.

Maximize Current Profit: Harvesting   At the other end of the life cycle, some product-markets decline rapidly as customer preferences change or new technologies and substitute products are introduced. Often it is too late to divest the product and earn a reasonable return, so firms facing this situation adopt a **harvesting** strategy to maximize short-term profits before demand for the product disappears. This typically involves cutting marketing, production, and operating costs of the product, while setting a relatively high price to maintain margins and maximize profits.[6] The opportunity to accomplish this ideal state depends largely upon exit barriers. If large barriers are present, then competitors will exert a downward pressure on prices. If few barriers are present, marginal competitors will exit and falling supplies may drive prices up.

The risk of maximizing short-run profits for a declining product is that demand can decline even faster as price-sensitive customers switch to competing brands or substitute products. Therefore, this is an appropriate strategy only where there is no way—such as by making product improvements or increasing promotion—to sustain market demand and the item's competitive position very far into the future.

Survival   Sometimes businesses with an established product in a market expected to grow or experience stable demand well into the future run into trouble because of strategic mistakes, such as failing to adapt to customers' changing desires or to competitive threats, or building excess capacity. If such mistakes are correctable, the firm may adopt a pricing objective of simply keeping the product alive while strategic adjustments are made. Because short-term profits are less important than survival for such products, this situation usually demands a low price to attract enough demand to keep the plant operating and maintain cash flow. So long as the price covers variable costs and at least contributes to fixed costs, the firm may be able to buy time to correct its competitive weaknesses.

Social Objectives   Some organizations may forgo possible profits—at least among some price-sensitive customer segments—by offering a low price to those customers to achieve some broader social purpose. This is most common among not-for-profit organizations such as performing arts organizations and public hospitals, especially if subsidized by government agencies, foundations, or private contributions and not relying on sales as their sole source of revenue. In reality, they are simply shifting the price "reduction" burden to organizations or individual contributors who are willing to subsidize one or more price-sensitive segments to achieve some social purpose. For example, performing arts organizations often offer substantial discounts to students. This is not just a strategy for building loyal future audiences. It also provides intellectual benefits to a customer group that would otherwise be unable to afford them.

Estimating Demand and Perceived Value

Demand sets the ceiling on the range of feasible prices for a product. Even before that ceiling is reached, however, the total number of customers willing to buy during a given period varies according to the price charged. The familiar **demand curve** depicts this variation in the quantity demanded at different prices.

In most cases there is an inverse relation between a product's price and the quantity demanded: the higher the price, the less people want to buy. Thus, the typical demand curve has a negative, or downward, slope. However, prestigious products (such as expensive wines and liquors) and those whose quality is difficult to objectively judge sometimes have positively sloping demand curves. Some customers use price as an indicator of the prestige or quality of such products, and they are induced to buy more as the price increases.

Factors Affecting Customers' Price Sensitivity   The demand curve sums the reactions of many potential buyers to the alternative prices that might be charged for a product. The curve's degree of slope reflects the fact that different buyers have different sensitivities to the product's price.

Thomas Nagle identified specific factors influencing variations in sensitivity to price across customers and products. Exhibit 12.3 summarizes these factors. Each factor reflects three basic phenomena that determine customers' willingness and ability to pay for a good or service. First, buyers' willingness to pay a given price for a product is influenced by their perceptions and preferences: their needs, desires, awareness of, and attitude toward, the item in question.

Second, the price, availability, and attractiveness of alternative brands and substitute products affect buyers' willingness to buy the product. So do the prices of complementary items that customers must buy to gain full value from the product. For example, the rising price of gasoline in the early years of the 21st century may dampen consumer demand for large, fuel-inefficient sport utility vehicles.

Finally, the size of their incomes relative to the price influences customers' ability to pay for a product or service. Taken together, these factors determine the **perceived value** a

Exhibit 12.3

FACTORS AFFECTING CUSTOMERS' SENSITIVITY TO PRICE

Buyer's perceptions and preferences

Unique-value effect	Customers are less price-sensitive when they perceive the product or service provides unique benefits; there are no acceptable substitutes.
Price-quality effect	Customers are less price-sensitive when they perceive the product or service offers high quality, prestige, or exclusiveness.

Buyer's awareness of and attitude toward alternatives

Substitute-awareness effect	Customers are less price-sensitive when they are relatively unaware of competing brands or substitute products or services.
Difficult-comparison effect	Customers are less price-sensitive when it is difficult to objectively compare the quality or performance of alternative brands or substitutes.
Sunk-investment effect	Customers are less price-sensitive when the purchase is necessary to gain full benefit from assets previously bought.

Buyer's ability to pay

Total-expenditure effect	Customers are less price-sensitive when their expenditure for the product or service is a relatively low proportion of their total income.
End-benefit effect	Customers—particularly organizational buyers purchasing raw materials or component parts—are less price-sensitive when the expenditure is a relatively small proportion of the total cost of the end product.
Shared-cost effect	Customers are less price-sensitive when part of the cost of the product or service is borne by another party (e.g., when part of the cost of medical services is covered by health insurance, or when a salesperson's travel costs are covered by an expense account).
Inventory effect	Customers are less price-sensitive in the short run when they cannot store large quantities of the product as a hedge against future price increases.

Source: Adapted from Thomas T. Nagle, *The Strategy and Tactics of Pricing.* Copyright © 1987. Reprinted by permission of Pearson Education, Inc., Upper Saddle River, NJ.

potential customer will associate with a given product-market entry, and thus the price he or she is willing to pay. Later in this chapter, we discuss how perceived value might be estimated for a given customer segment and used as a basis for setting a price level.

Price Elasticity of Demand   The larger the proportion of price-sensitive customers in a product's market, the more sensitive overall demand is to a change in the product's price. This degree of responsiveness of demand to a price change is referred to as the **price elasticity of demand.** The following formula calculates the price elasticity of demand for a product or service:

$$\text{Price elasticity of demand } (E) = \frac{\text{Percent change in quantity demanded}}{\text{Percent change in price}}$$

If, for instance, a seller raised the price of a product by 2 percent and demand subsequently fell by 6 percent, the price elasticity of demand for that product would be -3 (with the minus sign reflecting the inverse relationship between price and demand), indicating substantial **elasticity.** Conversely, if a 2 percent increase produced only a 1 percent decline in the quantity demanded, then price elasticity is $-\frac{1}{2}$ indicating that demand is **inelastic.** If a 2 percent price increase leads to a 2 percent decline in quantity, price elasticity is **unitary.** In such a case the seller's total revenue stays the same because the smaller quantity sold is offset by the higher price.

There are major problems in using price elasticity—as discussed above—to help set price in any precise way. These difficulties include the failure to consider the response of competitors to the company's change in price; that demand may be inelastic for a given price change, but elastic for a larger amount; that elasticity is measured in terms of sales revenues not profit margins (one reason being it doesn't take into account scale effects); that a lowering of price may affect the sales of other items in the company's product line (for example, cannibalization); and that it ignores any societal benefits accorded the company for benefiting low-income segments via a price reduction.

Methods for Estimating Demand   Many firms, particularly larger ones, attempt to estimate the demand curves for their products through marketing research. This is easier said than done, though, for two reasons: First, laboratory or test-market experiments can provide insights into the price–demand relationship for a product, but do not reflect the likely reactions of competitors to different prices or changes in price over time. Underestimating the aggressiveness and impact of such reactions can lead to debilitating price wars, particularly in mature industries suffering from excess production capacity.[7] A second problem researchers encounter when trying to empirically estimate demand curves is that *effects of nonprice factors,* such as changes in economic conditions or in other components of the marketing mix, must be controlled or measured. Thus, if a firm conducted a test market in which it increased advertising expenditures at the same time it lowered prices, researchers could not tell how much increased volume was a result of the sensitivity of demand to price and how much was a result of the heavier advertising.

Keeping these two problems in mind, there are a number of ways for marketers to estimate a product's demand curve. One approach is to survey a sample of consumers, or bring them into a laboratory setting, and ask them how much of the product they would buy at different possible prices. The artificiality of this approach, however, and the fact that respondents are not required to "put their money where their mouth is" leads to questions about the validity of the findings. More realistic approaches include estimating the price–quantity relationship via the regression analysis of historical sales using consumer panel data, in-store experiments where a product's price is systematically varied, or multiple test markets. The expense of the latter limits their use.

Estimating Costs

Demand and perceived value set the ceiling on the range of feasible prices a firm might charge for a product, but costs determine the floor. A firm's costs take two forms: fixed and variable. **Fixed costs** (or **overhead**) are constant in the short term, regardless of production volume or sales revenue. They include rent, interest, heat, executive salaries, and functional departments—such as purchasing and R&D—needed to support the products made by the firm. Because total fixed costs remain constant in the short term regardless of volume, the **fixed cost per unit** of a product declines as a firm produces and sells more of the product in a given period.

Variable costs vary in magnitude directly with the level of production, but they remain constant *per unit* regardless of how many units are produced. They involve such things as the costs of materials, packaging, and labor needed to produce each unit of the product.

Total costs equal the sum of fixed and variable costs for a given level of production. The product's price must cover this total cost figure—divided by the number of units produced—if it is to be economically viable in the long run.

Marketing mix costs, which may include both fixed and variable costs as well as other costs such as retailers' or distributors' markups that don't even appear on the company's books, must also be considered in determining the level at which a product's price will be set. For example, it is common for a greater portion of the consumer's dollar to be spent on **distribution channel markups** than for a product's actual manufacturing cost. Similarly, in some product categories—diet aids and colognes, among others—the cost to promote the product, establish its brand name, and acquire customers can be higher—sometimes far higher—than manufacturing costs. For new products in categories such as these, marketers are faced with a clear choice between setting a high price together with a substantial promotional budget to communicate the product's benefits and attract customers or a low penetration price along with little promotional support. Either strategy can be viable, depending on market and competitive conditions. Setting a high price with too little promotional support, however, is likely to lead to sales problems. Similarly, setting a low price alongside an aggressive promotional program can lead to profit and cash flow problems, as many dot-com retailers have learned the hard way. Thus, price setting for a product cannot occur in isolation. It requires considering the costs of the planned overall marketing mix for the product, including product, promotion, and distribution decisions.

Measuring Costs   The firm's cost accounting system provides managers with information about the fixed and variable costs associated with each of the company's products. Even though it is a relatively simple matter to measure each product's variable costs, fixed costs present a problem. The analyst has the option of using full costing (which involves allocating indirect costs) or direct costing (often referred to as the contribution margin approach because it takes into account only variable costs). These topics are covered in depth in Chapter 19 and will not be discussed here.

Examining the impact on a product's contribution is a useful way to evaluate the economic viability of marketing program components directly linked to a specific product. However, it does not provide enough detailed information for a manager to judge whether a given price is adequate to cover the total costs incurred by that product. Consequently, many firms are beginning to revise their cost accounting systems to provide more accurate product-cost information to managers. They often develop multiple systems for financial reporting, cost control, and product-cost measurement purposes. **Activity-based costing systems**—which allocate costs across individual products by directly observing the level of various functional activities such as shipping, receiving, supervising, and selling that are devoted to each item in the line—often generate very different estimates of the total costs associated with a given product than does the firm's standard cost control system. But such activity-based cost estimates are often more useful for making strategic marketing decisions, such as setting prices, because they reduce some of the distortions inherent in the allocation of indirect costs within standard cost accounting systems while avoiding the imprecision of the contribution margin approach.[8]

KEY OBSERVATION

Activity-based cost estimates are often more useful for making strategic marketing decisions, such as setting prices, because they reduce some of the distortions inherent in the allocation of indirect costs.

Cost and Volume Relationships   A product's average cost per unit—and the price necessary to cover that cost—varies with the quantity produced. Managers should take two different volume–cost relationships into account when making pricing decisions. The first relationship involves **economies of scale.** In the short run, scale economies result from more complete use of available capacity. In the long run, companies can gain further economies by constructing larger and more efficient facilities. The average cost per unit is high if few units are produced, but it falls as production approaches the plant's capacity because fixed costs are spread over more units. This is why excess capacity is anathema to the profitability and competitive cost position of a product, particularly in mature, commodity-like product categories where margins tend to be low. If, however, a company tries to produce more than capacity, average costs per unit would rise. The overworked machinery would break down more often, workers would get in each other's way, and other inefficiencies would occur.

The second volume–cost relationship involves the **experience curve**—the fall in production and marketing costs per unit as a firm gains accumulated experience. Regardless of a firm's plant size, its average costs per unit decline as it gains experience. Its production workers discover efficient shortcuts, procurement costs fall, and the accumulated impact of past advertising and marketing efforts may enable the firm to succeed with smaller per-unit marketing expenditures.

Analyzing Competitors' Costs and Prices

To achieve a desired strategic competitive position for a product or service in its target market, the manager must take competitors' costs and prices into account. To successfully implement a low-cost strategy, for instance, the manager must be sure that the product's costs are truly lower than any competitor's and that those lower costs are reflected in the product's relative price. Thus, the manager needs to learn and track the price, cost, and relative quality of each competitor's offer. For example, the continued success of Ryanair's low-price strategy obviously depends on the firm's ability to hold its total costs and prices well below those of other airlines—especially other no-frills carriers like EasyJet—while offering a reasonably comparable choice of destinations, flight times, and customer services.

Competitors' costs are harder to measure than their prices. Reverse engineering can be used to take apart competing products and estimate the cost of their components, packing, and production processes. Because the costs associated with services are often largely fixed, such as the costs of labor, physical facilities, and the like, a manager can estimate competitors' relative cost positions in a service industry by comparing their numbers of employees or the number and size of outlets and then looking at efficiency ratios like sales per employee or sales per square foot. And there is usually a relationship between costs and market share—the higher the relative share, the lower the relative cost is likely to be based on scale and learning effects.

Methods Managers Use to Determine an Appropriate Price Level

Given the complexity of the concerns involved in setting a price—and the frequent incompleteness of information about demand and costs—managers often rely on rules of thumb to set list prices. Although these practical pricing methods are unlikely to produce an optimal—or profit-maximizing—price, they are all based on a set of relevant considerations. These various pricing methods fall into three categories: cost-oriented pricing, competition-oriented pricing, and demand or customer-oriented pricing.

Cost-Oriented Methods

Perhaps the simplest and most commonly used pricing method is to add a standard markup to the cost of the product. This kind of **cost-plus** or **markup pricing** does not explicitly consider the price sensitivity of demand or the pricing practices of competitors. But it is convenient and easy to apply—important considerations when a firm faces hundreds or thousands of pricing decisions each year, as in the case of retail stores and wholesaling institutions. It is also widely used among firms that must submit competitive bids for a variety of projects, as is the case with construction firms.

The typical procedure for determining price under the markup approach is to first calculate the cost per unit by adding variable cost to fixed costs divided by an expected level of unit sales:

$$\text{Unit cost} = \text{Variable cost} + \frac{\text{Fixed cost}}{\text{Expected unit sales}}$$

To find the price, add a desired markup on retail to the unit cost (or divide unit cost by 1 minus the desired percent markup):

$$\text{Markup price} = \frac{\text{Unit cost}}{(1 - \text{Desired percent markup on retail})}$$

Suppose, for instance, that a small-appliance manufacturer produces a line of electric coffeemakers and expects to sell 50,000 in the coming period. Fixed costs of $500,000 are associated with producing the coffeemakers, and variable costs are $10 per unit. The unit cost for each coffeemaker would be

$$\text{Unit cost} = \$10 + \frac{\$500,000}{50,000} = \$10 + \$10 = \$20$$

Suppose further that the manufacturer wants to earn a markup (or margin on selling price) of 30 percent. The markup price would be

$$\text{Markup price} = \frac{\$20}{(1 - .30)} = \frac{\$20}{.7} = \$28.57$$

This approach largely ignores the price sensitivity of demand. It assumes a level of sales *before* the price is set. Furthermore, if the manager's assumption about likely sales volume is wrong, the desired markup is not achieved. A shortfall in units sold would mean that fixed costs would be spread over fewer units and the realized markup would be smaller than desired.

In the distributive trades, retailers and wholesalers often add standard markups to what they paid for the item to attain a margin sufficient to cover overhead and provide a profit. These standard markups do not explicitly consider variations in demand. However, they have evolved in a way that reflects general variations in price sensitivity across products. In supermarkets, for instance, markups on selling price range from as low as 10 percent on baby foods to more than 50 percent on some toiletries and greeting cards.[9] The products with the lowest markups tend to be frequently purchased, commodity-like items for which many consumers make price comparisons.

Rate-of-return or **target return pricing** is similar in principle to, but somewhat more sophisticated in practice than, markup pricing. This cost-oriented approach brings one more cost element into the pricing decision—the cost of capital tied up in producing and distributing the product. The objective is to set a price yielding a target rate of return on investment. This pricing approach is common at GM and other automobile companies that price their cars to achieve a target of 15 to 20 percent return on investment.

Operationally, this pricing approach demands that managers (1) estimate the unit sales volume of the product, (2) figure unit costs (variable costs plus overhead attributable to the product), (3) estimate the amount of capital involved in producing and selling the product, and (4) select a target rate of return on investment. They can then determine the price as follows:

$$\text{Target return price} = \text{Unit cost} + \frac{\text{Desired percent return} \times \text{Capital invested in product}}{\text{Unit sales}}$$

For example, suppose our small-appliance manufacturer has invested $1 million in facilities and equipment to produce and distribute its coffeemakers and wants to make a 20 percent return on that investment. The target return price for each coffeemaker would be

$$\text{Target return price} = \$20 + \frac{.20 \times \$1,000,000}{50,000 \text{ units}} = \$20 + \frac{\$200,000}{50,000} = \$24$$

When managers make these estimates accurately, the target return method results in a more rational pricing decision than the simpler markup method. As typically practiced, however, this method does not explicitly consider the interaction between alternative prices and demand.

What happens if the price is set on the basis of an overly optimistic sales estimate? As with markup pricing, the realized return falls below the target level because fixed costs have to be covered by a smaller unit volume. The impact of such variations in volume can be examined by preparing a **break-even analysis.** Suppose our appliance manufacturer decided to price its coffeemakers at $26. With variable costs of $10 per unit and fixed costs of $500,000, the break-even chart in Exhibit 12.4 indicates that the product's **break-even volume** is 31,250 units—the volume necessary to just cover total costs. To calculate this result, use the following formula:

Exhibit 12.4

BREAK-EVEN CHART SHOWING BREAK-EVEN AND TARGET RETURN VOLUME

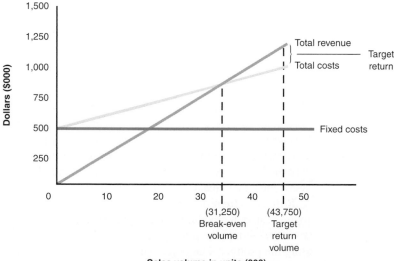

Sales volume in units (000)

$$\text{Break-even volume} = \frac{\text{Fixed cost}}{\text{Price} - \text{Variable cost}} = \frac{\$500,000}{\$26 - \$10} = 31,250 \text{ units}$$

If we also consider the $1 million of capital invested in the product and the manufacturer's target return of 20 percent (or $200,000), the chart shows that the firm must sell 43,750 to achieve the desired return. Break-even analysis can also calculate break-even and target return volumes at different price levels. Exhibit 12.5 indicates how these volumes vary for our product example over a range of prices. Break-even analysis, however, suffers from the same limitations as other cost-oriented pricing methods. It does not explicitly consider the price sensitivity of demand or the likely reactions of competitors. Therefore, managers must rely on their own judgment to decide how likely it is that the product's actual volume will reach or exceed the break-even level associated with each alternative price.

Competition-Oriented Methods

Some companies key their pricing decisions to what competitors are charging for similar offerings and pay relatively less attention to their own costs or demand schedules. This is not to say that their prices and competitors' prices are always the same; some firms may add a premium or discount their price below the industry average. Such competition-oriented pricing is also found in mature industries where little product differentiation and a few strong competitors make it difficult for one firm to change its price without precipitating a competitive reaction. Under such circumstances, a common industry price structure reflects the collective wisdom about finding the price that will yield a fair return and minimize the chances that a price war will jeopardize the profits of all industry firms.

Firms that pursue competition-oriented pricing approaches do not ignore cost or return-on-investment considerations. Instead, they try to control costs to make adequate returns at prices consistent with those of competitors. But if this cannot be done (for instance, because the firm is less efficient), the target rate of return may be the factor that is changed.

In some cases, firms adopt a **going-rate** or **competitive parity** pricing approach, where they try to maintain prices equal to those of one or more major competitors. This has been common in oligopolistic industries with little product differentiation and a few large competitors, as in steel, paper, and fertilizer. Price virtually ceases to be a controllable element of the marketing mix under such circumstances. No firm can increase its price without some assurance that others will follow, because most customers would switch to lower-priced competitors. Similarly, a firm would be reluctant to price below the competition lest other companies also cut their prices and reduce profits for all concerned. Consequently,

Exhibit 12.5

BREAK-EVEN AND TARGET RETURN VOLUMES FOR ALTERNATIVE SELLING PRICES

Selling price	Fixed costs ($000)	Per-unit average variable cost	Target return ($000)	Break-even volume (units)	Target return volume (units)
$18	$500	$10	$200	62,500	87,500
20	500	10	200	50,000	70,000
24	500	10	200	35,714	50,000
26	500	10	200	31,250	43,750
28	500	10	200	27,778	38,889
30	500	10	200	25,000	35,000

prices are usually quite stable in such industries until a **price leader** decides an increase in industry prices is necessary to meet increased costs and maintain returns.

The ability of a firm to be a price leader whose pricing decisions are emulated by other companies is not determined solely by its size or market share. The leader also tends to be one of the most efficient firms in the industry; that is, it is one of the last to feel the need for a price increase. Often leaders are also perceived to have good marketing expertise and have had past success in making price increases stick. Even so, there is no guarantee that a given price leader can maintain its position. "Follower" firms are particularly likely to cut prices below the leader during periods of overcapacity and to increase prices faster than the leader during periods of high inflation.

In industries where product quality, service, or availability vary across brands, a firm may still base its pricing on what its competitors are charging, but try to hold its prices either below or above the competition. Such **discount** or **premium price policies** usually reflect differences in positioning strategies. Ryanair's low-price strategy is a good example of a discount price policy. Once again, however, such a policy is sustainable only if the firm can maintain a total cost advantage over its competitors.

Sealed bidding is common in many businesses, especially in dealing with the government. In such situations buyers request a formal bid with no later opportunity for change. In public procurement the bids are opened publicly, enabling bidders to learn what competitors bid. Such is not typically the case with private bidding.

One approach used to set a bid price is an **expected value** model based on the following formula:

$$E(X) = P(X)Z(X)$$

where X = bid price, $Z(X)$ = the profit at the bid price, $P(X)$ = the probability of an award at the bid price, and $E(X)$ = the expected profit of a bid. The price the company bids is the one yielding the highest expected profit. But such models suffer because of the subjectivity of the probability estimates and objectives other than profit to take into account, such as the possibility of follow-on work, capacity availability, and need to keep the workforce intact.[10]

Internet Auction Sites Make Accurate Cost Estimates More Critical

The Internet might make old-fashioned sealed bidding procedures obsolete. Instead of asking for a single submission of sealed bids from alternative suppliers, government agencies are likely to turn to Internet auctions where suppliers can adjust their bids in response to those of competitors.

Recall that in Chapter 6 we discussed the rapid growth of auction websites, particularly in business-to-business markets.[11] Some business-to-business sites focus on **seller's auctions.** These sites are usually specialized by industry and facilitate global spot markets for relatively standardized materials, component parts, used equipment, and the like. On www.MetalSite.com, for example, a steelmaker such as LTV can offer a block of sheet or rolled steel whenever its plants have excess capacity and inventories grow too large. Potential buyers then enter bids for the steel over two or three days, and the highest bid wins. Similarly, www.acunet.com runs a popular wholesale auction for used cars.

More recently, **buyer's auction** sites have emerged in a number of industries where qualified suppliers are invited to compete for a contract where the buyer has specified all the technical requirements and purchase criteria in detail, except the price. Because the buyer must be able to specify all its requirements before suppliers can submit firm bids, such auctions are likely to work best for purchases where the buyer has past experience to draw on and where those requirements are unlikely to change rapidly, as, for example, when Ford buys seats or bumpers for one of its current car models.

Most analysts believe that, in markets where they are appropriate, both kinds of Internet auctions will work to increase price competition. Whether that turns out to be the case or not, one thing is clear: To be profitable selling goods or services at auction a firm must work to hold its costs down relative to its competitors, and it must have an accurate understanding of what those costs are.

When selling excess inventory on a seller's auction site, for instance, the firm may be willing to accept a bid that is below its full cost as long as that bid covers variable costs and makes a contribution to fixed costs. This is particularly true if the product or service would otherwise go unsold and contribute nothing to cover fixed costs, as is the case with empty seats on an airline flight or empty hotel rooms on weekends. Nevertheless, the selling firm must know what its fixed and variable costs are with some certainty before it can decide whether a given bid will provide enough revenue to cover variable cost and therefore be worth accepting.

The critical question facing managers bidding for contracts on a buyer's auction site is, How low should we go? Winning too many contracts by bidding prices that are too low to cover costs and provide a reasonable return on invested capital is a good recipe for failure in the long run.

Customer-Oriented Methods

Pricing to Capture the Value Perceived by the Customer   Perhaps the key concept in setting a price is the notion of *perceived value*. Whether the product offering is an industrial product or service that delivers primarily economic and functional benefits or a consumer item whose benefits are more psychological, potential customers usually have some idea of what constitutes a good or bad price. They develop such perceptions by comparing the prices being charged by a firm and its competitors to the benefits or value they think they can derive from purchasing the product or service. The essential purpose of the price level set by the marketing manager, then, should be to enable the firm to capture the value of the product as perceived in the mind of the customer.

While a firm's costs establish a minimum floor for long-term profitability, customers generally do not care what those costs are. The only thing important to them is the value they are likely to receive for the price they pay. Thus, one danger of cost-oriented (or even competition-oriented) pricing methods is that they can produce prices that are lower than perceived value, causing the firm to "leave money on the table." Such approaches might also result in prices that exceed many customers' perceptions of value, resulting in lost sales and competitive vulnerability.[12]

Of course, the perceived value of a given product offering can vary from customer to customer. When setting a price level within a strategic marketing program, however, the manager should try to determine an "average" perceived value for the customers in a particular target market segment. Such a determination typically requires research. Exhibit 12.6 summarizes a variety of methods for calculating customer value, ranging from reverse-engineering methods aimed at estimating the economic benefits generated by the product's performance to more common survey research approaches for measuring customers' perceptions.

Estimating Customer Value by Assessing Value-in-Use   One of the most useful ways to estimate customer value, particularly for industrial products and consumer durables, is by assessing the product's **value-in-use.** The value-in-use assessment process

Exhibit 12.6

METHODS FOR ESTIMATING PERCEIVED CUSTOMER VALUE

1. Industrial engineering methods:
   - Internal engineering assessment: Physical laboratory tests within the firm.
   - Field value-in-use assessments: Customer field trials or interviews determining economic benefits to using the product.
   - Indirect survey questions: Customer estimates of the effects of product changes on firm operations used to infer the value of product attributes.

2. Overall estimates of customer value:
   - Focus group value assessment: Willingness-to-pay questions in a small group setting.
   - Direct survey questions: Willingness-to-pay questions in a survey format.

3. Decomposition approaches:
   - Conjoint analysis: A method for estimating customer trade-offs of product attributes.
   - Benchmarks: Customer indication of willingness to pay for incremental (or fewer) attributes that can be compared to an example from the product category.

4. Compositional approach:
   - Direct customer questions about the value of product attributes.

5. Importance ratings:
   - Customer rank ordering or rating of the importance of product attributes as well as comparisons between competitors.

Source: James C. Anderson, Dipak C. Jain, and Pradeep K. Chintagunta, "Customer Value Assessment in Business Markets: A State-of-Practice Study," *Journal of Business-to-Business Marketing* 1 (1993), pp. 3–29. Used by permission.

Exhibit 12.7

THE "VALUE-IN-USE" APPROACH TO DETERMINING A CUSTOMER'S PERCEPTION OF VALUE

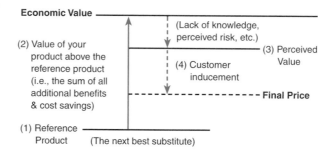

begins with the selection of a reference product, usually the product the customer is currently using or a major competitor's product. The manager then calculates the incremental benefits to the customer—in monetary terms—of using his or her product instead of the reference product. These benefits may be the result of improved performance and additional features, or improved efficiency and reduced costs over the life cycle of product. In either case, the additional monetary value of the manager's product added to the price of the reference product [(1) + (2) in Exhibit 12.7] equals the **economic value** of the manager's product to the customer: the maximum amount the customer should be willing to pay, assuming that she is fully informed about the product and the offerings of competitors.

For example, suppose New Holland introduces a new farm tractor to compete with a particular John Deere model. The John Deere is priced at $25,000. However, field use trials indicate that the New Holland tractor will use on average $2,000 less fuel over its 15-year productive life, and it has a more user-friendly hitch system that will save 100 hours of the farmer's time, worth (if we assume the farmer's time is valued at $20 an hour) another $2,000. Finally, the New Holland comes with a superior air-conditioned cab and a Bose stereo system, which a survey of farmers suggests is worth another $1,000 to potential buyers. Thus, if we add the additional cost savings and benefits provided by the New Holland model to the price of the reference product, we get $25,000 + $2,000 + $2,000 + $1,000 = $30,000. This is the total economic value-in-use to the average farmer of the New Holland tractor.

Therefore, $30,000 is the maximum amount a farmer should be willing to pay for the new tractor, *assuming* that he or she has all the relevant information. But while providing such "complete" information should obviously be the goal of New Holland's salesforce and promotional materials, it is unlikely such a state of complete information will usually exist. Therefore, the manager must anticipate some discounting on the customer's part due to lack of knowledge about the product's benefits, competitive offerings, the perceived risk of buying something new, and so on. Therefore, as indicated in Exhibit 12.7, the customer's actual *perceived* value of the New Holland tractor (3) is likely to be somewhat less than the tractor's actual economic value-in-use.

The difference between the value perceived by the customer and the manufacturer's marginal cost defines the range of possible prices. Suppose, for instance, that a farmer perceives the New Holland tractor to be worth $3,000 more than the John Deere, or $28,000, and that New Holland's marginal cost of producing another tractor (including the dealer's margin, etc.) is $20,000. New Holland's managers could set the price anywhere between those two figures.

KEY OBSERVATION

The difference between the value perceived by the customer and the manufacturer's marginal cost defines the range of possible prices.

From New Holland's perspective, it might seem desirable to set the price as close to the customer's perceived value as possible. The customer should be willing to pay such a price since the farmer would receive benefits equal to the cost. By capturing all of the incremental value the company has created, New Holland would fatten its profit margin and return on investment. However, there are sound strategic reasons for setting a price that shares at least some of the economic value with the customer [as indicated by (4) in Exhibit 12.7]. If New Holland's price is exactly equal to the perceived incremental value of the tractor in the customer's mind, then he or she will be indifferent between the two tractors; either tractor will leave the farmer equally well off after he pays for it. Therefore, passing some of the incremental value along to the customer in the form of a lower price provides an inducement to purchase the New Holland instead of the competing brand. Such inducements give the salesforce a strong argument to persuade potential purchasers. They also can be particularly important in achieving some strategic pricing objectives, such as when the firm is pursuing a penetration strategy to maximize sales growth.

Other Perceptual Pricing Issues   Often, a number of psychological factors can influence customers' perceptions of the relationship between a product's price and its value. Thus, many firms use such practices as customary pricing, price lining, psychological pricing, and promotional pricing. All of these are particularly popular in consumer nondurable product categories.

In some product categories consumers expect a single **customary price** for the product. Candy bars, for example, sold for many years at a customary price of 10 cents. When increasing costs put pressure on manufacturers' margins, they elected to reduce the size of the bar rather than upset customers' expectations by raising the price.

Price lining is another common customer-oriented pricing practice, especially among retailers. It involves selling all products in a category at one of several predetermined

ETHICAL PERSPECTIVE 12.1
When Is a "Sale" a Sale?

Because many customers in most product and service categories are price sensitive and are motivated to find the best value for their money, promotional pricing is both common and effective, particularly among retailers. Unfortunately, some firms engage in practices that attempt to deceive the customer. For instance, deception can occur when a retailer prices an item at an unusually high level for a short period and then discounts it for the remainder of the selling period and promotes it as being on sale. Since very little of the item is sold at the artificially high "regular" price, the "sale" price is in reality the regular price.

Bait-and-switch is another practice that is not only unethical but illegal as well. It involves a retailer advertising an unusually low price on one or more popular brands to attract customers. Once in the store, customers are told the sale items have been sold out or are otherwise dissuaded from buying the advertised items. Instead, the salesperson attempts to sell the customer a higher-priced/higher-margin substitute.

"price points" or levels. Each price line represents a different level of quality. For example, different brands of men's shirts in the same store might be priced at $29.95, $34.95, and $39.95. This practice helps customers make quality comparisons, assuming the price differences can be easily associated with differences in quality, including the number and type of features offered. It also simplifies pricing decisions for the retailer and guides the retail buyer in deciding which brands to stock.

In **psychological pricing** the firm takes advantage of the fact that many consumers use price as an indication of quality. For example, Heublein successfully repositioned its Popov brand of vodka by substantially raising its price. The 8 percent price increase reduced the brand's market share by 1 percent but produced a 30 percent increase in profit.[13] Some perfumes are priced high to elevate their status as a gift.

Another common psychological pricing practice is called *odd pricing*. For instance, a product or service might be priced at $29.95 instead of $30.00, 19 cents instead of 20 cents, or $39,950 instead of $40,000. Odd prices convey the psychological impression of a lower price. A final demand-oriented pricing practice is the use of **promotional pricing** to transmit a message about the product in conjunction with, or sometimes in lieu of, advertising or other forms of promotional activity. The most common form of promotional pricing is the familiar sale: the offer of a reduced price on the product for a limited time. Unfortunately, some firms are overly aggressive in their promotional pricing tactics, which can give rise to ethical concerns as discussed in Ethical Perspective 12.1.

Deciding on a Price Structure: Adapting Prices to Market Variations

Even though determining a product's price level is a complicated process, most firms do not stop with the selection of a single list price. Instead, the final step in the pricing process is usually to develop a **price structure** that adapts the price to variations in cost and demand across geographic territories, national boundaries, types of customers, and items within the product line.

Geographic Adjustments

Within a domestic market, firms with only one or a few plants must adjust prices for the variations in transportation costs of selling to customers in different parts of the country. One approach is called **FOB origin pricing:** The manufacturer places the goods "free on board" a transportation carrier. At this point the title and responsibility passes to the customer, who pays the freight from the factory to the destination. Advocates argue that this is the fairest way to allocate freight charges: Each customer picks up its own costs. The disadvantage, though, is that the manufacturer may be at a cost disadvantage when trying to sell to customers in distant markets.

The opposite alternative is **freight absorption pricing.** Here the seller picks up all or part of the freight charges. New competitors trying to penetrate new markets and smaller competitors in maturing industries trying to increase their share sometimes use this approach. Their rationale is that if they can obtain more business, their average unit costs will fall enough to compensate for the high freight costs.

Most firms use a compromise approach to deal with variations in transportation costs. One method is **uniform delivered pricing,** where a standard freight charge—equal to the average freight cost across all customers—is assessed every customer, regardless of location. This lowers the overall cost to distant customers, but raises costs for customers near the company's plant. Nevertheless, the approach is popular because it is easy to administer and enables the firm to maintain a single nationally advertised price. **Zone pricing** is another compromise approach that falls between FOB and uniform delivered pricing. Here the company divides the country into two or more pricing zones. It charges all customers within the same zone the same delivered price, but a higher price is set for distant zones than for those closer to the plant.

Global Adjustments

Geographic adjustments become even more complicated when the geographic areas involve different countries. In addition to reflecting transportation costs, prices in different countries may also have to be adjusted for different exchange rates, variations in competition, market demand, or strategic objectives (volume growth versus profit generation), and different governmental tax policies or legal regulations.

In some cases, firms attempt to minimize such adjustments by adopting a highly standardized global pricing policy similar to an FOB origin policy in the domestic market. They charge the same price around the world and require each customer to absorb all freight and import duties. Such a policy has the obvious virtue of simplicity, but it fails to respond to variations in local demand or competitive conditions.

Other firms charge a transfer price to their various national branches or subsidiaries but then give local managers in each country wide latitude to charge their customers whatever price they think most appropriate. Although sensitive to variations in local conditions, such a policy may lead to arbitrage involving the transshipment of goods across countries when price differences exceed the freight-and-duty costs separating the markets. There is also the question of control and whether the strategic objectives of local managers are always consistent with the higher business and corporate objectives.

For all the above reasons, most firms follow an intermediate approach to global pricing.[14] Corporate management establishes an acceptable range of prices. Local country managers are then given the flexibility to select the price within that range that is best suited to local demand and competitive conditions, though their decisions are often subject to strategic review and approval by top management. Thus, a firm might allow local managers to set a high price in countries where the product has a strong competitive position and high perceived value, but demand lower penetration pricing in less-established markets.

Countertrade   An additional pricing problem often arises when selling to customers in developing economies, which may lack sufficient hard currency to pay for their purchases.

Exhibit 12.8

GLOBAL COUNTERTRADE

Countertrade, which occurs in international transactions where the potential customer lacks sufficient hard currency to pay for a purchase, can take a variety of forms. These include:

- *Barter.* Barter involves the direct exchange of goods with no money and no third party involved. For instance, a German firm might agree to build a steel plant in Mexico in exchange for a given amount of Mexican oil.

- *Compensation deals.* Here the seller agrees to take some percentage of the payment in cash and the rest in goods, as when Boeing sells airplanes to Brazil for 70 percent cash and an agreed-upon number of tons of coffee.

- *Buyback arrangements.* Under such arrangements a seller offers a plant, equipment, or technical expertise to a customer and agrees to accept as partial payment products manufactured with the equipment or training supplied. For example, a U.S. chemical company built a plant for an Indian company in return for some cash and a volume of chemicals to be made in the plant.

- *Offsets.* The seller is compensated in cash but agrees to spend a substantial amount of that cash with the customer or its government over a stated time period. For instance, Pepsi sells its cola syrup to Russia for rubles and agrees to buy Russian vodka at a given rate for sale in the United States.

Source: Adapted from Stephen S. Cohen and John Zysman, "Countertrade, Offsets, Barter, and Buybacks," *California Management Review,* Winter 1986, pp. 41–56. Copyright © 1986, by The Regents of the University of California. Reprinted from the *California Management Review,* Vol. 28, No. 2. By permission of The Regents.

Such customers may offer items other than money as payment. While many companies dislike such deals, it is often in their best economic interest to facilitate them via a set of activities known as *countertrade.* For example, given the sharp devaluation of the Argentine peso and the resulting decline in new auto sales in 2002, Toyota began bartering pickup trucks in Argentina for a trade-in and 44 tons of soybeans.[15] Countertrade can take a variety of forms, several of which are discussed in Exhibit 12.8.

Discounts and Allowances

Firms relying on independent wholesalers and retailers to distribute their products must adjust their list prices to motivate and reward these firms to perform needed marketing activities.[16] We discuss programs for gaining reseller support in more detail in the next chapter, but briefly describe price discounts and allowances—basic tools used in creating such programs—in the next sections.

Trade Discounts   To induce wholesalers and/or retailers to carry a product and perform their usual marketing activities in its support, manufacturers offer **trade** (or **functional**) **discounts** from the suggested retail list price. Such discounts vary, depending on the intermediary's wholesale or retail level in the channel and the specific activities they are expected to perform. A manufacturer who distributes stereo speakers through a channel of independent wholesale distributors and retailers, for instance, might have a suggested retail price of $100 for each speaker and a trade discount schedule of 50/15. The 50 represents the percent discount from list price offered to retailers who carry the product. The 15 is the discount offered to the wholesaler. Thus, a retailer would pay $50 for each speaker ($100 − [.5 × $100]). The wholesaler would pay the manufacturer $42.50 ($50 − [.15 × $50]).

Quantity Discounts   To encourage channel members, or even ultimate customers, to purchase more of the product, a manufacturer might offer a price reduction for ordering in large quantities. The **quantity discount** often increases as order size increases. For example, a firm might offer no additional discount on orders of 50 units or less, a 2 percent discount off list on orders of 51 to 100 units, 4 percent off on orders of 101 to 500 units, and 5 percent off on orders of more than 500 units. To avoid charges of illegal price discrimination against smaller purchasers, the size of such discounts should be justified by the cost savings that manufacturers gain by filling larger orders. These savings include reductions in per-unit selling, order processing, transportation, and inventory carrying costs. In addition to cost savings, quantity discounts help move more inventory closer to the ultimate customer, thereby encouraging more impulse purchases and reducing the probability of stockouts occurring among wholesalers or retailers in the distribution system.

Cash Discounts   A **cash discount** is a price reduction to encourage customers to pay their bills promptly. A common example of such a discount is "2/10, net 30." This means that payment in full is due within 30 days, but the buyer can deduct 2 percent from the price if payment is made within 10 days. Such discounts help reduce the capital the seller has tied up in accounts receivable and lower collection costs and bad debts.

Allowances   Allowances are similar to discounts in that they are inducements to encourage channel members or final customers to engage in specific behaviors in support of the product. One common example in consumer durable goods categories—particularly automobiles—is the **trade-in allowance.** This is essentially a price reduction granted to customers for turning in an old item when buying a new one. Such allowances help customers recoup the value from their used products and thereby encourage more frequent replacement purchases. **Promotional allowances** such as cooperative advertising programs reward distributors or retailers for advertising the product at the local level. Other promotional allowances may induce retailers to devote more shelf space, personal selling effort, or point-of-purchase promotional material to the product. Payment of such allowances is often contingent upon the retailer's meeting a specific sales volume goal, but they can amount to substantial sums. For instance, Safeway Inc., a large supermarket chain, reported supplier promotion payments amounted to $2.1 billion in 2002.[17]

Price-Off Promotions   This is one of the simplest kinds of sales promotion since all that's involved is a temporary reduction in the product's price. A similar popular promotion increases the amount of product provided while holding the price constant—like Pepsi's offer of 15 cans of soda for the normal price of a 12-pack. Price-off promotions may be the most effective way to boost sales temporarily; however, they suffer from several disadvantages. Often they only transfer future sales to the present as loyal customers stock up. Another problem is that competitors can easily copy them. Also, they may lead consumers to the notion that the product should be bought only below the suggested retail price when a promotional deal is offered.

Coupons, Rebates, and Refunds   The proportion of consumer promotion dollars devoted to **cents-off coupons** declined somewhat during the 1990s. As redemption rates fell to about 2 percent and processing costs increased, many consumer goods manufacturers attempted to cut their couponing budgets and emphasize "value pricing" or "everyday low price" policies instead. Such actions were also motivated by other drawbacks of heavy reliance on coupons, including the potential for fraud—ranging from counterfeiting to misredemption by retailers—and the fact that it is difficult to gain a competitive advantage using such a ubiquitous tactic.

Nevertheless, couponing remains the dominant form of price-oriented promotion in the United States. Approximately 300 billion coupons are distributed each year, and a recent survey found that 100 percent of manufacturers who sell consumer goods through supermarkets still devote at least some of their promotion dollars to coupons.[18]

What accounts for the continuing popularity of coupons? Coupons can be an effective way to target discounts to specific customer segments, particularly as information technology makes it possible for firms to collect more detailed information about customers. For instance, by combining a computer database of purchase histories with a direct mail program, a marketer can direct coupons to the most price-sensitive households while maintaining higher regular prices for less price-oriented buyers.[19] Coupons are also useful for accomplishing specific strategic marketing objectives, such as motivating first-time buyers to try a product or encouraging the purchase of larger package sizes.

Rebates reduce the price of the product through a money refund offer. Such offers typically require the consumer to mail some proof of purchase to the manufacturer to receive the refund. In recent years rebates have been used extensively by producers of durable goods, including automobiles, major appliances, and cameras because they can move excess inventories quickly.

Premiums are attempts to attract buyers by offering a product or service free or at a substantially reduced price to encourage the purchase of another product. Premiums can be included in a package, sent by mail, or via another product (a free soft drink with the purchase of a pizza). Premiums can even be to some extent self-liquidating—as when the consumer sends in a package and 50 cents for a premium.

Differential Pricing

Differential pricing (also known as discriminatory pricing) occurs when a firm sells a product or service at two or more prices not determined by proportional differences in cost. This is usually done to adjust to differences in the price sensitivities or preferences of various customer segments. Prices may even vary on a customer-to-customer basis in organizational markets or consumer durable categories where the final price is determined through negotiation. For example, automobile retailers are noted for such pricing practices, although some manufacturers, such as Saturn, have moved toward a common list price with no bargaining.

Some common differential pricing adjustments targeted at particular customer segments include:

- *Time pricing.* Prices might be adjusted seasonally, across days of the week, or across hours of the day to capitalize on predictable fluctuations in demand over time. Movie theaters, for instance, often charge higher prices for evening shows than for early matinees, and hotels charge less for weekend occupancy.

- *Location pricing.* The same product or service might be priced differently at various retail locations to capitalize on local demand or the intensity of competition. Even within a single theater, seats in some locations are typically more expensive because many theater-goers are willing to pay more to sit near the stage.

- *Customer segment pricing.* Perhaps the most common differential pricing practice is to charge different prices to customer segments that vary in their willingness or ability to buy. Many arts organizations, for example, offer lower prices to senior citizens whose fixed incomes might otherwise prohibit their attendance.

Conditions Allowing Differential Pricing   It is not always possible or wise to set different prices for essentially the same product. For such a differential pricing policy to work, first there must be identifiable customer segments with different price sensitivities. Second, the customer segments must either be physically separated from one another or the firm must institute control procedures to ensure that the segment paying the lower price cannot resell the product to customers paying the higher price. Obviously, too, the cost to the manufacturer of segmenting and monitoring the market should not exceed the extra revenue generated by the discriminatory pricing. And the firm should be confident that resentment among customers asked to pay the higher price, or competitive conditions in the market, will not leave it vulnerable to competitive attacks in the high-price segments.

The Internet Facilitates Differential Pricing   As we have mentioned before, many analysts argue that the Internet will make product categories more price competitive. It is also making it easier to identify—and charge different prices to—customer segments with different price sensitivities. For example, there are software programs that let a Web-based seller examine the click-streams of visitors to its site. If the individual examines a number of alternatives without making a purchase, he or she might be identified as a high-involvement, price-sensitive shopper and therefore be offered lower prices.[20]

The Internet also enables firms, especially service firms, to do more differential pricing by allowing them to change prices quickly at different times of the day or week (i.e., time pricing) or in response to unused capacity, as when airlines make last-minute special fares available on their websites.

Legal Considerations[21]   Price discrimination is not the legal issue in the United States today that it was in the past. It is important to note, however, that the Robinson-Patman Act outlaws price discrimination among buyers of goods of "like grade and quality" where the effect may be to "injure, destroy, or prevent competition." Because individual consumers buy goods and services for their own use and are not competing with one another, the law usually does not prevent discriminatory pricing of consumer goods at the retail level because there is no injury to competition. To legally offer different prices for the same product to retailers, distributors, or industrial buyers, the manufacturer must be sure that the buyers involved are not in direct competition, or that the difference in prices offered is justified by differences in the cost of doing business with the different buyers. This cost defense, for example, is the rationale for offering the quantity discounts mentioned in the preceding section. Because transportation and order processing costs are usually lower for large orders, firms can legally pass those cost savings on to the buyer as a discount or lower price.

In addition to price discrimination, the Sherman Act prohibits both horizontal and vertical price fixing. In the case of the former, competitors agree to maintain a given price. The latter involves an agreement between manufacturers and retailers to sell products at a certain price. The Miller Tyding Act (1937) was passed to permit such vertical price fixing, but in 1976, Congress passed the Consumer Goods Pricing Act, which made such pricing once more illegal. Predatory pricing is also illegal under the Sherman Act because it involves selling below cost to drive one or more competitors out of the market.

In addition to legal concerns, differential price adjustments can raise some ethical issues as well. One such issue concerns the inherent "fairness" of charging higher prices to some customers simply because they are not very price sensitive. This is a particular concern in the pharmaceutical industry, as illustrated by the example in Ethical Perspective 12.2.

Product-Line Pricing Adjustments

Pricing decisions become even more complicated when a firm produces a line of several models or styles that potential customers perceive as bearing some relationship to one another. In such cases, firms need to adjust the prices of various models to reflect customers' perceptions of their relative value. In theory, producers should determine the prices for all the products in the line simultaneously, taking into account not only the price elasticity of demand for each model, but also the cross-elasticities among them. A **cross-elasticity** is the

ETHICAL PERSPECTIVE 12.2
Ethical Concerns over Differential Prices

While the issue of the equity or fairness of charging different prices to different customers is primarily a concern of the law, evaluating the fairness of the price charged to a particular customer can also involve ethical considerations. For instance, just because a customer attaches a high value to a given product or service and is therefore willing to pay a high price does not necessarily mean it is always ethical—or in the firm's best long-term interest—to charge such a price. Consider the case of AZT, a drug treatment for symptoms of AIDS. When the drug was first introduced

by Wellcome PLC, a yearlong treatment cost $10,000. The company argued that the high price was necessary to compensate for the heavy investment involved in developing such a drug for a relatively small market. In addition, potential customers attached a high value to any drug that offered promise for ameliorating AIDS symptoms. However, public reaction to AZT's high price was so negative that the company eventually reduced it substantially, but only after some damage had probably been done to the firm's image and reputation.

For a discussion of other ethical issues, see Gwendolyn K. Ortmeyer, "Ethical Issues in Pricing," in N. Craig Smith and John A. Quelch, eds., *Ethics in Marketing* (Burr Ridge, IL: Richard D. Irwin, 1993), p. 389.

percentage change in sales of one product induced by a 1 percent change in the price of another product that is assumed to be a close substitute.

Because of the difficulties in estimating such cross-elasticities, however, firms seldom use this approach. About the best that managers can do is to price each item separately and then adjust those prices to reflect the likelihood that customers will trade up or down and will perceive the prices of the related items to be fair and reasonable. Since some products require the use of other products (razors and razor blades or printers and ink cartridges), the seller may price one product lower to stimulate the sale of the other.

Many companies offer optional features with their basic product. Automobile companies offer such extras as bigger engines, special tires, sun roofs, higher-quality sound systems, and leather interiors—all for an extra cost. Luxury cars include most such features as standard equipment and many retailer's use them as a way of bargaining with consumers. Such practices make it difficult to price these options in any realistic way. A somewhat similar situation exists when firms sell a basic service for a fixed amount and then charge an additional amount based on the extent of usage (telephone companies and their long-distance charges).

Sellers often **bundle** the various items in their product line and sell the bundle at a price less than the total of the items if priced separately (McDonald's meals for children, season subscriptions to concerts, option packages offered by car companies). Since some customers may not want the bundle, provision must be made to allow purchase of individual items.

TAKE-AWAYS

- Pricing decisions involve an inherent conflict between (1) the need to win customers by allowing them to retain a portion of the value inherent in a product or service and (2) the need to maintain profit margins sufficient to compensate employees, fund growth, and satisfy the firm's various stakeholders.

- The price of a good or service must be high enough to cover per unit costs—at least in the long term—but cannot exceed its value as perceived by the customer. Therefore, the region between unit cost and perceived value represents the range of feasible prices.

- The decision about what price to select from within the range of feasible prices should be based on a careful analysis of competitors' costs and prices, the product's strategic objectives, and consistency with other components of the marketing plan.

- Perhaps the key concept in setting a price is the notion of perceived value. An essential purpose of the price set by a marketing manager should be to enable the firm to capture a fair share of the value of the product as perceived by the intended customer.

- The final step in deciding what price to charge for a product or service involves the development of a price structure that adapts the price to variations in cost and demand across geographic territories, national boundaries, customer segments, and items within the product line.

Self-diagnostic questions to test your ability to apply the analytical tools and concepts in this chapter to marketing decision making may be found at this book's website at www.mhhe.com/mullins05.

ENDNOTES

1. This case example is based on material found in Andrea Felsted, "The Ryanair Advantage: Airport Charges and Maintenance," and Daniel Dombey, Kevin Done, and Andrea Felsted, "As Regulators Launch an Inquiry into Suspected Illegal Subsidies, Is Cheap Air Travel in Europe Too Good to Last?" *Financial Times,* December 12, 2002, p. 19.

2. Robert J. Dolan, "How Do You Know When the Price is Right?" *Harvard Business Review,* September–October 1995, p. 174.

3. Dolan, "How Do You Know When the Price is Right?"

4. Y. K. Shetty, "Product Quality and Competitive Strategy," *Business Horizons,* May–June 1987, pp. 46–52; and David A. Garvin, *Managing Quality* (New York: Free Press, 1988), pp. 70–74.

5. Gerard J. Tellis, "Beyond the Many Faces of Price: An Integration of Pricing Strategies," *Journal of Marketing,* October 1986, p. 146.

6. To truly maximize current profit, of course, the product's price should be set exactly at the point where the marginal revenue gained from the last item sold equals the marginal cost of producing and selling that item. In reality, though, most firms do not have adequate knowledge of their demand and cost functions to determine the profit-maximizing price with such precision.

7. Akshay R. Rao, Mark E. Bergen, and Scott Davis, "How to Fight a Price War," *Harvard Business Review,* March–April 2000, pp. 107–16; and Thomas T. Nagel, "Managing Price Competition," *Marketing Management* 2 (Spring 1993), pp. 36–45.

8. Robin Cooper and Robert S. Kaplan, "Measure Costs Right: Make the Right Decisions," *Harvard Business Review,* September–October 1988, pp. 96–103.

9. "Supermarket 1998 Sales Manual," *Progressive Grocer,* July 1998.

10. H. Michael Hayes, Per V. Jenster, and Nels Erik Aaby, *Business Marketing* (Burr Ridge, IL: Richard D. Irwin, 1996), p. 306.

11. Spencer E. Ante, "Why B2B Is a Scary Place to Be," *Business Week,* September 11, 2000, pp. 34–37. Also see Steven Kaplan and Mohanbir Sawhney, "E-Hubs: The New B2B Marketplaces," *Harvard Business Review,* May–June 2000, pp. 97–103.

12. Lehmann and Winer, *Product Management,* chap.9; and Stephanie N. Mehta, "How to Thrive When Prices Fall," *Fortune,* May 12, 2003, pp. 131–34.

13. Jeffery H. Birnbaum, "Pricing of Products Is Still an Art, Often Having Little Link to Costs," *The Wall Street Journal,* November 25, 1981, p. 25.

14. Warren J. Keegan, *Global Marketing Management* (Englewood Cliffs, NJ: Prentice Hall, 1989), chap. 13.

15. Leslie Moore, "For Wary Argentines, the Crops Are Cash," *New York Times,* December 1, 2002, BU6.

16. Michael V. Marn and Robert L. Rosiello, "Managing Price, Gaining Profit," *Harvard Business Review,* September–October 1992, pp. 84–94.

17. David Henry, "Accounting Games in the Grocer's Aisle," *Business Week,* April 14, 2003, p. 64.

18. Cox Direct, *19th Annual Survey of Promtional Practices* (Largo, FL: Cox Direct, 1997).

19. "Targeting Couponing Slows Redemption Slide," *Marketing News,* February 12, 1996, p. 11.

20. Scott Woolley, "I Got It Cheaper Than You," *Forbes,* November 2, 1998, pp. 82–84.

21. For a more detailed discussion of the legal aspects of pricing, see Thomas T. Nagle and Reed K. Holden, *The Strategy and Tactics of Pricing* (Englewood Cliffs, NJ: Prentice Hall, 1995), chapter 14.

CHAPTER THIRTEEN

Distribution Channel Decisions

Changing Global Retail Trends Send a "Get Well" Greeting to Hallmark[1]

HALLMARK CARDS, THE privately held greeting card company in Kansas City, Missouri, enjoyed steadily increasing revenues and profits from its founding in the early 1890s through the mid-1990s. But then things started going wrong. By 1995 the firm's revenues had sagged by nearly half a billion dollars from their previous peak, and its share of the U.S. greeting card market slipped below 50 percent for the first time in decades.

Part of the problem was that Hallmark's cards and other merchandise began to look somewhat staid and dated next to hipper upstarts, such as Recycled Paper Greetings and Blue Mountain Arts (www. bluemountainarts.com). The firm was also slow to pursue expansion into other countries in Europe, Asia, and South America. But Hallmark's biggest challenge came from a change in customer buying patterns that favored mass merchandisers—and eventually the Internet—over the 9,000 specialty card stores the firm historically relied on to sell its products. While specialty shops once accounted for more than 65 percent of Hallmark's sales, their share had slipped below 30 percent by the mid-1990s, reflecting a trend occurring throughout the card industry.

The firm responded to its falling revenues and market share by first attempting to jazz up its product offerings. It formed cross-functional product teams and gave them greater creative control over the more than 20,000 card designs in 30 languages the company produces every year. It also created new product lines targeted at different ethnic and religious subcultures, such as cards for Hispanics, African-Americans, and Jewish religious holidays.

Hallmark also increased its presence in global markets, largely through the acquisition of domestic greeting card companies and by allocating substantial resources to product development, advertising, and promotion campaigns tailored to different countries. For instance, Hallmark launched a £3 million campaign in 2002 aimed at raising its profile and establishing it as the leading greeting card brand in the United Kingdom.

The firm's most vexing issue, however, was what to do with the thousands of independently owned Hallmark card shops now that discounters, supermarkets, and drugstores dominate the card market. Historically, those specialty shops agreed to carry mostly Hallmark merchandise in exchange for use of the Hallmark name, merchandising support, and designation as the primary outlet for the firm's products. The company's close relationship with those shops helped protect its brand's top-quality image.

Nevertheless, in recent years the firm has signed agreements with a number of large drugstore, supermarket, and discount chains—such as Target and Tesco—to carry the Hallmark line. As a result, there are now more than 22,000 mass-merchandise retail outlets selling Hallmark cards in the United States, and many more in Europe and elsewhere. The company also began marketing a specialized line of cards directly to businesses and organizations through its Business Expressions unit. It opened a website

(www.hallmark.com) where customers can purchase cards, gifts, flowers, and related merchandise or select and send e-cards over the Internet. And more recently the firm has been collaborating with Sony Ericsson to develop content that takes advantage of new mobile phone technologies such as MMS. Branded as Hallmark Hiya, the new content includes iMode greetings and screensavers in Japan, Germany, and the Netherlands, and picture messages and logos in the United Kingdom and southeast Asia.

All these actions went against decades of Hallmark culture and initially elicited howls of protest from the company's specialty retailers. In an attempt to resolve this conflict and retain the active support of its traditional retailers, Hallmark created a second brand, Expressions from Hallmark, that was offered exclusively through discount stores, while reserving its top-of-the-line products primarily for specialty shops. It also launched a $175 million advertising campaign promot-

ing its Gold Crown retail affiliates, began a customer loyalty program through which customers earn discounts and awards for purchases made in Gold Crown stores, and included a store locator on the company website.

Finally, Hallmark spent $30 million to develop a wholesale marketplace—www.ebizmix.com—where its retailers can purchase 70,000 different items ranging from candy to stuffed animals to stock their shelves. In addition to giving retailers quick access to a variety of suppliers who have agreed to offer discounts of up to 10 percent to members, the site also provides industry news and merchandising tips. "We figure we can immediately improve a retailer's bottom line by 10 to 15 percent," says Mark Ciaramitaro, sales and marketing chief for MIX, Inc., which handles the day-to-day operation of ebizmix.com on Hallmark's behalf. That fact has made the firm's longtime retailers much happier with its decision to distribute its cards in many new and different ways.

Marketing Challenges Addressed in Chapter 13

The importance of good distribution decisions in designing a marketing plan is simple: Customers won't buy your good or service unless it is readily available when and where they want to buy it. An effective distribution channel makes the right quantities of the right product available in the right place at the right time to satisfy the target customer. An efficient distribution channel also reduces the costs of marketing and acquiring the product.

KEY OBSERVATION

Customers won't buy your good or service unless it is readily available when and where they want to buy it.

As Hallmark's experience in recent years makes apparent, however, the manager really faces two separate but closely related sets of decisions concerning distribution channels. First come **channel design** decisions concerned with developing a channel structure that links the firm's marketing strategy with the needs of its target market. These decisions focus on questions such as how many levels of middlemen should be included in the distribution system and what types of institutions, and how many of each, should be included at each level. Thus, Hallmark's decisions to distribute its cards through discounters and to sell them directly to consumers through a company website and mobile phones changed the basic structure or design of its distribution system.

Once a product's distribution channel has been designed, a second set of decisions concerns how that channel should be managed. **Channel management** decisions involve the development of policies and procedures to gain and maintain the cooperation of—and often to form mutually beneficial long-term relationships with—the various institutions within the channel. Such decisions focus on selecting and recruiting individual channel members, motivating them to perform specific marketing functions on behalf of the supplier's product or service, coordinating their efforts, assessing their performance, and resolving conflicts that arise. Much of Hallmark's recent marketing activity has been aimed at encouraging its traditional retailers to continue to stock and promote the company's products despite conflicts emanating from increased direct competition from discounters and the firm's own website.

This chapter examines both the channel design and channel management decisions a marketer faces. We begin by discussing the economic rationale for having multiple institutions involved in distributing a given product or service. Why are channels involving networks of many independent firms often more efficient and effective than distributing things directly from the producer to the consumer?

Next, we discuss the various marketing objectives a distribution channel might be designed to accomplish. We then examine some alternative channel designs for both consumer and organizational goods and services, including the various types of institutions and the numbers of those institutions that might be included in a distribution channel given different objectives and strategic circumstances.

Finally, we examine the major issues involved in managing an existing channel, starting with various legal mechanisms, such as vertical integration and franchising, that some firms employ to control channel activities. However, because most channel systems consist of networks of legally independent firms, we devote most of our attention to examining the incentives that can be used to motivate those firms to act in concert with the manufacturer's marketing program. We conclude with a discussion of channel conflicts and the strategies firms employ to resolve them.

Why Do Multifirm Marketing Channels Exist?

As noted in our first chapter, someone must perform a number of marketing functions or activities before a producer and a customer can exchange goods or services—transportation and storage; communication of information via advertising, personal selling, and sales promotion; feedback (marketing research); financing; and such services as installation and repair. Sometimes the customer performs most of the marketing activities in an exchange, as when a family takes a drive through the country to buy vegetables at a farmer's roadside stand. In other cases, a producer may distribute goods or services directly to end users, for example, through mail-order catalogs or the Internet. Most goods are, however, distributed through systems consisting of a variety of middlemen such as retailers, wholesalers, and agents. Thus, a **marketing channel** is

> the set of interdependent organizations involved in the process of making a product or service available for consumption or use by consumers or industrial users.[2]

Many services are distributed through marketing channels, too. Due to their intangible nature, services often do not require the physical distribution activities, such as transportation and storage, that are necessary for goods. Nevertheless, many marketing activities are still necessary to facilitate exchanges with service customers, such as communicating information, customizing the service to a particular customer's needs, personal selling, and

Exhibit 13.1

WAYS BY WHICH USING MIDDLEMEN IMPROVES MARKET EFFICIENCY

- *Functional efficiency:* Middlemen can often perform one or more marketing activities more efficiently than manufacturers or their customers because of their specialization and greater economies of scale. For example, they can spread costs across different manufacturers and thus perform the selling function at a lower cost.

- *Scale efficiency:* By purchasing goods in large quantities, storing them, and then breaking them down into the smaller quantities their customers prefer, middlemen enable manufacturers and their customers to operate more efficiently. Rather than having to make small production runs to fill the orders of individual customers, manufacturers can achieve the economies of large-scale production. And their customers can buy smaller quantities without having their capital tied up in large inventories.

- *Transactional efficiency:* Through their various activities, wholesalers and retailers make it possible for customers to acquire wide assortments of products from a single source with one transaction. This reduces the time and effort that businesses and consumers expend in finding and purchasing the goods they need.

financing. Many of these activities are performed by independent middlemen; sometimes by franchised retailers such as McDonald's fast-food outlets, and in other cases by agent middlemen like insurance agents, travel agents, or stockbrokers.

The rationale for marketing channels lies in the trade-off between costs and benefits. Performing marketing activities costs money, which is reflected in the final selling price of the product or service. Such costs vary widely across products and customers, but are often substantial—on average about 50 percent of the retail price of most consumer package goods with about half that being the retailer's margin. The rest consists of the marketing expenses of the manufacturer and wholesale middlemen. Although the marketing costs for many industrial goods such as sheet steel or basic chemicals tend to be considerably lower since they are sold in large quantities to a smaller number of regular customers, they still account for 10 to 15 percent of the final selling price.

Would consumers be better off buying directly from the manufacturer and bypassing channel intermediaries? Usually not. It's a classic marketing truth that although middlemen can be eliminated, someone must still perform the marketing functions. Middlemen often perform the needed functions at a lower cost than either the customer or the manufacturer could by themselves. This is particularly true when a product must be distributed to large numbers of geographically dispersed customers. See Exhibit 13.1 for a discussion of the various ways marketing efficiency can be improved using middlemen.

However, not all middlemen perform a full range of marketing functions, nor are they equally efficient or effective. Therefore, the first step in designing a distribution channel for a given product is to determine what objectives the channel must accomplish and their relative importance.

Designing Distribution Channels: What Are the Objectives to Be Accomplished?

Managers can design distribution channels to accomplish one or more of the following objectives: (1) increase the availability of the good or service to potential customers, (2) satisfy customer requirements by providing high levels of service, (3) ensure promotional effort, (4) obtain timely and detailed market information, (5) increase cost-effectiveness, and (6) maintain flexibility. As summarized in Exhibit 13.2, the achievement of each of these objectives can be measured and thus can be used to evaluate the performance of a

Exhibit 13.2

DISTRIBUTION CHANNEL OBJECTIVES AND MEASUREMENT CRITERIA

Performance objective	Possible measures	Applicable products and channel level
Product availability:		
• Coverage of relevant retailers.	• Percent of all commodity volume (ACV).	• Consumer products (particularly convenience goods) at retail level.
• In-store positioning.	• Percent of shelf-facings or display space gained by product, weighted by importance of store.	• Consumer products at retail level.
• Coverage of geographic markets.	• Frequency of sales calls by customer type; average delivery time.	• Industrial products; consumer goods at wholesale level.
Meeting customer service requirements:		
• Installation, training, repair, reliability, order cycle time, etc.	• Number of service technicians receiving technical training; monitoring of customer complaints; customer satisfaction level.	• Industrial products, particularly those involving high technology; consumer durables at retail level; consumer and commercial services.
Promotional effort:		
• Effective point-of-purchase (P-O-P) promotion.	• Percent of stores using special displays and P-O-P materials, weighted by importance of store.	• Consumer products at retail level.
• Effective personal selling support.	• Percent of salespeople's time devoted to product; number of salespeople receiving training on product's characteristics and applications.	• Industrial products: consumer durables at all channel levels; consumer convenience goods at wholesale level.
Market information:		
• Monitoring sales trends, inventory levels, competitors' actions.	• Quality and timeliness of information obtained.	• All levels of distribution.
Cost-effectiveness:		
• Cost of channel functions relative to sales volume.	• Middlemen margins and marketing costs as percent of sales.	• All levels of distribution.
Flexibility:		
• Ability to switch to new channels or types of middlemen as conditions change.	• Amount of specialized assets or dedicated investments devoted to current channel.	• All levels of distribution; product or service categories experiencing rapid market development or technological change.
	• Number of long-term legal commitments to current channel members.	

particular channel. However, there are trade-offs among these various objectives, and they are not all equally relevant for all types of products or market circumstances. Consequently, we briefly discuss in the following sections each of these objectives and the conditions where each might be given greater emphasis.

Product Availability

The most important objective for any distribution channel is to make the product conveniently available for customers who want to buy it. For consumer goods, two aspects of availability must be considered. The first is to attain the desired level of coverage in terms of appropriate retail outlets. Because retailers differ in their sales volume, manufacturers need to weight the relative importance of each retailer on the basis of its percent of sales within the product category in question. The resulting figure is referred to as the percent of **all commodity volume (ACV).** For example, a packaged food item may be carried by only 40 percent of an area's food stores. But it may have 70 percent ACV because it is handled primarily by supermarkets accounting for a large proportion of the total sales of such products. The second important aspect of availability for consumer products is the item's positioning within the store. One way to measure performance here is the percentage of available shelf or display space devoted to the brand, weighted by the importance of the store.

For industrial products—and for assessing channel performance at the wholesale level for consumer products—the relevant issue of availability is whether the industrial customer or retailer has the opportunity to place an order and obtain the product when it is needed. This is a question of the adequacy of market coverage. Firms can assess coverage by measuring how often customers in a territory are called on by company or distributor salespeople *and* by the time required to fill and deliver an order (i.e., order cycle time).

Product availability is an important objective for all distribution channels. The appropriate *degree* of availability varies with the characteristics of the product and the target customers, particularly the product's importance to those customers and the amount of time and effort they will expend to obtain it. For example, consumer convenience goods, such as packaged foods and health products, demand immediate availability since most customers are unwilling to devote much effort to obtaining a particular brand. At the other extreme, immediate availability is less critical for unique and important products such as consumer specialty goods or major industrial equipment and installations.

Market and competitive factors also influence a firm's *ability to* achieve a desired level of availability for its product. When demand is limited or when the brand holds a small relative share of the total market, wholesalers or retailers willing to carry it may be difficult to find. The firm may have to offer extra incentives and inducements to achieve an adequate level of product availability. On the other hand, a brand's strong competitive position makes it easier to attain extensive retail coverage and shelf space. Also, as we'll discuss in more detail later, firms can enhance at least some aspects of availability through effective use of the Internet.

Meeting Customers' Service Requirements

A second channel objective, which is closely related to availability but broader in scope, is to achieve and maintain some target level of satisfaction in meeting the service requirements of target customers. This tends to be a particularly crucial objective for analyzer and defender businesses attempting to differentiate themselves from competitors on one or more service dimensions. Some service requirements that might be targeted for consumers, industrial end users, or other members of the distribution channel (e.g., the firm's "intermediate customers" such as distributors or retailers) include:

1. **Order cycle time,** which refers to how long it takes the manufacturer to receive, process, and deliver an order.

2. **Dependability,** which relates to the consistency/reliability of delivery. This is probably the most important element of distribution service, especially for those using just-in-time delivery systems.

3. **Communication** between buyer and seller, which enables both parties to resolve problems at an early stage.

4. **Convenience,** meaning that the system is sufficiently flexible to accommodate the special needs of different customers.

5. **Postsale services,** which help the customer attain full benefits over the life of the product. Such service might include installation, user training, help lines to resolve technical glitches, repair, and spare parts availability. Such services can be particularly important in the distribution of consumer durable goods and technically complex industrial products, like computer systems, major software applications, manufacturing machinery, and the like.

Monitoring customer complaints, and the ongoing measurement of customer (or channel member) satisfaction, retention, and loyalty levels are all appropriate measures of whether the firm is meeting its customer service targets.

Promotional Effort

Another common channel objective is to obtain strong promotional support from channel members for the firm's product, including the use of local media, in-store displays, and cooperation in special promotion events. Gaining broad retailer support for in-store promotions is particularly important for low-involvement, convenience goods. Both the amount and quality of personal selling effort that channel members devote to particular products can be critical. Strong selling support is particularly important when (1) firms are marketing technically complex and expensive consumer durables or industrial goods, (2) the market is highly competitive, or (3) a differentiated defender is trying to sustain a competitive advantage based on superior product quality or customer service.

Market Information

Because of their proximity to the marketplace, middlemen are often relied on for fast and accurate feedback of information about such things as sales trends, inventory levels, and competitors' actions. A high level of channel feedback is particularly important for firms in highly competitive industries characterized by rapid changes in product technology or customer preferences, such as the computer and fashion industries. Feedback is crucial for firms pursuing prospector business strategies since they depend on the early identification of new product and market development opportunities for their success.

Cost-Effectiveness

Channels must be designed to minimize the costs necessary to attain the firm's channel objectives. The cost-effectiveness of the distribution channel is of particular concern to businesses pursuing low-cost analyzer or defender strategies. However, there is often a trade-off between channel costs, particularly those associated with physical distribution activities such as transportation and inventory storage, and achieving high levels of performance on many of the other objectives we have examined, such as product availability and meeting customer service requirements. We will examine these trade-offs in more detail when we examine the pros and cons of alternative channel designs.

Flexibility

As Hallmark discovered, well-entrenched channels where the members have long-standing commitments or substantial mutual investments can be hard to change in response to shifting market or competitive conditions. Consequently, some firms, particularly those pursuing prospector strategies in new or rapidly growing or technically turbulent product categories, consider channel flexibility an important goal. A flexible channel is one where it is relatively easy to switch channel structures or add new types of middlemen (discount retailers and a direct-sales website in Hallmark's case) without generating costly economic or legal conflicts with existing channel members

Designing Distribution Channels: What Kinds of Institutions Might Be Included?

There are four broad categories of institutions that a manager might decide to include in the distribution channel: merchant wholesalers, agent middlemen, retailers, and facilitating agencies. Each of these categories is defined in Exhibit 13.3 and discussed below.

Merchant Wholesalers

Some types of merchant wholesalers engage in a full range of wholesaling functions while others specialize in only limited services. But both buy goods from various suppliers (that is, they take title) and then resell those goods to their commercial customers, either industrial buyers or other resellers such as a retailer. They are compensated by the margin between the price they pay and the price they receive for the goods they carry. Approximately 400,000 merchant wholesalers are operating in the United States, including sales branches maintained by manufacturing firms.[3]

Exhibit 13.3

INSTITUTIONS FOUND IN MARKETING CHANNELS

Institution	Definition
Merchant wholesalers	Take title to the goods they handle; sell primarily to other resellers (e.g., retailers), industrial and commercial customers rather than to individual consumers.
Agent middlemen	Include manufacturer's representatives and brokers. Also sell to other resellers, industrial or commercial customers, but do not take title to the goods. Usually specialize in the selling function and represent client manufacturers on a commission basis.
Retailers	Sell goods and services directly to ultimate consumers for their personal, nonbusiness use. Usually take title to goods they handle; are compensated by the margin between the price they pay for those goods and the price they receive from their customers.
Facilitating agencies	Include advertising agencies, marketing research firms, collection agencies, trucking firms, and railroads; specialize in one or more marketing functions, work on a fee-for-service basis to help clients perform those functions more effectively and efficiently.

Note: Terms such as *distributor* and *jobber* refer to wholesalers, especially those handling industrial goods. The term dealer may refer to either a wholesaler or retailer.

Source: Adapted from Louis W. Stern and Adel I. El-Ansary, *Marketing Channels,* 4th edition by Stern/El-Ansary, © 1992. Reprinted by permission of Pearson Education, Inc., Upper Saddle River, NJ.

Agent Middlemen

The primary role of agent middlemen is to represent other organizations in the sale or purchase of goods or services. Agents do not take title to, or physical possession of, the goods they deal in. Instead, they specialize in either the buying or selling function. There are about 45,000 agent middlemen in the United States, of which manufacturer's agents and sales agents are the two major types used by producers.[4]

Manufacturer's Agents or Manufacturer's Reps   These usually work for several manufacturers, carry noncompetitive, complementary merchandise in an exclusive territory, and concentrate only on the selling function. They are important where a manufacturer's sales are not sufficient to support a company salesperson in a particular territory. Manufacturer's reps are common in the industrial equipment, automotive supply, footwear, and toy industries.

Sales Agents   In contrast, **sales agents** usually represent only one manufacturer and are responsible for the full range of marketing activities needed by that producer. Because they have a wider range of responsibilities, their commissions are much larger than those of manufacturer's reps. Sales agents are used primarily by small firms or start-ups that have limited marketing capabilities. They are particularly common in the electronics, apparel, and home furnishing industries.

Brokers   These are independent firms whose purpose is to bring buyers and sellers together for an exchange. Unlike agents, brokers usually have no continuing relationship with a particular buyer or seller. The producers of seasonal products such as fruits and vegetables and the real estate industry use brokers extensively.

E-Hubs[5]   These emerging forms of business-to-business Internet sites serve the same major function as brokers; they help bring potential buyers and sellers together for an exchange. Also like a broker, the e-hub is usually compensated by commissions from one or both parties.

   Some hubs focus on broad product categories of frequently purchased goods and services that are not industry specific, such as office supplies, airline tickets, or janitorial supplies, and add value by giving buyers in a range of industries access to a "virtual catalog" of offerings from an array of suppliers. While the hub is not directly responsible for performing any of the physical distribution functions, such as transportation or storage, it may maintain relationships with third-party facilitating agencies such as UPS to help ensure that buyers get what they pay for in a timely manner. Examples of this kind of hub include W.W. Grainger and www.BizBuyer.com.

   Other hubs are more industry-specific, bringing buyers and sellers together within a single product category. They create value by enabling one-stop shopping by purchasers. For example, www.PlasticsNet.com allows plastics processors to issue a single purchase order for hundreds of plastics products sourced from a diverse set of suppliers. Because the products they offer tend to be specialized, industry-specific hubs often work with established merchant wholesalers (distributors) in their industry to ensure product availability and reliable delivery. Other examples include SciQuest in the life sciences industry and Chemdex in specialty chemicals.

Retailers

Retailers sell goods and services directly to final consumers for their personal, nonbusiness use. Because retailers usually take title to the goods they carry, their compensation is the margin between what they pay for the merchandise and the prices they charge their customers. Retailing is a major industry in the United States, with over 1.6 million retail establishments.

Retail stores can be categorized in many different ways, such as by the type of merchandise carried (supermarkets, drugstores), breadth of product assortments (specialty or department stores), pricing policies (discount or specialty stores), or nature of the business's premises (e-tailers, mail-order retailers, vending-machine operators, traditional stores). One useful classification scheme groups stores according to their method of operation—low margin/high turnover versus high margin/low turnover.

The former compete primarily on a price basis. To keep volume high while minimizing inventory investments, **low-margin/high-turnover** stores usually concentrate on fast-moving items—such as food, health and beauty aids, basic clothing items, and housewares—and carry a relatively limited selection in each product category. Examples of such retailers include mass-merchandise discounters, wholesale clubs, most supermarket and drug chains, and some specialty chains in such areas as women's clothing, shoes, hardware, office supplies, and building supplies (e.g., Home Depot and Lowe's).

To profit, low-margin/high-turnover retailers must minimize their costs. Their focus on standardized, prepackaged merchandise helps lower personnel costs by reducing or eliminating in-store sales assistance. It also enables them to centralize many purchasing and store operating decisions, thus reducing the number of administrative personnel needed. Many such operations—particularly the mass merchandisers—also minimize their capital investment by operating out of free-standing, no-frills facilities near major traffic arteries, locations where land costs, rents, and taxes are low. Many specialty store chains, however, operate out of sizable malls.

At the other extreme, **high-margin/low-turnover** retailers differentiate themselves with unique assortments, quality merchandise, good customer service, and a prestigious store image. They focus on shopping or specialty goods, usually carrying a narrow range of product categories but offering deep assortments of styles and sizes within each category. They also emphasize prestigious national brands or exclusive goods unavailable elsewhere. Tiffany's, for example, carries many one-of-a-kind crystal and jewelry items. This category includes most department stores, and upscale specialty stores.

Nonstore Retailing

These institutions fit the definition of a retailer, but we discuss them separately because they don't have a fixed brick-and-mortar physical location and most do not enable customers to personally inspect the merchandise or take immediate possession. This category includes direct selling (e.g., door-to-door sales and telemarketing), mail-order catalogs, TV shopping, vending machines, and websites.

There are several varieties of retail websites, including start-ups (Amazon.com, CD-Now), that exist solely on the Web and do not have any physical stores, websites developed by large catalog retailers (Lands' End, L.L. Bean) to leverage their direct-delivery operations, and websites developed by established bricks-and-mortar retailers (Wal-Mart, Target) to leverage their brand names and customer service skills.

An established brand name and customer base typically enables the catalog and bricks-and-mortar retailers to attract customers to their websites at much lower cost than the Web start-ups, as indicated in the top panel of Exhibit 13.4. However, the survey results shown in the middle panel of the exhibit suggest that retail websites in general have not done a great job of satisfying customers, particularly on basic customer service dimensions. Consequently, the proportion of visitors who end up buying something has been relatively low.

Exhibit 13.4

A COMPARISON OF THREE TYPES OF RETAIL WEBSITES

Despite huge expenditures on marketing . . .

	NET START-UPS	CATALOGERS ONLINE	BRICKS-AND-MORTAR STORES ONLINE
Cost per new customer	$82	$11	$31
Marketing as percentage of revenue	119%	6%	36%

DATA: BOSTON CONSULTING GROUP STUDY OF 221 ONLINE RETAILERS

. . . e-tailers fall short on key consumer desires . . .

CUSTOMER SATISFACTION WITH . . .

Customer service	41%
Easy returns	51%
Better product information	57%
Product selection/availability	66%
Price	70%
Ease of use	74%

DATA: JUPITER COMMUNICATIONS DECEMBER SURVEY OF 3,121 SHOPPERS

. . . so few customers hit the buy button . . .

	NET START-UPS	CATALOGERS ONLINE	BRICKS-AND-MORTAR STORES ONLINE
Percentage of visits leading to orders	1.7%	2.1%	1.4%
Percentage of individuals who ordered	3.5%	4.2%	1.8%
Repeat buyers	27%	20%	34%
Abandoned shopping carts	52%	66%	76%

DATA: BOSTON CONSULTING GROUP STUDY OF 221 ONLINE RETAILERS

Source: Heather Green, "Special Report: E-Tailing," Reprinted from the May 15, 2000 issue of *Business Week* by permission. Copyright The McGraw-Hill Companies.

As the third panel of Exhibit 13.4 points out, the start-ups have done a bit better job of converting visitors into buyers, but the bricks-and-mortar sites have been more successful at keeping those buyers coming back for repeat purchases.

Many of the start-ups began life as "virtual" businesses that outsourced many of the physical distribution functions such as inventory storage and delivery. But because of the critical importance of good customer service for developing a satisfied and loyal customer base, some of those start-ups have begun developing their own physical distribution and fulfillment competencies to gain tighter control over those activities. For instance, Amazon.com has invested hundreds of millions of dollars in warehouses and inventory to help ensure fast, reliable delivery. As a result, repeat customers now account for more than three-quarters of Amazon.com's orders.[6]

Channel Design Alternatives

Deciding which channel members to include when designing a distribution system depends in part on whether the good or service is to be sold to individual consumers or organizational customers. Therefore, we begin our examination of alternative channel designs by enumerating the options available for distributing consumer versus industrial goods. But the choice also depends, as we'll see in subsequent sections, on the firm's competitive strategy and resources and therefore on the relative importance of the various channel objectives we discussed earlier.

Alternative Consumer Goods Channels

Five channel designs are commonly used to distribute consumer goods and services, as shown in Exhibit 13.5. Channel A involves direct distribution from the producer to the consumer. This is becoming a more popular channel, particularly for products targeted at two-wage-earner households where time is of the essence. As noted earlier, a number of technologies can be employed to achieve direct distribution, including direct mail catalogs, telephone or door-to-door selling, interactive cable TV, and manufacturers' websites. Channel B in Exhibit 13.5 involves producers that sell directly to retailers, who in turn sell to consumers. Such channels are typically used when the retailers are large enough to perform their own wholesaling functions or to form efficient logistical alliances with the manufacturer, as is the case for chains like Wal-Mart, Sears, and Marks & Spencer. This kind of channel is also appropriate for distributing specialty goods such as designer fashions, expensive watches, or even greeting cards through selected retail outlets like Saks or Hallmark Card shops. Of course, the retailers involved in such channels may be traditional bricks-and-mortar operations, Internet start-ups, or some combination of the two.

Channel C uses both a wholesaler and a retailer and is most common for low-cost, frequently purchased items extensively distributed through a large number of retailers.

Exhibit 13.5

MARKETING CHANNELS FOR CONSUMER GOODS AND SERVICES

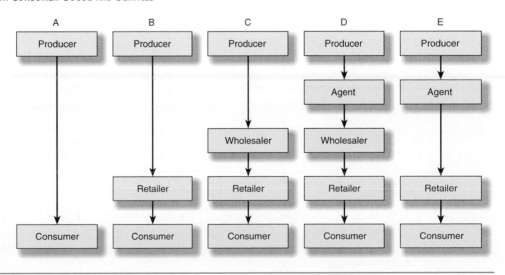

Because many of the retailers in such channels are small, the manufacturer's cost of dealing with them directly would be prohibitive. This channel system is common for such products as packaged food items, liquor, and health and beauty aids. Channel D, where an agent sells to wholesalers who in turn sell to retailer, is used when the manufacturer is too small, or its product line too narrow, to justify a company salesforce. In some cases, particularly where a small producer sells to retail chains that are large enough to take care of their own wholesaling functions, an agent may be employed to sell directly to the retailers', as shown in channel E.

Alternative Industrial Goods Channels

Exhibit 13.6 illustrates four alternative channel designs for distributing industrial goods. Direct distribution (channel A) is much more common for industrial goods and services than it is in the consumer sphere. It is particularly popular when buyers are large and well-known, the product or service is technically complex and of high unit value, and the selling function requires technical expertise or extended negotiation. For example, large computer systems, commercial aircraft, and consulting services are sold through direct distribution.

Many industrial goods manufacturers distribute through wholesalers (industrial distributors), as in channel B. While a manufacturer loses some control over such activities as the negotiation of sales contracts, installation, and maintenance by using distributors, wholesalers can improve distribution efficiency by lowering costs for such functions as selling, storage, and transportation. This is particularly likely when the product is standardized, there are many potential buyers with similar requirements, the average order value is relatively small, and the item is easy to handle and store.

The two other industrial goods channels involve the use of agents or brokers, either to sell directly to customers, as in channel C, or to wholesalers, as in channel D. Manufacturers too small to support a company salesforce most frequently use agents. For example, Stake Fastener Company, a small producer of industrial fasteners, uses agents to call on its customers rather than employing a company salesforce. Larger firms also employ agents, particularly to call on smaller customers or to cover low-potential geographic areas.

Exhibit 13.6

MARKETING CHANNELS FOR INDUSTRIAL GOODS AND SERVICES

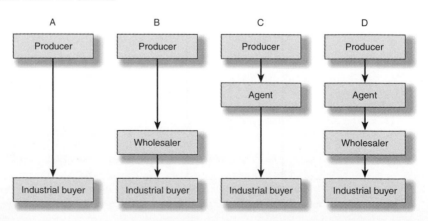

Which Alternative Is Best? It Depends on the Firm's Objectives and Resources

As we pointed out earlier, there are trade-offs among the various objectives a company might try to accomplish with its distribution channel; it's generally impossible to design a channel that performs well on all of them. In addition, each of the alternative designs outlined above are better suited for attaining some objectives than others. Therefore, the decision about which alternative to adopt depends on which distribution objectives are considered most important, which is influenced by the business's competitive strategy and the other components of the marketing program, including characteristics of the product itself.

KEY OBSERVATION

There are trade-offs among the various objectives a company might try to accomplish with its distribution channel; it's generally impossible to design a channel that performs well on all of them.

The following sections briefly examine the alternative channel designs most appropriate for the various objectives outlined earlier. For any given objective, channel design decisions may be further influenced by the availability of human and financial resources within the firm and by factors in the environment, such as technological developments.

Availability and the Satisfaction of Customer Service Requirements

Consumer Goods and Services For consumer goods and services, achieving a desired level of product availability is largely a matter of gaining the cooperation of appropriate numbers and types of retail outlets. A manufacturer can pursue three basic **strategies of retail coverage**—intensive, exclusive, or selective distribution (see Exhibit 13.7). The best strategy for a given product depends on the nature of the product, the target market pursued, and the competitive situation.

Intensive Distribution Such a strategy uses the maximum possible number of retailers and is most appropriate for low-involvement, frequently purchased convenience goods such as candy, soft drinks, deodorants, and razor blades. This strategy maximizes product

Exhibit 13.7

COMPARISON OF INTENSIVE, EXCLUSIVE, AND SELECTIVE RETAIL COVERAGE STRATEGIES

	Retail coverage	Major strength	Major weakness	Products most appropriate for
Intensive	Maximum	Maximizes product availability	Lack of retailer support	Low-involvement consumer convenience goods
Exclusive	Single	Matches retailer clientele with target market; facilitates close cooperation with retailer	Risk of relying on single retailer	High-involvement specialty or shopping goods
Selective	Limited	Provides adequate coverage but not at expense of manufacturer–retailer cooperation	Difficult to implement given interstore competition, especially where discounts may occur	Infrequently purchased shopping goods

availability, which generates greater product recognition and more impulse buying. However, firms that adopt intensive distribution often experience implementation and cost problems. Individual retailers may be more reluctant to carry the product or to cooperate fully with the manufacturer's marketing program than if they were given an exclusive right to carry the product in their territory. This was the problem Hallmark ran into with its traditional specialty retailers when the firm attempted to increase the intensiveness of its distribution by adding discounters and a website. Also, gaining cooperation from a large proportion of available retailers is a problem when total demand for the product is relatively small or when the brand is not the share leader in its product category.

Exclusive Distribution This strategy relies on only one retailer or dealer in a given geographic territory. It is most appropriate when the product is a high-involvement specialty or shopping good. Exclusive distribution is also useful when a firm wants to differentiate its product on the basis of high quality, prestige, or excellent customer service. The main advantages of exclusive distribution are that the manufacturer can choose retailers whose clientele match its target market, and that there will be close cooperation in implementing the producer's merchandising and customer service programs. Examples of products that are exclusively distributed include Ethan Allen furniture, and Rolls-Royce automobiles. The major disadvantage of exclusive distribution is the risk involved in relying on a single retailer in a given territory.

Selective Distribution This is a compromise between the other two extremes since it uses more than one but fewer than all available retailers in a geographic area. It is an appropriate strategy for shopping goods. Most brands of automobiles are distributed this way.

Implications for Channel Design

In general terms, the greater the strategic importance of availability and the more intensive the desired level of retail coverage, the more likely wholesalers and/or agents are to be used. Intensive distribution requires large numbers of retail outlets, many of which are small, independently owned operations. The personal selling, order processing, inventory storage, and delivery costs involved in servicing such a large network of retailers would be prohibitive for most manufacturers. Therefore, channel designs such as B and C in Exhibit 13.5 are most common for large, deep-pocketed firms seeking intensive distribution, while channel designs D and E are used by smaller firms needing intensive distribution. Firms with exclusive or selective distribution goals are likely to employ channel design B in order to interface directly with their retailers.

Industrial Goods and Services

In organizational markets, availability and customer service objectives tend to go together because it is order cycle time (the time it takes for customers to place orders and have the goods delivered to their plants or offices) and delivery dependability that tend to be most important for keeping customers satisfied. Historically, firms that wanted to provide fast and reliable delivery had to design channels with a relatively large number of "distribution points"—either wholesale distributors or company-owned warehouses and sales branches. Many distribution points were necessary to ensure adequate inventories would be available to avoid out-of-stock conditions and that those inventories would be close enough to the customer to allow quick delivery. Consequently, firms that tried to differentiate themselves on the basis of excellent customer service tended to rely on channels with substantial numbers of wholesale distributors, such as channel B in Exhibit 13.6 (for companies that could afford a field salesforce) or channel D (for those that could not). The reason, once again, had to do with the trade-offs between good customer service and physical distribution costs. Unless the producer was pursuing only a few very large customers or had sufficient sales volume and resources to make substantial investments in warehouses and field salespeople, the selling, storage, and transportation functions necessary to provide quick and reliable service could usually be performed more efficiently by independent distributors. As we'll see later, however, this historical trade-off between customer service levels and physical distribution costs is changing as the result of improved communication technologies and the logistical alliances they have made possible.

The Impact of the Internet on Availability and Customer Service   Some analysts argue that the Internet will lead to the "death of distance"; the geographic locations of sellers and their customers will no longer be relevant when they engage in transactions in cyberspace.[7] Consequently, they argue that the Internet will facilitate the availability of all sorts of goods and services—both consumer and industrial. Keep in mind, though, that there are two aspects of availability from the customer's point of view. The first has to do with product **search:** identifying available alternatives, collecting information about them, and placing an order. The second concerns product **acquisition** or order cycle time: how long it takes to gain physical possession of the product at the location where it is to be used or consumed.

Websites, whether sponsored by the manufacturer (as is the case with Hallmark's site) or by wholesalers, retailers, or e-tailers who are members of the distribution channel, have clearly enhanced the search aspect of availability. Potential customers can learn about available brands, compare features and prices, and make purchases any time of the day or week without ever getting up from their computer. And in many product categories, "aggregator" sites, or e-hubs, bring together many buyers and sellers under one virtual roof, enabling potential customers to compare alternatives and decide on a final purchase all at one site.

On the other hand, the Internet is not much help with the acquisition or physical distribution aspects of availability, at least not in most product categories. While it can help coordinate inventories and delivery schedules among channel members, it can't help move the physical product from the producer to the customer's home or plant, unless the product, like music or books, can be delivered in digital form. In fact, many e-tailers, such as RedEnvelope, outsource inventory storage and delivery activities to an established wholesaler or order fulfillment specialists. Therefore, channels incorporating traditional bricks-and-mortar wholesalers and retailers with the ability to provide quick delivery likely have a competitive advantage on the acquisition/order cycle time dimension;[8] particularly for consumer convenience and impulse items, fashion goods and big-ticket durables that need to be tried out or tried on before purchase, and industrial components where quick and reliable delivery are critical.

KEY OBSERVATION

The Internet is not much help with the acquisition or physical distribution aspects of availability, at least not in most product categories.

Promotional Effort, Market Information, and Postsale Service Objectives

As we shall see in a later section, one of the most vexing questions facing a manager who must rely on independent agents, wholesalers, and/or retailers is how to get them to do what he or she thinks is best for the product. This is particularly important when it comes to achieving high levels of promotional effort within the channel, collecting timely market information, and servicing customers after the sale. Achieving these objectives requires substantial effort and expense on the part of the middleman, but many of the benefits accrue to the manufacturer or service producer.

As we'll see, firms can attempt to control the activities related to these objectives by writing detailed legal contracts, such as franchise agreements, or to motivate voluntary effort from their channel members by providing appropriate incentives, such as cooperative advertising allowances or liberal service cost reimbursements. In many cases, though, firms can gain better control of such activities by using more direct, vertically integrated distribution channels, such as channel A in Exhibits 13.5 and 13.6. It's easier to control a company salesforce and company-owned warehouses, retail outlets, or websites than it is to monitor the behaviors of many independent middlemen[9] and find acceptable replacements for those who perform poorly.[10]

The replacement problem is particularly difficult when an intermediary must invest in specialized (or **transaction-specific**) assets, such as extensive product training or specialized capital equipment, in order to sell the manufacturer's good or service effectively. It's more difficult to find—or to develop—replacement channel members when such specialized assets are required. Thus, the theory of **transaction cost analysis** (TCA) argues that when substantial transaction-specific assets are involved, the costs of using and administering independent channel members are likely to be higher than the costs of managing a company salesforce and/or distribution centers. This is because TCA assumes independent channel members will pursue their own self-interest—even at the expense of the manufacturer they represent—when they think they can get away with it. For instance, they might provide only cursory postsale service or expend too little effort calling on smaller accounts because they are unlikely to earn big commissions from such activities. Because independent intermediaries are more likely to get away with such behavior when it is difficult for the manufacturer to monitor or replace them, the transaction cost of using independent agents or wholesalers under such circumstances is likely to be high.[11]

Recently, though, both managers and researchers have questioned TCA's assumption that independent intermediaries will always put their own short-term interests ahead of those of the manufacturer when they can avoid getting caught and replaced. Many argue that when both manufacturer and intermediary believe their relationship can be mutually beneficial for years into the future, norms of trust and cooperation can develop.[12] Such beliefs and norms are essential for the development of effective long-term relationships and alliances among channel partners.

Cost-Effectiveness

As pointed out earlier, firms often face a trade-off between high product availability and short order cycle times on one hand and higher distribution costs on the other. To service the large number of retailers necessary to provide intensive distribution of consumer products typically requires many salespeople, widely dispersed warehouses, and large inventories. Similarly, guaranteeing fast and reliable delivery to organizational customers, especially smaller ones, demands a relatively large number of wholesale distribution points. Therefore, the manager's task is to design a marketing channel that minimizes physical distribution costs subject to the constraint of achieving some target level of product availability and customer service.

Make-or-Buy Decisions   One issue that has a bearing on distribution costs is the choice among different types of institutions at each channel level. Would the firm be better off financially performing the functions necessary to achieve the desired level of customer service itself in a vertically integrated system or could independent intermediaries perform them more efficiently? In other words, for a given service level, are more direct, vertically integrated channel designs—such as channels A and B in Exhibit 13.5 or channel A in Exhibit 13.6—more cost-effective than channels incorporating independent, wholesalers and/or agent middlemen?

To answer this question, the manager needs to compare the relative costs of performing the necessary selling, storage, order processing, and transportation functions across the various alternative institutions for different levels of sales volume. For instance, at each sales level the margins that would have to be paid to wholesale distributors could be compared to the costs the firm would incur if it took over the sales and distributive functions necessary to support that level of volume. Similarly, the costs of maintaining a company salesforce can be compared to the commissions earned at various volume levels by external agents, such as manufacturer's reps.

The results of this analysis typically vary by the amount of sales projected. For physical distribution activities to be handled efficiently in-house, the firm's products must generate sufficient sales volume to achieve economies of scale. At lower volume levels, independent wholesale distributors are usually less costly because they can spread their fixed costs across the many different suppliers they represent, and the aggregated sales of all those suppliers' products enable greater scale economies.

Similarly, the fixed costs of using external agents are lower than those of using a company salesforce because there is usually less administrative overhead and agents do not receive a salary or reimbursement for selling expenses. But costs of using agents tend to rise faster as sales volume increases because agents usually receive larger commissions than company salespeople. Thus, agents are typically more cost efficient at lower levels of sales but less so as volumes increase. This helps explain why agents tend to be used by smaller firms or by larger firms in their smaller territories where sales are too low to justify a company salesforce.

Supply Chain Management—the Impact of New Technologies and Alliances

KEY OBSERVATION

New technologies are enabling firms to reengineer their distribution processes in ways that increase customer service levels while simultaneously reducing costs.

Recent developments may be changing the historical trade-offs between distribution costs and customer service levels. New data collection, communication, materials handling, and transportation technologies are enabling firms to reengineer their distribution processes in ways that increase customer service levels while *simultaneously* reducing costs. These new processes are commonly referred to as **supply chain management** (although consumer package goods firms that distribute through supermarkets have labeled them **efficient consumer response [ECR]** programs).

Much of the resulting improvement in customer service on dimensions such as order cycle time and dependability has been due to the electronic interchange of sales and inventory data—and the development of computerized ordering systems—between manufacturers and their channel partners. As we saw in Chapter 6, sales information from a retailer's checkout scanners can be sent directly to either a wholesaler's or a manufacturer's computer, which figures out when to replenish each product and schedules deliveries to appropriate warehouses or stores. Soon, it may even be possible to track each individual package via small microchips and wireless technology as it moves through a distribution channel.[13] And, as we saw in the relationship between Exel and Océ, logistics service firms or transportation agencies such as trucking or airfreight companies may also be included in these supply chain alliances to facilitate timely order processing and delivery.

Logistical alliances based on electronic data interchange are often able to reduce the total amount of inventory needed via improved coordination of the stocks kept at various levels in the distribution channel, quicker order processing, and speedier delivery. Thus, the number of wholesale distribution points required to provide a given level of customer service is often reduced. These reductions cut inventory carrying costs (the costs of capital tied up in inventory), storage costs, and damage to the stock. In most cases such reductions in inventory costs are more than sufficient to offset the costs of the computers and telecommunications equipment and the more costly modes of fast transportation usually involved in logistical alliances. For example, one study suggests that widespread adoption of such systems could reduce the average length of time it takes dry grocery products, such as cake mixes, soups, and pasta sauces, to reach the ultimate consumer from more than 100 days down to only 60 days. It is estimated that this would save consumers about 11 percent of their current grocery bills.[14]

Flexibility

Different channel designs involve different levels of commitment and loss of flexibility by manufacturers. Generally, vertically integrated systems are difficult to alter quickly, particularly when a firm has made substantial investments in physical (buildings) and human resources (salespersons). Channels involving independent middlemen are often more flexible, especially if the firm does not have to sign long-term contracts to gain their support. Manufacturers facing uncertain and rapidly changing market or competitive environments often rely on independent reps or wholesalers to preserve the adaptability of their distribution channels. Conversely, firms operating in relatively mature and stable markets, and defenders whose efficiency or good service is more critical than flexibility, might attach greater importance to the increased control inherent in vertical integration.[15] However, making major changes in channel design can lead to substantial conflict and resistance even when that channel is made up of independent middlemen, especially if channel members have had a long and profitable relationship with the supplier. Note, for instance, the reaction of Hallmark's traditional specialty retailers to the firm's addition of mass merchandisers, drugstores, and a company website to its channel.

Multichannel Distribution

Companies are increasingly using multiple channels. Some use **dual (two-channel) distribution** systems—as, for example, when a manufacturer of industrial goods uses wholesalers to sell small accounts and its own salesforce to handle large accounts. An increase in the number of target segments typically forces many companies to use more than two channels. For example, a manufacturer of brake fluid distributes its product (*a*) directly to General Motors, Ford, and BMW for use in new cars; (*b*) through major oil companies that wholesale the fluid to their retail stations for use in servicing cars; and (*c*) through auto parts wholesalers to retail auto parts stores to reach do-it-yourself customers.

Multichannel systems can create conflict and control problems. Conflicts can arise if different channel members try to pursue the same customer segment, and multiple channels are harder for the manufacturer to coordinate and control than a simpler system. Nevertheless, such systems often provide more complete market coverage with greater efficiency, which can provide a competitive advantage.

A variation of multichannel systems is the **hybrid system.**[16] While multichannel systems employ separate channels to reach different target segments (e.g., service stations versus do-it-yourselfers), the members of a hybrid system perform complementary functions for the same customer segment. As Exhibit 13.8 indicates, for example, a supplier might rely on its own website and salespeople to contact customers and generate sales, employ an independent wholesaler or fulfillment organization to deliver the goods, and then use a company help line and independent service centers to provide service after the sale. Some analysts expect such hybrid systems to become the most common channel design in the

Exhibit 13.8

EXAMPLE OF A HYBRID MARKETING CHANNEL

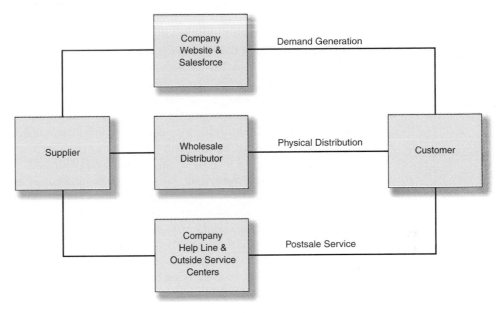

future, largely because the Internet is making it easier to effectively coordinate a large number of functional specialists.

Channel Design for Global Markets

When designing marketing channels to reach customers in more than one country, the manager faces a couple of additional issues. First, when entering a new national market for the first time, he or she must decide on an entry strategy. Subsequently, a decision must be made whether to rely on middlemen in the firm's home country that specialize in selling to foreign markets or to deal directly with foreign middlemen who operate in those markets.

Market Entry Strategies

There are three major ways of entering a foreign country—via export; by transferring technology and the skills needed to produce and market the goods to an organization in a foreign country through a contractual agreement; and through direct investment.

Exporting is the simplest way to enter a foreign market because it involves the least commitment and risk. It can be direct or indirect. The latter relies on the expertise of domestic international middlemen: **export merchants,** who buy the product and sell it overseas for their own account; **export agents,** who sell on a commission basis; and **cooperative organizations,** which export for several producers, especially those selling farm products. Direct exporting uses foreign-based distributors/agents or operating units (branches or subsidiaries) set up in the foreign country.

Contractual entry modes are nonequity arrangements that involve the transfer of technology and/or skills to an entity in a foreign country. In **licensing,** a firm offers the right to use its intangible assets (technology, know-how, patents, company name, trademarks) in exchange for royalties or some other form of payment. Licensing is less flexible and provides less control than exporting. Further, if the contract is terminated, the licensor may have developed a competitor. It is appropriate, however, when the market is unstable or difficult to penetrate.

Franchising grants the right to use the company's name, trademarks, and technology. Also, the franchisee typically receives help in setting up the franchise. It is an especially attractive way for service firms to penetrate foreign markets at low cost and to couple their skills with local knowledge and entrepreneurial spirit. Host countries are reasonably receptive to this type of exporting since it involves local ownership. American companies have largely pioneered franchising, especially such fast-food companies as McDonald's, Pizza Hut, Burger King, and Kentucky Fried Chicken. In recent years foreign franchisers have entered the United States—largely from Canada, England, and Japan—in a variety of fields, including food, shoe repair, leather furniture, and home furnishings.

Other contractual entry modes include **contract manufacturing,** which involves sourcing a product from a manufacturer located in a foreign country for sale there or elsewhere (auto parts, clothes, and furniture). Contract manufacturing is most attractive when the local market is too small to warrant making an investment, export entry is blocked, and a quality licensee is not available. A **turnkey construction contract** requires the contractor to have the project up and operating before releasing it to the owner. **Coproduction** involves a company's providing technical know-how and components in return for a share of the output, which it must sell. **Countertrade** transactions (as discussed in Chapter 12) include barter (direct exchange of goods—hams for aircraft), compensation packages (cash and local goods), counterpurchase (delayed sale of bartered goods to enable the local buyer to sell the goods), and a **buyback arrangement** in which the products being sold are used to produce other goods.

Overseas direct investment can be implemented in two ways—through joint ventures or sole ownership. **Joint ventures** involve a joint ownership arrangement (such as between a U.S. firm and one in the host country) to produce and/or market goods in a foreign country. Today, joint ventures are common because they avoid quotas and import taxes and satisfy government demands to produce locally. They also have the advantage of sharing investment costs and gaining local marketing expertise. For example, Motorola had difficulty penetrating the Japanese market until it formed an alliance with Toshiba to set up a joint chip-making venture. In addition, Toshiba provided Motorola with marketing help.[17]

A **sole ownership** investment entry strategy involves setting up a production facility in a foreign country. Direct investment usually allows the parent organization to retain total control of the overseas operation and avoids the problems of shared management and loss of flexibility. This strategy is particularly appropriate when the politics of the situation require a dedicated local facility.

High risks are associated with direct investment. Nevertheless, direct investments everywhere are accelerating because companies have concluded that capturing and retaining customers demands constant innovation and a rapid, flexible response to the dynamics of the environment.

Channel Alternatives[18]

Two major types of international channel alternatives are available to a domestic producer. The first involves the use of domestic middlemen who provide marketing services from a domestic base and the second is the use of foreign middlemen. These alternatives are discussed next.

Domestic Middlemen   While convenient to use, these may suffer from a lack of knowledge about a foreign market and their inability to provide the kind of local representation offered by foreign-based middlemen. The more common **merchant middlemen** (those taking title) include the **export merchant,** who takes physical possession of the goods (mostly manufactured), has a broad line, and sells in his own right; the **export jobber,** who handles mostly bulky and raw materials (but does not take physical control of them); and **trading companies,** which sell manufactured goods to developing countries and buy back raw materials and unprocessed goods.

Agent middlemen include **brokers; buying offices** (primarily concerned with searching for and purchasing merchandise upon request); **selling groups** (an arrangement by which various producers cooperate to sell their goods overseas); the **export management company,** which operates in the name of its principal; and the **manufacturer's export agent (MEA),** which specializes in only a few countries and has a short-term relationship with its clients.

Foreign Middlemen   In contrast to dealing with domestic middlemen, a manufacturer may decide to deal directly with **foreign middlemen.** This shortens the channel, thereby bringing the manufacturer closer to the market. A major problem is that foreign middlemen are some distance away, and therefore more difficult to control than domestic ones. Since many foreign middlemen, especially merchant middlemen, are prone to act independently of their suppliers, it is difficult to use them when market cultivation is needed.

Wholesalers around the world, while performing similar functions, vary tremendously in size, margins, and service quality. A broad generalization is that the less developed a country, the smaller the wholesaler and the more fragmented the wholesale channels. In recent years, however, the emergence of wholesaler-sponsored voluntary chains has tended to consolidate distribution power in the hands of a smaller number of wholesalers. Also, there is a worldwide trend of vertical integration from the wholesale or retail level to the manufacturer. And the growth of national wholesalers in many countries has made it easier for manufacturers to distribute their product(s) nationwide.

Retail Structures in Foreign Countries   These vary tremendously across countries because of differences in the cultural, economic, and political environments; for example, a generalization is that the size of retail stores increases as gross national product per capita increases. Both European and Japanese retailing are following a path similar to that pioneered by the United States with respect to store size, self-service, discounting, automation (use of electronic checkout counters), expansion of national chains, and direct marketing.

It is also becoming increasingly possible to promote and sell goods and services directly over the Internet almost anywhere. The online population was estimated to be 544 million in the year 2002, with 181 million in North America, 171 million in Europe, 157 million in the Asia-Pacific region, 25 million in South America, 4.2 million in Africa, and 4.7 million in the Middle East.[19] As we have seen, however, while the Internet enables firms to contact customers and generate orders, they must still rely on foreign middlemen to carry out the necessary physical distribution functions.

Channel Design for Services

Producers of services also face the problem of making their outputs available to targeted customer segments. In some cases, this results in forward vertical integration involving decisions about branch outlets—as in bank services that are accessible through branch banks (some of which may be located in supermarkets) and automatic tellers. Another example is a hospital that establishes outpatient clinics to serve the specific health needs of various community segments, such as high-stress or drug- or alcohol-dependent groups.

Ordinarily, the marketing of services does not require the same kind of distribution networks as does the marketing of tangible goods. Marketing channels for services tend to be short—direct from the creator or performer of the service to the end user—hence the emphasis on franchising (discussed later in this chapter).

Some services require the use of longer channels, however. Health care services use a variety of channel systems other than the traditional fee system employed by many doctors and hospitals in selling directly to the consumer. Health maintenance organizations (HMOs) sometimes use a vertically integrated system, where consumers pay a monthly charge to an organization (such as Baptist Medical Systems-HMO, Inc.) that coordinates the services of all the health care needs of its constituents. Hotels rely increasingly on indirect channels for their bookings. Intermediaries include travel agents who may deal directly with a hotel or contact another intermediary holding blocks of rooms, sales representatives who represent a number of noncompeting hotels or resorts, airlines that provide tour packages that include hotels, and automated reservation services that maintain a computerized inventory of available rooms travel agents can tap into for a fee, e-hubs that enable business buyers to reserve rooms online, and "name-your-own-price" sites such as www.priceline.com where hotels can dispose of excess capacity if potential buyers offer an acceptable price.[20]

Channel Management Decisions

Designing the perfect channel to accomplish the firm's objectives is one thing; getting the middlemen to carry the product and perform the desired functions is another. In recent years manufacturers—and in some cases large wholesalers and retailers—have developed **vertical marketing systems** (VMSs) to improve coordination among channel members, thereby improving their performance. Greater coordination and cooperation in VMSs have led to greater marketing effectiveness and distribution economies by virtue of their size, bargaining power, and the elimination of duplicated functions. As a result, VMSs have become the dominant form of channel arrangement, particularly in the distribution of consumer goods and services.

This section discusses the various types of VMSs and how firms can develop and maintain such systems. Next, we examine the sources of power and the inducements and incentives that channel members use to gain the support of other system members. Finally, we identify possible sources of conflict in VMSs and some resolution mechanisms that firms use to preserve cooperation within their channels.

Vertical Marketing Systems

Firms attempt to develop and manage integrated distribution systems in one of four ways: (1) a corporate VMS, which involves a vertically integrated system, (2) a contractual VMS, which formulates agreements spelling out a coordinated set of rights and obligations for members of the system, (3) an administered VMS, in which one firm uses its economic position or expertise to provide inducements for cooperation from other members, or (4) a relational VMS, where cooperation between two or more channel partners is based on norms of mutual trust and the expectation that cooperation will increase the total system's success and thereby make all members better off in the long term. Each of these four types is shown in Exhibit 13.9 and discussed next.

Exhibit 13.9

VERTICAL MARKETING SYSTEMS

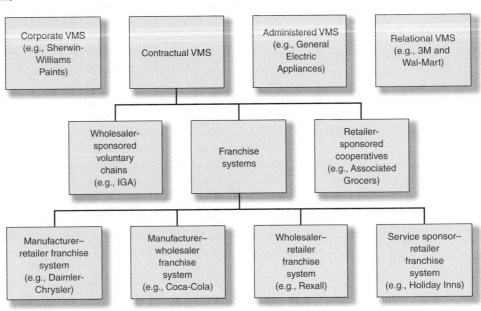

Corporate VMSs   In these systems firms achieve coordination and control through corporate ownership. In most cases, this is the result of forward integration by a manufacturer of the functions at the wholesale—and perhaps even the retail—levels. For example, many industrial firms have their own salesforces, warehouses, or branch sales offices. **Backward integration** occurs when a retailer or wholesaler assumes ownership of institutions that normally precede them in their distribution channels. Such integration is common among large supermarket chains.

The primary advantage of these systems is the tight control they provide over personal selling, promotion, distribution, and customer service activities. Such control is particularly important when the product is technically complex; when specialized knowledge or facilities are needed to sell, distribute, and/or service the product; and when few capable independent middlemen are available. Corporate VMSs are not without their disadvantages, which include the large capital investment required and less flexibility than conventional systems.

Contractual VMSs   In such systems independent firms at different levels of production and distribution coordinate their programs through contracts that spell out the rights and duties of each party. The intent is to obtain greater economies and market impact than they could achieve alone. Contractual VMSs have had the greatest growth of any channel system in recent years. There are many kinds of contractual systems, but the three basic types are **wholesaler-sponsored voluntary chains, retailer cooperatives,** and **franchise systems.**

Wholesaler-sponsored voluntary chains are formed by getting independent retailers to sign contracts in which they agree to standardize their selling practices and to purchase a certain portion of their inventories from the wholesaler. The Independent Grocers Alliance (IGA), Western Auto, and Ben Franklin are among the best-known wholesaler-sponsored voluntaries.

Retailer cooperatives are groups of independent retailers who form their own cooperative chain organizations. Typically, they agree to concentrate their purchases by forming their own wholesale operations. In many cases they also engage in joint advertising, promotion, and merchandising programs. Profits are passed back to the member retailers in proportion to their purchases. Such cooperatives are particularly common in the grocery field, where Associated Grocers and Certified Grocers are examples.

In *franchise systems*,[21] a channel member can coordinate two successive stages in the distribution channel by offering franchise contracts that give others the right to participate in the business provided they accept the agreement terms and pay a fee. Such contracts usually specify a variety of operational details—including which members of the system will perform specific functions and how—as well as mechanisms to evaluate members' performance and to terminate members who fail to perform adequately.

Franchising has great versatility. Such systems operate in almost every business area and cover a wide variety of goods and services. There are four major types of franchise systems.

1. **Manufacturer–retailer franchise systems** account for the largest number of franchisees and the largest volume of sales and are common in the automotive (DaimlerChrysler and Ford) and petroleum industries (Exxon, Shell, and BP).

2. **Manufacturer–wholesaler franchise systems** are exemplified by the soft-drink industry; Coca-Cola and Pepsi sell syrup concentrate to franchised wholesale bottlers who then carbonate, bottle, sell, and distribute soft drinks to retailers in their territories. In recent years, however, Coca-Cola has acquired several of its larger and previously independent bottlers to gain control over its distribution channel.

3. **Wholesaler–retailer franchise systems** are similar to wholesaler-sponsored voluntary chains, but the retail franchisees agree to conduct and coordinate their operations according to detailed standards specified by the franchise agreement. Examples include Rexall drugstores and SuperValu supermarkets.

4. **Service sponsor–retailer franchise systems** are the most familiar to consumers. Examples include McDonald's, Burger King, and Kentucky Fried Chicken in fast foods; Holiday Inn in lodging; Hertz and Avis in car rentals; Midas and Precision Tune in auto repair; and Manpower in employment services.

The popularity of franchise systems from a customer's point of view derives from their ability to deliver consistent quality at a convenient location and a reasonable price. From the franchiser's perspective, such systems provide a legal basis for exercising some control over franchisees without the large capital investments required by a vertically integrated system. On the other side, franchisees can gain access to the franchiser's operational expertise, brand recognition, and loyal customers in exchange for providing local capital and management oversight.

Administered VMSs   Firms using this system coordinate the necessary activities at successive stages of distribution through the informal guidance and influence of one of the parties (rather than through ownership or contractual agreements). The administrator is typically the manufacturer, but in some cases the role is performed by a large retailer or wholesaler (Wal-Mart). Usually, the administration of such systems develops a detailed merchandising program in which the manufacturer spells out shelf-space arrangements, a promotional calendar, pricing policies, and guidelines for other activities to be followed by its wholesalers and retailers.

To encourage the other members of the distribution channel to go along with its merchandising program, the channel administrator typically relies on its superior economic or expert power (as described in a later section) to provide incentives for cooperation. Therefore, administered VMSs are typically designed and managed by the most powerful member. As a result, however, the performance outcomes that are rewarded may be more reflective of the powerful member's objectives than of the interests of the system as a whole. And there is often a tendency for the administrator to use its power to "share the pain" when economic conditions are tough or to "hog the gain" during the good times.

Relational VMSs   Relational VMSs also rely on economic rewards—and often contractual agreements, as well—to specify what is expected of each channel member and to provide incentives for cooperation. However, in relational systems what is expected of each partner may change by mutual agreement as market or competitive conditions change, and the economic incentives depend more on the long-term market success of the entire system than on the power and largess of the strongest member.

As we have seen, such relational systems or alliances are often more effective and efficient than more traditional systems. This is largely because of the extensive and rapid sharing of information, cost savings resulting from better coordination of activities and less duplication of efforts, and the cooperative search for innovative ways for the system to gain a competitive advantage over other systems.

However, the open sharing of internal operating data and innovative ideas for improving efficiency and sales performance requires substantial mutual trust and long-term commitments from each partner. As we discussed in Chapter 6, trust tends to build slowly. Thus, the partners in a relational system must typically have some history of satisfying experiences with one another to provide a foundation for trust and a history of mutually rewarding performance outcomes to motivate continued commitment for the long haul.[22]

Sources of Channel Power

As mentioned, the channel leader in an administered VMS typically coordinates the actions of other members by exercising power over them. Channel member A has power over channel member B to the extent that A can get B to do something that B would not do if left alone.

The power of any firm within a distribution channel is inversely proportional to how dependent the other channel members are on that firm. Thus, the extent of Firm A's power over Firm B is determined by A's ability to deliver rewards desired by B, and by B's ability to attain those rewards outside of a relationship with A (that is, by the alternatives open to B). Thus, sources (or bases) of power within channel relationships include the following:

- **Economic power** exists when channel members perceive that a firm can mediate economic rewards for them if they follow its directives.
- **Coercive power** is based on a perception that one channel member will punish another for failure to cooperate. It is the inverse of economic power, since such punishments usually take the form of a reduction in or withholding of economic rewards. For example, a manufacturer might threaten to withdraw a retailer's exclusive territorial rights if the retailer's performance does not meet expectations.
- **Expert power** stems from a perception that one channel member has special knowledge or expertise that can benefit other members of the system. Because of the reputations of firms like Unilever and Procter & Gamble as savvy marketers, middlemen are often willing to abide by their merchandising suggestions.
- **Referent power** is based on the belief that the benefits generated are likely to continue. A channel member that has earned substantial profits from a manufacturer over the years may be willing to accede to its suggestions or requests, without demanding any additional rewards.
- **Legitimate power** flows from the belief that one channel member has the right to make certain decisions or demands and to expect compliance from other members. Legitimate power is usually the result of ownership or contractual agreements, but in some instances it is based on

moral authority or common beliefs about what is right and proper. For example, most middle-men would agree that a food manufacturer has the right to print expiration dates on its packages and to expect middlemen to remove outdated packages from the shelves as a means of protecting the product's quality and the consumer's health.

Of course, economic rewards and expertise are exchanged among partners in relational VMSs as well, but such exchanges tend to be relatively symmetrical—both parties benefit—rather than being dominated by one powerful member. Therefore, when one party in a relational VMS accedes to the requests or suggestions of a partner, that response often reflects the partner's referent power, a belief that the relationship will continue to be mutually beneficial in the future.[23]

Channel Control Strategies

Two strategies used by manufacturers to improve their perceived economic power and to gain better cooperation from channel members are a pull and a push strategy.

Pull Strategy   When pursuing this strategy, a manufacturer focuses primarily on building selective demand and brand loyalty among potential customers through media advertising, consumer promotions, extended warranties and customer service, product improvements, line extensions, and other actions aimed at winning customer preference. Thus, by building strong consumer demand, the manufacturer increases its ability to promote economic rewards in the form of large sales volumes to its channel members in return for their cooperation. A share leader or most prestigious brand in its category has substantial power to influence other channel members, particularly if the product is in the growth stage of its life cycle.

But what if the manufacturer is introducing a new product with no past sales history? In such situations, the manufacturer must convince prospective channel members that its marketing program can quickly build strong customer demand and loyalty for the new brand. Such efforts at persuasion are most likely to be successful when the manufacturer has substantial resources to devote to the new product's marketing program, is perceived to have a great deal of marketing expertise, and has an extensive track record of past new product successes. Thus, pull strategies are commonly employed by large consumer goods marketers such as Procter & Gamble, Gillette, Frito-Lay, and Diageo PLC. Such companies have the deep pockets necessary to implement pull strategies, and their products typically have sufficiently broad appeal to make an aggressive consumer promotion and advertising program worthwhile.

Push Strategy   Smaller firms with limited resources, those without established reputations as savvy marketers, and those attempting to gain better channel support for existing products with relatively small shares and volumes often have difficulty achieving cooperation solely on the promise of future sales and profits. In such situations firms usually adopt a **push strategy** in which much of the product's marketing budget is devoted to direct inducements to gain the cooperation of wholesalers and/or retailers. Typically, a manufacturer offers channel members a number of rewards, each aimed at motivating them to perform a specific function or activity on the product's behalf. The rationale is that by motivating more wholesalers or retailers to carry and aggressively sell the product, more customers are exposed and persuaded to buy it.

Most small and medium-sized marketers of consumer goods employ push strategies because they lack the necessary resources for, or sell products whose relatively narrow appeal cannot justify, the expense involved in a pull strategy. The growing number of energy bars—Clif bars, Luna bars, Balance bars, and others—are examples of products marketed largely through push strategies, even though some limited consumer promotion does appear for these products.

Trade Promotions—Incentives for Motivating Channel Members

Manufacturers typically use a combination of incentives to gain reseller support and push their products through the channel. Most of these incentives constitute **sales promotion** activities. As we shall see in the next chapter, sales promotions are incentives designed to stimulate the purchase or sale of a product in the short term. There are two categories of

sales promotion activities: (1) **consumer promotions,** such as coupons, rebates, and contests, aimed at stimulating consumer purchases, and (2) **trade promotions,** which encourage resellers to engage in activities that will support and increase local sales of the product. In the next chapter we will discuss how both types of sales promotion can be combined with other communications tools such as advertising, personal selling, and publicity to create integrated marketing communications programs. In this section, we focus on the variety of trade promotion incentives and their role in motivating reseller support.

Different trade promotion incentives motivate resellers to engage in different functions or activities on the manufacturer's behalf. By combining various rewards, manufacturers can tailor trade incentives to the specific marketing and distribution needs of a product and its target customers. Exhibit 13.10 lists a variety of reseller incentives along with the functional activities that each is appropriate for motivating.

Incentives to Increase Reseller Purchases and Inventories   For new products, the most critical objective is simply to get wholesalers or retailers to stock the new item. Manufacturers unable to build much pull for their products by stimulating selective demand often have to offer more direct inducements to build distribution. They can offer higher margins than are typical for the category, introductory discounts for a limited time, or even agree to give selected resellers exclusive rights to the product in their local territory

Exhibit 13.10

INCENTIVES FOR MOTIVATING CHANNEL MEMBER PERFORMANCE

Functional performance dimensions	Examples of channel incentives
Increased purchases/carry larger inventories	Larger margins, exclusive territories, buy-in promotions, quantity discounts, seasonal discounts, buy-back allowances, free goods, shelf-stocking programs, slotting allowances
Increased personal selling effort	Sales training programs, instructional materials, incentive programs for channel members' salespeople
Increased local promotional effort	
• Local advertising	Cooperative advertising; advertising allowances; print, radio, or spot TV ads for use by local retailers
• Increased display space	Promotion allowances tied to shelf space
• In-store promotions	Display racks and signs, in-store demonstrations, in-store sampling
• Price promotions	Off-invoice allowances
Improved customer service	Service training programs, instructional materials, high margins on replacement parts, liberal labor cost allowances for warranty service

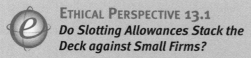

ETHICAL PERSPECTIVE 13.1
Do Slotting Allowances Stack the Deck against Small Firms?

The heavy reliance on trade promotions, which account for about two-thirds of the marketing budgets of U.S. consumer package goods firms, to gain channel member support can make it difficult for small firms to introduce new products. This is especially true for slotting allowances because the size of the allowance demanded by retailers tends to be larger for new products which have a relatively low probability of generating big sales volumes and profits. Since small firms and entrepreneurial start-ups tend to have limited promotional resources and unknown brands, they often have to pay bigger allowances to gain retailer acceptance than larger, well-established firms. While this practice makes good economic sense from the perspective of a retailer who must allocate scarce shelf space among a large number of new products, it may have a negative effect on new business formation, competition, and the availability of product innovations in the larger economy.

Source: Frank V. Cespedes, "Ethical Issues in Distribution," in N. Craig Smith and John A. Quelch, eds., *Ethics in Marketing* (Burr Ridge, IL: Richard D. Irwin, 1993), chap. 12. Reprinted with permission from The McGraw-Hill Companies. See also David Henry, "Accounting Games in the Grocer's Aisle," *Business Week,* April 14, 2003, p. 64.

(although exclusive territories are not appropriate for convenience goods requiring extensive distribution). In many cases, the manufacturer must also pay a onetime fee called a **slotting allowance** to induce retailers to stock the product on their shelves. The growing popularity of slotting allowances, however, raises ethical concerns, as discussed in Ethical Perspective 13.1.

Once a product has achieved adequate distribution, the manufacturer's purpose changes to one of maintaining adequate inventories of the product as close to the end customer as possible to minimize out-of-stock conditions. This usually involves offering some form of **quantity discount** tied to the volume of a reseller's purchases. Similar incentives include **buy-back allowances,** where the producer offers a discount on a future second order based on the size of the initial order, and **free goods,** where the manufacturer rewards volume purchases with additional merchandise at no cost. Of course, the manufacturer may also try to form logistical alliances or relationships involving electronic data interchange and computerized reordering with their larger resellers. As we have seen, such alliances help ensure that adequate stocks are available while reducing the volume of inventory (and the associated costs) that resellers must carry.

Incentives to Increase Personal Selling Effort
To motivate and assist resellers in upgrading the knowledge and professionalism of their salespeople, manufacturers can provide instruction manuals, training seminars, or detailed training programs held at the manufacturer's headquarters. Some firms also attempt to increase the amount of effort their resellers' salespeople devote to their products by offering incentives directly to those sales personnel. Such programs usually take the form of sales contests. The rewards may be monetary—sometimes called **push money** or **spiffs**—or in the form of merchandise or travel. However, manufacturers should obtain approval from each reseller before initiating such programs.

Incentives to Increase Local Promotional Effort
Middlemen can play an important role in advertising and promoting a manufacturer's product in their local areas, particularly for consumer goods. Thus, to stimulate more local advertising, many manufacturers offer **cooperative advertising programs** that pay a percentage of a reseller's expenses for local advertising up to some limit based on that reseller's sales of the product. Firms may also offer retailers **promotional allowances** tied to the amount of shelf or display space they devote to a product. To further encourage in-store promotions, many manufacturers offer free racks, signs, and other materials for use in point-of-purchase (P-O-P) displays.

Producers may also encourage periodic or seasonal price promotions featuring their product by providing **off-invoice discounts** for limited periods. The intention of such discounts is to encourage the reseller to pass along the savings to customers in the form of a special promotional price or sale event. One problem with such discounts, though, is that resellers may simply pocket the money as a means of increasing their own margins.

Incentives to Improve Customer Service

For consumer durables and industrial products, manufacturers often rely on distributors or retailers to provide product-related services, such as installation and repair, to the final customer. One way for firms to strengthen the quality of such service is to provide detailed instructional materials or company-sponsored training programs for their dealers' service technicians. Some firms, such as Caterpillar, are now making detailed repair guidelines and technical assistance available to dealers over the Internet.[24] Manufacturers also offer high margins on replacement parts or liberal labor cost reimbursements to reward resellers for performing warranty service.

The Changing Role of Incentives in Relational Distribution Systems

In channel systems where the manufacturer has forged successful long-term relationships with major resellers, the primary incentive for continued cooperation among the parties is focused on the improved sales volumes and reduced operating costs such cooperation can generate. Consequently, some of the specific trade promotion incentives discussed above are less important and less frequently used in such systems. As mentioned, for instance, logistical alliances and computerized reordering systems can reduce the amount of inventory that resellers must carry to avoid out-of-stock problems (though many manufacturers continue to offer quantity discounts to resellers based on their total sales volume during the year to encourage aggressive sales effort on behalf of their products). Similarly, some firms have reduced or eliminated off-invoice price promotions in favor of "everyday low prices" aimed at improving resellers' average margins. The purpose is to smooth out manufacturing schedules and inventories by discouraging resellers from stocking up during promotion periods. Some manufacturers continue to offer periodic price promotions, but they pay discounts to their resellers only on goods that were actually sold to consumers at a promotional price.[25]

Channel Conflicts and Resolution Strategies

Regardless of how well a manufacturer administers its channel system, some amount of **channel conflict** is inevitable. Some conflict is essential if members are to adapt to change. Conflict should result in more effective and efficient channel performance, *provided* it does not become destructive. Disagreements among channel members can occur for several reasons, including incompatible goals, unclear rights and responsibilities, and misperceptions and poor communication.

Because channel conflict is inevitable, the challenge is not to eliminate it but to manage it better. Firms can pursue several approaches aimed at recognizing and resolving potential conflicts early before they cause a breakdown of cooperation in the system. These include involving channel members in policy decisions (use of dealer advisory boards), increasing interaction among personnel at all levels (a manufacturer's salespersons making sales calls with each of its distributors), focusing on common goals, and the use of mediation and arbitration.

A manufacturer might also proactively adjust policy to defuse the source of conflict or increase the incentives and rewards available to channel members to lessen the economic consequences of contentious issues. For example, Hallmark created a separate line of greetings cards for sales through mass merchandisers to reduce the amount of direct competition

Exhibit 13.11

SUMMARY OF NONPRICE LEGAL CONSTRAINTS IN THE UNITED STATES

1. *Exclusive dealing.* The requirement that a channel member sell or lease only the seller's products is illegal if the requirement substantially lessens competition.

2. *Tying contracts.* This requires a buyer to take products other than the one wanted and, with some exceptions, is illegal per se. **Reciprocity,** wherein a buyer refuses to do business with a supplier unless that firm buys its products, is similar to tying contracts and is illegal when coercion is involved and substantial commerce is affected.

3. *Territorial restrictions.* This involves the granting of a geographical monopoly to a buyer for a given product. The decision here rests on the effect of intrabrand restrictions on interbrand competition. **Resale restrictions** on the type of customer the buyer can sell to are handled on much the same basis.

4. *Refusal to deal.* The right of a seller to select its customers—or to stop selling to one—is legal as long as it does not substantially lessen competition or foster a restraint of trade.

5. *Promotional allowances and services.* These must be offered to all resellers on proportionally equal terms and must be used for the purposes intended (e.g., advertising allowances must be used to pay for advertising).

6. *Incentives for resellers' employees.* Such incentives (e.g., push money) are generally acceptable, provided they do not injure competition substantially.

---

with its traditional retailers, and it created a website that helped those retailers attain discounts from other, noncompeting suppliers and thereby improve their profits.

There are legal constraints on how much and what kinds of power can be used to resolve conflicts or control channel members' actions. This is most apt to be the case when the firm uses an exclusive or selective distribution strategy and/or attempts to dictate how the channel intermediary will perform in marketing the product. In recent years, the U.S. courts have begun to use more of a rule-of-reason approach to potential offenses rather than finding specific practices inherently illegal. Even so, vertical relationships are covered by the major antitrust acts—Sherman, Clayton, and FTC. See Exhibit 13.11 for a brief discussion of the major nonprice legal constraints imposed by the federal government.

TAKE-AWAYS

- The importance of good distribution decisions in designing a marketing plan is simple: Customers won't buy your good or service unless it is conveniently available when and where they want to buy it.

- Distribution channel decisions have a major economic impact because distribution costs, many of which do not even appear in the firm's income statement, often exceed the costs of producing a good or service.

- Channel design involves decisions about the appropriate types and numbers of middlemen to include in the distribution channel in order to link the marketing strategy for the good or service to the needs of the target customers.

- Distribution channels can be designed to accomplish a number of objectives, including maximizing the product's availability, satisfying customer service

requirements, encouraging promotional effort, obtaining timely market information, minimizing distribution costs, and maintaining flexibility. However, each design alternative is better for achieving some objectives than others, and there are trade-offs across objectives; increasing availability and customer service, for example, tends to increase distribution costs. Therefore, good channel design decisions require compromise and careful judgment.

- A manufacturer or service provider can attempt to gain the support and direct the efforts of its channel partners through vertical integration, by legal contracts (e.g., franchise agreements), by providing economic incentives, and/or by developing mutually beneficial relationships based on trust and the expectation of future benefits. Given the large investments required for vertical integration and the difficulty of writing enforceable contracts when market conditions are changing rapidly, the development of effective incentives and long-term relationships with channel members is increasingly vital to the market success of most firms.

Self-diagnostic questions to test your ability to apply the analytical tools and concepts in this chapter to marketing decision making may be found at this book's website at www.mhhe.com/mullins05.

ENDNOTES

1. This case example is based on material found in Susan Chandler, "Can Hallmark Get Well Soon?" *Business Week,* June 19, 1995, pp. 62–63; Daniel Roth, "Card Sharks," *Forbes,* October 7, 1996, p.14; "Bringing Little Guys into the Loop," reported in "The Web Smart 50: a Business Week e.biz Special Report," *Business Week,* September 18, 2000, p. EB 72; Camilla Palmer, "Campaign: Soul to Build Hallmark Brand After Winning £3 million UK Brief," *Financial Times,* July 26, 2002; and the Hallmark website at www.hallmark.com.

2. Louis W. Stern and Adel I. El-Ansary, *Marketing Channels,* 3rd ed. (Englewood Cliffs, NJ: Prentice Hall, 1992), p. 1.

3. You can check the U.S. Census Bureau's most current wholesale and retail trade statistics at its website: www.census.gov/econ.

4. Ibid.

5. The following discussion is based largely on material found in Steven Kaplan and Mohanbir Sawhney, "E-Hubs: The New B2B Marketplaces," *Harvard Business Review,* May–June 2000, pp. 97–103.

6. Heather Green, "Special Report: E-Tailing," *Business Week,* May 15, 2000, pp. EB102; Heather Green, "How Hard Should Amazon Swing?" *Business Week,* January 14, 2002, p. 38.

7. Leyland Pitt, Pierre Berthon, and Jean-Paul Berthon, "Changing Channels: The Impact of the Internet on Distribution Strategy," *Business Horizons,* March–April 1999, pp. 19–28.

8. Ranjay Gulati and Jason Garino, "Get the Right Mix of Bricks and Clicks," *Harvard Business Review,* May–June, 2000, pp. 107–14.

9. Bernard J. Jaworski, "Toward a Theory of Marketing Control: Environmental Context, Control Types, and Consequences," *Journal of Marketing,* July 1988, pp. 23–39.

10. Allen M. Weiss and Erin Anderson, "Converting from Independent to Employee Salesforces: The Role of Perceived Switching Costs," *Journal of Marketing Research,* February 1992, pp. 101–15.

11. Transaction cost analysis was first developed in Oliver E. Williamson, *Markets and Hierarchies: Analysis and Antitrust Implications* (New York: Free Press, 1975). For empirical evidence that largely supports TCA's predictions about the conditions under which firms will employ independent agents versus company salespeople, see Erin Anderson, "The Salesperson as Outside Agent or Employee: A Transaction Cost Analysis," *Marketing Science* 4 (1985), pp. 234–54; Erin Anderson and Barton Weitz, "Make or Buy Decisions: Vertical Integration and Marketing Productivity," *Sloan Management Review,* Spring 1986, pp. 1–19; and Jan B. Heide and George John, "The Role of Dependence Balancing in Safeguarding Transaction-Specific Assets in Conventional Channels," *Journal of Marketing,* January 1988, pp. 20–35.

12. For example, see James C. Anderson and James A. Narus, "A Model of Distributor Firm and Manufacturer Firm Working Partnerships," *Journal of*

Marketing, January 1990, pp. 42–58; Jan B. Heide and George John, "Do Norms Matter in Marketing Relationships?" *Journal of Marketing,* 1992; and Erin Anderson and Barton Weitz, "The Use of Pledges to Build and Sustain Commitment in Distribution Channels," *Journal of Marketing Research,* February 1992, pp. 18–34.

13. Faith Keenan, "If Supermarket Shelves Could Talk," *Business Week,* March 31, 2003, pp. 66–67.

14. James Walsh, "Shortening the Supply Chain," *Minneapolis Star Tribune,* July 24, 1995, p. 1D. See also Ronald Henkoff, "Delivering the Goods," *Fortune,* November 28, 1994, pp. 64–78; and Joseph B. Fuller, James O'Conor, and Richard Rawlinson, "Tailored Logistics: The Next Advantage," *Harvard Business Review,* May–June 1993, pp. 87–98.

15. Robert W. Ruekert, Orville C. Walker, Jr., and Kenneth J. Roering, "The Organization of Marketing Activities: A Contingency Theory of Structure and Performance," *Journal of Marketing,* Winter 1985, pp. 13–25; and Melissa Campanelli, "Agents of Change," *Sales and Marketing Management,* February 1995, pp. 71–75.

16. Rowland T. Moriarity and Ursula Moran, "Managing Hybrid Marketing Systems," *Harvard Business Review,* November–December 1990, p. 146.

17. "Asia Beckons," *The Economist,* May 30, 1992, p. 63.

18. This section has benefited from Philip R. Cateora, *International Marketing,* 7th ed. (Burr Ridge, IL: Richard D. Irwin, 1990), chap. 4.

19. "2002 Marketing Factbook," *Marketing News,* July 8, 2002, p. 19.

20. See Louis W. Stern and Adel I. El-Ansary, *Marketing Channels,* 3rd ed. (Englewood Cliffs, NJ: Prentice Hall, 1992), chap. 13, for a discussion of the channels used by other service providers.

21. Ibid., pp. 348–58.

22. F. Robert Dwyer, Paul H. Schurr, and Sejo Oh, "Developing Buyer-Seller Relationships," *Journal of Marketing* 51 (April 1987), pp. 11–27; Robert M. Morgan and Shelby D. Hunt, "The Commitment-Trust Theory of Relationship Marketing," *Journal of Marketing* 58 (July 1994), pp. 20–38; and Shankar Ganesan, "Determinants of Long-Term Orientation in Buyer-Seller Relationships," *Journal of Marketing* 58 (April 1994), pp. 1–19.

23. Morgan and Hunt, "Commitment-Trust Theory." See also Donald V. Fites, "Make Your Dealers Your Partners," *Harvard Business Review,* March–April 1996, pp. 84–95.

24. Fites, "Make Your Dealers Your Partners."

25. For examples, see Zachary Schiller, Greg Burns, and Karen Lowry Miller, "Make It Simple," *Business Week,* September 9, 1996, pp. 96–104; and David Henry, "Accounting Games in the Grocer's Aisle," *Business Week,* April 14, 2003, p. 64.

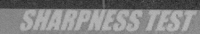
Integrated Promotion Decisions

Integrated Marketing Communication Takes on Some New Twists

MARKETERS HAVE LONG KNOWN that marketing communications of various kinds should be integrated, so that each communications effort builds on the others. Advertising campaigns, publicity, sales pitches delivered by the salesforce, even sales promotions—all should sing from the same hymnal. The advent of new digital media—from the Internet to e-mail to text messaging via mobile telephones—has opened a vast array of new opportunities to take integrated marketing communication—IMC for short—to a whole new level.

With today's technology, marketers can encourage radio listeners to e-mail the show. They can run a television campaign that drives audiences to a website. They can put radio or TV content on the Web to make it available any time, anywhere.

Larazade

Take, for example, the United Kingdom's garishly orange energy drink from GlaxoSmithKline (GSK), Lucozade. To coincide with the U.K. launch of the film *Tomb Raider* in 2001, GSK temporarily rebranded the drink as Larazade, using broadcast and new digital media to support the effort. In one television commercial, "Lara Croft, adventurer and archaeologist, flees through an underground cavern from a pack of pursuing dogs, only to find her way blocked by a chasm. Cornered, she reaches over her shoulder into her backpack, retrieves an orange bottle, and drinks its contents. Revitalised, she gives the dogs the slip and

springs to safety."[1] The television ads not only delivered Larazade messages directly; they also directed viewers to a website that reflected the film's theme.

Visitors to the Larazade website were encouraged to leave their mobile phone numbers and e-mail addresses to receive a message from Lara, the film's heroine. Drawing on the storyline in the film and in the video games of the same name, e-mail and text messages were then sent to drive *Tomb Raider* fans to a second and secret Larazade website. This multichannel approach targeted the hard-to-reach 18–24 market segment that GSK sought to address. A stunning 83 percent of those who received the text message from Lara went to her secret website.

Big Brother

In another example, the *Big Brother* TV program in the United Kingdom (like the somewhat similar program *Survivor* in the United States) used a voting engine that allowed viewers on Sky Digital to vote using their remote control. The voters decided which contestants should stay and which should go, thereby pruning the cast over time until a final winner was picked. The voting element converted typically passive television viewers into active participants, which was a plus for advertisers. In 2001, more than 5 million votes were cast using the voting engine to evict contestants from *Big Brother 2*. But instead of limiting itself to simply being a TV show, *Big Brother* broadcast the activities of its contestants in their own homes 24 hours

Courtesy GlaxoSmithKline

each day, live on the Web, thereby offering the show's advertisers yet another way to deliver messages to their audience.

What's Next?

What will integrated marketing communication planners think of next? Observers think that text, Web, radio, and television will become more and more integrated so viewers can go from, say, a TV program to a website or use text messages or e-mail to connect with the broadcaster. All these elements provide promotional opportunities that today's marketers are just beginning to learn to use. A critical link in making all this happen is implementing digital networks, which will make improved targeting and localized content possible. "It means that local radio can get even closer to its audience by being able to deliver services in a more localised way, as well as improving reliability and enhancing production values," says Sandy Milne, a digital products manager for the BBC.[2]

Thus, creating truly integrated marketing communication is not about simply linking advertising messages with the packaging and the sales pitch of the salesforce, as was often the case a decade or two ago. It's a digital game today, one best played by effectively combining—as did Larazade and *Big Brother*—traditional media like TV with what today's and tomorrow's new digital technologies offer.

Marketing Challenges Addressed in Chapter 14

Assessing markets, analyzing industries, and uncovering customers' unsatisfied wants and needs often leads to the development of new goods or services with huge potential—at least in the eyes of the marketing managers or entrepreneurs who introduce them. So far, we've seen how these activities, together with decisions about final product configuration, pricing, and distribution—three of the four Ps—bring companies to the brink of marketing success. With these important building blocks in place, a critical marketing task remains—to let a waiting world know of the new product and invite it to purchase. The entrepreneur with the new product is not alone; countless marketing managers face similar decisions every day, not only for new products of which customers are unaware, but also for established products trying to win in today's highly competitive markets.

In Chapter 14, we address the considerable challenges entailed in the last of the four Ps—**promotion**—and we provide tools and analytical frameworks for addressing several age-old marketing questions. To whom should marketing messages be directed, inside the company and outside, to consumers and other stakeholders? How can the marketing manager most effectively and efficiently inform the target market about the product? How can the manager persuade them to try or buy? What message should be delivered? How much should the firm spend to deliver it? In what media, or with what promotional tools? Finally, how might the manager assess whether the promotional strategy has been both effective and efficient? These are not easy questions to answer.

We begin by introducing the promotion mix, the collection of promotional elements from which marketers can choose. We then explore the communication process and the barriers that make it difficult to get promotional messages across to their intended

KEY OBSERVATION

How can the marketing manager most effectively and efficiently inform the target market about the product?

audiences. Finally, we provide tools for marketing managers or entrepreneurs to use in answering the questions just raised, in order to prepare evidence-based marketing plans that stand a good chance of meeting their marketing objectives.

The Promotion Mix: A Communication Toolkit

In deciding how to best promote their products, marketing managers must decide which promotional tools to use and with whom they wish to communicate. These decisions, as we shall see, must consider the objectives the marketer has in mind, as well as the merits of and costs entailed in using different tools in the **promotion mix.** In making these decisions, the marketer is developing a promotional or an **integrated marketing communication (IMC) plan.** Arens defines the IMC planning process as one of "building and reinforcing mutually profitable relationships with employees, customers, other stakeholders, and the general public by developing and coordinating a strategic communications program that enables them to make constructive contact with the company brand through a variety of media."[3]

The process by which the IMC plan is developed follows essentially the steps in the marketing management process that have served as the basis for the structure of this book.

KEY OBSERVATION

Of particular importance are the steps involving segmentation, targeting, and positioning.

Of particular importance are the steps involving segmentation, targeting, and positioning, which ideally would provide information on the choice criteria of the target audience. Setting marketing objectives and strategy for a product-market is also critical since it sets the stage for the development of the strategic marketing program, which establishes the role of the various elements in the marketing mix.

Successful execution of these steps and those concerned with the development of the promotion mix (as discussed in this chapter) should produce an effective IMC campaign. Also important is the development of message consistency over time, regardless of the form the message takes and the media vehicles used.

The principal tools from which a marketer can choose in developing an IMC plan, comprising the **promotion mix,** are **advertising, personal selling, sales promotion,** and **public relations,** though there are other promotional tools, such as sponsorships and staged events, that do not fall neatly into any of these categories. Definitions of these tools or promotional elements follow, and are elaborated in Exhibit 14.1.

- **Advertising**—Any paid form of *nonpersonal* (i.e. through some medium, such as radio, print, direct mail, or e-mail) presentation and promotion of ideas, goods, or services by an identified sponsor.
- **Personal selling**—A process of helping and persuading one or more prospects to purchase a good or service or to act on any idea through the use of an *oral* presentation (person-to-person communication).
- **Sales promotion**—Incentives designed to stimulate the purchase or sale of a product, usually in the short term.
- **Public relations**—Nonpaid, nonpersonal stimulation of demand for a product, service, or business unit by planting significant news about it or a favorable presentation of it in the media.

Firms spend substantial sums on their advertising and sales promotion activities. Advertising expenditures in all media, including the Internet, were estimated to be $233 billion in the United States alone in 2000. Spending levels in Europe were not far behind. Collectively this amounted to a per-capita expenditure of nearly $1,000 per year.[4] And the

Exhibit 14.1

EXAMPLES OF PROMOTIONAL ACTIVITIES

• **Advertising:**	Print ads (newspaper and magazine), radio, television, billboard, direct mail, brochures and catalogs, signs, in-store displays, posters, motion pictures, Web pages, banner ads, and e-mails.
• **Personal selling:**	Sales presentations, sales meetings, sales training and incentive programs for intermediary salespeople, samples, and telemarketing (either inbound or outbound).
• **Sales promotion:**	Coupons, sweepstakes, contests, product samples, rebates, tie-ins, self-liquidating premiums, trade shows, trade-ins, and exhibitions.
• **Public relations:**	Newspaper and magazine articles/reports, TV and radio presentations, charitable contributions, speeches, issue advertising, and seminars.

above totals do not include personal selling and public relations on which billions more are spent.

Developing an Integrated Marketing Communications Plan

There are many factors to consider in developing an effective promotion, or marketing communications, program, whether for goods or services. These include the objectives the marketer has in mind, the characteristics and decision processes of the target market(s) the communication is intended to reach, and the available budget. In addition, the product's positioning, its competitors' promotional strategies, the distribution channels through which it will be sold, the product's stage in the product life cycle, and the merits of the various elements of the promotion mix must be considered. Thus, promotional decision making is no simple task! Simply having a creative idea for an advertising campaign is not sufficient.

KEY OBSERVATION

Promotional decision making is no simple task!

Each of the four elements of the promotion mix—advertising, personal selling, sales promotion, and public relations—has its own unique strengths and weaknesses, though these vary for specific tools and media within each of the four elements. The marketer's challenge is to develop a budget that will accomplish the promotional objectives and distribute that budget across the elements of the promotion mix in the most effective and efficient manner. To do so, skilled marketers follow a five-step process like that outlined in Exhibit 14.2.

Step 1: Define the Audience(s) to Be Targeted

KEY OBSERVATION

Segmentation decisions are especially important to the marketing communications effort because they identify who the target market is.

In the market segmentation chapter, we identified three broad ways to segment both consumer and organizational markets: on the basis of demographic variables, geographic criteria, or behavioral descriptors of various kinds. Segmentation decisions are especially important to the marketing communications effort because they identify who the target market is, so those planning the communications effort can identify the best ways to reach the target customers. Making promotional decisions without a clear idea as to who the target market is can often lead to misdirection or waste of scarce marketing funds. Sometimes promotional messages in an integrated marketing communications program must target multiple audiences, such as for medical products. For example, Rogaine, the drug for male

Exhibit 14.2

DECISION SEQUENCE FOR DEVELOPING THE PROMOTION MIX

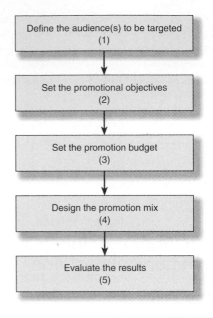

Define the audience(s) to be targeted
(1)

Set the promotional objectives
(2)

Set the promotion budget
(3)

Design the promotion mix
(4)

Evaluate the results
(5)

pattern baldness, was promoted to doctors, to encourage them to prescribe it, as well as to consumers, to encourage them to ask their doctors about the product.

Consider the Super Bowl, an annual football game that is the most watched sporting event in the United States, and is the top TV advertising opportunity for the country. The audience for this event averages 135 million, and the cost of a 30-second commercial is about $2.2 million. Two dot.com highfliers, Monster.com and HotJobs.com, advertised on the Super Bowl telecast in 1999 with considerable success. Their target markets were those who were looking for new jobs anywhere in the United States, a behavioral segment that crosses virtually all adult demographic and geographic groups. The Super Bowl, with its broad viewing audience, was a good way to reach this large target and get some press attention as well.

Now consider OurBeginning.com, a marketer of wedding invitations that advertised on the Super Bowl in 2000. Women ages 18 to 30 comprise the most attractive target market for wedding invitations, since women's families still plan most weddings and most weddings are still among couples in these age brackets. Was the Super Bowl an effective and efficient way to reach this target market? It may have been effective, since many young women do watch the Super Bowl, though they may be less glued to the screen at a Super Bowl party than are their male counterparts. But it was not efficient. Only a small portion of the total Super Bowl viewing audience fell into OurBeginning.com's target market, but OurBeginnings had to pay Super Bowl prices for the *entire* viewing audience. Thus, OurBeginning.com's cost to reach its *target* customers was very high.

Step 2: Set the Promotional Objectives

Having clearly identified the target audience for the marketing communication being planned, the marketer's next job is to decide exactly what the communication is supposed to accomplish, in measurable terms. Growth in sales and market share are often used as promotional objectives, but marketers should note that sales increases are a function of the entire marketing program, not just the promotion mix. Advertising a poorly designed or overpriced product or one that has little distribution is not likely to be successful. Appropriate promotional objectives, like other business objectives, should follow the SMART acronym: **s**pecific, **m**easurable, **a**ttainable, **r**elevant (to the firms' mission and overall market and competitive context), and **t**ime-bound. Thus, good promotional objectives should include four key elements:

- A statement defining the target audience.
- A statement of how some specific aspect(s) of the audience's perceptions, attitudes, or behavior should change.
- A statement of how quickly such a change is expected to occur.
- And a statement of the degree of change required.

Step 3: Set the Promotion Budget

There are a number of ways to prepare the promotion budget, most of which work from the top down (managers first determine the total amount to be budgeted and then allocate various amounts to the different mix components). The major budget-setting methods used are discussed briefly below.

The **percentage of sales** method is the most common. The procedure consists of setting this year's budget as a percentage of this year's anticipated sales. Under this approach, sales determine the promotional activity versus planning to achieve some desired sales objective. Even though illogical, this method has some advantages. It is simple to calculate and is risk-averse because spending is linked to sales.

The **competitive parity** method sets the relative level of promotional spending equal to the firm's market share or larger if an attempt is being made to increase share. Thus, if the firm's market share is 20 percent, then its budget would be its 20 percent of the total amount spent by the industry on promoting a given product-market entry. This method of budgeting tends to create stability in market shares among competitors and has the advantage of considering competition. Share of market budgeting is often used in connection with new products where one rule of thumb is to spend one and a half times the share objective at the end of the first or second year.[5]

One study suggests that firms with small shares tend to overspend, but as they gain share reduce their spending relative to their share of market.[6] Another study that concentrated on situations concerned with growing market share suggested that to do so managers should target market segments where competitors are weak and resist the temptation to take short-term profits.[7]

Because the **objective-and-task** method avoids most of the flaws inherent in the top-down budgeting approaches, it is the best one—though the most difficult—to use. It essentially involves three steps—first, define promotional objectives as specifically as possible; second, determine the strategies and specific tasks necessary to meet those objectives; and third, estimate the costs of performing those tasks and budget accordingly.

The objective-and-task method, has the advantage of forcing firms to set specific promotional objectives through careful analysis of the specific situation. It is most effective when the results obtained from a particular promotion activity can be measured (for instance, the awareness generated among members of the target audience or the number of persons who would be exposed to the product via sampling).

Step 4: Design the Promotion Mix

Designing the promotion mix is itself a three-step process.

- First, marketers decide which promotion components to use: advertising, personal selling, sales promotion, and/or public relations.
- Second, they choose the specific activities within each component. In advertising, this involves considering such media as TV, radio, newspapers, magazines, the Internet, or billboards. A consumer sales promotion could consist of coupons, free samples, or premiums, for example.
- Third, within each activity they must decide which specific vehicle to employ; for example, in advertising, this might require selecting a TV or radio program, while in sales promotion they must decide about the coupon specifics—its value, size and color, message format, and how it will be delivered.

These decisions are complex because the elements of the promotion mix are not independent; for example, a consumer sales promotion (perhaps a coupon or sweepstakes) often requires advertising to inform the target audience about the promotion. Making specific decisions about promotion mix elements requires examining the target audience, objectives, and budget, already established in Steps 1 though 3 (see Exhibit 14.3), as well as the company's overall strategic objectives and resources, the product's stage in the product life cycle, and various market characteristics and the other elements—the kind of product being promoted; its price and distribution—in the marketing mix. It also usually involves making a choice between advertising and personal selling as the principal driver of the promotion strategy (see Exhibit 14.3).

In practice, either advertising or personal selling generally plays a dominant role in the promotion mix, with sales promotion and/or publicity playing supporting roles. In marketing goods, especially consumer goods, when advertising dominates, the idea is to communicate with the consumer and encourage him or her to pull the product through the distribution channel, by demanding that the channel stock the product. As we saw in the previous chapter, this strategy is called a **pull strategy.** Major consumer goods marketers

KEY OBSERVATION

Making specific decisions about promotion mix elements requires examining the target audience, objectives, and budget. It also usually involves making a choice between advertising and personal selling as the principal driver of the promotion strategy.

Exhibit 14.3

STRATEGIC CIRCUMSTANCES AND THE RELATIVE IMPORTANCE OF ADVERTISING AND PERSONAL SELLING AS PROMOTIONAL TOOLS

Advertising relatively important		Personal Selling relatively important
	Number of customers	
Large		Small
	Buyers' information needs	
Low		High
	Size and importance of purchase	
Small		Large
	Postpurchase service required	
Little		Much
	Product complexity	
Low		High
	Distribution strategy	
Pull		Push
	Pricing policy	
Preset		Negotiated
	Resources available for promotion	
Many		Few

Source: Adapted from David W. Cravens, *Strategic Marketing* (Burr Ridge, IL: Richard D. Irwin, 1987), p. 508. Reprinted with permission from The McGraw-Hill Companies.

typically use pull strategies. For consumer goods when personal selling dominates, the marketer attempts to convince channel members to stock the product, so consumers will find it at their local store—a **push strategy.** Smaller consumer goods marketers who lack the budgets to pursue pull strategies typically use push strategies. Many little-advertised products found in supermarkets and mass merchants found their way to the shelf through effective push strategies.

Different elements in the promotion mix may be called on to meet different objectives. For example, advertising may be asked to develop awareness and brand recognition; the Internet may be used to build a contact list; personal selling may be used to complete the sale. Even when the strategic conditions and communications tasks faced by a firm favor the allocation of substantial promotional resources to the salesforce, the specific marketing objectives that salespeople are asked to pursue vary widely across firms facing different market and competitive situations. A company's sales personnel might be asked to focus on one or more of the following objectives:

- Winning acceptance of new products by existing customers.
- Developing new customers for existing products.
- Maintaining the loyalty of current customers by providing good service.
- Facilitating future sales by providing technical services to potential customers.
- Facilitating future sales by communicating product information to potential customers or influencers.
- Gathering market information.

An important part of designing the promotion mix is creating the messages to be communicated to the target audience(s). Preparing a successful message is difficult, if only because of the countless ways in which it can be constructed. Yet the payoffs from good messages are substantial. For example, simple changes in the wording of a print ad have been known to generate a substantial increase in sales for retail stores, mail-order houses, and direct mail sellers.

In concept, then, our discussion of this step highlights the remaining issues the marketer must consider in preparing a promotional plan. At the risk of being overly general, Exhibit 14.4 provides guidance in assessing some relative merits of the various elements of the promotion mix. But we have not yet provided enough specifics that the marketer charged with preparing a marketing or integrated marketing communications plan for a new or existing product can determine the specific budgets and activities necessary to meet a sales forecast. We address these important details in the balance of this chapter. First, however, comes Step 5, which assesses the results of the promotion plan, once it has been implemented.

Step 5: Evaluate the Results

This step involves finding out whether the objectives of the promotional activity have been met—usually via marketing research. For example, in advertising a new consumer product, the company could conduct a telephone survey after the promotional campaign had run for a designated period to determine whether the objective of generating a certain level of awareness among members of the target audience had been achieved. Further, the survey could determine what percent had tried the brand and of these how many had bought it two or more times. In this way management could obtain information about the relationship of trial to awareness. For example, assume a trial/awareness ratio of 25 percent and an awareness level of 50 percent among members of the target audience group. Under such conditions, management should seriously consider spending additional funds to increase

Exhibit 14.4

COMPARING THE MERITS OF THE PROMOTION MIX ELEMENTS

Promotion mix element	Amount of information communicated	Credibility	Control over the message	Cost to reach one customer	Strategic suitability
Advertising	Varies: little information in a radio or TV ad, to lots on a website	Low	Good	Low	Well-suited to a **pull strategy.**
Personal Selling	Lots of information	Depends on the credibility of the company and the personality and sales skills of the salesperson	Poor, but training helps	Very high in developed countries, can be low elsewhere	Well-suited to a **push strategy.**
Sales Promotion	Virtually no information	Not applicable	Good	Low and self-liquidating: generally pays for itself as the product is purchased	Consumer promotion supports a **pull strategy.** Trade promotion supports a **push strategy.**
Public Relations	Lots of information	High	Poor	Very low or nil	Supports both **pull** and **push** strategies.

awareness. Research can also provide important insights into whether the firm attained its distribution objectives.

The Nitty-Gritty of Promotional Decision Making

Faced with meeting a sales forecast, how should a marketer determine the specifics of his or her promotional program? How big an ad budget is needed? In which media should it be spent? What role should personal selling play? How might the Internet be used to best advantage? Are coupons or trade promotions called for? What about samples to encourage trial? Should we seek publicity through a public relations effort? We address these practical questions in this portion of the chapter.

Making Advertising Decisions

Advertising is a complex decision area and the changing macroenvironment has made it even more so. Major social and economic changes include a redefined family unit (fewer members, more single parents and two wage earners), which leads to less pressure to conform to traditional family values, more lifestyle options, and an increase in basic household needs; higher education levels leading to a demand for more meaningful information about products; an older population with the greatest wealth of any population segment; and an exploding media scene including a dramatic increase in the number of media options, not the least of which is the Internet and the emergence of the World Wide Web, where companies can advertise, provide demonstrations, answer questions, and even sell their products.

Advertising decision making is concerned with setting objectives and budgets, choosing which media types and vehicles to use with what frequency, deciding what the message should be and how to present it, and analyzing the effectiveness of the advertising program. We address these issues next.

Setting Advertising Objectives

Promotional objectives are important in developing an integrated promotion plan. They derive from the firm's marketing objectives and strategy and are concerned with communicating certain information about the company and its product(s) to target audiences. They help in the development of a promotion plan, which, in turn, facilitates decision making by a large number of diverse individuals both inside and outside the company. Promotional objectives serve as the basis for evaluating the advertising program once it is completed.

Advertising objectives must somehow relate to attitudes or behavior. Results can sometimes best be assessed by measuring the *process* by which the desired objectives are met. Hence the use of-hierarchy-of-effect models that move prospective buyers through a series of steps—awareness, comprehension, conviction, action—to the ultimate goal of purchasing the product.[8] Knowing the various steps in such models helps the marketer better set its advertising objectives. Thus, if most prospects are aware of the product *and* its advantages but not convinced of its uniqueness, one advertising objective would be to create conviction by demonstrating product superiority.

Another advantage of using the communication hierarchy as the basis for setting advertising objectives is that it is possible to measure the proportion of potential customers who are at each stage in the hierarchy. This means that advertising objectives can be set forth in numerical terms for a stated time period and pertaining to a defined audience group.

Thus, in setting advertising objectives, a clear understanding of precisely what the advertising is expected to accomplish, often measured in terms of attitude change, provides an ad agency or others who make the media choices and develop the ads with the direction they need to do their jobs. In large company settings, where advertising enjoys multimillion-dollar budgets, marketing research is used to assess whether the advertising is doing its intended job as we discuss later in this section. Setting SMART advertising objectives makes such an assessment possible.

KEY OBSERVATION

In setting advertising objectives, a clear understanding of precisely what the advertising is expected to accomplish, often measured in terms of attitude change, provides an ad agency or others who make the media choices and develop the ads with the direction they need to do their jobs.

Setting Advertising Budgets and Making Media Choices

Whether an advertising program consists of radio or television ads, banner ads on the Internet, print ads in magazines or newspapers, direct mail, or other media choices, setting budgets and choosing media comes down to making decisions about the extent to which a message is delivered to its target audience, or **reach,** and the **frequency** with which it does so. Thus, advertisers must choose some combination of *reach* and *frequency* to attain their advertising objectives. Reach is defined as the total number of individuals or households exposed to at least one ad during a given period—typically four weeks. The term can be used in connection with a single media vehicle (a specific TV show) or a media schedule comprising a number of different vehicles. Reach is typically expressed as a percent of the target audience; for example, if the target audience was 100,000 persons and the media schedule reached 70,000, then the reach would be 70 percent. Ordinarily, costs rise at an increasing rate as higher levels of reach are sought.

There are several problems in using reach and frequency to make media decisions. The first is defining the target audience and correlating it with the audiences reached by the various media vehicles. We discuss these problems later in this section. A second problem is defining exposure—is it an opportunity to be exposed to a given message or is it an actual reading of a print ad, actual watching of a TV commercial, or actual listening to an ad on radio? It is difficult to measure exposure no matter how it is defined. Third, not all who are exposed are of equal value to the advertiser, some may not even be prospects. Fourth, how should successive exposures be weighted? Is a second exposure worth more than a third? How much? And how much time should elapse between exposures?

Reach and frequency measures are used to prepare the advertising schedule, which, in turn, determines total advertising expenditures. In estimating the cost of a given schedule, media planners simplify their task by using gross rating points (GRPs), which are calculated by multiplying reach by average frequency. Assuming a reach of 70 percent and a desired average frequency of four, the number of GRPs would then be 280. By multiplying this by an estimated cost per GRP, the cost for a proposed media schedule can be estimated. A step-by-step procedure for setting an advertising budget for a new wine cooler brand is shown in Exhibit 14.5. This example also illustrates the use of the objective and task method to set an advertising budget.

Exhibit 14.5 shows that various assumptions must be made about desired levels of reach and frequency in order to prepare a media budget. On what are these assumptions based? In practice, marketers rely on their prior experience to determine how much reach and frequency is necessary to deliver a certain level of results. Thus, in preparing promotional plans, marketers must draw on either their own experience, that of others within their company, or that of experts, such as ad agency personnel, to determine how large a budget, or media buy, is necessary to meet a particular objective.

KEY OBSERVATION

Various assumptions must be made about desired levels of reach and frequency in order to prepare a media budget. On what are these assumptions based?

The costs of advertising in various media may be found from a variety of sources. Typically, an advertising medium provides to prospective advertisers upon request a **rate card,**

Exhibit 14.5

SETTING AN ADVERTISING BUDGET FOR A NEW WINE COOLER BRAND—A HYPOTHETICAL EXAMPLE

1.   Establish a market-share goal. By the end of the first year, achieve a 15 percent share of the estimated 40 million-case wine cooler market, which is expected to grow by 10 million cases per year for the next several years. This target of 6 million cases is to be obtained by attracting first-time wine cooler buyers and getting users to switch to the new brand. Assume some 10 million wine cooler drinkers and the net addition of 2.5 million new drinkers each year. The number of individual consumers needed to attain a 15 percent share is estimated to be 2 million.

2(a).   Determine the percent of the target audience that needs to be made aware of the new brand in order to induce a trial and repeat usage rate (three or more bottles) that will attract 2 million consumers. The agency estimates that 40 percent of those who try a bottle of the new brand will become long-term users. This means 5 million persons must try the product. The agency further assumes that 75 percent of those who become aware of the product will try it. This translates into a need to make 6.67 million—or some 53 percent of the 12.5 million total present and prospective buyers—aware of the brand.

2(b).   Determine the number of impressions needed to obtain an awareness level of 53 percent followed by trial and repeat buying. The agency estimates that 35 impressions on average will be needed for each of 12.5 million individuals in the target audience to bring this about (less than one per week). Thus, the total number of impressions needed is 35×12.5 million $= 437.5$ million.

2(c).   Determine the number of gross ratings points (GRPs) needed.[*] Based on needed reach and repetition (35), assume 3,500 GRPs are needed.

3.   Determine the cost of the needed 3,500 GRPs. The agency estimates an average cost per GRP of $4,000—hence, the advertising media budget would be $14 million. To this amount, the costs of ad production and marketing research have to be added.

[*]GRPs are computed by multiplying the *reach* by the average *frequency. Reach* means the different individuals (or households) exposed to an advertising schedule per time period. Reach measures the unduplicated audience exposed to a media schedule and is typically expressed as a percent of the target audience. *Frequency* is a measure of the number of times on average a person or household receives an advertising measure. Thus, it is a measure of repetition.

which specifies the nature and size of the audience it reaches and the costs of advertising in that medium. Costs are expressed in **cost per thousand** impressions (an impression is one person being exposed to the ad one time), or **CPM,** making comparisons across different kinds of media possible. Various industry sources compile such information and make it available to prospective advertisers for their use in planning promotional programs. Exhibit 14.6 provides several such sources and their Internet addresses. Most business libraries have copies of these or similar publications.

Traditional Media Types   Of the four major types of mass media, network and cable TV has the largest share in the United States at 32 percent, followed by newspaper advertising at 27 percent.[9] Direct marketing is on the rise globally; for example, the direct marketing industry in the United Kingdom grew by 10 percent in 2001, despite the slowdown in ad spending in other media.[10] Various Internet and e-mail media are taking market share, however, from these traditional media. Each media type offers unique advantages to the advertiser, but each also has limitations.

Television is best at communicating images and symbols because it can demonstrate product usage and consumer reactions. It is a particularly good medium to help sell a mass-market product. It has enormous reach—for example, in the United States almost all households have a TV set (98 percent have one set and nearly two-thirds have two or more). The average prime-time TV program in the United States reaches over 10 million homes at an average cost of $9 per thousand. Popular shows may attract audiences of over 30 million homes. Cable TV has experienced such substantial growth in the United States that it covers more than two-thirds of all households—nearly 70 million. While cable TV penetration is not as high in countries in Europe, satellite television is increasing in popularity and advertising on the free-to-air channels reaches all of the television households.

Radio is less involving than television, but offers economy and the opportunity to target specific audiences—particular ethnicities, teenagers, senior citizens. Radio advertising—while inexpensive compared with TV and newspapers—suffers in that it reaches people mostly when they are doing something else—working, driving, or walking. It is often used to reinforce TV advertising.

Exhibit 14.6

COMPREHENSIVE SOURCES OF MEDIA AUDIENCE AND RATE INFORMATION

Source	Website address	Description
Standard Rate and Data Service (SRDS)	www.srds.com	Provides rates and audience information for U.S. television, radio, newspaper, magazine (both consumer and business), and direct mail media
BPA International	www.bpai.com	Provides circulation and traffic information for newspaper, magazine (both consumer and business), trade show, website, industry database, and wireless communication media in 25 countries
DMPlaza	www.dmplaza.com	Provides web information relating to the direct marketing industry, including suppliers and call center services and products
A.C. Nielsen	www.nielsenmedia.com	Provides, on a fee basis, North American ratings and traffic data for television, cable television, and websites based on proprietary samples who report their viewing and Web traffic behavior

Print media are more involving than broadcast media. Readers select what advertising they want to read and take as much time as they wish to read it. Thus, print is effective in communicating detailed information about a product. This is particularly important for most industrial products and high-involvement consumer goods.

There are many types of magazines based on the nature of their content and the scope of their geographical coverage—local, regional, and national. And they can be categorized on the nature of their audience ranging from general or mass appeal (*The Economist, Newsweek*), to highly specific such as those dedicated to sports (football, golf, tennis), hobbies (gardening, stamp collecting, antiques), ethnic groups (Hispanic), age groups (teens, seniors), gender (working women), and financial (investment opportunities). In recent years more focused magazines in terms of market segments have gained circulation versus the larger more generalized ones.

Newspaper advertising consists mainly of retail and classified although it is an important medium for those national advertisers who want to communicate specific facts about their products.

Out-of-home, exhibition, and supplementary media cover a wide variety of media types.[11] These three categories are discussed briefly below.

- **Out-of-home.** Billboards are the most prominent media and come in a variety of shapes and sizes as well as location opportunities. These include spectacular electronic signs that feature moving messages and color graphics. Other outdoor media include transit shelters, terminals, and airports; transit vehicles—both inside and out—such as taxis, buses, and streetcars; sports stadiums (many carry the name and logo of a prominent advertiser); parking meters, public phones, and shopping malls.[12]

- **Exhibition.** This category is dominated by in-store display materials, which include signs, banners, video displays on shopping carts, and electronic ads on in-store screens.[13] Trade shows and exhibits are a favorite with many business-to-business marketers.

- **Supplementary.** Directories and yellow pages (both print and online) are the major media in this category.

Direct marketing using advertising media has been covered in part in Chapter 13 (distribution decisions). For consumer products, this approach typically involves direct mail (including catalogs and Internet marketing), TV, radio, and print ads with a toll-free phone number. Despite its high cost (per exposure) and despite typical response rates in the 1–2 percent range, direct mail's selectivity has enabled some companies to reap substantial profits.

New Media   Among the greatest challenges facing advertisers today is how to take best advantage of the opportunities presented by the new media made possible by advances in computing and communications technology. We address these challenges in considerable detail in Chapter 15, in which we examine an array of available strategic options in the Internet age. Here, we focus on the Internet and other new media as communication vehicles, where new developments are causing advertisers to rethink how they spend their advertising budgets.

In late 1998—eons ago in Internet time—J. William Gurley, a venture capitalist and columnist writing in *Fortune* magazine, predicted that Internet technologies would revolutionize advertising, largely because the performance of Internet ads is measurable. "On the Internet an advertiser can not only measure the number of people who see his ad but can also track the number of people who 'click through' an ad to get more information from the advertiser's own Web page. Armed with such data, an advertiser doesn't have to settle for spots that don't deliver customers. Unlike a print or television ad

KEY OBSERVATION

"On the Internet . . . an advertiser doesn't have to settle for spots that don't deliver customers. Unlike a print or television ad buyer—and like a direct marketer—he can pay only for messages that reach the most receptive audience."

buyer—and like a direct marketer—he can pay only for messages that reach the most receptive audience."[14]

Gurley's prediction has begun to play out, as Internet shopping takes off. Aided by recent software innovations, advertisers can now measure not only how many customers "click through" a banner ad, but they can also determine which customers bought online, how much they bought, and what the margins were on each sale. More traditionally, advertisers can also use the Internet for image-oriented brand building for both Web-based and traditional businesses.

Company **websites,** nearly as *de rigueur* for today's companies as having a fax machine, provide a cost-effective way to provide detailed product information about one's entire product line, as well as information of interest to investors and, unfortunately, to competitors. Websites are also good ways to build one-on-one relationships with customers, by giving them an easy place to go for information, day or night, and by offering opportunities to receive e-mail messages that might be of interest.

Banner ads and other forms of Internet ads, including buttons, text links, pop-up windows, and other new versions that are invented regularly, can be placed on Web portals or other websites. Ads can consist of text, graphics, audio, or video, and some are even interactive. In many cases, advertisers can choose how they wish to pay for such ads. They can pay for placements for a certain time period, like a billboard on a highway. They can pay on a cost per thousand impressions (CPM) basis, as they do for traditional print and broadcast media. They can pay for "click-throughs" or pay a fee only when the customer buys, thus bearing out Gurley's 1998 prediction.

Search keywords can be purchased by companies wanting to reach customers looking for their products based on their searches. For example, a search on popular search engine Google on this textbook and an author ("Marketing Management" Mullins) fetches a page with an embedded ad for several firms in marketing, including Claritas, which offers market research expertise. Similar placements can be purchased via other companies like Overture.

Portal deals, whereby marketers pay Web portals for prime or exclusive positions on the portals' websites, can establish competitive advantage for marketers by enhancing the likelihood that theirs will be the site in their product category or industry that customers find first on the Web. These deals are particularly popular with Web-based marketers, including travel, auction, and other services. A quick visit to the America Online home page (aol.com) makes clear who has paid AOL for prime space on its busy site.

E-mail is also a rapidly growing new advertising medium, one particularly well suited to building one-on-one relationships with customers. The best thing about e-mail as a medium, from an advertiser's view, is that it is virtually cost-free. Many airlines now send weekly e-mail updates on bargain weekend airfares to consumers who sign up for such services. On Tuesday or Wednesday, consumers are offered low-priced deals on flights the airlines need to fill. Those in a position to take short, spur-of-the-moment vacations appreciate the opportunities such services provide, and the airlines like having a way to fill seats, which would otherwise fly empty, without having to discount their fares to the general public. As Seth Godin in his book *Permission Marketing* points out, however, the considerable benefits attainable through e-mail marketing come only when the customer *gives his or her permission* to be sent marketing messages. Were this not the case, the system would be inundated with unwanted messages to the point that it would come to a screeching halt![15]

While the new media seem, on the surface, to be radically different from their more traditional counterparts—radio, television, and print—the logic entailed in planning their roles in promotional programs is no different than for other media. Considerations of reach, frequency, and cost—measured in cost per thousand impressions (or "hits" or "click-throughs" on the Web)—provide a means of comparing their value to one another and to traditional media. **Cost per acquisition,** another measure, is useful for Web advertising that results directly in actual customer purchases, a model familiar in the direct marketing industry. To the extent that new media performance can be measured (How many extra customers does a restaurant get for weekday lunches as a result of its ad, and at what cost per customer?), marketers will be encouraged to use them to their full economic potential.

The rapid growth of these and other new media has led to a variety of ethical issues marketers must address, including the security of Web transactions, privacy, and the sending of unwanted electronic messages, or SPAM, to unwilling customers. Some of these ethical issues are discussed in Ethical Perspective 14.1.

Developing the Creative Strategy

Creative strategy derives from the product's targeting and positioning decisions coupled with what the advertising must accomplish. From this information the major selling idea for communicating the key benefits must be developed. This, in turn, generates a strategy statement—often referred to as a copy platform (see Exhibit 14.7 for the contents of such a document). Deciding on the major selling idea or theme is the essence of the creative strategy process since it dictates the nature and scope of the various messages that collectively make up an advertising campaign, and it delivers on the positioning decisions already made as we saw in Chapter 9.

KEY OBSERVATION

Deciding on the major selling idea or theme is the essence of the creative strategy process.

Designing creative and effective marketing communications—regardless of media, whether traditional or new—is a task that requires creativity and special expertise. Copywriters, art directors, and others who ply this trade effectively are worth their weight in gold, for there are many ineffective ads in every medium. It is far beyond the scope of this book to explore how such messages are best created. The issues involved in managing the creative effort, however, include decisions about the **unique selling proposition** to be delivered (based on the desired positioning of the product), the **source** of the message (Should a company spokesperson or a celebrity be used?), the nature of the **appeal**

Exhibit 14.7

COPY PLATFORM CONTENTS

- Basic issue or problem advertising must address
- Advertising objective
- Target audience
- Major selling idea—or key benefits
- Creative strategy statement (campaign theme, appeal, and execution technique)
- Supportive information

Source: George E. Belch and Michael A. Belch, *Introduction to Advertising and Promotion* (Burr Ridge, IL: Richard D. Irwin, 1996), p. 278. Reprinted with permission from The McGraw-Hill Companies.

Exhibit 14.8

MARKETING DECISION SUPPORT TOOLS FOR PROMOTIONAL DECISION MAKING

Tool or service	Software packages, sources	Functions
Software for developing tag lines and slogans	Headliner® from The Namestormers, www.namestormers.com	Uses databases of idioms, clichés, titles, and expressions to assist the user in developing tag lines, slogans, and other promotional phrases.
Media buying software	Strata Buy Management System from Strata Agency Services, www.stratag.com	Does spot television, spot radio, local and national cable, network television, and print media analysis, planning, and buying based on the user's reach and frequency objectives.
Services for merging, purging, and cleaning data for direct marketing campaigns	datawash.com	Eliminates duplicate or out-of-date records, corrects abbreviations and spellings.
Software for managing co-op advertising and trade promotion programs	Co-opLink™ from Co-op Communications, www.coopcom.com	Provides Web-based tracking of co-op advertising funds and other trade promotion activities.

embodied in the message (Should it be primarily rational, emotional, or both? Should it compare one's own product with those of competitors? Should it use fear, humor, or music?). Effective creative strategies almost always contain at least some **emotional appeal,** and not only deliver the desired message, but also manage to attract the **attention** and **interest** of the target audience despite an extremely cluttered advertising environment. Some ads even include a **call to action,** in which the customer is asked to do something (like call a toll-free telephone number, clip a coupon, or click through to a website). Software tools that aid marketing managers in making advertising and other promotional decisions, including creative, media, and direct marketing decisions, are identified in Exhibit 14.8.

Several ethical issues are involved in developing advertising messages, including issues of morals, good taste, community values, and truth (or deception) in advertising. These issues are discussed in Ethical Perspective 14.2.

Measuring Advertising Results   Management must know to what extent the message was received, understood, and believed by the target audience, as well as what effect it had on the behavior of the receiver (trial, repeat buying). Message (copy) testing typically is concerned with alternative ways to present a message to the target audience. The

ETHICAL PERSPECTIVE 14.2
Ethical Issues in Advertising

To many, the ethical question is more than whether advertising is deceptive. Rather, the moral issue is seen as whether advertisers have the right to encourage the purchase of a product that might be harmful to certain individuals—for instance, the sale of tobacco and liquor products in general and, especially, to young people and certain minority groups. Seagram's decided to end the liquor industry's long practice of not doing television advertising. While all three major networks continue to refuse liquor ads, some of their affiliates will probably accept.

One of the most controversial areas is advertising to children, especially on TV, which is watched by children 2 to 11 years old an average of 26 hours a week. Critics argue that the advertising of toys creates unreasonable expectations, that children are encouraged to eat harmful foods (sugared cereals), and that the long-term effects of TV may negatively affect children's values, beliefs, and behavior (especially with respect to violence). Sweden and Canada prohibit any advertising aimed at children; France and Japan limit the use of cartoon characters in advertising to children; and the major networks have strict guidelines for children's ads. In the United States the Federal Trade Commission has taken a much less aggressive stance on this subject.

In the United States, both the federal government and a variety of industry groups have tried to regulate and control deception in advertising. For a given ad to be ruled illegal, it must have the potential to deceive a significant number of consumers as to the facts relating to a purchasing decision. However, deception is difficult to detect in many cases because of the subtle ways in which it can work. Enforcement is hindered by the fact that advertisers can legally employ *puffery*, which uses subjective claims (the "best" or "greatest") to promote the product. Many believe that since the role of advertising is to provide information relevant to the purchasing decision, puffery should be prohibited.

Deception can also occur via the use of mockups, which involve the alteration of a product or situation to get a realistic photograph of it (using mashed potatoes to represent ice cream, which melts under the photographer's lights). While the FTC has ruled that mockups are legal as long as they do not misrepresent the product's characteristics, some critics of advertising argue that many are misleading.

Endorsements and testimonials for products and services have increased in recent years. But do the individuals involved *really* use the products, or are they "hired guns"? Even though the FTC has rules governing their use, many such ads have the potential to deceive.

Partial disclosure concerning a product's attributes is yet another way consumers can be misled. An example is when an ad talks about a low cholesterol count but fails to mention the amount of fat the product contains.

---

discussion here is divided into two parts—tests made *before* the message is released on a full-run basis and tests done *after* the copy is run in the prescribed media.

Before Tests No copy pretest can simulate exactly the conditions of exposure and the long-run effects of repetition on a particular audience group. There are, however, a number of ways to pretest message effectiveness, including the following:

- **Recall tests** of proposed print ads are inserted into a simulated magazine and respondents are told to read whatever interests them. After doing so, they are asked to "play back" ads they remember. They are also asked questions about ad credibility and product usage. Using the results, researchers can determine the extent to which the message got through and to what extent it achieved the communicator's objective(s). Unfortunately, recall scores too often reflect a brand's popularity rather than message content.

- **Sales tests** as administered by commercial research firms such as BehaviorScan measure the effects of TV commercials through the use of consumer panels located in a number of small cities. Purchases are recorded electronically by scanners at supermarket checkout counters by panel members using special ID cards. BehaviorScan can insert test TV commercials into TV programs at the individual panel household level. They select household samples on the basis of their purchase behavior history. Thus, the consumer panel becomes a single source of both purchase and viewing behavior, thereby enhancing its value. Because alternative ad treatments can be shown to different balanced samples at the same time, it is possible to measure the sales effect of one copy treatment against another based on actual purchase data.

After Tests Measuring the effects of an advertising message after it has run is difficult because the results are confounded by the effects of the media used, the frequency with which the audience received the message and other factors, including competitive activity and even the weather!. *After* tests tend to measure the effectiveness of the total advertising effort. Here we look at only those *after* tests used primarily to measure message effects. Thus, for example, BMW's advertising agency reported that consumer research showed that consumers were getting the right message—namely, that a BMW is not only dynamic, but comfortable and affordable as well.

Advertisers design *after* tests in a number of ways, and they all rely on the respondent's memory, which raises the problem of how soon after running the ad the measurement should be taken. Also, testing that relies on a single measure in time does not reflect the learning that occurs with repeated exposure.

- **Recognition tests** are the most popular postexposure testing method for print media. Advertisers design these tests to measure the extent to which advertising copy is noted and read. Field workers interview people who say they have read a given issue of a magazine. Each respondent goes through the issue pointing out what was seen and read. When the respondent reports seeing an ad, the interviewer asks which parts were read. The interviewer starts each interview at a random point within the issue, so that the ratings are not affected by respondent fatigue.

- **Recall tests** are another common way to measure the effectiveness of an advertising message, especially a TV commercial, after it has been run. Respondents are typically aided in their recall. Interviewers show them a list of the advertisers and brands presented and ask which ones they have seen recently. Interviewers proceed to obtain playbacks of these ads from the respondents.

The industry has long raised questions of whether recall and recognition tests provide adequate measures of memory. Other postexposure ways of measuring the effectiveness of the message include sales tests similar to those used to test new products, inquiries (possible when coupons are used or a toll-free telephone number is made available for placing orders), and measurements of attitudinal change. The latter typically involve *before–after* measurements of the degree to which a given brand possesses certain salient features.

Where the objectives of an advertising effort involve increases in customer traffic, sales, market share, or other tangibly measurable outcomes, such measures should be taken to assess advertising effectiveness. Such measures—including cost per acquisition (to win a new customer) and cost per order (in absolute or percent of sales terms)—are commonly used in direct marketing and in many emerging Internet marketing contexts. Caution should be exercised, however, as other market and competitive factors—the product itself, its pricing or distribution, the weather, or competitive activities—may also have influenced the outcomes being measured. Blaming the advertising for unacceptable sales performance that really results from other causes is not uncommon!

KEY OBSERVATION

Blaming the advertising for unacceptable sales performance that really results from other causes is not uncommon!

International Media Global advertising has been aided by recent media developments. In TV, CNN reaches over 140 million households of which 81 million are outside the United States, and Viacom's MTV Networks estimates its audience worldwide at 250 million with only 25 percent in the United States. ESPN and NBC also have large international audiences.[16] The total number of TV channels in Europe has more than doubled in the past 10 years, and almost all are funded by advertising. China and India are expected to be the fastest growing TV advertising markets in the near future.[17]

The need to produce less-expensive advertising campaigns that have an effective reach has forced the growing use of nontraditional media in Europe.[18] In the United Kingdom, these include the use of supermarket receipts, bus tickets, and phone cards. PolyGram has promoted its new albums on the back of bus tickets while Image Promotions successfully introduced coupons on the back of supermarket receipts. Virgin Atlantic Airways, France Telecom, and British Telecommunications have advertised on phone cards. Other relatively new media include painted taxis and buses with ads (both inside and out), and direct-response TV on monitors at checkout counters.

Making Personal Selling Decisions

Advertising is one of the two principal elements in the promotion mix, as we saw in Exhibit 14.3. We now turn to the second key element, personal selling. As the top half of Exhibit 14.9 indicates, planning a sales program involves four sets of decisions. First, the sales-force must be **organized** to facilitate the most efficient allocation of effort. Second, **account management policies** should be developed as guidelines for the way different types of customers are approached, persuaded, and serviced. Third, **deployment** decisions must be made to define territories and assign salespeople to those territories. Fourth, performance expectations—**quotas**—should be developed for each sales rep based on forecasted demand in that territory. When these four aspects of a sales program are well planned and clearly communicated, they help the sales staff understand the job requirements and the role they are expected to play in implementing the firm's strategy. That improved understanding, in turn, should help the sales staff achieve desired levels of performance.

Space does not permit us to deal in any depth in this book with these four sets of decisions. For readers interested in additional detail, there are numerous books on salesforce management that treat these topics extensively.[19] But we do want to address several key strategic issues that marketing managers must consider in planning a marketing program or preparing a marketing plan: the sales cycle, organizing the sales effort in global markets, and managing customer service, an activity that new technology has the potential to influence dramatically, for better or worse.

The Sales Cycle   The sales cycle refers to the duration—expressed both in calendar time and number of sales visits—that it will take to meet with the various decision makers and convince them to try the product, perhaps on a limited basis at first, and then to adopt it more fully. As we saw in Chapter 6, in many business-to-business selling situations, numerous individuals in a typical client organization have influence over the purchase decision. Each of them will need to be contacted, often more than once. In some companies, annual budgeting cycles mean the purchasing window is open only at certain times of the year. Planning the sales program and determining how many—and what kind of—salespeople it will take to get the job done require a clear understanding of the length of the sales cycle, the number of sales calls it is likely to take to complete a sale, and the nature of the sales task at hand.

Organizing the Sales Effort in Global Markets

As firms expand their marketing and sales efforts into other countries, they face a critical decision concerning how to organize their selling efforts across national boundaries.

Exhibit 14.9

IMPLEMENTING THE STRATEGIC SALES PROGRAM

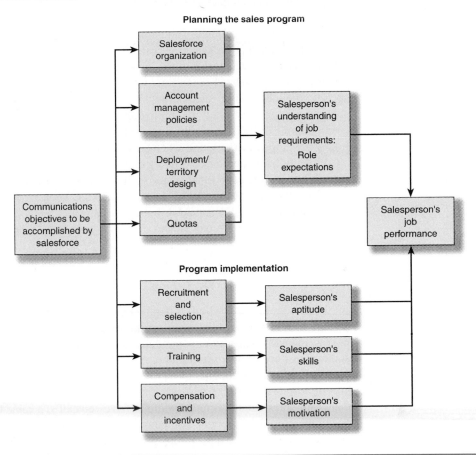

KEY OBSERVATION

While globalization obviously adds complexity to a firm's organizational design, the basic questions to be answered are the same as those faced in domestic markets.

While globalization obviously adds complexity to a firm's organizational design, the basic questions to be answered are the same as those faced in domestic markets. First, should the firm rely on independent agents to represent its interests in a foreign market or hire its own company salespeople? If the firm decides to establish its own subsidiary or sales office with a dedicated company salesforce in a foreign country, a second question arises concerning the appropriate horizontal structure for that salesforce. Should it be organized geographically, by product line, by type of customer, or some other way?

A survey of 14 large multinational corporations (MNCs) examined their sales management practices across 135 subsidiaries located in 45 countries.[20] The results indicate that about 25 percent of the MNCs' subsidiaries use independent agents, either alone or in combination with company salespeople. This is a somewhat lower percentage than found in the U.S. domestic market, where about one-third of all firms use manufacturer's reps. Note, however, that agents are used more frequently in developing markets than in more developed countries and in markets where the firm's sales volume is relatively small.

Industry factors are also related to the use of agents versus company salespeople. Firms selling complex, high-tech products such as computers and pharmaceuticals are significantly more likely to rely solely on their own salespeople than firms in other industrial or consumer goods industries. The higher levels of product knowledge and postsale service required to sell such high-tech products make it relatively more desirable for firms to employ their own salespeople. By doing so, they can maintain better control over the marketing and sales efforts devoted to their products and reduce their transaction costs.

Slightly more than half (51.5 percent) of the surveyed MNCs' subsidiaries report using simple geographic territories to organize their selling efforts within a given country. The rest use more specialized organizational structures, with different salespeople assigned to specific products and/or customer types. As you might expect from our earlier discussion, subsidiaries are most likely to employ specialized structures when they are selling relatively complex products, when their product lines are broad, when they are operating in highly developed markets, and when their sales volumes are relatively large.

While globalization makes the organization of the salesforce more complicated, firms tend to resolve organizational issues in international markets in largely the same way as they do in their native countries. The situational and strategic factors that influence firms' organizational decisions appear to be similar in both types of markets, and those factors seem to affect organizational choices in similar ways both at home and abroad.

Customer Service: An Increasingly Important Personal Selling Function

As the economies in developed countries have become more dominated by services businesses, the importance of customer service has grown. Even in today's manufacturing businesses, intense competition, sometimes from lower-cost providers, has made competent and responsive customer service a point of differentiation for companies seeking to provide complete customer solutions. Thus, just as marketing managers must make decisions about how to best manage their salesforce, they also must decide how best to provide the service that customers demand. How many times have you called a cable television provider, your bank—or even the telephone company itself!—only to have to wade through seemingly endless levels of voice-mail prompts. Finally, you're placed on "hold" at the end of the process! Is this any way to win loyal long-term customers?

Managing the customer service process is an important part of managing the personal selling function. Increasingly, responsibility for customer service and "outside" sales is being brought together on company organization charts, so the two functions can work together seamlessly to serve customers effectively and efficiently, before and after the sale. Managing customer service involves thinking carefully about the firm's objectives for serving customers before the sale and adding additional objectives for aftersale service, along with people and strategies for meeting these objectives. It is no longer sufficient to simply put some people at telephones and ask them to try to help the customers as best they can. Sophisticated systems now make it possible to identify customers as they call, so customer service representatives have their account information at their fingertips, and provide detailed product knowledge to answer the customers' questions, all electronically.

KEY OBSERVATION

Managing customer service involves thinking carefully about the firm's objectives for serving customers before the sale and adding additional objectives for aftersale service.

In the next section we discuss how modern technology is changing the way the customer service game is played. Modern **call centers** allow companies to place them in different time zones, following the sun, and calls made to a single number are automatically routed to the active call center. Technology also allows call centers to be located in places like India, which offer a lower cost basis and access to a large pool of highly skilled workers.[21]

Using Technology to Enhance Sales and Customer Service Performance[22]

Companies concerned about improving their personal selling, sales management, and customer service can turn to the latest computer technologies for help. **Salesforce automation, contact management software, call center software,** and other decision support tools are identified below and in Exhibit 14.10.

An early player in this domain was Siebel Systems, Inc.[23] Siebel, with revenues of $2 billion in 2001, and others provide software for managing field sales, telesales, and call centers, and related marketing functions in large companies. Such software enables field sales reps to track accounts, prospects, and inventories, either from the office PC or from a laptop on the road. The latest call center software enables customer service representatives to see customer account histories while talking with them and provides scripts to help solve common customer problems.

Other companies, like Kana Communications, Inc.,[24] offer software to manage e-mail-based customer service operations. Kana's customers include eBay and Lycos and other large Web-based consumer-to-consumer and business-to-consumer businesses. Use of such software is already paying some companies huge dividends. Companies are also using other software tools like Chat to help customers who are looking for help with their online shopping.[25]

All these innovations have just scratched the surface in making inside and outside sales and customer service people more efficient and effective. If one is not careful, however, some of these tools can enhance efficiency at the expense of effectiveness. Horror stories about endless waits for customer service reps in call centers or layer upon layer of keys to punch to obtain the desired automated information are not the best path to customer satisfaction. Astute marketing managers carefully assess such trade-offs. As these technologies develop, one thing is certain. Regardless of the size of one's company, selling with just a telephone, a company car, a frequent flyer card, and a pair of well-worn shoes is a thing of the past.

Exhibit 14.10

DECISION SUPPORT SOFTWARE FOR PERSONAL SELLING AND SALESFORCE MANAGEMENT

Tool	Software package	Functions
Contact Management Software	ACT, from Interact Commerce Corporation, at www.act.com Goldmine, available (along with other sales management software) from www.sales-tools.com	Keeps track of client lists—including addresses, phone numbers, and other idiosyncratic client information, such as birthdays—and organizes records of prior client contact and other customer-relevant information.
Sales Compensation Design Software	$alescom, from www.salesforcecompensation.com	Helps design base salary and/or incentive plans for any incentive-eligible position
Customer Relationship Management Software	Entice!, from www.multiactive.com	Integrates sales, marketing, and customer service, with e-commerce and wireless telephony, for online and offline marketing applications.

Recruiting, Training, and Compensating Salespeople: The Keys to Salesforce Performance

There is no guarantee that even a very well-designed and clearly communicated sales plan can be carried out effectively. Good implementation requires that the members of the salesforce have both the ability and the desire to meet management's expectations. Thus, as the bottom portion of Exhibit 14.9 indicates, implementing the sales program requires three more sets of management actions: First, management must **recruit and select** appropriate kinds of salespeople with the aptitude for effectively carrying out the activities involved in the job. Second, management must provide appropriate kinds and amounts of **training** to ensure that the salespeople have the knowledge and skills needed to do their jobs. Finally, management must design an attractive package of **compensation and other incentive rewards** to motivate the salesforce to expend the effort necessary to achieve good performance. For a more detail discussion of these key elements in sales program implementation see a text on salesforce management.[26]

Evaluating and Controlling Salesforce Performance to Ensure Delivery of Budgeted Results

Managers collect and evaluate information about their salespeople's performance and compare these data to the plan's objectives and forecasts to determine how well the salesforce is doing. The purpose is much like that of navigating a ship at sea. By determining where the ship is relative to its destination, the captain can see how well the ship is doing and make necessary corrections when it is off course.

Companies use three main approaches in monitoring the salesforce to evaluate and control sales performance.

1. **Sales analysis:** Managers monitor sales volume for each salesperson. In addition, they break down sales figures by geographic territory, by each product in the line, and by different types of customers. They compare results to the forecasts and quotas in the firm's sales plan to determine which salespeople are doing well and where adjustments may be needed.

2. **Cost analysis:** They can also monitor the costs of various selling activities such as travel and entertainment expenses. Managers often examine these across individual salespeople, districts, customers, and product types. However, this does present some difficult technical challenges about how certain costs, such as administrative costs and overhead, should be allocated. When put together with the results of a sales analysis, this procedure allows managers to evaluate the profitability of different territories, products, and customer types.

3. **Behavioral analysis:** When sales volume or profitability in a territory falls below expectations, managers may be uncertain as to the cause. Perhaps the salesperson in that territory is not working hard enough or is allocating effort to the wrong activities. Or the disappointing results could be due to factors beyond the salesperson's control, such as poor economic conditions or heavy competition in the territory. To gain a better understanding of the cause—and provide a better basis for taking corrective action—many managers believe it is necessary to monitor and evaluate the actual behavior of the salesperson as well as the outcomes of that behavior. They obtain much information for this kind of behavioral analysis from activity reports and call reports submitted by the salespeople. In addition, some firms use self-rating scales, field observations, and supervisor ratings to compile the needed information.

Many of these methods apply equally well to the evaluation and control of entire marketing programs, not just the salesforce, and we examine this topic in more detail in

Chapter 19. At this point, we have discussed the two principal elements in the promotion mix, advertising and personal selling. The two remaining elements, sales promotion and public relations, often play a secondary or supporting role to one or both of the first two elements. In some cases, however, especially in early-stage companies with limited marketing budgets, their roles can be more substantial.

Making Sales Promotion Decisions

The American Marketing Association defines **sales promotion** as "those marketing activities, other than personal selling, advertising, and publicity, that stimulate consumer purchasing and dealer effectiveness." Sales promotions typically offer an incentive to consumers and resellers to stimulate short-term demand for a product. As we saw in Chapter 13, sales promotion can be of two kinds: consumer promotion (targeted at consumers; often as part of a pull strategy) and trade promotion (targeted at channel members, often as part of a push strategy). More money is spent on sales promotion than on advertising in the United States. For example, Reebok launched a pan-European promotion for its new A6 shoe, using SMS, with several websites like mp3.com and Yahoo, running hip-hop and dance music ads.[27] More generally, expenditures for consumer promotions have lagged (especially for coupons) in recent years and are smaller than trade promotions.

Marketers use a variety of sales promotion techniques, the primary ones being price-off promotions, premiums, sampling, rebates, contests and sweepstakes, and trade promotions. The first four of these have been discussed earlier in Chapter 13 on pricing. The non–price-related promotion techniques are described below. As might be expected, trade allowances made to retailers by manufacturers dominate their promotional expenditures. More than half of all items sold by supermarkets are discounted.

- **Sampling** has become increasingly important because marketers have found more efficient ways to get samples to their target markets. Today's sampling promotions are cleverly designed so that shoppers who receive the samples use them right away. For example, Unilever handed out its personal hygiene products to students at the end of a sweaty fitness class, and Starbucks gave away free samples of its iced-coffee drink, Frappuccino, to commuters in Manhattan during a sweltering afternoon.[28]

- **Contests and sweepstakes** add interest to the sale of ordinary products. In a consumer contest, buyers compete for prizes on the basis of skill. Contests typically require proof of purchase to enter or the use of an entry form available only from a dealer. Popular formats for contests include naming new products or finding new uses for existing products as in the famous Pillsbury Bake-off in the Untied States. Sweepstakes, on the other hand, distribute prizes on the basis of chance and in many countries cannot require proof of purchase as a condition of entry. They are more popular than contests since no judges are required. But they do little to enhance the brand's image and often overshadow the product involved. Recently, several companies launched contests via text messages, where users send a text message with a code printed on products to be entered, for example, McDonald's in the United Kingdom to coincide with the launch of the new Disney movie *Monsters Inc.*[29]

- **Trade promotions** are used by manufacturers to stimulate resellers to improve their performance in a variety of ways, including contests and incentives for sales personnel, training a distributor's salesforce, and cooperative advertising and promotional allowances including in-store promotions. The latter is the most important. We discussed the role of trade promotions as incentives for distribution members in Chapter 13.

As is the case for advertising, designing a sales promotion program and budget involves choosing particular types of sales promotion and using experience to predict what the response rates are likely to be. Unlike advertising, for which considerable monies can be

KEY OBSERVATION

Sales promotion is less risky than advertising. Marketers also like it because its performance is usually easily measurable.

spent with little assurance that significant revenues will follow, many kinds of sales promotion require the customer to buy as the incentive is redeemed. This self-liquidating feature is true for coupons and rebates, for example, and for trade discounts to retailers who stock or display a new product. In this sense, sales promotion is less risky than advertising. Marketers also like it because its performance is usually easily measurable. As a result, and due also to scarce resources in small companies and to pressures on management in large public companies to deliver consistent short-term earnings, sales promotion is garnering an increasing share of many firms' total promotional budgets.

Making Public Relations Decisions

Public relations has many uses. One that is sometimes overlooked is its potential for marketing new products, whether goods or services. During the 1996 Christmas season in the United States, a publicist for Tyco Toys sent a Tickle-Me-Elmo (a Sesame Street character stuffed toy) to the son of a popular TV talk-show host, and several more to the producers of the show. The toy became an instant hit and the hottest toy of the season, and several stores across the country sold their entire stock within minutes. Tyco originally expected to sell 400,000 toys, but instead wiped out its inventory of a million, and projected it could have sold 2 million.[30]

KEY OBSERVATION

The major disadvantage is that publicity is beyond the company's control.

Public relations has several unique advantages (see Exhibit 14.4). It is credible; most people feel that the mass media have no reason to carry favorable information about a product unless it is true. Thus, public relations reinforces the firm's advertising campaign by increasing awareness and the believability of product claims. Publicity also makes it easier for the salesforce to present a case for the product. Also, it is low cost, in that there are few media costs. The major disadvantage is that publicity is beyond the company's control, not only as to whether the release will be run, but also what is finally said about the company and/or the product.

Of course, the media are not in business to provide free publicity to marketers. They only do so when they believe something is newsworthy because it is new, different, or tells an interesting story about a local person or organization. Because there is no cost entailed in having publicity picked up by the media, budgeting for public relations is easy—simply staff time to manage the effort—although many firms choose to use specialized public relations agencies to handle the media contacts. Fees for such activities, once negotiated, are easily budgeted, but whether a given public relations effort will actually attain the desired results is another story. Unfortunately, most public relations firms are unwilling to accept assignments in which they are paid based on performance.

Through public relations, firms communicate with a variety of publics, including the consumer (information about new products), the financial community and stockholders (improvement in the company's profitability), the community (the firm's being a good citizen), prospective employees (a good place to work), current employees (developing pride in the company), and suppliers (a good company with which to build an enduring relationship). This listing of audiences suggests that publicity can be used to accomplish different objectives among different groups. Such objectives range from simply increasing awareness of a company or its products to stimulating an actual response, such as sending for a free bulletin. Thus, public relations can play an important role in the development of an integrated marketing communication program.

Firms also use public relations to cope with an unexpected shock. This was the case with the public relations campaign Johnson & Johnson (J&J) mounted in the United States when seven people died from poisoned Tylenol capsules. In part because of its responsible and well-orchestrated public relations response, J&J was able to restore confidence in the company and its Tylenol brand. Whether Bridgestone/Firestone will be so fortunate in restoring long-term confidence in its tires and its service to consumers following its massive recall in the summer of 2000 (see Ethical Perspective 11.1 in Chapter 11) remains to be seen. Many observers felt at the time that its handling of the recall was not in the same league as that of Johnson & Johnson's handling of Tylenol's crisis.

TAKE-AWAYS

- Marketing managers in most companies face fundamental strategic decisions about whether to emphasize advertising or personal selling in their promotion mix. Identifying the strategic circumstances (see Exhibit 14.3) provides direction for these decisions.

- Getting marketing communications messages—of any kind, in any medium—noticed and understood is no easy task. Many ads and other communication attempts simply don't meet their objectives. Following the guidelines in this chapter will mitigate this risk.

- A clear understanding of one's target market is essential for planning and implementing an effective promotional program. Without such an understanding, money is likely to be wasted.

- Many marketing communications efforts are not easy to evaluate. Setting clear and measurable objectives up front facilitates doing so.

- New media, including the Internet, e-mail, and mobile telephones, are predicted to revolutionize ad spending, because their results—like those for direct marketing programs—can often be directly measured.

- In companies of all sizes, technology will play an increasingly meaningful role in managing sales and customer service efficiency and effectiveness. Caution must be exercised, however, to avoid sacrificing effectiveness for efficiency.

Self-diagnostic questions to test your ability to apply the analytical tools and concepts in this chapter to marketing decision making may be found at this book's website at www.mhhe.com/mullins05.

ENDNOTES

1. "Plug and Play," *The Economist,* July 24, 1999, p. 61.

2. Mark Vernon, "Integration of Media Content: The Key to Long Term Commercial Success," *Financial Times,* June 19, 2002, p. 5.

3. William F Arens, *Contemporary Advertising* (Burr Ridge, IL: Richard D. Irwin, 1996), pp. 198–203.

4. "2000 Marketing Fact Book," *Marketing News,* July 3, 2000, p. 13.

5. A study concerned primarily with packaged household goods raised considerable doubts as to whether increasing advertising budgets relative to competitors' increases sales. See Leonard Lodish, Magia Abraham, Stuart Kalmenson, Jeanne Levelsberger, Beth Lubetin, Bruce Richardson, and Mary Ellen Stevens, "How TV Advertising Works: A Meta-Analysis of 389 Real World Split Cable TV Advertising Experiments," *Journal of Marketing Research,* May 1995, p. 125.

6. John and Julian Simon, "Advertising and Economies of Scale: Critical Comments on the Evidence," *Journal of Industrial Consumers,* December 1983, pp. 229–41.

7. James Schroer, "Ad Spending: Growing Market Share," *Harvard Business Review,* January–February 1990, pp. 44–48.

8. Such a model was originally proposed by Russell H. Colley in *Defining Advertising Goals for Measured Advertising Results* (New York: Association of National Advertisers, 1961).

9. "No Surprise: Total Ad Spending Down 9.8% for 2001, Compared to Results in 2000, According to CMR," *Business Wire,* March 6, 2002.

10. Robert McLuhan, "Direct Marketing Bucks Slowdown—Below-the-Line Thrived in 2001 Despite Tough Conditions that Put . . . ," *Brand Republic,* July 5, 2002.

11. The structure of this section follows that used by William F. Arens in his book *Contemporary Advertising* (Burr Ridge, IL: Richard D. Irwin, 1996), chap. 14.

12. For a discussion of stadiums and vehicles as advertising vehicles, see William Spain, "For Stadiums the Game's the Dome Name," *Advertising Age,* March 4, 1996, p. S2; and Douglas Blackmon, "New Ad Vehicles: Police Cars, School Bus, Garage Truck," *The Wall Street Journal,* February 20, 1996, p. B1.

13. Ellen Newborne, "Brand Names Could Power On-Line Shopping Carts," *USA Today,* February 19, 1996, p. B1.

14. J. William Gurley, "How the Web Will Warp Advertising," *Fortune,* November 9, 1998, pp. 119–20.

15. Seth Godin, *Permission Marketing* (New York: Simon and Schuster, 1999).

16. Todd Pruzan, "Global Media," *Advertising Age International,* January 16, 1995, pp. 1–18.

17. "TV Advertising in India China Poised for Fastest Growth," *Financial Express,* June 23, 2002.

18. Based on an article by Allyson L. Steward-Alden, "Creative New Media in Europe Here to Stay?" *Marketing News,* June 3, 1996, p. 15.

19. See, for example, Gilbert A. Churchill, Jr., Neil M. Ford, and Orville C. Walker, Jr., *Sales Force Management,* 5th ed. (Burr Ridge, IL: Richard D. Irwin, 1997).

20. John S. Hill and Richard R. Still, "Organizing the Overseas Sales Force: How Multinationals Do It," *Journal of Personal Selling and Sales Management,* Spring 1990, pp. 57–66.

21. "Financial Express—WNS to Expand Ops, Plans to Open a Call Centre Down South," *Financial Express,* January 7, 2003; Jim O'Rourke, "News— IT Jobs Go Overseas for Lower Pay Rates," *Sun Herald,* December 29, 2002.

22. This section draws on information contained in a special report in *Business Week,* February 21, 2000, including Jay Greene, "Salesforce.com: An Ant at the Picnic," "A Guide to Customer Management Software," and "The Davids and Goliaths of Customer Service Software Square Off."

23. For more details see Siebel's website, http://www.siebel.com.

24. Kana Communications, http://www.kana.com.

25. Neiman Marcus added chat capability to its website so that its customers did not need to pick up the phone for a question. Ann Bednarz, "Retailers Poised for Seasonal Sales Rush," *Network World,* December 16, 2002.

26. See, for example, Churchill, Ford, and Walker, *Sales Force Management.*

27. Peter Crush, "Reebok Builds Email and SMS Database," *Brand Republic,* January 15, 2003.

28. Geoggrey A. Fowler, "Points of Sweat, Point of Thirst Marketing Offers Freebies When They Are Most Needed," *The Wall Street Journal,* August 12, 2001, p. B1.

29. "The Book of Lists—The 10 Best SMS Campaigns," *Brand Republic,* December 20, 2002.

30. Joseph Pereira, "Toy Story: How Shrewd Marketing Made Elmo a Hit," *The Wall Street Journal,* December 16, 1996, p. B1.

SECTION FOUR

STRATEGIC MARKETING PROGRAMS FOR SELECTED SITUATIONS

CHAPTER 15 Marketing Strategies for the New Economy

CHAPTER 16 Strategies for New and Growing Markets

CHAPTER 17 Strategic Choices for Mature and Declining Markets

CHAPTER FIFTEEN

Marketing Strategies for the New Economy

Chocolate Company Sweetens the Web[1]

WHAT CAN YOU GIVE for Christmas to the person who has everything? Chocolates, of course. But who has time these days to fight Christmas crowds in search of the perfect sweets? Thorntons, the longtime chocolatier, with more than 500 company-owned and franchised stores throughout the United Kingdom, has an online answer. And the Thorntons website at www.thorntons.co.uk doesn't stop at just chocolates. A variety of gift ideas from chocolates to flowers to teddy bears makes Thorntons a one-stop shopping destination for even the most perplexed of gift givers.

Thorntons Goes Online

After some experiments with the Internet in 1997 and 1998, Thorntons decided to get serious about its online effort in 1999. It asked the web design firm Clockworx to develop a site that would enable the venerable chocolate company to make its Internet strategy a centerpiece for growth. In February 1999, the Thorntons Gift Delivery Service was launched to provide an additional sales channel to complement the company's ubiquitous retail outlets and its mail order sales operation. After just a few months in business, it became clear that there was significant potential for growth. "It became necessary—and cost-effective—to develop a degree of integration with the back-end order system," said Clockworx managing director Robin Edwards.

"As this was a major step, we took the opportunity to further develop the customer experience at the front end. This work was based on our continual research into what makes a visitor become a customer, focusing on elements such as the ease of use, trustworthiness of the branding, site speed, overall design and presentation of the products themselves."

Sweet Rewards

Thorntons' website has delivered sweet rewards to Thorntons shareholders in many ways. It supports the company's offline marketing efforts. It directs retail shoppers to the location of the nearest Thorntons store, thereby increasing store traffic. Its biggest contribution, though, has been to fuel top-line sales growth through direct sales to consumers. In the year ended June 2002, Thorntons' e-commerce and mail order sales grew 89 percent over the prior year to £4.2 million, a figure that represents more than one-third of the company's overall growth from £158 to £163.8 million. How has this happened? "The conversion rate—a key measure of the effectiveness of the site—often exceeds 20 percent, compared with a typical one percent for many other large scale e-commerce sites," says Clockworx' Edwards. *New Media Age* ranked the Thorntons site as one of the fastest during the 2002 Valentine's season, an important usability issue for time-pressed consumers. Its overall speed and quick

Courtesy Thorntons PLC

transaction process encourage repeat purchases. Thorntons' head of e-commerce, David McQueen-Johnston, says the site "will continue to be our fastest growing sales channel," making Thorntons a true multichannel business.

Another key benefit has emerged as well. In the highly seasonal candy business, where sales soar around the key gift-giving holidays like Valentine's Day, the site has helped consumers and management alike get through peak seasons more easily and efficiently. "Without it our call centre would be twice the size," reports McQueen-Johnston. "We would struggle

at peak seasons. With over 50 percent of our high season daytime sales coming through the site," the operations benefits are as noteworthy as the added revenues.

Thorntons' experience with online sales highlights the potential that new-economy technologies can offer to long-established companies. As the United Kingdom's best-known confectioner, Thorntons is not about to rest on its laurels. Whether it's a box of chocolates at Valentine's Day, a teddy bear for Christmas, or corporate gifts for this year's best clients, Thorntons' new-economy solutions have made gift giving easy for U.K. consumers. And the chocolates still taste as good as ever!

Marketing Challenges Addressed in Chapter 15

As the Thornton's example shows, the opportunities presented by the Internet and other sectors of the new economy can transform old-economy companies and provide compelling opportunities for growth. Leaders of virtually every company today are, at a minimum, wondering what they should do about the Internet, the development of new communications media and technologies from broadband cable to mobile telephony, and other such developments. Some are committing significant resources in hopes of taking advantage of these new developments. But the optimal path through the new-economy maze is far from clear for most companies.

Thus, in Chapter 15, we address several timely and important questions that marketing managers in today's companies and entrepreneurs must ask. Does the company need a new-economy strategy? Do the technological advances of the new economy represent threats or opportunities? Most importantly, how should marketers address the development of strategies to take advantage of—or defend against—the rapid pace of change inherent in the new economy: What marketing roles can the Internet and other recent and future technological developments play, and which of these should be pursued?

KEY OBSERVATION

What marketing roles can the Internet and other recent and future technological developments play, and which of these should be pursued?

We begin by reviewing several trends that highlight the growing importance of the Internet and other new-economy technological developments. We then identify the key advantages and disadvantages inherent in new-economy phenomena, all of which every company must clearly understand. Next, we identify the marketing roles that new-economy technologies can plausibly play in marketing strategies, and we articulate a decision framework for managers to use to decide which of the growing array of new-economy tools their firms should employ—from Web-based marketing research to advertising on mobile phones to the delivery of digitized information, goods, and services over the Web. Finally, we examine what has gone wrong in the dot.com world to date, and we identify some key success factors in developing market offerings to successfully serve new-economy markets.

355

Does Every Company Need a New-Economy Strategy?

Like it or not, the **new economy** is here to stay, notwithstanding the dot.com bust at the dawn of the new millennium. But exactly what do people mean by this ubiquitous phrase? By new economy, we mean the industries that fuel the development of or participate significantly in electronic commerce and the Internet, develop and market computer hardware and software, and develop or provide any of the growing array of telecommunications services. The obvious players are dot.com retailers such as Amazon, Web portals like Yahoo! and America Online, companies like Cisco and 3Com that make much of the hardware on which the Internet runs, software firms such as Microsoft, and telecom companies like AT&T, Vodafone, and iMode whose communications networks permit the transmission of voice or data over various kinds of wire-line, wireless, and satellite networks in the United States, Europe, and Japan respectively.

However, many formerly old-economy companies are making increasingly significant commitments to new-economy technologies. Longtime bricks-and-mortar retailers like Gap and Wal-Mart, century-old manufacturing companies large and small whose electronic data interchange (EDI) systems are critical to their sourcing and/or selling, and service businesses such as Kinko's, the chain of print shops, are all committed to the new economy in one way or another. These days, every company is asking itself, "Do we need an Internet (or other new-economy-based) strategy?"

The growing adoption in both consumer and commercial sectors of the Internet, wireless telephony, and other new-economy technologies is making this question an imperative one. The growing penetration of broadband connections, which serve 18 percent of Internet users in the United States, 23 percent in Sweden, and a stunning 94 percent in South Korea means that new services that rely on high-speed data transfer are becoming viable.[2] Broadband connections, which permit data transmission dramatically faster than the more common 56K modems, will, according to Gartner, account for three-quarters of the $10,000 worth of goods and services that Gartner says will be bought online on average by each U.S. household in 2006.[3]

And the new economy is not just an American phenomenon. In 2000, nearly 400 million people worldwide had online access, of which only one-third were in the United States (see Exhibit 15.1).[4] Mobile telephones, more prevalent in Europe than in the United States, surpass 100 percent penetration in some countries. By 2003, new technologies had made the newest mobile phones able to receive images and advertisements and provide users with mobile access to the Web. Adding GPS (global positioning satellite) technology to the mix makes the possibilities even more intriguing, since marketers will know both *who* and *where* we are!

Online consumer spending also continues to grow. In certain markets like books, music, electronics, and toys, online shopping accounted for as much as 23 percent of U.S. retail sales in 2002, and online sales were growing at 30–40 percent per year, compared to 4 percent in conventional offline retailing.[5] American holiday shoppers spent $7.9 billion online during the Christmas season in 2002, up 23 percent from the comparable period the prior year, despite the fact that the Thanksgiving-Christmas period was six days shorter in 2002.[6]

The same sort of growth is also happening in business-to-business e-commerce. While **B2B (business-to-business)** e-commerce accounted for only $215 million in 1999 (not

Exhibit 15.1

TOP 10 COUNTRIES IN INTERNET USE

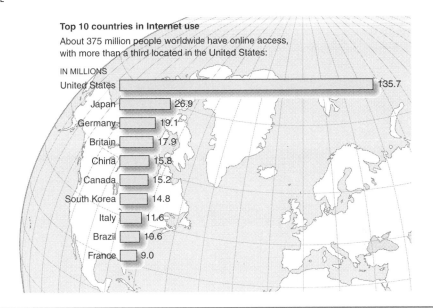

Top 10 countries in Internet use

About 375 million people worldwide have online access,
with more than a third located in the United States:

IN MILLIONS

United States	135.7
Japan	26.9
Germany	19.1
Britain	17.9
China	15.8
Canada	15.2
South Korea	14.8
Italy	11.6
Brazil	10.6
France	9.0

Source: *Newsweek*, "Top 10 Countries in Internet Use," October 2, 2000, p. 74L. © 2000 Newsweek, Inc. All rights reserved. Reprinted by permission.

counting business done via EDI channels), according to AMR Research Inc., or just 1.4 percent of all commercial transactions, it was expected to explode to $5.7 trillion by 2004.

What should marketers conclude from these trends? Notwithstanding the ups and downs of stock market valuations of new-economy companies, notwithstanding the difficulties many B2B and **B2C (business-to-consumer)** companies are having in developing business models that actually make money,[7] and notwithstanding the so-called digital divide, in which some segments of the population are still underrepresented in the Internet population, the long-term prospects for doing business in the new economy are still enormous. The growing market acceptance of and the inherent advantages that the Internet and other new-economy technologies bring, suggest that nearly every company needs to examine how it will be affected by and can take advantage of these new technol-

KEY OBSERVATION

Every company needs to examine how it will be affected by and can take advantage of these new technologies.

ogies (see Exhibit 15.2). The rapid pace of Internet adoption outside the United States suggests that the same can be said in most other developed and developing countries.

The outcome of such an examination should be the development of one's own new-economy strategy. The fact that one's competitors will surely develop and deploy such strategies is a further argument for doing so. But marketers should take heart, for the good news is this. "In the end, e-consumers and e-businesses aren't so different from traditional buyers and sellers after all. Customers are, by and large, pragmatists—be they individuals looking for a new shirt, or a big automaker looking for a new source of steel. When the e-way is easier, faster, and cheaper, it can win."[8] Today's well-educated business students can bring these insights—as well as new-economy expertise—to the companies they join.

Exhibit 15.2

CONVERTING BROWSERS TO BUYERS IN ONLINE RETAILING

Big Spenders
While online retail sales are projected to grow (figures in billions)...

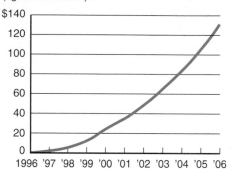

How Stores Score
The conversion rates of some big-name e-tailers.

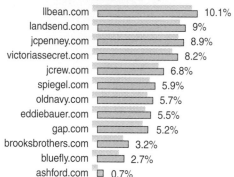

llbean.com	10.1%
landsend.com	9%
jcpenney.com	8.9%
victoriassecret.com	8.2%
jcrew.com	6.8%
spiegel.com	5.9%
oldnavy.com	5.7%
eddiebauer.com	5.5%
gap.com	5.2%
brooksbrothers.com	3.2%
bluefly.com	2.7%
ashford.com	0.7%

...But Few Spenders
...The percentage of browsers who actually buy something (the "conversion rate") remains slim in most categories.

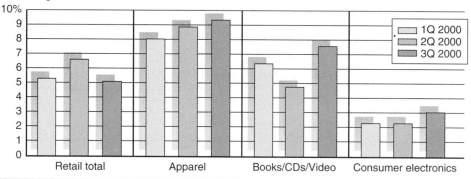

Source: Michael Totty, "Making the Sale," *The Wall Street Journal,* September 24, 2001, p. R6. Copyright 2001 by Dow Jones & Co., Inc. Reprinted by permission of Dow Jones & Co., Inc. via the Copyright Clearance Center.

Threats or Opportunities? The Inherent Advantages and Disadvantages of the New Economy for Marketers

What advantages do new-economy technologies provide to marketers and their customers? Seven potentially attractive elements characterize many new-economy technologies: the syndication of information, the increasing returns to scale of network products, the ability to efficiently personalize and customize market offerings, the ability to disintermediate distribution, global reach, round-the-clock access, and the possibility of instantaneous delivery.

The Syndication of Information[9]

Syndication involves the sale of the same good—typically an informational good—to many customers, who then combine it with information from other sources and distribute it. The entertainment and publishing worlds have long employed syndication, producing comic strips, newspaper columns, and TV shows that appear in many places at once. Without syndication, today's mass media would not exist as we know it. Though Internet marketers rarely use the word *syndication* to describe what they do, it lies at the heart of many e-commerce business models. Inktomi, an **originator** of syndicated content, provides its search engine technology to many branded search engine sites. Screaming Media, a **syndicator,** collects articles in electronic form and delivers relevant portions of this content to more than 500 sites, each of which appeals to a different target audience. E*Trade, a **distributor** of syndicated information, brings together from many sources content relevant to its investor clientele and packages it in ways useful to these clients. iMode, the mobile operator in Japan, syndicates an enormous variety of information—even cartoons.[10]

Why is syndication important? First, because syndication deals with informational goods (digitized text, music, photos, CAD/CAM files, and so on), rather than tangible goods, a company can syndicate the same informational goods or services to an almost infinite number of customers with little incremental cost. Variable costs approach zero. Producers of tangible goods and most services (Thornton's chocolates, for example, or haircuts) must spend money on sugar and chocolate or labor for each additional candy bar or haircut sold. Not so for information producers, where sending a digital copy of a photo or an Internet news feature to one more recipient is essentially free. Second, the syndication process can be automated and digitized, enabling syndicated networks to be created, expanded, and flexibly adapted far more quickly than would be possible in the physical world.

Syndication via the Internet—and soon, perhaps, via mobile phones or other mobile devices—opens up endless opportunities for marketers. It replaces scarcity with abundance. Information can be replicated an infinite number of times and combined and recombined in an infinite number of ways. It can be distributed everywhere, all at once, and be available all the time. Taking advantage of this potential, however, requires new thinking. Companies need to identify and occupy the most important niches in syndication networks. These are the ones that maximize the number and strength of links to other companies and customers, though shifting market conditions inevitably mean that these links must change as markets evolve. Bloomberg, the provider of syndicated information to stock traders and analysts, is an example of a company that has positioned itself well; many of its clients now regard their Bloomberg terminals as indispensable. Thus, almost any company can think of itself as part of a larger, interconnected world and seek ways to occupy originator, syndicator, or distributor roles in an appropriate syndication network.

KEY OBSERVATION

Syndication via the Internet—and soon, perhaps, via mobile phones or other mobile devices—opens up endless opportunities for marketers.

Increasing Returns to Scale of Network Products[11]

Any undergraduate economics student knows that an increased supply of a good leads to lower value, hence lower prices. But that was before fax machines, operating systems, and other products used in networks, where the second fax machine, for example, makes the first one more valuable, and so on. This characteristic of informational networks—a product becomes more valuable as the number of users increases—is often called a **positive network effect** or **network externality.** When combined with the syndication of informational products, this characteristic has led to the seemingly crazy strategy of giving one's Internet product away for free, often a strategy of choice for new-economy marketers! Hotmail, whose e-mail software costs users nothing, creates value for advertisers and others in the large network that it has created.

Companies that can identify and exploit opportunities where they can benefit from the **increasing returns to scale** that result from positive network effects can sometimes grow very quickly on relatively modest capital investment. If Thornton's is successful in building a community of chocolate lovers, the increasing returns of this growing community will benefit Thornton's as well as its customers.

The Ability to Efficiently Personalize and Customize Market Offerings

Amazon tracks the books I buy and, using a technology known as **collaborative filtering,** is able to compare my purchases with those of others and thereby recommend to me books they think I would like, personalized to my taste and reading habits, as Amazon understands them (see Exhibit 15.3). If they do this well, my purchases go up, and I become a happier customer because Amazon helps me find books I want to read. While collaborative filtering technology has a long way to go (the book I bought for my daughter when she was leaving for a semester in Ecuador does not make me a Latin American culture buff!) the potential of this and other new-economy technologies offers the promise of creating sharply targeted market segments—ultimately, market segments of one.

Collaborative filtering is but one way of personalizing a market offering to each customer. When formal decision rules can be identified in the way customers behave (for example, reminding customers of, or making special offers for, upcoming birthdays or offering supplementary items based on past purchases), **rules-based personalization** can

Exhibit 15.3

PERSONALIZATION THROUGH COLLABORATIVE FILTERING

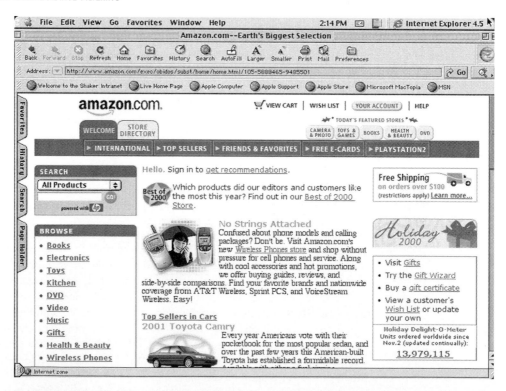

be done. The most predictive rules, however, may require customers to divulge information that they do not want to take the time, or are not willing, to divulge.

Customization techniques, which are user-driven instead of marketer-driven (as we have seen for personalization approaches), allow users to specify the nature of what is offered to them. Several office supply firms, for example, now offer corporate users the ability to create customized office supply catalogs tailored to their company. Such catalogs simplify ordering procedures, save time and money in the purchasing department, and help control expense by offering to perhaps far-flung employees only what the purchasing department has approved in advance. Similarly, some online music sellers offer consumers the opportunity to order customized CDs consisting of only the songs the customer chooses. In today's highly competitive markets, personalization and customization can help build customer loyalty and make it less likely for customers to switch to other suppliers.

Disintermediation and Restructuring of Distribution Channels

Many goods and services are sold through distribution channels, as we saw in Chapter 13. The Internet makes it possible for marketers to reach customers directly, without the expense or complication of distribution channels, a phenomenon known as **disintermediation.** Tina Lockwood, whose online crafts business SparkleCraft.com got started on the Web, says that without the Internet, "It would've taken a lot longer to get started, and with a store, you have to have a lot of money upfront for rent and utilities and fixtures and whatever else is involved with a storefront." At the beginning, Lockwood's virtual store cost just $15 per year for the domain name rights, plus a similar sum each month for Web hosting. She learned Web-page programming and built the site herself.[12]

Another firm to take advantage of the Internet in a similar way is Random House, the publisher, which has announced plans to offer electronic versions of 100 classic works in its literary library, such as James Joyce's *Ulysses,* for as little as $4.95 online.[13] Rather than selling direct, however, Random House will sell through specialty sites, such as Shakespeare.com, as well as through some established online book retailers. Thus, rather than disintermediating its channel for these books, Random House is simply restructuring it to take advantage of the Web's increasing reach.

Deciding to disintermediate or restructure one's channel, however, should not be done lightly. Levi Strauss, the jeans maker, angered its existing retailers by offering custom-fit

KEY OBSERVATION

Deciding to disintermediate or restructure one's channel, however, should not be done lightly.

jeans direct to consumers via the Web. Ultimately, the company withdrew the offering due in part to the howls of protest it heard from its regular retail channel members. Similar concerns have arisen in the travel industry, as airlines and others have sought to disintermediate travel agents by selling airline tickets and other travel services directly to consumers via the Web. Someone must perform the functions normally performed by channel members—taking orders, delivering products, collecting payment, and so on—so those who consider disintermediating their channels and selling direct must determine how they will perform these functions and must evaluate whether doing so is more effective and efficient than using intermediaries.

Global Reach, 24×7 Access, and Instantaneous Delivery

With the Internet and other new-economy technologies, typically there is no extra cost entailed in making information, digital goods, or services available anywhere one can gain access to the Web—literally, **global reach;** making them available 24 hours per day, seven days per week, 52 weeks per year; and, in some cases, providing instantaneous delivery. In our increasingly time-pressed world, access and service like this can be of great value to customers. Thornton's online store, for example, is always open. EasyJet, a rapidly growing low-priced airline in Europe, sells a large proportion of its tickets on its own website, many of them to international travelers who reserve flights from afar, even from another continent. Flight confirmations are delivered instantly. Software vendors whose products may be purchased and instantaneously downloaded from the Web provide similar responsiveness. As mobile telephony and GPS technologies develop, similar benefits will be available to customers and marketers whose products are well suited to mobile media. Is anyone up for portable music downloaded to one's cell phone from the Internet?[14] How about a free salad with a pizza, today only, at the restaurant just around the corner?

Are These New-Economy Attributes Opportunities or Threats?

Most marketers can choose to take advantage of one or more of the benefits offered by new-economy technologies, including those we have outlined above. To that extent, these technologies constitute opportunities available to marketers who employ them. Viewed differently, however, they raise complex ethical issues (see Ethical Perspectives 15.1 and 15.2) and they also present potentially significant threats.

First, the fact that the variable cost for syndicated goods approaches zero sounds like a good thing, until one realizes that for most products, price, over the long run, usually is not far from variable cost. If variable cost is zero, will prices drop to near zero, too? If so, such an outcome would represent disaster for information producers. Several companies once thought that providing lists of telephone numbers on CD-ROMs might be a good business. After all, it costs less than a dollar to produce a CD-ROM once the content is ready, and lists of phone numbers had already been compiled by the telephone companies. Alas for these marketers (or happily for consumers), numerous competitors rushed into the market,

ETHICAL PERSPECTIVE 15.1
Will E-Commerce Erode Liberty?

Cyberspace is evolving in ways that could threaten privacy and other constitutional rights. A vigorous debate has ensued over whether the government should put its finger in the Internet pie to protect these rights, or whether markets and consumers themselves are up to the task. To some, the Internet is a vast, out-of-control copying machine, spewing out an unlimited number of free copies of intellectual property rightfully owned by its creators. Further, they say, cyberspace is polluting households and schools with objectionable material too easily accessed by children. Others argue that the rapid progress in encryption technology will provide greater protection to copyright owners and families than has been available since Gutenberg's invention of the printing press. Whatever the outcome of the debate, there can be little doubt that the Internet has been an extraor-

dinary boon to free speech—for better or worse—as anyone with Web access is free to disseminate his or her ideas, before regulators or other watchdogs even know what has appeared.

A number of possible solutions to these problems have been proposed. One is to provide filters so that Internet surfers can block speech or other material they dislike. But if such filtering is done upstream—by portals or others—it could become a powerful form of censorship. Another has to do with the increasingly rich trove of information on consumer surfing behavior. Optimists wonder whether firms will compete for customers by using such data to better serve customers, while respecting their privacy, perhaps by using reputable third parties to vouch for their practices. Is it Big Brother? Or is it customer service? Who will decide—government or the marketplace?

Source: Carl Shapiro, "Will E-Commerce Erode Liberty," *Harvard Business Review,* May–June 2000, pp. 189–96.

and with undifferentiated products they were soon forced to compete on price alone. Prices plunged. CD phone books, originally priced in 1986 at $10,000 per copy, soon sold for a few dollars in discount software bins.[15]

Selling music on the Internet also seemed like a good idea to music publishers and even to artists. Imagine getting $12 to $15 for the music on a CD, with no retailers or distributors to take cuts of the revenue, and no costs to pay for fancy packaging! Disintermediation sounds good, if you are a music publisher, but it's a threat if you're a music retailer, even a Web-based one like Amazon! But Napster, Gnutella, and others developed ways to enable consumers to share and download music—and other kinds of files—for free.[16] The music labels and artists, of course, were less than excited about Napster's delivery of their music to consumers for free, fearing that such delivery would eliminate the need for consumers to buy CDs. Lawsuits ensued and Napster was required to remove copyrighted material from its site. While it is not clear at this writing how Internet distribution of music will play out, the fact that the variable cost of downloading the music on a CD is now essentially zero will likely have a profound effect on the pricing of recorded music in the long run, notwithstanding the current copyright laws that exist to protect the intellectual property of the musicians and songwriters.

> **KEY OBSERVATION**
>
> *The fact that the variable cost for syndicated goods approaches zero sounds like a good thing, until one realizes that for most products, price, over the long run, usually is not far from variable cost. If variable cost is zero, will prices drop to near zero, too?*

Another threat to new-economy technologies is that there are few barriers to entry, and most Internet strategies are easily imitated. Numerous book retailers are challenging Amazon. eBay's entry into European markets has made life difficult for QXL and other European online auction businesses. In 2002, eBay's German unit alone contributed 16 percent of eBay's total revenue.[17] Unless one can patent one's method of doing business on the Web, as has Amazon with its 1-Click® ordering system or Priceline.com with its approach to selling cut-rate airline tickets online, it is likely that one's competitive advantage in the online space will not be sustainable. Even for Amazon and Priceline, long-term success is by no means assured.[18]

Other threats include privacy and security issues, which can drive away customers rather than attract them if they are not handled with care. In Exhibit 15.4, we discuss the impact of the Internet's global reach on privacy issues. The most restrictive jurisdictions' privacy rules may eventually apply to Internet marketers anywhere. Privacy laws in Europe, compared to the United States, are substantially more strict, as is discussed in Exhibit 15.4.

Similarly for security, customers are wary of providing too much information to online marketers, even though that information might help the marketer tailor its offerings to the

---

ETHICAL PERSPECTIVE 15.2
Internet Scams Bring Government Lawsuits

Miracle products that don't do what they promise. Credit-card theft. Pyramid schemes. Bogus vacation bargains. All these old tricks are finding new life on the Internet, changing the way law enforcement agencies and consumer protection groups do business. The U.S. Federal Trade Commission and other governmental agencies brought more than 250 lawsuits against online scam artists in 2000. To deal effectively with the global reach that the Internet affords such scams,

the FTC is working to create an international network of consumer protection agencies, now comprised of more than 240 agencies around the globe. But differing laws in various jurisdictions make such efforts difficult. What's considered legal in one place may not be in another. But ethical? Who is to say? Jodie Bernstein, the FTC's director of consumer protection, is resolute in her efforts. "We want dot.con artists to know that consumer protection spans the globe, physically and in cyberspace," says Bernstein.

Source: Steve Raabe, "FTC Crackdown Details Internet Scams, Vows Crackdown on 'Dot-Cons,'" *Denver Post,* November 1, 2000, p. C1.

Exhibit 15.4   The Impact of Global Reach on Internet Privacy

Stefano Rodata is Italy's top privacy cop. His job, as president of the Italian Data Privacy Protection committee, is to ensure compliance with Italy's strict privacy laws. "People have a right to be left alone," says Rodata. A recent and uneasy truce between European authorities and the United States, a so-called "safe harbor" agreement, provides a set of privacy guidelines that U.S. firms doing online business in Europe can follow to avoid European Union legal action when Europeans fill out registration forms or make purchases on U.S. websites. Exporting personal data in this manner to countries that don't meet EU privacy standards is unlawful in Europe. The draft agreement, along with other information, can be found at http://europa.eu.int/comm/internal_market/en/media/dataprot/index.htm.

In the United States, Internet privacy has been dealt with largely through market forces, whereby consumers are expected to avoid sites where privacy is not handled to their liking. As firms attempt to take advantage of the global reach afforded by the Internet, will they run afoul of privacy laws in countries whose consumers they serve? In what jurisdictions will complaints be heard and dealt with? Will the most restrictive countries end up ruling the roost? These privacy questions are far from settled.

Source: Thomas E. Weber, "Europe and U. S. Reach Truce on Net Privacy, But What Comes Next?" *The Wall Street Journal,* June 19, 2000, p. B1. Copyright 2000 by Dow Jones & Co., Inc. Reprinted by permission of Dow Jones & Co., Inc. via the Copyright Clearance Center.

customer's benefit. Potential misuse of credit-card numbers and other personal information still concerns many users. The use of so-called **cookies,** electronic markers that enable websites to track whose computer visits them, for how long, and in what sequence, provides a wealth of consumer behavior data that marketers hope to use to personalize their offerings to customers. But how many customers want their **click-streams** tracked by an electronic Sherlock Holmes? Would a candidate for public office want the press to examine and make public his or her online shopping behavior?

Ultimately, a marketer's best defenses against these disadvantages are likely to take either of two forms. One defense is through the patent and copyright system, though as the Napster example shows, such protection may not be effective as new technologies are developed that make the protection of intellectual property problematic. A second defense is through what Carl Shapiro and Hal Varian call **versioning.**[19] Shapiro and Varian argue that, even for information products whose variable cost approaches zero, the value of information to different kinds of customers is likely to vary substantially. Marketers who determine which features will be valuable to some customers, but of little value to others, can package and repackage information differently and serve market segments with margins that need not fall to zero.

Versioning can be done on many dimensions: time (which users value getting the information sooner than others?); convenience (can we restrict the place or degree of access to some users?); comprehensiveness (which users need detail? Which only need the big picture?); manipulation (which users want to be able to manipulate, duplicate, process, store, or print the information?); community (which users want to discuss information with others?); support (who needs, and will pay for, support?). Other dimensions on which versioning can be based include freedom from annoyance, speed, user interfaces, image resolution (for visual images, such as stock photos), and more not yet imagined. By tailoring the same core information to the varied needs of different buyers, the unusual economics of information can work to the advantage of the seller, while providing excellent value to the buyer. Skills in market segmentation and targeting, differentiation, and positioning—skills developed earlier in this book—are needed to

KEY OBSERVATION

Skills in market segmentation and targeting, differentiation, and positioning—skills developed earlier in this book—are needed to enable marketers to best take advantage of new-economy technologies and mitigate their disadvantages.

enable marketers to best take advantage of new-economy technologies and mitigate their disadvantages.

First-Mover Advantage: Fact or Fiction?[20]

In the Internet gold rush in the late 1990s, the key to Internet success was said to be **first-mover advantage.** The first firm to establish a significant presence in each market niche would be the one that succeeded. Thus, Amazon would win in books. eBay would win in auctions. Autobytel would win in the automotive sector. And so on. Later followers need not bother. But is first-mover advantage real?

As we saw in Chapter 9, being the first mover does bring some potential advantages, but not all first movers are able to capitalize on those advantages. Thus, many are surpassed over time by later entrants. One thing a pioneer must do to hold on to its early leadership position is to continue to innovate in order to maintain a differential advantage over the many imitators likely to arrive late to the party but eager to get in.

Jim Collins, co-author of the best-sellers *Good to Great* and *Built to Last* is more blunt about the supposed rule that nothing is as important as being first to reach scale. "It's wrong," he says. "Best beats first."[21] As Collins points out, VisiCalc was the first major personal computer spreadsheet. Where is VisiCalc today? It lost the battle to Lotus 1-2-3, which in turn lost to Excel. What about the now-ubiquitous Palm Pilot? It came to market years after early leader Sharp and the Apple Newton. Palm Pilot's designers found a better way to design personal digital assistants—using one reliable script, instead of everyone's own script—and have sold 6 million units.[22] But its current advantage may not last, as Handspring and Blackberry have begun nipping at Palm Pilot's heels. America Online, another new-economy star, got to its leading position by being better, not first.

In the old economy, Wal-Mart didn't pioneer discount retailing. Nucor didn't pioneer the minimill for making steel from scrap. Starbucks didn't pioneer the high-end coffee shop. Yet all were winners, while the early leaders fell behind or disappeared. None of these entrants were first—they were *better.* Being first may help attract investors and may make some founders and venture capitalists rich, but it's hardly a recipe for building a great company. In his book *Digital Darwinism,* Evan Schwartz identifies seven strategies for surviving in the digital economy. Being the first mover is not among them.[23]

KEY OBSERVATION

Being first may help attract investors and make some founders and venture capitalists rich, but it's hardly a recipe for building a great company.

Developing a New-Economy Strategy: A Decision Framework

Most companies of substantial size or scope will need to develop strategies to take advantage of new-economy technologies, but doing so is easier said than done. This is new ground in most companies as it was for Thorntons. In several earlier chapters, we identified recent software applications with the potential for helping marketers be more effective and efficient in their marketing decision making and marketing activities. To some observers, such applications fall within the scope of the new economy. In this section, we examine areas in which even newer new-economy technologies have widespread marketing applications. While we recognize that other non-marketing applications may also be compelling for many companies, our focus remains on marketing, for which, as Peter Sealey points out, productivity gains have been hard to come by.[24] Sealey argues that major advances in marketing productivity will depend on the broader use of information. That will happen only when companies fully leverage the power of the Internet, he says. Thus, in this section we focus on how the Internet—and, for some applications, mobile telephony—can fruitfully be employed for marketing purposes.[25]

Marketing Applications for New-Economy Tools

In the first chapter of this book we pointed out that a number of activities have to be performed by somebody for an exchange transaction to occur between a selling firm and a potential customer. Retaining that customer for future transactions adds additional activities, such as providing effective and responsive customer service after the sale. From the customer's point of view, these necessary activities can be summarized in a six-stage **consumer experience process** that begins with communicating one's wants and needs to prospective sellers; moving through the awareness, purchase, and delivery processes; obtaining any necessary service or support after the purchase to support its use or consumption; and ultimately sometimes returning or disposing of the product (we identify the six stages from the marketer's perspective in Exhibit 15.5). Customers first provide information about their needs to sellers, whose **customer insight** permits them to develop goods or services intended to meet the customer's needs. This stage in the process requires that information flow from customer to seller, as shown in Exhibit 15.5. While there may be several back-and-forth iterations in the insight stage, as new product developers invent and refine their product ideas, ultimately some good or service is developed, and information about the new product—**promotion and brand building**—then flows to customers, to inform and encourage them to buy. If the customer likes what is offered, a **transaction** ensues, requiring that information about pricing, terms, delivery, and so on flow both ways. With a transaction consummated, **delivery** of the good or service is made, with the product flowing to the customer and money or other compensation flowing to the seller. But the seller's job is not yet done, for the customer may need some kind of **customer support or service** during use, in which case additional information may flow in either direction or additional goods or services may flow to the customer, possibly in exchange for additional revenue. Finally, the customer may need to **return, dispose** of, or discontinue use of the good or service, at which point the product may be returned to the seller, cash may flow

Exhibit 15.5

A CUSTOMER EXPERIENCE MODEL FOR NEW-ECONOMY MARKETING DECISION MAKING

Stage in customer experience process	Direction of information flows	Direction of product flows (goods or services)	Direction of cash flows (revenue opportunities)
Customer insight	P ◄—— C		
Product promotion and brand building	P ——► C		
Transaction	P ◄——► C		
Product delivery		P ——► C	P ◄—— C
Customer support and service	P ◄——► C	P ——► C	P ◄—— C
Product return or disposal		P ◄—— C	P ◄—— C

P = Producer
C = Customer

back to the customer (as a result of the product's return or some kind of trade-in, perhaps), and another transaction—with this or another seller—may ensue, thereby repeating much of the process.

The Internet and, to a more limited extent, mobile telephony offer applications at some or all of these stages. We now explore some of these applications; though in this fast-moving arena, new ones will undoubtedly arise before the ink is dry on this book. Then, in the next section, we set forth a decision framework to assist marketers in deciding for which of these stages, and with which applications, new-economy tools should become part of their strategies.

Internet Applications for Customer Insight

In Chapters 7 and 11, we discussed the role of marketing research in understanding customers and developing products—whether goods or services—to meet their needs. Marketers rely on a flow of information from customers or prospective customers about their wants and needs, however latent these may sometimes be, to generate the insight essential to the development of compelling new products (see Exhibit 15.5). How might the Internet facilitate this process?

Pollsters and other marketing researchers are increasingly turning to the Internet to conduct marketing research. Why? Just as Internet marketers see the potential for "easier, faster, and cheaper," so too do researchers when they consider the Internet. For example, in years past, when Hewlett-Packard wanted to know what customers thought about its printers, it sent thousands of surveys through the mail, either on paper or on a computer diskette. It was a cumbersome process and "very expensive," says H-P market analyst Anita Hughes.[26] Now, H-P sends customers to a website to gather feedback. The new approach saves time and money and allows greater depth in the research—targeting specific respondents with instant follow-ups, for instance, or showing product prototypes online. "The possibilities are just huge," says Hughes. H-P uses Greenfield Online, one of a growing number of firms that specialize in Web-based marketing research. In fact, some observers now view Internet-based quantitative research as the wave of the future, due to its cost-cutting, time-saving advantages over traditional telephone, mail and mall-intercept surveys.[27]

Nonetheless, using the Web for research is not without controversy. Traditional researchers debate the Web's merits on a number of dimensions: in terms of representativeness of the current makeup of the Web audience, largely whiter, richer, younger, and more educated than the population as a whole; in terms of self-selection biases, where people volunteer to participate in Web-based polls; and in terms of the randomness, or lack thereof, of Web samples. But many of these problems are present in other forms of research, too, especially as more people refuse to answer mail or telephone surveys. As is the case for these other forms, some of these problems can be mitigated (see Exhibit 15.6).

KEY OBSERVATION

Using the Web for research is not without controversy.

Where random sampling is not an issue, such as for small-scale qualitative research such as focus groups, the Web may be particularly attractive. Greenfield Online recently ran an online focus group for Ford Motor Company in which 17 people who drive sport utility vehicles participated in three live chat sessions. Juli Caltrider, the Ford Expedition brand manager, followed the discussion from her own computer and occasionally interjected questions herself. Was the effort successful for Ford? "I got information faster, [and] I got additional depth in the information that I don't believe I would have gotten otherwise," Caltrider says. The downside was her inability to see facial expressions or read the participants' body language.

Using Web-based research, both for qualitative studies like Ford's and for large-scale quantitative studies, is here to stay. The portion of total qualitative research done online could grow "to as high as 25 percent to 30 percent (of all money spent on qualitative

---

Exhibit 15.6   Conducting Marketing Research Online

Meticulous planning and measurement can make online research easy and productive. On the other hand, poorly designed Web surveys can reduce response rates and prompt early exits. Here are some guidelines to improve response rates for online surveys:

- Design surveys that take no more than 20 to 30 minutes to complete, the shorter the better. Less is more.
- Place open-ended questions toward the end of the survey, when the respondent is more likely to answer them.
- Do not ask questions of everyone that only brand-users can answer.
- Do not include large numbers of multiple-rating questions without keeping the respondent engaged.
- Do indicate progress made towards survey completion throughout the survey.

Do these guidelines get results? In a bold move, old-economy company Hershey moved all of its new product testing online in 1999 and 2000. This radical move was prompted by the company's discovery that doing so allowed it to cut its product development process time by two-thirds, a significant advantage in its marketplace.

Hershey did not make the change without careful planning and research, however. It first validated that online testing yielded results from a panel that shared the same demographics, product preferences, and price sensitivities as that of its historical samples based on mail surveys. Hershey's testing proved that the correlation between the mail and the online tests was about 0.9, an almost perfect match. Hershey also integrated its old research into a reporting and archival system that allowed all of its personnel to easily retrieve previous tests and results. Such testing allowed Hershey to continue to use its historical research and knowledge base.

Sources: Corinne Maginnis, "Design Net Surveys that Reduce Exits," *Marketing News*, November 25, 2002, p. 18; Catherine Arnold, "Hershey Research Sees Net Gain," *Marketing News*, November 25, 2002, p. 17. Used by permission of the American Marketing Association.

---

research) in the future," says Bill McElroy, president of the New York–based Internet Marketing Research Organization (IMRO).[28] For a demonstration of one provider's online research tools, see Interactive Tracking Systems Inc.'s website at www.iTracks.com.

New-Economy Applications for Product Promotion and Brand Building

There are three broad approaches for using the Internet to promote one's products or services, that is, to provide information about one's product to the intended target market and build brand awareness and equity (see Exhibit 15.5). One is to engage in **viral marketing,** whereby consumers are encouraged to spread the word about a Web-based marketer. Another is to place promotional content—**brochureware,** as it is sometimes called—on one's website and encourage customers to peruse it as they wish. A third approach is to place ads in various places on the Web.

Viral marketing was the way Hotmail.com, the largest free e-mail provider, won its success. It attached a message at the end of every e-mail sent by its users announcing its availability as a free provider. The more users sent e-mail, the faster the word about Hotmail spread. Viral marketing is a low-cost and potentially powerful technique for building brand awareness.[29]

Placing brochureware about a company's products, news development and press releases, or about other things on the Web is an easy and inexpensive first step toward a new-economy strategy. It provides answers to customer or prospective customer questions with global 24×7 access. It avoids looking technologically clueless: What company lacks a fax line or a website today? But it is not very proactive, and if a company doesn't otherwise promote the website where the information is placed, either on Web portals, search engines, or in offline media, no one will know it is there. "The Web cliché, 'if you build it, they will come,' has lulled many online marketers into a false sense of security," says Charles

Sayers, an Internet marketing consultant.[30] Unfortunately, brochureware also helps your competitors keep up with what you are doing.

To help customers find their websites, companies can use businesses such as Search Engine Watch to find software applications that help them appear among the first links the search engines return. Intelliquis is another such company. Some firms create so-called **hook-pages** or **doorway pages.** These pages offer information on specialized subjects that consumers are likely to search for. E*Trade, for example, offers a hook page with free online stock advice and links the page to its own home page.[31] Another way to attract customers to one's website is to put together **affiliate deals,** in which owners of other websites are paid—in flat fees or commissions on whatever the referred customers buy—to send customers your way. The largest portals, such as America Online and Yahoo!, earn a substantial portion of their revenues this way.

Internet (and, perhaps soon, mobile telephony) advertising is a more proactive strategy, but deciding whether and how to use it is not easy. A simple way to advertise on the Internet is to take advantage of the shift in power from marketers to consumers brought about by easy access to comparative information by making available information for comparison purposes. The Web-based luggage retailer eBags.com, for example, provides charts to make it easier for customers to compare different garment bags and other products to find the one that's right for them. Automakers and other automotive sites provide similar comparative information to help consumers choose makes and models of cars that best suit their needs. Comparative sites are likely to turn up in virtually every product category over time, and having one's goods or services included among those described by such sites will likely turn out to be increasingly important. Of course, if one's goods or services do not pass competitive muster, being included on such sites can work the other way!

A more proactive advertising strategy is to place ads on the Web. In the early days, 4 percent to 5 percent of viewers of **banner ads,** the colorful strips of ad content splashed across the top of a Web page, would click on the banner to read the additional information that followed. By 2000, though, as Web audiences widened beyond the early 'net-heads who frequented the Web and such ads become more pervasive, the click-through rate has plummeted to 0.3 percent to 0.5 percent, according to Jupiter Research, far below response rates for traditional direct mail, where about 2 percent of recipients typically respond.[32]

Once touted as a way to build brands on the Internet, whether for online or offline companies, there's growing concern that banner ads may simply not work. By 2001, amid an overall drop in ad spending across most media, online ad revenue had slid (see Exhibit 15.7) and the cost per thousand viewers for banner ads had dropped to about $10, about half the cost one year earlier.[33] In the first half of 2001, banner ads accounted for just 36 percent of online ad spending, down from 53 percent in the fourth quarter of 1999.[34]

Is advertising on the Internet dead? Probably not, as advertisers experiment with emerging formats for using this new medium. Century 21, a real estate firm, has run humorous superstitials to promote its services that help homebuyers find new homes. Travelocity.com, the Internet travel agency, uses Internet ads for promoting specific travel offers. Consumer response is measured several times a day, and the message is changed if the ad isn't boosting sales.[35]

The Century 21 and Travelocity ads reflect trends toward more compelling and, in some cases, more measurable ad vehicles. New techniques include **rich media** (short ads with video and sound), **cliffhangers** (rich media ads that leave the viewer "hanging" and direct them to a website to view the end of the ad); **superstitials** (rich media ads that show up unexpectedly on a viewer's screen); **streaming audio** (like a radio commercial); and **vFlash** (consumers can choose to place a vFlash icon on their screen from, say Blockbuster Video, which flashes when Blockbuster has an offer it wants to make. Clicking on a pop-up box

Exhibit 15.7

THE ONLINE PITCH

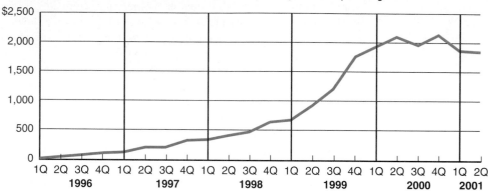

As Spending Eases...
Total internet ad revenue in millions has eased recently after years of explosive growth

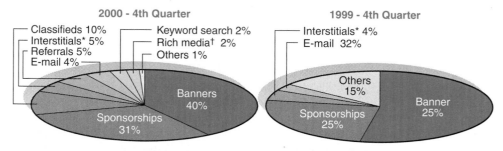

...Emerging Formats Gain
Internet ad revenue by format

2000 - 4th Quarter

Classifieds 10%   Keyword search 2%
Interstitials* 5%   Rich media† 2%
Referrals 5%   Others 1%
E-mail 4%

Banners 40%
Sponsorships 31%

1999 - 4th Quarter

Interstitials* 4%
E-mail 32%

Others 15%
Banner 25%
Sponsorships 25%

*Ads that appear between two content pages; also known as transition ads, intermercial ads, splash pages, and Flash pages.
†Generally includes a combination of animation, sound, video, and interactivity.

Source: "The Best Way to Advertise," by Vanessa O'Connell, *The Wall Street Journal,* November 12, 2001, p. R13. Copyright 2001 by Dow Jones & Co., Inc. Reprinted by permission of Dow Jones & Co., Inc. via the Copyright Clearance Center.

then takes the viewer to the Blockbuster website, where the offer is presented.). All these techniques, and new ones sure to be developed, hope to take advantage of growing Web penetration to reach consumers in new ways. If these approaches are not made more measurable, however, some observers say that big ad dollars are unlikely to flow their way.

There are several ways to use Internet advertising in a measurable manner. One way is to use **opt-in e-mail,** where consumers allow companies they are interested in to send them e-mail with new promotions. According to Seth Godin, such **permission marketing** (as opposed to interruption marketing, as Godin calls the current methods) offers the potential for companies to create trust, build long-term relationships with customers, and greatly improve their chances for making a sale.[36] By 2001, the average number of permission-based e-mails received by Internet users had increased to 36 per week, double the prior year figure.[37] For an example of how Harrah's, the resort casino operator, used e-mail marketing to fill its hotel rooms after the September 11, 2001, attacks on New York and Washington, see Exhibit 15.8.

Another way to make Web advertising more measurable is to have advertisers pay for performance, rather than for placement, regardless of the type of ad employed. The advertiser might pay for click-throughs, for leads generated, even commissions for actual orders

Exhibit 15.8   Harrah's Beats the House Odds to Fill Its Rooms

In the wake of the September 11, 2001 attack on America, Harrah's Entertainment, Inc. felt an immediate 25 percent downturn in its business in Las Vegas. Few people were in the mood to party, and fewer wanted to fly. By having already linked its 24 million-strong customer database with its website and e-mail marketing system, Harrah's was well positioned to counterattack. It targeted e-mails to customers it thought might want to take a trip to its tables and slot machines and, by the end of September, the hotel was back near 100 percent occupancy, filling almost 4,000 rooms that would otherwise have gone empty.

Harrah's data driven strategy has done more than just fill rooms when times are tough, however. Revenues have quadrupled since Chief Operating Officer Gary Loveman's data-driven strategy was put into place, and by late 2002, the stock price had neared an all-time high.

Source: Walker, Boyd, Mullins, Larreche. *Marketing Strategy: A Decision Focused Approach* (New York, NY: McGraw-Hill, 2003). Reprinted with permission from The McGraw-Hill Companies; David Rocks, "The Net As a Lifeline," *BusinessWeek*, October 29, 2001, p. EB 16. Simon London, "IT and Horsepower Are a Winning Formula," *Financial Times*, October 11, 2002, p. 12.

KEY OBSERVATION

Another way to make Web advertising more measurable is to have advertisers pay for performance, rather than for placement, regardless of the type of ad employed.

placed. Doing so, however, would require that extensive traffic data that follow a customer's **click-stream** be captured and analyzed. Jeff Forslund's job is to do just that for credit-card issuer NextCard, a major Web advertiser. For example, Forslund knows that a particular banner ad that appeared on Yahoo! on August 25, 2000 attracted 1,915 visits, 104 credit-card applications, and 22 approvals. He also knows that those 22 new customers transferred preexisting credit-card balances averaging $1,729 each.[38] With such data in hand, NextCard can determine the value of that banner ad and negotiate how much and on what basis—placement or performance—it is willing to pay Yahoo! to place another similar ad. Dan Springer, NextCard's chief marketing officer, believes that the Internet is better suited to getting measurable results than for branding efforts. He says current results indicate that today's Web ad prices are too high.[39]

Two additional factors, privacy and security concerns, are holding back development of the Web as a successful advertising medium. Consumer rights advocates are not certain that consumers want Jeff Forslund and others like him to have the click-stream data he needs to measure ad performance. What if someone's click-stream as he or she explores data about AIDS is gathered? Could such data be misused? Another deterrent is the glacial pace at which more interesting video and audio ads can download, given today's larger prevalence of 56K modems. Many people won't wait for such ads to load. As faster broadband connections become more common, this problem will fade, but it's hard to tell just how quickly broadband will penetrate the market.

While Internet advertising now seems almost "old hat," advertising on mobile phones is about to emerge as a significant new vehicle for promotion, especially in Europe and Japan, where mobile phone usage and technological development are far ahead of the United States. As DoCoMo's iMode and other high-speed mobile phone technologies penetrate various markets, the installed base of web-enabled mobile phones will grow large enough that ads will begin to make sense. The issues surrounding the use and effectiveness of this medium will parallel those for the Internet, and the pace at which applications become user-friendly enough to be valued by customers will determine how quickly this medium develops. In Europe and Japan, and subsequently elsewhere, these developments bear watching.

New-Economy Applications for Conducting Transactions   If promotional activities do their jobs, the hoped-for consequence is that some customers will decide to buy. Can the Internet or mobile telephony help transactions occur? Several Web-based companies are in the business of enabling client websites to handle transactions. Making the transition to a transaction-capable website was among the first tasks Thorntons had to do after they decided to get serious about the Internet. BroadVision Inc. (broadvision.com), for example, offers a wide range of software products that enable clients to conduct B2B or B2C commerce on their websites or via kiosks or mobile telephones. Such products typically provide back-end systems and inventory control, prepare warehouse and shipping documents, and bill the customer for the sale. Some such systems now allow companies to engage in **dynamic pricing,** a controversial system that gauges a customer's desire to buy, measures his means, and sets the price accordingly.[40] In this respect, target markets of one are now here, to the chagrin of some consumers!

An important step in facilitating Web transactions is making it easy for customers to pay, as PayPal does in the United States. In Europe, Click&Buy, a micro-payment system that enables consumers to make small transactions without using a credit card, had logged some 2 million transactions in Germany by late 2002.[41] Legislation in the United States has cleared the way for the use of **digital signatures** over the Web, and other countries may follow. Such digital authentication will pave the way for more efficient sale of insurance, mortgages, and other goods and services via the Web or mobile telephones. Imagine removing your car from your collision insurance policy when it's parked in the driveway for an extended period, and reinstating coverage with the click of a mouse. It will also lower the costs companies incur due to Internet fraud, which has been common, and thereby save consumers money. Brooks Fisher of Intuit Inc., a provider of a wide range of online financial services, says, "Less fraud means better pricing."[42]

More broadly, the Internet and wireless telephony are quickly removing constraints that limit sellers in terms of what they sell and how they sell it. Banks are moving all the transactions they can onto the Web, where a typical banking transaction costs just two cents, compared with 36 cents for an ATM transaction and $1.15 for a teller-assisted transaction.[43] In Scandinavia, 700,000 Finns use Sonera, the leading Finnish wireless carrier, to do everything from ordering chocolates from the back seat of a taxicab to getting a date. The 1999 mobile commerce and information revenues of Zed, a Finnish Internet site serving mobile phone users, totaled $126 million—in a country one-fortieth the size of the United States![44] Elsewhere, the Internet now offers buyers and sellers choices ranging from fixed-price online catalogs, to customer-tailored catalogs, to auctions, to negotiated prices, to Priceline.com's **demand collection system,** to barter and more.[45]

By enabling virtually frictionless movement among ways of doing business, these so-called **all-in-one markets** benefit both buyers and sellers. The trend toward multiple ways of transacting business on the Web runs counter to the conventional wisdom about e-commerce. Many observers had predicted that easy access to pricing information on the Internet would push all transactions toward a single mechanism—wide-open price competition in which the lowest-priced offer wins the order. For some commodity-like products that are easily compared—several Web **shopping bots** can tell a customer who has the lowest price on the latest Tom Clancy novel, for example—this may yet turn out to be the case. So far, however, this prediction has not come to pass.

New-Economy Applications for Delivering Digital Products

Many companies probably don't give much thought to it, but an increasing array of goods and services can be digitized and thereby delivered to customers via any digital medium, including the Internet, satellites, and mobile telephones. Fifty years ago, the then-current technological miracle was the analog delivery of sounds and images to consumers via the newfangled invention called television. Today, as we have seen earlier in this chapter, books, music, and more can be delivered digitally any time, at any digitally connected place. In 2, 5, or 10 years, what else will be digitally deliverable? Psychotherapy, with or without a live therapist, and legal advice are now available online from numerous providers.[46] Online postage is available at several websites, including that of the United States Postal Service. Unfortunately for their investors, e-postage pioneers Stamps.com and E-stamp.com squandered millions in start-up capital to pursue this market, with little so far to show for their efforts.[47] One new company is even rumored to be developing technology for delivering scents online. Who knows what's next? Beam me up, Scotty![48]

New-Economy Applications for Customer Service and Support

An increasingly important application on the Internet is for various sorts of customer service, replacing more costly—and sometimes more inconsistent and error prone—human support. Companies from Dell to the Denver Zoo use the Web to provide answers to frequently asked questions, from technical ones in Dell's case, to how to arrange a children's birthday party at the zoo. Savvy marketers know that, for all the hoopla about acquiring new customers, the real driver of the bottom line is the ability to profitably retain existing ones and that effective, responsive customer service is a key ingredient in doing so. They also know that **customer retention** is a competitive necessity. In nearly every industry, some company will soon figure out new ways to exploit the potential of the Internet to create value for customers. Without the ability to retain those customers, however, even the best-conceived business model on the Web will collapse.[49]

There are numerous examples of how Web-based customer service programs are providing customers with better service at lower costs, surely a win–win proposition. Michael Climo, purchasing director for e-tailer SmartHome.com, was seeking a supplier to provide fast delivery of its shipments to customers. United Parcel Service won the business by not only delivering SmartHome's parcels quickly, but also by cutting SmartHome's customer service costs while improving service. UPS helped redesign the SmartHome website so customers could track their shipments with a click of a mouse. SmartHome's call center now gets virtually no calls to check order status, down from 60 per day before the change, freeing its staff to make more sales calls. The Web-smart capabilities of UPS have made it the clear leader in delivering the $40 billion in merchandise bought online in 2000, with an estimated 55 percent of the business, compared to 10 percent for FedEx.[50] Attracting and retaining its business customers is what the UPS Web-based services are all about.

Benefits of an array of Web-based customer service applications are available to old- and new-economy companies alike, in both B2B and B2C contexts. Tracking shipments or answering other frequently asked questions is but one application. Building communities among users—using bulletin boards, chat rooms, or other e-techniques—is another one that can build customer loyalty and provide an important source of feedback on new product ideas, product problems, and other issues. Tom Lowe, founder of Playing Mantis, a maker of die-cast cars, plastic model kits, and action figures, credits his company's Web-based bulletin boards for feeding customer relationships that would be the envy of any company. As one customer posted to one of the Playing Mantis boards, "Polar Lights is very special to me. . . . You've rekindled the joy I once felt when buying these kits. . . . You're the ONLY company I feel a part of."[51]

The growing number of Web-based customer service applications offers the tantalizing combination of better service and significant cost savings. The trick is to focus on the customer service benefits first, rather than mere cost cutting. Customers are quick to discern when cost cutting takes precedence over genuine service responsiveness. Does anyone like the way call center software has changed the way consumers obtain phone numbers from directory assistance, or the fact that some banks won't provide bank-by-mail envelopes to those who prefer to do their banking the old-fashioned way?

KEY OBSERVATION

The growing number of Web-based customer service applications offers the tantalizing combination of better service and significant cost savings. The trick is to focus on the customer service benefits first, rather than mere cost cutting.

One myth some companies have bought into is that the Internet is a self-service medium. They assume that they can let customers do all the work, but most customers really don't want to do more. One solution is **coproduction,** in which companies carefully consider which burdens they can remove from the customer, using new-economy technologies, and which customers can perform, assessing costs and benefits to both parties. Doing so can provide insights into new ways to serve customers better, as Charles Schwab now does when it e-mails customers to alert them to big moves in their stocks.[52]

New-Economy Applications for Product Return and Disposal   Customers' experiences with goods and some services do not end until the products are consumed, returned, or disposed of. Some companies have found ways to use new-economy technologies to facilitate these processes. Dell, for example, provides an Internet space where Dell customers can sell their old computers when they upgrade to a new one. Both old- and new-economy companies can avail themselves of similar applications. In retailing, many retailers with both online and offline stores accept returns at any location. Concerns related to returning online purchases (the inability to see and touch the goods before purchase and inability to return goods easily) rank second and third on the list of factors that deter consumers from shopping online (see Exhibit 15.9).

Exhibit 15.9

WHY SHOPPERS ARE WARY

Concern about returning items is one of the main reasons cited by surveyed consumers for not shopping online. The leading responses:

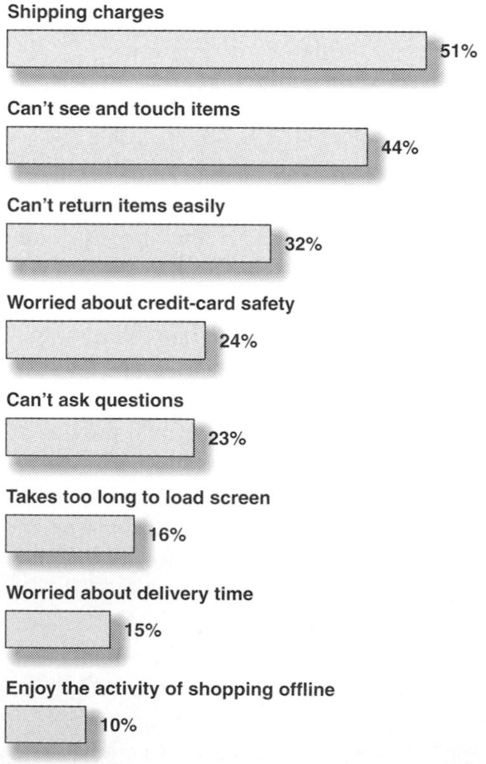

Shipping charges
51%

Can't see and touch items
44%

Can't return items easily
32%

Worried about credit-card safety
24%

Can't ask questions
23%

Takes too long to load screen
16%

Worried about delivery time
15%

Enjoy the activity of shopping offline
10%

Source: "Returns to Sender," by Rebecca Quick, *The Wall Street Journal,* July 17, 2000, p. R8. Copyright 2000 by Dow Jones & Co., Inc. Reprinted by permission of Dow Jones & Co., Inc. via the Copyright Clearance Center.

Developing New-Economy Marketing Strategies: The Critical Questions

Knowing what marketing arrows are available in one's new-economy quiver is one thing. Deciding which of these applications will deliver the best return on investment is quite another. Our flow model of the customer experience process (see Exhibit 15.4) facilitates such decision making by raising six important questions that should be asked about whether to employ new-economy tools at any or all stages of the process. These diagnostic questions are shown in Exhibit 15.10. We address each of these questions in this section.

Can We Digitize Any or All of the Necessary Flows at Each Stage in the Consumer Experience Process?   At the heart of the new economy is the reliance on digital means of transmitting *information,* some of which is recomposed into *goods*—CDs, books, and more. In considering whether to employ new-economy technologies at any stage of the consumer experience process, a company should ask whether any of the flows—information, goods or services, or cash—can be digitized.

For cash, the answer is an automatic yes, via credit cards or other forms of electronic payment, except where currency issues pose problems, such as in some international settings. And new forms of electronic payment will soon enhance the security of cash flows over the Web.

Exhibit 15.10

DIAGNOSTIC QUESTIONS FOR NEW-ECONOMY MARKETING DECISIONS

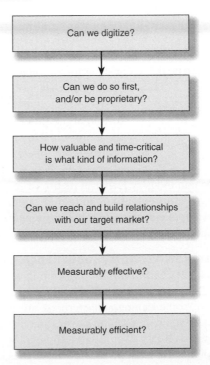

Can we digitize?

Can we do so first, and/or be proprietary?

How valuable and time-critical is what kind of information?

Can we reach and build relationships with our target market?

Measurably effective?

Measurably efficient?

For goods and services, the question is more difficult. Text, audio, and visual images (moving or still) can be digitized, as can books, music, photos, and, given enough bandwidth, movies and other videos. But what about the *soft hand* of a cashmere sweater? The *heft and balance* of a carpenter's hammer? The *taste* of fine European chocolate? The *fragrance* of a new cologne? Today, these important informational attributes of goods cannot be readily digitized. At present, most tangible goods and many services cannot easily be transmitted digitally. For others, however, such as legal advice, therapy for mental health patients, and other goods or services that can adequately be represented in words, sounds, or images, the possibilities are endless. Will technology soon make possible the digital transmission of physical goods? Who knows? When it happens, the many sci-fi buffs around the world will not be surprised!

When any of the flows at any stage of the consumer experience process can, given sufficient information and ingenuity, be digitized, the remaining questions in Exhibit 15.10 should then be considered to decide whether or not new-economy applications for a particular flow should be implemented.

Can We Do So First, and/or in a Proprietary Way

As we have seen, barriers to entry on the Web are low, and most good ideas can be quickly imitated. A key question in deciding whether or not to employ a new-economy application is whether one can do so in a proprietary way, thereby deterring imitation, or do so with a sufficient head start so that competitive advantage can be established before others follow. Amazon was early in the Internet retailing game and enjoyed a helpful head start. E-tailers of pet supplies, however, were not so fortunate.[53]

For old-economy companies, using the Internet for applications that do not reinvent the heart of the business—for brochureware or customer service, for example—speed to market may or may not be critical, depending on how quickly others in their industry are likely to move into similar applications. As always, competitor intelligence, some of which can be gleaned from competitors' websites, is essential.

How Valuable and How Time-Critical Are What Kinds of Information to the Recipient?

For the informational flows in Exhibit 15.4, a key question in making resource deployments is the importance of various kinds of information to the recipient, either the company or the customer, depending on the direction of the flow. The more valuable and time-critical the information, the more sensible it may be to invest in new-economy applications to provide easy, timely, and 24×7 access to those who can benefit from the information. Wal-Mart, arguably an old-economy company that has long been an industry leader in its use of information technology, now posts on the Web password-protected, up-to-the-minute, store-by-store, SKU-by-SKU sales information that its key suppliers can access, thereby enabling them to better ensure that Wal-Mart's stores remain in stock on their merchandise.

Can New-Economy Tools Reach and Build Relationships with Customers in the Target Market?

Making information, goods, or services available on the Web is of little use if the people to whom those flows are directed lack Web access. As we have seen, some demographic groups are underrepresented on the Internet. Web-based services targeted at senior citizens may have difficulty, given the current paucity of seniors who have easy Web access, though the number of seniors on the Web is now growing rapidly. Similarly, people and businesses in the third world are also underrepresented. New-economy applications that make the most business sense will be those targeting groups for whom use of the Web is relatively widespread.

Simply *reaching* customers with new-economy tools may not be enough, however, especially for marketers of commodity-like products. Going beyond reach to build mutually beneficial *relationships* may be what is needed. Amazon has begun to build loyal relationships with its growing customer base by focusing its efforts on exceptional customer service. While book lovers can often find books for lower prices elsewhere on the Web, many of them simply return to Amazon's site, with its easy 1-Click® ordering, customer reviews, and other customer-friendly features. Using new-economy tools for building customer relationships may be their most important application in the long run.

Are New Economy Tools Measurably Effective and Efficient Compared to Other Solutions?

Ultimately, given favorable answers to the first four questions in this section, deciding to invest in a particular new-economy marketing strategy or application comes down to two final questions. Is the new-economy solution effective, and is it more efficient than other solutions? As we have seen, UPS was able to sell SmartHome on its shipping because it was not only effective in getting SmartHome's parcels to their destinations on time, but also because SmartHome was able to improve on and save money on customer service at the same time.[54] Another example of using the Web for effectiveness and efficiency gains is Kinko's Internet order-taking system, Print to Kinko's. Customers can upload digital versions of documents to kinkos.com and have them delivered on paper at any Kinko's location within a few hours. Kinko's hopes the new system will capture some of the large market for corporate printing, thereby boosting sales, while enhancing productivity by reducing the error rate on printing orders from 10 percent to 1 percent, by cutting order handling costs, and by keeping Kinko's' copiers humming. Other dot.com printing players, such as iPrint and mimeo.com, were first to market, but Kinko's has the brand name and more than 1,000 stores. Will the digital strategy accelerate Kinko's' growth and increase earnings? CEO Joseph Hardin likes its potential. "We may be late to the market," he says, "but at the end of the day, he who executes wins."[55]

Marketers' concerns over the effectiveness and efficiency of their websites have led to the development of web analytics, software solutions that monitor and summarize website usage patterns. Web analytics is the equivalent of having a team of marketing researchers follow customers through a bricks-and-mortar retail store. The technology can uncover a variety of problems that can plague websites: cumbersome navigation, content that can't be easily found, underperforming search engine strategies, and unprofitable online marketing partnerships. The results of these analyses can improve customer satisfaction and response to the website, strengthen the marketer's hand in negotiating terms of partnership deals, and even identify new market segments that might be best served with tailored sites. "We're looking at the [Web analytics] every day, just like the guys on Wall Street look at daily stock quotes," says Jonathan Kapplow, corporate Internet marketing manager at Hanover Direct, a catalog and Web retailer of gifts and apparel.[56] Some observers, however, note that the ready availability of copious data can lead analysts into what Kate Delhagen, retail research director at Forrester Research, calls "data ratholes." "There are a lot of data flowing through [these] companies," she says, "but a lot of it is minutiae."[57] Deciding what metrics are the most important—to assess customer behavior on the site, not just traffic—is key.

In the final analysis, setting clear SMART objectives that new-economy tools or activities are intended to meet—specific, measurable, attainable, relevant, and timebound—and running cost-benefit analyses to assess their likely performance are necessary for making go/no-go decisions and for prioritizing which initiatives should be pursued first. Fortunately, the inherent measurability of many new-economy tools often provides clear and compelling feedback on whether they are meeting the objectives. In addition, attention must be given to a variety of business process issues that can get in the way of effective

Exhibit 15.11

THE 10 DEADLY MISTAKES OF WANNA-DOTS

1. Sprinkle Internet responsibilities throughout the company—a little Web site here, a little brochure-ware there. Let them all go forward, as long as they stay small and innocuous. If any look like they have potential, raise skeptical questions at executive meetings and repeat frequently that the Internet is overhyped.

2. Form a committee to create a new corporate Internet offering, staff it with people from unrelated areas who are already doing five other things, and don't release them from their regular jobs. give the leadership role to a bored executive as a reward for his years of loyal service. (Never mind that he has no Internet experience; he surfs the Web, doesn't he?)

3. Find the simplest, least-demanding thing you can do on the Web. Go for copyware that looks like what everyone else is doing. Instead of a killer app, create a "yawner app." (That will save time and money. And that way, you can cross the Internet off your to-do list quickly.)

4. To build the site, choose the vendors that are the most dismissive of your traditional business (they think you're dinosaurs) but whose abilities you're least capable of assessing. Then hand over the technical work to them (that way, nobody inside has to learn anything new) but refuse to take their advice about how the site should look (after all, you're the industry experts). Use more than one vendor—so you can have the fun of watching them slug it out.

5. Make sure what you do on the Web is exactly the same as what you do off-line. duplicate your traditional business assumptions on-line. (After all, the Internet is just a tool, isn't it?)

6. Insist that an Internet venture meet every corporate standard: cost controls, quarterly earnings, recruitment sources, compensation policies, purchasing procedures. Allocate just enough resources to keep it alive but not enough to risk its becoming an innovator—because that would require more investment.

7. Under the banner of decentralization and business unit autonomy, reward each unit for its own performance, and offer no extra incentives to cooperate in cyberspace. (Maintain your belief that conflict is a healthy spur to higher performance; let the victor get the spoils.) Keep reminding divisions that they are separate businesses because they are different, and that's that.

8. Compare your performance with your traditional industry competitors in the physical world. (That way you will always have someone to whom you can feel superior.) Dismiss on-line competitors as ephemeral fads. And don't even consider whether companies from unrelated industries could steal across the borders and poach your customers by using the Net. (Why worry about the hypothetical?)

9. Celebrate your conversion to e-business by giving people in the rest of the organization tools they are unable to use, requiring changes they are confused about making. Tell people this will help them do their work better. Schedule training classes at a distant location. Watch as the new tools take too much time and make it harder to get work done, then punish people for their resistance to make change.

10. And, last but not least, never forget that the company, not the customer, is in the driver's seat. The Internet is an opportunity for *us* to communicate with *them*.

execution of even the best intentions for a new-economy strategy in an old-economy company. Recent research by Rosabeth Moss Kanter identified ten common mistakes such companies commonly make (See Exhibit 15.11). Avoiding these errors is easier said than done, of course, but web analytics can help catch any errors that are made.

Developing Strategies to Serve New-Economy Markets

This chapter has, for the most part, addressed how companies of any kind, size, industry, or age can use new-economy tools and technologies for marketing purposes. No doubt, however, there are readers who see bigger fish to fry in the new-economy skillet. They see the new economy as offering the prospect for starting an entrepreneurial venture, in a new firm

KEY OBSERVATION

In this final section, we address some lessons learned from the dot.com crash of 2000, we provide a framework for thinking about where and how revenues might be generated in the new-economy marketspace, and we examine what it is likely to take to create enduring success in the new-economy ventures of tomorrow.

or within an existing one, to serve a market created by the advent of the Internet, wireless telephony, or other new or still-emerging technologies. Thus, in this final section, we address some lessons learned from the dot.com crash of 2000, we provide a framework for thinking about where and how revenues might be generated in the new-economy marketspace, and we examine what it is likely to take to create enduring success in the new-economy ventures of tomorrow.

What Lessons Can We Learn from the Dot.com Crash?

In April 2000 and the months that followed, the dot.com party ended. Many ventures with lofty market capitalizations stumbled and fell, in some cases losing more than 90 percent of their value by the end of 2000. Others shut their doors or were acquired, often on unfavorable terms. Venture capitalists slammed the funding window shut.[58] What went wrong?

In a lengthy cover story in October 2000, *Fortune* magazine identified a dozen lessons to be learned from the dot.com crash.[59] The 12 lessons, shown in Exhibit 15.12, indicate collectively that many fundamental strategic marketing principles were ignored in the mad

Exhibit 15.12

LESSONS LEARNED FROM THE DOT.COM CRASH OF 2000

If it doesn't make cents, it doesn't make sense.

Time favors incumbents.

The Internet isn't as disruptive as we thought?

Making a market is harder than it looks.

"Branding" is not a strategy.

Entrepreneurship cannot be systematized.

There is no such thing as "Internet time."

Investors are not your customers.

The Internet changes your job.

The real wealth creation is yet to come.

The Internet still changes everything.

The distinction between Internet companies and non-Internet companies is fading fast.

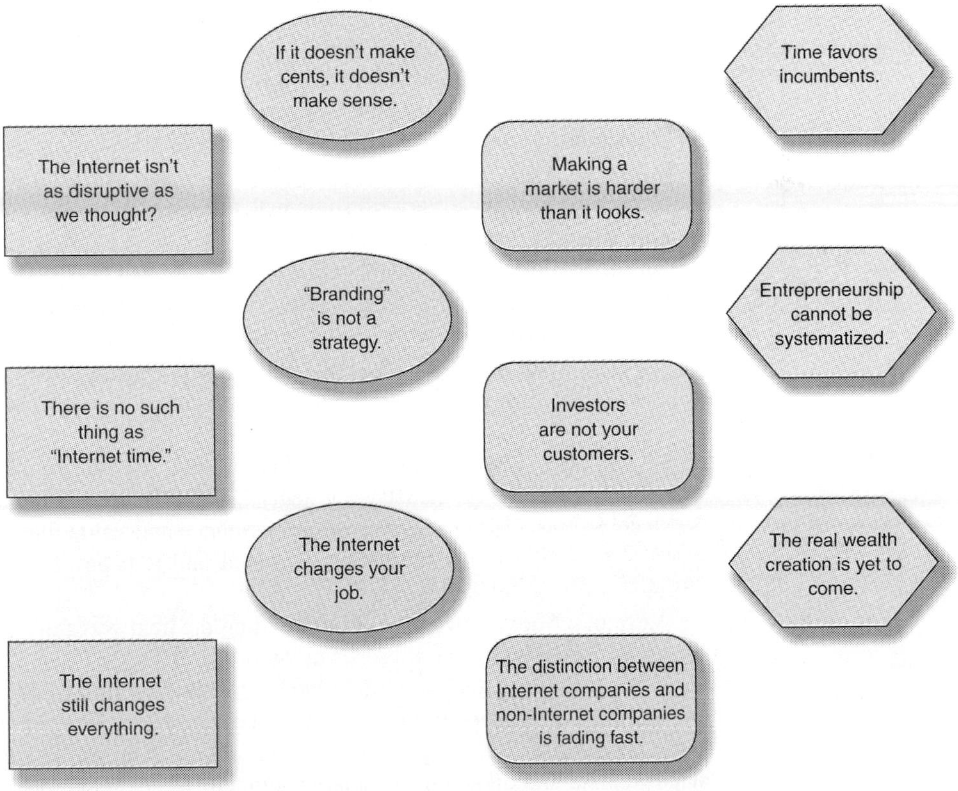

Source: Jerry Useem, "What Have We Learned?" *Fortune,* October 30, 2000, pp. 82–104. © 2000 Time, Inc. All rights reserved.

rush to what looked to be dot.com nirvana. Markets and market segments were not clearly identified and targeted. Low barriers to entry that made industries unattractive were ignored. First-to-market mania ruled, and the ability to sustain competitive advantage by offering better goods and services and better value was often overlooked. The basic economics of some businesses were ignored. Acquiring (at reasonable cost) and retaining satisfied customers matters. Profitability and positive cash flow matter (sooner rather than later, revenues should exceed expenses, including marketing expenses). Despite the carnage, however, *Fortune* concludes that, while the dot.com era is over, the Internet era is just getting started.

What Are the Key Success Factors in Serving the Dot.com Markets of Tomorrow?

What might tomorrow's entrepreneurs do to craft marketing strategies to serve these still enticing new-economy markets? For one, would-be Internet entrepreneurs should consider the various ways in which revenue can be generated on the Web or in other new-economy settings. Unless someone, a business or a consumer, is willing to fork over money for what a new business offers, its chances for success lie somewhere between slim and none. Exhibit 15.13 shows a number of ways in which revenue can be generated by Web-based businesses—from commerce, by selling content, by organizing communities, or from building the new-economy infrastructure. Understanding one's **business model** and being willing to change it as market and technological conditions warrant are essential.

Second, such entrepreneurs must ask not, What can I sell? but What do new-economy customers and markets need, whether through business-to-business (Grainger.com), business-to-consumer (Amazon.com or LandsEnd.com), consumer-to-consumer (eBay.com), or consumer-to-business (Priceline.com) business models, that my new company can provide better, easier, faster, or cheaper using new-economy tools and technologies? If a particular business idea does not fill some real, though perhaps currently latent, need identified by this question, there is no viable business.

Third, would-be entrepreneurs must now realize that barriers to entry are incredibly low in the new economy. For everyone who has the next latest and greatest Web-based idea, there are dozens of other prospective entrepreneurs likely to be exploring similar ideas concurrently. It's not really the ideas that count. As Bob Zider, president of the Beta Group, a Silicon Valley firm that develops and commercializes new technology, says, "Many entrepreneurs make the mistake of thinking that venture capitalists are looking for good ideas when, in fact, they are looking for good managers in good industry segments."[60] What matters is the team that will execute an idea to deliver the performance and value that customers, whether businesses or consumers, want and will pay for. Only then will investors make money.

As Intel's Andy Grove says about building the next wave of (it is hoped successful) Internet businesses, "It's work. Very unglamorous work . . . The heavy lifting is still ahead of us."[61] Much of this work is of the kind set forth in the first three-fourths of this book: understanding customers and the markets they comprise; understanding industries and the competitors that do daily battle in them; and developing strategic marketing programs that can establish and maintain sustainable competitive advantage.

But there's also the work of strategy execution. In this chapter, we've explored the new economy and how both existing and new firms can find ways—measured in terms of effectiveness and efficiency—to take advantage of the promise it offers. In the chapters that

Exhibit 15.13

E-BUSINESS MODELS

COMMERCE REVENUES

Revenue category	Description
Product sales	Sell or license physical or information-based products.
Commission, service or transaction fees	Charge a fee for services provided; can be a set fee or a % of the cost of a product or service.

CONTENT REVENUES

Revenue category	Description
Subscription fees	Charge for receipt of updated information on a particular topic or a broad range of topics for a specified period (e.g., annual).
Registration or event fees	Charge a fee for attendance at an online event, workshop, or course.

COMMUNITY REVENUES

Revenue category	Description
Advertising, slotting, affiliate and referral fees	Collect a fee for hosting a banner advertisement or special promotion. Collect a fee for an exclusive or nonexclusive partnership relationship. Collect a fee each time a visitor clicks through from your site to another company's site.
Membership fees	Charge a fee to belong to a private group or service.

INFRASTRUCTURE REVENUES

Revenue category	Description
Software/hardware sales	Sell or license a technology product.
Installation and integration fees	Charge either a set or variable fee for services provided; large-scale fixed-price projects are often broken into a series of discrete projects with well-defined time frames and deliverables; variable fees are often based on time, materials, and expenses incurred while working on a project.
Maintenance and update fees	Charge a fee for software/hardware maintenance and updates.
Hosting fees	Charge a fee for hosting a software application, website, data center, or network.
Access fees	Charge a fee for providing access to a network and/or to an Internet service.

Source: Lynda M. Applegate and Meredith Collura, as it appeared in *The E-Business Handbook* by Paul B. Lowry, Appendix B1, p. 29. © 2002, CRC Press. Used by permission.

follow, we examine the kinds of marketing strategies best suited to new and growing markets like those in the new economy, as well as those required in mature and declining markets, where new-economy tools and techniques can still play important roles. Finally, we close the book with chapters on how best to organize for the effective implementation of, and control over the results generated by, marketing strategies. "Give me "A" execution of a "B" plan over "B" execution of an "A" plan," is a common refrain heard from venture capitalists and other investors. Planning is important. But effective execution delivers the results, and results are what count.

TAKE-AWAYS

- Seven potentially attractive elements characterize many new economy technologies: the syndication of information, the increasing returns to scale of network products, the ability to efficiently personalize and customize market offerings, the ability to disintermediate distribution, global reach, 24×7 access, and the possibility of instantaneous delivery.

- First-mover advantage is simply wrong. Best beats first.

- Most observers now believe that the Internet is better suited for delivering measurable marketing results—as is direct marketing—than for brand building.

- Web-based customer service applications offer the tantalizing combination of better service and significant cost savings. The trick, of course, is to focus on the customer service benefits first, rather than mere cost cutting, since customers are quick to discern when cost cutting takes precedence over genuine service responsiveness.

- Keys to success in tomorrow's new-economy ventures include clearly understanding one's business model (Exactly where will revenue come from: commerce, content, community, or infrastructure?), filling real (though perhaps latent) customer needs, and putting together the right management team that can deliver the performance and value that customers want and will pay for. Only then will investors make money.

Self-diagnostic questions to test your ability to apply the analytical tools and concepts in this chapter to marketing decision making may be found at this book's website at www.mhhe.com/mullins05.

ENDNOTES

1. Sources for the Thorntons story include Richard Marshall, "New Media Choice/Thorntons," *Marketing* (UK), January 10, 2002; "E-volve: Chocolate Company with a Web Addiction," *FT Intelligence*, Financial Times Information Limited, May 23, 2002; "Chocs Away for Thorntons," *Food Manufacture*, August 2002.

2. Jim David Kim, "In Korea, the Cry of the Modem Falls Silent," *International Herald Tribune*, April 28, 2003, at www.iht.com/cgi-bin/generic.cgi?template=articleprint.tmplh&ArticleID=94597.

3. Allison Haines, "Gartner Says Consumers Will Spend 20 Times More on E-commerce with Broadband Access," at www.gartner.com/public/static/aboutgg/pressrel/pr20001017a.html.

4. "The New Economy Goes Global," *Newsweek*, October 2, 2000, p. 74L.

5. Fred Vogelstein, "What Went Right: E-Commerce," *Fortune*, December 30, 2002, p. 166.

6. "Holiday Online Sales Ride high," *Denver Post*, January 3, 2003, p. C2.

7. Spencer E. Ante and Arlene Weintraub, "Why B2B is a Scary Place to Be," *Business Week*, September 11, 2000, pp. 34–37.

8. Joseph B. White, "What Works?" *The Wall Street Journal*, October 23, 2000, p. R4.

9. This section is based on Kevin Werbach, "Syndication: The Emerging Model for Business in the Internet Era," *Harvard Business Review*, May–June 2000, pp. 85–93.

10. Yaeko Mitsumori, "NTT's iMode paves the way for wireless data services," *Radio Communications Report*, February 28, 2000, p. 108.

11. This section is based on Thomas Petzinger, Jr., "So Long, Supply and Demand," *The Wall Street Journal*, January 1, 2000; and W. Brian Arthur, *Increasing Returns and Path Dependence in the Economy* (Ann Arbor, MI: University of Michigan Press, 1994).

12. Erin Schulte, "Making It," *The Wall Street Journal Europe*, December 13–15, 2002.

13. Matthew Rose, "Random House Fires a Shot in E-Book Feud," *The Wall Street Journal*, November 1, 2000, p. B1.

14. Thomas E. Weber, "Web Music's Future: Turning Cell Phone into Wireless Walkman," *The Wall Street Journal*, July 10, 2000, p. B1.

15. Carl Shapiro and Hal R. Varian, "Versioning: The Smart Way to Sell Information," *Harvard Business Review*, November–December 1998, pp. 106–14.

16. Brad Stone, "Napster's Offspring," *Newsweek*, October 16, 2000, p. 58.

17. Fred Vogelstein, "What Went Right: E-Commerce," *Fortune*, December 30, 2002, p. 166.

18. Ibid.

19. Shapiro and Varian, "Versioning: The Smart Way to Sell Information."

20. Much of this section is based on Jim Collins, "Best Beats First," *Inc.*, August 2000, pp. 48–51.

21. Ibid, p. 48.

22. Ibid, p. 49.

23. Evan I. Schwartz, *Digital Darwinism* (New York: Broadway Books, 1999).

24. Peter Sealey, "How E-Commerce Will Trump Brand Management," *Harvard Business Review*, July–August 1999, pp. 171–76.

25. For a broader look at Internet marketing, see Ward Hanson, *Principles of Internet Marketing* (Cincinnati: South-Western College Publishing, 2000).

26. Rebecca Buckman, "A Matter of Opinion," *The Wall Street Journal,* October 23, 2000, p. R46.

27. Steve Jarvis and Deborah Szynal, "Show and Tell: Spreading the Word About Online Qualitative Research," *Marketing News,* November 19, 2001, p. 1.

28. Ibid, p. 13.

29. Seth Godin, *Unleashing the Ideavirus,* New York: Do You Zoom, 2000.

30. Joe Dysart, "Sites That Sell Themselves," *Financial Times,* April 4, 2000, p. 19.

31. Ibid, p. 19.

32. Jennifer Rewick, "Beyond Banners," *The Wall Street Journal,* October 23, 2000, p. R38; Suein Hwang and Mylene Mangalindan, "Yahoo's Grand Vision for Web Advertising Takes Some Hard Hits," *The Wall Street Journal,* September 1, 2000, p. A1.

33. Vanessa O'Connell, "The Best Way to Advertise," *The Wall Street Journal,* November 12, 2001, p. R13.

34. PricewaterhouseCoopers study for "Interactive Advertising Bureau (IAB) Reports Q1 & Q2 Internet Ad Revenue of $3.76 Billion in the United States," press release from IAB, September 24, 2001.

35. Ibid.

36. Seth Godin, *Permission Marketing* (New York: Simon and Schuster, 1999).

37. "E-mail Is Growing as a Communications Channel for the Marketer and the Consumer," www3.doubleclick.net/market/1.htm.

38. Hwang and Mangalindan, "Yahoo's Grand Vision for Web Advertising Takes Some Hard Hits," p. A6.

39. Ibid.

40. David Streitfeld, "On the Web, Price Tags Blur," *The Washington Post Online,* www.washingtonpost.com/wp-dyn/articles/A 15159-2000Sep25.html.

41. Marialuisa Taddia, "Pay as You Go for Bits on the Web," *Financial Times FT Creative Business,* September 17, 2002, p. 12.

42. Mark Wigfield, " 'Digital Signature' Bill Is Cleared by Congress," *The Wall Street Journal,* June 19, 2000, p. B12.

43. Youngme Moon and Francis X. Frei, "Exploding the Self-Service Myth," *Harvard Business Review,* May–June 2000, pp. 26–27.

44. Dennis K. Berman, "Killer Apps for a Wireless World," *Business Week e.biz,* September 18, 2000, p. EB 43.

45. Paul Nunes, Diane Wilson, and Ajit Kambil, "The All-in-one Market," *Harvard Business Review,* May–June 2000, pp. 19–20.

46. Rochelle Sharpe, "The Virtual Couch," *Business Week e.biz,* September 18, 2000, pp. EB 135–37; Richard B. Schmitt, "Lawyers vs. the Internet," *The Wall Street Journal,* July 17, 2000, p. B12.

47. Peter Gumbel, "Return to Sender," *The Wall Street Journal,* September 24, 2001, p. R19; Arlene Weintraub, "Dead Letter," *Business Week e.biz,* October 23, 2000, pp. EB 82–84.

48. From the science fiction movie *Star Trek,* in which it was routine to digitally transmit objects, including people, from place to place.

49. Frederick F. Reichheld and Phil Schefter, "E-Loyalty: Your Secret Weapon on the Web," *Harvard Business Review,* July–August 2000, pp. 105–13.

50. Charles Haddad, "Big Brown's Coup," *Business Week e.biz,* September 18, 2000, pp. EB 76–77.

51. Michael Warshaw, "The Thing That Would Not Die," *Inc. Technology,* no. 1 (March 2000), p. 89.

52. Youngme Moon and Francis X. Frei, "Exploding the Self-Service Myth," *Harvard Business Review,* May–June 2000, pp. 26–27.

53. Melanie Warner, "Fallen Idols," *Fortune,* October 30, 2000, pp. 108–21.

54. Charles Haddad, "Big Brown's Coup," *Business Week e.biz,* September 18, 2000, pp. EB 76–77.

55. Arlene Weintraub, "Late to the Party," *Business Week,* August 28, 2000, p. 254.

56. Steve Jarvis, "Follow the Money," *Marketing News,* October 8, 2001, p. 10.

57. Michael Totty, "So Much Information . . . ," *The Wall Street Journal Europe,* December 13–15, 2002, p. R3.

58. Warner, "Fallen Idols," *Fortune,* October 30, 2000, pp. 108–21.

59. Jerry Useem, "What Have We Learned?" *Fortune,* October 30, 2000, pp. 82–104.

60. Bob Zider, "How Venture Capital Works," *Harvard Business Review,* November–December 1998, pp. 131–39.

61. Useem, "What Have We Learned?"

CHAPTER SIXTEEN

Strategies for New and Growing Markets

Canon, Inc.—Success That Is Hard to Copy[1]

AT LAST COUNT, JAPAN'S ECONOMY had suffered through four recessions in about a decade. Consequently, many Japanese manufacturers—even some of the largest global competitors—have struggled to remain profitable and survive. However, a few firms have not only survived but grown and prospered in spite of the difficult domestic market environment. Canon, Inc., is one of those stellar performers. The company earned about $1.4 billion on consolidated net sales of approximately $25 billion in 2002, which gave it a third straight year of record profits and a nearly 12 percent return on equity.

How has Canon managed to wring so much money out of its copiers, printers, and cameras when other Japanese electronics firms have floundered? For one thing, Fujio Mitarai, the firm's CEO, has been willing to adopt some Western cost-cutting practices he learned during the 23 years he worked for Canon in America. First, he narrowed the company's strategic scope by concentrating on a few product markets where the firm had an established market presence and superior technological capabilities, while abandoning other businesses where it had a weaker competitive position, such as personal computers and liquid-crystal displays. Mr. Mitarai also scrapped the assembly lines in all 29 of Canon's Japanese plants, replacing them with small work teams—or "cells"—of about six employees who do the work of about 30 workers under the old system. These self-managed cells have not only reduced Canon's labor costs but enabled the firm

to cut its inventory of component parts by 30 percent and to close 20 of its 34 warehouses. In addition, Mr. Mitarai is gradually moving a larger portion of Canon's manufacturing outside of Japan to countries like Vietnam and China.

But a sharper market focus and increased manufacturing efficiency are not sufficient to explain the firm's strong performance. Other Japanese electronics firms have copied such cost-cutting actions without duplicating Canon's results. A second important strategic thrust underlying Canon's success is a heavy emphasis on developing and marketing a stream of new products, product improvements, and line extensions in order to sustain a leading share position in its core businesses.

As a first step toward implementing this product development strategy, the company plows nearly 8 percent of its total revenues back into product R&D. Some of that investment is targeted at continued improvement of Canon's offerings in businesses where it already holds a dominant market share. For instance, Canon's technical leadership has enabled it to maintain a 60 percent share of the global market for the core engines used to power laser printers, including printers developed through an alliance with Hewlett-Packard. In other cases, Canon's development efforts focus on innovative new-to-the-world products—like the development of a digital radiography system—or product modifications aimed at new applications segments, such as a wide-format bubble jet printer for the commercial printing industry.

Courtesy Canon USA

Of course, it is one thing to develop a bunch of new products on the cutting edge of technology, but making potential customers aware of those new products and their benefits—and actually generating sales revenues—requires effective and well-funded marketing and sales efforts as well. Consequently, Canon has restructured its global sales and marketing organization in recent years to decentralize decision making and make its marketing plans better adapted to local market conditions. This is particularly critical because the firm earns more than 70 percent of its sales revenues in markets outside of Japan. For example, in 2001 the company established Canon Europe Ltd. in the United Kingdom to help coordinate regional marketing efforts and strengthen its European sales network.

Marketing Challenges Addressed in Chapter 16

Canon's success illustrates several important points about new product and market development. First, both sales growth and cost cutting can help improve profits. But while it is often easier to cut costs in the short term, revenue growth—particularly growth generated by the development of innovative new products—can have a bigger impact on a firm's profitability and shareholder value over the long haul. This point is confirmed by a study of 847 large corporations conducted by Mercer Management Consulting. The authors found that the compound annual growth rate in the market value of companies that achieved higher-than-average profit growth but lower revenue growth than their industry's average—companies that increased profits mostly by cutting costs, in other words—was 11.6 percent from 1989 to 1992. By contrast, companies that achieved higher-than-average profits as the result of higher-than-average revenue growth saw their market value jump at an annual rate double that—23.5 percent.[2]

Canon's history also illustrates that new product introductions can involve products that differ in their degree of newness from the perspective of the company and its customers. Some of the products developed by the firm, such as its first office copier, presented a new technical challenge to the company but did not seem very innovative to potential customers who viewed the copiers merely as simpler and cheaper versions of Xerox's machines. But some of the firm's new product introductions—such as its digital radiology system—were truly innovations that were new to potential customers and the company alike.

In Chapter 11 we focused on the problems and processes involved in developing and evaluating product offerings that are *new to the company*. The first part of this chapter examines marketing strategies and programs appropriate for developing markets for offerings that are *new to the target customers*. Our primary focus is on programs used by the pioneer firm—or first entrant—into a particular product-market. Being the pioneer gains a firm a number of potential competitive advantages, but it also involves some major risks. Some pioneers capitalize on their early advantage and maintain a leading market share of the product category, earning substantial revenues and profits, well into the later stages of the product's life cycle.

Other pioneers are less successful. While Canon has pioneered some new product categories, for instance, it has not always ended up as the share leader in those categories as

KEY OBSERVATION

Being the pioneer gains a firm a number of potential competitive advantages, but it also involves some major risks.

they grew and matured. In some cases this was a consequence of Canon's strategy of withdrawing from markets where it could not sustain superior technical expertise, as in the case of liquid-crystal displays. But in other cases, followers have overtaken the pioneer by offering better products, superior customer service, or lower prices. This leads to an interesting strategic question: Is it usually better for a firm to bear the high costs and risks of being the pioneer in hopes of maintaining a profitable position as the market grows or to be a follower that watches for possible design or marketing mistakes by the pioneer before joining the fray with its own entry? We examine this question in the next section.

Not all pioneers are intent on remaining the overall share leader as the market grows. Some adopt a niche market strategy geared to making substantial profits from specialized market segments where they will face fewer large competitors. Others—like Canon—try to stay one jump ahead of the competition by introducing a constant stream of new products and withdrawing from older markets as they become more competitive. Which strategy is best? It depends on the firm's resources and competencies, the strength of likely future competitors, and characteristics of the product and its target market. Therefore, we will examine some alternative strategies that might be adopted by a pioneer and the situations where each makes most sense.

Finally, we'll examine how marketing strategies change as the product moves from the introductory to the growth stage of its life cycle. How should the pioneer adjust its strategy to maintain its position as market leader when new competitors arrive on the scene? And what marketing programs might those late-arriving followers employ to successfully challenge an entrenched market leader? We'll examine the strategic alternatives available to both parties—and the market and competitive conditions that make some of those alternatives more viable than others—in the last part of the chapter.

How New Is New?

A survey of the new product development practices of 700 U.S. corporations conducted by the consulting firm of Booz, Allen & Hamilton found that the products introduced by those firms over a five-year period were not all equally "new." The study identified six categories of new products based on their degree of newness as perceived by both the company and the target customers. These categories are discussed below and diagrammed in Exhibit 16.1, which also indicates the percentage of new entries falling in each category during the five-year study period. Notice that only 10 percent of all new product introductions fell into the new-to-the-world category.[3]

- *New-to-the-world products*—True innovations that are new to the firm and create an entirely new market (10 percent).

- *New product lines*—A product category that is new for the company introducing it, but not new to customers in the target market because of the existence of one or more competitive brands (20 percent).

- *Additions to existing product lines*—New items that supplement a firm's established product line. These items may be moderately new to both the firm and the customers in its established product-markets. They may also serve to expand the market segments appealed to by the line (26 percent).

- *Improvements in or revisions of existing products*—Items providing improved performance or greater perceived value brought out to replace existing products. These items may present moderately new marketing and production challenges to the firm, but unless they represent a technologically new generation of products, customers are likely to perceive them as similar to the products they replace (26 percent).

Exhibit 16.1

CATEGORIES OF NEW PRODUCTS DEFINED ACCORDING TO THEIR DEGREE OF NEWNESS TO THE COMPANY AND CUSTOMERS IN THE TARGET MARKET

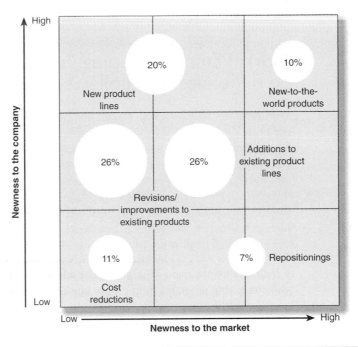

Source: New Products Management for the 1980s (New York: Booz, Allen & Hamilton, 1982). Used by permission.

- *Repositionings*—Existing products that are targeted at new applications and new market segments (7 percent).
- *Cost reductions*—Product modifications providing similar performance at lower cost (11 percent).

A product's degree of newness—to the company, its target customers, or both—helps determine the amount of complexity and uncertainty involved in the engineering, operations, and marketing tasks necessary to make it a successful new entry. It also contributes to the amount of risk inherent in those tasks.

Introducing a product that is new to both the firm and target customers requires the greatest expenditure of effort and resources. It also involves the greatest amount of uncertainty and risk of failure because of the lack of information and experience with the technology and the target customers.

Products new to target customers but not new to the firm (such as line extensions or modifications aimed at new customer segments or repositionings of existing products) are often not very innovative in design or operations, but they may present a great deal of marketing uncertainty. The marketing challenge here—as with new-to-the-world products—is to build **primary demand,** making target customers aware of the product and convincing them to adopt it. We investigate this marketing problem in the first half of this chapter.

Finally, products new to the company but not to the market (such as new product lines, line extensions, product modifications, and cost reductions) often present fewer challenges for R&D and product engineering. The company can study and learn from earlier designs or competitors' products. However, these products can present major challenges for process engineering, production scheduling, quality control, and inventory management. Once the company introduces such a product into the market, its primary marketing objective is to build selective demand and capture market share, convincing customers the new offering is better than existing competitive products. We discuss marketing programs a firm might use to accomplish these objectives later in this chapter.

Market Entry Strategies: Is It Better to Be a Pioneer or a Follower?

With products such as Word, Excel, and Powerpoint, Microsoft holds a leading share of most office application software categories. But in most of those categories, the firm was not the pioneer. Lotus 1-2-3 was the leading spreadsheet for many years, and WordPerfect and other programs led the word processing category. But as a follower, Microsoft developed improved product designs offering better performance, and it had superior financial resources to aggressively promote its products. Microsoft's Windows also held a commanding share of the operating systems market; a position the firm could leverage to convince personal computer manufacturers to bundle its applications software with their machines.

On the other hand, some of the software industry's pioneers have not fared so well in the marketplace. Lotus, for example, experienced financial difficulties and was ultimately acquired by IBM. While we have stressed the competitive importance of growth via the introduction of new products, the important strategic question is whether it always makes sense to go first. Or do *both* pioneer and follower market entry strategies have some particular advantages under different conditions?

Pioneer Strategy

Conventional wisdom holds that although they take the greatest risks and probably experience more failures than their more conservative competitors, successful pioneers are handsomely rewarded. It is assumed competitive advantages inherent in being the first to enter a new product-market can be sustained through the growth stage and into the maturity stage of the product life cycle, resulting in a strong share position and substantial returns.

Some of the potential sources of competitive advantage available to pioneers are briefly summarized in Exhibit 16.2 and discussed below.[4]

1. *First choice of market segments and positions.* The pioneer has the opportunity to develop a product offering with attributes most important to the largest segment of customers or to

Exhibit 16.2

POTENTIAL ADVANTAGES OF PIONEER AND FOLLOWER STRATEGIES

Pioneer	Follower
• Economies of scale and experience	• Ability to take advantage of pioneer's positioning mistakes
• High switching costs for early adopters	• Ability to take advantage of pioneer's product mistakes
• Pioneer defines the rules of the game	• Ability to take advantage of pioneer's marketing mistakes
• Possibility of positive network effects	• Ability to take advantage of the latest technology
• Distribution advantage	• Ability to take advantage of pioneer's limited resources
• Influence on consumer choice criteria and attitudes	
• Possibility of preempting scarce resources	

promote the importance of attributes that favor its brand. Thus, the pioneer's brand can become the standard of reference customers use to evaluate other brands. This can make it more difficult for followers with me-too products to convince existing customers that their new brands are superior to the older and more familiar pioneer. If the pioneer has successfully tied its offering to the choice criteria of the largest group of customers, it also becomes more difficult for followers to differentiate their offerings in ways that are attractive to the mass-market segment. They may have to target a smaller peripheral segment or niche instead.

2. *The pioneer defines the rules of the game.* The pioneer's actions on such variables as product quality, price, distribution, warranties, postsale service, and promotional appeals and budgets set standards that subsequent competitors must meet or beat. If the pioneer sets those standards high enough, it can raise the costs of entry and perhaps preempt some potential competitors.[5]

3. *Distribution advantages.* The pioneer has the most options in designing a distribution channel to bring the new product to market. This is particularly important for industrial goods where, if the pioneer exercises its options well and with dispatch, it should end up with a network of the best distributors. This can exclude later entrants from some markets. Distributors are often reluctant to take on second or third brands. This is especially true when the product is technically complex and the distributor must carry large inventories of the product and spare parts and invest in specialized training and service.

   For consumer package goods, it is more difficult to slow the entry of later competitors by preempting distribution alternatives. Nevertheless, the pioneer still has the advantage of attaining more shelf-facings at the outset of the growth stage. By quickly expanding its product line following an initial success, the pioneer can appropriate still more shelf space, thereby making the challenge faced by followers even more difficult. For consumer package goods, the pioneer can often attain more shelf-facings in retail stores than followers. And as many retailers are reducing the number of brands they carry in a given product category to speed inventory turnover and reduce costs, it is becoming more difficult for followers with unfamiliar brands and small market shares to gain extensive distribution.

4. *Economies of scale and experience.* Being first means the pioneer can gain accumulated volume and experience and thereby lower per unit costs at a faster rate than followers. This advantage is particularly pronounced when the product is technically sophisticated and involves high development costs or when its life cycle is likely to be short with sales increasing rapidly during the introduction and early growth stages.

   As we shall see later, the pioneer can deploy these cost advantages in a number of ways to protect its early lead against followers. One strategy is to lower price, which can discourage followers from entering the market because it raises the volume necessary for them to break even. Or the pioneer might invest its savings in additional marketing efforts to expand its penetration of the market, such as heavier advertising, a larger salesforce, or continuing product improvements or line extensions.

5. *High switching costs for early adopters.* Customers who are early to adopt a pioneer's new product may be reluctant to change suppliers when competitive products appear. This is particularly true for industrial goods where the costs of switching suppliers can be high. Compatible equipment and spare parts, investments in employee training, and the risks of lower product quality or customer service make it easier for the pioneer to retain its early customers over time.

   In some cases, however, switching costs can work against the pioneer and in favor of followers. A pioneer may have trouble converting customers to a new technology if they must bear high switching costs to abandon their old way of doing things. Pioneers in the development of music CDs, for instance, faced the formidable task of convincing potential buyers to abandon their substantial investments in turntables and LP record libraries and to start all over again with the new technology. Once the pioneers had begun to convince consumers that the superior convenience, sound quality, and durability of CDs justified those high switching costs, however, demand for CDs and CD players began to grow rapidly and it was easier for followers to attract customers.

6. *Possibility of positive network effects.* The value of some kinds of goods and services to an individual customer increases as greater numbers of other people adopt the product and the network of users grows larger. Economists say that such products exhibit **network externalities or positive network effects.** Information and communications technologies, such as wireless phones, fax machines, computer software, e-mail, and many Internet sites, are particularly likely to benefit from network effects.[6] For instance, the value of eBay as an auction site increases as the number of potential buyers and sellers who visit and trade on the site increase. If the pioneer in such a product or service category can gain and maintain a substantial customer base before competing technologies or providers appear on the market, the positive network effects generated by that customer base will enhance the benefits of the pioneer's offering and make it more difficult for followers to match its perceived value.

7. *Possibility of preempting scarce resources and suppliers.* The pioneer may be able to negotiate favorable deals with suppliers who are eager for new business or who do not appreciate the size of the opportunity for their raw materials or component parts. If later entrants subsequently find those materials and components in short supply, they may be constrained from expanding as fast as they might like or be forced to pay premium prices.

Not All Pioneers Capitalize on Their Potential Advantages

There is some evidence to suggest that the above advantages can help pioneers gain and maintain a competitive edge in new markets. For instance, some research has found that surviving pioneers hold a significantly larger average market share when their industries reach maturity than firms that were either fast followers or late entrants in the product category.[7]

On the other hand, some pioneers fail. They either abandon the product category, go out of business, or get acquired before their industry matures. One study, which took these failed pioneers into account and averaged their performance together with that of the more successful survivors, found that pioneers overall did not perform as well over the long haul as followers.[8]

Of course, volume and market share are not the only dimensions on which success can be measured. Unfortunately, there is little evidence concerning the effect of the timing of a firm's entry into a new market on its ultimate profitability in that market or the value generated for shareholders.[9]

In view of the mixed research evidence, then, it seems reasonable to conclude that while a pioneer may have some *potential* competitive advantages, not all pioneers are successful at capitalizing on them. Some fail during the introductory or shakeout stages of their industries' life cycles. And those that survive may lack the resources to keep up with rapid growth or the competencies needed to maintain their early lead in the face of onslaughts by strong followers.

Follower Strategy

In many cases a firm becomes a follower by default. It is simply beaten to a new product-market by a quicker competitor. But even when a company has the capability of being the first mover, the above observations suggest there may be some advantages to letting other firms go first into a product-market. Let the pioneer shoulder the initial risks while the followers observe their shortcomings and mistakes. Possible advantages of such a follower strategy are briefly summarized in Exhibit 16.2 and discussed below.

1. *Ability to take advantage of the pioneer's positioning mistakes.* If the pioneer misjudges the preferences and purchase criteria of the mass-market segment or attempts to satisfy two or more segments at once, it is vulnerable to the introduction of more precisely positioned products by a follower. By tailoring its offerings to each distinct segment, the follower(s) can successfully encircle the pioneer.

2. *Ability to take advantage of the pioneer's product mistakes.* If the pioneer's initial product has technical limitations or design flaws, the follower can benefit by overcoming these weaknesses. Even when the pioneering product is technically satisfactory, a follower may gain an advantage through product enhancements. For example, Compaq captured a substantial share of the commercial PC market by developing faster and more portable versions of IBM's original machine.

3. *Ability to take advantage of the pioneer's marketing mistakes.* If the pioneer makes any marketing mistakes in introducing a new entry, it opens opportunities for later entrants. This observation is closely related to the first two points, yet goes beyond product positioning and design to the actual execution of the pioneer's marketing program. For example, the pioneer may fail to attain adequate distribution, spend too little on introductory advertising, or use ineffective promotional appeals to communicate the product's benefits. A follower can observe these mistakes, design a marketing program to overcome them, and successfully compete head-to-head with the pioneer.

   Marketing mistakes can leave a pioneer vulnerable to challenges from later entrants even in product categories with substantial positive network effects. For example, Microsoft's Windows operating system was not the first user-friendly system on the market. However, Microsoft promoted and priced Windows very aggressively, it formed alliances with original equipment manufacturers (OEMs) in the personal computer industry to encourage them to install Windows on their machines, and it engaged in extensive licensing and cooperative agreements with other software developers. All these actions helped Windows capture a commanding share of the operating systems market, which in turn generated tremendous positive network effects for Windows and made it difficult for alternative systems to compete (perhaps *too* difficult, from the U.S. Justice Department's perspective).

4. *Ability to take advantage of the latest technology.* In industries characterized by rapid technological advances, followers can possibly introduce products based on a superior, second-generation technology and thereby gain an advantage over the pioneer. And the pioneer may have difficulty reacting quickly to such advances if it is heavily committed to an earlier technology. Consumer popularity of the newer VHS format, for instance, gave followers in the videocassette recorder market an advantage over pioneer Sony, which was locked in to the less-popular Beta format.

5. *Ability to take advantage of pioneer's limited resources.* If the pioneer has limited resources for production facilities or marketing programs, or fails to commit sufficient resources to its new entry, followers willing and able to outspend the pioneer experience few enduring constraints.

Determinants of Success for Pioneers and Followers

Our discussion suggests that a pioneering firm stands the best chance for long-term success in market-share leadership and profitability when (1) the new product-market is insulated from the entry of competitors, at least for a while, by strong patent protection, proprietary technology (such as a unique production process), substantial investment requirements, or positive network effects, or (2) the firm has sufficient size, resources, and competencies to take full advantage of its pioneering position and preserve it in the face of later competitive entries. Evidence suggests that organizational competencies, such as R&D and marketing skills, not only affect a firm's success as a pioneer, but may also influence the company's decision about whether or not to be a pioneer in the first place. Firms that perceive they lack the competencies necessary to sustain a first-mover advantage may be more likely to wait for another company to take the lead and to enter the market later.[10]

McDonald's is an example of a pioneer that has succeeded by aggressively building on the foundations of its early advantage. Although the firm started small as a single hamburger restaurant, it used the franchise system of distribution to rapidly expand the number of McDonald's outlets with a minimum cash investment. That expansion plus stringent quality and cost controls, relatively low prices made possible by experience-curve effects, heavy advertising expenditures, and product line expansion aimed at specific market segments (such as Egg McMuffin for the breakfast crowd) have all enabled the firm to maintain a commanding share of the fast-food hamburger industry.

On the other hand, a follower will most likely succeed when there are few legal, technological, or financial barriers to inhibit entry and when it has sufficient resources or competencies to overwhelm the pioneer's early advantage. For example, given Procter & Gamble's well-established brand name and superior advertising and promotional resources, the company was able to quickly take the market share lead away from pioneer Minnetonka, Inc., in the plaque-fighting toothpaste market with a reformulated version of Crest.

A study conducted across a broad range of industries in the PIMS database supports these observations.[11] The author's findings are briefly summarized in Exhibit 16.3 and discussed below. The author found that, regardless of the industry involved, pioneers able to maintain their preeminent position well into the market's growth stage had supported their early entry with the following marketing strategy elements:

- *Large entry scale*—Successful pioneers had sufficient capacity, or could expand quickly enough, to pursue a mass-market targeting strategy, usually on a national rather than a local or regional basis. Thus, they could expand their volume quickly and achieve the benefits of experience-curve effects before major competitors could confront them.
- *Broad product line*—Successful pioneers also quickly add line extensions or modifications to their initial product to tailor their offerings to specific market segments. This helps reduce their vulnerability to later entrants who might differentiate themselves by targeting one or more peripheral markets.

Exhibit 16.3

MARKETING STRATEGY ELEMENTS PURSUED BY SUCCESSFUL PIONEERS, FAST FOLLOWERS, AND LATE ENTRANTS

These marketers . . .	are characterized by one or more of these strategy elements:
Successful pioneers	• Large entry scale
	• Broad product line
	• High product quality
	• Heavy promotional expenditures
Successful fast followers	• Larger entry scale than the pioneer
	• Leapfrogging the pioneer with superior:
	product technology
	product quality
	customer service
Successful late entrants	• Focus on peripheral target markets or niches

- *High product quality*—Successful pioneers also offer a high-quality, well-designed product from the beginning, thus removing one potential differential advantage for later followers. Competent engineering, thorough product and market testing before commercialization, and good quality control during the production process are all important to the continued success of pioneers.

- *Heavy promotional expenditures*—Successful pioneers had marketing programs characterized by relatively high advertising and promotional expenditures as a percentage of sales. Initially the promotion helps to stimulate awareness and primary demand for the new product category, build volume, and reduce unit costs. Later, this promotion focuses on building selective demand for the pioneer's brand and reinforcing loyalty as new competitors enter.

The same study found that the most successful fast followers had the resources to enter the new market on a larger scale than the pioneer. Consequently they could quickly reduce their unit costs, offer lower prices than incumbent competitors, and enjoy any positive network effects. Some fast followers achieved success, however, by leapfrogging earlier entrants. These followers won customers away from the pioneer by offering a product with more sophisticated technology, better quality, or superior service.

Finally, the author found that some late entrants also achieved substantial profits by avoiding direct confrontations with more established competitors and by pursuing peripheral target markets. They often offer tailor-made products to smaller market niches and support them with high levels of service.

Followers typically enter a market after it is in the growth phase of its life cycle, and they start with low market shares relative to the established pioneer. Consequently, our discussion later in this chapter of marketing strategies for low-share competitors in growth markets is germane to both fast followers and later entrants. Before focusing on strategies for followers, however, we should first examine strategies that might be successfully employed by the first entrant in a new product-market.

Strategic Marketing Programs for Pioneers

The preceding discussion suggests that the ultimate success of a pioneering strategy depends on the nature of the demand and competitive situation the pioneer encounters in the market and on the pioneer's ability to design and support an effective marketing program.

KEY OBSERVATION

Success of a pioneering strategy depends on the nature of the demand and competitive situation the pioneer encounters in the market and on the pioneer's ability to design and support an effective marketing program.

It also depends on how the pioneer defines *success*—in other words, the objectives it seeks to achieve. Thus, a pioneer might choose from one of three different types of marketing strategies: mass-market penetration, niche penetration, or skimming and early withdrawal. Exhibit 16.4 summarizes the primary objectives of each strategy and the circumstances favoring their use. But, while specific conditions may favor a given strategy, they do not guarantee its success. Much still depends on how effectively a firm implements the strategy. Also, it is highly unlikely that all the listed conditions will exist simultaneously in any single product-market.

Mass-Market Penetration

The ultimate objective of a mass-market penetration strategy is to capture and maintain a commanding share of the total market for the new product. Thus, the critical marketing task is to convince as many potential customers as possible to adopt the pioneer's product quickly to drive down unit costs and build a large contingent of loyal customers before competitors enter the market.

Exhibit 16.4

MARKETING OBJECTIVES AND STRATEGIES FOR NEW PRODUCT PIONEERS

Situational variables	ALTERNATIVE MARKETING STRATEGIES		
	Mass-market penetration	Niche penetration	Skimming: early withdrawal
Primary objective	• Maximize number of triers and adopters in *total market*.	• Maximize number of triers and adopters in *target segment*.	• Recoup development and commercialization costs as soon as possible.
	• Maintain leading share position in *total market*.	• Maintain leading share position in *target segment*.	• Withdraw from market when increasing competition puts pressure on margins.
Market characteristics	• Large potential demand.	• Large potential demand.	• Limited potential demand.
	• Relatively homogeneous customer needs.	• Fragmented market; many different applications and benefit segments.	• Customers likely to adopt product relatively slowly; long adoption process.
	• Customers likely to adopt product relatively quickly; short diffusion process.	• Customers likely to adopt product relatively quickly; short adoption process.	• Early adopters willing to pay high price; demand is price inelastic.
Product characteristics	• Product technology patentable or difficult to copy.	• Product technology offers little patent protection; easily copied or adapted.	• Product technology offers little patent protection; easily copied or adapted.
	• Substantial network effects; value increases with growth of installed customer base.	• Limited or no network effects.	• Limited or no network effects.
	• Components or materials difficult to obtain; limited sources of supply.	• Components or materials easy to obtain; many sources of supply.	• Components or materials easy to obtain; many sources of supply.
	• Complex production process; substantial development and/or investment required.	• Relatively simple production process; little development or additional investment required.	• Relatively simple production process; little development or additional investment required.
Competitor characteristics	• Few potential competitors.	• Many potential competitors.	• Many potential competitors.
	• Most potential competitors have limited resources and competencies; few sources of differential advantage.	• Some potential competitors have substantial resources and competencies; possible sources of differential advantage.	• Some potential competitors have substantial resources and competencies; possible sources of differential advantage.
Firm characteristics	• Strong product engineering skills; able to quickly develop product modifications and line extensions for multiple market segments.	• Limited product engineering skills and resources.	• Strong basic R&D and new product development skills; a prospector with good capability for continued new product innovation.
	• Strong marketing skills and resources; ability to identify and develop marketing programs for multiple segments; ability to shift from stimulation of primary demand to stimulation of selective demand as competitors enter.	• Limited marketing skills and resources.	• Good sales and promotional skills; able to quickly build primary demand in target market; perhaps has limited marketing resources for long-term market maintenance.
	• Sufficient financial and organizational resources to build capacity in advance of growth in demand.	• Insufficient financial or organizational resources to build capacity in advance of growing demand.	• Limited financial or organizational resources to commit to building capacity in advance of growth in demand.

Mass-market penetration tends to be most successful when entry barriers inhibit or delay the appearance of competitors, thus allowing the pioneer more time to build volume, lower costs, and create loyal customers, or when the pioneer has competencies or resources that most potential competitors cannot match, as in the case of Canon's technical and R&D expertise in the copier industry. Other relevant competencies include product engineering, promotional and channel management skills, and the financial and organizational resources necessary to expand capacity in advance of demand. In some cases, though, a smaller firm with limited resources can successfully employ a mass-market penetration strategy if the market has a protracted adoption process and slow initial growth. Slow growth can delay competitive entry because fewer competitors are attracted to a market with questionable future growth. This allows the pioneer more time to expand capacity.

Mass-market penetration is also an appropriate strategy when the product category is likely to experience positive network effects. Since the value of such products increases as the number of users grows, it makes sense for the pioneer to quickly capture and maintain as large a customer base as possible.

Niche Penetration

Even when a new product-market expands quickly, however, it may still be possible for a small firm with limited resources to be a successful pioneer. In such cases, though, the firm must define success in a more limited way. Instead of pursuing the objective of capturing and sustaining a leading share of the entire market, it may make more sense for such firms to focus their efforts on a single market segment. This kind of **niche penetration** strategy can help the smaller pioneer gain the biggest bang for its limited bucks and avoid direct confrontations with bigger competitors.

A niche penetration strategy is most appropriate when the new market is expected to grow quickly and there are a number of different benefit or applications segments to appeal to. It is particularly attractive when there are few barriers to the entry of major competitors and when the pioneer has only limited resources and competencies to defend any advantage it gains through early entry.

Some pioneers may intend to pursue a mass-market penetration strategy when introducing a new product or service, but they end up implementing a niche penetration strategy instead. This is particularly likely when the new market grows faster or is more fragmented than the pioneer expects. Facing such a situation, a pioneer with limited resources may decide to concentrate on holding its leading position in one or a few segments, rather than spreading itself too thin developing unique line extensions and marketing programs for many different markets or going deep into debt to finance rapid expansion.

Skimming and Early Withdrawal

Even when a firm has the resources to sustain a leading position in a new product-market, it may choose not to. Competition is usually inevitable, and prices and margins tend to drop dramatically after followers enter the market. Therefore, some pioneers opt to pursue a **skimming** strategy while planning an early withdrawal from the market. This involves setting a high price and engaging in only limited advertising and promotion to maximize per-unit profits and recover the product's development costs as quickly as possible. At the same time, the firm may work to develop new applications for its technology or the next generation of more advanced technology. Then when competitors enter the market and margins fall, the firm is ready to cannibalize its own product with one based on new technology or to move into new segments of the market.

The 3M Company is a master of the skimming strategy. According to one 3M manager, "We hit fast, price high (full economic value of the product to the user), and get the heck out when the me-too products pour in." The new markets pioneered by the company are often smaller ones of $10 million to $50 million, and the firm may dominate them for only about five years or so. By then, it is ready to launch the next generation of new technology or to move the old technology into new applications.[12] An example of 3M's approach is described in Exhibit 16.5.

As Exhibit 16.4 indicates, either small or large firms can use strategies of skimming and early withdrawal. But it is critical that the company have good R&D and product development skills so it can produce a constant stream of new products or new applications to replace older ones as they attract heavy competition. Also, since a firm pursuing this kind of strategy plans to remain in a market only short term, it is most appropriate when there are few barriers to entry, the product is expected to diffuse rapidly, and the pioneer lacks the capacity or other resources necessary to defend a leading share position over the long haul.

Marketing Program Components for a Mass-Market Penetration Strategy

As mentioned, the crucial marketing task in a mass-market penetration strategy is to maximize the number of customers adopting the firm's new product as quickly as possible. This requires a marketing program focused on (1) *aggressively building product awareness and motivation to buy* among a broad cross-section of potential customers and (2) *making it as easy as possible for those customers to try the new product,* on the assumption that they will try it, like it, develop loyalty, and make repeat purchases.

Exhibit 16.6 outlines a number of marketing activities that might help increase customers' awareness and willingness to buy or improve their ability to try the product. This is by no means an exhaustive list; nor do we mean to imply that a successful pioneer must necessarily engage in all of the listed activities. Marketing managers must develop programs combining activities that fit both the objectives of a mass-market penetration strategy and the specific market and potential competitive conditions the new product faces.

Increasing Customers' Awareness and Willingness to Buy   Obviously, heavy expenditures on advertising, introductory promotions such as sampling and couponing, and personal selling efforts can all increase awareness of a new product or service among potential customers. This is the critical first step in the adoption process for a new entry. The relative importance of these promotional tools varies, however, depending on the nature of the product and the number of potential customers. For instance, personal selling efforts are often the most critical component of the promotional mix for highly technical industrial products with a limited potential customer base, such as Canon's new wide-format bubble

Exhibit 16.6

COMPONENTS OF STRATEGIC MARKETING PROGRAMS FOR PIONEERS

ALTERNATIVE STRATEGIC MARKETING PROGRAMS

Strategic objectives and tasks	Mass-market penetration	Niche penetration	Skimming: early withdrawal
Increase customers' awareness and willingness to buy	• Heavy advertising to generate awareness among customers in mass market; broad use of mass media.	• Heavy advertising directed at target segment to generate awareness; use selective media relevant to target.	• Limited advertising to generate awareness; particularly among least price-sensitive early adopters.
	• Extensive salesforce efforts to win new adopters; possible use of incentives to encourage new product sales.	• Extensive salesforce efforts focused on potential customers in target segment; possible use of incentives to encourage new product sales to target accounts.	• Extensive salesforce efforts, particularly focused on largest potential adopters; possible use of volume-based incentives to encourage new product sales.
	• Advertising and sales appeals stress generic benefits of new product type.	• Advertising and sales appeals stress generic benefits of new product type.	• Advertising and sales appeals stress generic benefits of new product type.
	• Extensive introductory sales promotions to induce trial (sampling, couponing, quantity discounts).	• Extensive introductory sales promotions to induce trial, but focused on target segment.	• Limited use, if any, of introductory sales promotions; if used, they should be volume-based quantity discounts.
	• Move relatively quickly to expand offerings (line extensions, multiple package sizes) to appeal to multiple segments.	• Additional product development limited to improvements or modifications to increase appeal to target segment.	• Little, if any, additional development within the product category.
	• Offer free trial, liberal return, or extended warranty policies to reduce customers' perceived risk of adopting the new product.	• Offer free trial, liberal return, or extended warranty policies to reduce target customers' perceived risk of adopting the new product.	• Offer free trial, liberal return or extended warranty policies to reduce target customers' perceived risk of adopting the new product.
Increase customers' ability to buy	• Penetration pricing; or start with high price but bring out lower-priced versions in anticipation of competitive entries.	• Penetration pricing; or start with high price but bring out lower-priced versions in anticipation of competitive entries.	• Skimming pricing; attempt to maintain margins at level consistent with value of product to early adopters.
	• Extended credit terms to encourage initial purchases.	• Extended credit terms to encourage initial purchases.	• Extended credit terms to encourage initial purchases.
	• Heavy use of trade promotions aimed at gaining extensive distribution.	• Trade promotions aimed at gaining solid distribution among retailers or distributors pertinent for reaching target segment.	• Limited use of trade promotions; only as necessary to gain adequate distribution.
	• Offer engineering, installation, and training services to increase new product's compatibility with customers' current operations to reduce switching costs.	• Offer engineering, installation, and training services to increase new product's compatibility with customers' current operations to reduce switching costs.	• Offer limited engineering installation, and training services as necessary to overcome customers' objections.

jet printer. Media advertising and sales promotion are usually more useful for building awareness and primary demand for a new consumer good among customers in the mass market. In either case, when designing a mass-market penetration marketing program, firms should broadly focus promotional efforts to expose and attract as many potential customers as possible before competitors show up.

Firms might also attempt to increase customers' willingness to buy their products by reducing the risk associated with buying something new. This can be done by letting customers try the product without obligation, as when car dealers allow potential customers to test-drive a new model, or when software developers allow customers to download a trial version and use it free for 30 days. Liberal return policies and extended warranties can serve the same purpose.

Finally, a firm committed to mass-market penetration might also broaden its product offerings to increase its appeal to as many market segments as possible. This helps reduce its vulnerability to later entrants who could focus on specific market niches. Firms can accomplish such market expansion through the rapid introduction of line extensions, additional package sizes, or product modifications targeted at new applications and market segments.

Increasing Customers' Ability to Buy

For customers to adopt a new product and develop loyalty toward it, they must be aware of the item and be motivated to buy. But they must also have the wherewithal to purchase it. Thus, to capture as many customers in as short a time as possible, it usually makes sense for a firm pursuing mass-market penetration to keep prices low (penetration pricing) and perhaps offer liberal financing arrangements or easy credit terms during the introductory period.

Pioneers introducing new information or communications technologies tend to be particularly aggressive in pricing their offerings for two reasons. First, as we have seen, such products can often benefit from positive network effects if enough customers can be induced to adopt them quickly. Second, the variable costs of producing and distributing additional units of such products is usually very low, perhaps even approaching zero. For instance, the costs of developing a new software product are high, but once it is developed copies can be made and distributed over the Internet for next to nothing. These two factors mean that it often makes sense for pioneers in such product categories to set their price very low to initial customers—perhaps even to give away trial copies—in hopes of quickly building a large installed base, capturing more value from later customers with higher prices, and maximizing the lifetime value of their customers by selling them upgrades and enhanced versions of the product in the future.[13]

Another factor that can inhibit customers' ability to buy is a lack of product availability. Thus, extensive personal selling and trade promotions aimed at gaining adequate distribution are usually a critical part of a mass-market penetration marketing program. Such efforts should take place before the start of promotional campaigns to ensure that the product is available as soon as customers are motivated to buy it.

A highly technical new product's incompatibility with other related products or systems currently used can also inhibit customers' purchases. It can result in high switching costs for a potential adopter. The pioneer might reduce those costs by designing the product to be as compatible as possible with related equipment. It might also offer engineering services to help make the new product more compatible with existing operations, provide free installation assistance, and conduct training programs for the customer's employees.

The above actions are suited not just to the marketing of products; most are essential elements of mass-market penetration strategies for new service, retail, and even e-commerce websites as well. The marketing actions of an e-tailer such as Amazon.com, discussed in

Exhibit 16.7   Amazon's Mass-Market Penetration Strategy

Founded in 1994 by Jeff Bezos as the first online bookstore, Amazon.com (www.amazon.com) has employed many of the marketing tactics we have listed as possible components of a mass-market penetration strategy. In the early days, the firm spent heavily on various promotional tools to attract buyers and build a base of loyal customers. In the late 1990s, the firm was spending an average of more than $50 for each new customer it attracted. The money was spent on banner advertising and alliances with other sites and Web portals, traditional media advertising, special consumer promotions, and an "associates" program through which sites that offer a link to Amazon get a cut of any sales they referred. As Amazon has built its customer base and increased public awareness, its acquisition costs per customer have declined substantially.

In the early years, many of Amazon's inventory-storage and order-fulfillment functions were outsourced, its fixed costs were low, and it had huge amounts of capital to play with. Consequently, it was able to attract customers from bricks-and-mortar bookstores by offering very low prices and a wide selection of titles.

To gain the loyalty of new customers it attracted, Amazon worked hard to constantly improve its customer service. It collected information from customers concerning their preferences, desires, and complaints, then launched a series of customer service innovations, such as one-click ordering and a popular best-seller list ranking sales on the site. More recently, it has invested hundreds of millions of dollars to build a network of six automated distribution centers around the United States to better control order fulfillment, ensure quick and reliable delivery, and lower fulfillment costs. Indeed, those fulfillment costs

were down to 10.6 percent of sales in 2002, compared to 12.8 percent the year before.

Finally, Amazon has greatly expanded its product lines over the years to include CDs, toys, electronics, tools, and a variety of other things. This move was motivated by the company's desire to become a one-stop shopping venue, and to increase the average annual revenues per customer.

By mid-2003 there were signs that Amazon's mass-market penetration strategy might succeed. Sales revenues were projected to grow to $4.5 billion. More importantly, early customers were returning to make repeat purchases. Repeat customers accounted for more than three-quarters of revenues in 2002, and the average annual revenue per customer was about $140.

While analysts and investors were concerned that the firm might never be able to recoup the heavy expenditures and investments involved in its strategy, Bezos and the believers were confident that the firm's expanding customer base and its ability to increase the loyalty and lifetime value of those customers would eventually pay big dividends. They were predicting the firm would become profitable on an annual basis for the first time in 2003, with an expected $200 million in earnings. It's too soon to know which side is right, but that is a very common state of affairs for any pioneering firm that opts to pursue a mass-market penetration strategy.

Source: Eryn Brown, "Nine Ways to Win on the Web," *Fortune,* May 24, 1999, pp. 112–25; Robert Hof, Debra Sparks, Ellen Neuborne, and Wendy Zellner, "Can Amazon Make It?" *Business Week,* July 10, 2000, pp. 38–43; David Shook, "Special Report: The 2002 E.Biz 25," *Business Week Online* (www.businessweek.com), October 1, 2002; Robert Hof, "Amazon: Heading for a Hangover?" *Business Week,* December 16, 2002, p. 87; and Fred Vogelstein, "Mighty Amazon," *Fortune,* May 26, 2003, pp. 60–74.

Exhibit 16.7, provide a textbook example of the elements of, as well as some of the risks inherent in, a mass-market penetration strategy.

Additional Considerations When Pioneering Global Markets   Whether the product-market a pioneer is trying to penetrate is domestic or foreign, many of the marketing tasks appropriate for increasing potential customers' awareness, willingness, and ability to buy the new product or service are largely the same. Of course, some of the tactical aspects of the pioneer's strategic marketing program—such as specific product features, promotional appeals, or distribution channels—may have to be adjusted to fit different cultural, legal, or economic circumstances across national borders. For Bausch & Lomb to develop the Chinese market for contact lenses, for instance, it first had to develop an extensive training program for the country's opticians and build a network of retail outlets, actions that were unnecessary in more developed markets.

Unless the firm already has an economic presence in a country via the manufacture or marketing of other products or services, however, a potential global pioneer faces at least one additional question to answer. What mode of entry is most appropriate? As we saw in Chapter 13 there are three basic mechanisms for entering a foreign market—exporting through agent middlemen (using local manufacturers reps or distributors), contractual agreements such as licensing or franchise arrangements with local firms, or direct investment.

Exporting lowers the financial risk involved for the pioneer when entering an unfamiliar foreign market. Unfortunately, such arrangements also afford the pioneer relatively little control over the marketing and distribution of its product or service, activities that are critical for winning customer awareness and loyalty in a new market. At the other extreme, investing in a wholly owned subsidiary typically makes little sense until it becomes clear whether the pioneering product will win customer acceptance. Consequently, intermediate modes of entry, such as licensing or forming a joint venture with a local firm in the host country, tend to be the preferred means of developing global markets for new products. Joint ventures are particularly appropriate in this regard because they avoid quotas and import restrictions or taxes, and they allow the pioneer to share financial risks while gaining local marketing expertise.[14] Thus, Bausch & Lomb established a joint venture with Beijing Optical as a basis for building contact lens factories in China and for gaining access to Chinese opticians. Consequently, the firm has been able to develop and maintain a leading market share in the world's most heavily populated country with a modest investment of only about $20 million.

Marketing Program Components for a Niche Penetration Strategy

Because the objectives of a niche penetration strategy are similar to but more narrowly focused than those of a mass-market strategy, the marketing program elements are also likely to be similar under the two strategies. Obviously, however, the niche penetrator should keep its marketing efforts clearly focused on the target segment to gain as much impact as possible from its limited resources. This point is evident in the outline of program components in Exhibit 16.6. For example, while a niche strategy calls for the same advertising, sales promotion, personal selling, and trade promotion activities as a mass-market program, the former should use more selective media, call schedules, and channel designs to precisely direct those activities toward the target segment.

Marketing Program Components for a Skimming Strategy

As Exhibit 16.6 suggests, one major difference between a skimming strategy and a mass-market penetration strategy involves pricing policies. A relatively high price is appropriate for a skimming strategy to increase margins and revenues, even though some price-sensitive customers may be reluctant to adopt the product at that price.[15] This also suggests that introductory promotional programs might best focus on customer groups who are least sensitive to price and most likely to be early adopters of the new product. This can help hold down promotion costs and avoid wasting marketing efforts on less profitable market segments. Thus, in many consumer goods businesses, skimming strategies focus on relatively upscale customers, since they are often more likely to be early adopters and less sensitive to price.

Another critical element of a skimming strategy is the nature of the firm's continuing product-development efforts. A pioneer that plans to leave a market when competitors enter should not devote much effort to expanding its product line through line extensions or multiple package sizes. Instead, it should concentrate on the next generation of technology or on identifying new application segments, in other words, preparing its avenue of escape from the market.

Now that we have examined some strategies a pioneer might follow in entering a new market, we are left with two important strategic questions. The pioneer is by definition the early share leader in the new market; hence the first question is, What adjustments in strategy might be necessary for the pioneer to *maintain its leading share position* after competitors arrive on the scene? The second is, What strategies might followers adopt *to take business away from the early leader and increase their relative share position* as the market grows? We examine these two issues next.

Growth-Market Strategies for Market Leaders

As a product-market enters the growth stage of its life cycle, the competitor with the leading market share is usually the pioneer or at least one of the first entrants. Often, that firm's strategic objective is to maintain its leading share position in the face of increasing competition as the market expands. Share maintenance may not seem like a very aggressive objective, because it implies the business is merely trying to stay even rather than forge ahead. But two important facts must be kept in mind.

First, the dynamics of a growth market—including the increasing number of competitors, the fragmentation of market segments, and the threat of product innovation from

within and outside the industry—make maintaining an early lead in relative market share very difficult. The continuing need for investment to finance growth, the likely negative cash flows that result, and the threat of governmental antitrust action can make it even more difficult. For example, 31 percent of the 877 market-share leaders in the PIMS database experienced losses in relative share, and leaders were especially likely to suffer this fate when their market shares were very large.[16]

Second, a firm can maintain its current share position in a growth market only if its sales volume continues to grow at a rate equal to that of the overall market, enabling the firm to stay even in *absolute* market share. It may, however, be able to maintain a relative share lead even if its volume growth is less than the industry's.

Marketing Objectives for Share Leaders

Share maintenance for a market leader involves two important marketing objectives. First, the firm must *retain its current customers,* ensuring that those customers remain brand loyal when making repeat or replacement purchases. This is particularly critical for firms in consumer nondurable, service, and industrial materials and components industries where a substantial portion of total sales volume consists of repeat purchases. Second, the firm must *stimulate selective demand among later adopters* to ensure that it captures a large share of the continuing growth in industry sales.

In some cases the market leader might pursue a third objective: stimulating primary demand to help speed up overall market growth. This can be particularly important in product-markets where the adoption process is protracted because of the technical sophistication of the new product, high switching costs for potential customers, or positive network effects.

The market leader is the logical one to stimulate market growth in such situations; it has the most to gain from increased volume, assuming it can maintain its relative share of that volume. However, expanding total demand—by promoting new uses for the product or stimulating existing customers' usage and repeat purchase rates—is often more critical near the end of the growth stage and early in the maturity stage of a product's life cycle. Consequently, we discuss marketing actions appropriate to this objective in the next chapter.

Marketing Actions and Strategies to Achieve Share-Maintenance Objectives

A business might take a variety of marketing actions to maintain a leading share position in a growing market. Exhibit 16.8 outlines a lengthy, though not exhaustive, list of such actions and their specific marketing objectives. Because share maintenance involves multiple objectives, and different marketing actions may be needed to achieve each one, a strategic marketing program usually integrates a mix of the actions outlined in the exhibit.

Not all the actions summarized in Exhibit 16.8 are consistent with one another. It would be unusual, for instance, for a business to invest heavily in new product improvements and promotion to enhance its product's high-quality image and simultaneously slash prices, unless it was trying to drive out weaker competitors in the short run with an eye on higher profits in the future. Thus, the activities outlined in Exhibit 16.8 cluster into five internally consistent strategies that a market leader might employ, singly or in combination, to maintain its leading share position: a **fortress,** or **position defense, strategy;** a **flanker strategy;** a **confrontation strategy;** a **market expansion strategy;** and a **contraction,** or **strategic withdrawal, strategy.**

Exhibit 16.9 diagrams this set of strategies. It is consistent with what a number of military strategists and some marketing authorities have identified as common defensive strategies.[17] To think of them as strictly defensive, though, can be misleading. Companies can use some of these strategies offensively to preempt expected future actions by potential competitors. Or they can use them to capture an even larger share of future new customers.

Which, or what combination, of these five strategies is most appropriate for a particular product-market depends on (1) the market's size and its customers' characteristics, (2) the number and relative strengths of the competitors or potential competitors in that market, and (3) the leader's own resources and competencies. Exhibit 16.10 outlines the situations in which each strategy is most appropriate and the primary objectives for which they are best suited.

Fortress, or Position Defense, Strategy

The most basic defensive strategy is to continually strengthen a strongly held current position—to build an impregnable fortress capable of repelling attacks by current or future competitors. This strategy is nearly always part of a leader's share-maintenance efforts. By shoring up an already strong position, the firm can improve the satisfaction of current customers while increasing the attractiveness of its offering to new customers with needs and characteristics similar to those of earlier adopters.

KEY OBSERVATION

The most basic defensive strategy is to continually strengthen a strongly held current position.

Strengthening the firm's position makes particularly good sense when current and potential customers have relatively homogeneous needs and desires and the firm's offering

Exhibit 16.8

MARKETING ACTIONS TO ACHIEVE SHARE-MAINTENANCE OBJECTIVES

Marketing objectives	Possible marketing actions
Retain current customers by:	
• Maintaining/improving satisfaction and loyalty.	• Increase attention to quality control as output expands.
	• Continue product modification and improvement efforts to increase customer benefits and/or reduce costs.
	• Focus advertising on stimulation of selective demand; stress product's superior features and benefits; reminder advertising.
	• Increase salesforce's servicing of current accounts; consider formation of national or key account representatives to major customers; consider replacing independent manufacturer's reps with company salespeople where appropriate.
	• Expand postsale service capabilities; develop or expand company's own service force, or develop training programs for distributors' and dealers' service people; expand parts inventory; develop customer service hotline or website.
• Encouraging/simplifying repeat purchase.	• Expand production capacity in advance of increasing demand to avoid stockouts.
	• Improve inventory control and logistics systems to reduce delivery times.
	• Continue to build distribution channels; use periodic trade promotions to gain more extensive retail coverage and maintain shelf-facings; strengthen relationships with strongest distributors/dealers.
	• Consider negotiating long-term requirements contracts with major customers.
	• Consider developing automatic reorder systems or logistical alliances.
• Reducing attractiveness of switching.	• Develop a second brand or product line with features or price more appealing to a specific segment of current customers (*flanker strategy*—see Exhibits 16.9 and 16.10).
	• Develop multiple-line extensions or brand offerings targeted to the needs of several user segments within the market (*market expansion*).
	• Meet or beat lower prices or heavier promotional efforts by competitors—or try to preempt such efforts by potential competitors—when necessary to retain customers and when lower unit costs allow (*confrontation strategy*).
Stimulate selective demand among later adopters by:	
• Head-to-head positioning against competitive offerings or potential offerings.	• Develop a second brand or product line with features or price more appealing to a specific segment of potential customers (*flanker strategy*).
	• Make product modifications or improvements to match or beat superior competitive offerings (*confrontation strategy*).
	• Meet or beat lower prices or heavier promotional efforts by competitors when necessary to retain customers and when lower unit costs allow (*confrontation strategy*).
	• When resources are limited relative to a competitor's, consider withdrawing from smaller or slower growing segments to focus product development and promotional efforts on higher potential segments threatened by competitor (*contraction or strategic withdrawal strategy*).
• Differentiated positioning against competitive offerings or potential offerings.	• Develop multiple-line extensions or brand offerings targeted to the needs of various potential user applications or geographical segments within the market (*market expansion*).
	• Build unique distribution channels to more effectively reach specific segments of potential customers (*market expansion strategy*).
	• Design multiple advertising and/or sales promotion campaigns targeted at specific segments of potential customers (*market expansion strategy*).

Exhibit 16.9

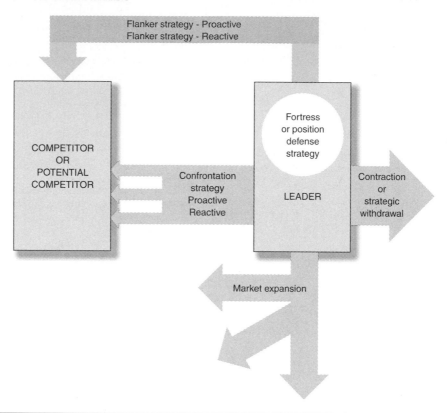

Source: Adapted from P. Kotler and R. Singh Achrol, "Marketing Warfare in the 1980's." Reprinted with permission from *Journal of Business Strategy,* Winter 1981, pp. 30–41. Used by permission of Thomson Media.

already enjoys a high level of awareness and preference in the mass market. In some homogeneous markets, a well-implemented position defense strategy may be all that is needed for share maintenance.

Most of the marketing actions listed in Exhibit 16.8 as being relevant for retaining current customers might be incorporated into a position defense strategy. Anything the business can do to improve customer satisfaction and loyalty and encourage and simplify repeat purchasing should help the firm protect its current customer base and make its offering more attractive to new customers. Some of the specific actions appropriate for accomplishing these two objectives are discussed in more detail below.

Actions to Improve Customer Satisfaction and Loyalty

The rapid expansion of output necessary to keep up with a growth market can often lead to quality control problems for the market leader. As new plants, equipment, and personnel are quickly brought on line, bugs can suddenly appear in the production process. Thus, the leader must pay particular attention to quality control during this phase. Most customers have only limited, if any, positive past experiences with the new brand to offset their disappointment when a purchase does not live up to expectations.

Exhibit 16.10

MARKETING OBJECTIVES AND STRATEGIES FOR SHARE LEADERS IN GROWTH MARKETS

SHARE MAINTENANCE STRATEGIES

Situational variables	Fortress or position defense	Flanker	Confrontation	Market expansion	Contraction or strategic withdrawal
Primary objective	Increase satisfaction, loyalty, and repeat purchase among current customers by building on existing strengths; appeal to late adopters with same attributes and benefits offered to early adopters.	Protect against loss of specific segments of current customers by developing a second entry that covers a weakness in original offering; improve ability to attract new customers with specific needs or purchase criteria different from those of early adopters.	Protect against loss of share among current customers by meeting or beating a head-to-head competitive offering; improve ability to win new customers who might otherwise be attracted to competitor's offering.	Increase ability to attract new customers by developing new product offerings or line extensions aimed at a variety of new applications and user segments; improve ability to retain current customers as market fragments.	Increase ability to attract new customers in selected high-growth segments by focusing offerings and resources on those segments; withdraw from smaller or slower-growing segments to conserve resources.
Market characteristics	Relatively homogeneous market with respect to customer needs and purchase criteria; strong preference for leader's product among largest segment of customers.	Two or more major market segments with distinct needs or purchase criteria.	Relatively homogeneous market with respect to customers' needs and purchase criteria; little preference for, or loyalty toward, leader's product among largest segment of customers.	Relatively heterogeneous market with respect to customers' needs and purchase criteria; multiple product uses requiring different product or service attributes.	Relatively heterogeneous market with respect to customers' needs, purchase criteria, and growth potential; multiple product uses requiring different product or service attributes.
Competitors' characteristics	Current and potential competitors have relatively limited resources and competencies.	One or more current or potential competitors with sufficient resources and competencies to effectively implement a differentiation strategy.	One or more current or potential competitors with sufficient resources and competencies to effectively implement a head-to-head strategy.	Current and potential competitors have relatively limited resources and competencies, particularly with respect to R&D and marketing.	One or more current or potential competitors with sufficient resources and competencies to present a strong challenge in one or more growth segments.
Firm's characteristics	Current product offering enjoys high awareness and preference among major segment of current and potential customers; firm has marketing and R&D resources and competencies equal to or greater than any current or potential competitor.	Current product offering perceived as weak on at least one attribute by a major segment of current or potential customers; firm has sufficient R&D and marketing resources to introduce and support a second offering aimed at the disaffected segment.	Current product offering suffers low awareness, preference and/or loyalty among major segment of current or potential customers; firm has R&D and marketing resources and competencies equal to or greater than any current or potential competitor.	No current offerings in one or more potential applications segments; firm has marketing and R&D resources and competencies equal to or greater than any current or potential competitor.	Current product offering suffers low awareness, preference, and/or loyalty among current or potential customers in one or more major growth segments; firm's R&D and marketing resources and competencies are limited relative to those of one or more competitors.

Perhaps the most obvious way a leader can strengthen its position is to continue to modify and improve its product. This can reduce the opportunities for competitors to differentiate their products by designing in features or performance levels the leader does not offer. The leader might also try to reduce unit costs to discourage low-price competition.

The leader should take steps to improve not only the physical product but customers' perceptions of it as well. As competitors enter or prepare to enter the market, the leader's advertising and sales promotion emphasis should shift from stimulating primary demand to building selective demand for the company's brand. This usually involves creating appeals that emphasize the brand's superior features and benefits. While the leader may continue sales promotion efforts aimed at stimulating trial among later adopters, some of those efforts might be shifted toward encouraging repeat purchases among existing customers. For instance, it might include cents-off coupons inside the package to give customers a price break on their next purchases of the brand.

For industrial goods, some salesforce efforts should shift from prospecting for new accounts to servicing existing customers. Firms that relied on independent manufacturer's reps to introduce their new product might consider replacing them with company salespeople to increase the customer service orientation of their sales efforts. Firms whose own salespeople introduced the product might reorganize their salesforces into specialized groups focused on major industries or user segments. Or they might assign key account representatives, or cross-functional account teams, to service their largest customers.

Finally, a leader can strengthen its position as the market grows by giving increased attention to postsale service. Rapid growth in demand can not only outstrip a firm's ability to produce a high-quality product, but it can also overload the firm's ability to service customers. This can lead to a loss of existing customers as well as negative word of mouth that might inhibit the firm's ability to attract new users. Thus, the growth phase often requires increased investments to expand the firm's parts inventory, hire and train service personnel and dealers, and improve the information content on the firm's website.

Actions to Encourage and Simplify Repeat Purchasing   One of the most critical actions a leader must take to ensure that customers continue buying its product is to maximize its availability. It must reduce stockouts on retail store shelves or shorten delivery times for industrial goods. To do this, the firm must invest in plant and equipment to expand capacity in advance of demand, and it must implement adequate inventory control and logistics systems to provide a steady flow of goods through the distribution system. The firm should also continue to build its distribution channels. In some cases, a firm might even vertically integrate parts of its distribution system—such as building its own warehouses, as Amazon.com and several other e-tailers have done recently—to gain better control over order fulfillment activities and ensure quick and reliable deliveries.

Some market leaders, particularly in industrial goods markets, can take more proactive steps to turn their major customers into captives and help guarantee future purchases. For example, a firm might negotiate requirements contracts or guaranteed price agreements with its customers to ensure future purchases, or it might tie them into a computerized reorder system or logistical alliance.

Flanker Strategy

One shortcoming of a fortress strategy is that a challenger might simply choose to bypass the leader's fortress and try to capture territory where the leader has not yet established a strong presence. This can represent a particular threat when the market is fragmented into major segments with different needs and preferences and the leader's current brand does not meet the needs of one or more of those segments. A competitor with sufficient resources and competencies can develop a differentiated product offering to appeal to the segment where the leader is weak and thereby capture a substantial share of the overall market.

To defend against an attack directed at a weakness in its current offering (its exposed flank), a leader might develop a second brand (a **flanker** or **fighting brand**) to compete directly against the challenger's offering. This might involve trading up, where the leader develops a high-quality brand offered at a higher price to appeal to the prestige segment of the market.

More commonly, though, a flanker brand is a lower-quality product designed to appeal to a low-price segment to protect the leader's primary brand from direct price competition. Pillsbury's premium-quality Hungry Jack brand holds the major share of the U.S. refrigerated biscuit dough market; however, a substantial number of consumers prefer to pay less for a somewhat lower-quality biscuit. Rather than conceding that low-price segment to competitors, or reducing Hungry Jack prices and margins in an attempt to attract price-sensitive consumers, Pillsbury introduced Ballard, a low-priced flanker brand.

A flanker strategy is always used in conjunction with a position defense strategy. The leader simultaneously strengthens its primary brand while introducing a flanker to compete in segments where the primary brand is vulnerable. This suggests that a flanker strategy is appropriate only when the firm has sufficient resources to develop and fully support two or more entries. After all, a flanker is of little value if it is so lightly supported that a competitor can easily wipe it out.

Confrontation Strategy

Suppose a competitor chooses to attack the leader head to head and attempts to steal customers in the leader's main target market. If the leader has established a strong position and attained a high level of preference and loyalty among customers and the trade, it may be able to sit back and wait for the competitor to fail. In many cases, though, the leader's brand is not strong enough to withstand a frontal assault from a well-funded, competent competitor. Even mighty IBM, for instance, lost 20 market-share points in the commercial PC market during the mid-1980s to competitors like Compaq, whose machines cost about the same but offered features or performance levels that were better, and to the clones who offered IBM-compatible machines at much lower prices. Later, the firm's share of the PC market eroded further as companies such as Dell and Gateway introduced more convenient and efficient Internet ordering and direct distribution systems and cut prices even more.

In such situations, the leader may have no choice but to confront the competitive threat directly. If the leader's competitive intelligence is good, it may decide to move proactively and change its marketing program before a suspected competitive challenge occurs. A confrontational strategy, though, is more commonly reactive. The leader usually decides to meet or beat the attractive features of a competitor's offering—by making product improvements, increasing promotional efforts, or lowering prices—only after the challenger's success has become obvious.

KEY OBSERVATION

Simply meeting the improved features or lower price of a challenger, however, does nothing to reestablish a sustainable competitive advantage for the leader.

Simply meeting the improved features or lower price of a challenger, however, does nothing to reestablish a sustainable competitive advantage for the leader. And a confrontation based largely on lowering prices creates an additional problem of shrinking margins for all concerned.[18]

Unless decreased prices generate substantial new industry volume and the leader's production costs fall with that increasing volume, the leader may be better off responding to price threats with increased promotion or product improvements while trying to maintain its profit margins. Evidence also suggests that in product-markets with high repeat-purchase rates or a protracted diffusion process, the leader may be wise to adopt a penetration pricing policy in the first place. This would strengthen its share position and might preempt low-price competitors from entering.[19]

The leader can avoid the problems of a confrontation strategy by reestablishing the competitive advantage eroded by challengers' frontal attacks. But this typically requires additional investments in process improvements aimed at reducing unit costs, improvements in product quality or customer service, or even the development of the next generation of improved products to offer customers greater value for their dollars.

Market Expansion

A market expansion strategy is a more aggressive and proactive version of the flanker strategy. Here the leader defends its relative market share by expanding into a number of market segments. This strategy's primary objective is to capture a large share of new customer groups who may prefer something different from the firm's initial offering, protecting the firm from future competitive threats from a number of directions. Such a strategy is particularly appropriate in fragmented markets if the leader has the resources to undertake multiple product development and marketing efforts.

The most obvious way a leader can implement a market expansion strategy is to develop line extensions, new brands, or even alternative product forms utilizing similar technologies to appeal to multiple market segments. For instance, although Pillsbury holds a strong position in the refrigerated biscuit dough category, U.S. biscuit consumption is concentrated among older, more traditional consumers in the South. To expand its total market, gain increased experience-curve effects, and protect its overall technological lead, Pillsbury developed a variety of other product forms that use the same refrigerated dough technology and production facilities but appeal to different customer segments. The expanded line includes crescent rolls, Danish rolls, and soft breadsticks.

A less-expensive way to appeal to a variety of customer segments is to retain the basic product but vary other elements of the marketing program to make it relatively more attractive to specific users. Thus, a leader might create specialized salesforces to deal with the unique concerns of different user groups. Or it might offer different ancillary services to different types of customers or tailor sales promotion efforts to different segments. Thus, performing arts groups often promote reduced ticket prices, transportation services, and other inducements to attract senior citizens and students to matinee performances.

Contraction or Strategic Withdrawal

In some highly fragmented markets, a leader may be unable to defend itself adequately in all segments. This is particularly likely when newly emerging competitors have more resources than the leader. The firm may then have to reduce or abandon its efforts in some segments to focus on areas where it enjoys the greatest relative advantages or that have the greatest potential for future growth. Even some very large firms may decide that certain segments are not profitable enough to continue pursuing. For example, IBM made an early attempt to capture the low end of the family market for personal computers with the introduction of the PC Jr. But the firm eventually abandoned that effort to concentrate on the more lucrative commercial and education segments.

Share-Growth Strategies for Followers

Marketing Objectives for Followers

Not all late entrants to a growing product-market have illusions about eventually surpassing the leader and capturing a dominant market share. Some competitors, particularly those with limited resources and competencies, may simply seek to build a small but profitable business within a specialized segment of the larger market that earlier entrants have overlooked. As we have seen, this kind of *niche strategy* is one of the few entry options that small, late entrants can pursue with a reasonable degree of success. If a firm can successfully build a profitable business in a small segment while avoiding direct competition with larger competitors, it can often survive the shakeout period near the end of the growth stage and remain profitable throughout the maturity stage.

Many followers, particularly larger firms entering a product-market shortly after the pioneer, have more grandiose objectives. They often seek to displace the leader or at least to become a powerful competitor within the total market. Thus, their major marketing objective is to attain *share growth,* and the size of the increased relative share such challengers seek is usually substantial. For instance, while Cisco Systems holds a dominant 80 percent share of the market for the routers that direct data to the right places on the Internet, it was a late entrant into the market for switching systems used by telephone companies to direct voice traffic. In 1999, Cisco held less than a 1 percent share of the $225 billion market for telephone equipment. Nevertheless, it announced its intention to become the global share leader in that market.[20]

Marketing Actions and Strategies to Achieve Share Growth

A challenger with visions of taking over the leading share position in an industry has two basic strategic options, each involving somewhat different marketing objectives and actions. Where the share leader and perhaps some other early followers have already penetrated a large portion of the potential market, a challenger may have no choice but to *steal away some of the repeat purchase or replacement demand from the competitors' current customers.* As Exhibit 16.11 indicates, the challenger can attempt this through marketing activities that give it an advantage in a head-to-head confrontation with a target competitor. Or it can attempt to leapfrog over the leader by developing a new generation of products with enough benefits to induce customers to trade in their existing brand for a new one. Secondarily, such actions may also help the challenger attract a larger share of late adopters in the mass market.

If the market is relatively early in the growth phase and no previous entrant has captured a commanding share of potential customers, the challenger can focus on *attracting a larger share of potential new customers* who enter the market for the first time. This may also be a viable option when the overall market is heterogeneous and fragmented and the current share leader has established a strong position in only one or a few segments. In either case, the primary marketing activities for increasing share via this approach should aim at *differentiating* the challenger's offering from those of existing competitors by making it more appealing to new customers in untapped or underdeveloped market segments.

Once again, Exhibit 16.11's list of possible marketing actions for challengers is not exhaustive, and it contains actions that do not always fit well together. The activities that do

Exhibit 16.11

MARKETING ACTIONS TO ACHIEVE SHARE-GROWTH OBJECTIVES

Marketing objectives	Possible marketing actions
Capture repeat/replacement purchases from current customers of the leader or other target competitor by:	
• Head-to head positioning against competitor's offering in primary target market	• Develop products with features and/or performance levels superior to those of the target competitor.
	• Draw on superior product design, process engineering, and supplier relationships to achieve lower unit costs.
	• Set prices below target competitor's for comparable level of quality or performance, but only if low-cost position is achieved.
	• Outspend the target competitor on promotion aimed at stimulating selective demand:
	Comparative advertising appeals directed at gaining a more favorable positioning than the target competitor's brand enjoys among customers in the mass market.
	Sales promotions to encourage trial if offering's quality or performance is perceptively better than target competitor's, or induce brand switching.
	Build more extensive and/or better-trained salesforce than target competitor's.
	• Outspend the target competitor on trade promotion to attain more extensive retail coverage, better shelf space, and/or representation by the best distributors/dealers.
	• Outperform the target competitor on customer service:
	Develop superior production scheduling, inventory control, and logistics systems to minimize delivery times and stockouts.
	Develop superior postsale service capabilities; build a more extensive company service force, or provide better training programs for distributor/dealer service people than those of target competitor.
• Technological differentiation from target competitor's offering in its primary target market.	• Develop a new generation of products based on different technology that offers superior performance or additional benefits desired by current and potential customers in the mass market (*leapfrog strategy*).
	• Build awareness, preference, and replacement demand through heavy introductory promotion:
	Comparative advertising stressing product's superiority.
	Sales promotions to stimulate trial or encourage switching.
	Extensive, well-trained salesforce; heavy use of product demonstrations in sales presentations.
	• Build adequate distribution through trade promotions and dealer training programs.
Stimulate selective demand among later adopters by:	
• Head-to-head positioning against target competitor's offering in established market segments.	• See preceding actions.
• Differentiated positioning focused on untapped or underdeveloped segments.	• Develop a differentiated brand or product line with unique features or prices that is more appealing to a major segment of potential customers whose needs are not met by existing offerings (*flanking strategy*).
	or
	• Develop multiple line extensions or brand offerings with features or prices targeted to the unique needs and preferences of several smaller potential applications or regional segments (*encirclement strategy*).
	• Design advertising, personal selling, and/or sales promotion campaigns that address specific interests and concerns of potential customers in one or multiple underdeveloped segments to stimulate selective demand.
	• Build unique distribution channels to more effectively reach potential customers in one or multiple underdeveloped segments.
	• Design service programs to reduce the perceived risks of trial and/or solve the unique problems faced by potential customers in one or multiple underdeveloped segments (e.g., systems engineering, installation, operator training, extended warranties, service hotline or website).

Exhibit 16.12

STRATEGIC CHOICES FOR CHALLENGERS IN GROWTH MARKETS

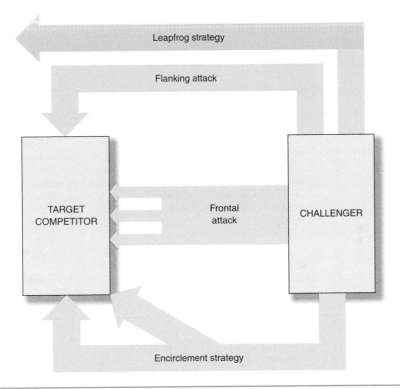

Source: Adapted from P. Kotler and R. Singh Achrol, "Marketing Warfare in the 1980's." Reprinted with permission from *Journal of Business Strategy,* Winter 1981, pp. 30–41. Used by permission of Thomson Media.

fit tend to cluster into four major strategies that a challenger might use singly or in combination to secure growth in its relative market share. As Exhibit 16.12 indicates, these four share-growth strategies are *frontal attack, leapfrog strategy, flanking attack,* and *encirclement.*[21] These strategies are basically mirror images of the share-maintenance strategies discussed earlier.

Which, or what combination, of these four strategies is best for a particular challenger depends on market characteristics, the existing competitors' current positions and strengths, and the challenger's own resources and competencies. The situations in which each strategy is likely to work best are briefly outlined in Exhibit 16.13 and discussed in the following sections.

Frontal Attack Strategy

Where the market for a product category is relatively homogeneous, with few untapped segments and at least one well-established competitor, a follower wanting to capture an increased market share may have little choice but to tackle a major competitor head-on. Such an approach is most likely to succeed when most existing customers do not have strong brand preferences or loyalties, the target competitor's product does not benefit from positive network effects, and when the challenger's resources and competencies—particularly in marketing—are greater than the target competitor's. But even superior resources are

Exhibit 16.13

MARKETING OBJECTIVES AND STRATEGIES FOR CHALLENGERS IN GROWTH MARKETS

	SHARE-GROWTH STRATEGIES			
Situational variables	Frontal attack	Leapfrog	Flank attack	Encirclement
Primary objective	Capture substantial repeat/replacement purchases from target competitor's current customers; attract new customers among later adopters by offering lower price or more attractive features.	Induce current customers in mass market to replace their current brand with superior new offering; attract new customers by providing enhanced benefits.	Attract substantial share of new customers in one or more major segments where customers' needs are different from those of early adopters in the mass market.	Attract a substantial share of new customers in a variety of smaller, specialized segments where customers' needs or preferences differ from those of early adopters in the mass market.
Market characteristics	Relatively homogeneous market with respect to customers' needs and purchase criteria; relatively little preference or loyalty for existing brands; no positive network effects.	Relatively homogeneous market with respect to customers' needs and purchase criteria, but some needs or criteria not currently met by existing brands.	Two or more major segment with distinct needs and purchase criteria; needs of customers in at least one segment not currently met by existing brands.	Relatively heterogeneous market with a number of small, specialized segments; needs and preferences of customers in some segments not currently satisfied by competing brands.
Competitor's characteristics	Target competitor has relatively limited resources and competencies, particularly in marketing and R&D; would probably be vulnerable to direct attack.	One or more current competitors have relatively strong resources and competencies in marketing, but relatively unsophisticated technology and limited R&D competencies.	Target competitor has relatively strong resources and competencies, particularly in marketing and R&D; would probably be able to withstand direct attack.	One or more competitors have relatively strong marketing, R&D resources and competencies, and/or lower costs; could probably withstand a direct attack.
Firm's characteristics	Firm has stronger resources and competencies in R&D and marketing and/or lower operating costs than target competitor.	Firm has proprietary technology superior to that of competitors; firm has necessary marketing and production resources to stimulate and meet primary demand for new generation of products.	Firm's resources and competencies are limited, but sufficient to effectively penetrate and serve at least one major market segment.	Firm has marketing, R&D, and production resources and competencies necessary to serve multiple smaller segments; firm has decentralized and adaptable management structure.

no guarantee of success if the challenger's assault merely imitates the target competitor's offering.

To successfully implement a frontal attack, a challenger should seek one or more ways to achieve a sustainable advantage over the target competitor. As discussed earlier, such an advantage is usually based on attaining lower costs or a differentiated position in the market. If the challenger has a cost advantage, it can cut prices to lure away the target competitor's customers—as Ryanair has done in the European air travel market—or it can maintain a similar price but engage in more extensive promotion.

Challenging a leader solely on the basis of low price is a highway to disaster, however, unless the challenger really does have a sustainable cost advantage. Otherwise, the leader might simply match the lower prices until the challenger is driven from the market. The problem is that initially a challenger is often at a cost *disadvantage* because of the experience-curve effects established competitors have accumulated. The challenger must have offsetting advantages like superior production technology, established relations with low-cost suppliers, the ability to share production facilities or marketing efforts across multiple SBUs, or other sources of synergy before a low-price assault makes sense.

A similar caveat applies to frontal assaults based solely on heftier promotional budgets. Unless the target competitor's resources are substantially more limited than the challenger's, it can retaliate against any attempt to win away customers through more extensive advertising or attractive sales and trade promotions.

One possible exception to this limitation of greater promotional effort is the use of a more extensive and better-trained salesforce to gain a competitive advantage. A knowledgeable salesperson's technical advice and problem-solving abilities can give additional value to a firm's product offering, particularly in newly developing high-tech industries.

In general, the best way for a challenger to effectively implement a frontal attack is to differentiate its product or associated services in ways that better meet the needs and preferences of many customers in the mass market. If the challenger can support those meaningful product differences with strong promotion or an attractive price, so much the better, but usually the unique features or services offered are the foundation for a sustainable advantage. For example, Dell has been successful as a follower in the PC market by offering *both* superior customer service and low prices. Customers can design their own computers on the company's website, get exactly the features they want, and have the equipment delivered to their doors in two or three days. Such excellent service is possible, in large part, due to the close coordination between Dell and its suppliers, coordination that minimizes inventories of parts and finished computers thereby lowering costs and prices and maximizes manufacturing flexibility and delivery speed. Dell's competitive advantage has proven to be sustainable, too, because its alliances with suppliers took years to develop and are hard for its competitors to match.

Variables that might limit the competitor's willingness or ability to retaliate can also improve the chances for successful frontal attack. For instance, a target competitor with a reputation for high product quality may be loath to cut prices in response to a lower-priced challenger for fear of cheapening its brand's image. And a competitor pursuing high ROI or cash flow objectives may be reluctant to increase its promotion or R&D expenditures in the short run to fend off an attack.[22]

Leapfrog Strategy

A challenger stands the best chance of attracting repeat or replacement purchases from a competitor's current customers when it can offer a product that is attractively differentiated from the competitor's offerings. The odds of success might be even greater if the challenger can offer a far superior product based on advanced technology or a more sophisticated design. This is the essence of a leapfrog strategy. It is an attempt to gain a significant advantage over the existing competition by introducing a new generation of products that significantly outperform or offer more desirable customer benefits than do existing brands. For example, the introduction of reasonably priced video cameras by Sony and other Japanese electronics manufacturers largely took over the market for home movie equipment and a large share of the market for Polaroid's self-developing photography equipment as well. And now digital cameras are beginning to do the same thing to the video market.

In addition, such a strategy often inhibits quick retaliation by established competitors. Firms that have achieved some success with one technology—or that have committed substantial resources to plant and equipment dedicated to a current product—are often reluctant to switch to a new one because of the large investments involved or a fear of disrupting current customers.

A leapfrog strategy is not viable for all challengers. To be successful, the challenger must have technology superior to that of established competitors as well as the product and process engineering capabilities to turn that technology into an appealing product. Also, the challenger must have the marketing resources to effectively promote its new products and convince customers already committed to an earlier technology that the new product offers sufficient benefits to justify the costs of switching.

Flanking and Encirclement Strategies

The military historian B. H. Liddell-Hart, after analyzing battles ranging from the Greek Wars to World War I, determined that only 6 out of 280 victories were the result of a frontal attack.[23] He concluded that it is usually wiser to avoid attacking an established adversary's point of strength and to focus instead on an area of weakness in his defenses. This is the basic premise behind flanking and encirclement strategies. They both seek to avoid direct confrontations by focusing on market segments whose needs are not being satisfied by existing brands and where no current competitor has a strongly held position.

KEY OBSERVATION

It is usually wiser to avoid attacking an established adversary's point of strength and to focus instead on an area of weakness in his defenses.

Flank Attack   A flank attack is appropriate when the market can be broken into two or more large segments, when the leader and/or other major competitors hold a strong position in the primary segment, and when no existing brand fully satisfies the needs of customers in at least one other segment. A challenger may be able to capture a significant share of the total market by concentrating primarily on one large untapped segment. This usually involves developing product features or services tailored to the needs and preferences of the targeted customers, together with appropriate promotional and pricing policies to quickly build selective demand. Japanese auto companies, for instance, penetrated the U.S. car market by focusing on the low-price segment, where domestic manufacturers' offerings were limited. Domestic car manufacturers were relatively unconcerned by this flanking action at first. They failed to retaliate very aggressively because the Japanese were pursuing a segment they considered to be small and unprofitable. History proved them wrong.

In some cases, a successful flank attack need not involve unique product features. Instead, a challenger can sometimes meet the special needs of an untapped segment by providing specially designed customer services or distribution channels. One major reason for the success of L'eggs pantyhose, for instance, was that it was the first U.S. brand to be distributed through an extensive channel of convenience goods retailers, such as grocery and drug stores, instead of more fashionable department and clothing stores. The greater shopping convenience provided by this new distribution channel appealed strongly to the

Exhibit 16.14   A Small Citrus Juice Co-op Squeezes Big Rivals

When a little-known farmers' cooperative called Citrus World Inc. started to market its own brand of pasteurized orange juice, it looked like an improbable player in the $3 billion juice market. Citrus World, an 800-employee operation in rural Florida, was up against a couple of established giants: Seagram Co., owner of the Tropicana brand, and Coca-Cola Co., with its Minute Maid line.

But Citrus World knew exactly what to do: Squeeze that folksy image for all it was worth. To sell its Florida's Natural brand, it ordered TV commercials featuring sunburned farmers gulping down juice. In one ad, growers holding boxes of oranges hold a "stockholders' meeting" in the back of a truck. Other workers cut "overhead" by chopping a branch from an orange tree.

Thanks to catchy ads, a quality product, and aggressive pricing, Citrus World made a splash. In 1995 Florida's Natural knocked Minute Maid out of the number 2 spot in the rapidly growing market for "premium," or pasteurized, not-from-concentrate orange juice, and the brand experienced a larger percentage sales increase than Tropicana. While Citrus World attacked its larger rivals' exposed flanks, in part, by offering lower prices, its success also demonstrates that a substantial segment of consumers prefers to deal with what they perceive to be small, "underdog" companies.

Source: Yumiko Ono, "A Pulp Tale: Juice Co-op Squeezes Big Rivals," *The Wall Street Journal,* January 30,1996, p. B1.

growing segment of working women. More recently, as Exhibit 16.14 recounts, a small citrus farmers' cooperative has stolen substantial market share from much bigger competitors by delivering a high-quality product and emphasizing its folksy, common-man image.

Encirclement   An encirclement strategy involves targeting several smaller untapped or underdeveloped segments in the market simultaneously. The idea is to surround the leader's brand with a variety of offerings aimed at several peripheral segments. This strategy makes most sense when the market is fragmented into many different applications segments or geographical regions with somewhat unique needs or tastes.

Once again, this strategy usually involves developing a varied line of products with features tailored to the needs of different segments. Rather than try to compete with Coke and Pepsi in the soft drink market, for example, Cadbury-Schweppes offers a wide variety of flavors such as cream soda, root beer and ginger ale—almost anything but cola—to appeal to small groups of customers with unique tastes.

Supporting Evidence

Several studies conducted with the PIMS database provide empirical support for many of the managerial prescriptions we have discussed.[24] These studies compare businesses that achieved high market shares during the growth stage of the product life cycle, or that increased their market shares over time, with low-share businesses. As shown in Exhibit 16.15, the marketing programs and activities of businesses that successfully achieved increased market share differed from their less-successful counterparts in the following ways:

- Businesses that increased the quality of their products relative to those of competitors achieved greater share increases than businesses whose product quality remained constant or declined.

- Share-gaining businesses typically developed and added more new products, line extensions, or product modifications to their line than share-losing businesses.

- Share-gaining businesses tended to increase their marketing expenditures faster than the rate of market growth. Increases in both salesforce and sales promotion expenditures were effective for producing share gains in both consumer and industrial goods businesses. Increased advertising expenditures were effective for producing share gains primarily in consumer goods businesses.

Exhibit 16.15

STRATEGIC CHANGES MADE BY CHALLENGERS THAT GAINED VERSUS LOST MARKET SHARE

Strategic changes	Share-gaining challengers	Share-losing challengers
Relative product quality scores	+1.8	−0.6
New products as a percent of sales	+0.1	−0.5
Relative price	+0.3	+0.2
Marketing expenditures (adjusted for market growth):		
Salesforce	+9.0%	−8.0%
Advertising:		
Consumer products	+13.0%	−9.0%
Industrial products	−1.0	−14.0
Promotion:		
Consumer products	+13.0%	−5.0%
Industrial products	+7.0	−10.0

Source: Reprinted with permission of The Free Press, a Division of Simon & Schuster Adult Publishing Group, from The PIMS Principles: Linking Strategy to Performance by Robert D. Buzzell and Bradley T. Gale. Copyright © 1987 by The Free Press. All rights reserved.

- Surprisingly, there was little difference in the relative prices charged between firms that gained and those that lost market share.

These findings are consistent with many of our earlier observations. For instance, they underline the folly of launching a frontal attack solely on the basis of lower price. Unless the challenger has substantially lower unit costs or the leader is inhibited from cutting its own prices for some reason, the challenger's price cuts are likely to be retaliated against and will generate few new customers. On the other hand, frontal, leapfrog, flanking, or encirclement attacks based on product improvements tailored to specific segments are more likely to succeed, particularly when the challenger supports those attacks with substantial promotional efforts.

Regardless of the strategies pursued by market leaders and challengers during a product-market's growth stage, the competitive situation often changes as the market matures and its growth rate slows. In the next chapter, we examine the environmental changes that occur as a market matures and the marketing strategies that firms might use to adapt to those changes.

TAKE-AWAYS

- Being the pioneer in a new product or service category gains a firm a number of potential advantages. But not all pioneers are able to sustain a leading position in the market as it grows. A pioneering firm stands the best chance for long-term share leadership and profitability when the market can be insulated from the rapid entry of competitors by patent protection or other means and when the firm has the necessary resources and competencies to capitalize on its first-mover advantages.

- Some pioneers attempt to penetrate the mass market and remain the share leader as that market grows. Others

adopt a strategy geared to making profits from specialized niche markets where they will face fewer direct competitors. Still others try to stay one jump ahead of competitors by introducing a stream of new products and withdrawing from older markets as they become more competitive. The appropriate strategy to adopt depends on the firm's resources and competencies, the strength of likely competitors, and the characteristics of the product and its target market.

- If a market leader wishes to maintain its number one share position as the product category moves through rapid growth, it must focus on two important objectives: (1) retaining its current customers, and (2) stimulating selective demand among later adopters. Marketing strategies a leader might adopt to achieve these objectives are position defense, flanker, confrontation, market expansion, and contraction. The best one to choose depends on the homogeneity of the market and the firm's resources and competencies relative to potential competitors.

- For a challenger to increase its market share relative to the leader, it must differentiate its offering by delivering superior product benefits, better service, or a lower price than the leader. Challenging a leader solely on the basis of price is a highway to disaster, however, unless the challenger has a sustainable cost advantage.

Self-diagnostic questions to test your ability to apply the analytical tools and concepts in this chapter to marketing decision making may be found at this book's website at www.mhhe.com/mullins05.

ENDNOTES

1. This example is based on information found in Irene M. Kunii, "Quick Studies," *Business Week,* November 18, 2002, pp. 48–49; "Hard To Copy," *The Economist,* November 2, 2002, pp. 63–64; and the company's website at www.canon.com.

2. These results are reported in Myron Magnet, "Let's Go for Growth," *Fortune,* March 7, 1994, pp. 60–72.

3. *New Products Management for the 1980s* (New York: Booz, Allen & Hamilton, 1982). More recent studies, though focusing on smaller samples of new products, suggest that the relative proportions of new-to-the-world versus less innovative product introductions have not changed substantially over the years. For example, see Eric M. Olson, Orville C. Walker, Jr., and Robert W. Ruekert, "Organizing for Effective New Product Development: The Moderating Role of Product Innovativeness," *Journal of Marketing* 59 (January 1995), pp. 48–62.

4. For a more extensive review of the potential competitive advantages of being a first mover, and the controllable and uncontrollable forces that influence a firm's ability to capitalize on those potential advantages, see Roger A. Kerin, P. Rajan Varadarajan, and Robert A. Peterson, "First-Mover Advantage: A Synthesis, Conceptual Framework, and Research Propositions," *Journal of Marketing* 56 (October 1992), pp. 33–52; for a more extensive review of the potential competitive advantages of being a first mover, and the controllable and uncontrollable forces that influence a firm's ability to capitalize on those potential advantages, see Roger A. Kerin, P. Rajan Varadarajan, and Robert A. Peterson, "First-Mover Advantage: A Synthesis, Conceptual Framework, and Research Propositions," *Journal of Marketing* 56 (October 1992), pp. 33–52; and David M. Szymanski, Lisa M. Troy, and Sundar J. Bharadwaj, "Order-of Entry and Business Performance: An Empirical Synthesis and Reexamination," *Journal of Marketing,* 59 (October 1995), pp. 17–33.

5. Thomas S. Gruca and D. Sudharshan, "A Framework for Entry Deterrence Strategy: The Competitive Environment, Choices, and Consequences," *Journal of Marketing* 59 (July 1995), pp. 44–55.

6. Carl Shapiro and Hal R. Varian, *Information Rules* (Boston: Harvard Business School Press, 1999), chap. 7.

7. For example, see William T. Robinson, "Market Pioneering and Sustainable Market Share Advantages in Industrial Goods Manufacturing Industries," working paper, Purdue University, 1984; and Robert D. Buzzell and Bradley T. Gale, *The PIMS Principles: Linking Strategy to Performance* (New York: Free Press, 1987), p. 183.

8. Peter N. Golder and Gerard J. Tellis, "Pioneer Advantage: Marketing Logic or Marketing Legend," *Journal of Marketing Research* 30 (May 1993), pp. 158–70.

9. Marvin B. Lieberman and David B. Montgomery, "First-Mover Advantages," *Strategic Management Journal* 9 (1988), pp. 41–59; and Michael J. Moore, William Boulding, and Ronald C. Goodstein, "Pioneering and Market Share: Is Entry Time Endogenous and Does It Matter?" *Journal of Marketing* 28 (February 1991), pp. 97–104.

10. Szymanski, Troy, and Bharadwaj, "Order-of-Entry and Business Performance."

11. Mary L. Coyle, "Competition in Developing Markets: The Impact of Order of Entry," unpublished doctoral dissertation, University of Toronto, 1986. Also see Kerin, Varadarajan, and Peterson, "First-Mover Advantage."

12. George S. Day, *Analysis for Strategic Marketing Decisions* (St. Paul, MN: West, 1986), pp. 103–4.

13. Shapiro and Varian, *Information Rules,* chap. 2.

14. Franklin R. Root, *Entry Strategy for International Markets* (Lexington, MA: D. C. Heath, 1987). Also see Jeremy Main, "Making Global Alliances Work," *Fortune,* December 17, 1990, pp. 121–26.

15. This assumes that demand is relatively price inelastic. In markets where price elasticity is high, a skimming price strategy may lead to lower total revenues due to its dampening effect on total demand.

16. Buzzell and Gale, *The PIMS Principles,* pp. 188–90.

17. For a detailed discussion of these strategies in a military context, see Carl von Clausewitz, *On War* (London: Routledge and Kegan Paul, 1908); and B. H. Liddell-Hart, *Strategy* (New York: Praeger, 1967). For a related discussion of the application of such strategies in a business setting, see Philip Kotler and Ravi Singh Achrol, "Marketing Warfare in the 1980's," *Journal of Business Strategy,* Winter 1981, pp. 30–41.

18. Thomas T. Nagle, "Managing Price Competition," *Marketing Management* 2 (Spring 1993), pp. 36–45; and Akshay R. Rao, Mark E. Bergen, and Scott Davis, "How To Fight a Price War," *Harvard Business Review,* March–April 2000, pp. 107–16.

19. Robert J. Dolan and Abel P. Jewland, "Experience Curves and Dynamic Demand Models: Implications for Optimal Pricing Strategy," *Journal of Marketing,* Winter 1981, p. 52.

20. Andy Reinhardt, "Meet Mr. Internet," *Business Week,* September 13, 1999, pp. 128–40.

21. There are some more specialized strategies that challengers may pursue under specific circumstances that are beyond the scope of this discussion. For a more detailed examination of such strategies see Orville C. Walker, Jr., Harper W. Boyd, Jr., John Mullins, and Jean-Claude Larreche, *Marketing Strategy: A Decision-Focused Approach,* 4th ed., (Burr Ridge, IL: McGraw-Hill/Irwin, 2003), chap.10.

22. For a more extensive discussion of factors that can limit a leader's willingness or ability to retaliate against a direct attack, see Michael E. Porter, *Competitive Advantage* (New York: Free Press, 1985), chap. 15.

23. Liddell-Hart, *Strategy,* p. 163.

24. Robert D. Buzzell and Federik D. Wiersema, "Successful Share-Building Strategies," *Harvard Business Review,* January–February 1981, pp. 135–43; Carl R. Anderson and Carl P. Zeithaml, "Stages in the Product Life Cycle, Business Strategy, and Business Performance," *Academy of Management Journal,* March 1984, pp. 5–25; and Buzzell and Gale, *The PIMS Principles,* chap. 9.

CHAPTER SEVENTEEN

Strategic Choices for Mature and Declining Markets

Johnson Controls—Making Money in Mature Markets[1]

AT FIRST GLANCE, Johnson Controls Inc. in Glendale, Wisconsin, appears to be the epitome of a staid, slow-growing, "old-economy" company. The firm's success and survival depend on several product and service categories that have not experienced much growth in the domestic market in recent years. Johnson's major businesses include batteries, seats and other internal components for automobiles, heating and cooling equipment for large commercial buildings and schools, and facilities management services.

But first glances can be deceiving. The firm's managers have developed a four-pronged strategy for making money in such mature markets. First, Johnson has acquired a number of weaker competitors in each of its product categories over the years in order to gain market share and remove excess capacity. Second, the firm has expanded sales volume by moving aggressively into global markets. The firm now operates in 500 locations around the world.

Most important, the firm has nurtured close relationships with established customers such as General Motors, DaimlerChrysler, BMW, and Toyota. Those relationships have enabled Johnson to maintain solid profit margins by improving customer retention and gaining operating efficiencies via logistical alliances, just-in-time delivery systems, and other process improvements. Finally, the firm's close customer relationships have provided it with market intelligence and facilitated joint development projects, both of which have helped the firm gain additional revenue from the introduction of new product and service offerings targeted at those customers.

A strong balance sheet and a long-term perspective have helped Johnson build market share—and expand into other countries—through the acquisition of competitors. In some cases, the firm has snapped up firms with product or service offerings that complement and extend Johnson's own product line in one of its established target markets. For instance, the firm spent $167 million to acquire Pan Am's World Services division, a facility management operation that does everything from mow the lawn to run the cafeteria. That acquisition, when combined with Johnson's existing heating and cooling systems business and some new products and services developed internally, turned the company into a full-service facilities operator. Johnson can now manage a client's entire building while offering highly customized heating and cooling systems and controls that minimize energy use. This combination of customized products and full service has both expanded the company's share of the commercial real estate market and enabled it to maintain relatively high margins in a highly competitive business.

In other businesses, Johnson has combined the economies of scale generated through savvy acquisitions with the knowledge gained from close customer relationships to both develop new products and drive down operating costs. For example, Johnson has

become the leading worldwide supplier of automotive seating and interior systems, such as floor consoles and instrument panels, by assisting manufacturers with the design and development, as well as the manufacture, of such components. As one engineer at Daimler-Chrysler pointed out, "Johnson is able to completely integrate the design, development, and manufacture of [our] seats," and do it for less than the auto companies could. On the design side, Johnson Controls has maintained its own industrial design department for many years. The firm's European design center in Cologne, Germany, alone has 70 staff members, more than the interior design teams of many car makers. The center includes an in-house market research department to help identify trends in consumer tastes in European markets, and pretest consumer reactions to possible design innovations.

On the manufacturing side, by closely coordinating inventories and production schedules, Johnson has reduced costs even further for both its customers and itself. For instance, by locating its plants close to a customer's production facility, Johnson is able to assemble seats to order, load them on a truck in a sequence that matches the cars coming down the assembly line, and deliver them to the customer all in as little as 90 minutes.

Despite the maturity of its markets, Johnson's strategy is paying off, both in terms of revenue growth and profits. In recent years the firm has experienced substantial annual revenue growth, with sales increasing from about $10 billion in 1996 to more than $20 billion in 2002. At the same time, the firm has increased annual dividends paid to shareholders for more than 25 years, and in 2002 it earned a 19 percent return on shareholder equity.

Marketing Challenges Addressed in Chapter 17

Many managers, particularly those in marketing, seem obsessed with growth. Their objectives tend to emphasize annual increases in sales volume, market share, or both. But the biggest challenge for many managers in developed nations in future years will be making money in markets that grow slowly, if at all. The majority of product-markets in those nations are in the mature or decline stages of their life cycles. And as accelerating rates of technological and social change continue to shorten such life cycles, today's innovations will move from growth to maturity—and ultimately to decline—ever faster.

A period of competitive turbulence almost always accompanies the transition from market growth to maturity in an industry. This period often begins after approximately half the potential customers have adopted the product and the rate of sales growth starts to decline. As the growth rate slows, many competitors tend to overestimate future sales volume and consequently end up developing too much production capacity. Competition becomes more intense as firms battle to increase sales volume to cover their high fixed costs and maintain profitability. As a result, such transition periods are commonly accompanied by a **shakeout** during which weaker businesses fail, withdraw from the industry, or are acquired by other firms, as has happened to some of Johnson Controls' competitors in the United States and European automotive seat and battery industries.

Challenges in Mature Markets

Businesses that survive the shakeout face new challenges as market growth stagnates. As a market matures, total volume stabilizes; replacement purchases rather than first-time buyers account for the vast majority of that volume. A primary market-ing objective of all competitors in mature markets, therefore, is simply to hold their existing customers—to sustain a meaningful competitive ad-vantage that will help ensure the continued satisfaction and loyalty of those customers. Thus, a product's financial success during the mature life-cycle stage de-pends heavily on the firm's ability to achieve and sustain a lower delivered cost or some perceived product quality or customer-service superiority.

Some firms tend to passively defend mature products while using the bulk of the rev-enues produced by those items to develop and aggressively market new products with more growth potential. This can be shortsighted, however. All segments of a market and all brands in an industry do not necessarily reach maturity at the same time. Aging brands such as Adidas, Johnson's baby shampoo, and Arm & Hammer baking soda experienced sales revivals in recent years because of creative marketing strategies. Thus, a share leader in a mature industry might build on a cost or product differentiation advantage and pursue a marketing strategy aimed at increasing volume by promoting new uses for an old product or by encouraging current customers to buy and use the product more often. Therefore, in this chapter we examine basic business strategies necessary for survival in mature markets and marketing strategies a firm might use to extend a brand's sales and profits, including the strategies that have been so successful for Johnson Controls.

Challenges in Declining Markets

Eventually, technological advances, changing customer demographics, tastes, or lifestyles, and development of substitutes result in declining demand for most product forms and brands. As a product starts to decline, managers face the critical question of whether to di-vest or liquidate the business. Unfortunately, firms sometimes support dying products too long at the expense of current profitability and the aggressive pursuit of future breadwinners.

An appropriate marketing strategy can, however, produce substantial sales and profits even in a declining market. If few exit barriers exist, an industry leader might attempt to in-crease market share via aggressive pricing or promotion policies aimed at driving out weaker competitors. Or it might try to consolidate the industry, as Johnson Controls has done in its automotive components businesses, by acquiring weaker brands and reducing overhead by eliminating both excess capacity and duplicate marketing programs. Alterna-tively, a firm might decide to harvest a mature product by maximizing cash flow and profit over the product's remaining life. The last section of this chapter examines specific mar-keting strategies for gaining the greatest possible returns from products approaching the end of their life cycle.

Strategic Choices in Mature Markets

The maturity phase of an industry's life cycle is often depicted as one of stability charac-terized by few changes in the market shares of leading competitors and steady prices. The industry leaders, because of their low per-unit costs and little need to make any further in-vestments, enjoy high profits and positive cash flows. These cash flows are harvested and diverted to other SBUs or products in the firm's portfolio that promise greater future growth.

Unfortunately, this conventional scenario provides an overly simplistic description of the situation businesses face in most mature markets. For one thing, it is not always easy to tell when a market has reached maturity. Variations in brands, marketing programs, and customer groups can mean that different brands and market segments reach maturity at different times.

Further, as the maturity stage progresses, a variety of threats and opportunities can disrupt an industry's stability. Shifts in customer needs or preferences, product substitutes, increased raw material costs, changes in government regulations, or factors such as the entry of low-cost foreign producers or mergers and acquisitions can threaten individual competitors and even throw the entire industry into early decline. Consider, for example, the competitive position of Timex, a brand that dominated the low-price segment of the American watch market in the 1970s. First the appearance of imported digital watches and later a shift in consumer preferences toward more fashionable and prestigious brands buffeted the firm and eroded its market share.

On the positive side, such changes can also open new growth opportunities in mature industries. Product improvements (such as the development of high-fiber nutritional cereals), advances in process technology (the creation of minimills for steel production), falling raw materials costs, increased prices for close substitutes, or environmental changes can all provide opportunities for a firm to dramatically increase its sales and profits. An entire industry can even experience a period of renewed growth.

Discontinuities during industry maturity suggest that it is dangerously shortsighted for a firm to simply milk its cash cows. Even industry followers can substantially improve volume, share, and profitability during industry maturity if they can adjust their marketing objectives and programs to fit the new opportunities that arise.[2] Thus, success in mature markets requires two sets of strategic actions: (1) the development of a well-implemented business strategy to sustain a competitive advantage, customer satisfaction, and loyalty, and (2) flexible and creative marketing programs geared to pursue growth or profit opportunities as conditions change in specific product-markets.

Strategies for Maintaining Competitive Advantage

As discussed in Chapter 10, both *analyzer* and *defender strategies* may be appropriate for units with a leading, or at least a profitable, share of one or more major segments in a mature industry. Analyzers and defenders are both concerned with maintaining a strong share position in established product-markets. But analyzers also do some product and market development to avoid being leapfrogged by competitors with more advanced products or being left behind in new applications segments. On the other hand, defenders may initiate some product improvements or line extensions to protect and strengthen their position in existing markets, but they spend relatively little on new product R&D. Thus, an analyzer strategy is most appropriate for developed industries that are still experiencing some technological change and may have opportunities for continued growth, such as the computer and commercial aircraft industries. The defender strategy works best in industries where the basic technology is not very complex or is unlikely to change dramatically in the short run, as in the food industry.

Both analyzers and defenders can attempt to sustain a competitive advantage in established product-markets through *differentiation* of their product offering (either on the basis of superior quality or service) or by maintaining a low-cost position. Evidence suggests the ability to maintain either a strongly differentiated or a low-cost position continues to be a critical determinant of success throughout both the transition and the maturity stage. One study examined the competitive strategies pursued by the two leading firms (in terms of return on investment) in eight mature industries characterized by slow growth and intense competition. In each industry, the two leading firms offered either the lowest relative delivered cost or high relative product differentiation.[3] Similarly, as we saw in Chapter 2, observations by Treacy and Wiersema found that market leaders tend to pursue one of three strategic disciplines. They either stress operational excellence, which typically translates into lower costs, or differentiate themselves through product leadership or customer intimacy and superior service.[4]

Generally, it is difficult for a single business to pursue both low-cost and differentiation strategies at the same time. For instance, businesses taking the low-cost approach typically compete primarily by offering the lowest prices in the industry. Such prices allow little room for the firm to make the investments or cover the costs inherent in maintaining superior product quality, performance, or service over time.

It is important to keep in mind, however, that pursuit of a low-cost strategy does not mean that a business can ignore the delivery of desirable benefits to the customer. Similarly, customers will not pay an unlimited price premium for superior quality or service, no matter how superior it is. In both consumer and commercial markets customers seek good *value* for the money, either a solid, no-frills product or service at an outstanding price or an offering whose higher price is justified by the superior benefits it delivers on one or more dimensions.[5] Thus, even low-cost producers should continually seek ways to improve the quality and performance of their offerings within the financial constraints of their competitive strategy. And even differentiated defenders should continually work to improve efficiency without sacrificing product quality or performance. This point is clearly illustrated in the diagram of the customer value management process in Exhibit 17.1, which shows that actions to improve customers' perceptions of quality (whether of goods or service) and to reduce costs both impact customer value. The critical strategic questions facing the marketing manager, then, are How can a business continue to differentiate its offerings and justify a premium price as its market matures and becomes more competitive? and How can businesses, particularly those pursuing low-cost strategies, continue to reduce their costs and improve their efficiency as their markets mature?

Methods of Differentiation

At the most basic level, a business can attempt to differentiate its offering from competitors' by offering either superior product quality, superior service, or both. The problem is that *quality* and *service* may be defined in a variety of different ways by customers.

Dimensions of Product Quality[6]
To maintain a competitive advantage in product quality, a firm must understand what *dimensions customers perceive to underlie differences across products* within a given category. One authority has identified eight such dimensions of product quality. These are summarized in Exhibit 17.2 and discussed below.

European manufacturers of prestige automobiles, such as Mercedes-Benz and Porsche, have emphasized the first dimension of product quality—**functional performance.** These automakers have designed cars that provide excellent performance on such attributes as handling, acceleration, and comfort. Volvo, on the other hand, has emphasized and aggressively promoted a different quality dimension—**durability** (and the related attribute of safety). A third quality dimension, **conformance to specifications,** or the absence of defects, has been a major focus of the Japanese automakers. Until recent years, American carmakers relied heavily on broad product lines and a wide **variety of features,** both standard and optional, to offset their shortcomings on some of the other quality dimensions.

Exhibit 17.1

THE PROCESS OF CUSTOMER VALUE MANAGEMENT

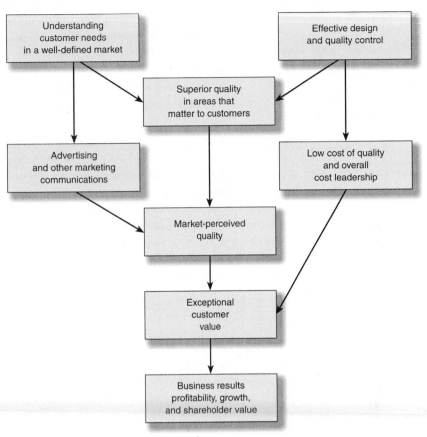

The **reliability** quality dimension can refer to the consistency of performance from purchase to purchase or to a product's uptime, the percentage of time that it can perform satisfactorily over its life. Tandem Computers has maintained a competitive advantage based on reliability by designing computers with several processors that work in tandem, so that if one fails, the only impact is the slowing of low-priority tasks. IBM had difficulty matching Tandem's reliability because its operating system was not easily adapted to the multiple-processor concept. Consequently, Tandem has maintained a strong position in market segments consisting of large-scale computer users, such as financial institutions and large retailers, for whom system downtime is particularly undesirable.

The quality dimension of **serviceability** refers to a customer's ability to obtain prompt and competent service when the product does break down. For example, Caterpillar has long differentiated itself with a parts and service organization dedicated to providing "24-hour parts service anywhere in the world."

Many of these quality dimensions can be difficult for customers to evaluate, particularly for consumer products. As a result, consumers often generalize from quality dimensions that are more visual or qualitative. Thus, the **fit and finish** dimension can help convince consumers that a product is of high quality. They tend to perceive attractive and well-designed

Exhibit 17.2

DIMENSIONS OF PRODUCT QUALITY

• Performance	How well does the washing machine wash clothes?
• Durability	How long will the lawn mower last?
• Conformance with specifications	What is the incidence of product defects?
• Features	Does an airline flight offer a movie and dinner?
• Reliability	Will each visit to a restaurant result in consistent quality?
	What percentage of the time will a product perform satisfactorily?
• Serviceability	Is the product easy to service?
	Is the service system efficient, competent, and convenient?
• Fit and finish	Does the product look and feel like a quality product?
• Brand name	Is this a name that customers associate with quality?
	What is the brand's image?

Source: Reprinted from "What Does 'Product Quality' Really Mean?" by David A. Garvin, *MIT Sloan Management Review,* Fall 1984, pp. 25–43 by permission of publisher. Copyright © 1984 by Massachusetts Institute of Technology. All rights reserved.

products as generally high in quality, as witnessed by the success of the Krups line of small appliances. Similarly, the **quality reputation of the brand name,** and the promotional activities that sustain that reputation, can strongly influence consumers' perceptions of a product's quality. A brand's quality reputation together with psychological factors such as name recognition and loyalty substantially determine a brand's **equity**—the perceived value customers associate with a particular brand name and its logo or symbol.[7] To successfully pursue a differentiation strategy based on quality, then, a business must understand what dimensions or cues its potential customers use to judge quality, and it should pay particular attention to some of the less-concrete but more visible and symbolic attributes of the product.

Dimensions of Service Quality   Customers also judge the quality of the service they receive on multiple dimensions. A number of such dimensions of perceived service quality have been identified by a series of studies conducted across diverse industries such as retail banking and appliance repair, and five of those dimensions are listed and briefly defined in Exhibit 17.3.[8]

The quality dimensions listed in Exhibit 17.3 apply specifically to service businesses, but most of them are also relevant for judging the service component of a product offering. This pertains to both the objective performance dimensions of the service delivery system, such as its **reliability** and **responsiveness**, as well as to elements of the performance of service personnel, such as their **empathy** and level of **assurance.**

The results of a number of surveys suggest that customers perceive all five dimensions of service quality to be very important regardless of the kind of service being evaluated. As Exhibit 17.4 indicates, customers of four different kinds of services gave reliability, responsiveness, assurance, and empathy mean importance ratings of more than 9 on a 10-point rating scale. And though the mean ratings for tangibles were somewhat lower in comparison, they still fell toward the upper end of the scale, ranging from 7.14 to 8.56.

The same respondents were also asked which of the five dimensions they would choose as being the most critical in their assessment of service quality. Their responses, which are shown in Exhibit 17.4, suggest that reliability is the most important aspect of service quality to the greatest number of customers. Both service reliability and responsiveness are

Exhibit 17.3

DIMENSIONS OF SERVICE QUALITY

- Tangibles   Appearance of physical facilities, equipment, personnel, and communications materials.
- Reliability   Ability to perform the promised service dependably and accurately.
- Responsiveness   Willingness to help customers and provide prompt service.
- Assurance   Knowledge and courtesy of employees and their ability to convey trust and confidence.
- Empathy   Caring, individualized attention the firm provides its customers.

Source: Adapted with the permission of The Free Press, a Division of Simon & Schuster Adult Publishing Group from *Delivering Quality Service: Balancing Customer Perceptions and Expectations* by Valarie A. Zeithaml, A. Parasuraman, Leonard L. Berry. Copyright © 1990 by The Free Press. All rights reserved.

Exhibit 17.4

PERCEIVED IMPORTANCE OF SERVICE QUALITY DIMENSIONS IN FOUR DIFFERENT INDUSTRIES

	Mean importance rating on 10-point scale*	Percentage of respondents indicating dimension is most important
Credit-card customers (n = 187)		
Tangibles	7.43	0.6
Reliability	9.45	48.6
Responsiveness	9.37	19.8
Assurance	9.25	17.5
Empathy	9.09	13.6
Repair-and-maintenance customers (n = 183)		
Tangibles	8.48	1.2
Reliability	9.64	57.2
Responsiveness	9.54	19.9
Assurance	9.62	12.0
Empathy	9.30	9.6
Long-distance telephone customers (n = 184)		
Tangibles	7.14	0.6
Reliability	9.67	60.6
Responsiveness	9.57	16.0
Assurance	9.29	12.6
Empathy	9.25	10.3
Bank customers (n = 177)		
Tangibles	8.56	1.1
Reliability	9.44	42.1
Responsiveness	9.34	18.0
Assurance	9.18	13.6
Empathy	9.30	25.1

*Scale ranges from 1 (not at all important) to 10 (extremely important).

Source: Adapted with the permission of The Free Press, a Division of Simon & Schuster Adult Publishing Group from *Delivering Quality Service: Balancing Customer Perceptions and Expectations* by Valarie A. Zeithaml, A. Parasuraman, Leonard L. Berry. Copyright © 1990 by The Free Press. All rights reserved.

proving to be particularly important for, and the Achilles' heel of, many e-commerce sites. This helps explain why Amazon.com has recently spent millions building distribution centers geared toward improving the reliability of its order fulfillment activities, and other e-commerce sites have shifted more attention to keeping existing customers happy than to blindly seeking new ones.[9]

The key to a differentiation strategy based on providing superior service is to meet or exceed target customers' service quality expectations and to do it more consistently than competitors. The problem is that sometimes managers underestimate the level of those customer expectations, and sometimes those expectations can be unrealistically high. Therefore, a firm needs to clearly identify target customers' desires with respect to service quality and to clearly define and communicate what level of service they intend to deliver. When this is done, customers have a more realistic idea of what to expect and are less likely to be disappointed with the service they receive.

Improving Customer Perceptions of Service Quality

The major factors that determine a customer's expectations and perceptions concerning service quality—and five gaps that can lead to dissatisfaction with service delivery—are outlined in Exhibit 17.5 and discussed next.

1. **Gap between the customer's expectations and the marketer's perceptions.** Managers do not always have an accurate understanding of what customers want or how they will evaluate a firm's service efforts. The first step in providing good service is to collect information—through customer surveys, evaluations of customer complaints, or other methods—to determine what service attributes customers consider important.

2. **Gap between management perceptions and service quality specifications.** Even when management has a clear understanding of what customers want, that understanding might not get translated into effective operating standards. A firm's policies concerning customer service may be unclear, poorly communicated to employees, or haphazardly enforced. Unless a firm's employees know what the company's service policies are and believe that management is seriously committed to those standards, their performance is likely to fall short of desired levels.

3. **Gap between service quality specifications and service delivery.** Lip service by management is not enough to produce high-quality service. High standards must be backed by the programs, resources, and rewards necessary to enable and encourage employees to deliver good service. Employees must be provided with the training, equipment, and time necessary to deliver good service. Their service performance must be measured and evaluated. And good performance must be rewarded by making it part of the criteria for pay raises or promotions, or by other more direct inducements, in order to motivate the additional effort good service requires.

4. **Gap between service delivery and external communications.** Even good service performance may disappoint some customers if the firm's marketing communications cause them to have unrealistically high expectations. If the photographs in a vacation resort's advertising and brochures make the rooms look more spacious and luxurious than they really are, for instance, first-time customers are likely to be disappointed no matter how clean or well-tended those rooms are kept by the resort's staff.

5. **Gap between perceived service and expected service.** This results when management fails to close one or more of the other four gaps. It is this difference between a customer's expectations and his or her actual experience with the firm that leads to dissatisfaction.

The above discussion suggests a number of actions management can take to close the possible gaps and improve customer satisfaction with a company's service. Achieving and sustaining high levels of service quality can present difficult implementation problems, however, because it usually involves the coordination of efforts of many employees from different functional departments and organizational levels. Some of these coordination problems are examined in Chapter 18.

Exhibit 17.5

DETERMINANTS OF PERCEIVED SERVICE QUALITY

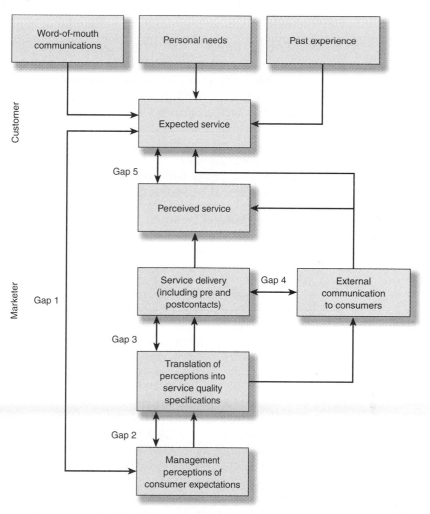

Source: Reprinted from A. Parasuraman, Valarie A. Zeithaml, and Leonard L. Berry, "A Conceptual Model of Service Quality and Its Implications for Future Research," *Journal of Marketing,* Fall 1985, p. 44. Used by permission of the American Marketing Association.

Methods of Maintaining a Low-Cost Position

Moving down the experience curve is the most commonly discussed method of achieving and sustaining a low-cost position in an industry. But a firm does not necessarily need a large relative market share to implement a low-cost strategy. For instance, Johnson Controls relies on close alliances with customers, as well as economies of scale, to hold down its inventory and distribution costs. And Michael Dell, as a small follower in the personal computer industry, managed to achieve costs below those of much larger competitors by developing logistical alliances with suppliers and an innovative, Internet-based direct distribution channel.

Some other means for obtaining a sustainable cost advantage include producing a no-frills product, creating an innovative product design, finding cheaper raw materials, automating or outsourcing production, developing low-cost distribution channels, and reducing overhead.[10]

A No-Frills Product   A direct approach to obtaining a low-cost position involves simply removing all frills and extras from the basic product or service. Thus, Ryanair's flights from secondary airports on the outskirts of major cities, warehouse furniture stores, legal services clinics, and grocery stores selling canned goods out of crates all offer lower costs and prices than their competitors. This lower production cost is often sustainable because established differentiated competitors find it difficult to stop offering features and services their customers have come to expect. However, those established firms may lower their own prices in the short run—even to the point of suffering losses—in an attempt to drive out a no-frills competitor that poses a serious threat. Thus, a firm considering a no-frills strategy needs the resources to withstand a possible price war.[11]

Innovative Product Design   A simplified product design and standardized component parts can also lead to cost advantages. In the office copier industry, for instance, Japanese firms overcame substantial entry barriers by designing extremely simple copiers, with a fraction of the number of parts in the design used by market-leading Xerox.

Cheaper Raw Materials   A firm with the foresight to acquire or the creativity to find a way to use relatively cheap raw materials can also gain a sustainable cost advantage. For example, Fort Howard Paper achieved an advantage by being the first major papermaker to rely exclusively on recycled pulp. While the finished product was not so high in quality as paper from virgin wood, Fort Howard's lower cost gave it a competitive edge in the price-sensitive commercial market for toilet paper and other such products used in hotels, restaurants, and office buildings.

Innovative Production Processes   Although low-cost defender businesses typically spend little on *product R&D,* they often continue to devote substantial sums to *process R&D.* Innovations in the production process, including the development of automated or computer-controlled processes, can help them sustain cost advantages over competitors.

In some labor-intensive industries, a business can achieve a cost advantage, at least in the short term, by gaining access to inexpensive labor. This is usually achieved by moving all or part of the production process to countries with low wage rates, such as China or Mexico. Unfortunately, because such moves are relatively easy to emulate, this kind of cost advantage may not be sustainable.

Low-Cost Distribution   When distribution accounts for a relatively high proportion of a product's total delivered cost, a firm might gain a substantial advantage by developing lower-cost alternative channels. Typically, this involves eliminating, or shifting to the customer, some of the functions performed by traditional channels in return for a lower price. In the consumer banking industry, for example, automated teller machines have helped reduce labor costs and investment in bricks-and-mortar branch banks. But they have also reduced the amount of personalized service banks provide to their customers, which may help explain why average customer satisfaction with banks fell by more than 8 percent from 1994 to 2000.[12]

Reductions in Overhead   Successfully sustaining a low-cost strategy requires that the firm pare and control its major overhead costs as quickly as possible as its industry matures. Many U.S. companies learned this lesson the hard way during the 1980s when high costs of old plants, labor, and large inventories left them vulnerable to more efficient foreign competitors and to corporate raiders.

Customers' Satisfaction and Loyalty Are Crucial for Maximizing Their Lifetime Value

Analyzer, and particularly defender, businesses are mostly concerned with protecting their existing positions in one or more mature market segments and maximizing profitability over the remaining life of those product-markets. Thus, financial dimensions of performance, such as return on investment and cash flow, are usually of greater interest to such businesses than are more growth-oriented dimensions, like volume increases or new product success. Businesses can achieve such financial objectives by either successfully differentiating their offerings or by maintaining a low-cost position.

While the primary emphasis in many businesses during the early 1990s was on improving efficiency through downsizing and reengineering,[13] there is substantial evidence that firms with superior quality goods and services also obtain higher returns on investment than do businesses with average or below average offerings.[14] The lesson to be learned, then, is that the choice between a differentiation or a low-cost strategy is probably not the critical determinant of success in mature markets. What is critical is that a business *continually work to improve the value* of its offerings—either by improving product or service quality, reducing costs, or some combination—as a basis for maintaining its customer base as its markets mature and become increasingly competitive.

Measuring Customer Satisfaction   To gain the knowledge necessary to continually improve the value of their offerings to customers, firms must understand how satisfied existing and potential customers are with their current offerings. This focus on customer satisfaction has become increasingly important as more firms question whether all attempts to improve *absolute* quality of their products and services generate sufficient additional sales and profits to justify their cost. This growing concern with the economic "return on quality" has motivated firms to ask which dimensions of product or service quality are most important to customers and which dimensions customers might be willing to sacrifice for lower prices. For instance, United Parcel Service recently discovered that many of its customers wanted more time to interact with the company's drivers in order to seek advice on their shipping problems, and they were willing to put up with slightly slower delivery times in return. Consequently, UPS now allows its drivers an additional 30 minutes a day to spend at their discretion to strengthen ties with customers and perhaps bring in new sales.[15]

Useful measures of customer satisfaction, then, should examine both (1) customers' *expectations and preferences* concerning the various dimensions of product and service quality (such as product performance, features, reliability, on-time delivery, competence of service personnel, and so on) and (2) their *perceptions* concerning how well the firm is meeting those expectations. Any gaps where customer expectations exceed their recent experiences may indicate fruitful areas for the firm to work at improving customer value and satisfaction. Of course, such measurements must be made periodically to determine whether the actions taken have been effective.[16]

Improving Customer Retention and Loyalty   As we discussed in Chapter 1, maintaining the loyalty of existing customers is crucial for a business's profitability. This is especially true as markets mature because loyal customers become more profitable over time. The firm not only avoids the high costs associated with trying to acquire replacement customers in an increasingly competitive market, but it also benefits because loyal customers (1) tend to concentrate their purchases, thus leading to larger volumes and lower selling and distribution costs, (2) provide positive word-of-mouth and customer referrals, and (3) may be willing to pay premium prices for the value they receive.[17]

Periodic measurement of customer satisfaction is important because a dissatisfied customer is unlikely to remain loyal over time. Unfortunately, the reverse is not always true: Customers who describe themselves as satisfied are not necessarily loyal. Indeed, one author estimates that 60 to 80 percent of customer defectors in most businesses said they were "satisfied" or "very satisfied" on the last customer survey before their defection.[18] In the interim, perhaps competitors improved their offerings, the customer's requirements changed, or other environmental factors shifted. Companies that measure customer satisfaction should be commended—but urged not to stop there. Satisfaction measures need to be supplemented with examinations of customer *behavior,* such as measures of the annual retention rate, frequency of purchases, and the percentage of a customer's total purchases captured by the firm.

Most important, defecting customers should be studied in detail to discover why the firm failed to provide sufficient value to retain their loyalty. Such failures often provide more valuable information than satisfaction measures because they stand out as a clear, understandable message telling the organization exactly where improvements are needed. The actions of MicroScan, as detailed in Exhibit 17.6, provide a good example of the intelligent use of such defector analysis.

Are All Customers Equally Valuable?[19]   While improving customer loyalty is crucial for maintaining market share and profitability as markets mature, an increasing number of companies are asking whether every customer's loyalty is worthy of the same level of effort and expense. In these firms, technology is creating a new business model that alters the level of service and benefits provided to a customer based on projections of that customer's value to the firm. With the development of extensive customer databases it is possible for companies to measure what different levels of customer service cost on an individual level. They can also know how much business a particular customer has generated in the past, estimate what she is likely to buy in the future, and calculate a rate of return for that individual for different levels of service.

KEY OBSERVATION

An increasing number of companies are asking whether every customer's loyalty is worthy of the same level of effort and expense.

Exhibit 17.6   MicroScan Examines Defectors to Improve Customer Loyalty

The MicroScan division of Baxter Diagnostics, Inc., makes instruments used by medical laboratories to identify microbes in patient cultures. In 1990 MicroScan was neck-and-neck with Vitek Systems, Inc., for market leadership, but its management knew it would have to do better to win the race. The firm analyzed its customer base, highlighting accounts that had been lost as well as those that remained active but showed a declining volume of testing. MicroScan interviewed all the lost customers and a large portion of the "decliners," probing deeply for the causes underlying their change in behavior. They found that such customers had concerns about the company's in-strument features, reliability, and responsiveness to their problems.

In response, MicroScan's management shifted R&D priorities to address specific shortcomings its lost customers had identified, such as test accuracy and time-to-result. It also redesigned customer service protocols to ensure that immediate attention was given to equipment faults and delivery problems. As a result, MicroScan's sales began to improve and it established a clear market-share lead within two years.

Source: Frederick F. Reichheld, "Loyalty and the Renaissance of Marketing," *Marketing Management* 2 (1994), pp. 10–21. Used by permission of the American Marketing Association.

The ability of firms to tailor different levels of service and benefits to different customers based on each person's potential to produce a profit has been facilitated by the growing popularity of the Internet. The Web has made it easier to track and measure individual transactions across businesses. It has also provided firms with new, low-cost service options; people can now serve themselves at their own convenience, but they have to accept little or no human contact in return.

The end result of this trend toward individually tailored service levels could be an increased stratification of consumer society. The top tier may enjoy unprecedented levels of personal attention. But those who fall below a certain level of profitability for too long may face increased service fees or receive reduced levels of service and benefits. For example, some credit-card companies now charge higher annual fees to customers who do not rack up some minimum level of interest charges during the year. In other firms, call center personnel route customers to different queues. Big spenders are turned over to high-level problem solvers while less profitable customers may never speak to a live person. Finally, choice customers may get fees waived or receive promotional discounts based on the value of their business, while less valuable customers may never know the promotions exist.

The segmentation of customers based on projections of their value, and the tailoring of different service levels and benefits to those segments, raises both ethical and strategic questions, some of which are explored in Exhibit 17.7. One possible way for a firm to resolve some of the dilemmas involved in dealing with less profitable customers is to find ways to increase their lifetime value by increasing the frequency and/or volume of their purchases. This is one strategy examined in detail in the following section.

Marketing Strategies for Mature Markets

Strategies for Maintaining Current Market Share

Since markets can remain in the maturity stage for decades, milking or harvesting mature product-markets by maximizing short-run profits makes little sense. Pursuing such an objective typically involves substantial cuts in marketing and R&D expenses, which can lead to premature losses of volume and market share and lower profits in the longer term. The business should strive during the early years of market maturity to *maximize the flow of profits over the remaining life of the product-market.* Thus, the most critical marketing objective is to *maintain and protect the business's market share.* In a mature market where few new customers buy the product for the first time, the business must continue to win its share of repeat purchases from existing customers.

In Chapter 16 we discussed a number of marketing strategies that businesses might use to maintain their market share in growth markets. Many of those same strategies continue to be relevant for holding on to customers as markets mature, particularly for those firms that survived the shakeout period with a relatively strong share position. The most obvious strategy for such share leaders is simply to continue strengthening their position through a *fortress defense.* Recall that such a strategy involves two sets of marketing actions: those aimed at improving customer satisfaction and loyalty, and those intended to encourage and simplify repeat purchasing. Actions like those discussed earlier for improving the quality of a firm's offering and for reducing costs suggest ways to increase customer satisfaction and loyalty. Similarly, improvements to service quality, such as just-in-time delivery arrangements or computerized reordering systems, can help encourage repeat purchases.

Since markets often become more fragmented as they grow and mature, share leaders may also have to expand their product lines, or add one or more *flanker* brands, to protect

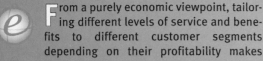

Exhibit 17.7   Pros and Cons of Varying Service Levels According to Customers' Profitability

From a purely economic viewpoint, tailoring different levels of service and benefits to different customer segments depending on their profitability makes sense, at least in the short run. In an era when labor costs are increasing while many markets, especially mature ones, are getting more competitive, many firms argue they cannot afford to provide extensive hands-on service to everyone. Companies also point out that they're often delivering a wider range of products and services than ever before, including more ways for customers to handle transactions. Thanks to the Internet, for example, consumers have better tools to conveniently serve themselves. And finally, service segmentation may actually produce some positive benefits for customers—more personalized service for the best customers and, in many cases, lower overall costs and prices for everyone else. For instance, Fidelity Investments now gets about 550,000 website visits each day and more than 700,000 daily phone calls, three-quarters of which go to automated systems that cost the company less than a dollar each, including research and development costs. The rest are handled by human operators, at a cost of about $13 per call.

From an ethical standpoint, however, many people question the inherent fairness and potential invasion of privacy involved in using a wealth of personal information about individual consumers as a basis for withholding services or benefits from some of them, especially when such practices are largely invisible to the consumer. You don't know when you're being shuttled to a different telephone queue or sales promotion. You don't know what benefits you're missing or what additional fees you're being charged. Some argue that this lack of transparency is unfair because it deprives consumers of the opportunity to take actions, such as concentrating their purchases with a single supplier, switching companies, or paying a service fee, that would enable them to acquire the additional services and benefits they are currently denied.

From a strategic view, there are also some potential dangers in cutting services and benefits to customers who have not generated profits in the past. For one thing, past behavior is not necessarily an accurate indicator of a customer's future lifetime value. The life situations and spending habits of some customer groups—college students, for instance—can change dramatically over time. In addition, looking only at a customer's purchases may overlook some indirect ways that customer affects the firm's revenues, such as positive word-of-mouth recommendations and referrals to other potential buyers. And some customers may not be spending much with a company precisely because of the lousy service they have received as a result of not spending very much with that company. Instead of simply writing off low-volume customers it may make more strategic sense to first attempt to convert them into high-volume customers by targeting them for additional promotions, by trying to sell complementary goods and services, or by instituting loyalty programs (e.g., the airlines' frequent-flier programs).

Finally, by debasing the satisfaction and loyalty of low-volume customers, firms risk losing those customers to competitors. In a mature industry, particularly one with substantial economies of scale, such a loss of market share can increase unit costs and reduce the profitability of those high-volume customers that do remain loyal. And, as the history of Commerce Bancorp (featured in Chapter 11) illustrates, a creative competitor may find ways to make other firms' cast-off customers very profitable after all.

Source: Diane Brady, "Why Service Stinks," Reprinted from the October 23, 2000 issue of *Business Week* by permission. Copyright The McGraw-Hill Companies.

their position against competitive inroads. Thus, Johnson Controls has strengthened its position in the commercial facilities management arena by expanding its array of services through a combination of acquisitions and continued internal development.

Small-share competitors can also earn substantial profits in a mature market. To do so, however, it is often wise for them to focus on strategies that avoid prolonged direct confrontations with larger share leaders. A *niche strategy* can be particularly effective when the target segment is too small to appeal to larger competitors or when the smaller firm can establish a strong differential advantage or brand preference in the segment. For instance, with only 36 hotels worldwide, the Four Seasons chain is a small player in the lodging industry. But by focusing on the high end of the business travel market, the chain has grown and prospered. The chain's hotels differentiate themselves by offering a wide range of amenities, such as free overnight shoeshines, that are important to business travelers. Thus, while they charge relatively high prices, they are also seen as delivering good value.

Strategies for Extending Volume Growth

Market maturity is defined by a flattening of the growth rate. In some instances growth slows for structural reasons, such as the emergence of substitute products or a shift in customer preferences. Marketers can do little to revitalize the market under such conditions. But in some cases a market only *appears* to be mature because of the limitations of current marketing programs, such as target segments that are too narrowly defined or limited product offerings. Here, more innovative or aggressive marketing strategies might successfully extend the market's life cycle into a period of renewed growth. Thus, *stimulating additional volume* growth can be an important secondary objective under such circumstances, particularly for industry share leaders because they often can capture a relatively large share of any additional volume generated.

A firm might pursue several different marketing strategies—either singly or in combination—to squeeze additional volume from a mature market. These include an *increased penetration strategy,* an *extended use strategy,* and a *market expansion strategy.* Exhibit 17.8 summarizes the environmental situations where each of these strategies is most appropriate and the objectives each is best suited for accomplishing. Exhibit 17.9 then outlines specific marketing actions a firm might employ to implement each of the strategies, as discussed in more detail in the following paragraphs.

Increased Penetration Strategy   The total sales volume produced by a target segment of customers is a function of (1) the number of potential customers in the segment, (2) the product's penetration of that segment; that is, the proportion of potential customers who actually use the product, and (3) the average frequency with which customers consume the product and make another purchase. Where usage frequency is quite high among current customers but only a relatively small portion of all potential users actually buy the product, a firm might aim at increasing market penetration. It is an appropriate strategy for an industry's share leader because such firms can more likely gain and retain a substantial share of new customers than smaller firms with less-well-known brands.

The secret to a successful increased penetration strategy lies in discovering why nonusers are uninterested in the product. Very often the product does not offer sufficient value from the potential customer's view to justify the effort or expense involved in buying and using it. One obvious solution to such a problem is to enhance the product's value to potential customers by adding features or benefits, usually via line extensions.

Another way to add value to a product is to develop and sell integrated systems that help improve the basic product's performance or ease of use. For instance, instead of simply selling control mechanisms for heating and cooling systems, Johnson Controls offers integrated facilities management programs designed to lower the total costs of operating a commercial building.

A firm may also enhance a product's value by offering services that improve its performance or ease of use for the potential customer. Since it is unlikely that people who do not know how to knit will ever buy yarn or knitting needles, for example, most yarn shops offer free knitting lessons.

Product modifications or line extensions will not, however, attract nonusers unless the enhanced benefits are effectively promoted. For industrial goods, this may mean redirecting

Exhibit 17.8

SITUATIONAL DETERMINANTS OF APPROPRIATE MARKETING OBJECTIVES AND STRATEGIES FOR EXTENDING GROWTH IN MATURE MARKETS

GROWTH EXTENSION STRATEGIES

Situation variables	Increased penetration	Extended use	Market expansion
Primary objective	Increase the proportion of users by converting current nonusers in one or more major market segments.	Increase the amount of product used by the average customer by increasing frequency of use or developing new and more varied ways to use the product.	Expand the number of potential customers by targeting underdeveloped geographic areas or applications segments.
Market characteristics	Relatively low penetration in one or more segments (i.e., low percentage of potential users have adopted the product); relatively homogeneous market with only a few large segments.	Relatively high penetration but low frequency of use in one or more major segments; product used in only limited ways or for special occasions; relatively homogeneous market with only a few large segments.	Relatively heterogeneous market with a variety of segments; some geographic areas, including foreign countries, with low penetration; some product applications underdeveloped.
Competitors' characteristics	Competitors hold relatively small market shares; comparatively limited resources or competencies make it unlikely they will steal a significant portion of converted nonusers.	Competitors hold relatively small market shares; comparatively limited resources or competencies make it unlikely their brands will be purchased for newly developed uses.	Competitors hold relatively small market shares; have insufficient resources or competencies to preempt underdeveloped geographic areas or applications segments.
Firm's characteristics	A market share leader in the industry; has R&D and marketing competencies to produce product modifications or line extensions; has promotional resources to stimulate primary demand among current nonusers.	A market share leader in the industry; has marketing competencies and resources to develop and promote new uses.	A market share leader in the industry; has marketing and distribution competencies and resources to develop new global markets or applications segments.

some sales efforts toward nonusers. The firm may offer additional incentives for new account sales or assign specific salespeople to call on targeted nonusers and convert them into new customers. For consumer goods, some combination of advertising to stimulate primary demand in the target segment and sales promotions to encourage trial, such as free samples or tie-in promotions with complementary products that nonusers currently buy, can be effective.

Finally, some potential customers may be having trouble finding the product due to limited distribution, or the product's benefits may simply be too modest to justify much purchasing effort. In such cases, expanding distribution or developing more convenient and accessible channels may help expand market penetration. For example, few travelers are so leery of flying that they would go through the effort of calling an insurance agent to buy an accident policy for a single flight. But the sales of such policies are greatly increased by making them conveniently available through vending machines in airport terminals.

Extended Use Strategy

Some years ago, the manager of General Foods' Cool Whip frozen dessert topping discovered through marketing research that nearly three-fourths of all U.S. households used the product, but the average consumer used it only four times per

Exhibit 17.9

POSSIBLE MARKETING ACTIONS FOR ACCOMPLISHING GROWTH EXTENSION OBJECTIVES

Marketing strategy and objectives	Possible marketing actions

Increased penetration

Convert current nonusers in target segment into users	• Enhance product's value by adding features, benefits, or services.
	• Enhance product's value by including it in the design of integrated systems.
	• Stimulate additional primary demand through promotional efforts stressing new features or benefits:
	    Advertising through selective media aimed at the target segment.
	    Sales promotions directed at stimulating trial among current nonusers (e.g., tie-ins with other products).
	    Some sales efforts redirected toward new account generation, perhaps by assigning some sales personnel as account development reps or by offering incentives for new account sales.
	    Improve product's availability by developing innovative distribution systems.

Extended use

Increase frequency of use among current users	• Move storage of the product closer to the point of end use by offering additional package sizes or designs.
	• Encourage larger volume purchases (for nonperishable products):
	    Offer quantity discounts.
	    Offer consumer promotions to stimulate volume purchases or more frequent use (e.g., multipack deals, frequent flier programs).
	• Reminder advertising stressing basic product benefits for a variety of usage occasions.

Encourage a wider variety of uses among current users	• Develop line extensions suitable for additional uses or applications.
	• Develop and promote new uses, applications, or recipes for the basic product.
	    Include information about new applications/recipes on package.
	    Develop extended use advertising campaign, particularly with print media.
	    Communicate new application ideas through sales presentations to current customers.
	• Encourage new uses through sales promotions (e.g., tie-ins with complementary products).

Market expansion

Develop differentiated positioning focused on untapped or underdeveloped segments	• Develop a differentiated flanker brand or product line with unique features or price that is more appealing to a segment of potential customers whose needs are not met by existing offerings. or • Develop multiple line extensions or brand offerings with features or prices targeted to the unique needs and preferences of several smaller potential applications or regional segments. • Consider producing for private labels. • Design advertising, personal selling, and/or sales promotion campaigns that address specific interests and concerns of potential customers in one or multiple underdeveloped segments to stimulate selective demand. • Build unique distribution channels to more effectively reach potential customers in one or multiple underdeveloped segments. • Design service programs to reduce the perceived risks of trial and/or solve the unique problems faced by potential customers in one or multiple underdeveloped segments (e.g., systems engineering, installation, operator training, extended warranties). • Enter global markets where product category is in an earlier stage of its life cycle.

year and served it on only 7 percent of all toppable desserts. In situations of good market penetration but low frequency of use, an extended use strategy may increase volume. This was particularly true in the Cool Whip case; the relatively large and homogeneous target market consisted for the most part of a single mass-market segment. Also, General Foods held nearly a two-thirds share of the frozen topping market, and it had the marketing resources and competencies to capture most of the additional volume that an extended use strategy might generate.

One effective approach for stimulating increased frequency of use is to move product inventories closer to the point of use. This approach works particularly well with low-involvement consumer goods. Marketers know that most consumers are unlikely to expend any additional time or effort to obtain such products when they are ready to use them. If there is no Cool Whip in the refrigerator when the consumer is preparing dessert, for instance, he or she is unlikely to run to the store immediately and will probably serve the dessert without topping.

One obvious way to move inventory closer to the point of consumption is to offer larger package sizes. The more customers buy at one time, the less likely they are to be out of stock when a usage opportunity arises. This approach can backfire, though, for a perishable product or one that consumers perceive to be an impulse indulgence. Thus, most super-premium ice creams, such as Häagen-Dazs, are sold in small pint containers; most consumers want to avoid the temptation of having large quantities of such a high-calorie indulgence too readily available.

The design of a package can also help increase use frequency by making the product more convenient or easy to use. Examples include single-serving packages of Jell-O pudding to pack in lunches, packages of paper cups that include a convenient dispenser, and frozen-food packages that can go directly into a microwave oven.

Various sales promotion programs also help move inventories of a product closer to the point of use by encouraging larger volume purchases. Marketers commonly offer quantity discounts for this purpose in selling industrial goods. For consumer products, multi-item discounts or two-for-one deals serve the same purpose. Promotional programs also encourage greater frequency of use and increase customer loyalty in many service industries. Consider, for instance, the frequent-flier programs offered by major airlines.

Sometimes the product's characteristics inhibit customers from using it more frequently. If marketers can change those characteristics, such as difficulty of preparation or high calories, a new line extension might encourage customers to use more of the product or to use it more often. Microwave waffles and low-calorie salad dressings are examples of such line extensions. For industrial goods, however, firms may have to develop new technology to overcome a product's limitations for some applications. For instance, Johnson Controls recently acquired Prince Automotive to gain the expertise necessary to develop instrument panels and consoles incorporating the sophisticated electronics desired by top-end manufacturers such as BMW and Mercedes-Benz.

Finally, advertising can sometimes effectively increase use frequency by simply reminding customers to use the product more often. For instance, General Foods conducted a reminder campaign for Jell-O pudding that featured Bill Cosby asking, "When was the last time you served pudding, Mom?"

Another approach for extending use among current customers involves finding and promoting new functional uses for the product. Jell-O gelatin is a classic example, having generated substantial new sales volume over the years by promoting the use of Jell-O as an ingredient in salads, pie fillings, and other dishes.

Firms promote new ways to use a product through a variety of methods. For industrial products, firms send technical advisories about new applications to the salesforce to present to their customers during regular sales calls. For consumer products, new use suggestions or recipes may be included on the package, in an advertising campaign, or on the firm's website. Sales promotions, such as including cents-off coupons in ads featuring a new recipe, encourage customers to try a new application. To reduce costs, two or more manufacturers of complementary products sometimes cooperate in running such promotions. A recent ad promoting a simple Italian dinner, for instance, featured coupons for Kraft's Parmesan cheese, Pillsbury's Soft Breadsticks, and Campbell's Prego spaghetti sauce.

In some cases, slightly modified line extensions might encourage customers to use the product in different ways. Thus, Kraft introduced a jalapeño-flavored Cheese-Whiz in a microwavable container and promoted the product as an easy-to-prepare topping for nachos.

Market Expansion Strategy

In a mature industry with a fragmented and heterogeneous market where some segments are less well developed than others, a market expansion strategy may generate substantial additional volume growth. Such a strategy aims at gaining new customers by targeting new or underdeveloped geographic markets (either regional or foreign) or new customer segments. Once again, share leaders tend to be best suited for implementing this strategy. But even smaller competitors can employ such a strategy successfully if they focus on relatively small or specialized market niches.

KEY OBSERVATION

In a fragmented and heterogeneous market where some segments are less well developed than others, a market expansion strategy may generate substantial additional volume growth.

Pursuing market expansion by strengthening a firm's position in new or underdeveloped **domestic geographic markets** can lead to experience-curve benefits and operating synergies. The firm can rely on largely the same expertise and technology, and perhaps even the same production and distribution facilities, it has already developed. Unfortunately, domestic geographic expansion is often not viable in a mature industry because the share leaders usually have attained national market coverage. Smaller regional competitors, on the other hand, might consider domestic geographic expansion a means for improving their volume and share position. However, such a move risks retaliation from the large national brands as well as from entrenched regional competitors in the prospective new territory.

To get around the retaliation problem, a regional producer might try to expand through the acquisition of small producers in other regions. This can be a viable option when (1) the low profitability of some regional producers enables the acquiring firm to buy their assets for less than the replacement cost of the capacity involved and (2) synergies gained by combining regional operations and the infusion of resources from the acquiring firm can improve the effectiveness and profitability of the acquired producers. For example, Heileman Brewing Company grew from the 31st largest U.S. brewer of beer in the mid-1960s to the 4th largest by the mid-1980s through the acquisition of nearly 30 regional brands. Heileman took control of strong regional brands such as Old Style, Carling, and Rainier, but because it had no dominant national brand it avoided antitrust opposition to its acquisition program. After acquisition, Heileman maintained the identity of each brand, increased its advertising budget, and expanded its distribution by incorporating it into the firm's distribution system in other regions. As a result, Heileman achieved a strong earnings record for two decades, until the firm was itself acquired by an Australian brewer.

In a different approach to domestic market expansion, the firm identifies and develops entirely **new customer** or **application segments.** Sometimes the firm can effectively reach new customer segments by simply expanding the distribution system without changing the product's characteristics or the other marketing-mix elements. A sporting goods manufacturer that sells its products to consumers through retail stores, for instance, might expand into the commercial market consisting of schools and amateur and professional sports teams by establishing a direct salesforce. In most instances, though, developing new market segments requires modifying the product to make it more suitable for the application or to provide more of the benefits desired by customers in the new segment.

One final possibility for domestic market expansion is to produce **private-label brands** for large retailers. Firms whose own brands hold relatively weak positions and who have excess production capacity find this a particularly attractive option. Private labeling allows such firms to gain access to established customer segments without making substantial marketing expenditures, thus increasing the firm's volume and lowering its per-unit costs. However, since private labels typically compete with low prices and their sponsors usually have strong bargaining power, producing private labels is often not a very profitable option unless a manufacturer already has a relatively low-cost position in the industry. It can also be a risky strategy, particularly for the smaller firm, because reliance on one or a few large private-label customers can result in drastic volume reductions and unit-cost increases should those customers decide to switch suppliers.

Global Market Expansion—Sequential Strategies

For firms with leading positions in mature domestic markets, less-developed markets in foreign countries often present the most viable opportunities for geographic expansion. As discussed in previous chapters, firms can enter foreign markets in a variety of ways, from simply relying on import agents to developing joint ventures to establishing wholly owned subsidiaries—as Johnson Controls has done by acquiring automotive seat and battery manufacturers in Europe.

Regardless of which mode of entry a firm chooses, it can follow a number of different routes when pursuing global expansion.[20] By *route* we mean the sequence or order in which the firm enters global markets. Japanese companies provide illustrations of different global expansion paths. The most common expansion route involves moving from Japan to developing countries to developed countries. They used this path, for example, with automobiles (Toyota), consumer electronics (National), watches (Seiko), cameras (Minolta), and home appliances, steel, and petrochemicals. This routing reduced manufacturing costs and enabled them to gain marketing experience. In penetrating the U.S. market, the Japanese obtained further economies of scale and gained recognition for their products, which made penetration of European markets easier.

A second type of *expansion path* has been used primarily for high-tech products such as computers and semiconductors. For the Japanese it consists of first securing their home market and then targeting developed countries. Japan largely ignored developing countries in this strategy because of their small demand for high-tech products. When demand increased to a point where developing countries became "interesting," Japanese producers quickly entered and established strong market positions using price cuts of up to 50 percent.

A home market—developed markets—developing markets sequence is also usually appropriate for discretionary goods such as soft drinks, convenience foods, or cosmetics. Coca-Cola, for instance, believes that as disposable incomes and discretionary expenditures grow in the countries of South America, Asia, and Africa those markets will drive much of the company's future growth. Similarly, firms such as the French cosmetics giant L'Oreal have positioned a number of different "world brands"—including Ralph Lauren perfumes, L'Oreal hair products, and Maybelline and Helena Rubinstein cosmetics—to convey the allure of different cultures to developing markets around the world.[21]

Strategies for Declining Markets

Most products eventually enter a decline phase in their life cycles. As sales decline, excess capacity once again develops. As the remaining competitors fight to hold volume in the face of falling sales, industry profits erode. Consequently, conventional wisdom suggests that firms should either divest declining products quickly or harvest them to maximize short-term profits. Not all markets decline in the same way or at the same speed, however; nor do all firms have the same competitive strengths and weaknesses within those markets. Therefore, as in most other situations, the relative attractiveness of the declining product-market and the business's competitive position within it should dictate the appropriate strategy.

Relative Attractiveness of Declining Markets

Although U.S. high school enrollment declined by about 2 million students from its peak in 1976 through the early 1990s, Jostens, Inc., the leading manufacturer of class rings and other school merchandise, achieved annual increases in revenues and profits every year during that period. One reason for the firm's success was that it saw the market decline coming and prepared for it by improving the efficiency of its operations and developing marketing programs that were effective at persuading a larger proportion of students to buy class rings.[22]

Jostens' experience shows that some declining product-markets can offer attractive opportunities well into the future, at least for one or a few strong competitors. In other product-markets, particularly those where decline is the result of customers switching to a new technology (e.g., more students buying personal computers instead of portable typewriters), the potential for continued profits during the decline stage is more bleak.

Three sets of factors help determine the strategic attractiveness of declining product-markets: *conditions of demand,* including the rate and certainty of future declines in volume; *exit barriers,* or the ease with which weaker competitors can leave the market; and factors affecting the *intensity of future competitive rivalry* within the market.[23] The impact of these variables on the attractiveness of declining market environments is summarized in Exhibit 17.10 and discussed below.

Conditions of Demand   Demand in a product-market declines for a number of reasons. Technological advances produce substitute products (such as electronic calculators for slide rules), often with higher quality or lower cost. Demographic shifts lead to a shrinking target market (baby foods). Customers' needs, tastes, or lifestyles change (the falling consumption of beef). Finally, the cost of inputs or complementary products rises and shrinks demand (the effects of rising gasoline prices on sales of recreational vehicles).

The cause of a decline in demand can affect both the rate and the predictability of that decline. A fall in sales due to a demographic shift, for instance, is likely to be gradual, whereas the switch to a technically superior substitute can be abrupt. Similarly, the fall in demand as customers switch to a better substitute is predictable, while a decline in sales due to a change in tastes is not.

As Exhibit 17.10 indicates, both the rate and certainty of sales decline are demand characteristics that affect a market's attractiveness. A slow and gradual decline allows an orderly withdrawal of weaker competitors. Overcapacity does not become excessive and lead to predatory competitive behavior, and the competitors who remain are more likely to make profits than in a quick or erratic decline. Also, when most industry managers believe market decline is predictable and certain, reduction of capacity is more likely to be orderly than when they feel substantial uncertainty about whether demand might level off or even become revitalized.

Not all segments of a market decline at the same time or at the same rate. The number and size of enduring niches or pockets of demand and the customer purchase behavior

Exhibit 17.10

FACTORS AFFECTING THE ATTRACTIVENESS OF DECLINING MARKET ENVIRONMENTS

	ENVIRONMENTAL ATTRACTIVENESS	
Conditions of demand	**Hospitable**	**Inhospitable**
Speed of decline	Very slow	Rapid or erratic
Certainty of decline	100% certain, predictable patterns	Great uncertainty, erratic patterns
Pockets of enduring demand	Several or major ones	No niches
Product differentiation	Brand loyalty	Commoditylike products
Price stability	Stable, price premiums attainable	Very unstable, pricing below costs
Exit barriers		
Reinvestment requirements	None	High, often mandatory and involving capital assets
Excess capacity	Little	Substantial
Asset age	Mostly old assets	Sizable new assets and old ones not retired
Resale markets for assets	Easy to convert or sell	No markets available, substantial costs to retire
Shared facilities	Few, freestanding plants	Substantial and interconnected with important businesses
Vertical integration	Little	Substantial
Single-product competitors	None	Several large companies
Rivalry determinants		
Customer industries	Fragmented, weak	Strong bargaining power
Customer switching costs	High	Minimal
Diseconomies of scale	None	Substantial penalty
Dissimilar strategic groups	Few	Several in same target markets

Source: Reprinted by permission of *Harvard Business Review.* From "End-Game Strategies for Declining Industries," by Kathryn Rudie Harrigan and Michael E. Porter, July–August 1983. Copyright © 1983 by the Harvard Business School Publishing Corporation, all rights reserved.

within them also influence the continuing attractiveness of the market. When the demand pockets are large or numerous and the customers in those niches are brand loyal and relatively insensitive to price, competitors with large shares and differentiated products can continue to make substantial profits. For example, even though the market for cigars shrank for years, there continued to be a sizable number of smokers who bought premium-quality cigars. Those firms with well-established positions at the premium end of the cigar industry have continued to earn above-average returns. And recently, the cigar market has been growing again.

Exit Barriers   The higher the exit barriers, the less hospitable a product-market will be during the decline phase of its life cycle. When weaker competitors find it hard to leave a product-market as demand falls, excess capacity develops and firms engage in aggressive pricing or promotional efforts to try to prop up their volume and hold down unit costs. Thus, exit barriers lead to competitive volatility.

Once again, Exhibit 17.10 indicates that a variety of factors influence the ease with which businesses can exit an industry. One critical consideration involves the amount of highly specialized assets. Assets unique to a given business are difficult to divest because of their low liquidation value. The only potential buyers for such assets are other firms who would use them for a similar purpose, which is unlikely in a declining industry. Thus, the firm may have little choice but to remain in the business or to sell the assets for their scrap value. This option is particularly unattractive when the assets are relatively new and not fully depreciated.

Another major exit barrier occurs when the assets or resources of the declining business intertwine with the firm's other business units, either through shared facilities and programs or through vertical integration. Exit from the declining business might shut down shared production facilities, lower salesforce commissions, damage customer relations, and increase unit costs in the firm's other businesses to a point that damages their profitability. Emotional factors can also act as exit barriers. Managers often feel reluctant to admit failure by divesting a business even though it no longer produces acceptable returns. This is especially true when the business played an important role in the firm's history and it houses a large number of senior managers.

Intensity of Future Competitive Rivalry   Even when substantial pockets of continuing demand remain within a declining business, it may not be wise for a firm to pursue them in the face of future intense competitive rivalry. In addition to exit barriers, other factors also affect the ability of the remaining firms to avoid intense price competition and maintain reasonable margins: size and bargaining power of the customers who continue to buy the product; customers' ability to switch to substitute products or to alternative suppliers; and any potential diseconomies of scale involved in capturing an increased share of the remaining volume.

Divestment or Liquidation

When the market environment in a declining industry is unattractive or a business has a relatively weak competitive position, the firm may recover more of its investment by selling the business in the early stages of decline rather than later. The earlier the business is sold, the more uncertain potential buyers are likely to be about the future direction of demand in the industry and thus the more likely that a willing buyer can be found. Thus, Raytheon sold its vacuum-tube business in the early 1960s even though transistors had just begun replacing tubes in radios and TV sets and there was still a strong replacement demand for tubes. By moving early, the firm achieved a much higher liquidation value than companies that tried to unload their tube-making facilities in the 70s when the industry was clearly in its twilight years.[24]

Of course, the firm that divests early runs the risk that its forecast of the industry's future may be wrong. Also, quick divestment may not be possible if the firm faces high exit barriers, such as interdependencies across business units or customer expectations of continued product availability. By planning early for departure, however, the firm may be able to reduce some of those barriers before the liquidation is necessary.

Marketing Strategies for Remaining Competitors

Conventional wisdom suggests that a business remaining in a declining product-market should pursue a harvesting strategy aimed at maximizing its cash flow in the short run. But such businesses also have other strategic options. They might attempt to maintain their

Exhibit 17.11

SITUATIONAL DETERMINANTS OF APPROPRIATE MARKETING OBJECTIVES AND STRATEGIES FOR DECLINING MARKETS

	STRATEGIES FOR DECLINING MARKETS			
Situational variables	Harvesting	Maintenance	Profitable survivor	Niche
Primary objective	Maximize short-term cash flow; maintain or increase margins even at the expense of a slow decline in market share.	Maintain share in short term as market declines, even if margins must be sacrificed.	Increase share of the declining market with an eye to future profits; encourage weaker competitors to exit.	Focus on strengthening position in one or a few relatively substantial segments with potential for future profits.
Market characteristics	Future market decline is certain, but likely to occur at a slow and steady rate.	Market has experienced recent declines, but future direction and attractiveness are currently hard to predict.	Future market decline is certain, but likely to occur at a slow and steady rate; substantial pockets of demand will continue to exist.	Overall market may decline quickly, but one or more segments will remain as demand pockets or decay slowly.
Competitors' characteristics	Few strong competitors; low exit barriers; future rivalry not likely to be intense.	Few strong competitors; but intensity of future rivalry is hard to predict.	Few strong competitors; exit barriers are low or can be reduced by firm's intervention.	One or more stronger competitors in mass market, but not in the target segment.
Firm's characteristics	Has a leading share position; has a substantial proportion of loyal customers who are likely to continue buying brand even if marketing support is reduced.	Has a leading share of the market and a relatively strong competitive position.	Has a leading share of the market and a strong competitive position; has superior resources or competencies necessary to encourage competitors to exit or to acquire them.	Has a sustainable competitive advantage in target segment, but overall resources may be limited.

position as the market declines, improve their position to become the profitable survivor, or focus efforts on one or more remaining demand pockets or market niches. Once again, the appropriateness of these strategies depends on factors affecting the attractiveness of the declining market and on the business's competitive strengths and weaknesses. Exhibit 17.11 summarizes the situational determinants of the appropriateness of each strategy. Some of the marketing actions a firm might take to implement them are discussed below and listed in Exhibit 17.12.

Harvesting Strategy   The objective of a harvesting or milking strategy is to generate cash quickly by maximizing cash flow over a relatively short term. This typically involves avoiding any additional investment in the business, greatly reducing operating (including marketing) expenses, and perhaps raising prices. Since the firm usually expects to ultimately divest or abandon the business, some loss of sales and market share during the pursuit of this strategy is likely. The trick is to hold the business's volume and share declines to a relatively slow and steady rate. A precipitous and premature loss of share would limit the total amount of cash the business could generate during the market's decline.

A harvesting strategy is most appropriate for a firm holding a relatively strong competitive position in the market at the start of the decline and a cadre of current customers likely to continue buying the brand even after marketing support is reduced. Such a strategy also works best when the market's decline is inevitable but likely to occur at a relatively slow

Exhibit 17.12

POSSIBLE MARKETING ACTIONS APPROPRIATE FOR DIFFERENT STRATEGIES IN DECLINING MARKETS

Marketing strategy and objectives	Possible marketing actions

Harvesting strategy

Maximize short-term cash flow; maintain or increase margins even at the expense of market share decline.

- Eliminate R&D expenditures and capital investments related to the business.
- Reduce marketing and sales budgets.
  Greatly reduce or eliminate advertising and sales promotion expenditures, with the possible exception of periodic reminder advertising targeted at current customers.
  Reduce trade promotions to minimum level necessary to prevent rapid loss of distribution coverage.
  Focus salesforce efforts on attaining repeat purchases from current customers.
- Seek ways to reduce production costs, even at the expense of slow erosion in product quality.
- Raise price if necessary to maintain margins.

Maintenance strategy

Maintain market share for the short term, even at the expense of margins.

- Continue product and process R&D expenditures in short term aimed at maintaining or improving product quality.
- Continue maintenance levels of advertising and sales promotion targeted at current users.
- Continue trade promotion at levels sufficient to avoid any reduction in distribution coverage.
- Focus salesforce efforts on attaining repeat purchases from current users.
- Lower prices if necessary to maintain share, even at the expense of reduced margins.

Profitable survivor strategy

Increase share of the declining market; encourage weaker competitors to exit.

- Signal competitors that firm intends to remain in industry and pursue an increased share.
  Maintain or increase advertising and sales promotion budgets.
  Maintain or increase distribution coverage through aggressive trade promotion.
  Focus some salesforce effort on winning away competitors' customers.
  Continue product and process R&D to seek product improvements or cost reductions.
- Consider introducing line extensions to appeal to remaining demand segments.
- Lower prices if necessary to increase share, even at the expense of short-term margins.
- Consider agreements to produce replacement parts or private labels for smaller competitors considering getting out of production.

Niche strategy

Strengthen share position in one or a few segments with potential for continued profit.

- Continued product and process R&D aimed at product improvements or modifications that will appeal to target segment(s).
- Consider producing for private labels in order to maintain volume and hold down unit costs.
- Focus advertising, sales promotion, and personal selling campaigns on customers in target segment(s); stress appeals of greatest importance to those customers.
- Maintain distribution channels appropriate for reaching target segment; seek unique channel arrangements to more effectively reach customers in target segment(s).
- Design service programs that address unique concerns/problems of customers in the target segment(s).

and steady rate and when rivalry among remaining competitors is not likely to be very intense. Such conditions enable the business to maintain adequate price levels and profit margins as volume gradually falls.

Implementing a harvesting strategy means avoiding any additional long-term investments in plant, equipment, or R&D. It also necessitates substantial cuts in operating expenditures for marketing activities. This often means that the firm should greatly reduce the number of models or package sizes in its product line to reduce inventory and manufacturing costs.

The business should improve the efficiency of sales and distribution. For instance, an industrial goods manufacturer might service its smaller accounts through telemarketing or a website rather than a field salesforce or assign its smaller customers to agent middlemen. For consumer goods, the business might move to more selective distribution by concentrating its efforts on the larger retail chains.

The firm would likely reduce advertising and promotion expenditures, usually to the minimum level necessary to retain adequate distribution. Finally, the business should attempt to maintain or perhaps even increase its price levels to increase margins.

Maintenance Strategy

In markets where future volume trends are highly uncertain, a business with a leading share position might consider pursuing a strategy aimed at maintaining its market share, at least until the market's future becomes more predictable. In such a maintenance strategy, the business continues to pursue the same strategy that brought it success during the market's mature stage. This approach often results in reduced margins and profits in the short term, though, because firms usually must reduce prices or increase marketing expenditures to hold share in the face of declining industry volume. Thus, a firm should consider share maintenance an interim strategy. Once it becomes clear that the market will continue to decline, the business should switch to a different strategy that will provide better cash flows and return on investment over the market's remaining life.

Profitable Survivor Strategy

An aggressive alternative for a business with a strong share position and a sustainable competitive advantage in a declining product-market is to invest enough to increase its share position and establish itself as the industry leader for the remainder of the market's decline. This kind of strategy makes most sense when the firm expects a gradual decline in market demand or when substantial pockets of continuing demand are likely well into the future. It is also an attractive strategy when a firm's declining business is closely intertwined with other SBUs through shared facilities and programs or common customer segments.

A strong competitor can often improve its share position in a declining market at relatively low cost because other competitors may be harvesting their businesses or preparing to exit. The key to the success of such a strategy is to encourage other competitors to leave the market early. Once the firm has achieved a strong and unchallenged position, it can switch to a harvesting strategy and reap substantial profits over the remaining life of the product-market.

A firm might encourage smaller competitors to abandon the industry by being visible and explicit about its commitment to become the leading survivor. It should aggressively seek increased market share, either by cutting prices or by increasing advertising and promotion expenditures. It might also introduce line extensions aimed at remaining pockets of demand to make it more difficult for smaller competitors to find profitable niches. Finally, the firm might act to reduce its competitors' exit barriers, making it easier for them to leave the industry. This could involve taking over competitors' long-term contracts, agreeing to supply spare parts or to service their products in the field, or providing them with components or private-label products. For instance, large regional bakeries have encouraged grocery chains to abandon their own bakery operations by supplying them with private-label baked goods.

The ultimate way to remove competitors' exit barriers is to purchase their operations and either improve their efficiency or remove them from the industry to avoid excess capacity. With continued decline in industry sales a certainty, smaller competitors may be forced to sell their assets at a book value price low enough for the survivor to reap high returns on its investment, as Heileman Brewing Company did on its acquisitions of smaller regional brewers during the 1970s and 80s.

Niche Strategy   Even when most segments of an industry are expected to decline rapidly, a niche strategy may still be viable if one or more substantial segments will either remain as stable pockets of demand or decay slowly. The business pursuing such a strategy should have a strong competitive position in the target segment or be able to build a sustainable competitive advantage relatively quickly to preempt competitors. This is one strategy that even smaller competitors can sometimes successfully pursue, because they can focus the required assets and resources on a limited portion of the total market. The marketing actions a business might take to strengthen and preserve its position in a target niche are similar to those discussed earlier concerning niche strategies in mature markets.

TAKE-AWAYS

- Strategic choices in mature, or even declining, markets are by no means always bleak. Many of the world's most profitable companies operate largely in such markets.

- A critical marketing objective for all competitors in a mature market is to maintain the loyalty of existing customers. To accomplish that goal, firms must pursue improvements in the perceived value those customers receive from their offerings—either by differentiating themselves on the basis of superior quality or service, by lowering costs and prices, or both.

- An important secondary objective for some firms, particularly share leaders, in mature markets is to stimulate further volume growth by taking actions to

convert nonusers into users, to increase use frequency among current users, or to expand into untapped or underdeveloped markets.

- Declining markets can still offer attractive opportunities for sales revenues and profits. Their attractiveness—and the appropriate marketing strategy to follow—depends on, among other things, the pace and certainty of market decline, the presence of exit barriers, the firm's competitive strengths, and the likely intensity of future competition.

Self-diagnostic questions to test your ability to apply the analytical tools and concepts in this chapter to marketing decision making may be found at this book's website at www.mhhe.com/mullins05.

ENDNOTES

1. This example is based on material found in Rick Tetzeli, "Mining Money in Mature Markets," *Fortune,* March 22, 1993, pp. 77–80; Edmund Chew, "Johnson Controls Inc. Displays Interior Concepts at Frankfurt Auto Show," *Automotive News,* October 29, 2001, p. 18; and in the *Johnson Controls Inc. 2002 Annual Report,* which can be found at the company's website at www.jci.com.

2. Cathy Anterasian and Lynn W. Phillips, "Discontinuities, Value Delivery, and the Share-Returns Association: A Re-Examination of the 'Share-Causes-Profits' Controversy," distributed working paper (Cambridge, MA: Marketing Science Institute, April 1988). Also see Robert Jacobson, "Distinguishing among Competing Theories of the Market Share Effect," *Journal of Marketing,* October 1988, pp. 68–80.

3. William K. Hall, "Survival Strategies in a Hostile Environment," *Harvard Business Review,* September–October 1980, pp. 75–85.

4. Michael Treacy and Fred Wiersema, *The Discipline of Market Leaders* (Reading, MA: Addison-Wesley Publishing, 1995).

5. Rahul Jacob, "Beyond Quality and Value," *Fortune,* Special Issue, Autumn–Winter 1993, pp. 8–11.

6. The following discussion is based on material found in David A. Garvin, "What Does 'Product Quality' Really Mean?" *Sloan Management Review,* Fall 1984, pp. 25–43; and David A. Aaker, *Strategic Market Management,* 5th ed. (New York: John Wiley & Sons, 1998), chap. 9.

7. For a more extensive discussion of brand equity see David A. Aaker, *Brand Equity* (New York: Free Press, 1991).

8. Valarie A. Zeithaml, A. Parasuraman, and Leonard L. Berry, *Delivering Quality Service: Balancing Customer Perceptions and Expectations* (New York: Free Press, 1990). See also Valarie A. Zeithaml and Mary Jo Bitner, *Services Marketing* (New York: McGraw-Hill, 1996).

9. Fred Vogelstein, "Mighty Amazon," *Fortune,* May 26, 2003, pp. 60–74; and Timothy J. Mullaney, Heather Green, Michael Arndt, Robert D. Hof, and Linda Himelstein, "The E-Biz Surprise," *Business Week*, May 12, 2003, pp. 60–68.

10. For a more detailed discussion of these and other approaches for lowering costs, see Aaker, *Strategic Market Management,* chap. 10.

11. Akshay R. Rao, Mark E. Bergen, and Scott Davis, "How To Fight a Price War," *Harvard Business Review,* March–April 2000, pp. 107–16.

12. This percentage decline is based on the University of Michigan's annual poll of customer satisfaction among a sample of 50,000 consumers, as reported in Diane Brady, "Why Service Stinks," *Business Week,* October 23, 2000, p. 120.

13. Ronald Henkoff, "Getting beyond Downsizing," *Fortune,* January 10, 1994, pp. 58–64.

14. Robert Jacobson and David A. Aaker, "The Strategic Role of Product Quality," *Journal of Marketing,* October 1987, pp. 31–44.

15. David Greising, "Quality: How to Make It Pay," *Business Week,* August 8, 1994, pp. 54–59.

16. For a discussion of various approaches to measuring customer satisfaction, see J. Joseph Cronin and Steven A. Taylor, "Measuring Service Quality: A Reexamination and Extension," *Journal of Marketing,* July 1992, pp. 55–68; and Susan J. Devlin and H. K. Dong, "Service Quality from the Customer's Perspective," *Marketing Research* 6 (1994), pp. 5–13.

17. Frederick F. Reichheld, "Loyalty and the Renaissance of Marketing," *Marketing Management* 2 (1994), pp. 10–21. Also see Rahul Jacob, "Why Some Customers Are More Equal than Others," *Fortune,* September 19, 1994, pp. 215–24.

18. Reichheld, "Loyalty and the Renaissance of Marketing." See also Thomas O. Jones and W. Earl Sasser, Jr., "Why Satisfied Customers Defect," *Harvard Business Review,* November–December 1995, pp. 88–99.

19. The following discussion is largely based on Brady, "Why Service Stinks," pp. 118–28.

20. The following discussion of sequential strategies is based largely on material found in Somkid Jatusripitak, Liam Fahey, and Philip Kotler, "Strategic Global Marketing: Lessons From the Japanese," *Columbia Journal of World Business,* Spring 1985, pp. 47–53.

21. Gail Edmonson, "The Beauty of Global Branding," *Business Week,* June 28, 1999, pp. 70–75.

22. Jaclyn Fierman, "How to Make Money in Mature Markets," *Fortune,* November 25, 1985, p. 47.

23. Kathryn Rudie Harrigan and Michael E. Porter, "End-Game Strategies for Declining Industries," *Harvard Business Review,* July–August 1983, pp. 111–20. Also see Kathryn Rudie Harrigan, *Managing Maturing Businesses* (New York: Lexington Books, 1988).

24. Harrigan and Porter, "End-Game Strategies," p. 114.

SECTION FIVE

IMPLEMENTING AND CONTROLLING MARKETING PROGRAMS

CHAPTER 18 Organizing and Planning for Effective Implementation

CHAPTER 19 Measuring and Delivering Marketing Performance

Organizing and Planning for Effective Implementation

Hewlett-Packard—Reorganizing to Implement a New Strategy[1]

THROUGHOUT MOST of the 1990s, Hewlett-Packard was one of the most successful and admired firm's in the computer industry. The firm's booming success in PCs and printers drove sales from $13 billion in 1990 to nearly $40 billion by 1996, with profits more than keeping pace.

A primary reason for HP's success during that period was its organization structure. The firm was managed like a conglomerate of small ventures, each responsible for its own success. More than 130 business units were focused on specific product lines such as UNIX computers or inkjet printers, each employing fewer than 1,500 people. And each SBU was granted substantial autonomy to pursue its own product and market development activities and to reinvest the capital generated by the unit.

Within HP's business units there was a heavy reliance on cross-functional teams. The PC unit, for example, was organized into small teams focused on different customer segments. The salesforce, too, was organized into teams focused on major accounts or application segments. HP's decentralized, team-based structure helped the firm stay in touch with changing customer needs and technical developments in each product category. And the SBUs were flexible enough to respond to those changes quickly. The result was a constant stream of product improvements and line extensions. More than half of the company's sales in 1995, for example, came from products that were not in existence two years earlier.

The Internet Changed the Firm's Market Environment

Paradoxically, the decentralized and flexible structure that enabled HP to be so successful at developing new generations of PCs and printers made it difficult for the firm to respond quickly to changes in the market environment brought about by the growing popularity of the Internet. For instance, as firms embraced the World Wide Web, system integration became critical. A company's computers, servers, routers and software all had to be designed—often with the help of experienced consultants—to work together seamlessly, both internally and with the Internet itself. Unfortunately, while the narrow product focus and high level of autonomy of HP's business units had enabled them to move quickly and creatively when bringing out the next generation of offerings within their own product domains, it hindered their ability to coordinate efforts across product categories. Consequently, while old competitors such as IBM and new ones like Sun Microsystems were designing and selling integrated

e-business systems, HP lacked the internal coordination mechanisms necessary to do so.

The autonomy and financial independence of HP's many business units also caused difficulty in developing innovative new technologies not directly related to an existing product category. A decision to devote substantial resources to a technology that fell outside the domain of existing SBUs required the consensus of the various unit managers; and gaining that consensus could take months or years, thereby giving competitors a head start. Worse, some promising new Internet technologies were never developed because the necessary consensus was never achieved.

As a result of the firm's lack of coordination and strategic focus, HP missed much of the early growth in Internet hardware, software, and e-services markets that occurred in the late 1990s. Sales and profits began to stagnate, the firm's share price dropped dramatically, and management got the message.

Reorganizing to Implement a New Strategy

One of the first steps toward correcting the problem taken by HP's board of directors was to bring in a new CEO from outside the company. Carly Fiorina was hired away from Lucent Technologies where she had gained substantial experience developing and marketing gear for the new economy. Fiorina and other top managers quickly took several actions aimed at improving the coordination and sharpening the strategic focus of the company. They created four divisions—each headed by a divisional manager with CEO-like powers—to provide closer coordination and oversight for businesses making complementary goods and services without constraining their entrepreneurial spirit. For example, the UNIX computer and software and support units are now components of an Enterprise Computing Solutions Division, which is charged with combining computers and software into simple problem-solving packages for buyers, such as technology for helping small businesses set up shop on the Web.

Other steps aimed at improving the coordination of HP's Internet-related goods and services include increasing emphasis on e-commerce consulting services aimed at designing customized solutions for customers that utilize a wide range of HP hardware and software, changes in the compensation and reward system that increase the proportion of managers' pay tied to company sales and profit performance via bonuses and stock options, and a $100 million advertising campaign aimed at increasing customer awareness of the full range of Internet goods and services HP offers and improving the company's image as an e-commerce provider.

Finally, Fiorina created a new organizational entity, the E-Services Solutions Group, whose domain cuts across all of the other business units and divisions in the company. Its charge is to get the various business units to work in innovative ways with each other—and with outside partners—to develop new Web-based goods, services, and ways of doing business. The manager of the new group was given a lot of authority to create, invest in, or acquire interesting Internet start-ups. And a large chunk of HP's $4 billion R&D budget was directed toward the development of new e-commerce systems and services. For example, the firm's research lab at Bristol, United Kingdom—its main research site in Europe—has been directed to focus its efforts on e-services and e-publishing.

It's too soon to know whether Carly Fiorina's attempts to reorganize and reorient Hewlett-Packard and turn it into a major e-services provider will be entirely successful. Matters have been complicated by a merger with Compaq, which was finally approved in 2002, and which nearly doubled the company's revenues to about $80 billion. Before the merger was finalized, HP's sales and earnings were battered during 2001 due to slackening demand in many computer equipment markets and Dell Computer's attempt to capture market share through very aggressive pricing tactics. Nevertheless, the company did experience 6 percent growth in revenues from e-services in 2001 and more than 20 percent sales growth overall in the fourth quarter of 2002 compared to the year before. But whether the firm's shift in direction is successful or not, the ongoing changes in HP's market, competitive, and internal environments will likely demand future adjustments in the firm's marketing strategies—and in the organizational structures needed to implement those strategies effectively.

Marketing Challenges Addressed in Chapter 18

Hewlett-Packard's fall from grace in the face of the dramatic Internet-driven shifts in its market environment and its subsequent attempts to remake itself into a major provider of e-commerce hardware and services illustrate that a business' success is determined by two aspects of strategic fit. First, its competitive and marketing strategies must fit the needs and desires of its target customers and the competitive realities of the marketplace. The emergence of the Internet increased companies' needs for closely integrated computer, network hardware, and software systems. Hewlett-Packard's balkanized approach of selling stand-alone products produced by many semiautonomous and entrepreneurial business units had once been extremely successful, but it was incapable of providing the integration customers were looking for in the Internet age. Consequently, the firm is scrambling to adjust its competitive strategy and product offerings to better fit the new realities of the marketplace.

But even if a firm's competitive strategy is appropriate for the circumstances it faces, it must be capable of implementing that strategy effectively. This is where the second aspect of strategic fit enters the picture. A business's organizational structure, internal policies, procedures, and resources must fit its chosen strategy or else implementation will fall short. Hewlett-Packard's highly decentralized structure and its policies of granting substantial control over financial resources to individual business units, for example, made it nearly impossible for the firm to implement a strategy of differentiating itself by providing tightly integrated and customized packages of Internet products and services to its customers. The company had to make major organizational changes to implement its new strategic direction.

KEY OBSERVATION

A business's organizational structure, internal policies, procedures, and resources must fit its chosen strategy or else implementation will fall short.

Therefore, in the next section we examine several questions related to the issue of **organizational fit**—the fit between a business' competitive and marketing strategies and the organizational structures, policies, processes, and plans necessary to effectively implement those strategies.

- For companies with multiple business units or product lines, what is the appropriate administrative relationship between corporate headquarters and the individual SBUs? How much autonomy should business unit managers be given to make their own strategic decisions, how much control should they have over the SBU's resources and programs, and how should they be evaluated and rewarded?

- Within a given business unit, whether it's part of a larger corporation or a one-product entrepreneurial start-up, what organizational structures and coordination mechanisms are most appropriate for implementing different competitive strategies? Answering this question involves decisions about variables such as the desired level of technical competence of the various functional departments within the business, the manner in which resources are allocated across those functions, and the mechanisms used to coordinate and resolve conflicts among the departments.

- How should organizational structures and policies be adjusted, if at all, as an organization moves into international markets?

However, even if a business has crafted brilliant competitive and marketing strategies, and it has the necessary organizational arrangements and wherewithal to implement them, implementation is unlikely to be very effective unless all of the business' people are following the same plan. This fact underlines the importance of developing formal, written marketing plans to document all the decisions made in formulating the intended strategy for a given good or service so it can be clearly communicated to everyone responsible for its implementation and to firmly establish who is responsible for doing what and when. And as we'll see in the next chapter, formal plans also establish the timetables and objectives that are the benchmarks for management's evaluation and control of the firm's marketing strategies. Thus, good planning is important.

Given the importance of formal plans as tools to aid implementation and control, we will return in the last part of this chapter to the planning framework we introduced briefly in Chapter 1. We will examine the content of effective marketing plans in more detail and review the many strategic decisions involved in formulating that content. The purpose of these planning decisions is to lay a well-conceived foundation that permits effective implementation of the marketing strategy. While good planning is important, effective implementation is crucial.

Designing Appropriate Administrative Relationships for the Implementation of Different Competitive Strategies

In Chapter 10 we pointed out that businesses, whether small independent firms or units within a larger corporation, compete in different ways depending on their intended rate of new product-market development (i.e., prospectors versus analyzers versus defenders) and whether they seek an advantage by differentiating themselves via superior product or service quality or by being the low-cost producer. For example, during the mid-1990s many of Hewlett-Packard's business units could be characterized as differentiated analyzers. They were defending well-established share positions within their product domains by offering quality products while simultaneously investing in the development of more technically advanced product improvements and line extensions.

The chosen competitive strategy tends to influence the marketing strategies pursued by individual product offerings within the business unit, at least in the short term. The differentiated analyzer strategies of Hewlett-Packard's businesses, for instance, demanded a willingness to cannibalize existing products in order to ensure the future. Consequently, the advertising and promotion budgets for many older products were slashed as more technically advanced models were introduced.

Because different competitive strategies seek to satisfy customers and gain a sustainable advantage in varying ways, different organizational structures, policies, and resources are necessary to effectively implement them. For one thing, the administrative relationships between the unit and corporate headquarters influence the ability of SBU managers, including its marketing personnel, to implement specific competitive and marketing strategies successfully. This section examines three aspects of the corporate–business unit relationship that can affect the SBU's success in implementing a particular competitive strategy:

1. The degree of autonomy provided each business unit manager.
2. The degree to which the business unit shares functional programs and facilities with other units.
3. The manner in which the corporation evaluates and rewards the performance of its SBU managers.

Exhibit 18.1

ADMINISTRATIVE FACTORS RELATED TO THE SUCCESSFUL IMPLEMENTATION OF BUSINESS STRATEGIES

	TYPES OF BUSINESS STRATEGY		
Administrative factor	Prospector	Differentiated defender	Low-cost defender
SBU autonomy	Relatively high level	Moderate level	Relatively low level
Shared programs and synergy	Relatively little synergy—few shared programs	Little synergy in areas central to differentiation—shared programs elsewhere	High level of synergy and shared programs
Evaluation and reward systems	High incentives based on sales and share growth	High incentives based on profits or ROI	Incentives based on profits ROI

Exhibit 18.1 summarizes how these variables relate to the successful implementation of different business strategies. Analyzer strategies are not included because they incorporate some elements of both prospector and defender strategies. The administrative arrangements appropriate for implementing an analyzer strategy typically fall somewhere between those best suited for the other two types. To simplify the following discussion we focus only on the polar types—prospector, differentiated defender, and low-cost defender strategies.

Business-Unit Autonomy

Prospector business units are likely to perform better on the critical dimensions of new product success and increased volume and market share when organizational decision making is relatively decentralized and the SBU's managers have substantial autonomy to make their own decisions. There are several reasons for this. First, decentralized decision making allows the managers closest to the market to make more major decisions on their own. Greater autonomy also enables the SBU's managers to be more flexible and adaptable. It frees them from the restrictions of standard procedures imposed from above, allows them to make decisions with fewer consultations and participants, and disperses power. All of these help produce quicker and more innovative responses to environmental opportunities.

One caveat must be attached to the above generalization, however. High levels of autonomy and independence can lead to coordination problems across business units. This can have a negative effect on market performance in situations where a firm's business units are narrowly defined and focused on a single product category or technology but the firm's customers want to buy integrated systems incorporating products or services from different units. This was the problem encountered by HP as the growing popularity of the Internet caused its customers to attach greater importance to system integration. One possible solution to this coordination problem is to redefine SBUs with a focus on customer or application segments rather than on narrowly defined product categories, as we discussed in Chapter 2. An alternative approach is to reduce the SBUs' autonomy somewhat by installing an additional level of managers—such as HP did with the appointment of divisional CEOs—responsible for coordinating the efforts of related business units. The risk inherent in this approach is that the essential flexibility and creativity of the individual business units may be compromised.

On the other hand, low-cost defender SBUs perform better on ROI and cash flow by giving their managers relatively little autonomy. For a low-cost strategy to succeed, managers must relentlessly pursue cost economies and productivity improvements. Such efficiencies are more likely to be attained when decision making and control are relatively centralized.

The relationship between autonomy and the ROI performance of differentiated defenders is more difficult to predict. On the one hand, such businesses defend existing positions in established markets and their primary objective is ROI rather than volume growth. Thus, the increased efficiency and tighter control associated with relatively low autonomy should lead to better performance. On the other hand, such businesses can maintain profitability only if they continue to differentiate themselves by offering superior products and services. As customers' wants change and new competitive threats emerge, the greater flexibility and market focus associated with greater autonomy may allow these businesses to more successfully maintain their differentiated positions and higher levels of ROI over time. These arguments suggest that the relationship between autonomy and performance for differentiated defenders (and probably for differentiated analyzers as well) may be mediated by the level of stability in their environments and by the proportion of offensive or proactive marketing strategies they employ. Units operating in relatively unstable environments and pursuing more proactive marketing programs (such as extended use or market expansion strategies) are likely to perform better when they have relatively greater autonomy.

Shared Programs and Facilities

Firms face a trade-off when designing strategic business units. An SBU should be large enough to afford critical resources and to operate on an efficient scale, but it should not be so large that its market scope is too broad or that it is inflexible and therefore cannot respond to its unique market opportunities. Some firms attempt to avoid this trade-off between efficiency and adaptability by designing relatively small, narrowly focused business units (as HP does), but then having two or more units share functional programs or facilities, such as common manufacturing plants, R&D programs, or a single salesforce.

Sharing resources poses a particular problem for prospector business units.[2] Suppose, for instance, a business wants to introduce a new product but shares a manufacturing plant and salesforce with other SBUs. The business would have to negotiate a production schedule for the new product, and it may not be able to produce adequate quantities as quickly as needed if other units sharing the plant are trying to maintain sufficient volumes of their own products. It may also be difficult to train salespeople on the new product or to motivate them to reduce the time spent on established products to push the new item. When Frito-Lay introduced Grandma's soft cookies, for instance, it relied on its 10,000 salty-snack route salespeople to attain supermarket shelf space for the new line. But because those salespeople were paid a commission based on their total sales revenue, they were reluctant to take time away from their profitable salty-snack lines to sell the new cookies. The resulting lack of strong sales support contributed to Grandma's failure to capture a sustainable share of the packaged cookie market.

One exception to this generalization, though, may be sharing sales and distribution programs across consumer package goods SBUs. In such cases, a prospector's new product may have an easier time obtaining retailer support and shelf space if it is represented by salespeople who also sell established brands to the same retail outlets. Similarly, as HP has recently discovered, sharing, or at least coordinating, sales, distribution, and customer service functions may be a good idea for business units that produce complementary goods or services that customers want to purchase as integrated systems rather than stand-alone offerings. In general, however, functional independence usually facilitates good performance for prospector businesses.

On the other hand, the increased efficiencies gained through sharing functional programs and facilities often boost the ROI performance of low-cost defender SBUs. Also, the inflexibility inherent in sharing is usually not a major problem for such businesses because their markets and technologies tend to be mature and relatively stable. Thus, Heinz, the cost leader in a number of food categories, uses a single salesforce to represent a wide variety of product from different business units when calling on supermarkets.

The impact of shared programs on the performance of differentiated defenders is more difficult to predict because they must often modify their products and marketing programs in response to changing market conditions to maintain their competitive advantage over time. Thus, greater functional independence in areas directly related to the SBU's differential advantage—such as R&D, sales, and marketing—tends to be positively associated with the long-run ROI performance of such businesses. But greater sharing of facilities and programs in less-crucial functional areas, such as manufacturing or distribution, may also help improve their efficiency and short-run ROI levels.

Evaluation and Reward Systems

Increasingly, U.S. firms are adopting some form of pay-for-performance compensation scheme. Some do it for individuals who meet specific goals (e.g., bonuses for salespeople who exceed their quotas), others on the basis of the performance of the SBU or the company as a whole (e.g., stock options). In either case, SBU managers are often motivated to achieve their objectives by bonuses or other financial incentives tied to one or more dimensions of their unit's performance. The question is, which dimensions of performance should be rewarded?

For defender businesses in relatively mature markets, particularly those competing as low-cost defenders, operating efficiency and profitability tend to be the most important objectives, for reasons discussed in Chapter 10. Consequently, tying a relatively large portion of managers' incentive compensation to short-term profits seems sensible. This can be done either through bonuses based on last year's profit performance or economic value added (EVA) or through options keyed to increases in the firm's stock price.

In prospector businesses, on the other hand, basing too large a portion of managers' rewards on current profitability may cause problems. Such rewards may motivate managers to avoid innovative but risky actions or investments that may not pay off for some years into the future.[3] Even successful new product introductions can dramatically increase costs and drain profits early in the product's life cycle. By the time the new product starts contributing to the unit's profits, the manager who deserves the credit may have been transferred to a different business. Therefore, evaluation and reward systems that place relatively more emphasis on sales volume or market share objectives, or on the percentage of volume generated by new products, may be more appropriate for businesses pursuing prospector strategies.

Designing Appropriate Organizational Structures and Processes for Implementing Different Strategies

Different strategies emphasize varying ways to gain a competitive advantage. Thus, a given functional area may be key to the success of one type of strategy but less critical for others. For instance, competence in new product R&D is critical for the success of a prospector business but less so for a low-cost defender.

Successful implementation of a given strategy is more likely when the business has the **functional competencies** demanded by its strategy and supports them with substantial **resources** relative to competitors; is organized suitably for its technical, market, and competitive environment; and has developed appropriate **mechanisms** for coordinating efforts and resolving conflicts across functional departments. Exhibit 18.2 summarizes the relationships between these organizational structure and process variables and the performance of different business strategies.

Functional Competencies and Resource Allocation

Competence in marketing, sales, product R&D, and engineering are critical to the success of prospector businesses because those functions play pivotal roles in new product and market development and thus must be supported with budgets set at a larger percentage of sales than their competitors. Because marketing, sales, and R&D managers are closest to the changes occurring in a business's market, competitive, and technological environments, they should be given considerable authority in making strategic decisions. This argues that bottom-up strategic planning systems are particularly well-suited to prospector businesses operating in unstable environments. Success here is positively affected by the extent to which customer orientation is an integral part of the unit's corporate culture.

In low-cost defender businesses, on the other hand, the functional areas most directly related to operating efficiency, such as financial management and control, production, process R&D, and distribution or logistics, play the most crucial roles in enabling the SBU to attain good ROI performance. Because differentiated defenders need to attain high returns on their established products, functional areas related to efficiency are also critical for their success. Similarly, such units also seek to improve efficiency by investing in process R&D, making needed capital investments, and maintaining a high level of capacity utilization. But because they must also maintain their differential advantage over time, functional departments related to the source of that advantage—the salesforce and product R&D for SBUs with a technical product advantage or sales, marketing, and distribution for SBUs with a customer service advantage—are also critical for the unit's continued success. As we have seen, for example, in an attempt to defend its leading share position, cement the loyalty of its growing customer base, and generate greater revenues from repeat purchases, Amazon.com has invested hundreds of millions of dollars to build its own distribution centers and improve the speed and reliability of its order fulfillment.[4]

Additional Considerations for Service Organizations

Given that service organizations pursue the same kinds of business-level competitive strategies as goods producers, they must meet the same functional and resource requirements to implement those strategies effectively. However, service organizations—and manufacturers that provide high levels of customer service as part of their product offering—often need some additional functional competencies because of the unique problems involved in delivering quality service.

This is particularly true for services involving high customer contact. Because the sale, production, and delivery of such services occur almost simultaneously, close coordination between operations, sales, and marketing is crucial. Also, because many different employees may be involved in producing and delivering the service—as when thousands of different cooks prepare Big Macs at McDonald's outlets around the world—production planning and standardization are needed to reduce variations in quality from

Exhibit 18.2

ORGANIZATIONAL AND INTERFUNCTIONAL FACTORS RELATED TO THE SUCCESSFUL IMPLEMENTATION OF BUSINESS STRATEGIES

Organizational factor	TYPE OF BUSINESS STRATEGY		
	Prospector	Differentiated defender	Low-cost defender
Functional competencies of the SBU	SBU will perform best on critical volume and share-growth dimensions when its functional strengths include marketing, sales, product R&D, and engineering.	SBU will perform best on critical ROI dimensions when its functional strengths include sales, financial management and control, and those functions related to its differential advantage (e.g., marketing, product R&D).	SBU will perform best on critical ROI and cash flow dimensions when its functional strengths include process engineering, production, distribution, and financial management and control.
Resource allocation across functions	SBU will perform best on volume and share-growth dimensions when percentage of sales spent on marketing, sales, and product R&D are high and when gross fixed assets per employee and percent of capacity utilization are low relative to competitors'.	SBU will perform best on the ROI dimension when percentage of sales spent on the salesforce, gross fixed assets per employee, percent of capacity utilization, and percentage of sales devoted to other functions related to the SBU's differential advantage are high relative to competitors'.	SBU will perform best on ROI and cash flow dimensions when marketing, sales, and product R&D expenses are low, but process R&D, fixed assets per employee, and percentage of capacity utilization are high relative to competitors'.
Decision-making influence and participation	SBU will perform best on volume and share-growth dimensions when managers from marketing, sales, product R&D, and engineering have substantial influence on unit's business and marketing strategy decisions.	SBU will perform best on ROI dimension when financial managers, controller, and managers of functions related to unit's differential advantage have substantial influence on business and marketing strategy decisions.	SBU will perform best on ROI and cash flow when controller, financial, and production managers have substantial influence on business and marketing strategy decisions.
SBU's organization structure	SBU will perform best on volume and share-growth dimensions when structure has low levels of formalization and centralization, but high level of specialization.	SBU will perform best on ROI dimension when structure has moderate levels of formalization, centralization, and specialization.	SBU will perform best on ROI and cash flow dimensions when structure has high levels of formalization and centralization, but low level of specialization.
Functional coordination and conflict resolution	SBU will experience high levels of interfunctional conflict; SBU will perform best on volume and share-growth dimensions when participative resolution mechanisms are used (e.g., product teams).	SBU will experience moderate levels of interfunctional conflict; SBU will perform best on ROI dimension when resolution is participative for issues related to differential advantage, but hierarchical for others (e.g., product managers, product improvement teams, etc.).	SBU will experience low levels of interfunctional conflict; SBU will perform best on ROI and cash flow dimensions when conflict resolution mechanisms are hierarchical (e.g., functional organization).

Source: Adapted from Orville C. Walker, Jr., and Robert W. Ruekert, "Marketing's Role in the Implementation of Business Strategies," *Journal of Marketing*, July 1987, p. 31. Used by permission of the American Marketing Association.

KEY OBSERVATION

Personnel management—particularly the activities of employee selection, training, motivation, and evaluation—is an important adjunct to the production and marketing efforts of high-contact service organizations.

one transaction to the next. Similarly, detailed policies and procedures for dealing with customers are necessary to reduce variability in customer treatment across employees. All of this suggests that personnel management—particularly the activities of employee selection, training, motivation, and evaluation—is an important adjunct to the production and marketing efforts of high-contact service organizations.

Competence in human resource development is more crucial for service businesses pursuing prospector strategies—and perhaps also for defenders and analyzers who differentiate their offerings on the basis of good service—than for those focused primarily on efficiency and low cost. In prospector service organizations, employees often play a critical role in identifying potential new service offerings and in introducing them to potential customers. Consequently, the effective implementation of such a strategy requires employees with superior communication and social skills and necessitates frequent employee retraining and performance feedback. For instance, banks pursuing a prospector strategy not only have more branches and engage in more market scanning, advertising, and new service development than those with other types of competitive strategies, but also devote more effort to screening potential employees and providing training and support after they are hired.[5]

Organizational Structures

Three structural variables—formalization, centralization, and specialization—are important in shaping both an SBU's and its marketing department's performance within the context of a given competitive strategy. **Formalization** is the degree to which formal rules and standard policies and procedures govern decisions and working relationships. **Centralization** refers to the location of decision authority and control within an organization's hierarchy. In highly centralized SBUs or marketing departments, only one or a few top managers hold most decision-making authority. In more decentralized units, middle- and lower-level managers have more autonomy and participate in a wider range of decisions. Finally, **specialization** refers to the division of tasks and activities across positions within the organizational unit. A highly specialized marketing department, for instance, has a large number of specialists, such as market researchers, advertising managers, and sales promotion managers, who perform a narrowly defined set of activities often as consultants to product managers.

Highly structured business units and marketing departments are unlikely to be very innovative or quick to adapt to a changing environmental circumstance. Adaptiveness and innovativeness are enhanced when (1) decision-making authority is decentralized, (2) managerial discretion and informal coordination mechanisms replace rigid rules and policies, and (3) more specialists are present. Thus, prospector business units and their marketing departments are likely to perform better when they are decentralized, have little formalization, and are highly specialized.

Differentiated defenders perform best when their organization structures incorporate moderate levels of formalization, centralization, and specialization. Those departments most directly related to the source of a differentiated defender's competitive advantage (sales, marketing, and R&D), however, should be less highly structured than those more crucial for the efficiency of the unit's operations (production and logistics).

Several common organizational designs incorporate differences in both the structural variables (formalization, centralization, and specialization) and in the mechanisms for resolving interfunctional conflicts. These include (1) functional, (2) product management, (3) market management, and (4) various types of matrix organizational designs.

Exhibit 18.3

FUNCTIONAL ORGANIZATION OF AN SBU AND ITS MARKETING DEPARTMENT

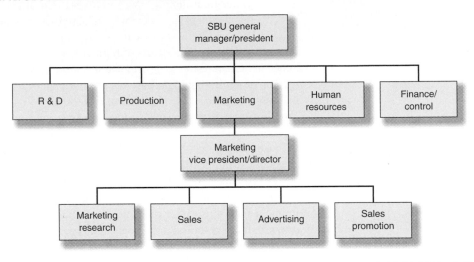

Functional Organizations   The functional form of organization is the simplest and most bureaucratic design. At the SBU level, managers of each functional department, such as production or marketing, report to the general manager. Within the marketing department, managers of specific marketing activity areas, such as sales, advertising, or marketing research, report to the marketing vice president or director, as shown in Exhibit 18.3. At each level the top manager coordinates the activities of all the functional areas reporting to him or her, often with heavy reliance on standard rules and operating procedures. This is the most centralized and formalized organization form and relies primarily on hierarchical mechanisms for resolving conflicts across functional areas. Also, because top managers perform their coordination activities across all product-markets in the SBU, there is little specialization by product or customer type.

These characteristics make the functional form simple, efficient, and particularly suitable for companies operating in stable and slow-growth industries where the environments are predictable. Thus, the form is appropriate for low-cost defender SBUs attempting to maximize their efficiency and profitability in mature or declining industries. For example, Ingersoll-Rand, a low-cost manufacturer of low-tech air compressors and air-driven tools such as jackhammers, uses a functional structure.

The simplicity of the functional organization also makes it the most common organizational form among entrepreneurial start-ups, including many dot.com companies. Even though the functional form is very hierarchical, such firms can still be nimble and innovative provided that (1) the company remains small enough that the entrepreneur can personally supervise and coordinate the various functions, (2) the firm is focused on a single product or product line targeted at one customer segment, and (3) the entrepreneur's personal vision is an adequate source of innovation to differentiate the entire company. As the start-up grows, its product offerings expand, and its markets fragment, however, it is usually wise to adopt a more decentralized and specialized organizational form. Unfortunately, some entrepreneurs find it difficult to delegate decision-making authority to their subordinates.

KEY OBSERVATION

The simplicity of the functional organization also makes it the most common organizational form among entrepreneurial start-ups, including many dot.com companies.

Exhibit 18.4

A MARKETING DEPARTMENT WITH A PRODUCT MANAGEMENT ORGANIZATION

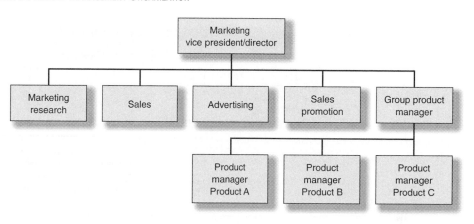

Product Management Organizations

When a company or SBU has many product-market entries, the simple functional form of organization is inadequate. A single manager finds it difficult to stay abreast of functional activities across a variety of different product-markets or to coordinate them efficiently. One common means of dealing with this problem is to adopt a product management organization structure. As Exhibit 18.4 illustrates, this form adds an additional layer of managers to the marketing department, usually called product managers, brand managers, or marketing managers, each of whom has the responsibility to plan and manage the marketing programs and to coordinate the activities of other functional departments for a specific product or product line.

A product management structure decentralizes decision making while increasing the amount of product specialization within the SBU. If the product managers are also given substantial autonomy to develop their own marketing plans and programs, this structure can also decrease the formalization within the business. Finally, although the product managers are responsible for obtaining cooperation from other functional areas both within and outside the marketing department, they have no formal authority over these areas. They must rely on persuasion and compromise—in other words, more participative methods—to overcome conflicts and objections when coordinating functional activities. These factors make the product management form of organization less bureaucratic than the functional structure. It is more appropriate, then, for businesses pursuing differentiated defender and analyzer strategies, particularly when they operate in industries with complex and relatively unstable market and competitive environments. Thus, many large consumer packaged-goods companies with multiple brands competing in diverse segments—such as Nestlé, Unilever, and Procter & Gamble—incorporate a product management structure.

When large firms target a number of brands at different market segments, a product management organization typically also includes one or more "group" or "category" marketing managers, on the level immediately above the product managers, who allocate resources across brands. Category management also provides an opportunity for the involvement of more experienced managers in brand management, particularly those concerned with coordinating pricing and other marketing efforts.[6]

Product management organizations have a number of advantages, including the ability to identify and react more quickly to the threats and opportunities individual product-market entries face; improved coordination of functional activities within and across

Exhibit 18.5

A MARKETING DEPARTMENT WITH A MARKET MANAGEMENT ORGANIZATION

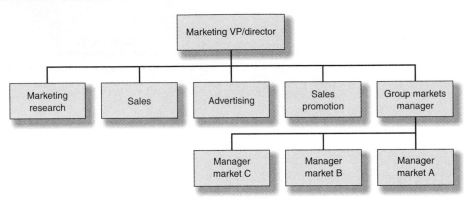

product-markets; and increased attention to smaller product-market entries that might be neglected in a functional organization. Consequently, about 85 percent of all consumer goods manufacturers use some form of product management organization.

Despite its advantages, a product management organization has shortcomings. The major one is the difficulty of obtaining the cooperation necessary to develop and implement effective programs for a particular product given that a product manager has little direct authority. Also, the environment facing product managers is changing drastically. They increasingly must face the fact that customers can quickly compare products and prices—and even suggest their own price—over the Internet; that customers are becoming more price sensitive and less brand loyal; that competition is becoming more global; that rapidly changing technologies are providing new ways to improve production and distribution efficiency, but also shortening product life cycles; and that the power of large retailers and distributors has increased due in part to their ability to collect and control information about the marketplace. These environmental trends have led to an increase in the sales of private-label brands and more aggressive bargaining by distributors.[7] As a result of these trends and the inherent weakness of the product manager type of organization, many companies have undertaken two major types of modifications—market management and matrix organization—discussed next.

Market Management Organizations

In some industries an SBU may market a single product to a large number of markets where customers have very different requirements and preferences. Pepsi-Cola, for example, is sold through restaurants, fast-food outlets, and supermarkets. The syrup needed to make Pepsi is sold directly to institutions such as Kentucky Fried Chicken and Taco Bell. But marketing Pepsi to consumers for home consumption involves the use of franchised bottlers who process and package the product and distribute it to a variety of retail outlets. The intermediaries and marketing activities involved in selling to the two markets are so different that it makes sense to have a separate market manager in charge of each. Such a company or SBU might organize itself along the lines shown in Exhibit 18.5. Some SBUs have adopted a combination of product and regional market management organization structures. A product manager has overall responsibility for planning and implementing a national marketing program for the product, but several market mangers are also given some authority and an independent budget to work with salespeople and develop promotion programs geared to a particular user segment or

Exhibit 18.6   Using Teams to Get the Job Done

Pillsbury, which has recently merged with General Mills, replaced its traditional marketing department with multiple discipline teams centered around a product group (pizza snacks). Each involves managers from marketing, sales, and production. Lever Brothers restructured in a similar fashion. It reorganized its marketing and sales departments into a series of business groups and set up a separate customer development team responsible for retailer relations across all the various SBU brands.

Source: "Death of the Brand Manager," *The Economist,* April 9, 1994, p. 67.

geographic market. This kind of decentralization or regionalization has become popular with consumer goods companies in their efforts to increase geographic segmentation and cope with the growing power of regional retail chains.

Matrix Organizations   A business facing an extremely complex and uncertain environment may find a matrix organization appropriate. The matrix form is the least bureaucratic or centralized and the most specialized type of organization. It brings together two or more different types of specialists within a participative coordination structure. One example is the product team, which consists of representatives from a number of functional areas assembled for each product or product line. As a group, the team must agree on a business plan for the product and ensure the necessary resources and cooperation from each functional area. This kind of participative decision making can be very inefficient; it requires a good deal of time and effort for the team to reach mutually acceptable decisions and gain approval from all the affected functional areas. But once reached, those decisions are more likely to reflect the expertise of a variety of functional specialists, to be innovative, and to be quickly and effectively implemented. Thus, the matrix form of organization particularly suits prospector businesses and the management of new product development projects within analyzer or differentiated defender businesses. Some examples are discussed in Exhibit 18.6.

Another form of matrix structure involves the creation of an additional organizational unit or managerial position responsible for coordinating the actions of other units within the firm. For example, nearly every business school has an MBA program director responsible for coordinating the courses offered by the functional departments in hopes of creating a tightly integrated and coherent curriculum. Similarly, Hewlett-Packard created an E-Services Solutions Group, a coordinating unit whose domain cuts across all the other SBUs and divisions in the company and who is charged it with encouraging the other SBUs to work with each other and with outside partners to develop new Web-based goods and services.

Recent Trends in Organizational Design

As we have stressed throughout this book, the dynamics of the marketplace are forcing companies to respond more quickly to their opportunities and threats if they hope to survive and prosper. This has spurred a search for organizational structures that are flexible, responsive, able to learn, and market oriented.[8] While we are only just beginning to gain insights into organizational structures of the future, certain aspects seem reasonably clear. We briefly discuss the more important of these.

Organizations will increasingly emphasize the **managing of business processes** in contrast to functional areas.[9] Every business has about six basic or core processes, such as, for example, new product development and supply chain management. The former would be staffed by individuals from marketing, R&D, manufacturing, and finance. The latter would contain people with expertise in purchasing, manufacturing, order delivery, and billing.

Managing processes will make the organization essentially horizontal—flat and lean versus a vertical or hierarchical model. Thus, executive positions will no longer be defined in terms of managing a group of functionally oriented people; instead, executives will be concerned with a process that strongly emphasizes the importance of customer satisfaction.[10] Process management is quite different from the management of a function because, first, it uses external objectives, such as customer satisfaction versus simple revenues. Second, people with different skills are grouped to undertake a complete piece of work; their work is done simultaneously, not in sequence. Third, information flows directly to where it is used. Thus, if you have an upstream problem, you deal with people involved directly rather than via your boss.

Next, the use of **self-managing teams** is increasing. Regardless of the form of worker self-management, all are based on the concept of *empowerment*—the theory that those doing the work should have the means to do what it takes to please the customer. In turn, this requires that performance objectives and evaluation of activities be linked to customer satisfaction. Successful teams can dramatically improve productivity; for example, Boeing used empowered teams to reduce the number of hang-ups by half when developing its 777 jet.[11] But many teams have failed because management was not serious about their empowerment, team members were poorly selected, or the team was launched in isolation with little training or support.[12]

In the future many companies will use teams as the basis for collaborative networks that link thousands of people together with the help of a variety of new technologies. Such networks enable businesses to form and dissolve relations quickly and to bring to bear on an opportunity or a threat the needed resources regardless of who owns them.[13] For example, AT&T used Japan's Marubeni Trading company as a means to link with Matsushita Electric Industrial Company to jump-start the manufacture of its Safari Notebook Computer, which was designed by Henry Dreyfuss Associates.[14]

But not all such collaborative networks are successful, especially those involving **joint ventures.** Partnering is at best a difficult and demanding undertaking requiring considerable managerial skills as well as a great deal of trust.[15] A major difficulty, especially for those involving companies from different parts of the world, is that "they cannot be controlled by formal systems, but require a dense web of interpersonal connections and internal infrastructures that enhance learning."[16]

Organizational Adjustments as Firms Grow and Markets Change

Managers often think of the design of their organization as stable and not subject to change. In rapidly growing entrepreneurial companies and in changing markets, however, such thinking can be dangerous. As the number of customers and the range of product lines grow, the best way to organize the marketing and sales functions should be subject to change.

An entrepreneurial start-up may begin with a simple functional structure, perhaps even simpler than that diagrammed in Exhibit 18.3. As it grows and its product offerings become broader and more complex, it may assign specialized product managers to coordinate the marketing efforts for the various products or product lines. Eventually, the firm might even split into several product divisions, each with its own sales and marketing departments. Or the firm's customers might fragment into a number of diverse segments with unique needs and requirement, favoring the adoption of a market management or matrix structure.

With each of these adjustments to a company's organization structure, however, comes added complexity and potential disadvantages. For instance, what if the new structure results in multiple salespeople, representing the company's different product lines, competing with each other for a customer's business? Such competition may be contrary to the company's self-interest as well as confusing and inconvenient for the customer. More importantly, such a lack of coordination would make it difficult to sell comprehensive solutions that cut cross the firm's product or divisional boundaries.

The above situation is where Hewlett-Packard found itself in 1999. Its various divisions, each with its own sales and marketing personnel, were ill-equipped to cooperate with each other or with outsiders to develop and market comprehensive systems and services geared to the new demands of the Internet, which HP viewed as crucial to its success. Consequently, new CEO Carly Fiorina reorganized the company and created the E-services Solutions Group, a new organizational entity whose domain cuts across all the other divisions.

How should managers decide when the time has come to restructure an organization, and what new structure should replace the old one? There are five key drivers and such decisions: (1) customer needs, (2) informational requirements of the sales and marketing personnel charged with meeting those needs, (3) ability of a given structure to motivate and coordinate the kinds of activities that market conditions require, (4) available competencies and resources, and (5) costs.

When customers all tend to use a narrow range of goods or services to satisfy similar needs, a simple functional structure may be sufficient. When customer segments use goods or services in different ways, either a product-focused or market-focused structure is likely to work well. If individual customers buy a broad range of the firm's goods or services, however, having multiple salespeople calling on those customers, unless they are organized into teams, is probably a bad idea. When a company's offerings are relatively simple and easy to understand, a single salesforce may be able to handle the entire line. But when products are technically complex or open to customization, each line may require its own specialized sales and marketing organization. When the firm is not well established or needs to educate potential buyers about the advantages of an innovative offering, it may need heavy incentives to encourage salespeople to expend the effort necessary to win new business. Under such circumstances, team-oriented selling arrangements are likely to be ineffectual. Finally, the fact that more highly specialized structures also tend to increase personnel and administrative costs should not be overlooked.

Thus, growing firms or those serving rapidly changing markets are likely to need to rethink—and perhaps change—the structure of their sales and marketing organizations frequently. Such changes can be disruptive to both internal and customer relationships, but as HP discovered, failure to adjust in the face of changing market conditions can make it impossible for the firm to implement its marketing strategy.

Organizational Designs for Selling in Global Markets[17]

An organization's complexity increases, often quite dramatically, as it "goes international" and especially so as overseas sales as a percentage of total sales increase. The issue is essentially one of deciding what organizational design is best for developing and implementing worldwide strategies while simultaneously maintaining flexibility with regard to individual markets. In evaluating the several types of international organizational structures discussed in this section, keep in mind two things: "first, that innovation is the key to success. An organization which relies on one culture for its ideas and treats foreign subsidiaries as dumb production-colonies might as well hire subcontractors."[18] Second, technology is making the world smaller.

Little or No Formal Organization

Early on in a firm's international involvement, the structure typically ranges between the domestic organization handling international transactions to a separate export department. The latter may be tied to the marketing department or may be a freestanding functional department.

An International Division

To avoid discriminating against international customers in comparison with domestic customers, an international division is often established to house all international activities, most of which relate to marketing. Manufacturing, engineering, finance, and R&D typically remain in their previous form to take advantage of scale effects. This type of organization serves best with a limited number of products that lack cultural sensitivity—for example, basic commodity types such as chemicals, metals, and industrial machinery.

Many Japanese firms historically emphasized low-cost manufacturing coupled with quality assurance as the essence of their international competitive strategy. Both of these require strong centralized control and, thus, the use of an export-based organizational structure. In recent years, though, Japanese firms have become more interested in global structures based on products or geographic areas.[19]

Global Structures

There are a variety of global types, of which the simplest replicates the firm's basic functional departments. A global company using the functional type of organization would have vice presidents (worldwide) for such areas as manufacturing, marketing, and finance—all reporting to the president.

By far the most common global structure is one based on products, which translates into giving SBUs worldwide control over their product lines. The main advantages of this type of structure are the economies derived from centralizing manufacturing activities and the ability to respond quickly to product-related problems originating in overseas markets. Marketing is usually localized at the country or regional level.

The *area structure* is another popular global organizational type and is especially appropriate when there is considerable variance across markets regarding product acceptance and marketing activities. Firms typically organize on a regional basis (North America, Latin America, Far East, Middle East, and Africa) using a central staff that coordinates worldwide planning and control activities.

Some companies use a hybrid organization that typically is some combination of the functional, product, or area types of structure. The global matrix is one such attempt. It has individual business managers reporting to both area and functional groups, or area managers reporting to business and functional groups, thereby enabling the company to balance the need for centralized efficiency and its responsiveness to local needs. But the dual reporting sets up conflicts and slows the management process to such an extent that many companies, including Dow and CitiCorp, have returned to more traditional organizational designs.[20]

Decision Making and Organizational Structure

Global organization structures can be centralized or decentralized in terms of decision making. In the case of the latter, controls are relatively simple and relations between subsidiaries and headquarters mainly financial. The logic here is that local management is closest to the market and can respond quickly to change. But multinationals faced with strong global competition require more centralization, which calls for headquarters to provide the overall strategy that subsidiaries (country units) implement within a range agreed upon with headquarters.[21]

Marketing Plans: The Foundation for Implementing Marketing Actions

As we pointed out in Chapter 1, preparation of a written plan is a key step in ensuring the effective execution of a strategic marketing program because it spells out what actions are to be taken, when, and by whom. Written plans are particularly crucial in larger organizations because a marketing manager's proposals must usually be reviewed and approved by higher levels of management, and because the approved plan then provides the benchmark against which the manager's and the marketing program's performances will be evaluated. Preparing formal, written marketing plans, however brief, is a useful exercise even in small firms because the discipline involved helps ensure that the proposed objectives, strategy, and marketing actions are based on rigorous analysis of the 4 Cs and sound reasoning.

Marketing plans can vary a good deal in content and organization, but they generally follow a format similar to the one outlined in Exhibit 1.7 and reproduced in Exhibit 18.7. To illustrate the kinds of information that might be included in each section of the plan, the contents of a marketing plan for a disguised Pillsbury refrigerated dough product are summarized in Exhibit 18.8.

Exhibit 18.7

CONTENTS OF AN ANNUAL MARKETING PLAN

Section	Content
I. Executive summary	Presents a short overview of the issues, objectives, strategy, and actions incorporated in the plan and their expected outcomes for quick management review.
II. Current situation and trends	Summarizes relevant background information on the market, competition and the macroenvironment, and trends therein, including size and growth rates for the overall market and key segments.
III. Performance review (for an existing product or service only)	Examines the past performance of the product and the elements of its marketing program (e.g., distribution, promotion, etc.).
IV. Key issues	Identifies the main opportunities and threats to the product that the plan must deal with in the coming year, and the relative strengths and weaknesses of the product and business unit that must be taken into account in facing those issues.
V. Objectives	Specifies the goals to be accomplished in terms of sales volume, market share, and profit.
VI. Marketing strategy	Summarizes the overall strategic approach that will be used to meet the plan's objectives.
VII. Action plans	This is the most critical section of the annual plan for helping to ensure effective implementation and coordination of activities across functional departments. It specifies • The target market to be pursued. • What specific actions are to be taken with respect to each of the 4 Ps. • Who is responsible for each action. • When the action will be engaged in. • How much will be budgeted for each action.
VIII. Projected profit-and-loss statement	Presents the expected financial payoff from the plan.
IX. Controls	Discusses how the plan's progress will be monitored: may present contingency plans to be used if performance falls below expectations or the situation changes.
X. Contingency plans	Describes actions to be taken if specific threats or opportunities materialize during the planning period.

Exhibit 18.8

SUMMARY OF AN ANNUAL MARKETING PLAN FOR A REFRIGERATED BREAD DOUGH PRODUCT

I. Analysis of current situation

  A. Market situation

  - The total U.S. market for dinner breadstuffs is enormous, amounting to about 10.5 billion servings per year.
  - Specialty breads, such as whole-grain breads are growing in popularity, largely at the expense of traditional white breads.
  - Pillsbury's share of the total dinner breadstuffs market, accounted for by several brands including Crescent rolls as well as refrigerated bread dough, is small, amounting to only about 2 percent of the total dollar volume.
  - Since its introduction several years ago, refrigerated bread dough (RBD) has been able to achieve only low levels of penetration (only about 15 percent of all households have used the product) and use frequency (nearly two-thirds of the product's volume comes from light users who buy only one or two cans per year).
  - RBD consumption is concentrated in the northern states and during the fall and winter months (about 75 percent of volume is achieved from September through February).
  - Marketing research results suggest consumers believe RBD is relatively expensive in terms of price/value compared to alternative forms of dinner breadstuffs.

  B. Competitive situation

  - RBD's share of the total dinner breadstuffs category is likely to remain low because of the wide variety of competing choices available to consumers.
  - The largest proportion of volume within the category is captured by ready-to-eat breads and rolls produced by supermarket chains and regional bakeries and distributed through retail grocery stores.
  - RBD's major competition within the refrigerated dough category comes from other Pillsbury products, such as Crescent rolls and Soft Breadsticks.
  - There are currently no other national competitors in the refrigerated bread dough category; but Merico, a small regional producer, was recently acquired by a major national food manufacturer. Evidence suggests Merico may be preparing to introduce a competing product line into national distribution at a price about 10 percent lower than Pillsbury's.

  C. Macroenvironmental situation

  - Changes in American eating habits may pose future problems for dinner breadstuffs in general, and for RBD in particular:
      More meals are being eaten away from home, and this trend is likely to continue.
      People are eating fewer starch foods.
      While total volume of dinner breadstuffs did not fall during the 1990s, neither did it keep pace with population growth.
  - Increasing numbers of women working outside of the home, and the resulting desire for convenience, may reduce consumers' willingness to wait 30 minutes while RBD bakes, even though the dough is already prepared.
  - Because RBD does not use yeast as a leavening agent, Food and Drug Administration regulations prohibit the company from referring to it as "bread" in advertising or package copy, even though the finished product looks, smells, and tastes like bread.

  D. Past product performance

  - While sales volume in units increased only slightly during the past year, dollar volume increased by 24 percent due to a price increase taken early in the year.
  - The improvement to gross margin was even greater than the price increase due to an improvement in manufacturing costs.
  - The improvement to gross margin, however, was not sufficient to produce a positive net margin due to high advertising and sales promotion expenditures aimed at stimulating primary demand and increasing market penetration of RBD.
  - Consequently, while RBD showed improvement over the last year, it was still unable to make a positive contribution to overhead and profit.

II. Key issues

  A. Threats

  - Lack of growth in the dinner breadstuff category suggests the market is mature and may decline in the future.
  - The large variety of alternatives available to consumers suggest it may be impossible for RBD to substantially increase its share of the total market.
  - Potential entry of a new, lower-priced competitor poses a threat to RBD's existing share and may result in lower margins if RBD responds by reducing its price.

  B. Opportunities

  - The largest percentage of RBD volume accounted for by light users suggests an opportunity of increasing volume among current users by stimulating frequency of use.
  - Trends toward increased consumption of specialty breads suggests possible line extensions, such as whole wheat or other whole grain flavors.

Exhibit 18.8

(CONCLUDED)

C. Strengths
   - RBD has a strong distribution base, with shelf-facings in nearly 90 percent of available retail outlets.
   - RBD sales have proved responsive to sales promotion efforts (e.g., cents-off coupons), primarily by increasing volume among existing users.
   - The fact that most consumers who try RBD make repeat purchases indicates a high level of customer satisfaction.

D. Weaknesses
   - RBD sales have proved unresponsive to advertising. Attempts to stimulate primary demand have not been able to increase market penetration.
   - Consumer concerns about RBD's price/value place limits on ability to take future price increases.

III. Objectives

A. Financial objectives
   - Achieve a positive contribution to overhead and profit of $4 million in current year.
   - Reach the target level of an average of 20 percent return on investment over the next five years.

B. Marketing objectives
   - Maintain market share and net sales revenues at previous year's levels.
   - Maintain current levels of retail distribution coverage.
   - Reduce marketing expenditures sufficiently to achieve profit contribution objective.
   - Identify viable opportunities for future volume and profit expansion.

IV. Marketing strategy
   - Pursue a maintenance strategy aimed at holding or slightly increasing RBD volume and market share primarily by stimulating increased frequency of use among current users.
   - Reduce advertising aimed at stimulation of primary demand/penetration and reduce manufacturing costs in order to achieve profit contribution objective.
   - Initiate development and test marketing of possible line extensions to identify opportunities for future volume expansion.

V. Marketing action plans
   - Improve the perceived price/value of RBD by maintaining current suggested retail price at least through the peak selling season (February). Review the competitive situation and the brand's profit performance in March to assess the desirability of a price increase at that time.
   - Work with production to identify and implement cost savings opportunities that will reduce manufacturing costs by 5 percent without compromising product quality.
   - Maintain retail distribution coverage with two trade promotion discount offers totaling $855,000; one offered in October–November to support peak season inventories, and another offered in February–March to maintain inventories as volume slows.
   - Reduce advertising to maintenance level of 1,100 gross ratings points during the peak sales period of September to March. Focus copy on maintaining awareness among current users.
   - Encourage greater frequency of use among current users through three sales promotion events, with a total budget of $748,000, that will stimulate immediate purchase:
        One free-standing insert (FSI) coupon for 15 cents off next purchase to appear in newspaper on September 19.
        One tear-off refund offer (buy three, get one free) placed on the retailer's shelves during November.
        A $1 refund with proof of purchase offer placed in women's service books (i.e., women's magazines like *Good Housekeeping*) during March.

VI. Contingency plans
   - Maintain the above marketing strategy and action plans without change during the planning period even if Merico (see item I.B) enters the market.
   - If Merico enters, carefully monitor its pricing and promotion actions, sales results, consumer perceptions, etc., and prepare recommendations for next year's plan.

Much of this book has focused on the planning process, the decisions that must be made when formulating a marketing strategy and its various components, the development of strategic marketing plans, and the analytical tools managers can use in reaching those decisions. Consequently, we will say little here about the processes or procedures involved in putting together a marketing plan. Instead, our purpose is to summarize how the topics we've covered can be integrated within a coherent marketing plan, and how the plan's content should be organized and presented to best ensure that the strategy will be effectively carried out.

The success of a marketing plan depends on effective communication with other parts of the organizations (such as production, engineering, and R&D) and a variety of marketing units, especially those concerned with sales, advertising, promotions, and marketing research. By using the experience of others (as consultants) in preparing the action programs (for instance, in-store promotions), the planner not only benefits from the expertise of specialists, but also increases their buy-in to the overall marketing plan, thereby increasing the likelihood of its success.

The action programs should reflect agreements made with other departments and marketing units as to their responsibilities over the planning period concerning the product. For example, if a special sale is to occur in a given month, the production department must commit to making sufficient product available and to the use of a special package; the promotion group agrees to develop and have available for use by the salesforce in-store displays; the salesforce must allocate the time necessary to do the in-store work; and so on. Thus, the annual plan serves as a means of allocating the firm's resources as well as a way of assigning responsibility for the plan's implementation.[22]

The Situational Analysis[23]

While many marketing plans start with a brief executive summary of their contents, this is typically the first substantive section in which the marketing manager details his or her assessment of the current situation. It is the "homework" portion of the plan where the manager summarizes his or her analysis of current and potential customers, the competitive environment and the company's relative strengths and weaknesses, trends in the broader macroenvironment that may impact the product, and past performance outcomes for existing products. This section also typically includes estimates of sales potential, forecasts, and other assumptions underlying the plan. Chapters 2 through 8 provide the principal tools and analytical frameworks for completing this section. Based on these analyses, the manager may then call attention to one or more key issues, major opportunities or threats that should be dealt with during the planning period.

Market Situation　　Here data are presented on the target market. Total market size and growth trends should be discussed, along with any variations across geographic regions or other market segments. Marketing research information might also be presented concerning customer perceptions (say, awareness of the brand) and buying-behavior trends (market penetration, repeat purchase rate, heavy versus light users). As Exhibit 18.8 indicates, for instance, information about the market situation presented in the plan for Pillsbury's refrigerated bread dough (RBD) not only includes data about the size of the total market for dinner breadstuffs and Pillsbury's market share, but also points out the low penetration and use frequency of RBD among potential users. Most of the kinds of customer analysis, market segmentation and targeting information discussed in Chapters 5, 6, and 8 would be relevant here.

Competitive Situation　　This section identifies and describes the product's major competitors in terms of their size, market share, product quality, marketing strategies, and other relevant factors as discussed in Chapter 4. It should also discuss the likelihood that other potential competitors will enter the market in the near future and the possible impact of such entry on the product's competitive position. Note, for instance, that while other Pillsbury

Exhibit 18.9

HISTORICAL AND PROJECTED FINANCIAL PERFORMANCE OF REFRIGERATED BREAD DOUGH PRODUCT

Variable	Last year	This year	Percent change	Next year	Percent change
Sales volume (cases)	2,290M	2,350M	3%	2,300M	(2%)
Net sales ($)	17,078M	21,165M	24	21,182M	0
Gross Margin ($)	6,522M	10,787M	65	11,430	5
Gross margin/net sales	38%	51%	—	54%	—
Advertising and sales promotion ($)	11,609M	12,492M	6	6,100M	(51)
Advertising & sales promotion/gross margin	178%	116%	—	53%	—
Net margin ($)	(5,087M)	(1,725M)	—	5,330M	—
Net margin/net sales	—	—	—	25	—
Product contribution ($)	(6,342M)	(3,740M)	—	4,017M	—

brands are the primary competitors for RBD in the refrigerated dough category, the potential entry of a new low-cost competitor could dramatically change the competitive situation.

Macroenvironmental Situation   This section describes broad environmental occurrences or trends that may have a bearing on the product's future. The issues mentioned here include any relevant economic, technological, political/legal, or social/cultural changes, as outlined in Chapter 3. As Exhibit 18.8 indicates, for example, lifestyle trends leading to more meals being eaten away from home and increased desires for convenience pose a threat to future demand for Pillsbury's RBD.

Past Product Performance   If the plan is for an existing product, this part of the situation analysis discusses the product's performance on such dimensions as sales volume, margins, marketing expenditures, and profit contribution for several recent years. This information is usually presented in the form of a table, such as the one for RBD shown in Exhibit 18.9. As the table indicates, even though RBD showed an improvement in gross margin due in part to reduced manufacturing costs, high advertising and sales expenditures prevented the product from making a positive contribution to overhead and profit.

The data contained in Exhibit 18.9 do not answer the question of whether the company's RBD prices and costs are competitive. Such information is critical since if a product's costs are not in line, then the product's market position is in jeopardy. This is especially true with commodity-type products, although even when products are differentiated it is essential that costs be maintained at competitive levels and any price premium charged provide a corresponding benefit to buyers. Some methods for measuring and monitoring costs and profitability are examined in the next chapter.[24]

Sales Forecast and Other Key Assumptions   Finally, the assessment of the current situation also typically includes estimates of sales potential, sales forecasts, and other evidence or assumptions underlying the plan. As we discussed in Chapter 7, such market measurements are particularly critical as the foundation for marketing plans for new goods or services were there is no past history to draw on. While the RBD plan does not explicitly report an estimate of total market potential, a sales forecast underlies the expected volume for next year reported in the fourth column of Exhibit 18.9.

Key Issues

After analyzing the current situation, the product manager must identify the most important issues facing the product in the coming year. These issues typically represent either threats to the future market or financial performance of the product or opportunities to improve those performances. This section should also highlight any special strengths of the product or weaknesses that must be overcome in responding to future threats and opportunities. Some of the key threats and opportunities faced by Pillsbury's RBD, together with the product's major strengths and weaknesses, are summarized in section II of Exhibit 18.8.

Objectives

Information about the current situation, the product's recent performance, and the key issues to be addressed now serve as the basis for setting specific objectives for the coming year. Two types of objectives need to be specified. **Financial objectives** provide goals for the overall performance of the brand and should reflect the objectives for the SBU as a whole and its competitive strategy. Those financial goals must then be converted into **marketing objectives** that specify the changes in customer behavior and levels of performance of various marketing program elements necessary to reach the product's financial objectives.

The major financial and marketing objectives for Pillsbury's RBD are summarized in section III of Exhibit 18.8. Sales volume and market share are not expected to increase, but the product is expected to make a $4 million contribution to overhead and profit through additional cost reductions.

Marketing Strategy

Because there may be a number of ways to achieve the objectives specified in the preceding section, the manager must now specify the overall marketing strategy to be pursued. It is likely to be one, or a combination of several, of the strategies discussed earlier in Chapters 15, 16, and 17. The chosen strategy should fit the market and competitive conditions faced by the product and its strategic objectives. It should also incorporate all of the necessary decisions concerning the 4Ps, as we have discussed in Chapters 11 through 14.

The RBD product manager recommends that a **maintenance strategy** be pursued. The intense competitive situation, uncertainty over the possible entry of Merico, and the past inability of primary-demand advertising to increase market penetration all suggest that it would be difficult to expand RBD's market by simply doing more of the same. Consequently, the recommended strategy seeks to maintain or slightly increase RBD volume and share primarily by stimulating repeat purchases among current customers. Reductions in advertising expenditures and continued improvements in manufacturing costs will be relied on to help the brand achieve its profit contribution objective. In addition, it is recommended that development and test marketing of several line extensions (for example, whole wheat and a French-style loaf) be initiated in an attempt to identify viable opportunities for future volume expansion.

Action Plans

The action plan is the most crucial part of the annual marketing plan for ensuring proper execution. Here the specific actions necessary to implement the strategy for the product are listed, together with a clear statement of who is responsible for each action, when it will be done, and how much is to be spent on each activity. Of course, actions requiring the cooperation of other functional departments should be included, but only after the product manager has contacted the departments involved, worked out any potential conflicts, and received assurances of support.

Here is where specific timelines and milestones are set forth. A variety of planning and project management tools—such at Gantt charts, stage-gate development processes, and others—may be used to illustrate and orchestrate the action steps entailed in the plan. Some of the action programs specified for RBD are outlined in section V of Exhibit 18.8.

Projected Profit-and-Loss Statement

The action plan includes a supporting budget that is essentially a projected profit-and-loss statement. On the revenue side, it forecasts next year's sales volume in units and dollars. On the expense side, it reflects manufacturing, distribution, and marketing costs associated with the planned actions. This budget is then presented to higher levels of management for review and possible modification. Once approved, the product's budget serves as a basis for the plans and resource allocation decisions of other functional departments within the SBU, such as manufacturing and purchasing, as well as other marketing units (e.g., marketing research). The projected financial results of RBD's annual plan are summarized in the second-to-last column of Exhibit 18.9.

Contingency Plans

Finally, the manager might also detail contingency plans to be implemented if specific threats or opportunities should occur during the planning period. The RBD product manager, for instance, recommended that no changes should be made in the product's overall marketing strategy nor in its pricing or promotion tactics in the event that Merico entered the national market. The rationale was that time should be taken to carefully analyze Merico's market impact and the magnitude of its competitive threat before crafting a response.

TAKE-AWAYS

- While much of this book has covered the various analytical tools and frameworks necessary to develop effective marketing strategies, such strategies are worthless without good implementation. Therefore, marketing managers, and general managers concerned about marketplace issues, must attend to organizational design issues. A business's structure, policies, procedures, and resources must fit its chosen strategy or else implementation will fall short.

- For firms with multiple businesses or product lines, different administrative relationships between the business unit and corporate headquarters are appropriate for different competitive strategies. Prospector businesses perform better with high levels of autonomy, fewer shared resources, and more top-line focused reward systems than defender businesses.

- Within a given business—whether it's part of a larger organization or a one-product entrepreneurial start-up—different functional competencies, levels of specialization, amounts of employee participation in decision making, and mechanisms for the resolution of internal conflicts are needed to effectively implement varying competitive strategies.

- Several different organizational designs incorporate differences in both structural variables (formalization, centralization, and specialization) and mechanisms for resolving interfunctional conflicts. These include functional, product management, market management, and various types of matrix organizational designs.

- Writing a formal marketing action plan is a key step toward ensuring the effective execution of a strategic marketing program because it spells out what actions need to be taken, when, and by whom. Written plans also provide the benchmarks by which the marketing strategy can be evaluated and controlled, as discussed in the next chapter.

Self-diagnostic questions to test your ability to apply the analytical tools and concepts in this chapter to marketing decision making may be found at this book's website at www.mhhe.com/mullins05.

ENDNOTES

1. This example is based on material found in Alan Deutschman, "How H-P Continues to Grow and Grow," *Fortune*, May 2, 1994, p. 90; Wendy Zellner, "The Go-Go Goliaths," *Business Week*, February 13, 1995, p. 64; Stratford Sherman, "Secrets of H-P's 'Muddled Team,'" *Fortune*, March 18, 1996; Peter Burrows and Peter Elstrom, "The Boss," *Business Week*, August 2, 1999, pp. 76–84; Eric Nee, "Hewlett-Packard's New E-vangelist," *Fortune*, January 10, 2000, pp. 166–68; Andrew Park and Peter Burrows, "Dell, the Conqueror," *Business Week*, September 24, 2001, pp. 92–102; Adam Lashinsky, "Now for the Hard Part," *Fortune*, November 18, 2002, pp. 95–106; and the Hewlett-Packard website at www.hp.com.

2. Robert W. Ruekert and Orville C. Walker, Jr., "The Sharing of Marketing Resources across Strategic Business Units: The Effect of Strategy on Performance," in *Review of Marketing 1990* (Chicago: American Marketing Association, 1990).

3. Bernard J. Jaworski, "Toward a Theory of Marketing Control: Environmental Context, Control Types, and Consequences," *Journal of Marketing*, July 1988, pp. 23–39.

4. Fred Vogelstein, "Mighty Amazon," *Fortune*, May 26, 2003, pp. 60–74; and Timothy J. Mullaney, Heather Green, Michael Arndt, Robert D. Hof, and Linda Himelstein, "The E-Biz Surprise," *Business Week*, May 12, 2003, pp. 60–68.

5. Daryl O. McKee, P. Rajan Varadarajan, and William M. Pride, "Strategic Adaptability and Firm Performance: A Market-Contingent Perspective," *Journal of Marketing*, July 1989, p. 19. For an interesting discussion of recent developments in the implementation of strategies for service organizations, see James L. Heskett, W. Earl Sasser, Jr., and Christopher W. L. Hart, *Implementing Strategy: Service Breakthroughs: Changing the Rules of the Game* (Cambridge, MA: The Mac Group, n.d.).

6. Michael J. Zenor, "The Profit Benefits of Category Management," *Journal of Marketing Research*, May 1994, p. 202.

7. Allen D. Shocker, Rajendra K. Srivastava, and Robert W. Ruekert, "Challenges and Opportunities Facing Brand Management," *Journal of Marketing Research*, May 1994, p. 149. Also see Donald R. Lehmann and Russell S. Winer, *Product Management* (Burr Ridge, IL: Richard D. Irwin, 1994) chap. 16.

8. For a discussion of firms as learning organizations and hence better able to cope with change, see "The Knowledge Firm," *The Economist*, November 11, 1995, p. 63; and Stanley F. Slater and John C. Narver, " Market Organization and the Learning Organization*," Journal of Marketing*, July 1995, p. 63.

9. Some analysts believe this may lead to a strategic advantage. See David A. Garvin, "Leveraging Processes for Strategic Advantage," *Harvard Business Review*, September–October 1995, p. 77.

10. Rahul Jacob, "The Struggle to Create an Organization for the 21st Century," *Fortune*, April 3, 1995, p. 90; Thomas A. Stewart, "Planning a Career in a World without Managers," *Fortune*, March 20, 1995, p. 72; and John A. Byrne, "Management by Web," *Business Week*, August 21, 2000, pp. 84–96; and Frederick E. Webster, "Marketing Management in Changing Times," *Marketing Management*, January–February 2002, pp. 18–23.

11. Brian Dumaine, "The Trouble with Teams," *Fortune*, September 5, 1994, p. 86.

12. Ibid.

13. Samuel E. Blucker, "The Virtual Organization," *The Futurist*, March–April 1994, p. 9. and Peter Coy, "The Creative Economy," *Business Week*, August 21, 2000, pp. 76–82.

14. John A. Byrne, Richard Brandt, and Otis Port, "The Virtual Corporation," *Business Week*, February 8, 1993, p. 98.

15. Rosabeth Moss Kanter, "Collaborative Advantage: The Art of Alliance," *Harvard Business Review*, July–August 1994, p. 97.

16. Ibid.

17. The discussion that follows draws heavily from Michael R. Czinkota, Pietra Rivali, and Idkka A. Ronkausen, *International Business* (New York: Dryden Press, 1992), pp. 536–45.

18. "The Discreet Charm of the Multicultural Multinational," *The Economist*, July 30, 1994, p. 57.

19. Christopher A. Bartlett and Sumantra Ghoshal, *Transnational Management* (Burr Ridge, IL: Richard D. Irwin, 1992) p. 520.

20. Ibid.

21. Czinkota et al., *International Business*, p. 545.

22. Donald R. Lehmann and Russell S. Winer, *Production Management* (Burr Ridge, IL: Richard D. Irwin, 1994), pp. 28–29.

23. While this example is based on the material contained in an actual marketing plan for a Pillsbury product, the name of the brand and some of the specific numbers included in this example have been disguised in order to protect proprietary information.

24. Robin Cooper and Robert S. Kaplan, "Measure Costs Right: Make the Right Decisions," *Harvard Business Review,* September–October 1988, pp. 96–103; and John K. Nrahk and Vijay Govindarajan, *Strategic Cost Measurement* (New York: Free Press, 1993), especially chaps. 2–6 and 10.

CHAPTER NINETEEN

Measuring and Delivering Marketing Performance

Controls Pay for Wal-Mart[1]

WAL-MART IS A DISCOUNT general merchandise retailer with sales of over $218 billion and operating income of over $15 billion in fiscal 2002. Founded some 40 years ago, it is America's largest, most-profitable, and one of its most-admired companies. Over the past decade it has continuously ranked as one of the best companies in its return on stockholders' equity.

As of January 2003 the company operated over 4,300 stores of which more than 1,100 were outside the United States (in Mexico, Canada, Europe, and Asia). Wal-Mart operates stores in several different formats apart from its original stores—some are supercenters (a combination supermarket and general merchandise store) and some are Sam's Clubs (a members-only warehouse store, selling high volumes, but at very low individual profit margins), and a smaller format, Neighborhood Markets, with a focus on groceries, in carefully chosen urban locations. Management had an aggressive plan for store growth in fiscal 2003—45 to 50 Wal-Mart stores, 200 to 210 supercenters, 20 to 25 Neighborhood Markets, and 40 to 45 Sam's Clubs. Internationally, the plan called for an additional 120 to 130 new stores. Wal-Mart stores serve more than 100 million customers per week, and the company employs more than 1 million people.

A major reason for Wal-Mart's success is its ability to control costs. In 2002 it was able to hold its operating, selling, and general administrative costs to 17.6 percent of sales. This was substantially below that of its closest competitors in the United States, Kmart and Target, and explains, in part, the company's excellent profitability record.

In the 1960s when he had only 10 stores, Sam Walton realized he couldn't expand successfully unless he could capture the information needed to control his operations. He became, according to one competitor, the best utilizer of control information in the industry. By the late 1970s Wal-Mart was using a storewide computer-driven information system that linked stores, distribution centers, and suppliers. Kmart started using a similar system only in the early 1990s.[2] In the late 1980s Sam Walton tapped David Glass to take over as CEO. Now the company's chairman, Glass, more than anyone, successfully engineered the development of Wal-Mart's advanced distribution and merchandise-tracking system, which were needed to handle the enormous sales increases as the company's stores spread throughout the United States. "Wal-Mart's incomparable systems are a secret of its success—the unadvertised contributor to the stock's 46.8 percent average annual return during the decade before Sam's death.[3]

Today, the company can convert information into action almost immediately. To do so required a massive investment (over $700 million) in computer and satellite systems, which collectively generate the largest civilian database of its kind in the world. In addition to automated replenishment, the system pro-

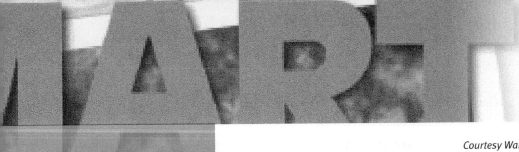

Courtesy Wal-Mart

vides up-to-the-minute sales of any item by region, district, and store. By looking at the computer screens in the satellite room, a manager can see systemwide data as the day's sales as they happen, the number of stolen bank cards retrieved that day, whether the seven-second credit card approval system is working properly, and the number of customer transactions completed that day.

Wal-Mart's philosophy has always been that its executives should spend part of their time in the field visiting with associates (employees) and customers. Thus, they board the company's prop planes in Bentonville on Monday each week, returning to share their findings with headquarters personnel and to prepare for a series of merchandise meetings Friday and Saturday. These are no-holds-barred sessions concerned with moving merchandise. For example, in one meeting it was suggested that Wal-mart was missing a great business opportunity in street-hockey gear because of the in-line skate craze. Others agreed, and within a few minutes appropriate action had been taken, including the development of an eight-foot-long display section.[4] This was, and similar decisions will be, communicated to all store managers by the following morning at the latest using Wal-Mart's computer-driven communications system.

By merging state-of-the-art computer communications technology with hands-on-management, Wal-Mart has developed a distribution system to the point that stores should, at least in theory, never be out of stock. Doing this better than its rivals has resulted in substantially more sales per square foot than competitors and, hence, a faster stock turn. This means less borrowing to carry fewer inventories and hence lower interest payments—several hundred million dollars lower than its nearest competitor. And lost sales because of stockouts are minimized.

Marketing Challenges Addressed in Chapter 19

In Chapter 18, we said that planning is important, and that effective implementation is crucial. The Wal-Mart example demonstrates how effective planning and implementation can play out in the performance of a company. Together, these two activities constitute the heart of most business endeavors. In the end, however, it is neither planning nor implementation that really counts. Results are what counts. Results are what managers and entrepreneurs are paid to deliver. Results are what attract investment capital to permit a company—whether a large public company such as Wal-Mart or an emerging dot.com start-up—to grow. Just watch what happens to a public company's stock price when the results are not what Wall Street expects. The share price plummets and, sometimes, heads roll. Weak sales and profit performance at Gap Inc. from late 1999 through 2002 cut Gap's stock price by half and led to a series of middle and upper management changes at the once high-flying retailer.[5] The focus on results is not restricted to for-profit organizations either. Exhibit 19.1 shows how some nonprofit organizations are adapting measurement methodologies to their own environments.

In Chapter 19, we address several critical questions that provide the link between a company's efforts to plan and implement marketing strategies and the actual results that those strategies produce. How can we design **strategic control systems** to make sure the strategies we are pursuing remain in sync with the changing market and competitive environment in which we operate? How can we design systems of **marketing metrics** to ensure

Exhibit 19.1   Measuring Results at Nonprofit Organizations

The mission of the Nature Conservancy, the world's largest conservation organization, is to preserve biodiversity by protecting the lands and waters that rare species need to survive. Historically, the Conservancy used a measure dubbed "bucks and acres" to gauge progress achieved every year. The "bucks" referred to charitable contributions raised and the "acres" to the number of acres under their control. During the 1990s, the Conservancy's total revenue grew at a rate of 18 percent compounded annually, and over the same period, acres protected in the United States grew from 5 million to more than 10 million. Despite this stellar progress as measured by this scale, the Conservancy realized that their mission of conserving biodiversity was becoming exponentially harder to achieve, and according to Harvard biologist E. O. Wilson, the species extinction rate today parallels that of the great epidemic of extinction that wiped out the dinosaurs 65 million years ago.

In their quest to develop more meaningful performance metrics that track progress toward their stated mission, the group researched issues that a host of other nonprofit groups were grappling with, and had found means (with varying degrees of success) for measuring their own progress toward their stated missions. The result, following a period of experimentation with new performance measures, was a system built around three themes: *impact, activity,* and *capacity.* The experience of the Nature Conservancy with developing its own metrics taught it that the important factors in achieving success in performance measurement are to derive measures aligned to its mission statements and to ensure that they are not too cumbersome to implement. While there is no one magic "profitability" measure that spans the broad spectrum of nonprofits, the Nature Conservancy has shown that measurement is indeed possible and more importantly, very desirable.

Source: John C. Sawhill, David Williamson, "Mission Impossible?: Measuring Success in Nonprofit Organizations," *Nonprofit Management and Leadership,* April 1, 2001, Vol. 11, Issue 3. Reprinted by permission of John Wiley & Sons, Inc.

that the marketing results we plan for are the results we deliver? In other words, if the ship gets off course during the journey, either strategically or in terms of execution of the marketing strategy, how can we make sure that we know quickly of the deviation so that midcourse corrections can be made in a timely manner? In today's rapidly changing markets, even the best-laid plans are likely to require changes as their implementation unfolds.

We begin by developing a five-step process for evaluating and controlling marketing performance on a continuous basis. We then apply the process to the issue of **strategic control:** How can we monitor and evaluate our overall marketing strategy to ensure that it remains viable in the face of changing market and competitive realities? Next, we apply the process to tracking the performance of a particular product-market entry and to the marketing actions taken to implement its marketing plan, or **marketing performance measurement.** Are we meeting sales targets, in the aggregate and for various products and market segments? Is each element of the marketing mix doing its job: Which items in the product line are selling best, are the ads producing enough sales leads, is the salesforce generating enough new accounts, and so on? Finally, we show how **marketing audits** can be used periodically to link the control process—that for both strategic control and for measuring current marketing performance—with marketing planning.

Designing Control Systems Step by Step

As the Wal-Mart example demonstrates, a well-functioning control and reappraisal system is critical to the success of a business. To be successful, it should be well integrated with the other steps in the marketing management process—setting objectives, formulating strategies, and implementing a plan of action. The control system monitors the extent to which the firm is achieving its objectives. When it is not, the firm determines whether the

Exhibit 19.2

THE CONTROL PROCESS

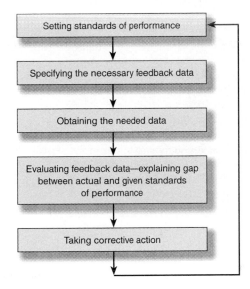

reason lies in the environment, the strategies employed, the action plans, the way the plans were being implemented, or some combination thereof. Thus, the control and reappraisal step is diagnostic, serving to start the marketing management process anew.

Control processes differ at each organization level. Thus, in a large diversified company, corporate management is concerned with how well its various SBUs are performing relative to the opportunities and threats each faces and the resources given them. Control here would be strategic. At the SBU level, or in smaller companies, concern is primarily with the unit's own strategy, especially as it pertains to its individual product-market entries. We will concentrate mainly on this latter organizational level since it constitutes the bulk of any control system.

Regardless of the organizational level involved, the control process is essentially the same. It consists of five steps: setting performance standards, specifying feedback, obtaining data, evaluating it, and taking corrective action (see Exhibit 19.2). Although the staff organization is typically responsible for generating the control data, the line organization administers the control process. Certainly, this is the case with Wal-Mart, as seen in the involvement of regional vice president, district managers, store managers, and department heads in obtaining and processing control data as well as taking corrective action. More importantly, line managers need to be closely involved with the development of the control system, so that they can be assured of getting the performance data they need, on a timely basis, and in a format they can easily use to support their long-term and day-to-day decision making.

Setting Standards of Performance

These standards derive largely from the objectives and strategies set forth at the SBU and individual product-market entry level. They generate a series of performance expectations for profitability (return on equity or return on assets managed), market share, and sales. At the product-market level, standards of performance also include sales and market-share

---

Exhibit 19.3   Are Drug Makers Addicted to Showing Profits?

In 2002, Bristol-Meyers Squibb faced the problem of two of its blockbuster products, the breast-cancer treatment drug Taxol and the antianxiety medication BuSpar coming off patent and losing market share to generics in the U.S. marketplace. When the drugs that the company had depended on to replace these were delayed, the company resorted to "stuffing the channel," that is, forcing its distributors to stock up on 56 weeks' worth of stock for these drugs. Such overselling into the channel is commonplace in this industry and normally goes unnoticed. However, when news of an SEC enquiry reached the marketplace, several top executives were forced to resign, and the stock price dropped by 37 percent. Schering-Plough ran into a similar issue when its anti-allergy drug Claritin came off patent.

Other industry giants like Merck and Johnson & Johnson reported that they monitor inventory levels. Johnson & Johnson said that it had put in place programs to reduce the volatility of inventories and that it was working closely with its largest distributors to forecast demand and restocking plans.

Source: Amy Tsao, "Drugmakers Struggle with an Addiction," Reprinted from the April 22, 2002 issue of *Business Week* by permission. Copyright The McGraw-Hill Companies.

---

determinants such as percent effective distribution, relative shelf-facings, awareness, consumers' attitude change toward a given product attribute, customer satisfaction, and the extent of price parity.

Similarly, for every line item in a marketing budget—product development costs, advertising and promotional expenses, costs for salespeople, and so on—specific and measurable standards of performance must be set so that each of these elements of marketing performance can be evaluated. We address the development of these standards later in this chapter. Without a reasonable set of performance standards, managers cannot know what results are being obtained, the extent to which they are satisfactory, or why they are or are not satisfactory. Performance-based control measures are often tied to the compensation of those individuals responsible for attaining the specified goals. Such a system can cause actions to be taken that in the short term may help attain the desired goals but in the longer term may be detrimental to the firm (see Exhibit 19.3).

KEY OBSERVATION

For every line item in a marketing budget—product development costs, advertising and promotional expenses, costs for salespeople, and so on—specific and measurable standards of performance must be set so that each of these elements of marketing performance can be evaluated.

Recent years have witnessed a shift from using primarily financially based performance measures to treating them as simply part of a broader array of measures. The now widely used balanced scorecard is one such approach.[6] While the use of nonfinancial measures is not new, giving them equal or greater status is. Thus, more and more companies are turning to measures they feel better reflect how their managers think about what decision areas drive the firm's success, such as customer satisfaction, product quality, market share, and new product development.

To be of any value, performance standards must be measurable; further, they must be tied to specific time periods, particularly when they concern a management compensation system. The SMART acronym (specific, measurable, attainable, relevant, and timebound), to which we have referred when discussing the setting of objectives in earlier chapters, is a useful framework for setting performance standards. Generally, control systems at the product-market level operate on a monthly, quarterly, and annual basis, with the monthly and quarterly data cumulated to present a current picture and to facilitate comparisons with prior years. In recent years, the trend has been for control systems to operate over shorter periods (weekly and even daily) and for control data to be more readily available. Wal-Mart's inventory control system, for example, provides instantaneous up-to-date data. Strategic control tends to operate over longer periods.

Of particular importance is whether the business unit as a whole and its individual product-market entries have set forth milestone achievement measures. For example, in a three-year strategic plan, a given SBU might have 12-month milestones such as annual sales of $100 million, profits of $20 million, and a return on assets managed of 14.5 percent. At the product-market entry level, milestones include such measures as product sales by market segments, marginal contributions, and operating margins. At the marketing functional area level, examples of milestone measures for a consumer good are level of awareness, trial, repeat purchases (brand loyalty) among members of the target audience, reduction in marketing costs as a percent of sales, and percent of stores stocking (weighted by sales).

In recent years, major multinationals such as DuPont, Ford, IBM, and Motorola have used a new performance type of measure—benchmarking. What this means is that the firm's performance in a given area is compared against the performance of other companies. Thus, Wal-Mart regularly compares itself with its competitors on merchandise assortments, service quality, and out of stocks. The comparison does not have to be with companies in the same industry. For example, Xerox benchmarked its order filling/shipping performance against L. L. Bean (a mail-order retailer catering to the outdoor set), which has a well-deserved reputation for fulfilling orders both quickly and accurately.[7] Small companies also use benchmarking to find out how they can better serve their customers and thereby increase sales. One small company found out that while customers in general were very happy with their financial advisory services, they felt that they did not get enough of the partners' time. A trucking company found out that their accounts receivables were much longer than the industry norm, simply because the truckers were not submitting their information soon enough after delivery.[8]

Profitability Analysis   Regardless of the organizational level, control involves some form of profitability analysis. In brief, **profitability analysis** requires that analysts determine the costs associated with specific marketing activities to find out the profitability of such units as different market segments, products, customer accounts, and distribution channels (intermediaries). Wal-Mart does this at the department and individual store levels as well as for individual lines of goods within a department. More and more managers are attempting to obtain profitability measures for individual products by market segments.

Profitability is probably the single most important measure of performance, but it has limitations. These are that (1) many objectives can best be measured in nonfinancial terms (maintaining market share); (2) profit is a short-term measure and can be manipulated by taking actions that may prove dysfunctional in the longer term (reducing R&D expenses); and (3) profits can be affected by factors over which management has no control (the weather). For a discussion of the newly discovered profitability religion in the dot.com world, see Exhibit 19.4.

KEY OBSERVATION

Profitability is probably the single most important measure of performance, but it has limitations.

Analysts can use direct or full costing in determining the profitability of a product or market segment. In **full costing,** analysts assign both direct, or variable, and indirect costs to the unit of analysis. **Indirect costs** involve certain fixed joint costs that cannot be linked directly to a single unit of analysis. For example, the costs of occupancy, general management, and the management of the salesforce are all indirect costs for a multiproduct company. Those who use full costing argue that only by allocating all costs to a product or a market can they obtain an accurate picture of its value.

Direct costing involves the use of **contribution accounting.** Those favoring the direct costing approach argue there is really no accurate way to assign indirect costs. Further, because indirect costs are mostly fixed, a product or market may make a contribution to profits even if it shows a loss. Thus, even though the company must eventually absorb its overhead costs, the contribution method clearly indicates what is gained by adding or

Exhibit 19.4　Is Profitability Important in the Dot.com World?

In the dot.com heyday of the late 1990s, it was said that profitability was not very important for dot.com companies. Other metrics, like first to market or first to scale, were thought to be sufficient. "We'll make money when we get big enough," said many a dot.com CEO. In April 2000, however, the sky-high dot.com stock market valuations came tumbling down, and the financing window for many dot.coms slammed shut. Suddenly, a newfound religion—profitability and positive cash flow—took its place on the dashboards of dot.com CEOs.

These CEOs found themselves thinking about more tangible, shorter-term performance metrics. The cost to acquire a customer was measured—and often found to be prohibitive—and new, lower-cost customer acquisition strategies were developed. The costs to deliver products sold in cyberspace but delivered on Maple Street were examined. Bags of dog food, for example, cost more to deliver one by one than they cost to buy in the first place. The efficacy and cost-effectiveness of banner ads for building brands was measured—and often found wanting—as we saw in Chapter 15.

In hindsight, most observers find these changes to have been healthy, in terms of directing investment capital to new-economy businesses that offer the potential to deliver real value for which customers are willing to pay. Today's dot.com entrepreneurs and those who fund them now know that measuring marketing performance and profitability is among the most important activities their firms undertake.

dropping a product or a customer. Exhibit 19.5 shows an example of full and direct costing. The difference in the results obtained is substantial—$370,000 using full costing versus $650,000 with the contribution method.

Contribution analysis is helpful in determining the yield derived from the application of additional resources (for instance, to certain sales territories). Using the data in Exhibit 19.6 we can answer the question, "How much additional profit would result from a marginal increase in sales of $300,000—assuming the gross margin remains at 19.62 percent and the only cost is $35,000 more in sales commissions and expenses?" As Exhibit 19.6 shows, the answer is a profit increase before taxes of $53,000.

Companies are increasingly turning from traditional accounting methods, which identify costs according to various expense categories, to activity-based costing (ABC), which bases costs on the different tasks involved in performing a given activity. ABC advocates have used it to improve product costing, thereby improving pricing parameters, providing better service, trimming waste, and evaluating quality initiative.[9]

Customer Satisfaction　So far, we have been discussing performance measures in essentially financial terms. But financial terms are insufficient since they fail to recognize the importance of customer satisfaction, which is an important driving force of the firm's future market share and profitability. As products and services become more alike in an already highly competitive marketplace, the ability to satisfy the customer across a variety of activities (of which the product is only one) will become an even greater success determinant. Thus, measures relating to customer preferences and satisfaction are essential as an early warning of impending problems and opportunities.

KEY OBSERVATION

Developing a meaningful measure of customer satisfaction requires the merging of two kinds of measures.

Developing a meaningful measure of customer satisfaction requires the merging of two kinds of measures. The first has to do with an understanding and measurement of the criteria used by customers to evaluate the quality of the firm's relationship with them. Knowing the product/

Exhibit 19.5

FINDING PRODUCT OR MARKET PROFITABILITY WITH FULL COSTING AND MARGINAL CONTRIBUTIONS METHODS ($000)

	Full costing	Marginal contribution
Net sales	$5,400	$5,400
Less: Cost of goods sold—includes direct costs (labor, material, and production overhead)*	3,800	3,800
Gross margin	$1,600	$1,600
Expenses		
Salesforce—includes direct costs (commissions) plus indirect costs (sales expenses, sales management overhead)[†]	510	450
Advertising—includes direct costs (media, production) plus indirect costs (management overhead)	215	185
Physical logistics—includes direct costs (transportation) plus indirect costs (order processing, warehousing costs)	225	190
Occupancy—includes direct costs (telephone) plus indirect costs (heat/air, insurance, taxes, building maintenance)	100	25
Management overhead—includes direct costs (product/brand manager and staff) plus indirect costs (salaries, expenses, occupancy costs of SBU's general management group)	180	100
Total	$1,230	$ 950
Profit before taxes	$ 370	
Contribution to fixed costs and profits		$ 650

*Production facilities dedicated to a single product.

[†]Multiproduct salesforce.

Exhibit 19.6

EFFECT OF $300,000 INCREASE IN SALES RESULTING FROM INCREASED SALES COMMISSIONS AND EXPENSES OF $35,000 (SAME DATA AS IN EXHIBIT 19.5) ($000)

Net sales	$5,700
Less: direct costs (29.62%)	4,012
	$1,688
Expenses	
Sales commissions and expenses	485
Advertising	185
Physical logistics	190
Occupancy	25
Management	100
	$ 985
Contribution to overhead and profits	$ 703
Increase in profit (before tax) = $703 − $650 =	$ 53

service attributes that constitute the customer's choice criteria as well as the relative importance of each should facilitate this task. These were developed in the process by which the firm identifies the target market for its product-market entries. Once these attributes are identified, they serve as the basis for developing **expectation measures.**

The second type of measurement is concerned with how well the firm is meeting the customer's expectations on an individual attribute as well as an overall basis. Thus, if the choice criteria of a cruiseline's target market included such attributes as food, exercise facilities, and entertainment, then a performance measure would be developed for each. By weighting these by the relative importance of each, an overall performance measure can be obtained. These two measures collectively serve as the basis for evaluating the company's performance on customer satisfaction.

In recent years more top-level executives are visiting their major accounts (whether they be end-use customers or intermediaries) to learn firsthand how to better serve them. Such visits frequently result in joint projects designed to reduce the costs incurred by both parties in the sale of a given set of products.

One of the high fliers in the Internet boom, Commerce One, rose to fame because of its partnership with General Motors to set up an online electronic marketplace.[10] The detailed customer understanding that Commerce One obtained through executive visits played an important role in its efforts.

Specifying and Obtaining Feedback Data

Once a company has established its performance standards, its next step is to develop a system that provides usable and timely feedback data on actual performance. In most cases someone must gather and process considerable data to obtain the performance measures, especially at the product-market level. Analysts obtain feedback data from a variety of sources, including company accounting records and syndicated marketing information services such as Nielsen. The sales invoice or other transaction records, such as those produced by retailers' point-of-sale systems, are the basic internal source of data because they provide a detailed record of each transaction. Invoices are the basis for measuring profitability, sales, and various budget items. They also provide data for the analysis of the geographic distribution of sales and customer accounts by type and size.

Another source, and typically the most expensive and time-consuming, involves undertaking one or more marketing research projects to obtain needed information. In-house research projects are apt to take longer and be more expensive than using an outside syndicated service. But there may be no alternative, as, for example, in determining awareness and attitude changes and obtaining data on customer service. Exhibit 19.7 gives an example of how Wal-Mart uses marketing research to help maintain its low-price image. A third source, and one we discussed above, involves the use of executives to gather information from their personal visits with customers.

Evaluating Feedback Data

Management evaluates feedback data to find out whether there is any deviation from the plan, and if so why. Wal-Mart does this in a variety of ways, including sending its regional vice presidents into the field on a regular basis to learn what's going on and why.

Typically, managers use a variety of information to determine what the company's performance *should* have been under the actual market conditions that existed when the plan was executed. In some cases this information can be obtained in measured form; examples include a shift in personal disposable income (available from government sources), a change in the demand for a given product type (obtained when measuring market share), the impact of a new brand on market share (reported by a commercial source), or a change in price by a major competitor. Often, however, the explanation rests on inferences drawn from generalized data, as would be the case in attributing poor sales performance to an improvement in a competitor's salesforce.

At the line-item level, whether for revenue or expenses, results are compared with the standards set in step one of the control process. A merchandise manager or buyer at an apparel retailer such as Gap, for example, would track sales results of each style or merchandise category in terms of its selling rate (How many weeks' supply is on hand overall and in which stores?) and its gross margin performance. For a district sales team of an industrial goods manufacturer, salespeople might be measured on the number of sales calls they make per week, the number of new accounts they generate, their sales volume in revenue and units, their travel expenses, and a variety of other metrics. A stylist in a beauty salon might be measured in terms of the number of haircuts or sales revenue she produces per day or per hour.

Taking Corrective Action

The last step in the control process concerns prescribing the needed action to correct the situation. At Wal-Mart, this is partly accomplished at its various congresses held every Friday and Saturday when managers decide what actions to take to solve selected problems. Success here depends on how well managers carry out the evaluation step. When linkages between inputs and outputs are clear, managers can presume a causal relationship and specify appropriate action. For example, assume that inputs consisted of an advertising schedule that specified the frequency of a given TV message. The objective was to change attitudes about a given product attribute (the output). If the attitude change did not occur, remedial action would start with an evaluation of the firm's advertising effort, particularly the advertising message and how frequently it ran.

But in most cases it is difficult to identify the cause of the problem. Almost always, an interactive effect exists among the input variables as well as the environment. There is also the problem of delayed responses and carry-over effects. For example, advertisers can rarely separate the effects of the message, media, frequency of exposure, and competitive responses in an attempt to determine advertising effects. Even if the company could determine the cause of a problem, it faces the difficulty of prescribing the appropriate action to take. Most control systems are "based on the assumption that corrective action is known should significant variations arise. Unfortunately, marketing still is not at a stage where performance deviations can be corrected with certainty."[11]

Sometimes the situation is so serious (shipping time lags competition by 30 percent) that radical change is needed. To more and more business managers this means "reengineering" or starting all over. This involves rethinking and resigning the relevant business processes "to achieve dramatic improvements in critical contemporary measures of performance such as cost, quality, service, and speed."[12] A business process uses a variety of activities to create an output that is of value to a customer. For example, the order-filling process exists only to deliver the right goods to a customer in good shape and in the time promised.

Sometimes the outcome is greater or better than management had planned; for example, when sales and market share exceed the schedule. In such cases, the marketers still need an evaluation to find out why such a variance occurred. Perhaps a more favorable environment evolved because demand was greater than expected and a major competitor failed to take advantage of it. Or perhaps the advertising message was more effective than expected. These different reasons would call for different marketing responses to maintain the new volume and to further exploit the favorable situation.

Design Decisions for Strategic Control Systems

Strategic control is concerned with monitoring and evaluating a firm's SBU-level strategies (see Exhibit 19.8 for the kinds of questions this type of control system is designed to answer). Such a system is difficult to implement because there is usually a substantial amount of time between strategy formulation and when a strategy takes hold and results are evident. Since both the external and internal environments are constantly evolving, strategic control must provide some way of changing the firm's thrust if new information about the environment and/or the firm's performance so dictates. Inevitably, much of this intermediate assessment is based on information about the marketplace and the results obtained from the firm's marketing plan.

KEY OBSERVATION

Strategic control must provide some way of changing the firm's thrust if new information about the environment and/or the firm's performance so dictates.

Identifying Key Variables

To implement strategic control, a company must identify the key variables to monitor, which are usually the major assumptions made in formulating the strategy. The key variables to monitor are of two types:

- Those concerned with external forces.
- And those concerned with the effects of certain actions taken by the firm to implement the strategy.

Exhibit 19.8

EXAMPLES OF QUESTIONS A STRATEGIC CONTROL SYSTEM SHOULD BE ABLE TO ANSWER

1. What changes in the environment have negatively affected the current strategy (e.g., interest rates, government controls, or price changes in substitute products)?
2. What changes have major competitors made in their objectives and strategies?
3. What changes have occurred in the industry in such attributes as capacity, entry barriers, substitute products?
4. What new opportunities or threats have derived from changes in the environment, competitors' strategies, or the nature of the industry?
5. What changes have occurred in the industry's key success factors?
6. To what extent is the firm's current strategy consistent with the preceding changes?

Examples of the former included changes in the external environment such as changes in long-term demand, the advent of new technology, a change in governmental legislation, and actions by a competitor. Examples of the latter types (actions by the firm) include the firm's advertising efforts to change attitudes and in-store merchandising activities designed to improve product availability.

The frameworks and analytical tools for market and competitive analysis that we discussed in Chapters 3 and 4 are useful in determining what variables to monitor in a strategic control system. Deciding exactly which variables to monitor is a company-specific decision; in general, it should focus on those variables most likely to affect the company's future position within its industry group.

Tracking and Monitoring

The next step is to specify what information or measures are needed on each of the key variables to determine whether the implementation of the strategic plan is on schedule—and if not, why not. The firm can use the control plan as an early-warning system as well as a diagnostic tool. If, for example, the firm has made certain assumptions about the rate at which market demand will increase, it should monitor industry sales regularly. If it has made assumptions about advertising and its effect on attitudes, it would be likely to use measures of awareness, trial, and repeat buying. In any event, the firm must closely examine the relevancy, accuracy, and cost of obtaining the needed measures.

The advent of e-mail, intranets, and other digital tools for disseminating information has made it easier for sometimes far-flung managers to monitor strategic developments. Critical strategic control information can now be monitored on a real-time basis anywhere in the world.

Strategy Reassessment

This can take place at periodic intervals—for example, quarterly or annually, when the firm evaluates its performance to date along with major changes in the external environment. A strategic control system can also alert management of a significant change in its external/internal environments. This involves setting triggers to signal the need to reassess the viability of the firm's strategy. It requires a specification of both the level at which an alert will be called and the combination of events that must occur before the firm reacts. For example, total industry sales of 10 percent less than expected for a single month would not be likely to trigger a response, whereas a 25 percent drop would. Or a firm might decide that triggering will occur only after three successive months in which a difference of 10 percent occurred in each.

In today's fast-changing world, strategy reassessment may happen much more quickly, as competitive and technological developments cause firms to quickly change their entire strategies and business models. Amazon, which started out as an online bookseller in the United States, has today grown to become an online shopping mall, with local presence in several countries across the globe. Its Marketplace area, started in November 2000, allows individuals and small businesses to sell their wares on the site. In 2000 and 2001, it entered into partnerships with other established retailers Toys "R" Us and Borders to run their online identities, respectively. In 2003, the company announced partnerships with several retailers to sell apparel in the United States. Thus, adapting its strategy to changing times allowed the company to beat Wall Street's profit and earnings estimates in the crucial holiday quarter in 2002.[13]

Design Decisions for Marketing Performance Measurement

Designing control systems to measure marketing performance at the product-market and line-item levels involves answering four essential questions.

- Who needs what information?
- When and how often is the information needed?
- In what media and in what format(s) or levels of aggregation should the information be provided?
- What contingencies should be planned for?

In essence, designing a marketing performance measurement system is like designing the dashboard of a car. Such a system needs to include the most critical metrics to assess whether the car or the business is progressing toward its objectives. Thus, for a car, the dashboard includes a speed gauge and odometer to measure progress toward the destination, a fuel gauge, warning lights for engine and braking system malfunction, and so on, but it typically does not indicate how much windshield wiper fluid remains, how much weight the car is carrying, or other relatively non-essential indicators. The same holds true for a business: The "drivers" who are managing the business need to know certain essential information while the "car"—or strategy—is running, while other less crucial indicators can be omitted or provided only when requested. We now address the four key questions, or **design parameters,** of marketing performance measurement systems.

KEY OBSERVATION

In essence, designing a marketing performance measurement system is like designing the dashboard of a car.

Who Needs What Information?

Marketing performance measurement systems are designed to ensure that the company achieves the sales, profits, and other objectives set forth in its marketing and strategic plans. In the aggregate, these plans reflect the outcomes of the company's or the SBU's planning efforts, which have specified how resources are to be allocated across markets, products, and marketing-mix activities. These plans, as we noted in Chapter 18, include line-item budgets and typically specify the actions expected of each organizational unit—whether inside or outside the marketing function or department—and deemed necessary to attain the company's financial and competitive positioning objectives. The first and foremost objective for marketing is the level of sales the company or the product-market entry achieves.

Who needs sales information? Top management needs it. Functional managers in other parts of the organization—manufacturing, procurement, finance, and so on—need it. Marketing managers responsible for the various marketing-mix activities, from product design to pricing to channel management to selling and other promotional activities, need it.

Sales Analysis   A sales analysis involves breaking down aggregate sales data into such categories as products, end-user customers, channel intermediaries, sales territories, and order size. The objective of an analysis is to find areas of strengths and weakness; for example, products producing the greatest and least volume, customers accounting for the bulk of the revenues, and salespersons and territories performing the best and the worst.

Sales analysis recognizes that aggregate sales and cost data often mask the real situation. Sales analysis not only helps to evaluate and control marketing efforts, but also helps management to better formulate objectives and strategies and administer such nonmarketing activities as production planning, inventory management, and facilities planning.

An important decision in designing the firm's sales analysis system concerns which units of analysis to use. Most companies assemble data in the following groupings:

- Geographical areas—regions, counties, and sales territories.
- Product, package size, and grade.
- Customer—by type and size.
- Channel intermediary—such as type and/or size of retailer.
- Method of sale—mail, phone, channel, Internet, or direct.
- Size of order—less than $10, $10-25, and so on.

These breakdowns are not mutually exclusive. Most firms perform sales analyses hierarchically; for example, by county within a sales territory within a sales region. Further, they usually combine product and account breakdowns with a geographical one; say, the purchase of product X by large accounts located in sales territory Y, which is part of region A. Only by conducting sales analysis on a hierarchical basis using a combination of breakdowns can analysts be at all sure that they have made every reasonable attempt to locate the opportunities and problems facing their firms.

Sales Analysis by Territory
The first step in a sales territory analysis is to decide which geographical control unit to use. In the United States, the county is the typical choice since it can be combined into larger units such as sales territories and it is also a geograph-

KEY OBSERVATION

Category and brand development indices are often used in assessing sales performance by territory.

ical area for which many data items are available, such as population, employment, income, and retail sales. Analysts can compare actual sales (derived from company invoices) by county against a standard such as a sales quota that takes into account such factors as market potential and last year's sales adjusted for inflation. They can then single out territories that fall below standard for special attention. Is competition unusually strong? Has less selling effort been expended here? Is the salesforce weak? Studies dealing with such questions as these help a company improve its weak and exploit its stronger ones. Category and brand development indices, such as those described in Chapter 7, are often used in assessing sales performance by territory.

Exhibit 19.9 illustrates a sales territory analysis. It shows that only one territory out of seven shown exceeded its 2002 quota, or standard of performance, and by just $18,112. The other six territories accounted for a total of $394,685 under quota. Territory 3 alone accounted for 55 percent of the total loss. The sales and the size of the quota in this territory suggest the need for further breakdowns, especially by accounts and products. Such breakdowns may reveal that the firm needs to allocate more selling resources to this territory. The company needs to improve its sales primarily in territories 3 and 5. If it can reach its potential in these two territories, overall sales would increase by $301,911, assuming that the quotas set are valid.

Without a standard against which to compare results, the conclusions would be much different. Thus, if only company sales were considered (column 1), White would be the best salesperson and Finch the worst. By using sales quotas as a performance standard, White was not the best but the worst salesperson, with a 77 percent rating.

Sales Analysis by Product
Over time, a company's product line tends to become overcrowded and less profitable unless management takes strong and continuous action to eliminate no-longer-profitable items. By eliminating weak products and concentrating on strong ones, a company can increase its profits substantially. Before deciding which products to abandon, management must study such variables as market-share

Exhibit 19.9

SALES ANALYSIS BASED ON SELECTED SALES TERRITORIES

Sales Territory	Salesperson	(1) Company Sales 2002	(2) Sales quota 2002	(3) Overage, underage	(4) Percent of potential performance
1	Barlow	$552,630	$585,206	−$32,576	94%
2	Burrows	470,912	452,800	+18,112	104
3	White	763,215	981,441	−218,226	77
4	Finch	287,184	297,000	−9,816	96
5	Brown	380,747	464,432	−83,685	82
6	Roberts	494,120	531,311	−37,191	93
7	Macini	316,592	329,783	−13,191	96

trends, contribution margins, scale effects, and the extent to which a product is complementary with other items in the line.[14]

A product sales analysis is particularly helpful when combined with account size and sales territory data. Using such an analysis, managers can often pinpoint substantial opportunities and develop specific tactics to take advantage of them. For example, one firm's analysis revealed that sales of one of its highest-margin products were down in all the New England sales territories. Further investigation showed that a regional producer was aggressively promoting a recently modified product with reduced prices. An analysis of the competing product revealed questionable reliability under certain operating conditions. The salesforce used this information to turn around the sales problem.

Sales Analysis by Order Size   Sales analysis by order size may identify which dollar-size orders are not profitable. For example, if some customers frequently place small orders that require salesforce attention and need to be processed, order picked, and shipped, a problem of some importance exists.

Analysis by order size locates products, sales territories, and customer types and sizes where small orders prevail. Such an analysis may lead to setting a minimum order size, charging extra for small orders, training sales reps to develop larger orders, and dropping some accounts. An example of such an analysis involved a nationwide needlework product distributor, which found that 28 percent of all its orders were $10 and under. A study revealed that the average cost of servicing such orders was $12.82. The analysis also showed that the company did not break even until the order size reached $20. Based on these findings, the company installed a $35 minimum order, charged a special handling fee of $7.50 on all orders below $35, and alerted its field sales reps and telephone salespeople to the problem. As a result, the company increased its profits substantially.

Sales Analysis by Customer   Analysts use procedures similar to those described earlier to analyze sales by customers. Such analyses typically show that a relatively small percentage of customers account for a large percentage of sales. For example, the needlework products distributor cited above found that 13 percent of its accounts represented 67 percent of its total sales. Frequently, a study of sales calls shows that the salesforce spends a disproportionate amount of its time with the small accounts as compared with the larger ones. Shifting some of this effort to the larger accounts may well increase sales.

Line-Item Margin and Expense Analysis   Sales data are not the only marketing performance information needed, of course. Gross and net margins must be tracked, and the effectiveness and efficiency of all line-item marketing expenses must be measured. The designers of marketing performance measurement systems must develop appropriate metrics to track the critical performance indicators for margins and expenses so that timely mid-course corrections can be made. Thus, the weeks-on-hand metric that tells a Gap sweater buyer how quickly each style is selling tells him or her whether to buy more of a particular style if it is selling well, or mark it down if it is not moving. Making such decisions on a timely basis can have a profound effect on gross margins. A not-so-pretty sweater may be more salable at 25 percent off before Christmas than at 60 percent off after December 26.

Because budgets project revenues and expenses for a given time period, they are a vital part of the firm's planning and control activities. They provide the basis for a continuous evaluation and comparison of what was planned with what actually happened. In this sense, budgeted revenues and profits serve as objective against which to measure performance in sales, profits, and actual costs.

Budget analysis requires that managers continuously monitor marketing–expense ratios to make certain the company does not overspend in its effort to reach its objectives. Managers also evaluate the magnitude and pattern of deviations from the target ratios. Managers of the various marketing units have their own control measures. For example, advertising managers track advertising costs per 1,000 target audience, buyers per media vehicle, print ad readership, size and composition of TV audiences, and attitude change. Sales managers typically track number of calls per salesperson, costs per call, sales per call, and new accounts. The major marketing expenses are those associated with marketing research, brand management, sales salaries, sales expenses, media advertising, consumer promotions, trade promotions, and publicity. Before taking corrective action on any of these expenses that are out of line, managers may need to disaggregate the data to help isolate the problem. For example, if total commissions as a percent of sales are out of line, analysts need to study them by each sales territory and product to determine exactly where the problem lies.

When and How Often Is the Information Needed?

Timeliness is a key criterion for the development of a marketing performance measurement system. As we have seen, Wal-Mart's systems provide sales information at the store and item level on an up-to-the-minute basis. More commonly, though, managers attend to performance information—whether for sales, margins, or expenses—on a periodic basis, since they don't have time or the need to assess the performance of every item at every minute of every day. Buyers and merchandise managers in retailing firms typically assess item and category sales performance on a weekly basis. In fashion categories, such as women's apparel, where timeliness is especially important, having sales information a couple of days, or even hours, ahead of competitors can make the difference between obtaining more of a hot-selling item or being left in a faster-moving competitor's dust. Store payroll expense, another key performance criterion for retailers that impacts both customer service and profitability, is typically measured on a weekly basis, though store managers may be encouraged to send employees home if business is unexpectedly slow on a given day or call in extra help when more is needed. The performance of industrial salespeople—in terms of number of sales calls, sales volume, expense control, and other indicators—is typically done on a monthly basis, though some firms may do so more or less frequently as they see fit. Strategic control indicators, such as changes in market share, macro trends, and so on, are likely to be measured and reported less frequently because these kinds of longer-term issues may not be readily apparent or may give false alarms at more frequent intervals.

In What Media and in What Format(s) or Levels of Aggregation Should the Information Be Provided?

Advances in information technology have made possible the measurement and reporting of marketing performance information with previously unheard-of ease of access and timeliness, without even printing the data! As we have seen, Wal-Mart's sales information is available on computer screens on an up-to-the-minute basis. In other companies, salespeople around the world now log on to company intranets to see the latest order status of a customer before they walk in the door on a sales call. But *having* good and timely information and *reporting* it in such a manner that it is easy and quick to use are different things. Imagine a Gap buyer having to manually add up the performance of various styles to determine how the category is performing. Reports should provide such aggregation, of course, but someone must decide what sort of aggregation is most useful for each information user.

> **KEY OBSERVATION**
>
> *Having good and timely information and reporting it in such a manner that it is easy and quick to use are different things.*

Even the format or medium in which performance information is presented can make a big difference to the manager using the data. Weekly weeks-on-hand sales reports that retail buyers and merchandise managers depend on are most usefully reported in order of how fast the styles are selling, rather than alphabetically or some other way. The styles at the top of the report (those with little stock on hand, as measured by their weeks-on-hand sales rate) are candidates for reorders. Styles at the bottom of the report (the ugly wool sweater in mid-November with 25 weeks of inventory on hand) are candidates for markdowns. The ones in between may need little attention. Once a season ends, a different report, aggregating styles by vendor, perhaps, might be useful to determine which suppliers have performed well and which have performed poorly across the assortment of styles they provide. Thoughtful attention to the format in which marketing performance information is reported, to the levels at which it is aggregated, for different kinds of decision purposes, and for different users can provide a company with a significant competitive advantage. As we noted earlier in this chapter, it took Kmart many years to come close to Wal-Mart's system of tracking and reporting store and item sales performance.

What Contingencies Should Be Planned For?

Because all strategies and the action plans designed to implement them are based on assumptions about the future, they are subject to considerable risk. Too often, assumptions are regarded as facts; and little attention is paid to what action or actions can be taken if any or all of the assumptions turn out to be wrong.

Managers, therefore, often follow a contingency planning process that includes the elements shown in Exhibit 19.10: identifying critical assumptions; assigning probabilities of being right about the assumptions; ranking the importance of the assumption; tracking and monitoring the action plan; setting the "triggers" that will activate the contingency plan; and specifying alternative response options. We discuss these steps briefly below.

Identifying Critical Assumptions   Because there are simply too many assumptions to track them all, contingency plans must cover only the more important ones. Assumptions about events beyond the control of the individual firm but that strongly affect the entry's strategic objectives are particularly important. For example, assumptions about the rate of

Exhibit 19.10

THE CONTINGENCY PLANNING PROCESS

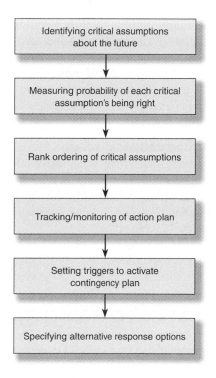

market growth coupled with the entry's market share will strongly affect the entry's profitability objectives. The effect of a wrong assumption here can be either good or bad, and the contingency plan must be prepared to handle both. If the market grows at a rate faster then expected, then the question of how to respond needs to be considered. Too often contingency plans focus only on the downside.

Another type of uncontrollable event that can strongly affect sales and profits is competitive actions. This is particularly true with a new entry (when a competitor responds with its own new product), although it can apply with more mature products (competitor's advertising is increased). Assumptions about industry price levels must be examined in depth because any price deterioration can quickly erode margins and profits.

Assumptions about the effects of certain actions taken by the firm to attain its strategic objectives also need to be considered in depth. Examples include the firm's advertising objectives, which are based on assumptions about an improvement or maintenance of consumer attitudes toward the product's characteristics compared with competing brands, or the monies allocated to merchandising to improve the product's availability. Further, once the targeted levels of the various primary objectives are reached, there are assumptions about what will happen to sales and share.

Assigning Probabilities   This step consists of assigning to the critical assumptions probabilities of being right. These probabilities must be considered in terms of the consequences of being wrong. Thus, assumptions that have a low probability of being wrong but could affect the firm strongly need to be considered in depth (for instance, gas shortages or high prices or the demand for large luxury automobiles).

Rank Ordering the Critical Assumptions   If assumptions are categorized on the basis of their importance, the extent to which they are controllable, and the confidence management has in them, then the basis for rank ordering the assumptions and drafting the contingency plan has been set forth. Ordinarily, these criteria will have screened out those assumptions that need not be included—those with a low impact on objectives and those about which there is a high confidence they will not occur. Assumptions that relate to uncontrollable events should, however, be monitored if they strongly affect the entry's strategic objectives since the firm can react to them. For example, if the assumption about the rate of market growth is wrong, then the firm can either slow or increase its investments in plant construction.

Tracking and Monitoring   The next step is to specify what information (or measures) are needed to determine whether the implementation of the action plan is on schedule—and if not, why not. The contingency plan is, therefore, an early warning system as well as a diagnostic tool. If, for example, the firm has made certain assumptions about the rate of market demand increase, then it would monitor industry sales on a regular basis. If assumptions were made about advertising and its effect on attitudes, then measures of awareness, trial, and repeat buying would be likely to be used. Relevancy, accuracy, and cost of obtaining the needed measures must be examined in depth. Some of the information needed in the contingency plan might have been specified in the control plan, in which case it is already available.

Activating the Contingency Plan   This involves setting the "triggers" to activate the contingency plan. It requires a specification of both the level at which an alert will be called and the combination of events that must occur before the firm reacts. If, for example, total industry sales were 10 percent less than expected for a single month, this would not be likely to trigger a response, whereas a 25 percent drop would. Or a firm may decide the triggering would occur only after three successive months in which a difference of 10 percent occurred. Triggers must be defined precisely and responsibility assigned for putting the contingency plan into operation.

Specifying Response Options   Actually, the term *contingency plan* is somewhat misleading. It implies that the firm know in advance exactly how it will respond if one or more of its assumptions go awry. This implication is unrealistic because there are a great many ways for critical assumptions to turn out wrong. To compound the problem, the firm's preplanned specific responses can be difficult to implement, depending on the situation and how it develops. This can lead to a set of responses that build in intensity. Thus, most firms develop a set of optional responses that are not detailed to any great extent in an effort to provide flexibility and ensure further study of the forces that caused the alert.

Global Marketing Control

Maintaining control over global marketing activities is more difficult than with domestic marketing, primarily because of the number of countries involved, each presenting a unique set of opportunities and threats. This makes it difficult to monitor simultaneously a variety of environments and to prescribe corrective action on an individual-country basis where appropriate. Differences in language and customs, accentuated by distance, further compound the control problem.

Nonetheless, global companies typically use essentially the same control system format for both their domestic and foreign operations, though report frequency and extent of detail can vary by the subsidiary's size and environmental uncertainties. The great advantage of using a single system is that it facilitates comparisons between operating units and communications between home office and local managers. On the surface, the use of electronic data interchange should simplify performance evaluation across countries. While this is true in terms of budget control, it leaves much to be desired in terms of understanding the reasons for any deviations.

A Tool for Periodic Assessment of Marketing Performance: The Marketing Audit

KEY OBSERVATION

While marketing performance measurement systems are essential for tracking day-to-day, week-to-week, and month-to-month performance to see that planned results are actually delivered, it is sometimes useful to step back and take a longer view of the marketing performance of an SBU or of the entire company.

While marketing performance measurement systems are essential for tracking day-to-day, week-to-week, and month-to-month performance to see that planned results are actually delivered, it is sometimes useful to step back and take a longer view of the marketing performance of an SBU or of the entire company. Marketing audits are growing in popularity, especially for firms with a variety of SBUs that differ in their market orientation. They are both a control and planning activity that involves a comprehensive review of the firm's or SBU's total marketing efforts cutting across all products and business units. Thus, they are broader in scope and cover longer time horizons than sales and profitability analyses.

Our concern here is at the individual SBU level or the entire company, for smaller or single business firms. Such an audit covers both the SBU's objectives and strategy and its plan of action for each product-market entry. It provides an assessment of each SBU's current overall competitive position as well as that of its individual product-market entries. It requires an analysis of each of the marketing-mix elements and how well they are being implemented in support of each entry. The audit must take into account the environmental changes that can affect the SBU's strategy and product-market action programs.[15]

Types of Audits

Audits are normally conducted for such areas as the SBU's marketing environment, objectives and strategy, planning and control systems, organization, productivity, and individual marketing activities such as sales and advertising. These areas are shown in Exhibit 19.11 with examples of the kinds of data needed and serve as the basis for the discussion that follows.

- The **marketing environment audit** requires an analysis of the firm's present and future environment with respect to its macro components, as discussed in Chapter 3. The intent is to identify the more significant trends to see how they affect the firm's customers, competitors, channel intermediaries, and suppliers.

- The **objectives and strategy audit** calls for an assessment of how appropriate these internal factors are, given current major environmental trends and any changes in the firm's resources.

- The unit's **planning and control system audit** evaluates the adequacy of the systems that develop the firm's product-market entry action plans and the control and reappraisal process. The audit also evaluates the firm's new-product development procedures.

- The **organization audit** deals with the firm's overall structure (can it meet the changing needs of the marketplace?); how the marketing department is organized (can it accommodate the planning requirements of the firm's assortment of brands?); and the extent of synergy between the various marketing units (are there good relations between sales and merchandising?).

Exhibit 19.11

SOME MAJOR AREAS COVERED IN A MARKETING AUDIT AND QUESTIONS CONCERNING EACH FOR A CONSUMER GOODS COMPANY

Audit Area	Examples of questions to be answered
Marketing environment	What opportunities and/or threats derive from the firm's present and future environment; that is, what technological, political, and social trends are significant? How will these trends affect the firm's target markets, competitors, suppliers, and channel intermediaries? Which opportunities/threats emerge from within the firm?
Objectives and strategy	How logical are the company's objectives, given the more significant opportunities/threats and its relative resources? How valid is the firm's strategy, given the anticipated environment, including the actions of competitors?
Planning and control system	Does the firm have adequate and timely information about consumers' satisfaction with its products? With the actions of competitors? With the services of intermediaries? Is the new product development process effective and efficient?
Organization	Does the organization structure fit the evolving needs of the marketplace? Can it handle the planning needed at the individual product/brand level?
Marketing productivity	How profitable are each of the firm's products/brands? How effective and efficient are each of its major marketing activities?
Marketing functions	How well does the product line meet the line's objectives? How well do the products/brands meet the needs of the target markets? Does pricing reflect cross elasticities, experience effects, and relative costs? Is the product readily available? What is the level of retail stockouts? What percentage of large stores carries the firm's in-store displays? Is the salesforce large enough? Is the firm spending enough on advertising?

- The **marketing productivity audit** evaluates the profitability of the company's individual products, markets (including sales territories), and key accounts. It also studies the cost-effectiveness of the various marketing activities.

- The **marketing functions audit** examines, in depth, how adequately the firm handles each of the marketing-mix elements. Questions relating to the *product* concern the attainability of the present product-line objective, the extent to which individual products fit the needs of the target markets, and whether the product line should be expanded or contracted. *Price* questions have to do with price elasticity; experience effects, relative costs, and the actions of major competitors; and consumers' perceptions of the relationship between a product's price and its value. *Distribution* questions center on coverage, functions performed, and cost-effectiveness. Questions about *advertising* focus on advertising objectives and strategies, media schedules, and the procedures used to develop advertising objectives and strategies, media schedules, and the procedures used to develop advertising messages. The audit of the salesforce covers its objectives, role, size, coverage, organization, and duties plus the quality of its selection, training, motivation, compensation, and control activities.

- The company's **ethical audit** evaluates the extent to which the company engages in ethical and socially responsible marketing. Clearly this audit goes well beyond monitoring to make sure the firm is well within the law in its market behavior. If the company has a written code of ethics, then the main purpose of this audit is to make certain that it is disseminated, understood, and practiced.

- The **product manager audit**, especially in consumer goods companies, seeks to determine whether product managers are channeling their efforts in the best ways possible. They are queried on what they're doing versus what they *ought* to be doing. They are also asked to rate the extent to which various support units were helpful.[16]

TAKE-AWAYS

- Most managers and entrepreneurs are evaluated primarily on the results they deliver. Effective design of control systems, whether for strategic control or for marketing performance measurement, helps ensure the delivery of planned results. A step-by-step process for doing so is provided in this chapter.

- Control systems that deliver the right information—in a timely manner and in media, formats, and levels of aggregation that users need and can easily use—can be important elements for establishing competitive advantage. Four key questions that designers of such systems should address are discussed in this chapter.

- From time to time, it is useful to step back from day-to-day results and take a longer view of marketing performance for a company or an SBU. A marketing audit, as outlined in this chapter, is a useful tool for conducting such an assessment.

Self-diagnostic questions to test your ability to apply the analytical tools and concepts in this chapter to marketing decision making may be found at this book's website at www.mhhe.com/mullins05.

ENDNOTES

1. Based on "Briefly....," *USA Today*, April 10, 1991, p. 28; Sam Walton, *Sam Walton: Made in America* (New York: Doubleday, 1992), pp. 85–86, 118, 212–27; David Smith, "One Step Ahead," *Arkansas Gazette*, September 30, 1991, pp. 7–9; Bill Saporito, "What Sam Walton Taught America," *Fortune*, May 4, 1992, p. 104; Wal-Mart's *1996 Annual Report*; Patricia Sellers, "Can Wal-Mart Get Back the Magic?" *Fortune*, April 29, 1996, p. 130; D. R. Stewart, "Wal-Mart Set to Open in China," *Arkansas Democrat-Gazette*, August 8, 1996, p. B1; and information from the company website at www.walmart-stores.com.

2. For a discussion of Kmart's new centralized replenishment system, see "Remote Control," *The Economist*, May 29, 1993, p. 90.

3. Sellers, "Can Wal-Mart Get Back the Magic?" p. 132.

4. Bill Saporito, "A Week aboard the Wal-Mart Express," *Fortune*, August 24, 1992. P. 77.

5. Calmetta Coleman, "Gap Inc. Stumbles as Respected CEO Loosens Reins," *The Wall Street Journal*, September 7, 2000, p. B4; Heesun Wee, "The Challenge in Store for Gap," *BusinessWeek Online*, October 9, 2002.

6. Robert S. Kaplan and David P. Norton, "Putting the Balanced Scorecard to Work," *Harvard Business Review*, September–October 1993.

7. Jeremy Mann, "How to Steal the Best Ideas Around," *Fortune*, October 19, 1992, p. 102.

8. Toddi Gutner, "Better Your Business: Benchmark It," *BusinessWeek Online*, April 27, 1998.

9. Terrence P. Paré, "A New Tool for Managing Costs," *Fortune*, June 14, 1993, p. 124.

10. Tere Hamm, "Way Down—In the Valley Commerce One Is Working to Escape from the Ranks of Tech Zombies," *BusinessWeek Online*, February 3, 2003.

11. Bernard J. Jaworski, "Toward a Theory of Marketing Control: Environmental Context, Control Types, and Consequences," *Journal of Marketing*, July 1988, p. 24.

12. "The Promise of Reengineering," Fortune, May 3, 1993, p. 94. This article is based on excerpts from Michael Hammer and James Champy, *Reengineering the Corporation: A Manifesto for Business Revolution* (New York: Harper Collins, 1993)

13. Allan Chernoff, "interview transcript—Amazon.com—Chairman and CEO," *CNNfn: Street Sweep,* January 23, 2003, 15:00; Allison Linn, "Amazon Striving to Widen Its Reach; E-Tailer Broadens Horizon from Book Trade to Everything," *Rocky Mountain News,* December 16, 2002; Neil Buckley, "Amazon Fights Back to Prove Pessimists Wrong," *Financial Times (FT.Com),* July 21, 2002.

14. Activity based accounting is particularly helpful to managers in determining product profitability since it allocates costs to products more accurately than traditional methods by breaking down overhead costs more precisely. See Paré, "A New Tool," p. 125.

15. Eric N. Berkowitz, Roger A. Kerin, Steven W. Hartley, and William Rudelius, *Marketing* (Burr Ridge, IL: Richard D. Irwin, 1994), pp. 630–32.

16. John A. Quelch, Paul W. Farris, and James M. Oliver, "The Product Manager Audit," *Harvard Business Review,* March–April 1987, p. 30. Based on their research, these authors conclude that product managers spend too much time on routine matters such as those relating to promotion execution and too little on product design and development.

INDEX

A

Aaby, Nels Erik, 293
Aaker, David A., 62, 266, 445, 446
Abell, D. F., 196
Abraham, Magia, 351
A.C. Nielsen, 337, 482
Accessory equipment, 149
Account management policies, 344
Achievers (psychographic
        segment), 124
Achrol, Ravi Singh, 29, 62, 404,
        411, 417
ACORN, 166
Acquisition product, 309
ACT software, 167, 347
Action plans, 470–471
Activity-based costing (ABC),
        277, 480
Adaptability, 230–231
Adapters (psychographic segment), 124
Adidas, 420
Adler, Robert, 167
Administered VMS, 316, 318
Administrative relationships, 451–452
Adoption
    categories of, 95–96
    comparison of adoption rate for
        cellular phones/personal
        computers, 97
    process, 94, 95
    rate of, 94–95
Advertising
    budgets, 335–337
    consumer buying behavior
        and, 118
    cooperative programs, 322
    creative strategy development,
        340–341
    defined, 328
    ethics in, 342
    examples of promotional
        activities, 329
    expenditures, 328–329
    IBM, 31, 32–33

Advertising—*Cont.*
    Integrated marketing
        communication (IMC) and,
        328, 330
    Internet, 369–371
    marketing functions audit and, 494
    mass-market penetration and
        media, 398
    mature markets and, 436
    measuring results, 341–343
    media choices, 337–340
    merits of, 334
    objectives, 335
    product life cycle stages and, 101
    as promotional tool, 332
    RedEnvelope and, 3
    social class and, 126
Aeppel, Timothy, 253
Affiliate deals, 369
Africa; *see also* African
        Communications Group (ACG);
        Tanzania Telecommunications
        Company Limited (TTCL)
    Coca-Cola and, 438
    demographic environment and, 69
    ethics and, 79
African Communications Group
        (ACG); *see also* Laguë, Côme;
        Monique, Maddy
    forecasting and, 155, 157–158, 161
    idea and development of, 152–153
    statistical methods of forecasting
        and, 156
Age (demographic descriptor), 185
Age of Us, 70
Agent middlemen, 22, 302, 306, 311,
        315, 345, 400
Agfa, 86
AIDS/HIV, 69, 292
Air France, 6
Airborne Express, 3, 13
Airbus, 254
Airline industry, 75
AirTouch, 84
Alcar Group, Inc., 55

Alcatel, 228
All commodity volume (ACV), 299
All-in-one markets, 372
All Sport, 187
Allowances, 289
Alreck, Pamela L., 178
Amazon.com, 303, 376, 377
    branding and, 250
    business to consumers sales and,
        26, 380
    collaborative filtering and, 360
    "cookies" and, 340
    differentiation and, 201, 202
    distribution channel decisions
        and, 304
    expansion and, 48
    first-mover advantage and,
        259, 365
    implementation/control and, 455
    marketing databases and, 164–165
    mass-market penetration and,
        398–399
    music and, 363
    new economy and, 356
    pioneer strategy and, 406
    price and, 228
    reliability and, 426
    repeat customers, 304
    search for information and, 113
    strategy reassessment and, 485
America Online
    affiliate deals and, 369
    first-mover advantage and, 365
    new economy and, 356
    portal deals and, 339
American Airlines, 26, 88, 89
American Association for Public
        Opinion Research, 167
American Express, 33, 226–227, 250
American Marketing Association
        (AMA)
    code of ethics and, 46, 63–64, 167
    definition of marketing, 28
    definition of sales promotion, 349
AMR Research Inc., 357

Analogy, 158–159
Analyzer strategy
    banking industry and, 227
    competitive strategy differences
        and, 229–230
    distribution channel decisions
        and, 300
    environment and, 233, 234
    global competitors and, 227
    implementation/control and, 451,
        452, 457, 459, 461
    mature markets and, 421, 429
    Pillsbury Company and, 240
    service businesses and, 227
    as strategic type, 223–225
Andean Common Market
    (ANDEAN), 73
Anderson, Carl R., 417
Anderson, Erin, 151, 325
Anderson, James C., 284, 325
Andreasen, Alan R., 28
Andrews, Katherine Z., 61
Annual requirements contract, 142
Annual Statement Studies, 171
"Annual Survey of Buying Power"
    (*Sales and Marketing
    Management*), 161
Ansberry, Clare, 253
Ante, Spencer E., 61, 293, 382
Anterasian, Cathy, 445
Any Given Sunday (movie), 183
Apian Software, Inc., 177
"Apparel Supplier of the Year," 183
Appeal, 340–341
Apple, 197, 259, 262, 365
Applegate, Lynda M., 381
Application segments, 437
Aquafina, 47
Area structure, 464
Arens, William F., 351
Arm & Hammer, 48, 254, 420
Armstrong, Gary, 29, 241
Arndt, Michael, 199, 446, 472
Arnold, Catherine, 368
Arnold, Stephen, 210, 213, 214, 218
Arthur, W. Brian, 382
Asia
    Coca-Cola and, 438
    demographic environment and,
        69, 70
    deregulation and, 75
    diversification and firms in, 50
    General Electric and, 48
    Star TV in, 198

Asia—*Cont.*
    statistical methods of forecasting
        and, 156
    VALS system and, 188
    Wal-Mart in, 474
Asia-Pacific Economic Cooperation
    (APEC), 73
Aspiration/expectation level, 115
Assael, Henry, 117, 128
Associated Grocers, 317, 318
Association of South-East Asian
    Nations (ASEAN), 73
Assumptions, 161, 162
Assurance, 248, 424
AT&T, 227, 356, 462
Attention, 120, 341
Attitudes, 114, 115, 121–123
Attributes
    customer preferences and, 211–212
    determinant, 207–208, 209–210,
        215, 217
    kinds of, 205
    perceptual, 205–206
    physical, 217
    product decisions and, 243
Auctions, 142–143, 144, 148
    new economy and, 363
    pricing and, 235, 282–283
Audits; *see* Marketing audits
Autobytel, 365
Autocar, 184
Automobile industry
    analyzer strategy and, 234
    pricing decisions and, 279,
        290, 292
Avis, 318
Awareness, 94, 162, 264
AZT (drug treatment for AIDS), 292

B

Babson College, 209
Baby boomers, 126
Backer Spielvogel & Bates ad
    agency, 123
Backward integration, 50, 317
Bait-and-switch, 286
Baker, Michael J., 199
Baker, Stephen, 103, 104
Banking industry, 227, 242–243, 315
    implementation/control and, 457
    Internet and, 372
    low-cost position and, 428
Banner ads, 339, 369

Baptist Medical Systems—HMO,
    Inc., 316
Barnes and Noble, 201–202
Barnett, F. William, 177
Barney, Jay B., 62
Barter, 288
Bartlett, Christopher A., 472
Bass, Frank M., 178
Bausch & Lomb, 399–400
Baxter Diagnostics, Inc., 430
BEA Systems, 33
Bednarz, Ann, 352
Behavioral analysis, 348
Behavioral descriptors, 187–189
BehaviorScan, 342
Beijing Optical, 400
Belch, George E., 341
Belch, Michael A., 341
Bell, Marie, 158, 160
Bellizzi, Joseph A., 151
Belvedere vodka, 225–226
Ben Franklin, 317
Benchmarking, 479
Benefits
    consumer buying behavior and,
        117–118
    defined, 244
    differentiation and, 229
    exchange relationships and, 10–11
    positioning and, 208, 216
    product design decisions and, 244
    sought, 187
Bennetton, 248
Bergen, Mark E., 293, 417, 446
Bergstrom, Robin Y., 151
Berkman, Robert I., 171
Berkowitz, Eric N., 137, 495
Berman, Dennis K., 383
Bernath, Ratma, 266
Bernenbeim, Ronald E., 45
Bernoulli Box, 9, 16
Bernstein, Jodie, 363
Bernstein, Peter L., 177
Berry, Leonard L., 248, 425, 427, 446
Berthon, Jean-Paul, 325
Berthon, Pierre, 325
Beta Group, 380
Bharadwaj, Sundar J., 417
Bias
    collector, 174–175
    in forecasting, 162
    market research and, 167
Bicycle industry, 101
Bidder's Edge, 113

Big Brother (TV program), 326–327
Big Brother 2 (TV program), 326
Billboards, 338
Billings, Hilary, 2, 5, 9
Birnbaum, Jeffrey H., 293
Bitner, Mary Jo, 61, 128, 151, 241, 427, 446
BizBuyer.com, 302
Black and Decker, 149
Blackberry, 365
Blackmon, Douglas, 351
Blattberg, Robert C., 167
Blazer brands, 66
Bleeke, Joel A., 82
Bloch, Peter H., 267
Blockbuster Video, 369–370
Bloom, Paul N., 167
Bloomberg, 359
Bloomingdale's, 210, 213, 214
Blucker, Samuel E., 472
Blue Mountain Arts, 294
Blue Ribbon Sports, 180–181, 182, 193–194; *see also* Bowerman, Bill; Knight, Phil; Nike brand
BMW, 6, 312
    advertising and, 343
    branding and, 250
    generic category levels and, 86
    Johnson Controls Inc. and, 418
    mature markets and, 436
    positioning and, 203, 209, 211
Boeing
    empowered teams, 462
    line extensions and, 254
    line stretching and, 254
Bonoma, Thomas V., 150
Booz, Allen & Hamilton, 256, 386
Borders, 485
Bose, 285
Boston Consulting Group (BCG), 51–52
Bots, shopping, 372
"Bots" software, 113
Boulding, William, 417
Bowerman, Bill, 180, 182, 183, 184, 187, 190, 193, 194, 196
Boyd, Harper W., Jr., 61, 417
Boynton, Andrew C., 198, 241
BP, 131, 318
BPA International, 337
Brady, Diane, 432, 446
Branch, Shelly, 128
Brand development indices (BDIs), 161

Brand New: How Entrepreneurs Earned Consumers' Trust from Wedgwood to Dell (Koehn), 186
Branding, 248–251
Brand(s)
    consumer buying behavior and, 114, 115, 121
    extensions, 254
    fighting, 407
    flanker, 407, 431
    loyalty, 116
    mark, 248
    multidimensional scaling and, 217
    name, 248
    new economy marketing applications for building, 368–371
    private-label, 438
    product decisions and, 248–251
    quality reputation of, 424
    Red Bull, 186
    RedEnvelope and, 3
    software for development of, 248
Brandt, Richard, 472
Branson, Richard, 85
Brauchli, Marcus, 141
Break-even analysis, 280, 281
Break-even volume, 280–281
Brekke, Dan, 28
Bribery, 141
Bridgestone Corp., 252, 253, 351
Bristol-Meyers Squibb, 478
Britches, 210, 213, 214
British Leyland, 211
British Market Research Association, 167
British Telecommunications, 344
BroadVision Inc., 372
Brochureware, 368, 369, 376
Brokers, 302, 306, 315
Brooke, Lindsay, 218
Brown, Eryn, 399
Brown, Shona L., 267
Bruss, Jill, 186
Bryan, Dawn, 61
B2B (business-to-business), 356–357
B2C (business-to-consumer), 357
Buckley, Neil, 495
Buckman, Rebecca, 383
Budgets
    marketing plans and, 471
    measuring results and, 489

Buena Vista Winery website, 37
Buglass, Craig, 181
Bundle, 292
Burberry, 251
Burger King, 89, 314, 318
Burley, James, 267
Burlington Northern Santa Fe Railroad, 44
Burns, Greg, 325
Burrows, Peter, 472
Business-level strategy, 15, 18, 40, 42, 455
Business model, 380
Business Periodicals Index, 171
Business services, 149–150
    product decisions and, 246
Business strategies, 220–240; *see also* Analyzer strategy; Defender strategy; Prospector strategy; Reactor strategy
    competitive strategies and single-business firms/start-ups, 225–226
    competitive strategy and marketing program fit, 239–240
    distribution policies and, 238
    environment and, 232–235
    generic business-level competitive strategies, 223–225
    for global competitors, 227–228
    how competitive strategies differ, 229–232
    influence over marketing decisions, 235–239
    Internet and, 228–229
    pricing policies and, 238
    product policies and, 237
    promotion policies and, 238–239
    for service businesses, 226–227
    3M, 220–223
BuSpar, 478
Buy-back allowances, 322
Buyback arrangements, 288, 314
Buyer's auction, 282–283
Buying centers, organizational, 135–137
Buying offices, 315
Buying Power Index (BPI), 161
Buying situation, 189
Buzzell, Robert D., 62, 241, 416, 417
Byrne, John A., 61, 472
Byrnes, Nanette, 128

C

Cable & Wireless Communications, 227
CACI, 165–166
Cadwalader, Wickersham, and Taft, 66
Calantone, Roger J., 178
Call centers, 346, 347, 373
Call to action, 341
Caltrider, Juli, 367
Campanelli, Melissa, 325
Campbell, P. B., 103
Campbell, 437
Canada, 46, 73, 342, 474
Canon Europe Ltd., 385
Canon, Inc., 22, 384–385, 385–386,
        396, 398
    mass-market penetration and, 395
Carbon dioxide, 77
Carey, John, 82
Cargill, 131
Carnation, 73
Carnival Corporation, 106, 108
Carnival Cruise Line, 106, 107, 108
Carrefour, 90
Carroll, J. Douglas, 218
Cash cows, 53, 231
Cash discounts, 289
Casual Corner, 210, 213, 214
Catalog marketers, 164, 303
Catalogs, customized, 361
Categorization, 120
Category development indices
        (CDIs), 161
Cateora, Phillip R., 246, 261, 325
Caterpillar, 198, 323, 423
Cecil Gee, 67
Cellular telephone business, 84–85; see
        also Mobile telephone service
    adoption factors and, 95
    comparison of adoption rate for
            cellular phones/personal
            computers, 97
    markets vs. industries and, 88
    Porter's competitive forces and,
            89–90, 91
    product life cycle stages and,
            100, 101
Central European Free Trade
        Agreement (CEFTA), 73
Centralization, 457, 458
Cents-off coupons, 289
Cereal market, 92
Certified Grocers, 318
Cespedes, Frank V., 322

Chaebol (Korean), 50
Chain ratio forecast, 160
Chambers, John C., 177
Champy, James, 495
Chandler, Susan, 325
Channel conflict, 323–324
Channel design, 295–296
Channel management, 295–296
Channels of distribution, 22; see also
        Distribution channels
Charles Schwab, 374
Chat (software), 347
Chernoff, Allan, 495
Chew, Bruce, 267
Chiagouris, Larry, 241
China
    Beijing Optical and, 400
    economic environment and, 74
    ethics and, 79
    Huawei Technologies Co. of, 228
    intellectual property and, 74
    physical environment and, 77
    television advertising and, 344
Chintagunta, Pradeep K., 284
Choice criteria, 114, 140, 187
Chrysler, 8, 73, 167
Chu, Wujin, 151
Churchill, Gilbert A., Jr., 352
Churches, 7
Ciaramitaro, Mark, 295
Circuit City, 30
Cisco Systems, 26, 87, 228, 409
    follower strategy and, 409
    new economy and, 356
CitiCorp, 464
Claritas, Inc., 171, 188, 189, 339
    PRIZM service, 165, 187
Claritin, 478
Clark, Bruce H., 103
Clark, Kim, 266
Clark, Kristen, 82
Clayton Act, 324
Click-streams, 364, 371
Click&Buy, 372
Cliffhangers, 369
Climo, Michael, 373
Clockworx, 354–355
CNN, 343
Co-op Communications, 341
Co-opLink™, 341
Cobranding, 250
Coca-Cola, 186, 187, 264, 317, 318
    brand, 250
    follower strategy and, 415

Coca-Cola—Cont.
    global market expansion and, 438
Code stores, 66, 67
Coercive power, 319
Cohen, Morris A., 267
Cohen, Stephen S., 288
Coleman, Calmetta, 495
Colgate-Palmolive, 123, 183, 233, 265
Collaborative filtering, 360
Collaborative networks, 462
Collector bias, 174–175
Collegiate Brand Managers, 186
Colley, Russell H., 351
Collins, Jim, 259, 365, 382
Collura, Meredith, 381
ColorStay Lipcolor (Revlon), 119
ComAlliance, 3, 13, 18
Commerce Bancorp, 432
Commerce One, 482
CommerceOne.com, 149
Commercial sources, 112
Commercialization, 265
Compaq, 8, 31
    follower strategy and, 391
    Hewlett-Packard and, 449
    pioneer strategy and, 407
Comparison, 208
Compensation, 288, 348, 454
Compensatory, 121
Competition; see also Business
        strategies; Market-
        attractiveness/competitive-
        position matrix/factors
    analyzing costs and prices of, 278
    business-level competitive
            strategies, 15, 223–225
    business's competitive position, 54
    cell phone service providers and, 85
    changing and industry evolution,
            91–92
    competitive strategies and single-
            business firms/start-ups,
            225–226
    competitive strategy and marketing
            program fit, 239–240
    contingency planning and, 491
    within cruise industry, 107
    declining markets and, 439, 440,
            441–445
    differentiation and, 202
    external environment and, 16
    how competitive strategies differ,
            229–232
    IBM and, 31–32

Competition—*Cont.*
  implementation/control and, 451–454
  industries and, 93
  industries vs. markets and, 86
  intelligence gathering and ethics, 93
  Internet and, 228–229
  Iomega Corporation and, 16
  market orientation and, 37
  marketing managers and, 15
  marketing plans and, 468–469
  marketing strategy and, 42
  markets and, 87
  mature markets and, 421–422
  Porter's competitive forces, 88–91
  positioning and, 207, 214
  pricing decisions and, 281–283
  product availability and, 299
  product design decisions and, 244–252
  product life cycles and, 99–100, 103
  relative market share and, 53
  service businesses and, 226–227
  strategic business units (SBUs) and, 58–59, 60
  strategic marketing programs and, 222
  strategies for global competitors, 227–228
  strategy and, 40, 41
  3M business strategies and, 221–222
Competitive intelligence (CI), 93, 166, 407
Competitive parity, 281, 331
Competitive situation, 91
Competitor intelligence, 376
Compiled databases, 166
Component materials/parts, 148
Comprehension, 120
Computer-aided design, 183
Computers; *see also* Internet
  comparison of adoption rate for cellular phones/personal computers, 97
  market segmentation and, 189
  positioning and, 217
Concentric diversification, 50
Conditions of demand, 439–440
Conformance, 247
Conformance to specifications, 422
Confrontation strategy, 402, 403, 404, 405, 407–408
Conglomerate diversification, 50

Conjoint analysis, 212, 217, 248
  perceived customer value and, 284
Conoco Phillips, 208
Consumer buying behavior, 106–128
  cruise industry and, 106–108
  demographics/lifestyle and, 123–124
  high-involvement purchase decisions and, 109–116, 117–119
  low-involvement purchase decisions and, 116–119
  need/attitudes and, 121–123
  perception/memory and, 119–121
  social influences and, 125–127
Consumer experience process, 366
Consumer goods and services
  customers and, 7
  declining markets and, 444
  distribution channel decisions and, 305–306, 307
  marketing-strategy implications of classifying, 246
  mature markets and, 434, 437
  pioneer strategy and, 389
  positioning and, 201
Consumer Goods Pricing Act, 291
Consumer need, 87
Consumer promotions, 321, 349
Contact management software, 347
Contests, 349
Contingency planning, 490–492
Contract manufacturing, 314
Contraction strategy, 402, 403, 405, 408
Contractual entry modes, 313
Contractual VMS, 316–318
Contribution accounting, 479–480
Convenience samples, 174
Cooke, Robert A., 61
Cookies, 340, 364
Cooper, Robert G., 262, 267
Cooper, Robin, 267, 293, 472
Cooperative advertising programs, 322, 349
Cooperative organizations, 313
Cooperman, Karen, 81
Copeland, Douglas, 81
Coproduction, 314, 374
Copy platform, 340–341
Corporate strategy, 40–42, 42–56
  allocating resources and, 51–56
  growth and, 48–51
  IBM and, 15
  mission and, 43–46

Corporate strategy—*Cont.*
  objectives and, 46–48
  scope and, 43–46
Corporate VMS, 316–317
Cosby, Bill, 436
Cost analysis, 348
Cost leadership, 202
Cost per acquisition, 340, 343
Cost per order, 343
Cost per thousand (CPM), 337, 339
Cost-plus pricing, 278–279
Cost reductions, 387
Costs
  global competition and, 23
  manufacturing, 23
  strategic business units (SBUs) and, 47
  who pays, 22–23
Council of American Survey Research Organizations, 167
Countertrade, 287–288, 314
Coupons, 289–290, 350
Coxe, Dale O., 177, 178
Coy, Peter, 472
Coyle, Mary L., 417
Cracker Jack, 50
Crandall, Bob, 89
Cravens, David W., 332
Crawford, C. Merle, 218, 266, 267
Cray computers, 187–188
Critical success factors, 92
Crockett, Roger O., 29, 128, 241
Cronin, J. Joseph, 446
Cross-elasticity, 291–292
Crossen, Cynthia, 167
Cruise industry
  benefits offered, 107
  competition within, 107
  consumer buying behavior and, 108, 121–122
  future challenges, 107–108
  growth and, 106–107, 108
  high-involvement purchase decisions and, 109, 111, 112, 113, 114, 115
  traditional target audience for, 107
  types of cruises, 107
Crush, Peter, 352
Crystal Cruises, 107
Culture, 125–126
Cunard cruise line, 106, 107
Customary price, 285
Customer relationship management (CRM), 164, 165

Customer Relationship Management
  Software, 347
Customer service(s), 366
  after the sale, 11
  customer perceptions of service
    quality, 426–427
  incentives to improve, 323
  Internet and, 373–374
  personal selling and, 346–347
  postsale, 406
Customer(s); *see also* Consumer
    buying behavior; Needs/wants;
    Organizational buying
  analysis, 16–17
  complaints, 11
  exchange relationships and, 7
  focus, 5, 9–10
  insight, 366
  on keeping current, 56
  retention, 373
  sales analysis by, 488
  segment pricing, 290
  support, 366
  value, 269
  value management, 423
  value of, 430–431
Customization, 361
Czinkota, Michael R., 472

D

DaimlerChrysler, 73, 317, 318
  Johnson Controls Inc. and,
    418, 419
Daniels, John D., 199
Danone, 159
Dant, Shirish P., 151
Data-mining, 166
Databases, 164–166
Datawash.com, 341
Davis, Scott, 293, 417, 446
Dawson, Chester, 241
Day, George S., 29, 62, 103, 104,
    196, 417
Days Inn, 226
De Chernatony, Leslie, 266
Deciders, 135
Declining markets, 438–445
  challenges in, 420
  divestment/liquidation and, 441
  marketing strategies for remaining
    competitors and, 441–445
  relative attractiveness of, 439–441
  strategies for, 438–439

Defender strategy; *see also*
    Differentiated defender strategy
  banking industry and, 227
  competitive strategy differences
    and, 230, 231
  distribution channel decisions
    and, 300
  environment and, 234
  flexibility and, 312
  implementation/control and, 451,
    454, 457
  mature markets and, 421, 429
  as strategic type, 223–225
Delhagen, Kate, 377
Delivery, 366
Dell, Michael, 427
Dell Computer, 22, 26, 31, 32
  follower strategy and, 413
  Hewlett-Packard and, 449
  Internet and, 373, 374
  pioneer strategy and, 407
  product life cycle stages and, 101
  warranties and, 252
Demand collection system, 372
Demand curve, 274–276
Demographic environment, 69–70
Demographics
  consumer buying behavior and, 123
  declining markets and, 439
  geodemographic descriptors and,
    186–187
  Internet and, 376
  market segmentation and, 173,
    184–186
  organizational vs. consumer markets
    and, 133
  target marketing and, 173, 189
Dempsey, Michael, 165
Denver Zoo, 373
Deployment, 344
Deregulation, 75
Derived demand, 133–134
Determinant attributes, 207–208,
    209–210, 215, 217
Deutschman, Alan, 472
Devine, Richard, 267
Devlin, Susan J., 446
Diageo PLC, 250, 251, 320
Dickson, Peter R., 82, 266
Differential pricing, 290–291,
    291–292
Differentiated defender strategy
  competitive strategy differences
    and, 230, 231

Differentiated defender strategy—*Cont.*
  distribution channel decisions
    and, 300
  distribution policies and, 238
  environment and, 233, 234–235
  implementation/control and, 452,
    453, 454, 455, 456, 457,
    459, 461
  mature markets and, 422
  pricing and, 238, 273
  product policies and, 237
  promotion policies and, 238
  3M and, 228
Differentiation, 201–203
  on basis of quality, 247
  Caterpillar and, 423
  Domino's Pizza and, 215
  environment and, 234–235
  follower strategy and, 413
  generic business-level competitive
    strategies and, 223
  Internet and, 228–229
  mature markets and, 421,
    422–427
  positioning and, 201
  pricing policies and, 238
  product decisions and, 247
  service and, 426
Diffusion of innovation, 94,
    96–97, 157
Digital Darwinism (Schwartz), 365
Digital networks, 327
Digital signatures, 372
Dillon, William R., 178
Direct costing, 479, 480, 481
Direct marketing, 337, 338, 343
Direct selling, 134, 303
Dischamps, Jean-Phillipe, 266
Discount price policies, 282
Discounted cash flow model, 55–56
Discovery Channel, 184
Discriminant analysis, 217
Discriminatory pricing, 290–291
Disintermediation, 361, 363
Disney, 107, 349
Displays, in-store, 102
Distribution; *see also* Distribution
    channel decisions; Distribution
    channels
  business strategies and, 236, 238
  consumer buying behavior
    and, 119
  product life cycle stages and, 102
  RedEnvelope and, 3

Distribution channel decisions, 294–325; *see also* Distribution; Distribution channels
  channel conflicts and, 323–324
  consumer/industrial goods alternative channels, 305–306
  cost-effectiveness and, 300, 310–311
  customer service requirements and, 299–300, 307–309
  facilitating agencies and, 301
  flexibility and, 301, 312
  global markets and, 313–315
  Hallmark Cards and, 294–295, 301, 305, 312, 323
  institutions and, 301–304
  legal constraints and, 324
  market information and, 300, 309–310
  measurement and, 298
  merchant wholesalers and, 301
  middlemen and, 301, 302, 306, 314–315
  multichannel distribution and, 312–313
  multifirm marketing channels, 296–297
  nonstore retailing, 303–304
  objectives and, 297–301, 307–313
  postsale service objectives and, 309–310
  product availability and, 299, 307–309
  promotions and, 300, 309–310
  retailers and, 301, 302–303
  for services, 315–316
  sources of power and, 319–320
  strategies for, 320–321
  supply chain management and, 311–312
  trade promotions and, 321–323
  vertical marketing systems (VMSs) and, 316–319, 319–320
Distribution channel markups, 277
Distribution channels, 22, 296; *see also* Distribution; Distribution channel decisions
  for agricultural materials, 147
  follower strategy and, 414–415
  industries vs. markets and, 86
  low-cost position and, 428
  market expansion strategy and, 437–438
  marketing functions audit and, 494

Distribution channels—*Cont.*
  for natural materials, 147
  new economy and, 361
  penetration strategy and, 434
  pioneer strategy and, 389, 406
  product decisions and, 263
  Wal-Mart, 475
Distribution coverage, 162
Distributor, 301, 359
Diversification, 48, 49–50, 51
DMPlaza, 337
Dochat, Tom, 199
DoCoMo, 371
Dodd, AnnMarie, 81
Dogs, 53
Dolan, Robert J., 178, 293, 417
Dombey, Daniel, 293
Domestic geographic markets, 437
Domestic middlemen, 314–315
Domino's Pizza, 215
Donaldson, Gordon, 61, 241
Donath, Bob, 150
Done, Kevin, 293
Dong, H. K., 446
Donnelley's DQI database, 165
Doorway pages, 369
Dot.coms, 355, 356, 379–380
  organizational structures and, 458
  profitability analysis and, 479, 480
Dow, 464
Dress Barn, 210, 213, 214
Drucker, Peter, 5
Dual (two-channel) distribution, 312
Dumaine, Brian, 267, 472
Dun and Bradstreet Million Dollar Directory, 171
DuPont, 240, 479
Durability, 247, 422
Duracell, 254
Dwyer, F. Robert, 150, 151, 325
Dychtwald, Ken, 81
Dynamic pricing, 372
Dysart, Joe, 383

E

E-Commerce; *see also* Internet
  categories of, 26
  IBM and, 32
  technological trends and, 77
E-exchanges, 142–143
E-hubs, 302
E-mail, 339, 340, 370, 371
E-stamp.com, 373

E-Steel.com, 138
EasyJet, 75, 187, 268
  new economy and, 362
  pricing decisions and, 278
EBags.com, 369
EBay, 26, 113, 347, 380
  first-mover advantage and, 365
  pioneer strategy and, 390
Economic environment, 72–73
Economic power, 319
Economic value, 284
Economic value added (EVA), 55, 454
Economies of scale, 277–278, 389
Economist, The, 184, 338
EDI channels, 357
Edison Brothers, 66
Edmonson, Gail, 446
Education (demographic descriptor), 185
Edwards, Cliff, 104
Edwards, Robin, 354
Effectiveness, 230
Efficiency, 23–24, 25, 230
Efficient consumer response (ECR) programs, 311
Egg, 242–243
  differentiation and, 247
  multichannel strategy, 242
  new product development process decisions and, 255
  positioning and, 247
Einhorn, Bruce, 241
Eisenhardt, Kathleen M., 267
El-Ansary, Adel I., 301, 325
Elasticity, 275–276
Electronic data interchange (EDI), 356
Electronics, 76
Elgin, Ben, 76, 151, 241
Elstrom, Peter, 103, 472
Emerson Electric, 232, 239
Emotional appeal, 341
Empathic design, 248, 249
Empathy, 248, 424
Empowerment, 462
Encirclement strategy, 410, 411, 412, 415, 416
Encyclopedia of Associations, 171
Endorsements, 208
Eng, Paul, 9
Entice! (software), 347
Entrepreneurial start-ups, 59–60, 225–226, 239, 458, 462

Environment; *see also* Environmental
    context
  business strategies and, 232–235
  external, 15, 16–17, 43
  physical, 77–78, 79
  product attributes and, 114
  product decisions and, 261
Environmental context, 67–81, 91;
    see also Environment;
    Macroenvironment
  demographic environment, 69–70
  economic environment, 72–73
  macro trend analysis, 79–80
  marketing audits and, 493
  political/legal environment, 73–75
  prioritizing trend categories,
    78–79
  proenvironment, 208
  sociocultural environment, 70–72
  strategic control systems and, 485
  technological environment, 75–77
Equity, 424
Ericsson, 84
ESPN, 343–344
ESPN Magazine, 183
Esthetics, 247
Ethan Allen furniture, 308
Ethical audit, 494
Ethics, 44–46
  advertising and, 342
  audits and, 494
  codes of, 46, 63–64, 93, 167
  competitive intelligence and, 93
  databases and, 166, 167
  defined, 44
  differential pricing and, 291, 292
  idea generation/screening and,
    260, 261
  importance of, 44–45
  Internet and, 113, 167, 340
  macro trend analysis and, 79
  market research and, 167
  market segmentation based on
    customer value and,
    431, 432
  new economy and, 362–365
  organizational buying and, 141
  positioning and, 215
  product decisions and, 252, 253
  promotional pricing and, 286
  slotting allowances and, 322
  statements, 45
  target marketing and, 191, 192
E*Trade, 26, 359, 369

Europe; *see also* European Union (EU);
    names of individual countries
  advertising expenditures in, 328
  Amazon.com in, 363
  branding and, 250–251
  cell phone industry and, 84–85
  Click&Buy in, 372
  Danone in, 159
  deregulation and, 75
  diversification and companies in, 50
  EasyJet airline of, 187, 268
  eBay in, 363
  economic environment and, 72, 73
  ethics and companies in, 46
  Excel Company and, 130
  Hewlett-Packard and, 449
  Johnson Controls Inc. and, 419, 438
  media in, 344
  mobile telephony and, 371
  new economy and, 356
  retail structures in, 315
  Ryan Air of, 268–269
  services and, 245
  television advertising and, 337, 344
  VALS system and, 188
  Wal-Mart in, 474
European Trade Associations, 171
European Union (EU); *see also* Europe
  free-trade agreements and, 73
  government regulation and, 74
  Internet privacy and, 364
  macro trend analysis and, 79
Eurostat, 79
Evaluating/legitimizing functions, 112
Evaluation
  adoption process and, 94, 96
  consumer buying behavior and, 115
  implementation/control and, 454
  integrated marketing
    communication plans and,
    333–334
  organizational buying and, 143–144
Evoked set, 114
Excel Company, organizational buying
    and, 130–131, 311
  decision-making process, 139
  derived demand and, 133
  long-term buyer-supplier
    relationships, 145
  selling and, 150
  trust and, 145
Exchange relationships, 5–13, 27
Exclusion/inclusion, 192
Exclusive dealing, 324

Exclusive distribution, 307–308
Exit barriers, 439, 440–441, 444–445
Expansion, 48–50
Expectation measures, 482
Expected value, 282
Experian MOSAIC database, 166
Experience curve, 278
Experiment, marketing research
    and, 173
Experimental test markets, 159
Expert power, 319
Export agents, 313
Export jobber, 315
Export management company, 315
Export merchants, 313, 315
Exporting, 313
Exposure, 119–120
Extended use strategy, 434, 435
Exxon, 318

F

Facilitating agencies, 22
Factor analysis, 217
Fahey, Liam, 29, 61, 62, 446
Family, 127
Family branding, 250
Family life cycle, 127
Faris, Charles W., 151
Farndon, Lucy, 81
Farrelly, Glen, 76
Farris, Paul W., 495
Features, 207–208, 216
  defined, 244
  goods and, 247
  product decisions and, 244, 247–248
Federal Trade Commission (FTC), 324,
    342, 363–364
FedEx, 373
Feedback
  distribution channel decisions
    and, 300
  implementation/control and, 19
  Iomega Corporation and customer, 9
  organizational buying and, 143–144
  RedEnvelope and customer, 3
Felsted, Andrea, 293
Fidelity Investments, 432
Field test market, 263
Fierman, Jaclyn, 13, 241, 446
Fighting brand, 407
Filters, 362
Financial objectives, 470

Finkelman, Daniel P., 61
Fiorina, Carly, 449, 463
Firestone Inc., 73, 351
First-mover advantage, 259, 365
Firtle, Neil H., 178
Fishbein, Martin, 121
Fisher, Brooks, 372
Fisher, Marshall L., 156, 178
Fit and finish, 423
Fitch PLC, 9
Fites, Donald V., 325
Fixed cost per unit, 276
Fixed costs, 276
Flanker (brand), 407, 431
Flanker strategy, 402, 404, 405,
    406–407
Flanking attack, 410, 411, 412,
    414–415, 416
Flextronics Corp., 74
FOB origin pricing, 286–287
Focus, 202, 223, 224
Focus groups
    FocusVision Online and, 177
    Internet and, 367
    perceived customer value and, 284
    positioning and, 209
    qualitative research and, 170–171
FocusVision Online, 177
Follower strategy, 390–391, 409–416;
    see also New product
    development; Pioneer strategy
    advantages of, 388
    determinants of success for,
        391–393
    encirclement strategy, 410, 411,
        412, 415, 416
    flanking strategy, 410, 411, 412,
        414–415, 416
    frontal attack strategy, 411–413, 416
    leapfrog strategy, 410, 411, 412,
        413–414, 416
    marketing objectives and, 409
    share growth and, 409–412,
        415–416
Ford Motor Company
    auctions and, 283
    benchmarking and, 479
    categories of E-Commerce and, 26
    customer needs/wants and, 8
    derived demand and, 134
    distribution and, 312
    focus groups and, 367
    franchise systems and, 318
    General Motors and, 102

Ford Motor Company—*Cont.*
    international trade and, 73
    physical positioning and, 203
    positioning and, 211
Ford, Neil M., 352
Forecasting
    African Communications Group
        (ACG) and, 152, 153–154
    analogy and, 158–159
    biases in, 162
    chain ratio forecast, 160
    evidence-based, 155–156
    Gap Inc. and, 156
    judgment and, 159
    keys to good, 161
    market tests and, 159–160
    marketing plans and, 468
    mathematics in, 160
    observation and, 157
    sales and diffusion of innovation
        theory, 96–97
    statistical methods, 156–157
    surveys and, 157–158
    SWAG method of, 156
    wrongness of, 154–155
Foreign middlemen, 314–315
Formalization, 457, 458, 459
Forrester Research, 377
Forslund, Jeff, 371
Fort Howard Paper, 428
Fortress/position defense strategy, 402,
    404–406, 431
Fortune magazine, 338, 379–380
Forward vertical integration, 50, 238
Four Seasons, 432–433
4Cs
    marketing plans and, 20
    what they are, 15
4 Ps; *see also* Place; Price; Product(s);
    Promotion(s)
    elements of, 18
    marketing plans and, 20–21
    marketing strategy and, 42
Foust, Dean, 253
Fowler, Geoggrey A., 352
France, 342
France Telecom, 344
Franchising, 314, 316, 317–318,
    392, 400
Frank, Steve, 103
Free goods, 322
Freedman, Felix M., 192
FreeMarkets, Inc., 138, 142, 148
Frei, Francis X., 383

Freight absorption pricing, 287
French winemakers; *see* Wine industry
Frequency, 335–336
Frito-Lay, 43, 320, 453
Frontal attack strategy, 416
Fruit of the Loom Inc., 143
Fuji, 86
Full costing, 479, 480, 481
Fuller, Joseph B., 325
Functional competencies, 455
Functional discounts, 288
Functional efficiency, 23
Functional organizational design, 457,
    458, 460
Functional performance, 422
Functional strategies, 40

G

Gale, Bradley T., 62, 241, 416, 417, 423
Gale Directory of Publications, 171
Ganesan, Shankar, 150, 151, 325
Gantt charts, 471
Gap Inc./The Gap
    casual dress trend and, 68
    feedback data and, 483
    forecasting and, 156, 161
    margins and, 489
    measuring results and, 490
    new economy and, 356
    perceptual map and, 210, 213, 214
    results and, 475
Garfinkels, 210, 213, 214
Garino, Jason, 325
Gartner, 356
Garvin, David A., 247, 293, 445, 472
Gary Fisher, 187
Gatekeepers, 135
Gates, Bill, 82
Gateway, 407
Gatignon, Hubert, 104
Gatorade, 187
General Electric, 35, 39, 250, 317
    growth strategies and, 48
    Hungary and, 74
    organizational buying and, 140
    product decisions and, 265
General Foods Corporation, 57, 434–435
General Mills Company, 92, 234, 263,
    265, 461
General Motors, 26, 73, 102, 279, 312
    Commerce One and, 482
    Johnson Controls Inc. and, 418
    market segmentation and, 183

Generation X, 70–71
Generic category, 86
Genysys Sampling System, 177
Geodemographic descriptors, 186–187
Geographic descriptors, 186
Georgeoff, David M., 177
Germany
    branding and, 250
    cell phone service providers and, 84–85
    economic environment and, 73
    ethics and, 44
    Johnson Controls Inc. and, 419
    physical environment and, 77
    strategic planning and, 35
Gersick, Connie J. G., 241
Gerstner, Lou, 32, 33, 40
Ghingold, Morry, 150
Ghoshal, Sumantra, 472
Gillette, 255, 320
Gladwell, Malcolm, 178
Glascock, Ned, 199
Glass, David, 475
GlaxoSmithKline (GSK), 326
Glazer, Rashi, 167
Glenton, Bill, 128
Global cruise industry; *see* Cruise industry
Global market(s)
    control systems and, 492–493
    exchange relationships and, 11
    Johnson Controls Inc. and, 418
    organizational designs for, 463–464
    segmentation, 197–198
Global matrix, 464
Global reach, 362
Global Scan, 123–124
Globalization
    advertising and, 343–344
    branding and, 250–251
    competition and, 23, 227–228
    distribution channel decisions and, 313–315
    economy and, 5–6
    Hallmark Cards and, 294, 295
    market orientation and, 38–39
    marketing management and, 24, 25
    mature markets and, 438
    new economy and, 361–362
    organizational buying and, 143
    PepsiCo and, 43
    pioneer strategy and, 399–400
    pricing decisions and, 287–288
    sales efforts and, 344–346

Globalization—*Cont.*
    services and, 246
    trade and, 73
Gnutella, 363
Goals, strategy and, 40, 41
Godin, Seth, 339, 351, 370, 383
Going-rate, 281
Goldberg, Stephen M., 218
Golden Valley Microwave, 240
Golder, Peter N., 417
Goldman Sachs, 66
Goldmine software, 167, 347
Good to Great and Built to Last (Collins), 365
Goods, dimensions of quality for, 247
Goods manufacturers, 6, 8
Goodstein, Ronald C., 417
Goodyear Tire and Rubber, 146, 188
Google, 76, 79, 339
Goss, Jon, 199
Government markets, 145–146
Govindarajan, Vijay, 472
GPS (global positioning satellite) technology, 356, 362
Grainger.com, 380
Great Plains Software, 36
Green, Heather, 62, 304, 325, 446, 472
Green organizations, 79
Green, Paul E., 218
Green products, 77–78
Greenberger, Robert, 141
Greene, Jay, 29, 128, 241, 352
Greenfield Online, 367
Greenhouse effect, 77, 79
Greeting card industry, 294
Greising, David, 446
Greyser, Stephen, 253
Griffin, Abbie, 178
Gross domestic product (GDP), 72
Gross rating points (GRPs), 336
Grove, Andy, 380
Growth
    Boston Consulting Group (BCG) and, 51–52
    cell phone industry and, 85
    corporate strategies for, 48–51
    cruise industry and, 106–107, 108
    opportunity and, 85
Growth markets, 196–197, 401, 402, 404, 405
Growth-share matrix, 51–52, 53
Gruca, Thomas S., 417
Gulati, Ranjay, 325
Gumbel, Peter, 383

Gurley, J. William, 338–339, 351
Gutner, Toddi, 495

H

Häagen-dazs, 250, 436
Haddad, Charles, 383
Haines, Allison, 382
Hall, William K., 445
Halliburton, Christ, 266
Halliday, Jean, 199
Hallmark Cards, 294–295, 296, 301, 305, 308, 309, 312, 323–324
Hallmark Hiya, 295
Hambrick, Donald C., 28, 237, 241
Hamel, Gary, 28, 61, 178, 241
Hamm, Steve, 29, 104
Hamm, Tere, 495
Hammer, Michael, 495
Hammond, J. S., 196
Hammond, Janice H., 178
Han, Sang-Lin, 151
Handspring, 365
Hanna Andersson, 13
Hanover Direct, 377
Hanson, Ward, 382
Hardie, Bruce G. S., 266
Hardin, Joseph, 377
Harrah's Entertainment, Inc., 370–371
Harrigan, Kathryn Rudie, 440, 446
Hart, Christopher W. L., 472
Hartley, Steven W., 137, 495
Hartmarx, 66
Harvesting, 102, 272, 273, 442–444
Hassan, Salah S., 199
Hauser, John R., 218
Hayes, H. Michael, 293
Headliner®, 341
Health care services, 316
Health maintenance organizations (HMOs), 316
Hecht's, 210, 213, 214
Hedley, Barry, 51
Heide, Jan B., 151, 325
Heileman Brewing Company, 437–438, 445
Heinz, 454
Helena Rubinstein, 438
Hello (magazine), 184
Henkoff, Ronald, 29, 241, 325, 446
Henry, David, 293, 322, 325
Henry Dreyfuss Associates, 462
Hershey, 368

Hertz, 318
Heskett, James L., 241, 472
Hewlett-Packard, 32, 86, 254, 255
    Canon, Inc. and, 384
    differentiated analyzers and, 451
    E-Services Solutions Group, 449,
        461, 463
    implementation/control and, 452,
        453, 463
    organizational structures and, 463
    reorganization for, 448–450, 463
High-definition television
        (HDTV), 159
High-margin/low-turnover, 303
Hill, Don, 151
Hill, John S., 352
Himelstein, Linda, 76, 151, 446, 472
Hirakata, Noriaki, 253
Hit or Miss, 210, 213, 214
Hitchens, R. E., 196
Ho, Teck H., 267
Hof, Robert D., 29, 399, 446, 472
Hofer, Charles W., 61
Hogan, Mark, 199
Holden, Reed K., 293
Holiday Inns, 211, 317, 318
Holland America cruise line,
        106, 107
Holmes, Stanley, 29, 128, 241
Homburg, Christian, 35, 61
Home Depot, 303
Honda, 197, 234
Honeywell MICRO SWITCH
        division, 137
Hook-pages, 369
Hoover's Online Business, 171
Hopkins, David S., 29
Horovitz, Bruce, 266
Hotels, 316
HotJobs.com, 330
Hotmail, 359
Hotmail.com, 368
Hrebiniak, Lawrence G., 241
Huawei Technologies Co., 228
Hughes, Anita, 367
Hugo Boss, 67
Hulland, John S., 267
Hungary, 74
Hunt, Shelby D., 151, 325
Hurdle, 46
Hwang, Suein, 383
Hybrid organization, 464
Hybrid system, 312–313
Hyster, 149

I

IBM; see International Business
    Machines (IBM)
Idea generation, 258, 260, 261
Ihlwan, Moon, 103
Image Promotions, 344
IMode, 356, 359, 371
Implementation/control, 19–20,
    448–471
    business-unit autonomy and,
        452–453
    evaluation and reward systems
        and, 454
    functional competencies/resource
        allocation and, 455
    global markets and, 463–464
    Hewlett-Packard and, 448–450, 452,
        453, 461
    marketing plans and, 465–471
    organizational adjustments for
        growth and market changes
        and, 462–463
    organizational/interfunctional
        factors related to, 456
    organizational structures and,
        457–461
    service organizations and, 455, 457
    shared programs/facilities and,
        453–454
    trends in organizational design and,
        461–462
Importance Scale, 172
Impulse buying, 116–117
In Style, 200
Incentives, 321–323, 348
Inclusion/exclusion, 192
Income (demographic descriptor), 185
Increasing returns to scale, 359
Independent Grocers Alliance
        (IGA), 317
India, 344
Indices, 161
Indirect costs, 479
Individual branding, 249
Industrial goods and services, 7
    declining markets and, 444
    distribution channel decisions and,
        305–306, 308–309
    mature markets and, 433–434,
        436–437
    positioning and, 201
    product availability and, 299
    product life cycle stages and, 102

Industrial markets, market
        segmentation and, 185, 188
Industries
    changing competition and evolution
        of, 91–92
    competition and, 93
    critical success factors and, 92
    defined, 86
    defining markets and, 86–88
    markets vs., 85–86
    Porter's competitive forces and,
        88–91
Inelastic, 276
Inertia, 39, 116
Influencers, 135
Informing function, 112
ING (European bank), 165
Ingersoll-Rand, 458
Ingredients, 208
Inktomi, 359
Innovation, 94
Innovators, 95
Installations, 148
Institutions, marketing, 21–22
Intangibles, 226, 245
Integrated marketing communication
        (IMC), 326–351
    advertising decisions and, 334–344
    Big Brother and, 326–327
    developing a plan for, 328, 329–334
    Larazade and, 326
    personal selling decisions and,
        344–349
    promotion mix and, 328–329, 330,
        332–333, 334
    public relations decisions and,
        350–351
    sales promotion and, 349–350
    Thorntons and, 372
Integration, 50, 120
Intel, 6, 380
Intellectual property, 74
Intelliquis, 369
Intensive distribution, 307–308
Intention-to-Buy Scale, 172
Interact Commerce Corporation, 347
Interactive Tracking Systems Inc., 368
Interest, 94, 96, 341
Internal records systems, 163–164
Internal Revenue Service, installations
        and, 148
International Business Machines
        (IBM), 30–33, 60, 197, 250
    advertising, 31, 32–33

International Business Machines
    (IBM)—*Cont.*
  alliances, 50
  Apple and, 197
  benchmarking and, 479
  competition and, 31–32
  corporate strategy and, 40–41
  economic environment and, 74
  follower strategy and, 391
  Hewlett-Packard and, 448–449
  integration and, 50
  Lotus and, 388
  market orientation and, 36
  new business/marketing strategies
    for, 32–33
  new corporate strategy for, 32
  organizational buying and, 137
  pioneer strategy and, 407, 408
  product decisions and, 265
  reliability and, 423
  strategic business units (SBUs)
    and, 58
  strategic inertia and, 39
  synergy and, 42
  technology changes and, 31–32
Internet; *see also* Auctions; Dot.coms;
    E-Commerce; E-mail; New
    economy, marketing strategies
    for the; RedEnvelope; World
    Wide Web
  advertising and, 335, 337, 338–340,
    343, 369–371
  Cisco Systems and, 87
  competition and, 228–229
  conducting transactions and,
    371–372
  customer insight and, 367–368
  customer service and, 309, 323,
    373–374
  delivering digital products and,
    372–373
  Dell Computer and, 22
  differential pricing and, 291
  digitization and, 375–376
  distribution channels and, 361
  dot.coms and, 379–380
  E-Business models, 381
  E-hubs, 302
  Egg and, 242
  ethics and, 362–365
  future for, 380–381
  globalization and, 315, 361–362
  Hallmark Cards and, 294–295
  Hewlett-Packard and, 448–449

Internet—*Cont.*
  hybrid systems and, 313
  IBM and, 32
  implementation/control and, 450
  market segmentation based on
    customer value and, 431
  market tests and, 160
  marketing mistakes, 378
  marketing research and, 171,
    367–368
  measuring effectiveness/efficiency
    of marketing on, 377–378
  nonstore retailing, 303–304
  online consumer spending, 356–357
  online retailing, 358
  organizational buying and, 142–143
  privacy and, 371
  product availability and, 299, 309
  product information and ethics, 113
  product promotion/brand building
    and, 368–371
  product return/disposal and, 374
  sales, 26–27
  security and, 363–364, 371
  selling music on, 363
  syndication and, 359
  taxes and, 75
  technological environment and, 76
  Thorntons and, 354–355
  top 10 countries in use of, 357
Internet Marketing Research
    Organization (IMRO), 368
Interviews, qualitative research
    and, 170
Intuit Inc., 372
Iomega Corporation
  competition and, 16
  customer needs/wants and, 9
  implementation/control and, 19
  market segments and, 17
  strategies/resources and, 15
IPrint, 377
Ireland, 130
Italy, 364

J

J. D. Edwards & Co., 32
Jacob, Rahul, 28, 241, 445, 446, 472
Jacobs, Peter, 178
Jacobson, Robert, 62, 266, 445, 446
Jain, Dipak C., 284
Japan
  advertising to children and, 342

Japan—*Cont.*
  automobile industry and, 234,
    414, 422
  Canon of, 384–385
  culture and, 126
  economic environment and, 72, 73
  global market expansion and
    companies in, 438
  IMode in, 359
  lifestyles and, 124
  low-cost position and firms in, 428
  Marubeni Trading company of, 462
  Mitsubishi Heavy Industries
    and, 198
  mobile telephony and, 371
  new economy and, 356
  observation in marketing research
    and, 173
  organizational design and firms
    in, 464
  retail structures in, 315
  services and, 245
Jarvis, Steve, 383
Jatusripitak, Somkid, 446
Jaworski, Bernard J., 61, 325, 472, 495
JC Penney, 210, 213, 214, 254
Jennings, Richard G., 151
Jenster, Per V., 293
Jewland, Abel P., 417
JIT management systems, 148
Jobber, 301
Jocz, Katherine E., 28
John, George, 151, 325
John Deere, 284
Johnson & Johnson (J&J), 350–351,
    420, 478
Johnson Controls Inc., 418–419, 420,
    427, 432, 433, 436, 438
Johnson, Mark W., 151
Johnson, Wesley J., 151
Joint ventures, 314, 400, 462
Jones, Thomas O., 446
Jordan, Michael, 181, 203, 206
Jostens, Inc., 439
Judgment, 159
Jupiter Research, 369

K

Kahneman, Daniel, 178
Kalmenson, Stuart, 351
Kambil, Ajit, 383
Kana Communications, Inc., 347
Kanter, Rosabeth Moss, 378, 472

Kaplan, Robert S., 61, 293, 472, 495
Kaplan, Steven, 293, 325
Kapplow, Jonathan, 377
Kataris, Lea P., 199
Keegan, Warren J., 293
Keenan, Faith, 29, 104, 128, 241, 325
Keiretsu (Japanese), 50
Kellogg, 92, 250
Kentucky Fried Chicken, 314, 318, 460
Keon, John W., 218
Kerin, Roger A., 62, 137, 417, 495
Kerstetter, Jim, 76
Kim, Jim David, 382
Kim, W. Chan, 87
Kinko's, 356, 377
Kleinschmidt, Elko, 267
Klerks, Jos, 131
Kletter, Melanie, 81
Kmart, 209–210, 213, 214, 475, 490
Knight, Phil, 180–181, 182, 183, 184,
     187, 190, 193, 196
Knowlton, Christopher, 396
Kodak, 86, 250
Koehn, Nancy F., 186
Kohli, Ajay, 61
Komatsu, 198
Koppleman, Frank S., 218
Korea, South, 72, 356
Kotler, Philip, 28, 29, 62, 241, 404,
     411, 417, 446
Kraft, 437
Krishnan, Trichy V., 178
Krohmer, Harley, 35
Krups, 424
Kumar, V., 178
Kunii, Irene M., 253, 266, 417
Kuppenheimer chain, 66

L

L&T, 210, 213
Laboratory test markets, 263–264
Lacey, Roger, 260
Laggards, 95
Laguë, Côme, 152–154, 155, 157–158,
     161, 168–169, 170, 173, 174; see
     also African Communications
     Group (ACG)
Lambert, Denis, 259
Lambert's Pasta and Cheese, 158
Lambkin, Mary, 103, 104
Lamont, Douglas, 199
Lampe, John, 253
Lancet, The, 215

Landau, Meryl Davids, 101
Landro, Laura, 61
Lands' End, 164, 229, 303, 380
     categories of E-Commerce and, 26
     Internet and, 303
     warranties and, 252
Lanning, Michael J., 218
Larreche, Jean-Claude, 61, 417
Lashinsky, Adam, 472
Latin America, 48, 69
Laura Ashley, 251
Laurence, Henry, 199
Lay's (potato chips), 47
Lead user research, 260
Lead users, 260
Leapfrog strategy, 410, 411, 412,
     413–414, 416
Legal advice, 373, 376
Legal/political environment, 73–75
L'eggs pantyhose, 414–415
Legitimate power, 319–320
Lego, 32
Lehmann, Donald R., 28, 29, 293, 472
Lei, David, 28
Leigh, Thomas W., 218
Leonard, Dorothy, 249, 266
Levels of analysis, 86
Levelsberger, Jeanne, 351
Lever Brothers, 461
Levi Strauss, 254, 361
Levine, Mark, 199
Levitt, Theodore, 43, 61, 241
Levy, Michael, 210
Lewin, Jeffrey E., 151
Li, Tiger, 178
Licensing, 313–314
Liddell-Hart, B. H., 414, 417
Lieberman, Marvin B., 417
Lifestyle Market Analyst, 171
Lifestyles, 123–124, 188
Lifetime customer value, 11–12
Lii, Jane H., 82
Likert Scale, 172
Limited, The, 210, 213, 214, 251
Lincoln, D. J., 136
Line extensions, 243, 253, 254, 387
     Canon, Inc. and, 384
     skimming and, 401
Line filling, 253
Line stretching, 254
Linn, Allison, 495
Liquidation, 441
Little, John D. C., 167
L.L. Bean, 115, 164, 303, 479
Location, 92, 290

Lockwood, Tina, 361
Lodging industry, 226
Lodish, Leonard, 266, 351
Loehmann's, 210, 213, 214
Logistical alliances, 143, 229, 311–312,
     322, 323
Logistics, reverse, 131
London, Simon, 371
Long-term memory, 120
L'Oreal, 438
Lotus 1-2-3, 388
Lovelock, Christopher H., 266
Loveman, Gary, 370–371
Low-cost strategies
     implementation/control and, 451,
          452–453, 454, 455,
          456, 458
     mature markets and, 421, 422,
          427–429
Low-margin/high turnover, 303
Lowe, Tom, 373
Lowe's, 303
Loyalty
     Amazon.com and customer, 377
     brand, 116
     consumer buying behavior and, 116
     customers' service requirements
          and, 300
     differentiation and, 229
     exchange relationships and, 11–12
     Hallmark Cards and program for
          customer, 295
     information technology and, 26
     Internet and customer, 373
     marketing management and, 25
     mature markets and, 429–431
     new products and, 398
     organizational buying and, 145
     pioneer strategy and, 404
     share maintenance objectives
          and, 403
Lubetin, Beth, 351
Lucent Technologies, 449
Lucozade, 326
Lutheran Hour Ministries, 7
Lycos, 347
Lynn, Susan, 150
Lyons, Steve, 218

M

Mack (trucks), 86
Macroenvironment, 78–80, 256–257,
     469; see also Environmental
     context

Macrosegmentation, 185
Macy's, 210, 212, 213, 214
Madden, Thomas J., 178
Maddy, Monique, 152–154
Magazines, 338
Maginnis, Corinne, 368
Magnet, Myron, 103, 417
Mahajan, Vijay, 62, 266
Main, Jeremy, 417
Maintenance strategy, 442, 443,
        444, 470
Majaro, Simon, 199
Malkani, Gautam, 81
Managing of business processes, 461
Mangalindan, Mylene, 383
Mankiw, N. Gregory, 82
Mann, Jeremy, 495
Mannesmann, 85
Manpower, 318
Manufacturer-retailer franchise
        systems, 318
Manufacturer-wholesaler franchise
        systems, 318
Manufacturer's agents, 302
Manufacturer's export agent
        (MEA), 315
Manufacturer's reps, 302, 345
Manufacturing process, 208
March, Artemus, 267
Margin of error, 174, 175
Margins, gross/net, 489
Market, defined, 12
Market-attractiveness/competitive-
        position matrix/factors,
        190–196
Market channels; *see also* Distribution
        channels
Market expansion strategy, 402, 403,
        404, 405, 408, 434, 435,
        437–438
Market knowledge, 162–163
Market knowledge systems, 163–168
    client contact/salesforce automation
        systems, 166–168
    competitive intelligence and, 166
    internal records systems, 163–164
    marketing databases and, 164–167
Market management organizational
        design, 457, 460–461
Market measurements, 17
Market orientation, 33, 35–37, 248
    across industries, 38
    competition and, 37
    corporate strategy and, 42
    globalization and, 38–39

Market orientation—*Cont.*
    guidelines for, 36
    product orientation vs., 38
Market positioning analysis, 211
Market potential, 154, 155, 160, 161
Market research, 162–163
    computers and, 217
    demand curve and, 276
    ethics and, 167
    product decisions and, 247–248
Market Research Society, 167
Market segmentation, 12–13, 17,
        180–198
    based on customer value, 430–431
    behavioral descriptors and, 187–189
    consumer needs and, 187–188
    demographics and, 173, 184–186
    geographic, 186–187, 461
    geographic descriptors and, 186
    global, 197–198
    heterogeneous markets and, 182–183
    importance of, 183–184
    innovative, 189–190
    macrosegmentation, 185
    marketing communications and, 329
    media and, 184
    microsegmentation, 183, 186
    Nike brand and, 181
    objectives, 184
    positioning and, 182, 212–213
    process of choosing attractive
        market segments, 190–196
    product life cycle stages and, 100
    social class and, 189
    target marketing and, 182–184
    target strategies and, 196–198
    ways of dividing markets into
        segments, 184
Market Share Reporter, 171
Market space, 87
Market tests, 157, 159–160
Marketing audits, 476, 493–494
Marketing channels, 22, 296
Marketing communication; *see*
        Integrated marketing
        communication (IMC)
Marketing concept, 33, 35, 36–37, 38
Marketing decision support
        systems, 176
Marketing, defined, 5, 28
Marketing environment audit, 493–494
Marketing functions audit, 494
Marketing management
    defined, 13
    process, 13–15, 19

Marketing managers
    influence of, 34
    role of, 24
Marketing metrics, 475–476
Marketing mix; *see also* Distribution;
        Pricing; Product(s);
        Promotion(s)
    costs, 277
    critical success factors and, 92
    defined, 18
    differentiation and, 203
    elements of, 19
    market segmentation and, 184
    marketing strategy and, 42
    product life cycle stages and,
        99–100, 100–102
Marketing News, 177
Marketing performance
        measurement, 476
Marketing plan(s), 19–20, 465–471
    action plans and, 470–471
    contents of, 465
    contingency plans and, 471
    importance of written, 20
    key issues and, 470
    macroenvironment and, 469
    major parts of, 20–21
    market situation and, 468
    marketing strategy and, 470
    objectives and, 470
    past product performance and, 469
    profit-and-loss statements and, 471
    sales forecasts and, 469
    summary of annual, 466–467
Marketing productivity audit, 494
Marketing research, 17, 154
    advertising and, 335
    analyzing data, 175
    collecting data and, 174–175
    contact methods and, 173–174
    data collections methods and, 173
    data sources and types, 169–172
    designing the, 172–174
    evaluation and, 333–334
    Internet and, 367–368
    marketing plans and, 468
    objectives and, 168–169, 175
    process (steps), 168–175
    sampling plans and, 174
    sources, 171
    Wal-Mart and, 482
    web-based, 355
    what users should ask, 176
Marketing Research Association, 167
Marketing strategy, 15–16, 470

Markets
    defining industries and, 86–88
    industries vs., 85–86
Marks & Spencer, 6, 305
Markup pricing, 278–279
Marlboro, 250
Marn, Michael V., 293
Marriott, 226
Marshall, Greg W., 151
Marshall, Richard, 382
Marshalls, 210, 213, 214
Martin, Justin, 28
Marubeni Trading company, 462
Mass-market, 196–197
Mass-market penetration, 393–395,
    396–400
Massachusetts Institute of Technology
    (MIT), 11
Mateschitz, Dietrich, 186
Mathematics, in forecasting, 160
Matrix organizational designs, 457
Matsushita Electric Industrial
    Company, 91, 462
Mature markets, 418–438
    challenges in, 420
    competitive advantage and,
        421–422
    current market share strategies and,
        431–433
    customer satisfaction/loyalty and,
        429–431
    differentiation and, 422–427
    extending volume growth strategies
        and, 433–438
    Johnson Controls Inc. and,
        418–419, 420, 427, 432, 433,
        436, 438
    low-cost position and, 427–429
    strategic choices in, 420–421
Mauborgne, Renée, 87
Maybelline, 438
MBTI® Creativity Index, 259
McCarthy, E. Jerome, 61
McClelland, Anna Sheen, 156
McCracken, Grant, 178
McDonald's, 6, 87, 89, 292, 297
    branding and, 248, 250
    customer wants/needs and, 8
    environment and, 78, 79
    franchising and, 314, 318
    implementation/control and,
        455, 457
    pioneer strategy and, 392
    promotions and, 349

McElroy, Bill, 368
McEnroe, John, 182, 203
McGahan, Anita M., 177, 178
McGee, Gail W., 61, 151
MCI, 227
McKay, David M., 218
McKee, Daryl O., 241, 472
McKinsey new product studies, 257
McLuhan, Robert, 351
McQueen-Johnson, David, 355
McWilliams, Robert D., 136, 150
Me-too products
    differentiation and, 215
    pioneer strategy and, 389
    product decisions and, 256, 261
    skimming and, 396
Measuring results, 474–494
    contingency planning and, 490–492
    corrective action and, 483–484
    feedback data and, 482–483
    global marketing and, 492–493
    marketing audits and, 493–494
    media for, 490
    at nonprofit organizations, 476
    standards of performance and,
        477–482
    strategic control systems and,
        484–486
    strategy reassessment and, 485
    timeliness and, 489–490
    tracking/monitoring and, 485
    who needs what information for,
        486–489
Mechanisms, 455
Media
    advertising and, 337–340
    international, 343–344
Memory, 120
Menswear market, 66–67
Mercedes-Benz, 203, 208, 250, 253
    line stretching and, 254
    mature markets and, 436
    product quality and, 422
Mercer Management Consulting, 385
Merchant middlemen, 315
Merchant wholesalers, 22
Merck, 478
Merico, 470, 471
Merrill Lynch, 66
MetalSite, 142
Mexico, 39, 73, 474
Meyer, Dale, 7
Michelin, 156
MicroScan, 430

Microsegmentation, 183, 186
Microsoft
    economic environment and, 75
    follower strategy and, 391
    new economy and, 356
    pioneer strategy and, 388
Midas, 318
Middlemen, 297, 314–315, 322
Miles, Robert E., 62, 223, 224,
    227, 241
Milibank, Dana, 141
Miller, Cyndee, 218
Miller, Karen Lowry, 325
Miller Tyding Act (1937), 291
Milne, George R., 167
Milne, Sandy, 327
Mimeo.com, 377
Minnesota Mining and Manufacturing
    Company (3M); see 3M
Minnetonka, Inc., 59, 232–233, 392
Minolta, 438
Mission, 40
Mission statements, 43–44, 45
Mitarai, Fujio, 384
Mitsubishi Heavy Industries, 198
Mitsumori, Yaeko, 382
MIX, Inc., 295
Mobile telephone service, 362, 366,
    369, 371–372; see also Cellular
    telephone business
    advertising and, 371
    digitization and, 372
    new economy and, 356, 359
Mockups, 342
Modified rebuy, 138, 189
Monique, Maddy, 155, 157–158, 161,
    168–169, 170, 173, 174; see
    also African Communications
    Group (ACG)
Monsanto, 134
Monster.com, 330
Monsters Inc. (movie), 349
Montague, Bill, 82
Montgomery, David B., 103, 417
Moody's Industrial Manual, 171
Moon, Youngme, 383
Moore, Geoffrey, 96
Moore, Leslie, 293
Moore, Michael J., 417
Moorman, Christine, 28
Moran, Ursula, 325
Morgan, Robert M., 151, 325
Morgan Stanley, 66
Moriarity, Rowland T., 325

Morita, Akio, 8
MOSAIC database, 166
Moss Brothers, 66, 67
Motorola, 84, 314, 479
MTV networks, 343
Muir, Patrick, 242–243
Mullaney, Timothy J., 446, 472
Mullick, Satinder K., 177
Mullins, John, 61, 81, 103, 417
Multidimensional scaling, 217
Multinational corporations (MNCs),
     344–346
Murdick, Robert G., 177
Murray, Keith B., 128
My Yahoo! website, 229

N

Nabisco, 33
Nagle, Thomas T., 274, 293, 417
Naisbitt, John, 81
NamePro®, 248
Namestormers, 248, 341
Napster, 363, 364
Narayandas, Das, 61
Narus, James A., 325
Narver, John C., 28, 61, 472
National, 438
Natural products, 146–147
Nature Conservancy, 476
Naumann, Earl, 136, 150
Nayak, P. Ranganath, 266
NBC, 343–344
Nedungadi, Prakash, 62
Needs/wants, 7–10
     consumer need, 87
     customer analysis and, 16
     global market segmentation and, 198
     high-involvement purchase
          decisions and, 109
     market segmentation and, 12, 181,
          187–188, 192
     marketing managers and, 15
     organizational buying and, 138–139
Negotiation, 150
Neighborhood Markets, 474
Neiman Marcus, 186–187, 209–210,
     213, 214
Nescafé brand, 250
Nestlé, 131, 250
     forecasting and, 158, 160
     organizational design and, 459
Netherlands, 130
Network externality, 359, 390

Networks, organizational, 50
Neuborne, Ellen, 399
New customer segments, 437–438
New economy, marketing strategies for
     the, 354–382
     advantages/disadvantages of new-
          economy technologies, 358
     developing, 365–366, 375–379
     distribution channels and, 361
     dot.coms and, 379–382
     ethical issues and, 362–365
     first-mover advantage and, 365
     globalization and, 361–362
     marketing applications for new-
          economy tools, 366–375
     on need for, 356–357
     networks and, 359–360
     online retailing and, 358
     personalizing/customizing and,
          360–361
     syndication of information and,
          358–359
     Thorntons and, 354–355, 359, 360,
          362, 365
New Holland, 284–285
New Media Age, 354
New product development, 243,
     384–388; see also Pioneer
     strategy
New-task buying, 138, 139, 189
New-to-the-world products, 243,
     386–387
New Yorker, The, 200
Newborne, Ellen, 351
Newman, William H., 241
Newspaper advertising, 338
Newsweek, 338
NextCard, 371
Niche-market, 196–197, 386
Niche penetration, 394, 395, 397, 400
Niche strategy, 409, 432, 442, 443, 445
Nike brand, 181, 189, 208, 250;
          see also Bowerman, Bill;
          Knight, Phil
     differentiation and, 203
     positioning and, 206
     product decisions and, 250
     UnderArmour and, 183
Nine West Group, 159, 163
911Gifts; see RedEnvelope
Nissan, 247
Nokia, 84, 185
Noncompensatory attitude models, 122
Nonprobability sampling, 174

Nordstrom, 209–210, 212, 213, 214
Norelco, 208
North American Free Trade Agreement
     (NAFTA), 73
Norton, David P., 61, 495
Norwegian Cruise Line, 107
Nova Cruz Products, 264
Nrahk, John K., 472
Nucor, 365
Nunes, Paul, 383

O

Obermeyer, Walter R., 178
Objective-and-task, 331
Objectives
     competitive strategy differences
          and, 230–231
     corporate, 46–48
     follower strategy and, 409
     market research and, 168–169, 175
     marketing plans and, 470
     pioneer strategy and, 401–402
     promotional, 330–331
     research, 169
     social, 274
     strategic marketing programs and, 18
     strategy and, 40, 41
Objectives and strategy audit, 493–494
Observation, marketing research
     and, 173
Observation-based forecasting, 157
Occupation (demographic
     descriptor), 185
Océ; see Excel Company,
     organizational buying and
"Ocean Village" cruises, 107
O'Connell, Vanessa, 370, 383
O'Connor, Paul, 258, 267
O'Conor, James, 325
Odd pricing, 286
O'Dell, John, 253
Off-invoice discounts, 323
Office Depot Inc., 11, 149
Offsets, 288
Ogilvy and Mather (advertising
     agency), 188
Oh, Sejo, 150, 151, 325
Old Navy, 156
Olesen, Douglas E., 82
Oliver, James M., 495
Olson, Eric M., 241, 266, 417
Olson, Jerry, 128
1-Click® ordering system, 363, 377

Onitsuka Tiger, 180, 182
Ono, Yumiko, 128, 415
Operating supplies, 149
Opportunity, 85
Opportunity cost, 112
Opportunity/threat matrix, 80
Opt-in e-mail, 370
Oracle Corp., 26, 33
Order cycle time, 299, 308, 309
Order fulfillment, 3
Organization, 120
Organization audit, 493–494
Organization Mabe, 39
Organization of Petroleum Exporting
        Countries (OPEC), 147
Organizational buying, 130–150; see
        also Excel Company,
        organizational buying and
    buying centers and, 135–137
    decision-making process, 138–144
    derived demand and, 133–134
    different kinds of goods/services
        and, 146–150
    ethics and, 141
    evaluation/feedback, 143–144
    government markets and,
        145–146
    high-involvement purchase
        decisions and, 137, 138
    logistical alliances and, 143
    long-term buyer-supplier
        relationships, 145
    marketing implications of,
        144–145
    organizational markets and, 134
    organizational vs. consumer markets
        and, 132–133
    participants in, 135
    purchase agreements, 142
    suppliers and, 140–142, 144–145
    technology and, 142–143
    trust and, 145
    types of buying situations,
        137–138
Organizational customers, 7, 11
Organizational design, 461–462
Organizational fit, 450
Organizational markets, 189
Organizational structures, 457–461
O'Rourke, Jim, 352
Ortmeyer, Gwendolyn K., 292
Orwall, Bruce, 218
OurBeginning.com, 330
Overhead, 276

Overseas direct investment, 314
Overture, 339
Ozaki, Ritsuko, 81

P

P&O Princess, 107
Packaging decisions, 251
Page, Albert L., 266
Palm Pilot, 365
Palmer, Camilla, 325
Palmieri, Jean, 81
Pan Am, 418
Panera, 89
Papa John's, 215
Papows, Jeff, 178
Parasuraman, A., 248, 425, 427, 446
Paré, Terrence P., 62, 495
Parentage, 208
Park, Andrew, 472
Parry, Mark E., 266
Pascual, Aixa M., 128
PayPal, 372
PDSA (UK), 165
Penetrated market, 155
Penetration pricing, 100, 271
Penetration strategy, 433–434, 435
Penn Central, 43–44
PeopleSoft, 36
PepsiCo, 60, 289, 318, 460
    All Sport, 187
    corporate objectives and, 47
    diversification and, 50
    growth-share matrix and, 53
    mission of, 43
Perceived value, 274–276, 283
Percentage of sales, 331
Perception, 119–120, 121
Perceptual attributes, 205–206
Perceptual defense, 120
Perceptual map, 209
Perceptual organization, 120
Perceptual positioning, 204–205
Perceptual positioning analysis, 204
Perceptual vigilance, 120
Perdue, Carlos, 253
Pereira, Joseph, 352
Performance, 247
Periodic discounting, 273
Permission marketing, 370
Permission Marketing (Godin), 339
Perreault, William D., Jr., 61
Personal characteristics, 108, 114,
        119, 120

Personal selling, 101, 322, 333; see
        also Sales
    accessory equipment and, 149
    business services and, 150
    customer service and, 346–347
    decision-making, 344–349
    defined, 328
    examples of promotional
        activities, 329
    expenditures, 329
    Integrated marketing
        communication (IMC)
        and, 328
    merits of, 334
    as promotional tool, 332
Personal sources, 112
Personalization, 360–361
Peter, J. Paul, 128
Peteraf, Margaret A., 62
Peterson, Robert A., 417
Petzinger, Thomas, Jr., 382
Pharmaceutical industry, 215, 291, 292
Phillips, Lynn W., 445
Phillips Petroleum, 208
Physical environment, 77–78, 79
Picaro, Gary P., 266
Pichery, JeanMarc, 199
Pillsbury, 126, 234, 248, 349
    marketing plans and, 465, 466–467,
        468–469, 470, 471
    mature markets and, 437
    pioneer strategy and, 407, 408
Pillsbury Company, 240
PIMS database, 392, 401, 415
Pine, Joseph B., II, 198, 241
Pioneer strategy, 388–390; see also
        Follower strategy; New product
        development
    advantages of, 388–390
    confrontation and, 405, 407–408
    contraction and, 405, 408
    determinants of success for,
        391–393
    flanker strategy, 405, 406–407
    fortress/position defense and, 402,
        404–406
    global markets and, 399–400
    growth-market strategies and, 401
    market expansion and, 405, 408
    mass-market penetration and,
        393–395, 396–400
    niche penetration and, 394, 395,
        397, 400
    repeat purchasing and, 406

Pioneer strategy—*Cont.*
  share maintenance objectives and, 401–402, 403, 405
  skimming/early withdrawal and, 394, 395–396, 397, 400–401
  on strategic marketing programs for, 392
  strategic withdrawal and, 405, 408
Pitt, Leyland, 325
Pizza Hut, 43, 314
Place, 18, 19, 92
Plank, Kevin, 183
Plank, Richard E., 151
Planning and control system audit, 493–494
PlasticsNet.com, 138
Playing Mantis, 373
Plummer, Joseph, 71
Poer, Christopher, 267
Polaroid, 414
Political/legal environment, 73–75
Polk Company, 165
Pollution, 77
PolyGram, 344
Population, 69–70
Porsche, 422
Port, Otis, 472
Portal deals, 339
Porter, Michael E., 62, 82, 103, 202–203, 218, 223, 224, 241, 417, 440, 446
Porter's competitive forces, 88–91, 169
Portfolio models, 51, 53–54
Position defense, 402
Positioning, 17, 182
  analytical tools for decision making for, 216–217
  constraints imposed by intense position, 211
  consumer buying behavior and, 117–118
  defined, 201
  differentiation and, 201–203, 215
  ethics and, 215
  follower strategy and, 391
  grid, 209
  Hanna Andersson and, 13
  levers to establish, 205–206
  perceptual, 204, 205
  physical, 203–204, 205
  process, 206–216
  product decisions and, 247

Positioning—*Cont.*
  statements/value propositions, 214–216
  wine industry and, 200–201
  women's clothing retailers and, 209–210, 212–214
Positive network effects, 359, 390, 391
Power, sources of distribution channel, 319–320
Power, Stephen, 253
Powerade, 187
Prahalad, C. K., 28, 61, 178, 241
Precision Tune, 318
Predatory pricing, 291
Predicast F&S Index United States, Europe and International, 171
Premium price policies, 282
Premiums, 290
Pressured (psychographic segment), 124
Prêt A Manger, 89
Price elasticity of demand, 275–276
Price fixing, 291
Price leader, 282
Price lining, 285–286
Price-off promotions, 289
Price/quality, 208
Price structure, 270
Priceline, 26
Priceline.com, 363, 372, 380
Pricing; *see also* Pricing decisions
  business services and, 149–150
  business strategies and, 236, 238
  competition and, 228–229, 231, 232, 239
  consumer buying behavior and, 118
  critical success factors and, 92
  dynamic, 372
  as element of marketing mix, 19
  environment and, 233, 235
  follower strategy and, 413, 416
  marketing functions audit and, 494
  markup, 278–279
  odd, 286
  as one of 4 Ps, 18
  overall cost leadership and, 223
  penetration, 100, 271
  pioneer strategy and, 400
  positioning and, 215
  predatory, 291
  product decisions and, 263
  product life cycle stages and, 100, 101, 102
  product policies and, 237
  promotion policies and, 239

Pricing—*Cont.*
  psychological, 286
  time, 290
  uniform delivered, 287
Pricing decisions, 268–293; *see also* Pricing
  adapting prices to market variations, 286–292
  allowances, 289
  analyzing competitors' costs/prices, 278
  cash discounts, 289
  competition-oriented methods of pricing, 281–283
  cost-oriented methods of pricing, 278–281
  coupons/rebates/refunds, 289–290
  customer-oriented methods of pricing, 283–286
  demand curve and, 274–276
  differential pricing, 290–291
  discounts, 288–289
  estimating costs, 276–278
  factors affecting customers' sensitivity to price, 275
  geographic adjustments, 286–287
  global adjustments, 287–288
  Internet auction sites and, 282–283
  legal considerations of, 291
  methods to determine price level, 278–286
  perceived value and, 274–276
  perceptual pricing issues, 285–286
  price-off promotions, 289
  process of price setting, 270–278
  product-line pricing adjustments, 291–292
  promotional pricing ethics, 286
  Ryan Air, 268–269, 270, 278, 282
  strategic pricing objectives, 270–274
Pride, William M., 241, 472
Primary data, 169–170
Primary demand, 387
Primary research, 261
Prince Automotive, 436
Princess cruise line, 106
Print media, 338
Privacy, 362, 363, 364, 371, 432
Private-label brands, 438
PRIZM service, 187
Probability sampling, 174
Problem children, 52
Process management, 462

Procsal, Bob, 137
Procter & Gamble, 26, 232–233, 263,
  319, 320
  branding and, 249–250, 251
  follower strategy and, 392
  organizational design and, 459
  supply chain management
    alliances, 143
Product decisions, 242–266; *see also*
    Product(s)
  attributes and, 243
  benefits/features and, 244
  branding and, 248–251
  for competitive advantage, 244–252
  features and, 247–248
  goods vs. services, 245–247
  packaging, 251
  process for new products, 255–265
  product lines and, 252–255
  quality and, 247–248
  services and, 242–243, 251–252
  support tools for, 248
  warranties and, 251–252
Product life cycle (PLC)
  competition and, 103
  curves, 97–98
  stages, 97, 99–102
  strategic implications and
    limitations of, 102–103
Product-line extensions, 256
Product manager audit, 494
Product offering
  as element of marketing mix, 19
  as one of 4 Ps, 18
Production orientation, 37
Product(s); *see also* New product
    development; Product decisions
  acquisition, 309
  availability and distribution channel
    decisions, 299
  behavioral descriptors and, 188
  business strategies and, 236, 237
  class, 86–87
  consumer buying behavior and
    design of, 117–118
  defined, 10, 244
  development of, 255–265
  dimensions/attributes, 114
  dropping, 255
  expansion strategies, 252–253
  global markets and, 464
  as goods and services, 246
  improvements, 256
  launch, 258

Product(s)—*Cont.*
  lines, 243
  management organizational design,
    457, 459–460
  marketing functions audit and, 494
  me-too, 215, 256–261, 389, 396
  modifications, 243
  needs/wants and development of,
    9–10
  orientation, 37, 38
  positioning, 182
  positioning analysis, 211
  quality (dimensions of), 422–424
  sales analysis by, 487–488
  scoring model for, 262
  search, 309
  systems, 255
  types, 86, 87
  usage, 188
Profitability analysis, 479–480
Profitable survivor strategy, 442, 443,
    444–445
Promotion and brand building, 366
Promotional allowances, 289, 322,
    324, 349
Promotion(s); *see also* Integrated
    marketing communication
    (IMC); Sales promotion
  budgeting, 331
  business strategies and, 236,
    238–239
  consumer buying behavior and,
    118–119
  costs, 277
  critical success factors and, 92
  distribution channel decisions and,
    300, 309–310, 321–323
  as element of marketing mix, 19
  market orientation and, 37
  mix, 327–329, 330, 332–333, 334
  new economy marketing
    applications for product,
    368–371
  as one of 4 Ps, 18
  pricing decisions and, 286
  product life cycle stages and, 100,
    101, 102
  RedEnvelope and, 3
Prospector strategy
  banking industry and, 227
  competitive strategies and, 229,
    230, 231, 239
  distribution and, 238, 300, 301
  environment and, 232–233

Prospector strategy—*Cont.*
  implementation/control and, 451,
    452, 453, 455, 456, 457, 461
  marketing policies/programs
    and, 236
  pricing policies and, 238
  product policies and, 237
  promotion policies and, 238
  as strategic type, 223–225
  3M and
Protectionism, 246
Prudential (British insurer), 242; *see
    also* Egg
Pruzan, Todd, 351
Psychographics, 123–124, 188
Psychological costs, 112
Psychological pricing, 286
Psychotherapy, 373, 376
Public relations
  decision-making, 350–351
  defined, 328
  examples of promotional
    activities, 329
  expenditures, 329
  Integrated marketing
    communication (IMC)
    and, 328
  merits of, 334
Public sources, 112
Publicity, 350
Puffery, 342
Pull strategy, 320, 332–333,
    334, 349
Purchase agreements, 142
Purchase influence, 188
Purchasing; *see* Organizational buying
Purchasing agent, 135
Purchasing manager, 135
Purchasing power party (PPP), 72
Purchasing structure, 189
Push money, 322, 324
Push strategy, 320–321, 333, 334, 349

Q

QFD/CAPTURE, 248
Quaker Oats, 48
Qualcomm, 84
Qualitative research; *see also*
    Marketing research
  Internet and, 367–368
  marketing research data and, 170
  positioning and, 209
  techniques, 170–171

Quality
   dimensions of (for goods), 247
   dimensions of service, 248,
      424–427
   mature markets and product,
      422–424
   pricing decisions and, 271, 273
   product decisions and, 247–248
   prospector strategy and, 237
Quality Rating Scale, 172
Quality reputation of the brand
   name, 424
Quantitative research; *see also*
   Marketing research
   Internet and, 367
   marketing research data and, 170
   statistical methods of forecasting
      and, 156–157
   techniques, 172
Quantity discounts, 288–289, 322
Quelch, John A., 192, 292, 322, 495
Question marks, 52, 53
Quick, Rebecca, 374
Quotas, 344
Qwest Communications, 156
QXL, 26, 363

R

Raabe, Steve, 363
Race/ethnic origin (demographic
   descriptor), 185
Radebaugh, Lee H., 199
Radio, 337
Ralph Lauren, 251, 438
Raman, Ananth, 156, 178
Random House, 361
Random sampling, 174
Rangan, V. Kasturi, 61, 158, 160
Rao, Akshay R., 293, 417, 446
Rappaport, Alfred, 55, 62
Rate card, 336–337
Rate-of-return, 279
Raw materials, 146–147
Rawlinson, Richard, 325
Rayport, Jeffrey F., 249, 266
Reach, 335–336
Reactor strategy, 223–225, 227
Rebates, 289–290, 350
Recall tests, 342, 343
Reciprocity, 141, 324
Recognition tests, 343
Recruit and select, 348
Recycled Paper Greetings, 294

Red Bull, 186, 189, 248
Red Herring magazine, 171
RedEnvelope, 6, 26, 115, 153
   alliances, 50
   distribution channel decisions
      and, 309
   exchange relationships and, 13
   importance of sales revenue and, 5
   marketing strategy, 15
   new marketing plan, 2–4
   positioning, 17
   start-ups and, 60
   strategic marketing programs
      and, 18
Reebok, 183, 349
Reference groups, 126
Referent power, 319
Refunds, 289–290
Refusal to deal, 324
Regan, Mary Beth, 82
Regulatory environment, 73–75
REI outdoor gear retailer, 113
Reichheld, Frederick F., 28, 383,
   430, 446
Reinhardt, Andy, 104, 417
Related (or concentric)
   diversification, 50
Relational distribution systems, 323
Relational VMS, 316, 318–319
Relationships; *see* Exchange
   relationships
Relative market share, 52, 53
Reliability, 247, 248, 423, 424, 426
Repeat buying, 264
Repositionings, 387
Request for quotes (RFQs), 142
Resale restrictions, 324
Research; *see* Marketing research
Research and development (R&D)
   Hewlett-Packard, 449
   implementation/control and, 453,
      454, 455, 456
   Iomega Corporation and, 15, 19
   needs/wants and, 8–9
   profitability analysis and, 479
   service levels and, 432
Research objectives, 169
Resource deployments, 230, 231
Resources
   allocating corporate, 51–56
   implementation and, 455
   strategic business units (SBUs)
      and, 58
   strategy and, 40, 41

Respondents, 174
Responsiveness, 248, 424, 426
Results; *see* Measuring results
Retail coverage, 307
Retailer cooperatives, 317–318
Retailers, 6, 22, 302–303
Retention, 120
Return on investment (ROI), 452–453,
   454, 455, 456
Returns, 13, 366–367, 374
Revlon, 119
Reward systems, 454
Rewick, Jennifer, 383
Rexall, 317, 318
Rich media, 369
Richardson, Bruce, 351
Ries, Al, 201, 218, 250, 266
Ries, Laura, 266
Riggings stores, 66
Rink, David R., 61, 98, 104, 151
Risk Management Association
   (formerly Robert Morris and
   Associates), 171
Ritchie, Karen, 81
Rivali, Pietra, 472
Robertson, Thomas S., 104
Robinson, Patrick J., 151
Robinson, S. J., 196
Robinson, William T., 417
Robinson-Patman Act, 291
Robots, Web-crawling "bots," 113
Rocks, David, 101, 371
Rockwell, 146
Rodata, Stefano, 364
Rodgers, Anni Layne, 186
Roering, Kenneth J., 325
Rogaine, 329–330
Rogers, Everett M., 104
Rolls-Royce automobiles, 308
Romanelli, Elaine, 241
Ronkausen, Idkka A., 472
Root, Franklin R., 417
Rose, Matthew, 382
Rosenau, M. D., 178
Rosiello, Robert L., 293
Roth, Daniel, 113, 325
Rothman, Andrea, 103
Royal Caribbean cruise line, 106, 107
Rudelius, William, 137, 495
Ruekert, Robert W., 266, 325, 417,
   456, 472
Rules-based personalization, 360–361
Running shoes; *see* Blue Ribbon Sports
Russell, Jack, 128

Rust, Roland T., 28
Ryan Air, 75, 268–269, 270, 282
    follower strategy and, 413
    installations and, 148
    low-cost position and, 428
    pricing decisions and, 278, 282

S

Safeway Inc., 289
Sager, Ira, 61
Saks, 209–210, 213, 214, 305
Sales; *see also* Forecasting; Personal
        selling; Sales promotion
    agents, 302
    analysis, 348, 486–488
    cycle, 344
    force automation, 347
    forecasting, of new products/firms,
        96–97
    managers, 34
    orientation, 37–38
    revenue, 5
    tests, 342–343
Sales and Marketing Management, 161
Sales Compensation Design
        Software, 347
Sales promotion, 321; *see also*
        Promotion(s)
    decision-making, 349–350
    defined, 328, 349
    examples of promotional
        activities, 329
    Integrated marketing
        communication (IMC) and,
        328
    mass-market penetration and, 398
    mature markets and, 437
    merits of, 334
$alescom (software), 347
Salesforce, 348–349, 494
Sampling, 174, 349
Sam's Clubs, 474
Samsung, 91
Sandbagging, 162
Sanders, Edmund, 253
Sanderson, George F., 82
Saporito, Bill, 495
Sassafras, 210, 213, 214
Sasser, W. Earl, Jr., 446, 472
Satisfaction, customer, 11, 404
    information technology and, 26
    marketing management and, 25
    mature markets and, 429–431

Satisfaction, customer—*Cont.*
    performance measurement and,
        480, 482
Savoy Taylors Guild, 66
Sawhill, John C., 476
Sawhney, Mohanbir, 293, 325
Sawtooth Software, Inc., 217, 248
Sawtooth Technologies, 177
Sayers, Charles, 368–369
Scandinavia, 372
Schefter, Phil, 383
Schendel, Dan, 61
Schenker, Jennifer L., 62
Schering-Plough, 478
Schiller, Zachary, 325
Schine, Eric, 103
Schleifer, Arthur, Jr., 177
Schlesinger, Leonard A., 241
Schmitt, Richard B., 383
Schroer, James, 351
Schulte, Erin, 382
Schurr, Paul H., 150, 151, 325
Schwartz, Evan I., 365, 382
SCIP; *see* Society of Competitive
        Intelligence Professionals (SCIP)
Scope, 39–40, 41, 42
    corporate strategy and, 43–46
    how competitive strategies differ in,
        229–230
    strategic business units (SBUs)
        and, 58
Scott, Stan, 136, 150
Screaming Media, 359
Screening, 260, 261
Seabourn Cruise Line, 107
Seagram Co., 342, 415
Sealed bidding, 282
Sealey, Peter, 365, 382
Search Engine Watch, 369
Search engines, 76, 79
Search keywords, 339
Search (product), 309
Sears, 26, 210, 213, 214, 305
Secondary data, 169–170
Security, 363–364, 371
Segmentation; *see* Market
        segmentation
Seiko, 438
Selective distribution, 307–308
Selectivity, 120
Self-managing teams, 462
Sellers, Patricia, 12, 28
Seller's auctions, 282, 283
Selling groups, 315

Semantic Differential Scale, 172
Seniors, 376
Sensus, 177
Sequoia Capital, 2
Service sponsor-retailer franchise
        systems, 318
Serviceability, 247, 423
Service(s)
    businesses, 226–227, 242–243
    defined, 10, 226
    distribution channel decisions and,
        315–316
    Europe and, 245
    implementation/control and,
        455–456
    importance of, 25
    industries, 38
    international, 246
    Japan and, 245
    positioning and, 201
    producers, 6
    quality (dimensions of), 424–427
    sector, 24–25
    segmentation, 432
Settle, Robert B., 178
Sex (demographic descriptor), 185
Shakeout, 419–420
Shakespeare.com, 361
Shannon, Elaine, 183
Shapiro, Carl, 362, 364, 382, 417
Sharp, 365
Sharpe, Rochelle, 383
Shell, 318
Sherman Act, 291, 324
Sherman, Stratford, 472
Shervani, Tasadduq A., 29, 61
Sherwin-Williams Paints, 317
Sheth, Jagdish, N., 29
Shetty, Y. K., 61, 293
Shocker, Allen D., 472
Shoes, running; *see* Blue Ribbon Sports
Shook, David, 399
Shop.org, 113
Shopping bots, 372
Short-term memory, 120
SIC codes, 185
Siebel Systems, Inc., 347
Silbert, Theodore H., 177
Silversea Cruises, 107
Simon, John, 351
Simon, Julian, 351
Sisodia, Rajendra S., 29
Skimming, 100, 395–396, 397,
        400–401

Skimming price policy, 272, 273
Sky Sport (cable TV), 184
Slater, Stanley F., 28, 61, 241, 259, 472
Sloan, Pat, 82
Slogans, 216
Slotting allowances, 322
Slywotzky, Adrian J., 103
SMART (specific, measurable, attainable, relevant, time-bound), 331, 335, 377, 478
SmartHome.com, 373, 377
Smith, David, 495
Smith, Donald D., 177
Smith, N. Craig, 192, 292, 322
SMS, 349
Snow, Charles C., 62, 223, 224, 227, 241
Social class, 126, 189
Social influences, 108, 114, 125, 140–141
Social institutions, 6–7
Social objectives, in pricing decisions, 274
Society of Competitive Intelligence Professionals (SCIP), 93
Sociocultural environment, 70–72
Software
    ACT, 167
    for advertising, 341
    brand development, 248
    call center, 347, 373
    campaign management, 165
    contact management, 347
    Goldmine, 167
    new economy and, 362
    salesforce automation, 166–167
    tools for marketing, 176–177
    tools for positioning decision making, 217
Sole ownership, 314
Somassundarm, Mora, 199
Sonera, 372
Song, Michael, 266
Sonnack, Mary, 260
Sony, 6, 86, 91, 248, 250
    customer needs/wants and, 8
    follower strategy and, 391, 414
    music on Internet and, 76
    Walkman and, 9
Sony Ericsson, 295
Source (of message in advertising), 340
Sourcebook of County Demographics, 171

Sourcebook of Zip Code Demographics, 171
South America
    Coca-Cola and, 438
    economic environment and, 72
Southern Common Market (MERCOSUR), 73
Spain, William, 351
SPAM, 340
SparkleCraft.com, 361
Sparks, Debra, 399
Specialization, 457
Specialized, 187
Spekman, Robert, 150
Spiffs, 322
Sporting Goods Business, 183
Sports beverages, 187
Sports utility vehicles (SUVs), 203
Springer, Dan, 371
SPSS MR, 177, 217
SRI International, 124
Srivastava, Rajendra K., 29, 61, 472
Stage-gate systems, 258–265, 471
Stake Fastener Company, 306
Stalk, George, Jr., 267
Stamps.com, 373
Standard Rate and Date Service (SRDS), 337
Stanford Research Institute (SRI), 188
Star TV, 198
Starbucks, 183, 250, 349, 365
Stars, 52, 53
Statistical Abstract of the United States, 171
Statistical methods of forecasting, 156–157
StatPac, Inc., 177
Steenkamp Jan-Benedict, E. M., 218
Steere, John, 128
Stern, Gabriella, 102
Stern, Louis W., 301, 325
Stevens, Greg, 267
Stevens, Mary Ellen, 351
Steward-Alden, Allyson L., 352
Stewart, D. R., 495
Stewart, Thomas, 472
Still, Richard R., 352
Stone, Brad, 382
Stone, Oliver, 183
Store brands, 250–251
Straight rebuy, 137–138, 144, 189
Strata Agency Services, 341
Strata Buy Management System, 341

Strategic business units (SBUs), 47, 56–59, 60
    business strategies and, 235–236
    competition and, 223
    control systems and, 477
    global markets and, 464
    growth-share matrix and, 53
    Hewlett-Packard, 448–449
    implementation/control and, 450, 452, 453–454, 456
    marketing audits and, 493
    organizational structures and, 458, 460
    3M, 220–221
Strategic control, 476
Strategic control systems, 475, 484–486
Strategic fit, 222, 260, 450
Strategic marketing programs; see also Business strategies
    adopter categories and, 95
    competition and, 222
    consumer buying behavior and, 117
    formulating, 17–19
    institutions and, 21
    3M business strategies and, 221–222
Strategic planning, 34, 35, 39
Strategic withdrawal strategy, 402, 403, 404, 405, 408
Strategies/resources, company's, 15–16
Strategy; see also Business-level strategy; Corporate strategy
    components of, 39–40, 41
    defined, 39
    hierarchy of, 40
    marketing, 42
    resource allocation and, 52–53
Strategy statements, 340
Strauss, Gary, 82, 266
Streaming audio, 369
Streitfeld, David, 383
Strivers (psychographic segment), 124
Subcultures, 126
Sudharshan, D., 417
Suit Company, 66
Sultan, Fareena, 178
Summers, John O., 218
Sun Microsystems, 31, 32, 33, 448–449
Super Bowl, 330
Super 8, 226
Superstitials, 369
Supply chain, 134
Supply chain management, 311–312

Supply chain management
    alliances, 143
Survey of buyers' intentions, 157, 158
Survey of Buying Power in *Sales and*
    Marketing Management, 171
Survey of salesforce opinion, 157
Survey Pro, 177
Surveys, 177
    evaluation and, 333
    forecasting and, 157–158
    Internet and, 368
    marketing research and, 173
    perceived customer value and, 284
    positioning and, 209
    as primary data, 170
Survivor (TV program), 326
Swan, John E., 61, 98, 104, 151
Swan Hellenic, 107
Sweden, 342, 356
Sweepstakes, 349
Swire, Donald J., 62
Switching costs, 389
Syndication, 358–359, 362
Syndicator, 359
Synergy, 40, 41, 42, 231–232
    competitive strategy differences
        and, 230
    corporate missions and, 43
    strategic business units (SBUs)
        and, 57
SyQuest, 16
Szymanski, David M., 417
Szymanski, Troy, 417
Szymczak, Robert, 241
Szynal, Deborah, 383

T

Taco Bell, 43, 460
Taddia, Marialuisa, 383
Tag lines, 216
Talbots, 210, 213, 214
Tandem Computers, 423
Tangibles, 226, 245
Tangil, 248
Tanzania Telecommunications
    Company Limited (TTCL),
    152–153; *see also* African
    Communications Group (ACG)
Target marketing, 182–184, 214
Target markets
    business strategies and, 236
    defining, 12–13
    demographics and, 173, 189

Target markets—*Cont.*
    differentiation and, 202
    forecasting and, 155
    Gatorade and, 187
    Hanna Andersson and, 13
    innovation and, 94
    marketing communications and,
        329–330
    marketing mix and, 19
    marketing plans and, 21
    marketing strategy and, 42
    Nova Cruz Products and, 264
    positioning and, 207
    RedEnvelope and, 2–3
    strategic marketing programs and, 18
Target (retail store), 143, 303, 474
Target return pricing, 279, 280, 281
Taxol, 478
Taylor, Steven A., 446
Technological environment, 75–77
Technology
    declining markets and, 439
    IBM and changes in, 31–32
    information, 25–26
    marketing management and
        communications, 25
    organizational buying and, 142–143
    sales and customer service and, 347
Telecommunications, 76, 80; *see also*
    Tanzania Telecommunications
    Company Limited (TTCL)
Telephones; *see* Cellular telephone
    business; Mobile telephone
    service
Television, 303, 337, 344
Tellis, Gerard J., 293, 417
Ten Berge, Jos M. F., 218
Territorial restrictions, 324
Tesco (UK), 165
Test markets, 159, 263, 264, 265
Tetzeli, Rick, 445
Thomke, Stefan, 260
Thorntons, 354–355, 359, 360, 362,
    365, 372
3Com, 356
3M
    competitive strategy and marketing
        program fit and, 239–240
    competitive strategy differences
        and, 232
    differentiated defender strategy
        and, 237
    global competition strategies
        and, 228

3M—*Cont.*
    government markets and, 146
    growth strategy of, 220–223
    information technology and, 26
    lead user research at, 260
    product decisions and, 257
    promotion policies and, 238
    prospector strategy and, 223,
        229, 237
    skimming and, 396
    strategic business units (SBUs) of,
        220–223
    Wal-Mart and, 27
Tigert, Douglas, 210, 213, 214, 218
Time pricing, 290
Time to market, 257
Timex, 421
Timplin, Neal, 102
T.J. Maxx, 210, 213, 214
Tomb Raider (film), 326
Toshiba, 314
Total costs, 277
Totty, Michael, 358, 383
Toyota, 86, 234
    bartering and, 288
    branding and, 249
    global market expansion
        and, 438
    Johnson Controls Inc. and, 418
    line stretching and, 254
Toys "R" Us, 485
Tracking studies, 168
Trade agreements, free, 73
Trade area, 186
Trade-category code, 185
Trade discounts, 288, 350
Trade-in allowance, 289
Trade promotions, 321–323, 349
Trademark, 248
Trading companies, 315
Traditional (psychographic
        segment), 124
Training, 348
Transaction, 366
Transaction cost analysis (TCA), 310
Transaction-specific, 310
Transactional efficiency, 23
Travel industry, 361
Travelocity.com, 369
Trawick, I. Frederick, 61, 151
Treacy, Michael, 59, 60, 62, 422, 445
Trend(s)
    demographic, 70
    economic, 73

Trend(s)—*Cont.*
in electronics/
telecommunications, 76
macro, 68
macro trend analysis, 79–80
macroenvironmental, 66–67, 68
in menswear, 66–67
in physical environment, 78
prioritizing categories of, 78–79
sociocultural, 71–72
technological, 76–77
unexpected, 66
Trials, 94, 96, 264
Trout, Jack, 201, 218
Troy, Lisa M., 417
Trust, organizational buying and, 145
Tsao, Amy, 478
Tully, Shawn, 62, 151
Turnkey construction contract, 314
Tushman, Michael L., 241
Tversky, Amos, 178
20th Century Fox, 6
Tyco Toys, 350
Tying contracts, 324
Tylenol brand, 350–351

U

UK Trade Association Forum, 171
Ulrich, Karl, 264
Ultimate customers, 7
UnderArmour, 183
Uni-Marts, Inc., 186
Uniform delivered pricing, 287
Unilever, 319, 459
Unique selling proposition, 215, 340
Unitary, 276
United Kingdom; *see also* Excel
Company, organizational
buying and
banking industry, 242–243
branding and, 250
Canon in, 385
cell phone service providers and, 85
databases and, 165–166
direct marketing industry in, 337
economic environment and, 73
Hallmark Cards and, 294, 295
Hewlett-Packard and, 449
Lucozade, 326
market research and, 167
market segmentation and, 184
McDonald's in, 349
media in, 344

United Kingdom—*Cont.*
PDSA in, 165
Prêt A Manger in, 89
Prudential of, 242
Tesco in, 165
Thorntons in, 354–355
Trade Association Forum, 171
Waterstones in, 202
United Parcel Service (UPS), 302, 373,
377, 429
United States Postal Service, 373
United Technologies, 44
Universal, 73, 76
Unrelated (or conglomerate)
diversification, 50
Urban, Glen L., 267
US WEST (now Qwest
Communications), 156
Useem, Jerry, 241, 379, 383, 480
Users, 135

V

VALS system, 188
VALS 2, 124, 188
Value analysis, 140
Value-based planning, 51, 54–56
Value drivers, 56
Value-in-use, 283–284, 285
Value propositions, 214–216, 247
Value(s)
defined, 11
social class and, 126, 189
sociocultural environment and,
70–71
Van der Linde, Clas, 82
Van Engelen, Erik, 130–131
Van Tripp, Hans C. M., 218
Vanity Fair, 200
Varadarajan, P. Rajan, 62, 241, 417, 472
Variable costs, 276
Varian, Hal R., 364, 382, 417
Variety of features, 422
Vavra, Terry G., 29
Vending machines, 303
Verg, Jehoshua Elias, 267
Verity, John W., 28, 143
Vernon, Mark, 351
Versioning, 364
Vertical integration, 22, 50
Vertical marketing systems (VMSs),
316–319, 319–320
Vertu, 185
VFlash, 369

Viacom, 343
Victor, Bart, 198, 241
Vierling Group, 228
Villanueva, Pilar, 215
Viral marketing, 368
Virgin Atlantic Airways, 344
Virgin Group, 85
Virgin Telecom, 85
Visa, 183
VisiCalc, 365
Vitek Systems, Inc., 430
Vodafone, 84–85, 356
Vogelstein, Fred, 382, 399, 446, 472
Volvo, 187, 203, 215
durability and, 422
positioning and, 215, 216
Von Clausewitz, Carl, 417
Von Hippel, Eric, 260
Voyle, Susanna, 81
VWR Corp., 11

W

Wade, D. P., 196
Wal-Mart, 6, 26, 90, 143
administered VMSs and, 318
benchmarking and, 479
branding and, 251
channel design alternatives and, 305
control systems and, 474–475,
476–477, 478, 489, 490
corrective action and, 483
distribution channel decisions
and, 305
feedback data and, 482
first-mover advantage and, 365
Golden Valley Microwave and, 240
Internet and, 303, 376
low-price positioning and, 212
market knowledge systems and, 163
market segmentation and, 187
marketing research and, 482–483
new economy and, 356
positioning and, 208, 212
profitability analysis and, 479
3M and, 27
vertical marketing systems (VMSs)
and, 317
websites and, 303
Walker, Chip, 128
Walker, Orville C., Jr., 61, 266, 325,
352, 417, 456, 472
Walkman, 9
Wall Street Journal, 167, 203

Walsh, James, 325
Walton, Sam, 483, 495
Wanderlust, 184
Wansley, Brant, 241
Wants/needs; *see* Needs/wants
Ward, Andrew, 81
Wardell, Charles, 177
Ward's Business Directory, 171
Warner, Fara, 7
Warner, Melanie, 383, 480
Warner Music, 76
Warranties, 251–252
Warshaw, Michael, 383
Water, 77, 79
Waterstones, 202
Watkins, James D., 240
Web portals, 339
Weber, Thomas E., 167, 364, 382
Websites, 339; *see also* World
    Wide Web
Webster, Frederick E., Jr., 28, 36, 61,
    104, 150, 218, 472
Weinberg, Bruce D., 267
Weintraub, Arlene, 382, 383
Weiss, Allan M., 151
Weiss, Allen M., 325
Weitz, Barton A., 151, 210, 325
Welch, Colin, 178
Welch, David, 199
Wellcome PLC, 292
Welsh, Jonathan, 203, 218
Wendy's, 89
Werbach, Kevin, 382
Western Auto, 317
Weston Presidio, 2
Wheelwright, Steven C., 266
White, Erin, 28

White, Joseph B., 382
Wholesaler-retailer franchise
    systems, 318
Wholesaler-sponsored voluntary
    chains, 317
Wholesalers, 143, 306
Wiersema, Frederik D., 59, 60, 62, 417,
    422, 445
Wigfield, Mark, 383
Williams-Sonoma, 2
Williamson, David, 476
Williamson, Oliver E., 325
Williamson, Peter, 199
Wilson, David T., 150, 151
Wilson, Diane, 383
Wilson, E. O., 476
Wind, Jerry, 266
Wind, Yoram, 62, 151
Wine industry, 200–201, 204, 211
Wine Spectator, The, 200
Winer, Russell S., 29, 293, 472
Wise, Jeff, 128
Wolkomer, Richard, 267
Women's clothing retailers, 209–210,
    212–214
Woodward & Lothrop, 210, 213, 214
Woolley, Scott, 293
WordPerfect, 388
Workman, John P., Jr., 35, 61
World Wide Web; *see also*
    Amazon.com; Internet
    auctions, 142–143, 144, 148, 235,
        282–283, 363
    catalog sites, 149
    consumer buying behavior and,
        112–113
    exchange relationships and, 13

World Wide Web—*Cont.*
    macro trend analysis and, 79
    marketing efficiency and, 24
    marketing research data and, 170
    modified rebuys and, 138
    organizational buying and, 142–143
    robots "bots," 113
    sales, 26
    technological environment and, 76
Wright, Adrian, 67
W.W. Grainger, 302

X

Xerox, 149, 385, 428, 479

Y

Yahoo!, 356, 369, 371
Yip, George S., 266
Yoshino, Michael Y., 199

Z

Zaltman, Gerald, 178
Zara, 6
Zaun, Todd, 253
Zed, 372
Zeithaml, Carl P., 417
Zeithaml, Valarie A., 61, 128, 151, 241,
    248, 425, 427, 446
Zellner, Wendy, 103, 399, 472
Zenor, Michael J., 472
Zider, Bob, 82, 380, 383
Zip drives, 9, 17
Zone pricing, 287
Zysman, John, 288